Fodor's

W9-BDO-523

BALLPARK VACATIONS

Great Family Trips to Minor League and Classic

Major League Baseball Parks Across America

BY BRUCE ADAMS & MARGARET ENGEL

Fodor's Travel Publications, Inc.

New York • Toronto • London • Sydney • Auckland

http://www.fodors.com/

First Edition

ISBN 0–679–03152–9

Fodor's Ballpark Vacations

Editor: Nancy van Itallie
Creative Director: Fabrizio La Rocca
Cartographer: David Lindroth
Cover Photograph: Mickey Pfleger
Cover Design: Guido Caroti

About the Writers

Margaret Engel, co-author of Food Finds: America's Best Local Foods and the People Who Produce Them, is a former reporter for the Washington Post. She runs the Alicia Patterson Journalism Foundation. Bruce Adams is a lifelong baseball and history fan and the co-author of two books on political issues. He is coach of his son's Little League baseball team.

Authors' Dedication

We dedicate this book to our children, Emily and Hugh. Without their unquenchable enthusiasm for baseball and extraordinary energy and endurance, there would be no book.

Editor's Note

While every care has been taken to ensure the accuracy of the information in this guide, the passage of time will always bring change, and consequently Fodor's cannot accept responsibility for errors that may occur. All prices and opening times quoted here are based on information supplied to us at press time. Hours and admission fees may change, however, and the prudent traveler will avoid inconvenience by calling ahead.

Fodor's wants to hear about your travel experiences, both pleasant and unpleasant. Send your letters to: Editor, Ballpark Vacations, 201 East 50th Street, New York, NY 10022. Also check out Fodor's Web site at http://www.fodors.com/. We look forward to hearing from you, and have a wonderful trip!

Special Sales

Contents

INTRODUCTION

" **T**ake me home, momma, and put me to bed. I have seen enough to know I have seen too much." That was the announcer's reaction when the Racine Belles upset the Rockford Peaches in the bottom of the ninth in the 1992 classic film *A League of Their Own*.

That's the way the four members of the Adams family—Bruce, Peggy, Emily, and Hugh—felt when we returned to our home in Bethesda, Maryland, on July 3, 1996. We had driven 25,000 miles, been in 44 states, seen 85 baseball games in 82 different stadiums, gotten 11 foul balls, and seen three rainbows. Remarkably, we had only two rainouts and no traffic tickets, breakdowns, or accidents. As Larry King said, "If you have to have an obsession, make it baseball."

What's in the Book

The Ballparks

This is a great time to be a baseball fan who likes to travel. Fabulous new stadiums are being built all across America for major and minor league teams alike. Not since the golden age of major league stadiums, in the early 20th century, and the bumper crop of municipal stadiums built by the Works Progress Administration in the 1930s, have baseball players and fans been so blessed.

After decades of concrete and steel bowls and artificial turf at the major-league level and neglect and mediocrity at the minor-league level, there has been an extraordinary turnabout in the quality and fan-friendliness of baseball stadium architecture. Each year's new ballparks seem better than those of the year before. Fans are the big winners.

Something for Everyone in the Family

Baseball is a wonderful way to see and experience America. We saw it all—from the extraordinary beauty of our country to the shameful neglect of our downtowns.

One of the first things we saw in every small town we visited was a baseball field. The sport is a basic part of America's fabric, and its tentacles reach into all parts of life. In Memphis, patrons got free admission if they brought in a

bulletin from any house of worship. No matter how many times we witnessed it, it was hard not to get teary when teams would let Little Leaguers stand next to the players for the "Star Spangled Banner."

We wrote this book to help families plan realistic vacations that include baseball. It's a departure from the usual "guy trip" books that emphasize steakhouses, baseball trivia, and sports bars. Hey, we love those guys, but it's nice to know a restaurant with milk and apple juice. We've included kids' entertainments, from hands-on science museums to waterparks, and history stops that, for the most part, kids will want to see, like Indian pueblos, battlefields, and a corny Boston tea party.

We divided the book into trips that could be accomplished over a long weekend. They can be stretched into a week, taking advantage of all the sights and entertainments in each town. Our interest is in economy, so we tried to keep lodgings to under $50 a night for four people, except in large cities, where we aimed at a $100 a night limit. Lodgings $60 and under are listed by a $ symbol; those $60–$125 are $$; those over $125 have $$$.

In most cases, we listed the hotels used by the visiting baseball clubs first, as staying there gives you a chance to run into the players. But if we particularly liked a non-team hotel, we listed it first. Also, please realize that these visiting team hotels change frequently, as ballclubs switch whenever they get a better deal. So if it's important to stay at a team hotel, call the club and check which one they're using this season.

We chose restaurants that are high on charm and regional flavor and low on price. We listed the restaurant closest to the ballpark first. Nearly every restaurant listing ends with a $ symbol, which means meals are under $10 per person. Many are under $5 per person. Those few that are more expensive have the $$ symbol.

In the information box for each team, you'll find seven different designations that indicate the level of play. The top level is the *Major Leagues*. Next, there are five designations for the members of baseball's National Association, the organization of the minor leagues. Top among the minors are the three *Triple AAA leagues*, where many of the players are heading to the major leagues or have already been there. Each major-league team has only one Triple AAA affiliate. Players in the three *Double AA leagues* have distingushed themselves at the lower levels and are attempting to show they have major-league talent. In the seven *Single A leagues,* major-league teams affiliate with more than one team. Two Single A leagues play a *Short Season* beginning in June. Most of the players are just out of college and recently drafted to play professional baseball. The game's youngest, rawest recruits play at the *Rookie* level.

Independent leagues do not belong to the National Association and their members are not affiliated with major-league teams.

The College World Series, in Rosenblatt Stadium in Omaha, Nebraska, held the first Friday after Memorial Day, determines the best college baseball team in the country. Many of the stars from this competition immediately join one of the seven summer *college-level leagues.*

Why Did We Do It?

This all began a very long time ago. Bruce's dad, Tinsley, was a young baseball fan with a very famous neighbor. Walter Johnson, perhaps the greatest right-handed pitcher of all time, lived nearby in Bethesda, Maryland. While managing the Washington Senators from 1929 to 1932, after his pitching days were over, Johnson took his son, Eddie, and Tinsley to Griffith Stadium to sit in the dugout. Bruce grew up going to Griffith Stadium for Saturday ball games.

In the Engel household, the sound of Herb Score announcing the Indians game on the radio was a summertime constant. The late, lamented *Cleveland Press* used to give students 16 pairs of Indians tickets if they got straight A's the last marking period. Peggy and her twin sister, Allison, would turn on the juice for the last 10 weeks. It was safe enough for 12-year-old girls to ride the rapid transit downtown to watch a game in cavernous Municipal Stadium on Cleveland's Lakefront.

Bruce rediscovered baseball after a 25-year lapse in 1983 watching "Orioles Magic" bring a World Championship to Baltimore. By August of 1991, Bruce was completely hooked and went off for a classic "guy baseball trip"—four guys in a van going 3,000 miles to 11 major league games in 10 cities in 9 days. Soon Peggy and the children joined the road trips. Our friends with young children would marvel. That sounds like fun, but how do you know where the teams are? How do you know when the games are? From those questions, this book was born.

Emily & Hugh's Excellent Adventure

The key to fan attraction to the minor leagues, especially for children, is the small scale and the resulting intimacy. In the minor leagues, you are right near the action. At most of the parks we visited, you could talk with the players before the game and kibitz with the guys in the bullpen during the game. The kids could run around and be semi-independent in a way you would never allow in a major-league stadium.

Before, during, and after the games, there were balls—well-worn practice balls and pristine official league balls. Many minor-leaguers find smiling young kids with dirty caps and beat-up mitts irresistible. Emily and Hugh collected 60 balls and countless autographs. There were tons of give-aways and endless contests. We came home with enough backpacks to supply half the students in an elementary school class.

We were awash in community spirit in the many stadiums where the fans enthusiastically sing "Take Me Out to the Ball Game." There's no denying the magic of the perpetual game on "The Field of Dreams" in Dyersville, Iowa. As for the games, we will never forget the thrilling finishes of the Northern League game at Saint Paul and the Babe Ruth League 16-year-old World Series in Jamestown. We doubt we will soon see three runners score on a wild pitch as we did in Idaho Falls or a mascot hip-hop dancing with the home plate umpire as we did in Stockton, California.

There were some special personal moments as well. Watching Hugh, in the awkward scrawl of a 5-year-old, write his name on a ball over and over again, Bruce asked, "Hugh, what are you doing?" "Practicing," he responded with the confidence of a kid who thinks he has a big league future. Our 8-year-old daughter Emily's column on her summer vacation for our community newspaper ended in a way that should bring a tear to any parent: "This was the best summer of my life because my mommy and daddy were with me every day of the whole summer. The end."

Share Your Favorites With Us

When you travel, please remember that baseball leagues shift constantly. Each season brings new mascots, new logos, new management, and sometimes new teams. Do call in advance and make sure the team is still playing in its customary stadium and check on the home games.

Please share your favorite mascots, stadiums, attractions, lodgings, and restaurants with us. We are especially interested in learning of child-friendly activities near the ballparks. Write to us: Bruce Adams and Peggy Engel, 7211 Exeter Road, Bethesda, MD 20814. And have a great time at the ballparks!

Acknowledgments

Who would imagine that an 8-year-old and a 5-year-old could travel 25,000 miles in a van in one summer and still be fun to be with? So first things first—thanks to Emily, to Hugh, and to our 1993 Dodge Caravan for incredible adventures that went amazingly well.

Our thanks also are due to many people who helped us along our big baseball adventure. Three stand out. Brother-in-law and baseball aficionado Sandy Horwitt had the idea of our spending an entire summer on the road in our van. Glenn Orlin, an otherwise sane and mild-mannered government policy analyst, years ago set for himself the goal of visiting every single ballpark where professional baseball is played. Glenn was a constant source of information and encouragement. Our friend Ira Lechner joined us for 13 of the games from Rancho Cucamonga to Harrisburg and cheered us on every step of the way.

Our special thanks to Julian Bach and Carolyn Krupp, our agents, and Nancy van Itallie, our editor at Fodor's/Random House. Kevin Nealon is the brains behind our computers. Becca Peck gets credit for the wonderful idea of including discount ticket coupons with the book. Our thanks to all the owners, general managers, public relations staffs, reporters, players, and fans who took the time to share their insights and stories with us.

To all the people who went to games with us, helped get us tickets, gave us tips, let us stay a night at their homes, fed our cat while we were away, and told us stories, we are grateful to you: Ragan Adams, Nick Allard, Linda Anderson, Susan Bennett, Jim Bettinger, Claudia Biron, John Blazer, Jeff Booser, Tom Boyle, Gene Callahan, Wayne Christensen and his *Baseball Parent* newsletter, Russ Clemings, Carol and Curtis Cole, Kate and Willie Coleman, Rod Dalton, Eleanor Engel, Frank Eschenbacher, Frank and Sam Garry, Susie and Michael Gelman, Heidi and Peter Grunwald, Eileen Haag, Doug, Carol, and Elizabeth and Wade Henton, Joan Horwitt, Karen and Sara Jaffe, Joanne Johnson, Jordan Family, Kitty Kelley, Lynn and Chris Kelly, Kirkpatrick Family, NYPD Officer Love, Marty Laufer, Don and Ann Lieder, Donald Lindamood, Coke Matthews, Dallas Miller, Wade Nelson, Joseph Overfield, Dottie Paponetti, Richard Peabody, Molly Peter, the Petty family, Jim and Sandi Risser, Dave Roberts, Alvin Rosenbaum, John Ross, Harry and Barbara Sanders, Carol Scott, Salley Shannon, Harrison Sokoloff, Heather Spyker, Lisa Stevenson and Larry Latourette, Howard and JoAnn Symons, Cathy Trost, Sharon and Sam Varnum, Ellen Warren, the Watts family, Polly Webster, Howard Weinberg, William Winter, and Ed Zuckerman. Thanks, also, to Billy Elrod, of Riddle, Oregon, who solved our only car trouble, a punctured tire, for $3.

Tips for Your Ballparks Trip

Travel Tips

The words "long car trip" evoke fear in many families. We found a few ingredients are key in making trips enjoyable.

A mechanical lifesaver for long trips was the 9-inch combination TV/VCR that a neighbor lent us. It plugs into the cigarette lighter and we lashed it with a bungee cord on top of the driver and passenger's armrests. A towel covered it as a rustic anti-theft device when we parked. The children never watched the TV, but the VCR worked miracles in reducing the sniping and complaints during six-hour drives. Carry the tapes (and any cameras and film) in an empty insulated cooler, so summer heat doesn't ruin them. What were the favorites? Baseball tapes, of course:

- *A League of Their Own* (1992, Columbia) — Emily and Bruce

- *Field of Dreams* (1989, Universal), *Pride of the Yankees* (1942, The Samuel Goldwyn Co.) — Peggy

- *The Sandlot* (1993, Twentieth Century-Fox), *Angels in the Outfield* (1994, Disney), *Rookie of the Year* (1993, Twentieth Century-Fox) — Hugh

A molded fiberglass roof luggage carrier was useful for the bats, balls, programs, and extras we collected. Two warnings—the extra height may put some parking garages out of reach, and you must have sufficient weight in the carrier to prevent it from bouncing. We also kept the kids' sleeping bags and pillows up top and used them during late night and early morning drives.

You are going to stop every hour and 45 minutes or two hours if you have children under 10. Insist on bathroom visits at each stop. Bring a baseball, frisbee, or football to throw during rest stops to burn off energy.

Carry a container of baby wipes and a roll of paper towels. Both will be well-used.

In addition to a first-aid kit, carry scissors, can opener, flashlight, tape, and stapler. We used them all.

Join AAA. You'll get significant savings on family admissions at many museums, zoos, amusement parks, even restaurants. The AAA rate at motels is usually the best discount, and there are special family AAA rates at many lodgings. Always ask. Serious money can be saved at DisneyWorld and Disneyland with the AAA discount, but you must buy the passes from AAA, not at Disney ticket windows. Use the AAA trip-tickets and ask for maps of the cities you'll be visiting, too. Buying AAA traveler's checks on the road is not as easy as advertised. In many cities, you pay an extra fee for your out-of-town check. You'll have no trouble using them—AAA checks are accepted everywhere as cash.

Consider joining your hometown zoo, as the 60-plus members of the American Zoological Society extend free admission to members of other zoos. This can be a real savings if you visit more than two zoos a year. Many museums have a free day or evening each week.

Call or write to each city's visitor's bureau before traveling; kids often like to do this so as to receive packages addressed to them in the mail. Most visitors' bureaus have coupon books with decent savings on lodging, food and attractions.

Ball Game Tips

After you pass through the turnstiles, you may want to pin your child's ticket to a jacket or pocket, so that if you become separated, children or ushers can find you. Always instruct children to go to the game-announcing booth if they can't find you—ushers also will help.

In the southeastern leagues during early summer, carry Avon Skin So Soft or children's strength bug deterrent to ward off chiggers and other bugs. Keep clear of the dugouts, as players often spray them with near-toxic doses of DEET-based bug repellent.

Always take a baseball hat or sun visor and sunscreen to games.

Take a sweater or jacket to night games, no matter how hot the afternoon sun was when you left for the park. Once the sun is down and winds pick up, many ballparks can be chilly. We carried a canvas bag of sweaters, sweatpants, and socks, as many times the kids would wear shorts and sandals until the late innings.

If you don't always pay attention to the game, sit behind the screen behind home plate to avoid foul balls.

Children 3 and under may be frightened by baseball mascots. Don't force them to say hello or be photographed. There's always next year.

In major-league parks, write down where you parked the car. In the excitement of arrival, you can forget. Watch kids carefully in the parking lots. Don't park in the surprisingly vacant spaces close to minor-league stadiums unless you want a cracked windshield. The spaces are empty because they're foul-ball heaven. Check with locals in the parking lot if you're unsure where balls frequently land.

Weather Tip

Don't worry about the weather. You can't do anything about it, and the odds are there will be a game. In 82 cities, we had only two rain-outs. New parks have incredible drainage systems, and even old parks get tarps on the field pronto.

Fun Tips

A large measure of the success of minor-league baseball in the 1980s and '90s is the result of aggressive promotions, give-aways, and constant between-innings contests.

Buy a program and enter the crazy games. Some stadiums have a very visible table soliciting contestants near the entrance, but at most parks this process is obscure. So, don't be bashful; ask how to enter.

Get there early. The minor leagues are where the players still enjoy talking with the fans and signing autographs. There's no telling what will happen before the game. Five-year-old Hugh spent 10 minutes warming up a Warthog catcher from the bullpen mound in Winston-Salem before the game with an entire team of uniformed little leaguers looking on with envy.

Hugh & Emily's Tips on Getting Foul Balls

1. Don't ask the bat girl or ball boy for a foul ball. It is their job to keep the ball. You'll just make them feel bad, and you won't get one.

2. It's sort of hard—and sometimes dangerous—for five- and eight-year-olds to catch foul balls.

3. The very best place to go for a foul ball is near the bullpen. At many stadiums, you can stand right behind where the pitchers and catchers sit just past first and third bases. Lots of kids go there and ask the players for balls. Here's some of what does not work: "Hey, number 28, give me a ball!", "Smith, may I have a ball?" "Gimme a ball!" The players aren't supposed to give away their practice balls. They are professionals at work. Respect them. Here's what does work: Between innings, go up behind one of the players and say: "Sir, if you get a foul ball, may I have it?" Then sit patiently until a ball comes. This might take a few innings. When it does come, stand and remind the player of your interest: "Sir, may I have the ball?"

4. Always say "Thank you."

Motel Tips

When packing, consider bringing some of the following items, which can smooth the way:

• a night-light, or better yet, a night-light attached to a 16-foot extension cord. Turning the bathroom light on for middle-of-the-night illumination is not an option in many motels, as the light also activates an aged, raspy ceiling fan.

• a roll of quarters. For tolls, newspaper vending boxes, telephone calls, coin laundries.

• a box of laundry soap, in a plastic bag with a twistie, so you're not at the mercy of the over-priced soap vending machines.

• an oversized safety or diaper pin, to hold together the curtain edges of the drapes that let in the dawn sunlight.

• a separate bathroom bag for each family member, with his or her name on it.

• a six-pack-size cooler for drinks and/or medicines.

• children's pain-relief medicine, cough syrup, Band-Aids, creams, and a bottle of ipecac (for accidental poisoning) in your bathroom bag.

• a watch with a luminous dial that lets you tell time in the dark, without having to rely on the absent or broken motel clock radio.

• a flashlight, to discern the user-unfriendly air-conditioning and heating apparatus, which often goes awry in the middle of the night.

On arrival, make a quick sweep of the motel room, removing any matches, ash trays, drinking glasses, and so on, that could be a problem for children. For children who aren't totally reliable in the wet-bed department, bring a rubber-backed flannel crib pad to place on the mattress.

If you need an all-night pharmacy and the Yellow Pages and front desk staff of your hotel aren't helpful, call the emergency room of a local hospital. The nurses there will know.

Consider joining Super 8 Motel's VIP club. It costs $3 and allows you to hold reservations without tying up your credit card. (You are on the honor system to cancel any unneeded rooms 24 hours in advance.) Super 8 Motels were the unexpected find of our trip—clean, inexpensive, and surprise-inspected four times yearly by management. Don't expect landscaping or interesting surroundings, but the rooms were equal or superior to chain motels charging $20 more a night.

Hotels and motels are slowly getting family-friendly, but you're still going to find rickety cribs with no baby linens. The Westin chain has taken the lead and offers potty seats, bed railings, and night-lights. About half of all Radisson hotels are "Family Approved," which includes cots, cribs, playpens, family movies, and child-proofing kits. You'll have to haul your own baby and safety equipment for most stays. Most lodging chains' efforts toward encouraging children are financial (no extra charge or free meals) or promotional (lots of cheap travel games or playing cards). Arranging baby-sitting through the front desk is no longer the rarity it once was, but it's still expensive. Some motels and hotels will give a discount on adjoining rooms if your children are old enough to sleep separately. These usually aren't advertised, so ask.

Ask in advance if your hotel or motel gives free or discounted tickets to the ball game. Several team hotels do this. Saving $18 on admission is a powerful persuader to use that hotel.

Choose lodgings with pools. There will be moments of meltdown, as there always are on long family vacations. It is amazing what a quick swim will do to revive children for a night of baseball. Carry a bag of swim suits and towels so you can get in and out quickly.

If quiet is a concern, ask for a room away from the soda and ice machines, away from the elevator, away from the train tracks. Motels usually block-book rooms to help the cleaning staff. Ask for the quietest part of the motel. In a two-story motel, the top rooms are quieter, but you must haul luggage up and down stairs.

800 NUMBERS OF FREQUENTLY USED HOTELS AND MOTELS

Best Western 800/528–1234
Courtyard by Marriott 800/321–2211
Days Inns 800/325–2525
Econo Lodges 800/424–6423
Embassy Suites 800/362–2779
Hampton Inns 800/426–7866
Hilton Inns 800/445–8667
Holiday Inns 800/465–4329
Howard Johnson's Motor Lodges 800/654–2000
Hyatt Hotels 800/233–1234
La Quinta 800/551–5900
Quality Inns 800/424–6423
Radisson Hotels 800/333–3333
Ramada Hotels 800/228–2828
Super 8 Motels 800/800–8000
Travelodge 800/578–7878

Restaurant Tips

Kids' menus usually have the same four items, all heavy on the fried food. Discover the world of appetizers and a beverage for children—it's usually the right amount of food. Encourage children to try soup.

On long driving days, skip dessert and make an ice-cream stop two hours later.

Remember, peanuts, hot dogs, and grapes all pose problems for children under 5. Avoid Popsicles and lollipops if your kids are going to be running around a ballpark.

Non-soda beverages aren't as obvious in ballparks, but they are there. Fruit juices often are in barrels holding cans of beer. Bottled water is everywhere. Don't automatically get soda in kid's meal specials in ballparks and elsewhere—even McDonald's will substitute orange juice or milk if you ask.

We avoided fast food chain restaurants and chose diners, cafeterias, Mom and Pop restaurants, and city markets' cafés instead. The service is nearly as fast and you have a much better chance of getting a fruit or vegetable into your child's mouth. The surroundings are more interesting and reflect the region.

Reading Resources

Any and all of the books on roadside America by our friend John Margolies, the premier photographer of Main Street America (*Signs of Our Time, Ticket to Paradise, Pump and Circumstance,* and *Hitting the Road*), are good background. We've dogeared three copies of Jane and Michael Stern's *Roadfood* (HarperCollins, 1992) and would eat anywhere they recommend. Other important books include *Historic Black Landmarks, A Traveler's Guide,* by George Cantor (Visible Ink, 1991); *The Book of America: Inside Fifty States Today* by Neal R. Peirce and Jerry Hagstrom (Norton, 1983); *America's Heritage: Capitols of the United States* by Willis J. Ehlert (State House Publishing of Madison, WI, 1994). Also vital was *The Amusement Park Guide,* by Tim O'Brien (Globe Pequot, 1991).

Baseball America's Directory (Baseball America, Box 2089, Durham, NC 27702, tel. 800/845–2726; $10.95) is the indispensable guide for baseball travelers. It comes out in March each year. In addition to schedules, the Directory includes phone numbers, addresses, and directions to the ballparks.

The Minor League Baseball Book, by writers associated with *USA Today* (published by Macmillan), is a great book for what we call "guy trips," with a heavy dose of baseball trivia and sports bars. *Mud Hens and Mavericks* by Judith Blahnik and Philip S. Schulz (Viking Studio Books) profiles the 116 full-season minor-league teams. *Ballparks of North America* by Michael Benson (McFarland & Company, 1989) provides a comprehensive reference book of baseball yards and stadiums since 1845 in almost 400 cities.

Diamonds: The Evolution of the Ballpark From Elysian Fields to Camden Yards by Michael Gershman (Houghton Mifflin, 1993); *Green Cathedrals: The Ultimate Celebration of All 271 Major League and Negro League Ballparks Past and Present* by Philip J. Lowry (Addison-Wesley, 1992); *Lost Ballparks: A Celebration of Baseball's Legendary Fields* by Lawrence S. Ritter (Viking Studio Books, 1992); and *Take Me Out to the Ball Park* by Lowell Reidenbaugh with illustrations by Amadee (The Sporting News, 1983) are also valuable.

David Lamb's *Stolen Season: A Journey Through America and Baseball's Minor Leagues* (Random House, 1991) was an inspiration to us to make the journey as well as a source of things to explore that we might have missed. Two other baseball trip books made our journey more fun—Bob Wood's *Dodger Dogs to Fenway Franks* (McGraw-Hill, 1988), taking you to all the major-league stadiums, and Ernest J. Green's *The Diamonds of Dixie* (Madison Books, 1995), a trip through the Southern minor leagues.

For an overview of baseball history, we suggest: *Baseball: An Illustrated History* by Geoffrey C. Ward and Ken Burns (Knopf, 1994) and two superb, readable, and elegantly illustrated histories by Bruce Chadwick—*Baseball's Hometown Teams: The Story of the Minor Leagues* (Abbeville Press, 1994) and *When the Game Was Black and White: The Illustrated History of Baseball's Negro Leagues* (Abbeville Press, 1992).

Books about specific minor leagues include: *Wild and Outside: How a Renegade Minor League Revived the Spirit of Baseball in America's Heartland* by Stefan Fatsis (Walker and Company, 1995), about the Northern League; *Separating the Men From the Boys: The First Half-Century of the Carolina League* by Jim L. Sumner (John F. Blair, 1994); and a series of league histories by Bill O'Neal on the American Association, International League, Pacific Coast League, Southern League, and Texas League (all published by Eakin Press).

The Ballplayers, edited by Mike Shatzkin (Arbor House, 1990), provides brief biographies of more than 6,000 ballplayers; *The Negro Leagues Book,* edited by Dick Clark and Larry Lester (Society for American Baseball Research, 1994), is the most complete record of the Negro Leagues ever published; *The Minor League Register,* edited by Lloyd Johnson (Baseball America, 1994), provides the year-by-year records of more than 800 top minor-leaguers; *The Encyclopedia of Minor League Baseball,* edited by Lloyd Johnson and Miles Wolff (Baseball America, 1993), is the definitive minor-league record book; and *Great Baseball Films,* by Rob Edelman (Citadel Press, 1994), covers that subject thoroughly. To follow minor-league baseball on a regular basis, subscribe to *Baseball America* and *USA TODAY Baseball.*

DURHAM BULLS AND OTHER TAR HEEL TREATS

DURHAM, GREENSBORO, WINSTON-SALEM

North Carolina is a mecca for baseball fans, with 10 minor-league teams and some of baseball's best stadiums and favorite mascots. You can combine baseball with three of the state's extraordinary science centers in Durham, Greensboro, and Winston-Salem.

Aim first for Durham, where the 1980s minor-league revival began, thanks to the hit movie, *Bull Durham*. Now there's a thrilling new baseball cathedral, a $16-million beauty with a hand-operated scoreboard and a trademark snorting bull.

After a night in the Durham/Chapel Hill area (with its many colleges to visit), drive 55 miles west to Greensboro, where the stadium is ancient and character-laden. There's historic barbecue in this city, too, and the state's sprawling zoo is but 26 miles south, near Asheboro.

As you continue west, you may succumb to the lure of the country's epicenter for home furnishings in High Point, 20 miles southwest of Greensboro. Winston-Salem is another 20 miles northwest of High Point, with its home-run hitters' ballpark, Wally the Warthog mascot, and exceptional science center. Staying overnight gives you the time to visit Old Salem, a Moravian village that has a new children's section and a living history center.

The Kinston Indians and the Carolina Mudcats in Zebulon are among Carolina's many other options for vacationing baseball fans. (We visit Asheville in Chapter 2.)

DURHAM BULLS

League: Carolina • **Major League Affiliation:** Atlanta Braves • **Class:** A • **Stadium:** Durham Bulls Athletic Park • **Opened:** 1995 • **Capacity:** 9,033 • **Dimensions:** LF: 305, CF: 400, RF: 327 • **Surface:** grass • **Season:** Apr.–Labor Day

STADIUM LOCATION: 409 Blackwell St., Durham, NC 27701

TEAM WEB SITE: http://www.dbulls.com

GETTING THERE: From I–85, Downtown Durham/Mangum St. exit 2 mi and follow signs. From I–40, I–40 W. to Durham Freeway (Hwy. 147). 8 mi on Durham Freeway to Mangum/Roxboro St. exit and follow signs to ballpark.

TICKET INFORMATION: Box 507, Durham, NC 27702, tel. 919/687–6500, fax 919/687–6560

PRICE RANGE: Box seats $6.25; reserved seats $5.25; general admission $4.25 adults, $3.25 children, senior citizens, and students, under 5 free

GAME TIME: Mon.–Sat. 7:30 PM, Sun. 6:05 PM

TIPS ON SEATING: All seats have good views with ample leg room and cup holders. Call ahead and buy box or reserved seats. 2,300 seats are under cover. Only 25% of 6,340 permanent seats are general admission. Best are down foul lines at first and third.

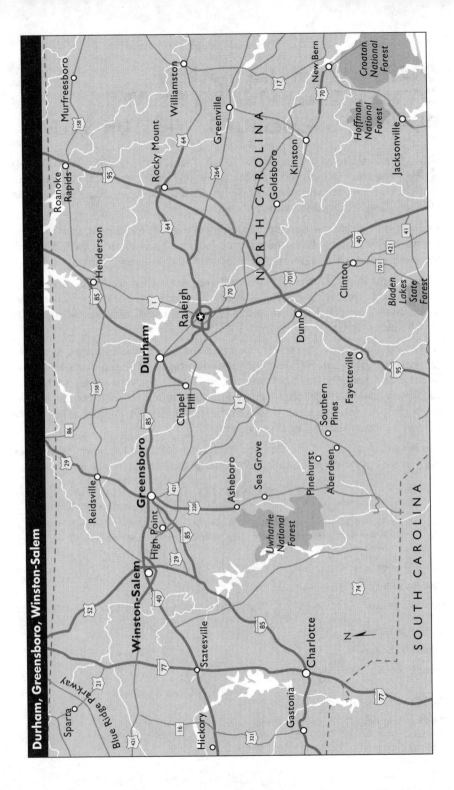

Durham, Greensboro, Winston-Salem

SEATING FOR PEOPLE WITH DISABILITIES: Down first- and third-base lines and behind home plate.

STADIUM FOOD: This park has some of the best food in baseball. **Dillard's BBQ** still sells its buck-a-bone ribs. They're meaty and worth the calories. Other highlights are caramelized pecans and almonds, sold in cones for $3; an excellent steak and onion sandwich for $3.50, and raspberry Italian soda for $1.75. There's great ice cream, a bakery stand, and espresso carts. Avoid the fake lemonade. Several concessions and an international food court are near the main entrance. Try the **Flying Burrito Brothers** stand, but stick to the standards; some of the weird burrito combinations, such as sauerkraut, don't work. Picnic areas adjoin each foul line.

SMOKING POLICY: Smoking prohibited in seating areas and on concourse; permitted in designated areas.

PARKING: Get to game early. Limited free parking on street near ballpark. Three downtown garages north of ballpark have shuttle service.

VISITING TEAM HOTEL: Red Roof Inn (I-85 at Guess Rd., Durham, N.C. 27705, tel. 919/471–9882 or 800/843–7663)

TOURISM INFORMATION: Durham Visitors' Information Center (101 E. Morgan St., Durham, NC 27701, tel. 919/687–0288 or 800/446–8604)

Durham: Durham Bulls Athletic Park

Every baseball fan knows of the Durham Bulls, made famous by the 1988 baseball movie classic *Bull Durham*, starring Kevin Costner, Susan Sarandon, and Tim Robbins.

The Bulls—named for a popular brand of tobacco—first played professional baseball in Durham in 1902. Legend has it that the term "bullpen" was coined here. Pitchers would warm up in the shade of the "Genuine 'Bull' Durham Smoking Tobacco" signs that sported huge replica bulls in many turn-of-the-century ballparks.

The Carolina League, founded in 1944, has been a significant part of the roller-coaster ride that has been the history of the minor leagues these last 50 years. Durham, Greensboro, and Winston-Salem were three of the eight original teams. The golden age of minor-league baseball after World War II ended abruptly in the early 1950s when television brought the major leagues into the living rooms of fans across the nation. The minor leagues hit bottom in the 1970s. Durham was not immune, and the team folded after the 1971 season.

Baseball entrepreneur Miles Wolff paid $2,500 for the franchise rights to bring baseball back to Durham in 1980 and helped lead a national minor-league renaissance. Wolff, who sold the Bulls in 1990 for several million dollars, looks

like a genius. Not so, he says—"Minor-league baseball was dead. But it was what I did for a living. It was the only team I could buy. I was buying the right to lose money." Eight years later *Bull Durham* was a hit, and Wolff had to open a store to handle the national demand for Durham Bulls memorabilia. Within a few more years, minor-league baseball was approaching the attendance records of the late 1940s as the baby boomers rediscovered baseball.

If the 1980s were the years baseball fans rekindled their appreciation for the minor leagues, the 1990s will be remembered for the return to classic stadium architecture. The highly praised redbrick Oriole Park at Camden Yards in Baltimore triggered a move to build stadiums like they once were and to locate them downtown, where they belong.

Many of us fell in love with the Durham Athletic Park we saw in *Bull Durham*. First constructed in 1926 and rebuilt after a 1939 fire, the DAP is a national symbol of baseball nostalgia. The 1988 movie crew installed a huge smoking, snorting bull in right field complete with a HIT BULL WIN STEAK sign. It was a wonderful place to see a game, but it was hopelessly unsuited for the huge crowds that came in response to the hit movie. The choice between staying in the DAP with all its faults or building a soulless aluminum and concrete stadium like Five County Stadium, built in nearby Zebulon for the Carolina Mudcats, would be easy. Durham, to its credit, chose a third path—a modern facility with a traditional brick and steel feel.

In *Bull Durham*, Kevin Costner's character, Crash Davis—the real Crash Davis led the Carolina League in doubles in 1948—remarks from his time in the majors: "The stadiums are like cathedrals." In 1995, a new baseball cathedral opened in Durham. The Durham Bulls Athletic Park, with a view of downtown Durham over the left-field fence, is a $16-million masterpiece designed by the architects of Camden Yards, HOK Sport of Kansas City. A tobacco warehouse à la Camden Yards runs parallel to the third-base line. Durham's "Blue Monster," the 26-foot-high left-field wall, and hand-operated scoreboard evoke memories of Boston's Fenway Park. The attractive navy blue seats are roomy with plenty of legroom, complete with a cup holder for every fan. The Bulls' owners pressed hard for a grandstand roof and they got a beauty, the largest cantilevered roof in the minors, covering 2,300 seats without an obstructed view. To complete the new-old feel, there is a human organist playing baseball tunes.

We usually buy general admission seats for minor-league games, but we made an exception here. They are packing them in these first seasons. We recommend calling ahead and buying reserved seats. Come early and eat at the park. The food is excellent, the music first-rate, and the parking limited. Walk along the concourse and find the three brick murals—including one of Hall of Famer and former Bull Joe Morgan—among the many tributes to the illustrious history of baseball in Durham.

This ballpark is made for kids. Birthdays are announced, and there is a children's playground in the park's northwest corner beyond the third-base line. Take your kids to visit Cathy Sokal, who operates the bull beyond the right-field fence. She will let your child wag the mechanical bull's tail if you are there for a good play by the Bulls or turn on the blazing red eyes and smoking snout if a Bull hits a home run.

Durham will be the Triple AAA affiliate of the Tampa Bay Devil Rays beginning in 1998. The stadium will be expanded to 10,000 seats.

More Durham Baseball

Durham Athletic Park. The historic ballpark where the movie *Bull Durham* was filmed is not far from the new stadium. A player was married in the stadium in the movie and in real life. *428 Morris St., tel. 919/687–6500. From I-85 take Downtown Durham/Mangum St. exit and turn right at Geer St.*

Where to Stay

Visiting Team Motel: Red Roof Inn. This is an ordinary interstate exit motel, with no pool but low rates. *2000 I-85 Service Road, Durham 27705, tel. 919/471–9882 or 800/843–7663, fax 919/477–0512. 120 rooms. AE, D, DC, MC, V. $*

Omni Durham Hotel & Civic Center. Within walking distance of the ballpark, it is an impressive, nine-story downtown convention hotel. There also are shuttle buses to the park from the nearby city parking garage. *201 Foster St., Durham 27701, tel. 919/683–6664 or 800/843–6664, fax 919/683–2046. 187 rooms. Facilities: restaurant, indoor pool. AE, D, DC, MC, V. $$*

Where to Eat

Pop's. This imaginative Italian restaurant is in a former commercial laundry. Entrées include mussels, five pastas, fish, and chicken. There's also a children's pizza and pasta menu. It's across the street from Brightleaf Square, less than a mile from the ballpark. *810 W. Peabody St., Durham, tel. 919/956–1677. Reservations accepted for lunch only. AE, MC, V. $*

A Southern Season. This is one of the premier regional food emporiums in the country. Its Weathervane restaurant has a large umbrella-shaded outdoor patio as well as indoor service. Children are given crayons and a healthy kid's menu, including pasta, grilled chicken, and turkey sandwiches, as well as unusual treatments of lunch and dinner standards. *Eastgate Shopping Center, Chapel Hill, tel. 919/929–9466 or 800/253–3663. AE, MC, V. $*

Breadman's. In this comfy restaurant, you can get breakfast all day. The blueberry pancakes and waffles are standouts. The portions are huge; children get junior-size plates and prices. *224 W. Rosemary, Chapel Hill, tel. 919/967–7110. No credit cards. $*

Elmo's Diner. A family restaurant with breakfast all day, it serves outstanding apple pie, mashed potatoes, and sandwiches. There is a children's menu. Carrboro is adjacent to Chapel Hill. *100 N. Greensboro St., Carrboro, tel. 919/929–2909. D, MC, V. $*

Allen and Son Pit-Cooked Barbecue. Here you can get very good North Carolina–style barbecue, with Brunswick stew. There are wooden floors and a comfortable atmosphere. They serve fruit cobblers for dessert. *Airport Rd. (Rte. 2), Chapel Hill, tel. 919/942–7576. No credit cards. $*

Entertainments

Museum of Life and Science. At this spectacular, fascinating science center, you can stand in the center of a tornado, cup a cloud in your hand, or try launching a rocket to Mars. The well-designed museum emphasizes aerospace, weather, and scientific theories. A small zoo and aquarium focus on Carolina wildlife, including bats, snakes, flying squirrels, and river otters. A KidLab is for younger visitors, with bubble machines and climbing apparatus. For an extra $1.50, you can ride an outdoor train through a farmyard, a nature park, and bear, lion, and wolf habitats. *433 Murray Ave., Durham, tel. 919/220–5429. Admission: $5.50 adults, $3.50 ages 3–12 and senior citizens. Open Memorial Day–Labor Day, Mon.–Sat. 10–6, Sun. 1–6; Sept.–May, Mon.–Sat. 10–5, Sun. 1–5.*

Morehead Planetarium. This former NASA training center has wonderful programs for younger children. Its projector shows nearly 9,000 stars. Films roll daily in the 68-foot-high domed theater. Exhibits of planet life and basic astronomy are free. *E. Franklin St., Chapel Hill, tel. 919/549–6863. Admission to shows: $3 adults, $2.50 children and senior citizens. Open Sun.–Fri. 12:30–5 and 7:30–9:30, Sat. 10–5 and 7:30–9:30.*

Sites to See

Sarah P. Duke Gardens. Here children can run and appreciate the fountains, gazebos, and nooks and crannies of a beautiful Italian garden. It lies on 55 acres on Duke University's West Campus and includes 5 miles of paths, as well as fishponds and a Japanese pond. *Anderson St., Durham, tel. 919/684–3698. Admission free. Open 8–dusk.*

Carolina Theatre. See Greensboro's sister theater, built in 1926 and restored to its former glory. A variety of classic films and stage shows are presented, including children's films and shows. *309 Morgan St., Durham, tel. 919/530–3060.*

GREENSBORO BATS

League: South Atlantic League • **Major League Affiliation:** New York Yankees • **Class:** A • **Stadium:** War Memorial Stadium • **Opened:** 1926 • **Capacity:** 7,500 • **Dimensions:** LF: 327, CF: 401, RF: 327 • **Surface:** grass • **Season:** Apr.–Labor Day

STADIUM LOCATION: 510 Yanceyville St., Greensboro, NC 27405

GETTING THERE: I–40/I–85 to Exit 125, Elm-Eugene St. North on Elm St. 2 mi, right on Market St. Left on Dudley 1 mi to corner of Lindsay and Yanceyville Sts.

TICKET INFORMATION: 510 Yanceyville St., Greensboro, NC 27405, tel. 910/333–2287, fax 910/273–7350

PRICE RANGE: Box seats $7; reserved seats $5; general admission $4 adults, $3 ages 4–21 and senior citizens

GAME TIME: Mon.–Sat. 7:15 PM, Sun. 6:15 PM

TIPS ON SEATING: Plenty of good general admission seats; most food and bathroom facilities are on third-base side.

SEATING FOR PEOPLE WITH DISABILITIES: Along fence in picnic area, in Family Section, and in the Grand Stand.

STADIUM FOOD: This park sells Cheerwine, a regional cherry cola favorite. Add a burger from the **Bats Sidewalk Cafe** behind the third-base stands. There's pan pizza for $3.75, soft-serve ice cream, and warm Vinnie's pretzels. **The Grand Stand** atop the left field stands offers a bar within a ballpark complete with beverages and television. A picnic area down the left-field line is called **Lefty's Grove.**

SMOKING POLICY: Alcohol and smoking prohibited in small Family Section with general admission seats and 2 rows of box seats.

PARKING: Get to game early. Limited $2 parking adjacent to ballpark and across street.

VISITING TEAM HOTEL: Travelodge (2112 W. Meadowview Rd., Greensboro, NC 27403A, tel. 910/292–2020 or 800/578–7878)

TOURISM INFORMATION: Greensboro Visitor Information Center (317 S. Greene St., Greensboro, NC 27401-2615, tel. 919/274–2282 or 800/344–2282)

Greensboro: War Memorial Stadium

We often drive by a stadium a few hours before a game just to make sure we have the time right and know when the gates open. Imagine our surprise at three o'clock in the afternoon when we saw streams of pink and white balloons out in front of Greensboro's War Memorial Stadium. Yes, a wedding reception was in full swing in the Grand Stand, a huge multilevel deck that sits atop the left-field stands. Four hours later the bride, still in her wedding gown, tossed out the first ball after muttering to a friend, "I'm so embarrassed." This was a first for us and for War Memorial.

This really looks like a war memorial—fortress architecture complete with flags top towers and an arched concrete coliseum front. Built in 1926 for football and track, the stadium is shaped like a J, with the stem going down the left-field line to the end of the track.

Professional baseball first came to Greensboro in 1902, but the first minor-league baseball game wasn't played in War Memorial until 1930, when a roof for the grandstand, a press box, and dugouts were added. Greensboro was one of the eight original teams when the Carolina League formed in 1944. Greensboro dropped minor-league baseball for 10 years after the 1968 season, apparently in part because of the condition of War Memorial Stadium. In 1978 baseball returned, this time in the South Atlantic League. New York Yankee star Don Mattingly was the Sally League MVP in 1980, hitting .358 for the league champion Greensboro Hornets.

Bizarre is the only word for War Memorial's right field. A stream runs under fair territory along the first-base line, and wires hang over it. Because of the odd J shape of the stadium and the stream, the right-field foul pole was 248 feet from home plate when the stadium opened for baseball in 1930. The foul pole is now 327 feet from home, but the stream forces a short porch that is a left-handed hitter's dream.

The Old South is still in evidence at War Memorial. Take a close look at the war-memorial plaque listing Greensboro's dead from World War I on the first-base side at the front gate. Above the last six or so names something has been filed off crudely. It had said "Colored" for the separate listing of blacks who had given their lives for their country.

The owners have substantially invested in making aging War Memorial Stadium a good place to watch baseball. They funded a significant upgrade in 1993, including construction of the popular left-field bar, the Grand Stand. They moved seats originally from Yankee Stadium and Philadelphia's Connie Mack Stadium from behind home plate to the Grand Stand. The souvenir stand is called the Bats Belfry, and the bathrooms are called Bat Rooms in honor of Greensboro's distinctive Bat mascot. There is entertainment on and off the field every moment you are here.

In spite of recent renovations and improvements, War Memorial's future is uncertain. Parking is extremely limited, the plumbing old, and the lighting inadequate.

Where to Stay

Biltmore Greensboro Hotel. This elegant, European-style hotel downtown has reasonable rates and free limousine rides to the nearby ballpark. There are complementary afternoon beer and wine tastings here as well. *111 W. Washington St., Greensboro 27401, tel. 910/272–3474 or 800/332–0303. 25 rooms. Facilities: parking (fee). AE, D, DC, MC, V. $$*

The Greensboro Hilton. This 11-story downtown hotel is the largest in town and often runs weekend specials. Child care is available in the athletic club. The rooms are good-sized and newly renovated. *304 N. Greene St., Greensboro 27401, tel. 910/379–8000 or 800/533–3944, fax 910/275–2810. 283 rooms. Facilities: restaurant, sports bar, indoor pool, hot tub, sauna, health club, parking (fee). AE, D, DC, MC, V. $$*

Where to Eat

Macado's Restaurant and Delicatessen. The overstuffed sandwiches and decor (planes suspended from ceilings, dinosaurs crashing through walls) appeal to kids. It's 2 miles from the ballpark. *125 Summit Ave., Greensboro, tel. 910/373–0600. AE, D, MC, V. $*

Stamey's Barbecue. The city's premier barbecue mecca since 1930, it serves pork and chicken cooked over axe-handle wood in 12 huge ovens. Don't miss the red coleslaw and fruit cobblers with ice cream. *2206 High Point Rd., Greensboro, tel. 910/299–9888. No credit cards. $*

Entertainments

North Carolina Zoological Park. This is a natural-habitat zoo, which means lots of walking and few animals in cages for close viewing. Small children may be frustrated. African animals—like the warthog—are featured, in open fields and in a tropical rain-forest pavilion. The other major habitat, North America, has polar bears, sea lions, black bears, and cougars. Trams take you between habitats, but they run full, and you cannot see animals while riding. Shuttle buses return you to parking lots. The 300-acre park is

6 miles southeast of Asheboro. *Zoo Parkway (NC Rte. 159), Asheboro, tel. 910/879–7000 or 800/488–0444. Admission: $6 adults, $4 ages 2–12. Open daily 9–5.*

Natural Science Center. Another of North Carolina's good hands-on children's centers, this one has a planetarium, a zoo, and a petting barn. Kids like the dinosaur gallery and sea lab's touch tank. The adjoining Country Park has pedal boats, bicycling and hiking trails, and two fishing lakes. *4301 Lawndale Dr., Greensboro, tel. 910/283–3769. Admission: $4.50 adults, $3.50 ages 4–13. Open Mon.–Sat. 8–5, Sun. 1–5.*

Emerald Pointe Water Park. This 45-acre park has 22 rides, and you'll get wet on most of them. There are height restrictions on the thrill rides. Pools and slides keep younger children occupied. *3910 S. Holden Rd., Exit 121 off I-85, Greensboro, tel. 910/852–9721 or 800/555–5900 (in NC and VA). Admission: $17.95 adults, $12.95 children under 45". Open June–Aug., Mon.–Thurs. 10–7, Fri.–Sun. 10–8; late May and early Sept., weekends 10–6. AE, MC, V.*

Carolina Theater. The sister theater to the Carolina Theater in Durham, this restored vaudeville house showcases theater, dance, concerts, and films. It has a genuine theater organ and is listed on the National Register of Historic Places. *310 S. Greene St., Greensboro, tel. 910/333–2600.*

Sites to See

Woolworth's Lunch Counter Sit-in. This downtown F. W. Woolworth store closed in 1994 but is still intact. Portions of the lunch counter are in the Smithsonian and in the Greensboro Historical Museum, but you can still see where four black students from North Carolina A&T State University staged a sit-in at the whites-only lunch counter. Their February 1, 1960, protest sparked civil rights demonstrations in 50 cities. There is a plaque and a photo of the four young men. The side street where they exited has been renamed February One Place. *132 South Elm St., Greensboro.*

WINSTON-SALEM WARTHOGS

League: Carolina • **Major League Affiliation:** Chicago White Sox • **Class:** A • **Stadium:** Ernie Shore Field • **Opened:** 1956 • **Capacity:** 6,280 • **Dimensions:** LF: 325, CF: 400, RF: 325 • **Surface:** grass • **Season:** Apr.–Labor Day

STADIUM LOCATION: 401 Deacon Blvd., Winston-Salem, NC 27105

TEAM WEB SITE: http://www.arolinaleague.com/baseball/winston

GETTING THERE: Ernie Shore Field is next to Wake Forest football stadium; I–40 Business to Cherry St. exit, north through downtown, right on Deacon Blvd.

TICKET INFORMATION: Box 4488, Winston-Salem, NC 27115, tel. 910/759–2233, fax 910/759–2042

PRICE RANGE: Box seats $6; reserved seats $5; general admission $4 adults, $3 under 13, students, senior citizens, and military personnel

GAME TIME: Mon.–Sat. 7:15 PM, Sun. 2:05 PM

TIPS ON SEATING: There are plenty of good general admission seats.

SEATING FOR PEOPLE WITH DISABILITIES: On concourse along rail on first- and third-base sides

STADIUM FOOD: The food is several cuts above most parks, in both variety and quality. The pizza slices are huge, with a thick crust. There are Buffalo wings, a good BBQ sandwich, and your choice of Winston Cup hard-dipped or soft-serve ice cream or frozen yogurt. For adults, there's an assortment of 12 beers, including Warthog ale. Lemonade is fresh-squeezed for $2. Locally made Texas Pete Hot Sauce is available in all the condiment stands. Warm pretzels, topped with either cinnamon or parmesan cheese, make a good snack for $2. A new tree-shaded picnic area is down the left-field line. The concession stand area has plenty of space for watching the game while you eat.

SMOKING POLICY: Smoking and alcohol prohibited in Family Section of box seats

PARKING: Ample free parking

VISITING TEAM HOTEL: Holiday Inn-North (3050 University Pkwy., Winston-Salem, NC 27105, tel. 910/723–2911 or 800/465–4329).

TOURISM INFORMATION: Winston-Salem Visitor Center (601 N. Cherry St., Winston-Salem, NC 27101, tel. 800/331–7018)

Winston-Salem: Ernie Shore Field

Ernie Shore was Babe Ruth's roommate on the Yankees. They went together from Baltimore to Boston to New York. On June 23, 1917, starting pitcher Babe Ruth was ejected from a game for protesting a walk to the first batter. Shore relieved, the runner was thrown out trying to steal, and Shore pitched a perfect game, retiring 26 straight batters. He was ineffective after returning from military service in World War I. Shore moved back to his native North Carolina and served as Forsyth County sheriff from 1936 to 1970. He led the fundraising campaign to build a new baseball stadium in Winston-Salem.

When it opened in 1956, the city named it for Shore.

Ernie Shore probably wouldn't know what to make of the team's new mascot—Wally the Warthog—or all the hoopla at Warthog games, but he would be proud of this fine old stadium. The ballpark sits next to Grove Stadium, Wake Forest University's football field. An extensive face-lift for the 1993 season included an attractive brick front entrance and a brick wall between the bases behind home plate à la Chicago's Wrigley Field. Two thousand seats were added and a new clubhouse built.

You walk through the brick arches and down into an amphitheater to your seats. Many of the seats under the grandstand are the original

1956 seats styled after those then in use in Yankee Stadium. Ernie Shore Field is a home-run hitter's park. The prevailing winds carry balls over the fence in record-setting numbers.

The minor leagues are noted for contests and entertainment between the innings. In most parks, it is something of a mystery how people get chosen for these contests, as the forms are usually scattered throughout the program. When you enter this stadium, you are greeted by friendly staff at a table with forms that allow you to sign up for the various contests.

Wally the Warthog made his debut as the Winston-Salem mascot in 1995. Wally was an unusual choice. The fans voted for a camel, but management wisely scrubbed that choice because of the controversy over the infamous Joe Camel. Alliteration won out with Wally the Winston-Salem Warthog. The warthog had been a strong contender because of notoriety over recent misdeeds of several of the new residents of the nearby North Carolina Zoo in Asheboro. Wally has turned out to be a winner. Somehow we can't imagine Ernie Shore's Yankees advertising "There's no SNOUT about it. The Most BOARing logo in baseball!" But Wally is energetic and seemingly ever-present atop the dugout, leading the fans in cheering on the home team. He only lost his poise once, when the winner of the dizzy bat contest hoisted him onto his shoulders, spun him around, and dropped him on his stomach.

Smoking is allowed through most of the ballpark, as this is RJR country. A massive RJR factory sits just over the right-field wall. Beyond the trees past the left-field fence is Planters, the peanut people, a subsidiary of RJR/Nabisco.

Where to Stay

Visiting Team Motel: Holiday Inn–North. The standard, four-story motel is a half-mile from the ballpark and offers free transport to the airport. *3050 University Pkwy., Winston-Salem 27105, tel. 910/723–2911 or 800/465–4329, fax 910/777–1003. 193 rooms. Facilities: restaurant, pool, exercise room. AE, D, DC, MC, V. $*

Courtyard by Marriott. This pleasant, new motel offers free entry to a nearby Gold's gym and free greens fees at a local golf course. It is a half-mile to the ballpark. *3111 University Pkwy.,* *Winston-Salem 27105, tel. 910/727–1277 or 800/321–2211, fax 910/722–8219. 123 rooms. Facilities: restaurant, pool, exercise room. AE, D, DC, MC, V. $*

Where to Eat

The Village Tavern. Sit outside on the patio for fresh salads, sandwiches, and pizza and marvel over the beautifully restored village and grounds of the R. J. Reynolds estate. *221 Reynolds Village, Winston-Salem, tel. 910/748–0221. MC, V. $*

Mayberry Restaurant. Next door to the Old Salem Visitor's Center, this family restaurant serves breakfast and lunch. Walk a bit of Old Salem and have lunch here. *201-B West St., Old Salem Village, Winston-Salem, tel. 910/721–4801. No credit cards. $*

Entertainments

SciWorks. This superlative science center is well kept, imaginative, and aimed at kids' interests. The hands-on saltwater aquariums, sea lions, and insects are a hit. You can hunt fossils, get next to a stuffed leopard and lion, and learn about chemical reactions. There's a 120-seat planetarium with laser shows and kids' programs and a play room for preschoolers. *400 Hanes Mill Rd., Winston-Salem, tel. 910/767–6730. Admission: $7 adults, $5 ages 6–19, $3 ages 3–5. Open Mon.–Sat. 10–5, Sun. 1–5.*

Old Salem. The emphasis on artifacts and architecture may not hold children's interest through a full exploration of this German Moravian town. View 90 buildings, walk historic streets, and watch costumed staff reenact how people lived. You may walk the streets for free and patronize Winkler's Bakery, circa 1800, and get a free ginger cookie. A new, interactive history museum for ages 4 to 12 opened in 1996, with a climbing sculpture and a backward-running clock. *Old Salem Rd., Winston-Salem, tel. 910/721–7300 or 800/441–5305. Two-day admission: $12 adults, $6 ages 6–14, $30 family. Open Mon.–Sat. 9–5, Sun. 1:30–5.*

Unusual Shopping

High Point Furniture Outlet Clearance Centers. Call the High Point Convention Bureau (tel. 910/884–5255) to get a full listing and discount coupons.

BLUE RIDGE BASEBALL

2

ASHEVILLE, BLUEFIELD, LYNCHBURG, SHENANDOAH VALLEY LEAGUE

Thehe Blue Ridge Mountains are the stunning backdrop for three mountain ballparks, beginning with Asheville, North Carolina, with its intimate, modern park set into a green hillside. The city also has the attraction of the spectacular Biltmore Estate, the largest private home in America. Its gardens, walking paths, and sumptuous architecture make this a memorable family excursion. Driving 200 miles north to tiny Bluefield, West Virginia, takes you through high-altitude scenery and several tunnels under solid rock. Bowen Field, in Bluefield, literally straddles West Virginia and Virginia. A stream and deep forest lie beyond center field. The seating is rustic, and games here are one of baseball's biggest bargains. The attractions of Bluefield are physical—its mountain beauty and a nearby coal mine in a partial ghost town that visitors can explore.

Eastward 150 miles in central Virginia is Lynchburg, a city of seven hills that wisely put its Carolina League stadium on one of them. The city has several unusual kid-friendly restaurants and a central city market. One of the wonders of the world—Natural Bridge—is nearby. Just an hour north of Lynchburg, you'll find the Shenandoah Valley League, a summer college league. The endearing stadiums have basic seating, attractive views, and a competitive level of play. In the cities you'll find vintage downtowns, plus many B&Bs in historic homes that welcome children and are near the Valley's famed caverns and river sports.

ASHEVILLE TOURISTS

League: South Atlantic League • **Major League Affiliation:** Colorado Rockies • **Class:** A • **Stadium:** McCormick Field • **Opened:** 1924/92 • **Capacity:** 3,400 • **Dimensions:** LF: 328, CF: 406, RF: 300 • **Surface:** grass • **Season:** Apr.–Labor Day

STADIUM LOCATION: 30 Buchanan St., Asheville, NC 28801

GETTING THERE: From I–240, take Charlotte St. exit south. Turn left on McCormick Place just after you pass brick city government buildings on right. You'll see stadium as you turn left onto Buchanan St.

TICKET INFORMATION: Box 1556, Asheville, NC 28802, tel. 704/258–0428, fax 704/258–0320

PRICE RANGE: Box seats $6 adults, $5 children and senior citizens; general admission $4 adults, $3 children 3–12 and senior citizens

GAME TIME: Mon.–Sat. 7 PM, Sun. 2 PM; gates open 1 hr before game.

TIPS ON SEATING: Only 800 box seats. General admission seats are aluminum benches with backs, close to action.

SEATING FOR PEOPLE WITH DISABILITIES: Behind home plate just behind box seats

STADIUM FOOD: Two chains provide most of the food, which includes ice cream and pizza. The other offerings are ordinary: a decent grilled chicken sandwich for $2.75, brats for $2.50, and burgers, fries, and chili-cheese nachos. Tropical snow-cones use fruit juice instead of lurid-colored flavorings.

Asheville, Bluefield, Lynchburg, Shenandoah Valley League

SMOKING POLICY: General admission and box seat family sections behind home plate on third-base side where smoking and alcohol are prohibited.

PARKING: Parking at stadium free, but lot is tiny. Additional parking up hill in front of Asheville Municipal Stadium.

VISITING TEAM HOTEL: Days Inn (199 Tunnel Rd., Asheville, NC 28805, tel. 704/254–4311 or 800/325–2525)

TOURISM INFORMATION: Asheville Convention & Visitors Bureau (Box 1010, Asheville, NC 28802, tel. 704/258–6111 or 800/257–1300)

Asheville: McCormick Field

McCormick Field in Asheville, North Carolina, is one of the most beautiful little fields in all of baseball. From the grandstand, fans look out over the green outfield grass to a gorgeous stand of tall trees on the hillside beyond the outfield fence.

Built in 1924 near the city's downtown, the ballpark had no outfield fence for much of its history. A hillside sloping sharply up to a city football field above served the purpose. When we visited, we heard the story of rival teams complaining that the home-team Tourists hid balls in the bushes before games. When the visitors hit a ball into the woods, the home-team outfielder would find it in short order. The visiting team outfielders never had such luck.

The Buncombe County commissioners authorized a $3-million reconstruction of the ballpark for the 1992 season, replacing the wooden grandstand with brick and steel. Local architects Bowers, Ellis, and Watson produced a baseball jewel. The new McCormick Field retains the classic feel of its historic predecessor. We fell in love with this redbrick ballpark just walking up the hill from the small parking lot below. The brick exterior is carried inside with brick behind home plate and down the base lines as in Chicago's Wrigley Field. Asheville's short right field has tempted ballplayers ever since McCormick Field's opening exhibition game in 1924. Ty Cobb hit a home run, one of six hit that day. Outfield fences were put in during the 1950s, and today the right-field fence, although only 300 feet from home, is 35 feet high. The entire hill beyond the fences is covered with a gorgeous stand of tall trees. The wide con-course, with tall brick arches and a picnic and play area, fits nicely below the field level.

Babe Ruth was a big fan of McCormick Field, but his first visit to Asheville produced "the belly-ache heard 'round the world!" In April of 1925, the Yankees and the Dodgers, barnstorming north from spring training, played exhibition games in Chattanooga and Knoxville. After a train ride from Knoxville, Ruth collapsed at the Asheville station. Teammates carried the uncon-scious Ruth to a hotel, and he missed the exhibi-tion game against the Dodgers. The doctor reported a case of flu. Others suspected too much beer and too many hot dogs. There were even rumors that the Babe had died in Asheville. Whatever the problem, it was more than indigestion, as Ruth missed all the games in April and May. He returned to Asheville for two exhibition games in 1931 and hit a home run in each.

McCormick Field has seen more than its share of stars. In addition to Cobb and Ruth, Jackie Robinson played two exhibition games here in 1948, one year after he broke through baseball's color line. Future Hall of Famer Willie Stargel hit 22 home runs for Asheville in 1961, and Sparky Anderson managed the Tourists to first place in 1968. Future Hall of Famer Eddie Murray played here when Asheville was a Baltimore Orioles franchise in the 1970s. Cal Ripken Sr. was the manager and Cal Ripken Jr., baseball's iron man, was the bat boy.

In the 1988 movie *Bull Durham*, Crash Davis, the character played by Kevin Costner, needed one more home run to set the all-time minor-league record. The record-breaking home run was filmed in McCormick Stadium. Costner's signed uniform is framed and on display in the Tourists' office at the ballpark.

McCormick Field got its name from Dr. Lewis M. McCormick, a local hero who had died two years before the ballpark opened. McCormick, a bacteriologist, arrived in town in 1904. He was horrified at the large number of houseflies in town. McCormick pushed to have the livery stables cleaned up and started a campaign in town to "Swat That Fly." His movement spread nationwide, and we've all been swatting flies ever since. Despite McCormick Field's great history, it was endangered when the region's Tri-State League folded after the 1955 season. To keep the stadium from falling down, the city leased it for weekly stock-car races for three summers. They tore out the quarter-mile asphalt track and started playing minor-league baseball in McCormick Field again in 1959, this time in the South Atlantic League.

There is a fine souvenir shop at the entrance selling all the regular baseball memorabilia plus blankets, which can come in handy. It can be cool even on an August night. Asheville's logo is a lively Ted E. Tourist bear complete with sunglasses, a flowered shirt, and a suitcase.

Where to Stay

Holiday Inn–Tunnel Rd. This ordinary, well-kept two-story motel is one block from a shopping mall and a half-mile from downtown. Child care is available. *201 Tunnel Rd., Asheville 28805, tel. 704/252–4000 or 800/465–4329, fax 704/258–0359. 131 rooms. Facilities: restaurant, pool. AE, D, DC, MC, V. $*

Grove Park Inn Resort. This is worth seeing, even if you can't splurge to stay here. Built from local stone in 1913, it includes a massive Great Hall lobby. Rock in a wooden chair on the veranda and view the Blue Ridge mountains. A crafts museum, mountain crafts, and an antique-car museum are next door. *290 Macon Ave., Asheville 28804, tel. 704/252–2711 or 800/ 438–5800, fax 704/253–7053. 510 rooms. Facilities: 4 restaurants, indoor and outdoor pools, golf, health club. AE, D, DC, MC, V. $$$*

The Log Cabin Motor Court. In this collection of rustic log cabins, some have fireplaces and living rooms and about half have kitchens. There's a two-night minimum stay. *330 Weaverville Hwy., Asheville 28804, tel. 704/645–6546. 18 cabins. Facilities: pool, coin laundry, playground. D, MC, V. $*

Where to Eat

Biltmore Dairy Bar. Famous for its ice cream (from the Biltmore herd), this sandwich-and-soup restaurant dates from 1957. Don't miss the homemade tomato soup, tipsy spiced fruit, and Dagwood sandwich. *115 Hendersonville Rd., 2 blocks from Biltmore estate, Asheville, tel. 704/274–2370. AE, MC, V. $*

Lil Pigs BBQ. Baseball and other sports memorabilia and antiques fill the walls. The delectable hickory-smoked pork is cooked for 14 hours. Half-orders are available. *1916 Hendersonville Rd., 2½ mi south of town, Asheville, tel. 704/684–0500. No credit cards. $*

Picadilly Cafeteria. This is part of a fine southern cafeteria chain. Kids can pick vegetables they like (even carrot soufflé), and there's good pink lemonade and homemade pie. *Asheville Mall, Asheville, tel. 704/298–5048. AE, D, DC, MC, V. $*

Entertainments

Pack Place Education, Arts and Science Center. Take a scavenger hunt inside the body, hear a transparent woman talk, and try hands-on health and science exhibits. A Cultural Center celebrates African-American life. The center also has art, gem, and mineral museums. *2 S. Pack Sq., Asheville, tel. 704/257–4500. Admission to all museums: $5.50 adults, $3.50 ages 4–15. Single passes available. Open Tues.–Sat. 10–5, Sun. 1–5.*

Old Presley Gem Mining. Travel 30 minutes from town and try your hand at finding a sapphire, a garnet, or quartz from a flume trough. Even preschoolers enjoy this. *240 Presley Mine Rd. Take I-40 west. Exit 33 to Newfound Rd., bear left on New Harmony Rd., left on Presley Mine Rd., Canton, tel. 704/648–6320. Admission: $5, plus 50¢ per bucket of ore. Open daily 9–6.*

Sites to See

Downtown Walking Tour. See the wedding-cake Art Deco **City Hall** and have a ginger beer at the 1891 **Morrison General Store.** The 1-hour, 45-minute tours leave from Pack Place. For a self-guided tour, the Preservation Society (tel. 704/251–9973) publishes an "Urban Trail" guide. *Pack Place, 2 S. Pack Sq., Asheville, tel. 704/255–1093. Admission: $7.50 adults, $3.50 ages 12 and under. Tour daily at 10 AM.*

Thomas Wolfe House. View the 29-room boardinghouse that the novelist's mother ran. It's "Dixieland," which Wolfe described in *Look Homeward, Angel*. Children may be amazed at how travelers lived and that, as a child, Wolfe had no room but roamed nightly to find an empty bed. *48 Spruce St., Asheville, tel. 704/253–8304. Admission: $1 adults, 50¢ students. Open Mon.–Sat. 9–5, Sun. 1–5.*

Biltmore Estate. Your children will know this as the mansion in the film *Richie Rich*. You may recall Peter Sellers strolling the grounds in *Being There*. This is not a movie set but the largest private home in the United States. It's George Washington Vanderbilt's American version of a European estate. As the grandson of "Commodore" Cornelius Vanderbilt, the fabulously wealthy railroad industrialist and investor, young Vanderbilt was able to retain the finest architects and devote extraordinary resources to the task. The result is a masterpiece. In 1888, Vanderbilt commissioned Richard Morris Hunt and landscape architect Frederick Law Olmsted to design his dream estate on 125,000 acres in the Blue Ridge Mountains. An army of stonecutters and artisans labored for six years before completing the 250-room mansion. Vanderbilt himself collected much of the art, furniture, and rugs, including paintings by Auguste Renoir and John Singer Sargent. The gardens and grounds are every bit as breathtaking and meticulously kept as the main house. Look particularly at the Winter Garden, the Tapestry Gallery, and the Walled Garden. Because our children had watched Macaulay Culkin pretend to be the world's wealthiest child in *Richie Rich*, they were fascinated as they went from room to room describing what Richie had done in each scene. Visitors can tour the estate on their own. This child-friendly practice made for a relaxed two-hour visit. See the gardens and the walking paths to the pond, stop for sherbet at the old stable, and tour the mansion. You can eat at the Stable Cafe and Deerpark restaurants. There's also a winery, with free tastings, and gift shops on the grounds. *Hwy. 25, One N. Pack Sq., just north of Exit 50 or 50B off I–40, Asheville 28801, tel. 704/255–1700 or 800/543–2961. Admission: $25.95 adults, $22.50 ages 10–15, under 10 free with paying adult. Open daily 9–6.*

Blue Ridge Parkway and Folk Art Center. The parkway entrance is 4 miles from Asheville. The center, operated by Southern Highland Handicraft Guild, has wooden toys, crafts, and demonstrations of music and dance. *Milepost 382; take I–40 to U.S. 70W, Exit 55 to parkway; follow parkway ½ mi north to Milepost 382; ½ mi north of U.S. 70; Asheville, tel. 704/298–7928. Admission: Donations. Open Apr.–Dec., daily 9–6; Jan.–Mar., daily 10–5.*

BLUEFIELD ORIOLES

League: Appalachian League • **Major League Affiliation:** Baltimore Orioles • **Class:** Rookie/Short Season • **Stadium:** Bowen Field • **Opened:** 1939/75 • **Capacity:** 3,000 • **Dimensions:** LF: 335, CF: 365, RF: 335 • **Surface:** grass • **Season:** mid-June–Aug.

STADIUM LOCATION: Stadium Dr., Bluefield, WV 24701

GETTING THERE: From Route 460, take West Gate Shopping Center exit (look for sign for Bluefield College). Turn right onto Leatherwood Lane. Take left at first stop light onto College Ave. and then first right onto Stadium Dr. into parking lot.

TICKET INFORMATION: Box 356, Bluefield, WV 24701, tel. 540/326–1326, fax 540/326–1318

PRICE RANGE: General admission $2.50 adults, $1 students, under 7 free

GAME TIME: Mon.–Sat. 7 PM, Sun. 6 PM; gates open for batting practice.

TIPS ON SEATING: Come early and get one of the few folding chairs or bring a cushion or your own folding chair. No reserved or box seats. All seats are general admission and close to action.

SEATING FOR PEOPLE WITH DISABILITIES: On walking concourse just inside dugouts on first and third

STADIUM FOOD: This is bargain baseball fare, where you can feed the whole family for under $10. The hot dogs are $1, and soft drinks and popcorn are 50¢. Pizza slices are only $1, as are nachos. Good hamburgers are $1.50. No alcohol is sold or allowed in Bowen Field.

SMOKING POLICY: Non-smoking section designated behind screen just on third-base side of home

PARKING: Ample free parking

VISITING TEAM HOTEL: Ramada Inn East River Mountain (3175 East Cumberland Rd., Bluefield, WV 24701, tel. 304/325–5421 or 800/228–2828)

TOURISM INFORMATION: West Virginia Tourist Information Center (I–77 and Rte. 460, Princeton, WV 24740, tel. 304/487–2214)

Bluefield: Bowen Field

This Appalachian League park is a mountain gem. Built in 1939, Bowen Field sits at the edge of a city park on West Virginia's southern border with Virginia. A ball hit to right field goes out of the state, as the state line crosses the field. A stream runs by, and a deep-green forest lies just beyond the outfield wall. This beautiful natural setting is marred only by the Marlboro Man cutout advertisement that stands near a scoreboard in center field.

Thankfully, not much has changed here in the last 50 years. This nostalgia trip back to the '40s is the perfect setting for the Appalachian League's rookie-level baseball. The park's high elevation can make for cool evenings, even in August. Bowen Field can accommodate 3,000 fans in wide concrete benches arranged in a horseshoe shape behind home plate under a rust-color roof. The seats let you see the almost-perfect arch of trees on a green hill beyond the close-in fences and give you a clear view of your wandering children. A wide wooden ramp makes the stadium accessible to wheelchairs and baby carriages, a rarity among the older minor-league stadiums.

No skyboxes here. In fact, there aren't even any box or reserved seats. Come early if you want to sit on one of the few metal folding chairs. Bring a seat cushion or your own folding chair if you want to be comfortable. Bowen Field is the best bargain in baseball, with $2.50 tickets, $1 for students, and kids six and under free. The policy under long-time general manager George Fanning has always been "If you don't have the money, we'll let you in for free." The night we were there, a local business bought all the tickets and everyone got in free.

The best treat for children is the easy access to the dugouts before and after the game. The gates were open hours before the game for batting practice. Our children wandered through the home-team dugout before the game, getting their baseballs signed by nearly every player and coach. Club security was a kindly older man who gently shooed the children back up to the stands as game time approached.

For decades, this ballpark has been run as George Fanning thought a ballpark should be run—it's open, friendly, and inexpensive. You won't find the legions of recent college grads in T-shirts with team logos running around the stadium with walkie-talkies imbedded in their ears. The small staff is virtually invisible, but the job gets done. When the third-base coach got a birthday cake the night we were there, the fans all sang "Happy Birthday." A bunch of veteran Orioles' fans sit in the "Railbirds" box on the third-base side.

George Fanning and his wife, Catherine, ran the show from a small office near the entrance and the concession stands on the third-base side. When we visited shortly before Mr. Fanning's death in 1995, he reminisced about the 1920s, when the parking lot was a dirt airstrip and the miners' league played baseball right there in front of a grandstand from the old fairgrounds.

Future Hall of Famers Eddie Murray and Cal Ripken, Jr., played here in the 1980s. The field is named for Joe Bowen, a coal-company executive who bought the land and donated it to the city of Bluefield. The Fannings told us the story of the early-morning call they got in the summer of 1973. Lightning had hit a transformer and set the stadium roof on fire. The wooden grandstand was quickly destroyed. For a season, fans brought their chairs and the team played without a grandstand. Then in 1975, the city of Bluefield rebuilt the grandstand with concrete and cinderblock.

A huge orange-and-black Baltimore Orioles logo with bird welcomes visitors to Bowen Field, a symbol of the longest-running affiliation in professional baseball. Local churches and civic clubs take turns at the refreshment stand. The cinderblock construction that looks tacky in the fancy new stadiums fits right in here. Bluefield doesn't promise anything very fancy—just a good, solid all-American night at a beautiful mountain ballpark.

Where to Stay

Visiting Team Hotel: Ramada Inn East River Mountain. This two-story brick hotel nestles into a mountain. Its rooms are larger than usual but are ordinary. You are away from road noise. *3175 E. Cumberland Rd., Bluefield 24701, tel. 304/325–5421 or 800/228–2828. 158 rooms. Facilities: restaurant, indoor pool, sauna, hot tub, billiards. AE, D, DC, MC, V. $*

Holiday Inn. This standard roadside motel sits along the town's commercial strip. Its rooms are conventional and clean. *Rte. 460, Exit 1 off I–77, Bluefield 24701, tel. 304/325–6170 or 800/465–4329, fax 304/325–6170. 120 rooms. Facilities: 2 restaurants, no-smoking rooms, pool, sauna. AE, D, DC, MC, V. $*

Where to Eat

Johnston's Inn and Restaurant. Here, in a small commercial crossroads amid the mountains, you can eat country ham, homemade bread, and rolls. It's known for its coconut cream and peanut butter pies. There is a children's menu. *Oakvale Rd., Princeton, WV, tel. 304/425–7591 or 800/424–7591. Exit 9 off I–77, west on Rte. 460 to Pipestem/Bluestone exit; inn is at first stop sign. AE, D, DC, MC, V. $*

Roma III. At this Italian family restaurant, the homemade lasagna and ravioli are especially good. There is homemade cannoli. A children's menu is available. *140 Brick St., Princeton, WV, tel. 304/487–2568 or 304/425–7662. AE, MC, V. $*

Entertainments

Pocahontas Exhibition Mine. A fascinating walk-through coal mine, it has tours conducted by men who once dug coal out of its 13-foot-high seam. The work was dirty and dangerous. This prodigious mine heated homes throughout America until it closed in 1955. Wear sweaters, as it's a cool 52° inside. An adjoining education room with artifacts and a movie carries an extra $1 fee. Afterward, walk the streets of this old mining town and view the Opera House and log schoolhouse. Bluefield's Craft Memorial Library (600 E. Commerce St., tel. 304/325–3943) contains the history of this mine in its Eastern Regional Coal Archives. *Pocahontas, VA, tel. 540/945–2134. Admission: $5 adults, $3 children. Open May–Oct., Mon.–Sat. 10–5, Sun. noon–6.*

The Science Center of West Virginia. Here hands-on exhibits on electricity, computers, and geology are housed in actual jail cells. Try playing basketball with Virtual Hoops. The center shares space in the city's original municipal building with an arts-and-crafts center that displays authentic mountain handwork. *500 Bland St., Bluefield, tel. 304/325–8855. Admission: $3. Open Tues. and Thurs.–Sat. 9:30–5.*

Unusual Shopping

West Virginia Tourist Information Center. One of four centers along I–77 between Princeton and Charleston, it contains "West Virginia Made" food, crafts, art, unusual jewelry, and books. *I–77 N and Rte. 460, Princeton exit, Princeton, tel. 304/487–2214.*

LYNCHBURG HILLCATS

League: Carolina League • **Major League Affiliation:** Pittsburgh Pirates • **Stadium:** City Stadium • **Opened:** 1940 • **Capacity:** 4,000 • **Dimensions:** LF: 325, CF: 390, RF: 325 • **Surface:** grass • **Season:** Apr.–Labor Day

STADIUM LOCATION: City Stadium, Fort Ave. and Wythe Rd., Lynchburg, VA 24501

TEAM WEB SITE: http://www.cl.org/baseball/lynchburg

GETTING THERE: U.S. 29 South to exit 4, City Stadium or U.S. 29 North to exit 6, City Stadium. Follow signs to stadium.

TICKET INFORMATION: Box 10213, Lynchburg, VA 24506, tel. 804/528–1144 or 804/846–0768

PRICE RANGE: Reserved box seats $5; general admission $4 adults, $3 senior citizens and students

GAME TIME: Mon.–Sat. 7:05 PM, Sun. 2:05 PM (Apr.–June), 6:05 PM (July–Sept.)

TIPS ON SEATING: Best view of Blue Ridge Mountains is from first-base visitors' side. Stadium is windy, so bring jackets no matter how warm the day.

SEATING FOR PEOPLE WITH DISABILITIES: Special ramp for wheelchairs at right field entrance gate (Wythe Rd. entrance).

STADIUM FOOD: A grill on parking lot level mimics a neighborhood picnic—great burgers with tubs of tomatoes, lettuce, pickles, and onions. It's at the stadium entrance—watch for foul balls. Vendors carry newsboy bags, selling Cracker Jack and peanuts. At concession stands at top of seating, you can get bar-becued chicken and pork sandwiches, corn dogs, french fries, nachos, foot-long hotdogs, a "Big Cat" quarter-pound hot dog, and pizza.

SMOKING POLICY: No smoking or alcohol in section 5.

PARKING: Free

VISTING TEAM HOTEL: Best Western (2815 Candlers Mountain Rd., Lynchburg, VA 24502, tel. 804/237–2986 or 800/528–1234)

TOURISM INFORMATION: Visitors Center (216 12th St., Lynchburg, VA 24504, tel. 804/847–1811 or 800/732–5821)

Lynchburg: City Stadium

Baseball has deep roots in Lynchburg. Professionals played ball here as far back as 1886. In 1895, the Lynchburg Tobacconists finished in second place in the 150-game Virginia State League. Since 1966, Lynchburg has played in the Carolina League. The Lynchburg Mets won the 1983 league title behind 18-year-old Dwight Gooden's 19 wins and 300 strikeouts. In 1995 the team became affiliated with the Pittsburgh Pirates and acquired a new name—the Hill-cats—and a sporty new logo.

Lynchburg's historic City Stadium reflects the city's long baseball tradition. With the exception of a gorgeous new coat of Camden Yards dark green paint, City Stadium must look much like it did when it opened in 1940. We asked Hillcats general manager Paul Sunwall how he could maintain this wonderful 1940s feel in the face of pressure from professional baseball to upgrade facilities. He pointed to the new foul poles and the fact that the chicken wire had been replaced

behind home plate. The appeal, in fact, is that so little has changed. The city needs to add a few lights, improve access for people with disabilities, spruce up the bathrooms, and otherwise leave this '40s gem as is.

With a general admission ticket, you'll be right near the action. There are only 208 reserved seats in this cozy, scenic 4,000-capacity stadium. In this, "the Hill City," the stadium has the Blue Ridge Mountains as its backdrop. The best view of the Blue Ridge is from the visitors' first-base side. The ubiquitous Marlboro Man appears to be looking incredulously at a STRIKE OUT TOBACCO USE! sign among the ads for local merchants stacked two deep along the outfield wall.

Most of the concession stands are at the top of the seating, so you can get your basic food and drinks without missing any of the action. The big exceptions are the excellent grill on the parking-lot level near the stadium entrance, the souvenir stand, and the bathrooms.

Minor-league baseball provides a friendly, relaxed ambience all too absent in the high-stakes major leagues. A Hillcat player talked with five-year-old Hugh for 10 minutes before the game and gave him a ball. We saw a fast-paced, error-free game played in just over two hours. A Hillcat player hit a home run, but no one collected the $500 for hitting a ball through the basketball net in right-center field.

With children it's easier to drive than to walk Lynchburg's seven hills. Tour its historic cemetery, city market, and former warehouse district before the game. It's worth getting the useful Visitor's Bureau (216 12th St.; open daily 9–5) brochures on the cemetery and warehouse district.

Where to Stay

Lynchburg Mansion Inn. Call first to stay on historic Garland Hill in an unforgettable B&B that accepts children. The rooms, all with private baths, are large and beautifully decorated. *405 Madison St., Lynchburg 24504, tel. 804/528–5400 or 800/352–1199. 5 rooms. Facilities: outdoor spa pool, solarium. AE, DC, MC, V. $$*

Federal Crest Inn. This B&B accepts children, if you call first. In the mansion district, it has bedrooms with private baths appointed with comfy terry robes. *1101 Federal St., Lynchburg 24504, tel. 804/845–6155 or 800/818–6155. 5 rooms. Facilities: soda shop, meeting room. AE, D, MC, V. $$*

Days Inn. At one of the chain's nicest properties you get free breakfast and a free game of bowling at the adjacent alley. Rooms are freshly decorated. The hotel is 15 minutes from the ballpark and next to the River Ridge Mall. Children under 18 stay free. *3320 Chandlers Mountain Rd., Exit 8B off I–29, Lynchburg 23502, tel. 804/847–8655 or 800/329–7466, fax 804/846–3297. 131 rooms. Facilities: restaurant, pool, playground. AE, D, DC, MC, V. $$*

Where to Eat

Spanky's. Crammed with roadside art, neon signs, and circus memorabilia, this visual fun fest is a rollicking place to eat. There's an inexpensive kid's menu (49¢ macaroni and cheese!), a separate soda fountain, and a huge menu of sandwiches and salads. *908 Main St., Lynchburg, tel. 804/846–4146. AE, MC, V. $*

Billy Joe's Ice Cream Parlor. The Wurlitzer here is filled with records from the '50s and '60s. Sandwiches, pizza, pita, burgers, and ice cream creations are on the menu. *4915 Fort Ave., Lynchburg, tel. 804/237–7825. AE, D, MC, V. $*

Pearson's Rexall Drugs. There's a working soda fountain here. Let your children see what real drugstores from the 1950s contained. *2259 Langhorne Rd., Lynchburg, tel. 804/847–4431. No credit cards. $*

Entertainments

City Pest House Medical Museum and Cemetery. Walking among the 2,071 Confederate headstones brought history alive for our children. Look inside the tiny Pest House, a re-creation of the miserable quarters given to those suffering from malaria and smallpox. You can also see the former office of Quaker doctor John Jay Terrell, who worked with these shunned patients. The cemetery has artistic ironwork and Old Garden roses throughout. *4th and Taylor Sts., Lynchburg. Admission: Free. Open sunrise–sunset.*

Community Market. Buy flowers, cheap and beautiful produce, and wooden toys. A few stalls are open during the week, but the market comes alive on Friday and Saturday, plus a few summer Sundays. *Main and 12th Sts., Lynchburg, tel. 804/847–1499. Open Mar.–Dec., Mon.–Sat. 7–2.*

Sites to See

Poplar Forest. Fifteen minutes west of Lynchburg is the elegant, octagonal home Thomas Jefferson designed as a country retreat in 1806. It's being restored, and kids like viewing the rats' nests as archivists explain the clues the rodents hid. *Rte. 661; take U.S. 221 to Rte. 811, left on Rte. 661 to front gate; Forest 24551, tel. 804/525–0419. Admission: $5 adults, $1 ages 2–18. Open Wed.–Sun. 10–3:45.*

Natural Bridge. The James River has carved 36,000 tons of limestone into a bridgelike wonder. The view is free; a nightly light show and daily cavern tours are extra. To get here, follow mansion-lined Rivermont Avenue (Rte. 501) out of Lynchburg and make a left onto Route 130. *Rte. 130, Natural Bridge, tel. 800/533–1410.*

Shenandoah Valley League

If you like the small-town, family atmosphere of minor-league baseball, you'll be taken by the endearing Shenandoah Valley League. This summer college league is even more intimate and genuine than the entry-level rookie leagues of professional baseball. Here, many of the nation's top college baseball players move in with local families, get jobs, and play baseball almost every night in June and July. The league motto is "Gateway to the Major Leagues," and there may be a major-league scout, holding a speed gun and a stat book, in the audience when you visit. The Valley League has been an officially NCAA-sanctioned league for 35 seasons.

America's community spirit is alive and well in the Valley League. The players rake, line, and water the fields before the games. Club officers walk through the crowd selling 50–50 raffle tickets (the winner splits the proceeds with the team). It's a county-fair atmosphere, complete with volunteers operating the concession stands. There aren't any big shots here. When a larger-than-expected crowd shows up on a steamy summer night and the ice cream starts to melt, the owner goes out for the ice. When a player's family and girlfriend are in town for a game, they are announced on the public address system, and the several hundred loyal fans in attendance give them a warm cheer of welcome. The players from the opposing teams still shake hands after the game, just like in Little League.

Don't come here looking for Camden Yards. In the Valley League, you will find the wonderful, scruffy little ballparks that professional baseball has tried hard to eliminate. For three bucks, you can sit right next to the baseball action. A program costs a quarter. Hot dogs are about a dollar, and the parking is free. In our trips through the minor leagues, we thought we had seen every imaginable contest until we heard of "Best Decorated Lawn Chair Night," held each year at Waynesboro's Kate Collins Field.

We enjoyed visiting all six teams in the Valley League. The league can be reached through its president, Dave Biery (tel. 540/885–8901).

The **Front Royal Cardinals** play in Bing Crosby Stadium, named for the crooner who contributed $1,000 toward building the ballpark in 1948 when he visited as grand marshal of the Apple Blossom Festival. The cinderblock wall in center field is only 330 feet from home plate.

The **Harrisonburg Turks** play in Veterans' Memorial Stadium, an aging, ex–minor-league park. Why Turks? Harrisonburg is the self-described Turkey Capital of the World.

The home of the **New Market Rebels** is Rebel Park, a small ballpark at the old high school, with a stunning mountain view beyond the outfield fences. The crowd sings "Take Me Out to the Ballgame" a cappella in the seventh inning unless an accordion-player fan shows up. Most of the park's fences are farm fences.

The **Staunton Braves** play in John Moxie Stadium, adjacent to the magnificent Gypsy Hill city park. The ballpark has an unusual blue grandstand with a mansard roof. If a player hits a ball through the o in the Coke ad in center field, some lucky fan wins $3,000.

The **Waynesboro Generals** play in Kate Collins Field, at Kate Collins Elementary School, which has seats for only about 300 fans in the aluminum bleachers. Bring a lawn chair or a blanket. There's plenty of room on the hill that runs along the first-base side.

The **Winchester Royals** play in Bridgeforth Field, perhaps the best baseball facility in the league. The ballpark sits on a hill above a city park full of recreational activities.

The Shenandoah Valley is a gorgeous region of trails, rivers, and historic small towns in western Virginia, lying between the Blue Ridge Mountains to the east and the Allegheny Mountains to the west. It's a perfect place for hiking, camping, fishing, and antiquing. The 105-mile Skyline Drive runs the entire length of the Shenandoah National Park (tel. 540/999–3500). We especially like Luray Caverns (tel. 540/743–6551), Staunton's Woodrow Wilson Birthplace and Museum (tel. 540/885–0897) and Museum of American Frontier Culture (tel. 540/332–7850), and New Market's Civil War Battlefield Historical Park (tel. 540/740–3101). For travel information, contact the Shenandoah Valley Travel Association (tel. 540/740–3132).

THE OPRY AND ELVIS
CHATTANOOGA, NASHVILLE, MEMPHIS

3

Tennessee is blessed with three exciting cities in which to watch baseball, in easy proximity for a three-game weekend. Historic Engel stadium in Chattanooga is the best-restored minor-league park in America, with its handsome brick walls, wide concourse, and covered grandstand. A smoke-puffing Chattanooga Choo-Choo emerges from behind the scoreboard for home runs and game wins. The lively downtown includes a hotel at the renovated Beaux Arts Terminal Station where you can sleep in a train car, interesting aquatic ecosystems at the freshwater Tennessee Aquarium, and a hundred-year-old incline railroad that speeds up Lookout Mountain.

Northwest 120 miles, on Interstate 24, is Nashville, America's country music citadel. Greer Stadium has the best scoreboard in baseball—a 60-foot-long guitar. Drive 20 minutes west of town to eat in the legendary Loveless Cafe and plan a non-baseball night to take in the timeless and engaging Grand Ole Opry. During the day, you can spend several hours at the Country Music Hall of Fame.

Drive west for 206 miles to Memphis on Interstate 40 for an eye-popping visit to Elvis's mansion, a staggering number of remarkable down-home restaurants, and a game at Tim McCarver Stadium. The plain baseball park is in the fairgrounds, within sight of the Libertyland amusement park, where Elvis's favorite, the Zippin Pippin wood roller coaster, still runs. You'll need to spend at least two days to do justice to the many attractions here—the gripping National Civil Rights Museum, the Beale Street Historic District, the Mud Island theme park, and the Pink Palace children's museum.

CHATTANOOGA LOOKOUTS

League: Southern League • **Major League Affiliation:** Cincinnati Reds • **Class:** AA • **Stadium:** Historic Engel Stadium • **Opened:** 1930 • **Capacity:** 7,500 • **Dimensions:** LF: 325, CF: 471, RF: 318 • **Surface:** grass • **Season:** Apr.–Labor Day

STADIUM LOCATION: 1130 E. 3rd St., Chattanooga, TN 37403

GETTING THERE: From I–24, I–27 north to 4th St. exit; right on 4th, 1½ mi to stadium.

TICKET INFORMATION: Box 11002, Chattanooga, TN 37401, tel. 423/267–2208, fax 423/267–4258

PRICE RANGE: Dugout box seats $7 adult, $5 children and senior citizens; box seats $6 adult, $4 children and senior citizens; reserved $5 adult, $3 children and senior citizens; general admission $4 adult, $2 children and senior citizens

GAME TIME: Mon.–Tues. and Thurs.–Sat. 7 PM, Wed. 12:30 PM, Sun. 2 PM; gates open 1½ hrs before game.

TIPS ON SEATING: 12 rows of box seats; large roof over grandstand held up by poles that can obstruct view. To be close to action, buy box seat. General admission seats fine if you avoid poles.

SEATING FOR PEOPLE WITH DISABILITIES: Space behind screen and non-smoking box seats in section D on first-base side

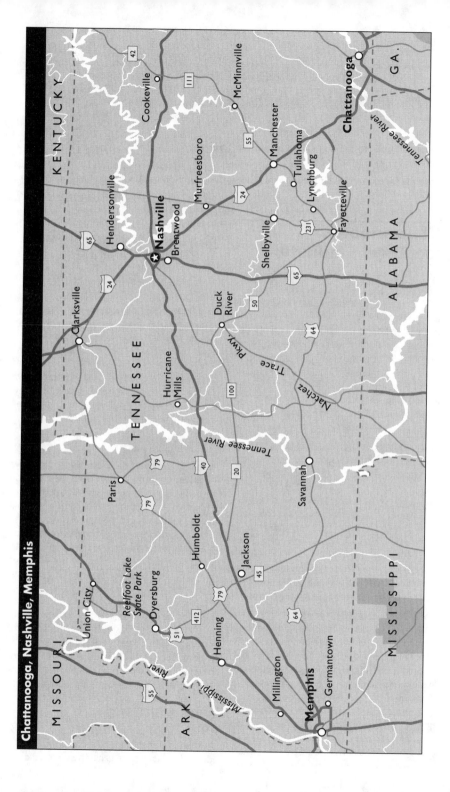

Chattanooga, Nashville, Memphis

STADIUM FOOD: Popsicles and slush puppies cost $1–1.50. The family-sized popcorn is a bargain at $2, as are whole pizzas for $6.50. Very good bratwursts are only $3 in the main concourse.

PARKING: Ample parking, $2.

SMOKING POLICY: Smoking prohibited in section D of box seats behind screen on first-base side and in section A in general admission down first-base line.

VISITING TEAM HOTEL: Days Inn Convention Centre (1400 Mac Smith Rd., East Ridge, TN 37412, tel. 423/894–0440 or 800/325–2525)

TOURISM INFORMATION: Chattanooga Visitors Center (2 Broad St., Chattanooga, TN 37402, tel. 423/266–7070)

Chattanooga: Joe Engel Stadium

We can't figure out why the sign out front calls this HISTORIC ENGEL STADIUM. No one coming to a Chattanooga Lookouts game here would have the slightest doubt that this is the real thing. With $2 million of city and county money and the leadership of former owner Richard Holtzman, this fabulous stadium was restored to its 1930 look for the 1990 season. The historic brick walls remain, along with the green awnings. The wide concourse under the grandstand is beautifully restored with antique street lights and black wrought-iron frame design.

The grandstand roof goes out as far as first and third bases. The mechanical fans hanging from the grandstand roof evoke the 1930s more than they cool off those in attendance. Under the roof are wonderful old brownish-red straight-back wooden chairs that make a fearsome noise when the crowd bangs them up and down to try to get or keep a Lookouts rally going. There are 1,604 dark green box seats in the 7,500-capacity stadium. Two small wooden bleachers down the third-base line and past the outfield fence in left round out the seating.

The outfield is particularly interesting in Engel Stadium. The older stadiums had high concrete walls far from home plate. When the home run became popular, wooden fences were built within the concrete walls. Center field in the original Engel Stadium was 471 feet from home plate. Only future Hall of Famer Harmon Killebrew cleared the wall at the 471-foot mark. The cinderblock wall still stands, now painted with ads on a tan background. The field inclines 5 feet in center to a longstanding Coca-Cola sign, creating

a porch planted with flowers that spell out LOOK-OUTS. The porch was in play until 1987, when a chain-link fence was installed. In 1995, the new owner of the Lookouts, Frank Burke, had the fence taken out, adding excitement and authenticity to the Engel Stadium experience.

Chattanooga has one of the most famous logos in minor-league baseball—a pair of big eyes looking out of a large letter C. Unfortunately, Lookout Mountain—the site of a famous Civil War battle and the landmark for which the Lookouts are named—sits behind home plate and cannot be seen from the stands. The view beyond the outfield wall is uninspiring—dominated by a bridge over railroad tracks.

We had been impressed with the stadiums that set off fireworks when the home team hits a home run or wins the game. But nothing we have seen compares with Frank Burke's creation here. By luck, we came the first day the fireworks gadgetry was installed, and the very first Lookout up to bat hit a home run. A huge, colorful Chattanooga Choo-Choo emerges from behind the left-field scoreboard, puffing smoke and blaring its horn. Burke got the idea from his father, Daniel Burke, whose Portland Sea Dogs have an exploding lighthouse. Burke also set up a barbershop at the top of the grandstand behind home plate for the novelty of fans' getting their hair cut in a stadium. The Trash Monster has scores of kids eager to help keep Engel Stadium clean. The mascot, Looie the Lookout, is a red creature resembling a tomato. And in a pen behind center field, two camels—Larry and Lumpy—wear Lookout helmets and watch the games. Fans bring stuffed camels to the park in their honor.

Holtzman and Burke deserve credit for their leadership in restoring and enhancing Engel Stadium. But the ultimate genius here is celebrated in several plaques at the stadium entrance. In 1929, Clark Griffith, the future Hall of Fame owner of the Washington Senators, sent his top baseball scout, Joe Engel, to take over the Chattanooga franchise he had recently acquired. Engel's first job was to oversee the construction of a new ballpark. We ran into Clark Griffith's son Calvin at a game in Helena, Montana, and the first question he asked was "Are you going to Engel Stadium?" He assured us, "Bill Veeck got all his ideas from Joe Engel." Engel was the P. T. Barnum of Baseball.

A sample of Joe Engel stories: On May 1, 1936, Engel drew more than 24,000 fans by raffling off a $10,000 house. It was standing room only in the outfield. Engel had another stunt—freezing baseballs before the game, which cut down their loft. This was not to protect the fans but to make sure he didn't lose too many balls. On opening day 1938, the former vaudevillian Engel staged a wild-elephant hunt. Only after the shots were fired did the fans realize that each of the falling elephants was two men inside an animal suit. He once traded shortstop Johnny Jones for a 25-pound turkey. He also fed thousands of people free meals at Engel Stadium during the Depression.

Where to Stay

Visiting Team Hotel: Days Inn Convention Centre. This two-story motel at an Interstate exchange on the Georgia–Tennessee line is 6 miles from downtown Chattanooga. The rooms are small. The motel offers lodging packages that include admission to the Tennessee Aquarium. *1400 Mack Smith Rd., Exit 1 off I–75 S, East Ridge 37412, tel. 423/894–0440 or 800/325–2525, fax 423/899–5819. 210 rooms. Facilities: restaurant, pool. AE, D, DC, MC, V. $*

Chattanooga Choo-Choo Holiday Inn. Created in Chattanooga's Beaux Arts Terminal Station, the inn lets you sleep in a sleeping-parlor car or in a regular room. All have been newly renovated. A model-train museum is part of the reuse of this 1909 train station. The hotel offers discount tickets to area attractions and a free downtown shuttle to the aquarium. *1400 Market St., Chattanooga 37402, tel. 423/266–5000 or 800/465–4329, fax 423/265–4635. 315 rooms, 48 parlor-car rooms. Facilities: 3 restaurants,* indoor and outdoor pools, waterslide, hot tubs, tennis courts. AE, D, DC, MC, V. $$

Radisson Read House Hotel and Suites. This historic downtown hotel is on the National Register of Historic Places. Most of the rooms in the 10-floor hotel are suites with dining alcoves and sitting rooms. Parking is $4 per day. The "AAA Family Adventure" rate includes two tickets to the Tennessee Aquarium. *827 Broad St., Chattanooga 37402, tel. 423/266–4121 or 800/333–3333, fax 423/267–6447. 238 rooms. Facilities: restaurant, pool, wading pool. AE, D, DC, MC, V. $$*

Where to Eat

Big River Grille & Brewing Works. At this boisterous microbrewery you can eat family meals of shepherd's pie, salads, soups, and fish. Vegetables are good. It serves homemade root beer, ginger ale, and cream soda, as well as alcoholic brews. *222 Broad St., Chattanooga, tel. 423/267–2739. AE, D, DC, MC, V. $*

Silver Diner. In a real dining car parked in the former train station, you can order pizza, baked potatoes, and nachos. The adjacent **Dinner in the Diner** is for more formal meals, dinner only. *Chattanooga Choo-Choo Holiday Inn, 1400 Market St., Chattanooga, tel. 423/266–5000. AE, MC, V. $, $$*

Mt. Vernon Restaurant. At this old-fashioned family restaurant, in business for 40 years, you'll find southern cooking with homemade pies. A children's menu is available. *3509 S. Broad St., Chattanooga, tel. 423/266–6591. MC, V. $*

Entertainments

Tennessee Aquarium. An imaginative, downtown fresh-water aquarium, it has child-height tanks for close encounters with gigantic catfish, piranhas, alligators, sharks, and stingrays. It's arranged by ecosystem, with two forests, a 60-foot canyon, and more than 7,000 animals. *1 Broad St., Chattanooga, tel. 800/262–0695. Admission: $9.75 adults, $5.25 ages 3–12. Open 10–6; extended hrs weekends Memorial Day–Labor Day.*

Creative Discovery Children's Museum. Here you'll find colorful, inviting exhibits, including an inventor's workshop, an artist's studio, and a musician's workshop. Kids can experiment with water, color, light, and motion. There's a preschoolers' section and an optics tower. *321 Chestnut St., Chattanooga, tel. 423/756–2738. Admission: $7.50 adults, $4.75 ages 2–12. Open May–Aug., daily 10–5; Sept.–Apr., Tues.–Sun. 10–5.*

Lookout Mountain Incline Railway No. 2. On November 24, 1863, Union troops led by General U. S. Grant crossed Lookout Creek and began an advance up the steep slope of Lookout Mountain. Amazingly—with the help of midday clouds that covered the summit and confused the Confederates—Grant took the mountain in what has come to be called the Battle Above the Clouds. Today, we can gain this extraordinary view of the Tennessee River valley a lot easier than Grant and his men. Incline No. 2 takes you a mile up Lookout Mountain, 2,200 feet above the valley, in about 10 minutes. Chattanooga became a major trading center in 1850 when the first railroad opened from Atlanta to Chattanooga. As other rail lines opened, the Lookout Mountain area became popular with Southerners wanting to escape the hot summer. In the 1880s, an incline and a broad-gauge railroad were constructed. The present Incline No. 2 opened for business in 1895 and has a perfect safety record. It is the steepest passenger incline in the world. *St. Elmo Ave., Chattanooga, tel. 423/821–4224. Admission: $6 adults, $3 ages 3–12. Open Memorial Day–Labor Day, daily 8:30 AM–9 PM; Labor Day–Memorial Day, daily 9–6.*

Sites to See

Chattanooga Regional History Museum. A woman striking out Babe Ruth? No way, you say—you won't believe it unless you see it. The ever-enterprising Joe Engel signed 17-year-old Jackie Mitchell to a contract for the Southern Association's 1931 season. When the Yankees came through Chattanooga for an exhibition game, the left-handed Mitchell came in to the game in relief and struck out Ruth and Lou Gehrig. When Judge "Kenesaw Mountain" Landis, the commissioner of baseball, learned what Engel had done, he voided Mitchell's contract, blocking women from professional baseball. The wonderful Jackie Mitchell video is one of several historic videos in the museum's permanent collection, accessible at the touch of the screen. It lasts only about two minutes, and it's worth watching several times. The video shows all three of Ruth's strikes, with Ruth throwing the bat down in disgust after the third strike. Our eight-year-old left-handed daughter, Emily, cheered every pitch. The Chattanooga Regional History Museum displays a replica locker full of baseball memorabilia going back to 1895 in its permanent collection. The museum also contains a Chattanooga Sports Hall of Fame. *400 Chestnut St., 1½ mi from Historic Engel Stadium, just off I–27, Chattanooga 37402, tel. 423/265–3247. Admission: $2.50 adults, $1.75 senior citizens, $1.50 ages 5 and up. Open weekdays 10–4:30, weekends 11–4:30.*

Chattanooga Visitors Center. Start your day at this friendly one-stop shop with the information you need to plan your visit. The visitor center is next to the Tennessee Aquarium. A 22-minute slide presentation provides basic perspective on Chattanooga for a small fee. *2 Broad St., Chattanooga 37402, tel. 423/266–7070. Open daily 8:30–5:30.*

NASHVILLE SOUNDS

League: American Association • **Major League Affiliation:** Chicago White Sox • **Class:** AAA • **Stadium:** Herschel Greer Stadium • **Opened:** 1978 • **Capacity:** 17,000 • **Dimensions:** LF: 327, CF: 400, RF: 327 • **Surface:** grass • **Season:** Apr.–Labor Day

STADIUM LOCATION: 534 Chestnut St., Nashville, TN 37203

GETTING THERE: From downtown, I–65 south to Wedgewood exit. Go west one block, right on 8th Ave. At next light, right on Chestnut.

TICKET INFORMATION: Box 23290, Nashville, TN 37202, tel. 615/242–4371, fax 615/256–5684

PRICE RANGE: Box seats $7; reserved grandstand $5; left field corner $4; general admission $3 adults, $2 children

GAME TIME: Mon.–Sat. 7:15 PM, Sun. 2:05 (Apr.–May), Mon.–Sat. 7:15 PM (June–Sept.); gates open 1 hr before game.

TIPS ON SEATING: General admission seats not very good. Buy reserved seats, even though they are relatively expensive for minor leagues. $2 children's general admission seats are recommended if your children tend to roam about.

SEATING FOR PEOPLE WITH DISABILITIES: Space for 20 people in wheelchairs in box seat section L behind home plate. General admission is charged. Companions can pay for box seat in front of this section or general admission behind it.

STADIUM FOOD: The food is inexpensive, but not very good. The best bets are the $2 root beer floats and $1.50 hard dip ice cream or frozen yogurt. Avoid the chicken sandwich. The hamburgers and cheeseburgers ($2.50) are slightly better bets. Spring water is $1. The **Stadium Club Restaurant** above the press box behind home plate is open to the public. It's worth the extra dollars to eat here.

SMOKING POLICY: Section QQ, small box seat section in back of grandstand on third-base side of home, is only family section with no smoking and no alcohol.

PARKING: Ample parking, $2.

VISITING TEAM HOTEL: Ramada Inn–Governor's House (737 Harding Place, Nashville, TN 37211, tel. 615/834–5000 or 800/228–2828)

TOURISM INFORMATION: Nashville Convention & Visitors Bureau (161 4th Ave. N, Nashville, TN 37219, tel. 615/259–4700 or 800/950–4418)

Nashville: Greer Stadium

There is one reason to go to Nashville's Herschel Greer Stadium: the scoreboard. It would be the best scoreboard in baseball if it weren't, as our daughter, Emily, pointed out, dominated by eight beer ads. It is shaped like a guitar—not just any guitar, a 60-foot-long guitar that is 53 feet high. A 35,825-pound guitar. A guitar that explodes with fireworks when the home team hits a home run or wins a game. A half-million-dollar guitar. The inning-by-inning score is kept horizontally along the neck of the guitar. Balls, strikes, and outs are registered vertically on the peghead. There are two electronic scoreboards on the body of the guitar. It is spectacular.

Once you stop gawking at the scoreboard, this is a pretty mediocre ballpark. Built in 1978 on land of the metropolitan park district, the stadium was entirely financed with private funds. It is clean and constantly upgraded. But it is a 1970s stadium—too big, too heavy, too dull. With seats for 17,000 fans, it is the wrong scale for minor-league baseball, lacking the intimacy of the best old and new ballparks. Most of the seats are comfortable—new, blue, and plastic. All cost top dollar; there aren't any good bargain seats here. The uncovered grandstand forms an L shape with the long end down the first-base line. There are aluminum bleacher seats down the third-base line and beyond the wall in right field.

The entryway is colorful and inviting, with pennants flying, although it lacks the grand architectural statement of the newer stadiums or the classic look of the old-time ballparks. The team's logo—a baseball player swinging a guitar for a bat—is among our favorites. The logo enhances both the entrance and the scoreboard. There is a fine souvenir shop at the entrance. Inside, a formidable structure above the seating area contains 18 large skyboxes, the press box, and the Stadium Club Restaurant. Unfortunately, from the entrance to the stadium, this complex looks like the back of a run-down 1960s motel.

Champ, the mascot, is a friendly green dinosaur who signs autographs at the end of the game. The team is named the Sounds and the music here is fine, but not as exceptional as you would expect in the capital of country music. There is a barbershop at the top of the seating area behind home plate, making Nashville one of several stadiums where fans can get haircuts. The concourse is large and serviceable, with large white baseballs honoring former players and coaches along the walls. This includes future Hall of Famer Don Mattingly, who hit .316 for Nashville in 1981. The Nashville Sounds are famous as the team Michael Jordan would have played for in 1995 had he not resumed his career as one of the greatest professional basketball players in history.

There isn't any doubt who is in charge here. The man you see working the crowd with the smoothness and skill of a master politician is not a candidate for mayor working the crowd. That's Larry Schmittou, president of the Sounds, methodically working the ballpark section by section, taking as much time with a five-year-old as a U.S. senator's spouse. Schmittou, a former baseball coach at Vanderbilt University, put together the ownership group that built the stadium and brought professional baseball back to Nashville in 1978 after a 15-year absence. Herschel Greer, a local business leader who had been active in the Nashville Vols in the early 1960s, was part of Schmittou's group, and the stadium is named for him.

Greer Stadium was built in parkland south of the city. Fort Negley, a key point in the defense of the city in the Battle of Nashville on December 15, 1864, once stood just behind where the stadium was built. Railroad tracks run behind the stadium's left-field wall.

Other Baseball Sites

There is a state-government parking lot just north of the capitol where Nashville's most historic ballpark once stood. First used for baseball in 1876, the field was in the old Sulphur Spring Bottom. The famed *Tennessean* sports writer Grantland Rice named it Sulphur Dell. The ballplayers sometimes called it Suffer Hell, for the fumes from the nearby city dump. Only 440 yards from the Cumberland River, the ballpark flooded in the spring. Philip Lowry, the author of *Green Cathedrals*, said, "Sulphur Dell had the greatest and craziest right field in history." The incline in right field rose 25 feet, sometimes at an angle as steep as 45 degrees. The most successful outfielder in handling this short right-field porch was Doc Wiseman, who got the nickname the Goat for his heroic running sidehill catches.

Wilson Park, in the Trimble Bottom section of South Nashville, was named for the president of the Negro National League. Roy Campanella played here before becoming a Dodger and, later, a Hall of Famer. After the field's stint with baseball, a dog-racing track stood here and later the Paradise Ballroom, which hosted Cab Calloway, Lionel Hampton, and Sarah Vaughn.

Where to Stay

Quality Inn–Hall of Fame. This convenient downtown hotel is within walking distance of the Country Music Hall of Fame. Some rooms in the five-story property have extra sofa beds. *1407 Division St., Nashville 37203, tel. 615/242–1631 or 800/424–6423, fax 615/244–9519. 103 rooms. Facilities: pool, free parking. AE, D, DC, MC, V. $*

Union Station Hotel. In the restored downtown train station, this seven-story stone hotel has a spectacular lobby. Rooms range from standard to deluxe. Parking is $8 daily. *1001 Broadway, Nashville 37203, tel. 615/726–1001 or 800/331–2123, fax 615/248–3554. 124 rooms. Facilities: 3 restaurants. AE, D, DC, MC, V. $$*

Wilson Inn. In this five-story chain hotel, many rooms have kitchens. There are some junior and regular suites. The hotel is 3 miles from Opryland. A Continental breakfast is served in the lobby. Free popcorn and punch are offered all day. Kids up to 18 stay free. *600 Ermac Dr., Elm Hill Pike exit from Briley Pkwy., Nashville 37214, tel. 615/889–4466 or 800/333–9457, fax 615/889–0484. 110 rooms. AE, D, MC, V. $*

Where to Eat

Elliston Soda Shop. At this small, 1939-era fountain restaurant, you'll find good soups, fried oysters, orangeade, pie, and 14 kinds of vegetables. *2111 Elliston Pl., Nashville, tel. 615/327–1090. No credit cards. $*

Loveless Cafe. One of America's best country meals is served in this former motel dining room, which is 20 minutes west of town. It's a genuine café, with oilcloths, metal chairs, and generous portions. The biscuits and preserves are to sing about. Try the spectacular fried chicken and country ham. You can even buy blackberry jam to take home. *8400 Hwy. 100, Nashville, tel. 615/646–9700. AE, MC, V. $*

Belle Meade Buffet. In a ritzy neighborhood of megamansions, 7 miles from the ballpark, you'll find a grand Southern cafeteria in a shopping center. Established in 1961, it attracts all ages and incomes. There are miniplates for children, as well as catfish, okra, mackerel, and brownie pie. *Harding Rd., Belle Meade Plaza, Nashville, tel. 615/298–5571. MC, V. $*

Entertainments

Opryland. This country-music-theme amusement park includes a kiddie park and a petting zoo. Many live shows and entertainers appear throughout the park. There are museums featuring Roy Acuff and Minnie Pearl. A steam locomotive takes passengers. The Chaos indoor roller coaster, the Wabash Cannonball, and raft rides appeal to teens. *2802 Opryland Dr., Nashville, 9 mi northeast of downtown; take the Briley Pkwy. exit east from I–65; tel. 615/889–6600. Admission: $31.38 adults, $20.56 ages 4–11, $28.13 senior citizens; $10 second-day ticket; $4 parking. Open late Mar.–Oct., daily 9–9. AE, D, MC, V.*

Nashville Zoo. White tigers, snow leopards, pythons, giraffes, and a new arrival, a red panda, are in this 135-acre zoo. *1710 Ridge Rd. Circle, Exit 31 off I–24 W, New Hope Rd. W., tel. 615/370–3333. Admission: $5.50 adults, $3.50 ages 3–12. Open Apr.–Oct., daily 9–6 (June–Aug., Fri. 9–8), Nov.–Mar. daily 10–5.*

Grand Ole Opry. Be a part of the weekly radio broadcast by attending a show in this cavernous 4,400-seat theater. This is radio's longest-running regularly scheduled show. Write or call several weeks in advance for summer broadcasts. The box office sells walk-up tickets starting Tuesday for the weekend shows. Even small children enjoy the bouncy program, held at the Opryland complex, 9 miles northeast of downtown. River taxis ($9.95 adults, $6 ages 4–11) shuttle between Riverfront Park downtown and Opryland on the half hour, 9:30 AM to 12:30 AM. *Opryland Reservations, 2808 Opryland Dr., Nashville 37214, tel. 615/889–6611. Admission: $14–$16 evening shows, $12–14 matinees. Shows: early May–late Oct., Fri.–Sat. at 6:30 and 9:30 PM (matinees, late May–late Aug., Tues. and Thurs. at 3); Nov.–Apr., Fri. at 7:30, Sat. at 6:30 and 9:30.*

Sites to See

Ryman Auditorium. The downtown home of the Grand Ole Opry from 1943 to 1974 has been renovated and is again used as a performance hall. Its museum contains colorful concert posters and artifacts from its Opry years. *116 5th Ave. N, Nashville, tel. 615/254–1445. Admission: $2.50 adults, $1 ages 6–12. Open daily 8:30–4:30.*

Country Music Hall of Fame. This is a thorough and touching museum of the hardships and triumphs of America's country music stars. Elvis's gold Cadillac is here, along with costumes from Loretta Lynn and Patsy Kline. It has many mementos, vintage photographs, and audiovisual exhibits. The Music Row area contains several studios, music company offices, the Gospel Music Association, and individual stars' museums (Hank Williams Jr., Randy Travis, Barbara Mandrell). *4 Music Square E, Demonbreun St. exit (209-B) from the I–40 loop, Nashville, tel. 615/255–5333. Admission: $7.50 adults, $2 ages 6–11. Open June–Aug., daily 8–7; May and Sept.–Oct., Mon.–Thurs. 9–5, Fri.–Sat. 8–6, Sun. 8–5; Nov.–Apr., daily 9–5.*

Parthenon. If Greece is not in your travel plans, come to Centennial Park and see a full-size reproduction of the Parthenon on the Acropolis. Built for the city's centennial celebration in 1897, it has the largest bronze doors in the world. Imagine slamming 7½ tons. The interior houses the city's art collection, including a 42-foot-tall sculpture of Athena and castings from the Elgin Marbles. *West End Ave., Nashville, tel. 615/862–8431. Admission: $2.50 adults, $1.25 ages 4–17. Open Apr.–Sept., Tues.–Sat. 9–4:30, Sun. 12:30–4:30; Oct.–Mar., Tues.–Sat. 9–4:30.*

The Hermitage. This huge estate is the home and burial site of President Andrew Jackson and his wife, Rachel Jackson. You can see a film of the president's life, and cassettes explain the grounds, garden, and living quarters. Tulip Grove, the home of Jackson's nephew, is also included. There are original log cabins and slave quarters. *2850 Rachel's La., 15 min from Nashville, Hermitage 37076, tel. 615/889–2941. Admission: $7 adults, $3.50 ages 6–18; free Jan. 8 and Mar. 15. Open daily 9–5. Closed 3rd wk of Jan.*

Capitol. The Tennessee Capitol sits on a prominent site overlooking Nashville. The 206-foot-high Capitol is modeled after a Greek Ionic temple. *Charlotte Ave., next to Capitol Plaza, Nashville, tel. 615/741–2692. Open daily 8–5.*

MEMPHIS CHICKS

League: Southern League • **Major League Affiliation:** Seattle Mariners • **Class:** AA • **Stadium:** Tim McCarver Stadium • **Opened:** 1963/80 • **Capacity:** 10,000 • **Dimensions:** LF: 323, CF: 398, RF: 325 • **Surface:** artificial turf infield • **Season:** Apr.–Labor Day

STADIUM LOCATION: 800 Home Run La., Memphis, TN 38104

GETTING THERE: I–240 south to Poplar Ave. west exit, left on Highland, right on Central, and left on Early Maxwell in State Fairgrounds complex next to Liberty Bowl.

TICKET INFORMATION: tel. 901/272–1687, fax 901/278–3354

PRICE RANGE: Box seats $6 adults, $4 children, over 59, and military personnel; general admission $5 adults, $3 children, senior citizens, and military personnel; left-field bleachers, $1.96

GAME TIME: Mon.–Sat. 7:15 PM, Sun. 2:15 (Apr.–and May) or 6:15 (June–Sept.); gates open 45 min before game.

TIPS ON SEATING: Setting sun hits eyes of fans sitting on first-base side. Box seats are worth extra dollar here, as kids get discount.

SEATING FOR PEOPLE WITH DISABILITIES: Spaces to accommodate 22 people in wheelchairs; 13 reserved parking spaces near home plate entrance are reserved for cars with handicapped license plates.

STADIUM FOOD: The best bet is the barbecue pork sandwiches, under the stands behind home plate. The barbecue is mild and costs $5 with slaw and beans. The chicken sandwich ($3.50) is better than most and so is the pizza ($2 a slice, $12 whole). There are regular and foot-long hot dogs, with onions, relish, and sauerkraut. There are also vendors who bring covered trays of hot funnel cakes around the stadium. Low-fat ice cream is advertised, but it's just the usual high-fat machine-chilled mix in vanilla and chocolate.

SMOKING POLICY: Sections A, B, O, and P no-smoking in both reserved and general admission areas

PARKING: At stadium, $2

VISITING TEAM HOTEL: Quality Hotel–Airport (3222 Airways Blvd., Memphis, TN 38116, tel. 901/332–3800 or 800/424–6423)

TOURISM INFORMATION: Memphis Convention & Visitors Bureau (47 Union Ave., Memphis, TN 38103, tel. 901/543–5333)

Memphis: Tim McCarver Stadium

Frankly, we came to Memphis for Elvis. We had heard that the baseball stadium has an artificial-turf infield, and we had promised to avoid recommending fake grass wherever possible. But we simply could not resist Graceland, the National Civil Rights Museum, the barbecue, and the other fabulous attractions of this great city.

When the history of professional baseball is written sometime in the middle of the next century, Tim McCarver Stadium will be the forgettable field used between the classic old Russwood Park and the state-of-the-art 21st-century

facility the Memphis Chicks now envision for the year 2000.

Don't get us wrong—we admire Tim McCarver, the Hall of Fame catcher turned broadcaster for whom this stadium is named. This stadium simply does not do him justice. The Memphis native, who hit .347 for the Chicks in 1960, is a member of the team of celebrity owners of the current Chicks.

The stadium that took McCarver's name in 1978 is one of those 1960s ballparks utterly lacking charm or consciousness of history. Built in 1963 for American Legion baseball with a covered grandstand and 2,300 seats, it was expanded to 5,447 in 1968 and to its current capacity of 10,000 in 1980. The 1980 expansion added aluminum bleacher seats with backs beyond the grandstand down the first- and third-base lines as well as a bleacher section beyond the left-field wall. A large play and picnic area under the bleachers on the third-base side has a batting cage and several amusements. From the outside, the stadium looks second-rate, with white aluminum siding above a blue wall foundation. There is no scenic view beyond the outfield wall, unless you count the Liberty Bowl over the right-field foul pole or the airplanes that fly out of left field directly over the infield on a regular basis.

There is also the artificial turf. It's not just bad, it's odd. The outfield is real grass. But when the Kansas City Royals affiliated with Memphis in 1984, they wanted their prospects to play ball on a carpet as they then did in Royals Stadium. The new owners spent a bundle to replace the infield carpet in 1993, and they don't seem willing to tear it out as the Royals have done in Kansas City. Too bad.

The 1993 renovation included all new box seats, a new scoreboard in right field, and a new Stadium Club behind home plate. But this stadium was conceived and built and rebuilt in the 1960s—when architects built cold, ugly concrete stadiums that are not nice places for fans to watch baseball. They play great music here and shoot water balloons into the stands with a giant slingshot, but there simply isn't much you can do to make this poorly designed stadium an exciting place to play or watch baseball. The ownership group is correct to focus on what it needs next—a new, fan-friendly stadium.

Unfortunately, there is not a trace left of Memphis's really great baseball stadium, **Russwood Park**. Built in 1899 and expanded to hold 13,000 after the Chicks won the Southern Association championship in 1921, Russwood Park was a charming, lopsided old ballpark of the sort now in favor with fans and stadium architects alike. After a 1950s renovation, Russwood measured 335 feet to left, 301 feet to right, 380 feet to center, and a whopping 425 feet to right center.

A who's who of baseball stars from Babe Ruth to Stan Musial played in this park, as major-league exhibitions were often staged here before the final game on April 17, 1960. John Guinozzo, then a 10-year-old fan and for the last quarter of a century the official scorer at McCarver Stadium, remembers going to the game that day with his grandfather and seeing Rocky Colavito hit a home run in a 2–1 Cleveland Indians victory over the Chicago White Sox. That evening, Guinozzo and others throughout the Memphis region watched a red glow from the five-alarm fire that destroyed Russwood Park. The site is now the Medical Center Complex, directly across the street from the Baptist Memorial Hospital.

Memphis also hosted a long-running team in the Negro Leagues from 1920 through the late 1950s. In highly segregated Memphis, the black team played at a separate field—Martin Stadium (at what is now the corner of Danny Thomas and Crump)—named for the prominent family that owned the team. Future Hall of Famers Leroy "Satchel" Paige and James "Cool Papa" Bell played for the Memphis Red Sox.

The Martin family offered its field to the Chicks after the disastrous fire of 1960. Memphis being Memphis, the Chicks turned them down and played at a converted high school football stadium. In November, they gave up their franchise, and the Southern Association folded after the 1961 season, as the major-league teams pressured their southern affiliates to play all their best prospects, not just the whites. As a result, Memphis was without professional baseball for seven seasons.

Some progress has been made. Now when you enter McCarver Stadium, you will find yourself on "Bo Jackson Boulevard," the concourse to the concession stands on the third-base side. Jackson caused a sensation here in 1986 when the Heisman Trophy football star selected baseball over football and blasted a colossal home run over the light pole in left field and onto a football practice field more than 500 feet from home plate. Jackson's first home run in McCarver Stadium on July 16, 1986, is marked with a red sign in the outfield bleacher section. He struck out 81 times in 184 at bats and made some astonishing overthrows into the stands beyond third as he learned to adjust to the small ball.

Next to the Russwood fire, Denny McLain was the biggest disaster to hit Memphis baseball. The former Detroit Tiger pitching great was the general manager in 1976. He built fancy offices and a stadium club lounge that bankrupted the club. Memphis had no professional baseball in 1977. Locals speculate about what was going on down the left-field line in the building Denny built. In the 1980s, McLain spent time in jail after being convicted of racketeering and smuggling cocaine.

The mascot is a Native American chief. The nickname Chicks was first used in 1912 to honor the Chickasaw Indians.

Where to Stay

Brownstone Hotel. This downtown, 11-story hotel is a four-block walk from Mud Island. Nicely landscaped, it has standard-size rooms. *300 N. 2nd St., at I–40, Memphis 38103, tel. 901/525–2511, fax 901/525–2511. 240 rooms. Facilities: restaurant, pool, free parking. AE, D, DC, MC, V. $*

Hampton Inn–Medical Center. Kids stay free at this four-story brick hotel on the medical-center campus. A free Continental breakfast is served. Rooms are small and clean. *1180 Union Ave., I–240 at Exit 30, Memphis 38104, tel. 901/276–1175 or 800/426–7866, fax 901/276–4261. 126 rooms. Facilities: pool. AE, D, DC, MC, V. $*

Where to Eat

Buntyn Cafe. The place to eat "meat and three" in Memphis, it's along the railroad tracks. Booths and tables crowd this family restaurant and so do customers, as its fried chicken, okra, banana pudding, and cornbread are superlative. It's a small place and fills up fast. *3070 Southern Ave., Memphis, tel. 901/458–8776. No credit cards. $*

Arcade Restaurant. At Memphis's oldest lunch counter, the food has been fast and filling since 1919. Don't miss the black-walnut ice cream, but you may want to pass on the pork brains for breakfast. It's at Calhoun Street, by a trolley stop. There's free parking in the rear. *540 S. Main St., Memphis, tel. 901/526–5757. No credit cards. $*

Corky's. One of Memphis's standout purveyors of slow-smoked barbecue, it serves wet and dry ribs. Its slogan is "Bad to the bone!" There's meltingly good beef brisket, as well as tamales, onion loaves, and fudge pie. *5259 Poplar Ave., Memphis, tel. 901/685–9744. AE, D, MC, V. $*

Rendezvous. This cozy restaurant offers great barbecue pork and ribs. The Greek owners have been serving eaters hungry for Tennessee barbecue since 1948. *52 S. 2nd St. Rear, Memphis, tel. 901/523–2746. MC, V. $*

Wiles-Smith Drug Store. In this midtown classic, you can get great milk shakes, sandwiches, and homemade vegetable soup. *1635 Union St., Memphis, tel. 901/278–6416. No credit cards. $*

Leonard's Restaurant. It was for a time the world's largest barbecue drive-in restaurant and serves good ribs, slaw, and chicken. Founder Leonard Heuberger bartered a Model-T for a seven-stool sandwich place in 1922. Four decades later, Elvis was a regular customer. *5465 Fox Plaza Blvd., Memphis, tel. 901/360–1963. AE, D, DC, MC, V. $*

Entertainments

Mud Island. On the Mississippi River, this 52-acre theme park has a swimming pool, a beach, and an amphitheater. You can walk a miniature version of the 900 miles of the Mississippi along a River Walk, one footstep per mile. You can take a tour of the World War II bomber, *Memphis Belle*, which is housed in a pavilion (donation requested), or eat in one of several restaurants. You reach the island by footbridge or monorail. *125 Front St., Memphis, tel. 901/576–7212. Admission to all attractions: $6 adults, $4 ages under 13. Entry to grounds and monorail: $2 adults, $1 ages 12 and under; free Thurs. after 4. Open June–Aug., daily 10–8; Apr.–May and Sept.–Nov., Tues.–Sun. 10–5.*

Memphis Zoo and Aquarium. This huge zoo in Overton Park has 2,800 animals in Cat Country, the Primate Canyon, and Animals of the Night. There are also kiddie rides. *2000 Galloway Ave., Memphis, tel. 901/726–4775. Admission: $5 adults, $3 ages 2–11; free Mon. 3:30–5. Open Apr.–Sept., daily 9–6, Oct.–Mar., daily 9–5.*

Memphis Pink Palace Museum and Planetarium. The mansion of Clarence Saunders, the founder of Piggly Wiggly, the first large-scale self-service grocery, has an insect zoo and the world's largest mechanical miniature circus. *3050 Central Ave., Memphis, tel. 901/320–6320. Museum admission: $5.50 adults, $3.50 ages 5–12, free Sat. Planetarium admission: $3 adults,*

$2.50 ages 5–12; laser shows extra. Open Tues.– Thurs. 9–5, Fri.–Sat. 9 AM–10 PM, Sun. 1–6.

Libertyland. At this amusement park adjoining the ballpark, you can ride Elvis's favorite, the Zippin Pippin wooden roller coaster. A paddleboat and a 1909 Dentzel carousel are among the 22 rides. Get $3-off coupons at Graceland. Admission covers a show, the carousel, a train, and kiddie rides. It's in the Mid-South Fairgrounds. *940 Early Maxwell Blvd., Memphis, tel. 901/274–1776. Admission: $7; senior citizens and ages 3 and under free; thrill-ride ticket, $15; twilight ticket (after 4 PM), $4. Open Sat. 10–9, Sun. noon–9.*

Sites to See

National Civil Rights Museum. This spectacular, not-to-be-missed museum is in the Lorraine Motel, where Martin Luther King Jr. was slain. It creatively tells civil wrongs and rights throughout the South. Artifacts from the struggle include a burned-out bus, crosses, posters, and prayer books. A replica bus instructs riders to move to the back. Exhibits make a big impression on children. It ends emotionally with a view of King's room and the balcony where he fell. *450 Mulberry St., Memphis, tel. 901/521–9699. Admission: $5 adults, $4 ages 13–18, $3 ages 6–12; free Mon. 3–5. Open June–Aug., Mon.–Sat. 10–6; Sept.–May, daily 1–5.*

Graceland Mansion Tour. You can save yourself an hour of waiting by calling ahead for reservations. Plan to arrive 15 minutes before your ticket time. If you walk in, use a pay phone in the visitor center to cut the wait. Buses take you to the Presley home, which is modest in size but not in scope. It has vintage '60s furnishings, costumes, gold records, movie posters, and family photographs. Many somber fans visit his gravesite and eternal flame. Touring Elvis's jets, the auto museum, and the Sincerely Elvis museum is extra. *3717 Elvis Presley Blvd., 12 mi southeast of city, Memphis, tel. 901/332–3322 or 800/238–2000. Admission: $9 adults, $8.10 senior citizens, $4.75 ages 5–11. Open Memorial Day–Labor Day 9–6, Labor Day–Memorial Day 9–5. AE, MC, V.*

Beale Street Historic District. On the street where W. C. Handy established the blues, the **Center for Southern Folklore** (130 Beale St.) has films, tours, and exhibits. *Beale St. between 2nd and 4th Sts., Memphis, tel. 901/526–0125.*

The Peabody Ducks. To the strains of the "King Cotton March," five famous ducks waddle on a red carpet from the swank Peabody Hotel fountain to an elevator to their penthouse home twice a day. Tourists flock to the lobby at 11 and 5 for the free show. *149 Union Ave., Memphis, tel. 901/529–4000.*

BOURBON STREET TO BIRMINGHAM

4

NEW ORLEANS, JACKSON, LITTLE ROCK, BIRMINGHAM

In the deep South, politics and baseball are serious subjects. Both are played to win. A visit to New Orleans, Jackson, Birmingham, and Little Rock is a living history excursion with good baseball into the bargain.

In New Orleans, a new $20-million stadium opens in 1997. Plan to spend your day walking or taking the historic streetcars through this magical city, eating at any of the casual restaurants serving authentic regional food. The city's aquarium is one of the nation's finest, and you can combine your visit with a riverboat excursion and tour of the impressive Audubon Park Zoo. You'll need to spend two nights minimum so you can take children for an evening of jazz at Preservation Hall, a safe and appropriate French Quarter destination.

Driving west on Route 10 and north on Route 55, you'll reach Jackson in 3½ hours. Its ballpark adjoins Mississippi's new Sports Hall of Fame, which should be explored, along with the free Museum of Natural Science, which is downtown. The elegant and affordable Edison Walthall Hotel lets you stay within walking distance of the Beaux Arts Capitol.

It's an easy, flat drive on Route 20 east and north to Birmingham, four hours from Jackson. You'll need to visit its downtown separately, as baseball has moved to the suburbs, in Hoover. The 1988-era ballpark is attractive, but you may want to explore its predecessor inside the city limits, Rickwood Field, the oldest ballpark in America. Downtown also houses a superlative Civil Rights Institute, with vivid exhibits. Birmingham has a unique city landmark, a 50-foot iron figure of Vulcan, the god of fire, in which you can take an elevator to its top.

Stay in Birmingham or Hoover overnight, but for history's sake, consider a 90-mile detour south on Route 65 to Montgomery, for the state capitol, the Civil Rights Memorial, Martin Luther King, Jr.'s Dexter Avenue Baptist Church, and the marked site where Rosa Parks refused to give up her bus seat.

From Montgomery, you can travel west on Route 80 through Selma, then pick up Route 20 west to Jackson. If speed is an issue, take Route 55 north to Memphis and then go west on Route 40 to Little Rock. It's a long drive from Montgomery— 510 miles—but Little Rock is worth the trip. At Ray Winder Field, there is a real organist, Alfreda Wilson, who's been playing at Travelers' games since 1970. You'll also want to see Central High School, site of one of America's most famous school integration battles. Its football stadium was used by the Travelers before Winder Field was built. At the state capitol, be sure to see the portrait of "boy" governor Bill Clinton, painted when he was just 27 years old.

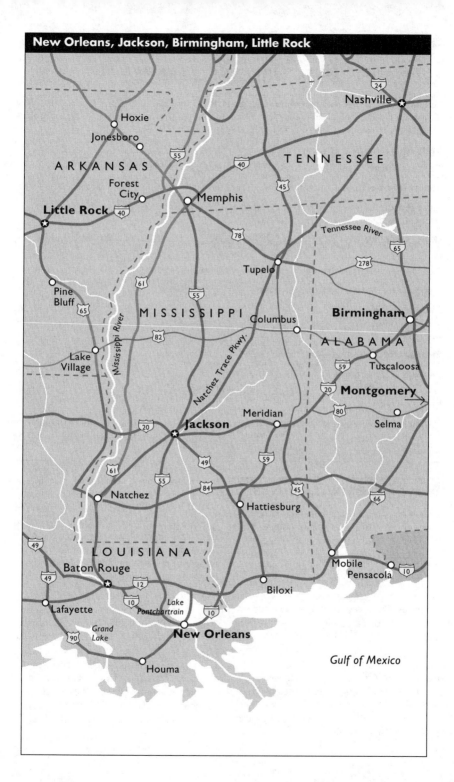

New Orleans, Jackson, Birmingham, Little Rock

NEW ORLEANS ZEPHYRS

League: American Association • **Major League Affiliation:** Houston Astros • **Class:** AAA • **Stadium:** Unnamed as yet • **Opened:** 1997 • **Capacity:** 10,500 • **Surface:** grass • **Season:** Apr.– Labor Day

STADIUM LOCATION: Airline Hwy. and Elise Lane, Metairie, LA 70003

GETTING THERE: From city, I–10 west to Clearview Pkwy. south, right on Airline Hwy.; ballpark on left.

TICKET INFORMATION: 6000 Airline Hwy., Metairie, LA 70003, tel. 504/734–5155, fax 504/734–5118

PRICE RANGE: Reserved box, $8 adults, $7 children 12 and under; reserved seats, $7 adults, $6 children; reserved grandstand, $6 adults, $5 children.

GAME TIME: Mon.–Sat. 7:05 PM, Sun. 6:05 PM; gates open 1 hr before game, 90 min before Saturday games.

TIPS ON SEATING: Seating on grass hill beyond outfield wall

SEATING FOR PEOPLE WITH DISABILITIES: Throughout stadium

STADIUM FOOD: This is a park that wisely emphasizes regional food specialties. It sells cups of jambalaya and Kate Latter's pralines. There is terrific fresh-squeezed lemonade and orangeade for $2. The main concession stand sells the more standard pizza, hot dogs, and soda.

SMOKING POLICY: No smoking in seating areas.

PARKING: Ample parking, $3

VISITING TEAM HOTEL: Holiday Inn–I–10 (6401 Veterans Blvd., Metairie, LA 70003, tel. 504/885– 5700 or 800/465–4329)

TOURISM INFORMATION: New Orleans Metropolitan Convention and Visitors Bureau (1520 Sugar Bowl Dr., New Orleans, LA 70112, tel. 504/566–5011). Louisiana State Visitors Center (529 St. Ann St., New Orleans, LA, tel. 504/568–5661)

New Orleans Zephyrs

When the Louisiana State Base Ball Association dissolved in 1873, the *New Orleans Daily Picayune* declared baseball dead. In truth, the relationship between baseball and New Orleans has been rocky ever since. New Orleans fancies itself a big-league town, but baseball here hasn't had the continuous community following that other cities have provided. The New Orleans Pelicans joined the Southern League in 1887 and were in the Southern Association from 1902 through 1959. The most famous slugger to play here was Shoeless Joe Jackson, who led the Southern Association in batting with a .354 average in 1910. Negro League teams played here only sporadically. Between 1960 and 1993, New Orleans had a professional baseball team for only one season, 1977.

In 1993, the Triple A minor-league team that left Denver to make way for the Colorado Rockies moved to New Orleans. The team played for several years at Privateer Park, a college stadium near Lake Pontchartrain and the Lakefront Arena of the University of New Orleans. The team was named the Zephyrs for the gentle breezes that blow off the lake.

The $20-million baseball park that opens in 1997 is about 20 minutes west of downtown New Orleans near the airport in Jefferson Parish. The stadium, built in conjunction with a new training facility for the New Orleans Saints NFL football team, was developed by the Louisiana Stadium and Exposition District for the state. It was designed by Perez, Ernst, Farnet Architects and Planners of New Orleans in collaboration with HOK Sport of Kansas City.

The new stadium was built to hold 10,500 fans, with future expansion to 15,000 possible. One-third of the stands are covered, and fans can visit the concession stands while continuing to watch the ball game. There are 14 skyboxes, as well as picnic and family areas. Fans can sit in a grass area beyond the outfield wall. There is a swimming pool and a hot tub beyond the outfield for use by ticketholders with club seating.

Abner Powell came to New Orleans to manage and play for the Pelicans in 1887. Because of the frequent summer thundershowers in New Orleans, Powell came up with the ideas of covering the infield and giving fans a raincheck if the game wasn't finished.

Where to Stay

June through August are bargain months for New Orleans hotels, when rates are often half the usual cost.

Holiday Inn Chateau Le Moyne. This quaint small hotel on a quiet French Quarter street has a heated pool in a shady central courtyard. Rooms in this historic hotel with character are nicely furnished. There is convenient pay parking in a guarded lot across the street. *301 Dauphine St., New Orleans 70112, tel. 504/581–1301 or 800/465–4329, fax 504/523–5709. 171 rooms. Facilities: restaurant. AE, D, DC, MC, V. $$*

Dauphine Orleans Hotel. On a quiet French Quarter street, this hotel offers free drop-off service in the quarter and in the Central Business District (CBD). You can stay in historic cottages dating from the 1700s, in rooms adjoining a patio, or in the more conventional three-story main section. All rooms freshly decorated. There's a free Continental breakfast. *415 Dauphine St., New Orleans 70112, tel. 504/586–1800 or 800/521–7111, fax 504/586–1409. 109 rooms. Facilities: coffeeshop, pool, hot tub, parking (fee). AE, D, DC, MC, V. $$*

Avenue Plaza Suite Hotel/Eurovita Spa. This antiques-filled 12-story hotel has charming one-bedroom suites with a living room. All contain a full kitchen, with a refrigerator, a microwave, and a stove. It's 2 miles west of the French Quarter and 15 minutes from the ballpark. *2111 Saint Charles Ave., New Orleans 70130, tel. 504/566–1212, fax 504/525–6899. 40 suites. Facilities:*

restaurant, pool, sauna, hot tub, health club. AE, D, DC, MC, V. $$

Where to Eat

Mother's. Order at the grill for turtle soup, crawfish étouffée, authentic po'boys, bread pudding, and sweet potato pie. You get huge portions of genuine Creole dishes. *401 Poydras St., at Tchoupitoulas St., New Orleans, tel. 504/523–9656. No credit cards. $*

Acme Oyster House. You can eat exquisite fresh oysters, po'boy sandwiches, gumbo, jambalaya, and bread pudding at this noisy, character-filled restaurant founded in 1910. The food is casual and served on plastic. *724 Iberville St., New Orleans, tel. 504/522–5973. AE, MC, V. $*

Camellia Grill. At this wonderful vintage counter restaurant, cooks and waiters wear white and customers get linen napkins. The fast food, cooked before your eyes, includes heavenly burgers, salads, waffles, and turkey omelettes. Its "freeze" drinks resemble thin sodas, not milk shakes. There are only 29 stools, so go at off-peak hours. It's stop No. 44 (Riverbend) on the Saint Charles Avenue streetcar. *626 Carrollton Ave., New Orleans, tel. 504/866–9573. No credit cards. $*

Café du Monde. A famous people-watching sidewalk café on Jackson Square in the French Market, it serves irresistible hot beignets covered with powdered sugar. There's chicory coffee for adults, orange juice for children. *Decatur and Saint Ann Sts., New Orleans, tel. 504/525–4544. No credit cards. $*

Central Grocery. Here, you can choose from a two-item menu: stuffed artichokes or muffuletta—a filling sandwich of cold meats, marinated vegetables, mozzarella, pickles, and olives. *923 Decatur St., New Orleans, tel. 504/523–1620. No credit cards. $*

Entertainments

Aquarium of the Americas. On the French Quarter's riverfront, this aquarium is one of the nation's best. The white alligators are a big draw, but no section lets you down. Feel the shock of an electric eel. Walk through a Caribbean reef and an Amazon rain forest. Combine your entry with an ecology tour on the Riverboat *John*

James Audubon, departing at the aquarium's front door. *Canal St., New Orleans, tel. 504/565–3033. Admission: $9.75 adults, $5 children. Open Memorial Day–Labor Day, Sun.–Thurs. 9:30–7, Fri.–Sat. 9:30–9; Labor Day–Memorial Day, Sun.–Thurs. 9:30–6, Fri.–Sat. 9:30–7.*

Audubon Park Zoo. You can see endangered species and exhibits on extinct creatures as well as kangaroos, wallabies, and a miniature train (extra fee). Feed the sea lions, pat the creatures in the petting zoo, and take elephant and camel rides. A Louisiana swamp exhibit highlights white alligators. A combination ticket is available with the aquarium and riverboat tour. *6500 Magazine St., New Orleans, tel. 504/861–2537. Admission: $7.75 adults, $3.75 ages 2–12. Open weekdays 9:30–5, weekends 9:30–6.*

Sites to See

Walking Tours. The National Park Service Folklife Center conducts free tours. Sign-up opens at 9 AM. You need reservations for the Garden District tour, which leaves from First Street and Saint Charles Avenue at 2:30. *916 N. Peters St., New Orleans, tel. 504/589–2636.*

Louisiana Superdome. You may agree with us that baseball and football should be played outside on grass. That shouldn't stop you from visiting the Louisiana Superdome. As a sports facility, it may not be attractive, but as an amazing piece of architecture, it is worth a look. The Superdome opened in 1975 after four years of construction. The ceiling is 273 feet high, the roof is 9.7 acres, it has 400 miles of electrical wiring, and it seats 63,524. It takes 40 hours to prepare the field for baseball. When we visited, you could see the metal cutouts for home plate and the three bases. The Superdome is downtown near I–10. The entrance for tours is on Poydras Street at Gate A. *Sugar Bowl Dr., New Orleans 70112, tel. 504/587–3810. Admission: $6 adults, $4 ages 6–10, $5 senior citizens. 30-min. tours daily 10–4 except during some events.*

Jackson Square. In the historic heart of the French Quarter, artists of every sort—from mime to painting to balloons—set up shop around the beautifully landscaped square.

The Cabildo. This Jackson Square building is a good place for children to discover the gumbo of cultures that has evolved into modern-day New Orleans. Completed in 1799 to house the governing body of Spanish Colonial New Orleans, the present structure sits on a site associated with the first official buildings of the city. The Louisiana Territory was transferred to the United States in this building on December 20, 1803. The Cabildo has showcased Louisiana's history as part of the Louisiana State Museum since 1911. One of the most famous items in the museum is a death mask of Napoleon, one of only four in existence. For us, the most moving display was the slave auction block. Slaves were sold at public auction with no regard for keeping families together. There is a Children's Visitor's Guide to the Cabildo. The Cabildo is part of the Louisiana State Museum and can be included in a package with the Old U.S. Mint, the Presbytère, the 1850 House, and the Arsenal. *Jackson Sq., Box 2448, New Orleans 70176, tel. 504/568–6968. Admission: $4 adults; $3 senior citizens, students, and military personnel; children under 13 free. Admission package (all buildings): $10 adults; $7.50 senior citizens, students, and military personnel; children under 13 free. Open Tues.–Sun. 9–5.*

Old U.S. Mint. This stuffy-sounding building has some of the liveliest exhibits in New Orleans. "New Orleans Jazz" documents the evolution of jazz from the earliest influences to today. "Who invented jazz?" the exhibit asks. "The City of New Orleans did," it answers without equivocation. "Carnival in New Orleans" displays the costumes, masks, and crown jewels of what is known around the world as Mardi Gras. Both exhibits come alive with music. The Mint is part of the Louisiana State Museum; ask about the package admission fee. *400 Esplanade Ave., New Orleans, tel. 504/568–6968. Admission: $4 adults, $3 students and senior citizens, children under 13 free. Open Tues.–Sun. 9–5.*

Preservation Hall. This is jazz in its purest form, and they make you suffer a little for it. There are no cocktail waitresses, no food, and no air-conditioning. Many of the legends who made Preservation Hall famous are dead now, but the music continues to be exceptional. Expect to wait in line, as Preservation Hall is a tiny, dingy, wonderful little place that attracts people from the world over. Unlike most of what's going on at night on and around Bourbon Street, Preservation Hall is fine for kids, and ours loved it. The music starts at 8:30 PM and ends at midnight. The sign behind the performers reads just as it has for decades: TRADITIONAL REQUESTS $1, OTHERS $2, THE SAINTS $5. *726 Saint Peter St., just off Bourbon St., New* *Orleans, tel. 504/522–2841 or 504/523–8939. Admission: $3. Open 8 PM–midnight.*

JACKSON GENERALS

League: Texas League • **Major League Affiliation:** Houston Astros • **Class:** AA • **Stadium:** Smith-Wills Stadium • **Opened:** 1975 • **Capacity:** 5,052 • **Dimensions:** LF: 330, CF: 400, RF: 330 • **Surface:** grass • **Season:** Apr.–Labor Day

STADIUM LOCATION: 1200 Lakeland Dr., Jackson, MS 39216

GETTING THERE: From I–55, Lakeland Dr. exit east for ¼ mi. Look for sign for parking for Agriculture and Forestry Museum, left on Cool Papa Bell Rd. to stadium lot.

TICKET INFORMATION: Box 4209, Jackson, MS 39296, tel. 601/981–4664, fax 601/981–4669

PRICE RANGE: Box seats $7; lower reserved $6; upper reserved $5; general admission $4 adult, $3 students, senior citizens, and military personnel, under 6 free.

GAME TIME: Mon.–Sat. 7 PM, Sun. 2:30 PM; gates open 1 hr before game.

TIPS ON SEATING: Family section of general admission bleachers well situated behind dugout on first-base side. You can rent chair with back for 50¢.

SEATING FOR PEOPLE WITH DISABILITIES: On top of dugout on first-base side; area is screened.

STADIUM FOOD: The best item here is the frozen Pepsi for $1. Skip the hot dogs and pizza. The **Hardball Grill** behind the first-base bleachers serves grilled chicken sandwiches and a Big Smokey grilled sausage. They are only fair, but there is table seating under umbrellas.

SMOKING POLICY: No smoking/no alcohol family section in bleacher area behind first-base dugout

PARKING: Ample free parking

VISITING TEAM HOTEL: Northside Days Inn (4651 I–55N, Jackson, MS 39206, tel. 601/982–1044 or 800/329–7466)

TOURISM INFORMATION: Metro Jackson Convention & Visitors Bureau (921 N. Presidents St., Jackson, MS 39202, tel. 601/960–1891 or 800/354–7695)

Jackson: Smith-Wills Stadium

The trees. Smith-Wills Stadium in Jackson, Mississippi, is an unremarkable ballpark with a remarkable backdrop of southern pine trees. When everything else about this stadium has blurred in your mind, you will remember these trees. This is a soothing, relaxing place to watch a ball game.

The history of baseball in Jackson is sporadic, with professional teams as far back as 1904. The stadium was built in 1975 when the New York Mets' minor-league franchise came to town, ending a 22-year absence of professional baseball. The most memorable event in the history of Smith-Wills Stadium was on June 22, 1978,

when future Met star Mookie Wilson married Rosa Gilbert at home plate. After the ceremony, they walked back to the dugout under an archway of bats held by Wilson's teammates.

The stadium was built on a city dump site that was then fairly far out of town. Now it is right in the growth corridor, sharing a parking lot with the popular Agriculture and Forestry Museum and the brand-new Mississippi Sports Hall of Fame. The stadium was named for two young local athletes—Johnny Smith and Doug Wills—killed in separate automobile accidents. After the New York Mets complained about the stadium and took their minor league franchise from Jackson, the city and county governments shared in a $2.5 million complete renovation of the stadium for the 1992 season.

The stadium design is straightforward. The entranceway is festive, with flags flying and attractive landscaping. The architecture is underwhelming. The covered grandstand has 1,652 new seats in tan and blue, all behind the screen and between the dugouts. There are large high-school-football-style aluminum bleachers behind the dugouts on first and third. The bleacher seats don't have backs, but for 50¢ you can rent a seat that hooks into the bleacher and adds more than 50 cents' worth of comfort. And there is an odd little wooden bleacher on a deck down the right-field line past the picnic and play area. This is a 1970s-style symmetrical outfield. The scoreboard in right center field encourages the fans in the bleachers to stomp their feet, and the sound can really rock you.

In 1982, Con Maloney, a local business and political leader, bought the team from the Mets and held a contest to give the team a name with local flavor. Fittingly, the favored choice in a town named for Andrew Jackson was the Generals. The mascot is G.J. (General Jackson), and General Manager Bill Blackwell made sure he's not a fierce General who will scare your kids.

The lively, eclectic musical repertory includes a Three Stooges number. Here, they introduce by name the little leaguers who run out onto the field with the big guys for the national anthem, as only a few other teams do. The annual Diamond Dig contest is a groundskeeper's nightmare and a fan's delight. The first 500 women through the gate are given small spades. After the game, they line up along the outfield wall and on signal race to the infield, where a $4,500 diamond ring is buried. It is quite a sight, and the field is back in shape in a remarkably short time. If it rains, you can volunteer to help put down or take up the tarp. The stadium is open when batting practice begins three hours before the game. The stadium is cleared and the gates open officially one hour before the game.

In 1994, the City Council renamed the road into the parking lot Cool Papa Bell Road after the Hall of Fame Negro League star. The legendary Satchel Paige once said that Bell was so fast "he could turn out the light and jump in bed before it got dark." A Starkville, Mississippi, native, Bell is one of the members of the Mississippi Sports Hall of Fame honored in a brand-new building near Smith-Wills Stadium, opened in 1996. The exterior is decorated with replica sports balls 5 feet in diameter atop 24-foot-high columns.

Where to Stay

Edison Walthall Hotel. The rooms are spacious in this glorious downtown historic hotel. Built in 1928 and renovated in the 1990s, this hotel has charm and great service. There are irons and boards in every room. Parking is free. *255 E. Capitol St., Jackson 39201, tel. 601/948–6161 or 800/932–6161, fax 601/948–0088. 208 rooms. Facilities: restaurant, pool, exercise room. AE, D, DC, MC, V. $$*

Visiting Team Hotel: Northside Days Inn. This three-story Interstate hotel with standard rooms is 2½ miles from the ballpark. *4651 I–55 N, Exit 100, Jackson 39206, tel. 601/982–1044 or 800/329–7466. 300 rooms. Facilities: restaurant, pool. AE, D, DC, MC, V. $*

Wilson Inn. This five-story motel is near the fairgrounds and the coliseum. Many of the standard-size rooms have kitchens, and a free Continental breakfast is served in the lobby. *310 Greymont Ave., Jackson 39202, tel. 601/948–4466 or 800/333–9457, fax 601/948–4466. 110 rooms. AE, D, DC, MC, V. $*

Where to Eat

Museum Cafe. This one-story wooden restaurant resembles a dining hall at a summer camp. It is on the grounds of the ballpark and the state agriculture museum. State-owned, it is run by prisoners and is famous for its traditional Southern cooking and large portions. Order from a menu for breakfast, or choose from the buffet lunch, where fried chicken and banana pudding are the big draws. *1150 Lakeland Dr., Jackson, tel. 601/981–1465. MC, V. $*

Frank's Restaurant. Owner Frank Latham claims his 120-seat downtown restaurant is world famous for his flaky biscuits. We agree there's no better way to ruin your diet with breakfast. There are great grits, waffles, and preserves. For lunch, focus on his pot pies, catfish, and peanut butter pie. *219 N. President St., Jackson, tel. 601/354–5357. D, MC, V. $*

Farmers Market Restaurant. This casual restaurant is adjacent to the city's impressive and extensive farmer's market. The truck farmers eat here, along with Jacksonians seeking a hearty breakfast and fresh-from-the-farm food. The owners raise the vegetables and smoke the pork barbecue daily. It's buffet-only for lunch, with homemade meatloaf and fried chicken as standouts. *352 E. Woodrow Wilson Ave., Jackson, tel. 601/353–4735. MC, V. $*

Gridley's Fine BBQ. This casual barbecue restaurant is operated by Dave Cunningham, a San Francisco '49ers running back in '69, '70, and '73. The walls are complete with team photos and a grip-and-grin photo with Joe Montana. The hearty, messy ribs are served on Formica tables with plenty of napkins. There is a children's menu. *1428 Old Square Rd., Jackson, tel. 601/362–8600. AE, D, MC, V. $*

Cock of the Walk. Get your fried pickles here, along with fried catfish and tasty chicken dinners. This casual restaurant overlooks Ross Barnett Reservoir. There is a standard children's menu. *1 Dyke Rd., Jackson, tel. 601/856–5500. AE, MC, V. $*

Entertainments

Mississippi Sports Hall of Fame and Museum. This museum includes the collection formerly housed in the Dizzy Dean Museum. It is much more than a standard-fare sports museum of old uniforms, bats, and programs. There's a participation area, where you can pitch against a batter, kick a football, and play golf against a computerized screen. This facility is across a parking lot from the ballpark. For information, write the Mississippi Sports Foundation, Inc. (Box 16021, Jackson, MS 39236). *1152 Lakeland Dr., Jackson, tel. 601/982–8264 or 800/280–3263. Admission: $5 adults, $3.50 ages 6–17, $3 senior citizens. Open Tues.–Sat. 10–4.*

Mississippi Museum of Natural Science. This excellent free museum near the state fairgrounds is great for gator watchers, as the central courtyard exhibit is filled with them. Well-done displays on the state's geologic areas show flora and fauna. There is a small aquarium section with native fish. *111 N. Jefferson St., Pearl St. exit off I–55, Jackson, tel. 601/354–7303. Open weekdays 8–5, Sat. 9:30–4:30.*

Jim Buck Ross Mississippi Agriculture and Forestry/National Agricultural Aviation Mu- seum. The exhibits are interesting, especially the vivid crop-dusting sections. The complex is staffed by prison labor, all wearing white-striped pants and "convict" across the backs of their shirts. They add tragic realism to the re-creation of a 1910-era Small Town, Mississippi. There's a working general store, a school, a petting zoo, and a gristmill. The main museum has an oversize rocking chair that fits the entire family and is good for a souvenir photo. The Chimneyville Crafts Gallery carries works from the Craftsmen's Guild of Mississippi. *1150 Lakeland Dr., Exit 98-B off I–55, Jackson, tel. 800/844–8687. Admission: $3 adults, $1 children. Open Mon.–Sat. 9–5, Sat. 1–5.*

Jackson Zoo. This 70-year-old zoo has a primate section, peacocks, lions, elephants, and a petting zoo. There's also a Children's Discovery Zoo with hands-on exhibits. You are admitted free if you are a member of a zoo in the national zoo-aquarium association. *2918 W. Capitol St., Jackson, tel. 601/352–2585. Admission: $3.50 adults, $1.75 ages 3–12. Open May–Labor Day, daily 9–6; Sept.–Apr., daily 9–5.*

Sites to See

Smith-Robertson Museum. This heritage museum is housed in a former elementary school, the first public school for African-American children in Jackson. Saved from demolition in 1977, it houses artifacts, quilts, and photographs concerning African-American life and commerce. Its location indicates the huge disparities in Jackson—only three blocks from the State Capitol, it is surrounded by boarded-up shotgun shacks. *528 Bloom St., Jackson, tel. 601/960–1457. Admission: $1 adults, 50¢ children. Open weekdays 9–5, Sat. 9–noon, Sun. 2–5.*

Medgar Evers Memorial Site. At the rear of Medgar Evers Library is a bronze statue of Mississippi's most prominent civil rights leader. He was assassinated in his nearby home, at 2332 Margaret Walker Alexander Drive, on June 12, 1963. A World War II army veteran, he became the field secretary for the NAACP in Jackson after his application to the University of Mississippi's law school was denied because of his race. The statue was built as a result of five years of efforts by Mirtes Gregory, a Jackson civic worker and beautician. Notable, too, is the downtown **Farish Street Historical District** (bounded by Amite,

Fortification, Mill, and Lamar streets), where African-American commerce, music, and civil rights flourished. The Metro Jackson Convention & Visitors Bureau (tel. 601/960–1891 or 800/354–7695) has a good African-American heritage guide. *4215 Medgar Evers Blvd., Jackson, tel. 601/982–2867.*

Mississippi's Old Capitol. This building has served as the State Historical Museum since 1961. Construction began on the elegant Greek Revival structure in 1833, one year after Jackson was made the permanent capital. The building, which nearly faced the wrecking ball on several occasions, is now a National Historic Landmark. Here in 1839, the legislature passed the first law in America giving property rights to women. The exhibits on the first floor trace Mississippi's early history. The state built an extraordinarily strong economy on the technology of the cotton gin, slave labor, rich soil, and cheap river transportation. The exhibit pulls few punches: "The south-

ern dream of a separate nation was replaced with a separate society," reads a display caption. *State and Capitol Sts., Jackson 39205, tel. 601/359–6920. Open weekdays 8–5, Sat. 9:30–4:30, Sun. 12:30–4:30.*

State Capitol. The present State Capitol, built on the site of the old state penitentiary, was completed in 1903. Restored from 1979 to 1982, the Beaux Arts building is notable for the domes over the House and Senate chambers and for the 8-foot-high, 15-foot-wide gold-leaf eagle on top of the dome. The interior walls are Italian marble on a base of New York jet-black marble. Above the rotunda, notice the four blindfolded ladies representing Blind Justice. Free tours are available year round, weekdays at 9, 10, 11, 1:30, 2:30, and 3:30. A printed, self-guided walking tour is available, as well. *President and West Sts., Jackson 39205, tel. 601/359–3114. Open weekdays 8–5, Sat. 10–4, Sun. 1–4.*

ARKANSAS TRAVELERS

League: Texas League • **Major League Affiliation:** St. Louis Cardinals • **Class:** AA • **Stadium:** Ray Winder Field • **Opened:** 1932 • **Capacity:** 6,083 • **Dimensions:** LF: 330, CF: 390, RF: 345 • **Surface:** grass • **Season:** Apr.–Labor Day

STADIUM LOCATION: War Memorial Park, Little Rock, AR 72205

GETTING THERE: From downtown, Markham Ave., turn south on Monroe St; stadium ½ mi away. From I–630, stadium is at Fair Park Blvd. exit (not Stadium exit; that sign is for football stadium). From Memphis, I–40 across Arkansas River Bridge to I–630.

TICKET INFORMATION: Box 5599, Little Rock, AR 72215, tel. 501/664–1555, fax 501/664–1834

PRICE RANGE: General admission $4 adults, $3 military personnel, $2 under 15; box seats $2 extra.

GAME TIME: 7:30 PM; gates open 1 hr before game.

TIPS ON SEATING: Box seats are right at field level and amazingly close to action. 2 warnings: setting sun can shine in your eyes if you sit on third-base side; 4 poles that hold up grandstand roof can obstruct view from some general admission seats.

SEATING FOR PEOPLE WITH DISABILITIES: Spaces for wheelchairs in box seat sections at general admission prices. Fixed seats for companions next to all wheelchair locations.

STADIUM FOOD: The menu is very limited and lines can be long. The grilled chicken ($2.75) is the best of the average choices. Hot dogs are better than most at $1.75, but there's only yellow mustard and no relish.

SMOKING POLICY: Smoking allowed throughout

PARKING: Stadium parking free, but not well organized.

VISITING TEAM HOTEL: Holiday Inn–City Center (617 Broadway, Little Rock, AR 72201, tel. 501/376–2071 or 800/465–4329)

TOURISM INFORMATION: Little Rock Convention & Visitors Bureau (1 State Health Plaza, Little Rock, AR 72201, tel. 501/376–4781)

Little Rock:
Ray Winder Field

You won't find one of those sleek new stadiums here in Little Rock, Arkansas. Ray Winder Field is a baseball place, good ol' boy style. The entrance sits almost hidden in War Memorial Park, a complex that includes the zoo, an amusement park, and the football stadium where the University of Arkansas Razorbacks play. The baseball stadium was built with private funds in 1932, and in many ways it seems unchanged. Almost 2,000 of the green-and-orange seats in the grandstand are the original straight-backed ones installed in 1932.

The covered grandstand forms the letter L with the stem down the first-base line. A press box hangs from the roof above home plate. Aluminum bleachers stretch down the third-base line to a comfortable bowl-like picnic area. The ballpark's most distinctive feature is a 55-foot-high chain-link fence above the outfield wall from center to right, known to locals as Screen Monster. It used to be that a player had to hit a ball 400 feet to get a home run here. That was until the mid-1970s, when the state highway department turned a residential street into a six-lane highway and took a big chunk of Ray Winder Field's right field. About once a month, someone knocks one over the screen.

The Travelers get their nickname from the legend of a 19th-century trader who rode throughout Arkansas telling yarns and selling wares. The Travelers have their own legend, Bill Valentine, the general manager since 1976. His roots are deep: "I was born eight blocks from this ballpark. I grew up here, cutting the grass and sorting the soda bottles." Valentine had been a major-league umpire until he was fired in 1968 for trying to organize an umpire's union. Valentine coined what we think is the best slogan in baseball—"the greatest show on dirt." The circus folks threatened a lawsuit, and the Travelers' slogan now reads "the greatest game on dirt."

Originally called Travelers Field, the park was renamed Ray Winder Field in 1966 after the man who led Little Rock baseball for more than 30 years. Winder was the *Sporting News*'s "No. 1 Minor League Executive" in 1960. One of the two plaques to Winder at the entranceway calls him "a .400 hitter in the game of life." There is a small but fine collection of Winder and Travelers baseball memorabilia back to 1932 in a glass case next to the office on the first-base side of the entryway.

Now playing in the Double A Texas League as an affiliate of the St. Louis Cardinals, the Travelers have a long history in professional baseball. Little Rock was a charter member of the Southern Association in 1901. Future Hall of Famer Tris Speaker was the league's leading hitter at .350 in 1908. Not surprisingly, Little Rock had its problems integrating baseball in the 1960s.

We will take an old stadium with charm and history over the new stadiums almost every day, but there are some serious shortcomings here. The entranceway seemed incapable of dealing easily with the crush of the 5,000 people who showed up at the bat give-away night we attended. There were not enough concession stands to serve a large crowd. There is not a single nonsmoking section in the place—and there are a lot of Travelers fans who like to smoke.

Alfreda Wilson sits way up under the grandstand roof behind home plate. She had been a part-time teacher at the music shop where the team bought its first organ in 1970. The team signed her up, and she has been playing the organ at Travelers games ever since. Wilson says she gets through all 1,200 songs in her repertory during the course of each season. It was refreshing to find a Double A team that limits its contests and focuses on baseball. But we were disappointed with the nonstop commercials by the public address announcer, who pitched discount souvenirs between batters. We wanted more of Alfreda Wilson on the organ and fewer ads.

Other Baseball Sites

Lamar Porter Field. There is a special treat awaiting baseball fans in Little Rock, a classic diamond in the rough that lies between the Capitol and Ray Winder Field. The field was used in the 1983 movie *Soldier's Story* because it so strongly evoked the ballparks of the 1940s. Alert to other movie producers: This is an absolutely enchanting, scruffy little place full of charm—white exterior with a covered green grandstand of old wooden benches with backs. John Ross, a former minor-league umpire, gave us a tour and let the kids play on the field. According to Ross, the field was built by the Works Progress Administration (WPA) in 1936. Professional baseball was never played here. Ross was the batboy for the Little Rock Doughboys of American Legion baseball when future Hall of Famer Brooks Robinson was the shortstop. Bill Valentine, now the general manager of the Arkansas Travelers and a former major-league umpire, got his start umpiring here at the age of 14. Still in use today, Lamar Porter Field is part of the Billy Mitchell Boys Club complex of fields and recreation facilities. *7th and Johnson Sts., Little Rock. Take I–630 to Woodrow St. exit south and go left on 7th St.; field is across street from elementary school.*

Where to Stay

La Quinta Inn–Fair Park. The rooms are small and the wooden staircases creak, but this clean motel has a cheery lobby with a free Continental breakfast. The two-story motel is four blocks from the ballpark and convenient to I–630. *901 Fair Park Blvd., Little Rock 72204, tel. 501/664–7000 or 800/551–5900, fax 501/223–2833. 122 rooms. Facilities: pool. AE, D, DC, MC, V. $*

Arkansas Excelsior Hotel. This sprawling luxury hotel faces the Arkansas River, next to the Old State House. The 20-story structure dominates the city skyline. *3 Statehouse Plaza, Little Rock 72201, tel. 501/375–5000 or 800/527–1745, fax 501/375–7320. 418 rooms. Facilities: 3 restaurants, fitness center. AE, D, DC, MC, V. $$*

Markham Inn. This ordinary, inexpensive three-story brick hotel is one block from the ballpark. Its rooms are small and clean. *5129 W. Markham Ave., Little Rock 72205, tel. 501/666–0161, fax 501/666–3348. 150 rooms. Facilities: coin laundry. AE, MC, V. $*

Where to Eat

Franke's Cafeterias. This is one of three good cafeteria chains in the city, along with Wyatt's and the Dixie Cafe. Founded in 1919, it still has many classic items on the menu, such as eggplant casserole and egg custard pie. It has three locations in Little Rock. *First Commercial Bank Bldg., 400 Broadway, downtown, Little Rock, tel.* *501/372–1919; weekday lunch only. University Mall, 300 S. University Ave., Little Rock, tel. 501/666–1941. Market Place Shopping Center, 11121 Rodney Parham Rd., Little Rock, tel. 501/225–4487. AE, MC, V. $*

Catfish City. Little Rock is crazy for catfish and has two dozen restaurants devoted to this farm-raised "crop." This casual one-story restaurant in a commercial strip also serves shrimp, chicken, hush puppies, and frogs' legs. There is a children's menu with corn dogs and shrimp. *1817 S. University Ave., Little Rock, tel. 501/663–7224. AE, MC, V. $*

Entertainments

Little Rock Zoo. This is a small zoo of 600 animals, including 30 endangered species. A zoo train circles the waterfowl ponds. Look for the lion house, monkey island, the white tiger, giant anteaters, and the animal nursery. *War Memorial Park, Fair Park Blvd. exit off I–630, Little Rock, tel. 501/666–2406. Admission: $3 adults, $1 children under 13. Open Memorial Day–Labor Day, daily 9–5, Labor Day–Memorial Day, daily 9:30–4:30.*

War Memorial Amusement Park. This tiny park next to the zoo in War Memorial Park has seen better days, but the price is right. There are 16 kiddie rides and a concession stand. The park owns an extremely rare "Over the Jumps" carousel, in which carousel horses jump, but it's under repair until 1998. *Jonesborough Dr., Little Rock, tel. 501/663–7083. Admission: free; rides 50¢–$1; free parking. Open weekdays 10–4, weekends 10–6.*

Children's Museum of Arkansas. In the city's historic Union Station, this frenzied place has bubble machines, a farmer's market, and a computerized stock market. Children can make their own pretzels and peanut butter. It includes a toddler climbing area and drop-in arts area. *1400 W. Markham Ave., Little Rock, tel. 501/374–6655. Admission: $3; free parking. Open Tues.–Thurs. and Sat. 10–5, Fri. 10–9, Sun. 10–5.*

Wild River Country. This pretty water park has a wave pool, a lazy river float, inner-tube rapids, and a wading pool. *6801 Crystal Hill Rd., Crystal Hill Rd. exit off I–430, at I–40, North Little Rock, tel. 501/753–8600. Admission: $13.95 adults, $11.95 ages 4–11. Open June–Sept., daily 11–6.*

Sites to See

Central High School. Cross I–630 to visit this historic high school, where the most celebrated case of integration occurred. Three years after the Supreme Court in essence ended school segregation in 1954, Arkansas governor Orville Faubus used the National Guard to turn away black students from Central High. President Eisenhower sent federal troops to Little Rock, and the nine children entered school with soldiers holding back jeering crowds with bayonets. The courage of the young students crossing through a hostile crowd to reach this imposing Art Deco building is memorable. The school is now 63% black. There are no plaques at the school or signs to direct you. The fortresslike football stadium at Central High School was the site of Kavanaugh Field, home of the Travelers before Travelers Field, now called Ray Winder Field, was completed for the 1932 season. *Park Ave. and 14th St., Little Rock.*

State Capitol. Arkansas has a traditional Greek Revival Capitol patterned after the United States Capitol. It was constructed between 1899 and 1915 on the site of the former state penitentiary. Give Arkansas credit for candor. There is a detailed display on the history of the building near the House of Representatives chamber, with every twist and turn in a bizarre 16-year story of Arkansas politics, power, and corruption. Look in the Governor's Conference Room at the portrait of the boy wonder Governor Bill Clinton, who looks impossibly young. Also, note the chandeliers in the rotunda, the legislative chambers, and the stained glass in each chamber. *W. Capitol Ave., Little Rock, tel. 501/682–5080. Open weekdays 7–4:30, weekends and holidays 10–4; guided tours, weekdays 9–4 by reservation.*

Old State House. What Arkansans call the Old State House is now a museum of Arkansas history. They take politics seriously in Arkansas. Here in the second-floor House chamber in 1837, the Speaker of the House killed a state representative in a knife fight during a legislative session. The Old State House is downtown, next to the Convention Center. *300 W. Markham St., Little Rock 72201, tel. 501/324–9685 Admission: $2 adults, $1 senior citizens, 25¢ ages 6–18; free Mon. Open Mon.–Sat. 9–5, Sun. 1–5.*

BIRMINGHAM BARONS

League: Southern League • **Major League Affiliation:** Chicago White Sox • **Class:** AA • **Stadium:** Hoover Metropolitan Stadium • **Opened:** 1988 • **Capacity:** 10,800 • **Dimensions:** LF: 340, CF: 405, RF: 340 • **Surface:** grass • **Season:** Apr.–Labor Day

STADIUM LOCATION: 100 Ben Chapman Dr., Birmingham, AL 35244

TEAM WEB SITE: http://www.spectra.net/mall/bmets

GETTING THERE: From I–65 or Hwy. 280, I–459 toward Tuscaloosa. Go past Galleria to Hwy. 150 exit in Hoover, turn left, ¼ mi to Stadium Trace Parkway, right to stadium.

TICKET INFORMATION: Box 360007, Birmingham, AL 35236, tel. 205/988–3200, fax 205/988–9698

PRICE RANGE: Box seats $6; general admission $4, $3 ages under 15, over 59, and military personnel

GAME TIME: Mon.–Sat. 7:10 PM, Sun. 2 PM; gates open 90 min before game.

TIPS ON SEATING: Box seats not expensive for such a modern facility and discounts available for children.

SEATING FOR PEOPLE WITH DISABILITIES: Near front entrance of stadium behind home plate on concourse level

STADIUM FOOD: The best buy is soft serve ice cream for $1 per cone, available on the third-base side. If you haven't reached your quota of fried food, the $3.50 chicken tenders are large and come with french fries. One order may be sufficient for two youngsters. The best drinks are the frozen cherry Coke for $2.50 and the fresh lemonade for $2. There are chicken breast sandwiches and pizza, each for $3.25, and Italian sausage for $3.50, but all are undistinguished.

SMOKING POLICY: General admission sections 205 (on first-base side) and 210 (on third-base side) are no smoking/no alcohol family areas.

PARKING: Ample parking, $2

VISITING TEAM HOTEL: Riverchase Inn (1800 Riverchase Dr., Hoover, AL 35244, tel. 205/985–7500 or 800/239–2401)

TOURISM INFORMATION: Greater Birmingham Convention and Visitors Bureau (2200 9th Ave. N, Birmingham, AL 35203, tel. 205/252–9825)

Birmingham: Hoover Metropolitan Stadium

Hoover Metropolitan Stadium is the baseball equivalent of a suburban shopping mall—big, safe, clean, and efficient. It is a fine place to play and watch a baseball game, but, the product of white flight and suburban sprawl, almost completely lacking the character of its predecessor, Birmingham's Rickwood Field.

Happily, the trend in baseball stadiums in the 1990s is back toward preservation and the center city. The trend in the late 1980s was different—new stadiums in the suburbs. Of this genre, the Hoover Met stadium is a first-class effort. It was built a dozen miles from downtown Birmingham in a fast-growing suburb at a cost of $14.5 million. Opened in 1988, the Met is owned by the city of Hoover and was designed by local architects Gresham, Smith & Partners in collaboration with HOK of Kansas City.

As you drive to the stadium and emerge from the tree-lined roadway of a suburban development, Hoover Metropolitan Stadium appears enormous. This place must seat 20,000 people, we thought. Well, it doesn't. It has seats for 10,800. Once you get into the stadium, you can see that the large, slanted concrete roof high above the sky boxes creates the effect of a much larger facility. It is a rather imposing place for a minor-league ballpark. Initial plans contemplated the possibility of a second deck for Triple A baseball.

There are a dozen luxury skyboxes, 3,202 red box seats, and room for another 7,500 general admission fans on blue aluminum benches with backs. They can squeeze more in because of seating in well-conceived grass hillsides beyond the first- and third-base lines. More than 16,000 showed up for a fireworks night the season bas-

ketball superstar Michael Jordan decided to find out if he could play a game with a smaller ball.

Here in the suburbs, the automobile is king, and there is plenty of parking right at the entrance to the stadium. A car dealer even has a creative ad on a wall over the left center-field fence with a small piece of glass for a windshield of a car: A player, whether visitor or home team, whose home run breaks the glass takes home a truck. There are trees beyond the outfield fence in right and center and an athletic field beyond the left-field wall.

The music is lively, and the Barons have a giant dog named Babe Ruff for a mascot. There are plenty of souvenirs at a store right at the entranceway. Most of the stands and facilities were built on the wrong side of the concourse, backing up to the seating area. They cannot open the concourse to the field as several of the most successful 1990s stadiums have done.

Other Baseball Sites

Rickwood Field. Future Hall of Fame relief pitcher Rollie Fingers—as noted for his great handlebar mustache as for his tremendous pitching—was the main attraction for the "Mustache Madness" game we attended at the Hoover Met. Fingers played for the 1967 Southern League champion Birmingham Athletics with teammates Reggie Jackson and Tony LaRussa. We asked Fingers what memories he has of playing at Rickwood Field. "Getting hit in the face and being out six weeks," he said good-naturedly as he signed "Save Rickwood!" over his autograph.

Our Sunday-morning visit to Rickwood Field was the highlight of our trip to the Deep South. Rodney Dalton, one of a legion of fans working to preserve Rickwood, arranged to get us into the stadium to meet with Coke Matthews, a local advertising executive who is working relentlessly as a volunteer to put Rickwood Field into its 1948 prime form. Matthews explained that in 1948 the Birmingham Black Barons had a championship season and the white Barons—shortened from the original nickname Coal Barons—won the Dixie Series Championship. The Barons set an attendance record not surpassed until their Michael Jordan year.

What's so special about Rickwood? Everything. The stadium, listed on the National Register of Historic Places, is the oldest baseball park in America, according to the National Park Service. Nothing we have seen so evokes the spirit of baseball in its glory days of Cobb, Johnson, and Ruth. You can almost hear the organ music and smell the cigar smoke.

Birmingham industrialist Rick Woodward built the stadium in 1910; the stadium name is a contraction of his name. Woodward was determined to build a great stadium, the first minor-league park of concrete and steel. He had family friend Philadelphia's legendary Connie Mack come down and lay out the field. The lights, some of the first installed in a minor-league ballpark, hang some 20 feet out from the roof over the field.

The field evokes magnificent memories. Future Hall of Famers Hank Aaron, Ty Cobb, Reggie Jackson, Jackie Robinson, Pie Traynor, and Ted Williams all played here. It is Rickwood lore that the longest home run in history was hit here—a blast by Babe Ruth that was said to have landed in a freight train moving along the tracks just beyond the right-field wall and not to have stopped until it got to Nashville, 200 miles away.

Coke Matthews took us past the wooden outfield wall to show us the other most legendary blast in Rickwood history. Before Babe Ruth reinvented baseball, the home run wasn't a big deal. The balls were dead and the fences were deep. The concrete wall in Rickwood was 405 feet from home in left, 470 feet in center, and 334 in right. In many of these stadiums, wooden fences were installed within the original field. At Rickwood, a huge scoreboard was installed in left center. In 1948, Baron Walt Dropo blasted a towering shot that went over the left corner of the scoreboard and hit the top of the concrete wall in deep center field. Beyond the trashed scoreboard and beneath the vines, there is an X painted where Dropo's shot hit the wall.

Willie Mays was discovered here. Bull Connor, before he became internationally infamous for turning dogs loose on civil rights activists, was a broadcaster for the white Barons. The white and black Barons shared Rickwood for decades, but until 1966 a city ordinance prohibited black and white players from playing together. In 1967, Reggie Jackson helped Birmingham win the Southern League championship.

Coke Matthews's Friends of Rickwood have begun the essential restoration and have an ambitious master plan. The producers of the 1995 movie *Cobb* replaced the modern scoreboard with a larger, hand-operated one and painted period ads on the wooden outfield walls. Restoration of the press box, vintage-style seats, and the repainting of the official government green with a dark baseball green are high on Matthews's list and may have been accomplished by the time you visit.

We wish the investment in the Hoover Met had been made to restore Rickwood. But you should visit both and decide for yourself. Consider this: From the 1880s, big-time baseball in Birmingham was played at the **Slag Pile**, a 600-seat stadium hard by the railroad tracks. Adults who could not get into the small grandstand sat on the slag pile—waste from the mining process—above and outside the outfield fence. Kids cut holes in the fence to get a view. After several decades at the Slag Pile, the decision was made that the Birmingham area needed a new, state-of-the-art facility. They built it out in the then suburbs: They built Rickwood Field.

Rickwood Field is still in constant use by high school, industrial, and senior-citizen leagues, and for an occasional movie. If you are lucky, you might find it open for a game. To get to Rickwood Field from downtown Birmingham, drive out 3rd Avenue West about 2 miles past I–65 and take a left on 12th Street West for one block to the stadium. For information, call or write Friends of Rickwood (2100 Morris Ave., Birmingham, AL 35203, tel. 205/458–8161).

Where to Stay

Visiting Team Hotel: Riverchase Inn at the Galleria. This new, two-story motel is on the edge of a shopping mall. The view is of parking lots and a gas station, but the motel is clean and convenient to the ballpark. It offers a free Continental breakfast. *1800 Riverchase Dr., Hoover 35244, tel. 205/985–7500 or 800/239–2401, fax 205/733–8122. 139 rooms. Facilities: pool. AE, D, DC, MC, V.* $

Courtyard by Marriott. This three-story hotel is modern and 1 mile from the Galleria mall. The rooms are standard size and freshly decorated. *1824 Montgomery Ave. S, Hoover 35244, tel. 205/988–5000 or 800/443–6000, fax 205/988–4659. 153 rooms. Facilities: restaurant, pool, exercise room, coin laundry, baby-sitting. AE, D, DC, MC, V.* $$

Holiday Inn Redmont City Centre. This historic downtown hotel has high ceilings, a marble lobby floor, and a sidewalk café. Ask for a room close to the top of its 14 floors for a nice city view. *2101 5th Ave. N, at 21st St., Birmingham 35203, tel. and fax 205/324–2101 or tel. 800/465–4329. 110 rooms. Facilities: restaurant, café, sauna, hot tub. AE, D, DC, MC, V.* $$

Where to Eat

John's Restaurant. This venerable seafood restaurant has tables and banquettes that ooze history. A must-try is the unique shredded cabbage with its signature red dressing. Portions are generous, and there's a wide variety of vegetables. A children's menu is available. *112 21st St. N, Birmingham, tel. 205/322–6014. Closed holidays. AE, D, DC, MC, V.* $$

Ollie's BBQ. A huge world globe advertises this longtime restaurant from 1–65. It's been selling great barbecue, baked ham, chili, six kinds of pies, and six types of Bibles since 1926. There are children's BBQ or chicken plates. *515 University Blvd., Birmingham, tel. 205/324–9485. D, MC, V.* $

Browdy's Fine Foods. This new, neon-filled incarnation of a 52-year-old restaurant and deli is popular before and after games. It offers New York deli food, especially corned beef, Reuben, and pastrami sandwiches. There are also po'boys on homemade buns, brownies, and cookies. Box lunches can be packed. It is 10 miles from the stadium, near the zoo and botanical gardens. *2713 Culver Rd., Birmingham, tel. 205/879–8585. Zoo exit off I–280 to Mountain Brook Shopping Center. AE, D, DC, MC, V.* $

Dreamland BBQ. This 115-seat downtown restaurant has a one-item menu—pork ribs—and the apt slogan "Ain't Nothin' Like 'Em Nowhere!" There's tea, soft drinks, or beer to wash them down and some white bread to mop up sauce, but that's it. The ribs are meaty and flavorful, and eating them on wooden tables is a happy, messy time. Nostalgic eaters can order the sauce long-distance at 800/752–0544. *1427 14th Ave. S, Birmingham, tel. 205/933–2133. AE, D, MC, V.* $

Entertainments

Discovery Place of Birmingham. Many entertaining hands-on exhibits fill this modest children's center. Young visitors can dress up like a policeman or assemble a skeleton. *1320 22nd Ave. S, Birmingham, tel. 205/933–4153. Admission: $2 adults, $1.50 children. Open Tues.–Fri. 9–3, Sat. 10–4, Sun. 1–4.*

Sites to See

Birmingham Civil Rights Institute. This modern, exhibit-filled museum presents a vivid description of America's civil rights movement. A 12-minute film covers Birmingham history. A "barriers gallery" includes replicas of a segregated streetcar, a classroom, a courtroom, and a church. The Confrontation Gallery illustrates the violence surrounding black liberation. Voting rights efforts, the March on Washington, Dr. King's "Letter from a Birmingham Jail," and other milestones are shown. A window overlooks the 16th Street Baptist Church, with photographs describing the four African-American children attending Sunday school who were killed here in 1963 when the church was bombed. *520 16th St. N, Birmingham, tel. 205/328–9696. Suggested donations: $3 adults, $1 college students. Open Tues.–Sat. 10–5, Sun. 1–5.*

Vulcan Statue. Travel to the top of the city's landmark, a 50-foot iron figure of Vulcan, god of fire, on Red Mountain. Created for the 1904 Louisiana Purchase Expo in St. Louis, it lay in ruins on Rickwood Field until it was reassembled as a monument to the iron ore that built Birmingham. Take an elevator to the top and view the city. There are great photo ops with children sitting on Vulcan's sandaled foot at the base. Vulcan's torch is green normally, but it burns red for 24 hours if there's been a traffic fatality in the city. The last tickets are sold at 10:30 PM. The adjacent gift shop has low-price kitsch souvenirs that are affordable and irresistible to children. *U.S. 31,*

Birmingham, tel. 205/328–2863. Admission: $3. Open 8 AM–11 PM.

Red Mountain Museum. Geology comes alive in a walkway carved into Red Mountain. It also houses the country's only solar telescope that's open to the public. Here's one place where you can look safely at the sun's surface. Tickets in combination with Discovery Place are available. *1421 22nd St. S, Birmingham, tel. 205/933–4104. Admission: $3 adults, $2 ages under 16. Open Tues.–Sat. 10–4:30, Sun. 1–4:30.*

Montgomery, Alabama

We couldn't conceive of being in Birmingham and not going the extra 90 miles to Montgomery, the Alabama state capital. Here in Montgomery, the forces of white supremacy and equal rights have battled toe to toe. Both efforts are celebrated here. The Dexter Avenue King Memorial Baptist Church, where the decision to launch a bus boycott was made in 1955, is just one block from the State Capitol building that served as the first capitol of the Confederacy for three months before the move to Richmond. Martin Luther King, Jr. ended the historic 1965 Selma-to-Montgomery civil rights march on the steps of the Capitol building. Not far away, on the west portico of the Capitol, there is a bronze star that marks the spot where Jefferson Davis took his oath of office as president of the Confederacy just more than 100 years before. The First White House of the Confederacy is next door to the State Archives and History Museum, which displays busts of George Washington Carver and Booker T. Washington.

State Capitol. Montgomery became Alabama's capital city in 1846. The first Capitol was built in 1847 and burned in 1849. The present Capitol was built on the same site—known as Goat's Hill—in 1850 and 1851. The handsome Greek Revival–style building has six Corinthian columns on each facade and a distinctive clock over the front portico. The state has done an outstanding job of restoring most of the Capitol to the style of the 1870s and 1880s. Note also the eight large murals just under the Capitol dome. A self-guided tour of the Capitol is available. The real legislative business of the state is now done in the Alabama Statehouse, just down the hill from the Capitol on Union Street. *Washington Ave., Mont-*

gomery, tel. 205/242–3184 or 800/252–2262. Open Mon.–Sat. 9–4, Sun. noon–4.

State Archives and History Museum. This is less interesting than most similar museums, but it does have a Children's Gallery that provides hands-on learning opportunities. Our kids enjoyed trying on old clothes in "Grandma's Attic" and working on a pattern for a quilt. It's across from the Capitol. *624 Washington Ave., Montgomery, tel. 205/242–4363. Open weekdays 8–5, Sat. 9–5.*

The First White House of the Confederacy. The first and only President of the Confederacy, Jefferson Davis, and his family lived in this townhouse leased by the Provisional Confederate Congress. The wood Italianate home was built by an ancestor of Zelda Sayre, who married F. Scott Fitzgerald. Furnished with some Davis relics and period furniture, it tells the story of how a new government was formed. *644 Washington Ave., tel. 334/242–1861. Donations appreciated. Open weekdays 8–4:30, weekends 9–4:30.*

Civil Rights Memorial. This unusual waterfall was built by the Southern Poverty Law Center and designed by Maya Lin, the architect of the Vietnam War Memorial in Washington, D.C. A stone is inscribed with the names of 40 civil rights martyrs. Water flows over black marble with a quote from Martin Luther King, Jr.: "... until justice rolls down like waters and righteousness like a mighty stream." *400 Washington Ave., near Hull St., Montgomery, tel. 205/263–3970.*

The Dexter Avenue King Memorial Baptist Church. Here, around the corner from the memorial, is the church where Martin Luther King, Jr. served as pastor. *454 Dexter Ave., Montgomery, tel. 334/263–3970. Donations appreciated for church tours. Church tours Mon.–Thurs. 10–2, Fri. 10, Sat. 10–2.*

Rosa Parks Marker. Rosa Parks and Hank Williams share a historic marker in front of the once popular and now deserted Empire Theatre. Parks, a seamstress, refused to give up her bus seat to a white man in 1955 and was arrested. The incident sparked a citywide boycott of buses for one year and launched the Rev. Martin Luther King, Jr. into leadership as chairman of the boycott committee. Williams won a contest at the Empire in 1938 that began his country music career. *Molton and Montgomery Sts., Montgomery.*

PLANTATIONS AND PALMETTOS
CHARLESTON, SAVANNAH

I t is convenient to watch baseball in the beautiful coastal cities of Charleston and Savannah in one weekend, as they are only 100 miles apart. Members of the Sally League, the South Atlantic League, they represent the best of the new and old stadiums.

The Ashley River is the dramatic backdrop for Charleston's new gem of a small ballpark. You can watch the sun set over the river in the early innings of a night game. Its RiverDogs have a kid-friendly mascot, Charlie, who has his own hometown ice cream at the park. During the day, you can delight your eyes and appetite at the Old City Market. It is tolerable even on steamy days to walk through the city's elegant, shady streets to the Battery at Charleston Harbor and take a boat ride to Fort Sumter.

The views are of lush, overgrown oaks along sections of Route 17 South as you head to Savannah. The Spanish moss hangs in the trees, giving a languid look to Savannah, a city you can explore in a horsedrawn carriage that takes you to many of the city's 21 squares. The entire downtown is a National Historic Landmark District, and it's easier to concentrate on the architecture and ambience if someone else is driving. The baseball field is beautiful, too, with an inspiring tree-lined entrance, a brick archway, and a pine-tree backdrop to the outfield. Savannah's City Market is lively, and the swimming is perfect for children on the Tybee Island beaches, 18 miles to the east.

CHARLESTON RIVERDOGS

Stadium: Charleston Ballpark • **Major League Affiliation:** Tampa Bay Devil Rays • **Opened:** 1997 • **Capacity:** 5,500 • **Dimensions:** LF: 303, CF: 386, RF: 336 • **Surface:** grass • **Season:** Apr.–Labor Day

STADIUM LOCATION: Lockwood Blvd. and Fishbourne St., Charleston, SC 29403

TEAM WEB SITE: www.awod.com/riverdogs/

GETTING THERE: From I-26, exit at Hwy. 17S, drive to Lockwood Blvd. Right on Lockwood; ballpark is at boulevard's end. From Hwy. 17 in the downtown, exit onto Lockwood Blvd., go ½ mi to the stadium.

TICKET INFORMATION: Box 20849, Charleston, SC 29413, tel. 803/723–7241, fax 803/723–2641

PRICE RANGE: Reserved box seats $6; general admission $4 adults, $3 under 13, over 60, and military personnel

GAME TIME: Mon.–Sat. 7:15 PM, Sun. 5 PM; gates open 75 min before games except Sun., when they open 1 hr before game.

TIPS ON SEATING: Fans in second level on third-base side have spectacular view of sunset over Ashley River behind first-base (home team) dugout toward left field.

SEATING FOR PEOPLE WITH DISABILITIES: Areas designated throughout stadium.

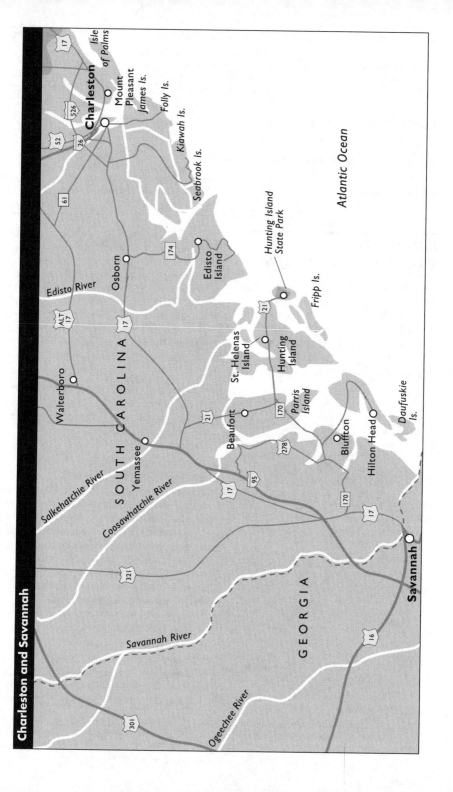

Charleston and Savannah

STADIUM FOOD: A **First Bites** stand offers fried popcorn shrimp, jalapeño poppers (too hot for young children), mozzarella sticks, and chicken fingers. There are sauces to accompany each fried item. Just inside the main gate is a grill serving brats, Italian sausage, steak and chicken sandwiches, and burgers. Your kids can even turn their lips and mouth RiverDog purple by eating mint RiverDog Ripple ice cream.

SMOKING POLICY: Smoking prohibited in seating areas but allowed in concourse.

PARKING: Ample pay parking

VISITING TEAM HOTEL: Howard Johnson Riverfront (250 Spring St., Charleston, SC 29403, tel. 803/722–4000 or 800/654–2000)

TOURISM INFORMATION: Charleston Trident Convention & Visitors Bureau (Box 975, Charleston, SC 29402, tel. 803/853–8000)

Charleston:
Charleston Ballpark

Baseball fans in Charleston are in for a double treat in 1997—a new downtown stadium on the Ashley River and a new club president, Mike Veeck, the enthusiastic and imaginative son of baseball's premier promoter, Bill Veeck.

The new 5,500 seat stadium, Charleston Ballpark, was designed by the HOK Sports Facilities Group. The most striking feature of the new ballpark is its location adjacent to Brittlebank Park along the Ashley River. Fans sitting in the second level on the third-base side have a spectacular view of the sunset over the river. The seats have backs and are as close to the field as rules allow, providing an intimate baseball experience. A roof covers 40% of the seats.

Two picnic areas overlook the field, and a wide variety of foods, including seafood, as well as Mexican, Italian, German, and American standbys, is available.

Fans who visited Charleston's College Park will find two friends from the past. With a general manager who worked for the Durham Bulls, Charleston has a huge, snorting mechanical bull trained to blow smoke and go wild when a RiverDog hits a home run. The bull made the move to the new stadium.

Baseball entrepreneur Marvin Goldklang decided the Charleston Rainbows needed a spicy new nickname when the team moved to its new riverfront stadium. "RiverDogs" won in a local contest, and Charlie the RiverDog became the team mascot in August of 1993. Charlie stands 6 feet, 3 inches tall and weighs

285 pounds wringing wet. For several years he lived at the Dog House down the left-field line at College Park, where he signed autographs for the kids during the sixth inning of every River-Dogs game. Charlie moved to the new ballpark and got a new dog house as a reward for years of fan-friendly behavior. One of the real treats of RiverDog baseball is watching Charlie boogie to "Whoop, There It Is" and other tunes before each game.

The Citadel College Bulldogs will share the new stadium with the RiverDogs and host the Southern Conference Baseball Tournament. The old stadium gets its name—College Park—from its location next to the Citadel. If you're a ballpark aficionado, take the time to visit the classic 1930s stadium. Happily, it will continue in use as a Citadel practice field.

College Park, with its wooden grandstands and intimate seating, has always been one of our favorites. The seats directly behind the plate are dug down below field level, giving the first-row fans an unusual ankle-eye view of the game. In past years, we met distinguished conservative journalist James J. Kilpatrick and a pot-bellied pig at this ballpark. (They weren't together.) Our trip for this book got off to a great start here, as Hugh left with a South Atlantic League ball signed by Nolan Ryan's son Reid.

This is hallowed ground, and not just for baseball fans. Elvis performed at College Park in 1956. He didn't blow the roof off the joint, but Hurricane Hugo did blow the press box off the stadium roof in 1988.

Ted Williams and Bob Feller played exhibition games here. When former major leaguer Sandy Alomar coached the Rainbows in 1985, he had two sons in the lineup—second baseman Roberto and catcher Sandy Jr.

Make sure you bring child-strength bug deterrent to Charleston. The sand gnats are fierce in early summer. Long pants, or at minimum, socks, can help.

Where to Stay

Music and dance lovers take over the city during its Spoleto Festival (tel. 803/722–2764), from late May to mid-June. Reservations are a must then and for most other weeks during the summer.

Visiting Team Motel: Howard Johnson Riverfront. This eight-story motel is on a busy commercial road, about 1 mile from the ballpark. It is not on the water, but the waterfront is nearby and visible. The rooms are slightly larger than average, but some are worn. *250 Spring St., Charleston 29403, tel. 803/722–4000 or 800/654–2000, fax 803/569–1608. 151 rooms. Facilities: restaurant, pool. AE, D, DC, MC, V. $$*

Sheraton Inn Charleston. This spacious, 13-story hotel overlooks the city park and the Ashley River. The rooms are large and light-filled. It is walking distance from the new ballpark. *170 Lockwood Dr., Charleston 29403, tel. 803/723–3000 or 800/325–3535, fax 803/723–3000, ext. 1595. 333 rooms. Facilities: restaurant, pool, health club, coin laundry. AE, D, DC, MC, V. $$*

Days Inn Historic. This two-story downtown hotel is within walking distance of the city market and is on a trolley stop. Its location and price make it essential to book early for this 124-room hotel. There's no charge for children under 12. *155 Meeting St., Charleston 29401, tel. 803/722–8411 or 800/325–2525, fax 803/723–5361. 124 rooms. Facilities: restaurant, pool, parking (free). AE, D, DC, MC, V. $$*

Where to Eat

Kitty's Fine Foods. This venerable Old South restaurant serves grits, flounder, and banana pudding. It's a small, stand-alone restaurant with Formica tables and serious eaters. It's 1 mile from the Visitor's Information Center. *1137 Morrison Dr., Charleston, tel. 803/722–9370. No credit cards. $*

Hyman's Seafood Company. One firm owns three popular Meeting Street restaurants, all at the same address: Hyman's is a fish feast of fresh oysters, clams, scallops, and she-crab soup. It has a large appetizer list, including shrimp and clam strips, plus a children's menu. Hyman's Half-Shell is a raw bar restaurant, and at Aaron's Deli, good corned beef and soups are dispensed. *215 Meeting St., Charleston, tel. 803/723–6000. AE, D, MC, V. $*

Nathan's Deli. Just down the street is one of three locations of this deli selling overstuffed corned beef sandwiches, homemade chicken noodle soup, and salads. *229 Meeting St., Charleston, tel. 803/723–3354. AE, D, MC, V. $*

Poogan's Porch. Housed in a turn-of-the-century home with creaky floors and character, this is sufficiently casual for children. Newly rebuilt after a fire in 1991, the Porch has outdoor dining on a rear patio, not the porch. Try the Low Country soups and novelty dishes of alligator, squirrel, and rabbit. A children's menu is available. *72 Queen St., Charleston, tel. 803/577–2337. AE, DC, MC, V. $$*

Entertainments

There are several pedal-carriage companies, but it's too dangerous to be in traffic with children armed only with a modified bicycle. You can take the DASH transit to the City Market and Historic King Street areas. There are many carriage and horse-drawn wagon tours of the city, as well as organized and self-made walking tours.

CharlesTowne Landing. In this state park 3 miles northwest of Charleston, you can watch wild animals—wolves, bobcats, pumas—in their natural habitats. You can rent bicycles or take a $1 tram through the 80 landscaped acres of Charleston's first settlement, circa 1670. There are a replica village and a 17th-century ship to explore. *Hwy. 171, 1500 Old Towne Rd., Charleston, tel. 803/852–4200. Admission: $5 adults, $2.50 ages 6–14. Bicycles $2 per hr. Open daily 9–6.*

Magnolia Plantation. A petting zoo, a 50-acre garden, miniature horses, and a maze will interest children here. A nature train ride around the huge estate lasts 45 minutes. *Ashley River Rd. (S.R. 61), 10 mi north of U.S. 17, Charleston, tel.*

803/571–1266. Admission: $9 adults, $7 ages 13–18, $4 ages 4–12; train admission: $3 adults, $2 ages 6–12, $1 ages 4–6. Open 8–dusk; train runs 9–5.

Sites to See

The Battery. View Charleston Harbor at the place where the Ashley and Cooper rivers meet. Also known as White Point Gardens, this is a good place to climb on cannons and view history. *Battery Point, where E. Battery St. and Murray Blvd. meet and Meeting St. deadends, Charleston.*

Fort Sumter. Boats leave from Charleston City Marina and Patriots Point (Mt. Pleasant side of Cooper River Bridge) to tour the fort where the Civil War began on April 12, 1861. Artillery captain Abner Doubleday, the man wrongly credited with inventing baseball, did fire the first Union shot of the Civil War from Fort Sumter. The tour spends an hour on Fort Sumter and another 75 minutes on Charleston Harbor. *Fort Sumter Tours, City Marina, 17 Lockwood Dr., Charleston, tel. 803/722–1691. Admission: $9 adults, $4.50 children under 13.*

Black History Tours. See the Battery, the Old Slave Mart Museum, Catfish Row, and the site of the Denmark Vesey Slave Uprising. One- and two-hour bus tours depart from the Charleston Visitor Center (375 Meeting St.). *Sites and Insights Tours, Charleston, tel, 803/782–0051. Admission: $10.*

SAVANNAH SAND GNATS

League: South Atlantic League • **Major League Affiliation:** Los Angeles Dodgers • **Class:** A • **Stadium:** Grayson Stadium • **Opened:** 1941 • **Capacity:** 8,500 • **Dimensions:** LF: 290, CF: 400, RF: 310 • **Surface:** grass • **Season:** Apr.–Labor Day

STADIUM LOCATION: 1401 E. Victory Dr., Savannah, GA 31404

GETTING THERE: Take I–16 to 37th St. exit. Turn left on 37th, right on Abercorn St., and left on Victory Dr.; 2 mi on right is Daffin Park. Stadium is on a city bus line; for schedule information, call 912/233–5767.

TICKET INFORMATION: Box 3783, Savannah, GA 31414, tel. 912/351–9150, fax 912/352–9722

PRICE RANGE: Reserved box seats $5.50; reserved loge seats $4.50; general admission $3.75 adults, $3 children, senior citizens, and military personnel.

GAME TIME: Mon.–Sat. 7:15 PM, Sun. 2 PM; gates open 1 hr before game.

TIPS ON SEATING: Only 500 seats are reserved. General admission seats in grandstand have backs. Bleachers are benches without backs.

SEATING FOR PEOPLE WITH DISABILITIES: In grandstand and bleachers; ramps for wheelchairs on third-base side

STADIUM FOOD: You'll find dinner food at **Big Will's Grill,** near the picnic area on the third-base side. The nicely grilled hamburgers are merely $2; brats and Polish and Italian sausages are $2.50. The meats are good; the mustard isn't. There's good pink lemonade for $1.25 and no-fat, no-cholesterol Arctic Cream soft-serve for $1.50. The funnel cakes at the concession stand on the third-base side are a special treat. They're not healthy, but they're hot and fresh. A Southern specialty, boiled peanuts, is sold in brown bags for $2. They're an acquired taste and are reminiscent of black-eyed peas.

SMOKING POLICY: City ordinance prohibiting smoking is widely disregarded.

PARKING: Ample free parking

VISITING TEAM HOTEL: Holiday Inn Midtown (7100 Abercorn St., Savannah, GA 31406, tel. 912/352–7100 or 800/465–4329)

TOURISM INFORMATION: Savannah Area Convention & Visitors Bureau (Box 1628, Savannah, GA 31402, tel. 912/944–0456 or 800/444–2427)

Savannah: Grayson Stadium

The drive to Savannah's Grayson Stadium is one of the best in all of baseball. The approach from downtown is through a beautiful oak-tree-lined neighborhood. The Spanish moss hanging from the trees is magical for kids and parents alike. The stadium is in Daffin Park, a large city park full of ball fields and basketball courts. The magic continues as you approach the redbrick stadium's arched entranceway. GRAYSON STADIUM is etched in stone in large letters. The oak trees and Spanish moss surround the stadium.

Savannah's baseball roots are deep. The city was a charter member of the South Atlantic League in 1904. Shoeless Joe Jackson led the league in hitting with a .358 average in 1909, just a decade before being accused of throwing the 1919 World Series in the Black Sox scandal that rocked baseball.

Built to accommodate football as well as baseball, Grayson Stadium is the largest-capacity stadium in Single A baseball. The concrete football-stadium construction dates from 1901 and gives Grayson thousands of bleachers seats down the third-base line and beyond the left-field fence. As a result, this is a home-run hitter's park, with some of the shortest home-run alleys in professional baseball, at 290 feet down the left-field line and 310 feet down the right-field line. Center field is deep, at 400 feet. They have been playing minor-league baseball on this spot since the mid-1920s. The stadium you visit, built in 1941, is named for Spanish-American War hero General William Grayson.

Tall pine trees dominate the scene beyond the concrete left-field bleachers. There is a large scoreboard in center field. Recent renovations replaced an ancient press box and provided new bathrooms and bullpens. If you worry about foul balls, you'll be safe here, as the entire first-base grandstand is screened.

This setting is so perfect that the producers of The Bingo Long Travelling All-Star & Motor Kings (Universal), a 1976 movie with James Earl Jones, Richard Pryor, and Billy Dee Williams about black barnstormers, was filmed here.

You shouldn't have much trouble with restless kids in this stadium. There is a batting cage and a speed pitch on the third-base side. There is plenty of space for the kids to race around in the treed area beyond the picnic area. If you want a foul ball, the best place appears to be along the fence on the third-base side past the picnic area.

The atmosphere is fun and the sound system lively. The sound effects go way beyond the traditional broken-windshield-on-a-foul-ball-out-of-the-stadium gag. Listen for everything from themes from The Wizard of Oz to The Three Stooges. When an opponent got a hit, we heard the Stooges' "Oh, a wise guy, eh?!"

These folks have a sense of humor. About the only thing anyone could complain about here are the bugs. The sand gnats are ferocious in the spring and fall. When the Los Angeles Dodgers took over the franchise from the St. Louis Cardinals for the 1996 season, the team changed its nickname. Now it's called—you guessed it—the Savannah Sand Gnats. As the temperature grows warmer, the gnats are less of a problem. But mosquitoes may appear in the summer. Wear long pants and a long-sleeved shirt. The locals swear by Avon's bath oil Skin-So-Soft, but the team does not have large quantities to sell. Plan ahead (Avon, tel. 800/858–8000). By the time you are in the stadium, it's too late to get the protection you need.

Where to Stay

Visiting Team Motel: Holiday Inn–Midtown. This ordinary two-story hotel is 5 miles from downtown and 15 minutes west of the ballpark. It's one block from the Oglethorpe Mall. Kids stay free and eat free with paying adults in the hotel restaurant. 7100 Abercorn St., Savannah 31406, tel. 912/352–7100 or 800/465–4329, fax 912/235–6408. 174 rooms. Facilities: restaurant, pool. AE, D, DC, MC, V. $

Days Inn–Savannah Historic Riverfront. At this imposing seven-story redbrick hotel between the Savannah River and City Market, kids 12 and under eat free. No-smoking rooms are available. The ballpark is 10 minutes north. 201 West Bay St., Savannah 31401, tel. 912/236–4440 or 800/325–2525, fax 912/232–2725. 196 rooms.

Facilities: restaurant, pool, parking (free). AE, D, DC, MC, V. $$

The Mulberry–Holiday Inn Hotel. This hotel began in 1846 as a livery stable, became a cotton warehouse, and, in the 1960s, a Coca Cola bottling plant. It's been completely renovated, with a formal Georgian exterior and three floors of spacious rooms. It stands on Washington Square in the Historic District, overlooking Emmitt Park. *601 E. Bay St., Savannah 31401, tel. 912/238–1200 or 800/465–4329, fax 912/236–2184. 120 rooms. Facilities: 2 restaurants, pool, hot tub, parking (fee). AE, D, DC, MC, V. $$*

Where to Eat

Crystal Beer Parlor. This family-friendly place dispenses more root beer floats than alcohol. It's been serving exemplary oyster sandwiches, crab stew, seafood gumbo, and Brunswick stew since 1933. The milk shakes and homemade potato chips are winners, too. Padded wooden booths stand against walls decorated with old photos of the city. It's three blocks south of the Civic Center. *301 W. Jones St., Savannah, tel. 912/232–1153. AE, D, MC, V. $*

Mrs. Wilkes Boarding House. You'll wait in line for at least 20 minutes before you're grouped with others at tables for a genuine Southern feed. The all-you-can-eat lunches are a groaning board of fried chicken, cornbread, cobblers, grits, and red rice. Only a tiny sign on the wall of this residential neighborhood indicates the restaurant—you'll see the line first. *107 W. Jones St., Savannah, tel. 912/232–5997. No credit cards. $*

Morrison's Cafeteria. This nicely furnished downtown restaurant is another of the South's exemplary cafeterias. The choice of vegetables and salads is extensive, and there is a less expensive children's menu. It's on Johnson Square in the Historic District. *15 Bull St., Savannah, tel. 912/232–5264. AE, D, MC, V. $*

The Seashell House. This casual family seafood house arranges its tables sensibly—with a hole in the middle over a trash container, for all the crab shells, shrimp tails, claws, and corn cobs. Crabs and ribs are the mainstays here, and oysters, crawfish, clams, and conch also are served. There is a children's menu. *3111 Skidaway Rd., Savannah, tel. 912/352–8116. AE, MC, V. $*

The Pirate's House. This gigantic restaurant in the historic district has 23 dining rooms, including the original Pirate's House, dating from the 1700s, and a house once owned by city founder James Oglethorpe that's the oldest residence in Georgia. It's a popular tourist stop, despite the pricey menu. The service is speedy for a restaurant this size, and the seafood, pasta, steaks, and chicken dishes are pleasing. Jambalaya, pecan-fried chicken, and praline sundae pie are standouts. There is a children's menu. *20 E. Broad St. at Bay St., Savannah, tel. 912/233–5757. AE, D, DC, MC, V. $$*

Entertainments

City Market. There are four blocks of shops, restaurants, and art galleries in this restored city market. Low Country basket weavers work and sell their wares in open-air sheds, sharing space with produce sellers. *Jefferson and W. Saint Julian Sts., Savannah, tel. 912/232–4903. Open mid-Mar.–Sept., Mon.–Sat. 10–9, Sun. noon–5; Oct.–early Mar., Mon.–Sat. 10–6, Sun. noon–5.*

Juliette Gordon Lowe Girl Scout National Center. Any Brownie or Girl Scout in your family gets a $1 discount when visiting the home of the girl-scouting movement. Lowe's home includes memorabilia on the origins of scouting and its links to Europe's "girl guides." There is a child-oriented gift shop. *142 Bull St., Savannah, tel. 912/233–4501. Admission: $5 adults, $4 ages 6–8. Open Mon.–Tues. and Thurs.–Sat. 10–4, Sun. 12:30–4:30.*

Sites to See

This city is memorable. The oaks, covered with Spanish moss, make its distinctive squares beautiful and mysterious. There is street after street of Federal and Regency homes, wrought iron, and sweeping porches—the entire downtown is a National Historic Landmark District.

It was the women of the city who saved it from bulldozers and modernization in the 1950s. Ask children to pick their favorite among the 21 squares originally laid out by city founder General James Oglethorpe.

Historic Savannah. You can go by horse and carriage, or by foot, bus, or trolley through the 2.2-mile historic downtown. The cheapest way is on the county's CAT shuttle buses. They depart from the visitor center every 20 minutes Monday through Saturday from 7 to 6, and every 40 minutes Monday through Saturday from 6 to 10 and Sunday from 9:30 to 5. The one-way fare is 50¢; an all-day pass is $1.50. Children under 40 inches ride free, with no more than two children per paying adult. The buses are accessible to people in wheelchairs. *Savannah Visitor Center, 301 Martin Luther King, Jr. Blvd., Savannah, tel. 912/233-5767.*

Carriage tours. Fourteen tour companies operate in the city, including a haunted-history trolley, a black heritage trail, riverboat cruises, and a ghost walk. There's much to be said for seeing the city by horse-drawn open carriage. Pick-up sites are at the Hyatt Hotel in Bay Street, Jefferson Street in the City Market, and at the visitor center. Those with reservations are seated first. The tours last 50 minutes and leave on the hour. *Carriage Tours of Savannah, Savannah, tel. 912/*

236–6756. Admission: $13 adults, $6 ages 4–11. Open daily 9–3 and 6–9.

King-Tisdell Cottage and Tours. The city's black history museum conducts a tour of African-American historic sights (admission: $10 adults, $5 children under 12) arranged by the Association for the Study of Afro-American Life and History. One day's advance registration is required. The tour departs from the Savannah Visitor Center (see *Historic Savannah* in *Sites to See, above*) at 10 and 1. The compact museum itself is filled with mementos of the achievements and history of local residents. *514 E. Huntington St., Savannah, tel. 912/234–8000. Admission: $2.50. Open weekdays noon–4, weekends 1–4:30.*

Tybee Island Lighthouse. This beach resort of barrier islands is 18 miles east of Savannah on U.S. 80 (Victory Dr.). You can climb the 128 steps to the lighthouse's top. There is great swimming on Tybee's beautiful beaches. *Meddin Dr., Tybee, tel. 912/786–4077. Admission: $1.50 adults, 50¢ ages 6–12. Open daily 10–6.*

FLORIDA: AFTER THE MAJOR 6
LEAGUERS HEAD NORTH
KISSIMMEE, LAKELAND, TAMPA,
ST. PETERSBURG

The home of major-league baseball's Grapefruit League spring training, Florida is synonymous with the game. There are dozens of parks on the ocean coast, in interior Florida, and on the Gulf shores, allowing snowbirds to get a jump on their hometown team's new rosters each spring.

But those same fields are home to the Single A Florida State League after the majors head north. For one trip, try starting in Kissimmee, right next door to Disney World, Universal Studios, MGM Grand, and Epcot, among other attractions. There are true bargains in lodging in this over-built area. The Kissimmee Cobras play in a stadium with palm trees past its outfield and a kid's playground.

Drive 40 miles west on Interstate 4 to Lakeland and its Tigertown, spring home of the Detroit Tigers and the summer home of the Lakeland Tigers. The renovated stadium is laden with character. Another 30 miles west on Interstate 4 is Tampa, with its sparkling new, state-of-the-art ballpark for the New York Yankees in spring and the Tampa Yankees in summer. Yankees legends are recalled here, in banners and columns. Tampa has one of the nation's best zoos, with just the right scale for children. The city's new $84-million, three-level aquarium is a marvel. The historic Ybor City is a must for authentic Cuban food and a look at the city's colorful past.

Continuing on Interstate 4 west to U.S. 19 South brings you to St. Petersburg, where during spring training you can enjoy sea breezes in Al Lang Stadium. This intimate downtown park is right on Tampa Bay. The sand and water at nearby St. Petersburg Beach are a lovely respite. Another must-see is one of the famed Old Timers Softball games, where the youngest players are 75 years old.

KISSIMMEE COBRAS

League: Florida State League • **Major League Affiliation:** Houston Astros • **Class:** A • **Stadium:** Osceola County Stadium • **Opened:** 1985 • **Capacity:** 5,100 • **Dimensions:** LF: 330, CF: 410, RF: 330 • **Surface:** grass • **Season:** Apr.–Labor Day

STADIUM LOCATION: 1000 Bill Beck Blvd., Kissimmee, FL 34744

GETTING THERE: From Florida Turnpike, exit 244, right on U.S. 192, right on Bill Beck Blvd. to stadium. From I–4, exit to U.S. 192E, 12 mi to stadium. From 17/92S, left on U.S. 192, 3 mi to stadium.

TICKET INFORMATION: Box 422229, Kissimmee, FL 34742, tel. 407/933–5500, fax 407/847–6237

PRICE RANGE: Box seats $5; grandstand $4; general admission $3.50 adults, $2.50 students and over 63

GAME TIME: Mon.–Sat. 7 PM, Sun. 6 PM

TIPS ON SEATING: Sit on third-base side to be near playground behind left field grandstand.

Kissimmee, Lakeland, Tampa, St. Petersburg

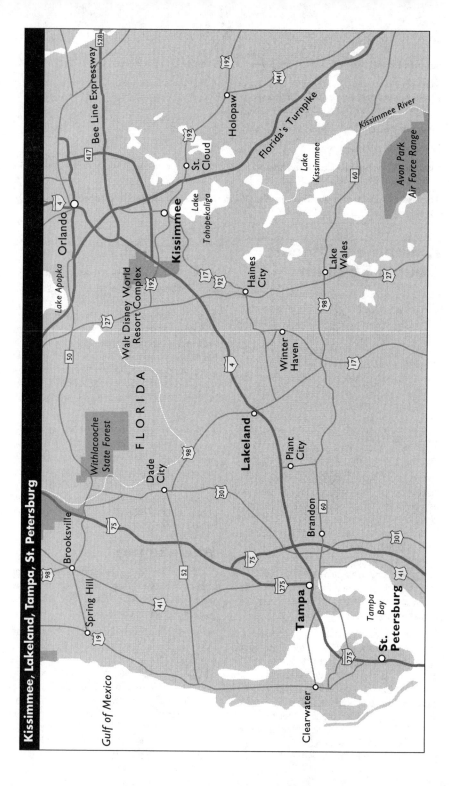

SEATING PEOPLE WITH DISABILITIES: Behind on-deck circles on both first and third-base sides

STADIUM FOOD: The menu has the usual stadium hot dogs and popcorn, but the smoked sausages, at $3, are fair, and the lemonade ($1.25) is a welcome switch from the soda-only choices for children. For indulgences, the park sells ice cream bars ($3).

SMOKING POLICY: Smoking and alcohol prohibited in section 203 of grandstand

PARKING: Ample free parking

VISITING TEAM HOTEL: Stadium Inn and Suites (2039 E. Irlo Bronson Hwy., Kissimmee, FL 34743, tel. 407/846-7814 or 800/221-2222)

TOURISM INFORMATION: Kissimmee–St. Cloud Convention & Visitors Bureau (Box 422007, Kissimmee, FL 34742, tel. 407/847-5000 or 800/327-9159)

Kissimmee: Osceola County Stadium

Baseball doesn't stop in Florida when the major-leaguers pack their bags and head north in the spring. But you wouldn't know it by looking at the attendance figures from the Single A Florida State League. The league was the only full-season league in the National Association of Professional Baseball Leagues that drew fewer than 1 million fans in 1996. That is barely more than 1,000 fans per game. And it is not for lack of teams—there are 14 of them spread all through central Florida. It may be because many of the teams are owned by major-league teams that care more about having a spring-training facility than promoting community events.

Kissimmee, the Florida State League team nearest to Walt Disney World, isn't a new team. Until 1995, it was known as the Osceola Astros. Happily, in recent years market-oriented teams have adopted names and logos that promote community identity rather than major-league loyalty. The Osceola Astros are now the Kissimmee Cobras. The team's metallic silver, dark green, and midnight blue is one of the best color combinations in baseball.

The new Kissimmee logo is a cobra coiled around a baseball, ready to strike. The fans hiss to let the opponents know they are in "the Snake Pit." Osceola County Stadium is part of the Houston spring-training complex, which includes four practice fields. The $5.5 million stadium complex was completed for the Astros in 1985. Palm trees and a large pond sit beyond the outfield wall. The best reason to come here is not the stadium but nearby Walt Disney

World, Epcot, MGM, Sea World, and Universal Studios.

There's an endearing tradition in most minor-league cities—team fan clubs that help the young players set up their apartments, give them home-cooked meals, help their families, and ease these young players into becoming professional sportsmen. Here, Helen Knowling has rung a cowbell for the team for the last 11 years and makes cookies three times a year for the players, who adore her. "Thanks for the cookies, Helen," we heard player after player tell her.

A former knothole kid from New Jersey, she says, "I just live for the Lord and for baseball." The Cobras were one of the first teams to build a screened playground for younger kids to let off steam. The nicely netted Elinor Moser Cobraland Playground is behind the left-field grandstand. It should become a model for others to follow.

Where to Stay

You'll find terrific bargains on lodging, as this area competes for customers. You save a bundle by staying outside Walt Disney World, but you sacrifice some convenience.

Howard Johnson's Fountain Park Plaza Hotel. A pretty lake and picnic area are the backdrop for this highway hotel with resort features. There's a free Continental breakfast, and refrigerators may be rented for $10 daily. Efficiencies are available. This 10-story hotel is 11 miles east of the stadium and 3½ miles west of Walt Disney World. U.S. 192, Orlando 34746, tel. 407/396-1111 or 800/654-2000, fax 407/248-0266. 400 rooms. Facilities: restaurant, ice cream parlor, pool, kiddie wading pool, sauna, hot tub, 2 tennis courts, game room. AE, D, DC, MC, V. $

Visiting Team Motel: Stadium Inn and Suites. This stand-alone apartment motel composed of three two-story buildings has kitchens in half of the rooms. Some rooms have Murphy beds, a treat for children. 2039 E. Irlo Bronson Hwy., U.S. 192. 1 mi east of stadium, 14 mi east of Walt Disney World, at Rte. 441, Kissimmee 34741, tel. 407/846–7814 or 800/221–2222, fax 407/ 846–1863. 114 rooms. Facilities: pool, hot tub. AE, D, DC, MC, V. $

Wynfield Inn–Main Gate. This sprawling motel is built around the large swimming pool. Four miles east from Walt Disney World, the motel has a free shuttle to it, Epcot, and MGM Studios. Children 17 and under stay free, and the two adjacent restaurants give a 10% discount to guests. 5335 W. Irlo Bronson Hwy., U.S. 192, 8 mi west of ballpark, 4 mi east of Walt Disney World, Kissimmee 43745, tel. 407/396–2121 or 800/ 346–1551, fax 407/396–1142. 216 rooms. Facilities: snack bar, pool, kiddie wading pool, coin laundry. AE, D, DC, MC, V. $

Ramada Inn Orlando Westgate. This two-story motel shuttles you the 6 miles to Walt Disney World, Epcot, and MGM parks for free. It is 20 minutes southwest of the ballpark. Kids eat free at the restaurant. 9200 W. Irlo Bronson Hwy., U.S. 192, Orlando 34742, tel. 941/424–2621 or 800/228–2828, fax 941/424–4360. 200 rooms. Facilities: restaurant, pool, playground, game room, coin laundry. AE, D, DC, MC, V. $

Gator Motel. This clean, two-story bargain motel is next door to Jungleland, a small zoo, and across a playfield, with picnic benches, from Medieval Times, a dinner theater. The motel has a stone exterior, and stucco walls. All rooms have two standard beds and air-conditioning. 4576 W. Irlo Bronson Hwy., U.S. 192, 3 mi west of U.S. 17 and 441, 5 mi east of Walt Disney World and 8 mi west of the ballpark, Kissimmee 34746, tel. 407/396–0127, fax 407/396–6262. 38 rooms. Facilities: pool. MC, V. $

Where to Eat

Morrison's Cafeteria. This large, nicely decorated cafeteria has a children's menu and good renditions of American favorites. It is in the Osceola Square Mall, 5 minutes west of the ballpark. 3831 W. Vine St., Kissimmee, tel. 407/846–6011. AE, D, MC, V. $

Entertainments

For all the huge Orlando-area attractions for kids, some precautions make the days more fun. Use sunscreen, bring drink boxes, get a stroller for any child six or under, and don't feel you have to get your money's worth by seeing it all.

Walt Disney World. It is good to follow a system, rather than just wandering. The basic Walt Disney World plan: Prepurchase your tickets at a AAA office to get a discounted rate and make reservations for lunch and dinner; write down where you parked; arrive a half hour before the gates open, see the most popular rides first, eat lunch early, at 11 AM; force yourself to leave the park from 1 to 4 when the crush is heaviest. Go back to your hotel for a swim and a nap. Return to the park until closing, eating dinner late on the front patio of a restaurant along the parade route. For our money, "Pirates of the Caribbean" is the top ride and Fantasyland the best area in Walt Disney World. Older children flock to the Blizzard Beach water park.

Epcot Center. Epcot is 3 miles south of the Magic Kingdom. There are long waits, and adults may chafe at the commercialization of exhibits. Children may find "Wonders of Life-Body Wars" too intense. The new Circle of Life film is a winner, and so is the 3-D Honey I Shrunk the Audience. You may want to skip the beautiful indoor restaurants in favor of the less expensive ones outside.

Disney–MGM Studios. This is an imaginative, flashy park. Some attractions ("Tower of Terror," "Star Tours") may be too intense for younger children. The Indiana Jones stunt special is unique. Try to visit the "Honey, I Shrunk the Kids" playland before dusk, as it closes early for insurance reasons. There are many clever theme restaurants on the grounds. The park is 2 miles north of U.S. 192.

There are one-day, one-park tickets (to Magic Kingdom, Epcot, or Disney-MGM Studios) listed below, or multiday passes. Parking is $5 at any of the Walt Disney World properties. U.S. 192 and I–4, Lake Buena Vista, tel. 407/824–4321. Admis-

sion: $40.81 adults, $32.86 ages 3–9. Open 9–9, with some variation in closing times. AE, MC, V.

Sea World of Florida. Children love the various touch pools; the whale and waterskiing shows are exciting. Sharks, sea lions, and dolphins also get huge exhibits. The "Penguin Encounter" lets you view hundreds of king and Adélie penguins. Parking is $5. Discount tickets to Busch Gardens and Cypress Gardens are available here. *7007 Sea Harbor Dr., Bee Line exit (S.R. 528) from I–4, then exit for Sea World/International Dr., Orlando, tel. 407/351–0021. Admission: $37.95 adults, $31.80 ages 3–9. Open 9–7. AE, D, MC, V.*

Gatorland. It may seem odd to eat fried alligator, but watching a man wrestle a gator is a permanent memory. You'll see dozens of gators and learn about their behavior. This attraction works hard at education, with a zoo that puts you very close to poisonous snakes. *14501 S. Orange Blossom Terr., 3½ mi north of Kissimmee on U.S. 17; Exit 28 east from I–4, then south 5 mi on Rte. 17; Orlando, tel. 407/855–5496. Admission: $10.95 adults, $7.95 ages 3–11. Open Apr.– Sept., daily 8–7; Oct.–Apr., daily 8–5:45.*

Universal Studios–Nickelodeon. View back lots, fly on a bicycle through the "E.T. Adventure" (too scary for our five-year-old), and take an informative tram tour. If your kids want to be part of a Nickelodeon show audience, call the production hot line (tel. 407/363–8586) one week early and find out what shows are filming. Audiences are filled on a first-come, first-served basis. Parking costs $5 for a car, $7 for an RV. *1000 Universal Studios Plaza, Exit 30B from I–4*

onto S.R. 435, Orlando, tel. 407/363–8000 or 800/232–7827. Admission: $38.50 adults, $31 ages 3–9. Open 9–7.

Other Baseball Sites

Ted Williams Larger-than-Life Art. You're driving along I–4, and there he is—Ted Williams swinging a bat several times larger than life on the side of a hotel. You can't resist pulling over at the Baseball City Stadium exit and checking this out. Sure enough, it is the Ted Williams Best Western Inn, with huge flashing letters: GREAT TRUCKER RATES. The Splendid Splinter himself was a part-owner. If you're a baseball memorabilia collector, ask for a sheet of the hotel letterhead, with a smaller version of the hotel mural. *I–4 and U.S. Hwy. 27 S, Exit 23 from I–4 onto Rte. 27, Baseball City, tel. 813/424–2511.*

Ted Williams Museum and Hitters Hall of Fame. At the Ted Williams Best Western Inn (see *above*), they'll give you directions to Williams's museum in Hernando, which is arranged like a baseball diamond, with memorabilia, television tapes on his career in baseball and the Marines, and a bat collection—including one from Shoeless Joe Jackson—lining the walls. One wing includes a 20-member Hitters Hall of Fame, as chosen by Williams. *2455 N. Citrus Hills Blvd.; Exit 66 (Wildwood/Inverness) from I–75 N; left on Hwy. 44 for 15 mi, then right on Hwy. 41; in Hernando, left on Hwy. 486 to museum a few mi ahead on left; Hernando, tel. 352/527–6566. Admission: $3 adults, $1 children under 13. Open Tues.–Sun. 10–4.*

LAKELAND TIGERS

League: Florida State League • **Major League Affiliation:** Detroit Tigers • **Class:** A • **Stadium:** Joker Marchant • **Opened:** 1967 • **Capacity:** 7,000 • **Dimensions:** LF: 340, CF: 420, RF: 340 • **Surface:** grass • **Season:** Apr.–Labor Day

STADIUM LOCATION: 2301 Lakeland Hills Blvd., Lakeland, FL 33805

GETTING THERE: From I–4, exit 19 to Lakeland Hills Blvd., turn left, go 1½ mi; stadium is on left.

TICKET INFORMATION: Box 90187, Lakeland, FL 33804, tel. 941/688–7911, fax 941/688–9589

PRICE RANGE: Box seats $4; general admission $3 adults, $2 under 12 and senior citizens.

GAME TIME: Mon.–Sat. 7 PM, Sun. 2 PM (Apr.–June) and 6 PM (July–Aug.); gates open 1 hr before game.

TIPS ON SEATING: Best view of Lake Parker and palm trees beyond right-center-field fence is from high up in general admission bleachers on third-base side. Minor league team closes bleachers except on Fourth of July.

SEATING FOR PEOPLE WITH DISABILITIES: Near box seats on third-base side

STADIUM FOOD: The best bargain is the whole pizza ($7). Ask the help to cut them in more than four pieces. There are burgers, hot dogs, and fries, but they are ordinary. The kielbasa is a better bet, but may be too spicy for children. Avoid the watery sodas and choose the bottled fruit juices. The Italian ices on a push-up stick ($1.50) are refreshing and not too messy.

SMOKING POLICY: Smoking prohibited in seating area

PARKING: Ample free parking

VISITING TEAM HOTEL: Wellesley Inn (3520 Hwy. 98N, Lakeland, FL 33805, tel. 941/859–3399 or 800/444–8888)

TOURISM INFORMATION: Central Florida Convention & Visitors Bureau (Box 1839, Bartow, FL 33831, tel. 813/534–4372)

Lakeland: Joker Marchant Stadium

One morning, we were driving from Orlando to St. Petersburg on I–4 and stopped at Tigertown, the spring home of the Detroit Tigers. We loved the atmosphere and looked for an open gate. Once inside, we saw a white-haired man hitting golf balls from the bullpen near right field into left field. Emily grabbed a Florida State League ball lying near the dugout and got an autograph from Sparky Anderson, the first manager to win world championships with both American and National League teams.

Who is Joker Marchant, we wondered? It turns out he was the long-time city recreation director who pressed to have the stadium built. Why Joker? His name was Marcus Thigpen Marchant; we understood. The Tigers have been in Lakeland since 1933 and had outgrown the 3,500-capacity Henley Field long before the 7,000-capacity, $500,000 Marchant Stadium was opened for the 1967 spring-training season.

They call it Tigertown; the stadium is on Al Kaline Drive, named for Mr. Tiger, the Gold Glove home-run-hitting Hall of Famer. The structure of the stadium is quite like that of the ordinary Florida State League stadiums in Kissimmee, Clearwater, and elsewhere. But the feel is different. The city and the Tigers did a wonderful $600,000 renovation in 1994 that gives this stadium real character. Tiger flags and huge pictures of Tiger stars fly among the umbrellas and picnic tables, creating a warm and friendly atmosphere at minimal cost. The con-

cession stands are lit in neon. Southpaw the Tiger is a fan-friendly mascot who takes part in the contests.

From high up in the general admission bleacher seats on the third-base side, you get the best view of Lake Parker beyond the right-center-field fence and a brightly lighted power plant in the distance. Unfortunately, the minor-league team allows seating in the bleachers only on the Fourth of July. We were struck by the absence of advertising signs on the walls. There was something soothing and dignified about the uncluttered navy blue walls with palm trees and water behind. Paul Dash, the former grounds-keeper for 19 years, explained: "Joker said the signs looked tacky."

Where to Stay

Visiting Team Hotel: Wellesley Inn. This new six-story peach stucco motel is on the edge of the Lakeland Square Mall. Rooms are bright and nicely decorated. Guests receive a free Continental breakfast. It's 10 minutes from the stadium. *3520 Hwy. 98 N, Exit 18 off I–4, Lakeland 33805, tel. 941/859–3399 or 800/444–8888, fax 941/859–3483. 106 rooms. Facilities: pool. AE, D, DC, MC, V. $*

Best Western Diplomat Inn. This courtyard inn was redone in 1994, with pretty landscaping throughout the grounds. Many rooms have sofas and desks. There is a free Continental breakfast. It is one exit from the ballpark. *3311 U.S. 98 N, Exit 18 from I–4, Lakeland 33805, tel. 941/688–7972 or 800/528–1234, fax 941/688–8377. 120 rooms. Facilities: restaurant, pool, exercise room, game room. AE, D, DC, MC, V. $$*

Scottish Inns. Several rooms in this two-story downtown motel have a view of one of the city's many lakes. It is walking distance from the Historic District. The rooms are basic and inexpensive. *244 N. Florida Ave., ½ mi south of U.S. 98 and 92, Lakeland 33801, tel. 941/687–2530 or 800/251–1962, fax 941/688–1961. 50 rooms. Facilities: pool, coin laundry. AE, D, MC, V. $*

Where to Eat

Landmark Restaurant. Housed in a former dry-goods building in the Munn Park Historic District, this is an endearing mix of mismatched tables, cheery "found" art, and great breakfasts. Don't miss the strawberry pancakes, cheese grits, and French toast. There are salads and fish for lunch. *228 E. Pine St., Lakeland, tel. 941/682–7691. Closed dinner. MC, V.*

Sites to See

Munn Park Historic District. Bookstores, more than 60 antiques shops, and renovated storefronts are clustered along Kentucky Avenue and Pine Street in downtown Lakeland. Self-guided tours are available through the Lakeland Chamber of Commerce (35 Lake Morton Dr., Lakeland, tel. 941/688–8551).

Frank Lloyd Wright Buildings. The largest collection of architect Frank Lloyd Wright's work outside of Oak Park, Illinois, is at Florida Southern College. The 12 Wright buildings are made of cypress, copper, and coquina shells. Self-guided tour maps are available in the administration building, where you may also join the docent tour at 11 on Thursdays for $5. *Ingraham Ave. and McDonald St., Lakeland, tel. 941/680–4111. Administration building open weekdays 8–5.*

TAMPA YANKEES

League: Florida State League • **Major League Affiliation:** New York Yankees • **Class:** A • **Stadium:** Legends Field • **Opened:** 1996 • **Capacity:** 10,387 • **Dimensions:** LF: 318, CF: 408, RF: 314 • **Surface:** grass • **Season:** Apr.–Labor Day

STADIUM LOCATION: 3802 W. Martin Luther King Blvd., Tampa, FL 33614

GETTING THERE: From I–275S or N, take N. Dale Mabry (exit 23) north 3 mi; Legends Field is on left. From airport, take exit to Spruce St.; in approximately 2 mi, turn left onto N. Dale Mabry for 1 mi; Legends Field is on left.

TICKET INFORMATION: 3802 W. Martin Luther King Blvd., Tampa, FL 33614, tel. 813/879–2244, fax 813/673–3186

PRICE RANGE: For Florida State League games, all seats reserved: lower box $5; upper box $3. Yankees spring training tickets: $12, $10, $8, and $6.

GAME TIME: Mon.–Sat. 7 PM, Sun. 1 PM; gates open 90 min before game; most Yankees spring training games 1:05 PM

TIPS ON SEATING: All seats are excellent. Sit on third-base side for a view of Tampa Stadium (view beyond left field is a car dealership). Third-base side is in the sun during day games. Section 200 seats are not at second level.

SEATING FOR PEOPLE WITH DISABILITIES: 240 seats; companion rest rooms on both third- and first-base sides. 80 reserved parking spaces with access to seating area by elevator

STADIUM FOOD: The food choices are more varied and much better at the spring training games. Both have 12-inch pizzas for $11 on the first-base side. The Clipper Italian Sausage is $3.25. There are microbrews and imported beers for $4.

SMOKING POLICY: Smoking prohibited in seating areas

PARKING: Free for Florida State League games; for spring training, all parking near ballpark is reserved. Ample parking ($5) at Tampa Stadium, across N. Dale Mabry from Legends Field and accessible by footbridge over highway.

VISITING TEAM HOTEL: Holiday Inn Express (4732 N. Dale Mabry Hwy., Tampa, FL 33614, tel. 813/872–6061 or 800/465–4329)

TOURISM INFORMATION: Tampa/Hillsborough Convention & Visitors Center (111 Madison St., Suite 1010, Tampa, FL 33602, tel. 813/223–1111 or 800/448–2672)

Tampa: Legends Field

George Steinbrenner, the man baseball fans love to hate, has produced a winner in his hometown of Tampa. After three decades in Ft. Lauderdale, the New York Yankees have returned to Tampa Bay, where they trained from the 1920s until the early 1960s, moving into a splendid new Tampa ballpark for spring training 1996. The Tampa Yankees of the Class A Florida State League play here, too.

The $17.5 million Legends Field was designed by Lescher and Mahoney of Tampa to evoke Yankees tradition. Part of an exquisitely landscaped $30 million, 31-acre spring-training complex that includes two other baseball fields, Legends Field is owned and operated by the Tampa Sports Authority. The Yankees have a 30-year lease. The football Tampa Bay Buccaneers play in Tampa Stadium, directly across Dale Mabry Highway from right field. There are 10,387 very comfortable and attractive Yankee-blue seats, each with an excellent view of the action.

Huge blue and white banners spell out YANKEES and help give the impression that this is a two-level major-league ballpark. The replica of the classic Yankee Stadium facade along the grandstand roof was a great idea executed less successfully than it might have been. The outfield dimensions are identical to those in Yankee Stadium.

Three of the four columns in front of the gift shop honor past Yankees greats—Babe Ruth, Lou Gehrig, and Miller Huggins, the manager of the 1927 world champions. The fourth column is being saved for the next Yankees legend. Fans walk up steps to the main entrance. The six main entryways to the seating area each highlight a legendary Yankees team with a team photo and banners of the stars—from the "Murderers' Row" team of 1927 to the Reggie Jackson–Thurman Munson champions of 1977.

Legends Field is state-of-the-art, with a great sound system and a first-class scoreboard-videoboard in left center field. The landscaped plaza, the practice field, and the community field are behind the stadium and hidden from view from the stands. The view from inside the ballpark looking to left and center fields is of a highway and a commercial strip. Tampa Stadium dominates the view past right field. The concessions and rest rooms are on a wide, handsome, and convenient concourse.

Where to Stay

Visiting Team Hotel: Holiday Inn Express–Stadium. This pretty new hotel is only two blocks from the ballpark. Its two floors overlook the adjoining small man-made Lake Holiday, where ducks swim. The rooms are standard doubles, and there is a free Continental breakfast bar for guests. *4732 North Dale Mabry Hwy., exit 23A off I–275, Tampa, tel. 813/877–6061 or 800/465–4329, fax 813/876–1531. 200 rooms. Facilities: pool, fitness center, game room, coin laundry. AE, D, DC, MC, V. $$*

Where to Eat

Columbia Restaurant. It's hard to tear yourself from the terrific Cuban bread, wrapped in paper for each diner, at this venerable Ybor City restaurant, decorated in Spanish tile and greenery. There is an open courtyard in its center, with a balcony, plus three huge dining rooms, two with stages for the nightly flamenco shows. The all-male wait staff is formal, but the dining for lunch is casual. Its signature 1905 salad, with olives, ham, and cheese is special, as are all fish dishes. *2117 E. 7th Ave., Tampa, tel. 813/248–4961. AE, D, DC, MC, V. $$*

Bern's Steak House. This well-known meat palace is frequented by tourists eager to see just how good the steaks are. They're excellent, expensive, and accompanied by superb vegetables grown on the restaurant's farm. After your dinner, you can tour the restaurant and wine room before you go upstairs to a room devoted entirely to desserts. Customers sit at booths in this room, decorated with wine vats, and choose from among 80 desserts. Bern's plain warehouse facade does not look appealing from the outside, and the overdone red velvet interior downstairs is a bit much, but the food is excellent. *1208 S. Howard Ave., Tampa, tel. 813/251–2421. Closed lunch. AE, DC, D, MC, V. $$*

Entertainments

Lowry Park Zoo. One of our favorite small zoos in the country, this shaded, peaceful park keeps animals at children's eye-level and keeps the walking times manageable. Its 29 acres are packed with animals in their own habitats, from primates to birds. There is a petting zoo. *North Blvd. and Sligh Ave., Tampa, tel. 813/935–8552. Admission: $6.50 adults, $4.50 children 3–11, $5.50 senior citizens. Open daily 9:30–5.*

Fun Forest. This small amusement park has a storyland park, with lovely hand-painted murals of the Wizard of Oz, Snow White, and others on some rides. *North Blvd. and Sligh Ave., adjoining Lowry Park Zoo, Tampa, tel. 813/935–5503. Admission: Free; rides 50¢–$1. Open weekdays 11–5, Sat. 11–6, Sun. 12–6.*

Florida Aquarium. This new $84-million three-level aquarium has Florida's water resources as its theme, from coral reefs to limestone caves and wetlands. Overlooking the Port of Tampa, visitors walk under a huge glass dome resembling a seashell. The emphasis is on habitats; visitors are given audio wands that provide descriptions of the various sections. The facility is home to more than 4,300 animals and plants. *701 Channelside Dr., Tampa, tel. 813/273–4000. Admission: $13.95 adults, $12.55 ages 13–18 and senior citizens, $6.95 ages 3–12; parking $3; reduced-price tickets with free parking some summer Fri. after 5 PM. Open daily 9–5; mid-June–mid-Aug., Fri. until 9 PM.*

Museum of Science and Industry. This multipurpose science center contains a planetarium, nature trails, an IMAX dome theater, and hundreds of hands-on exhibits, including many space shuttle displays. Visitors wearing goggles and earplugs can sit through a two-minute hurricane in a special room where a 75-mph wind velocity and noise are duplicated. The museum is light-filled, with the open-air design popular in the early 1980s that exposed service pipes—painted in bright colors—overhead. *4801 E. Fowler Ave., Tampa, tel. 813/987–6300. Admission: $8 adults, $7 ages 13–18 and senior citizens, $5 ages 2–12. Open Sun.–Thurs. 9–5, Fri.–Sat. 9–9.*

Busch Gardens. An extensive zoo with endangered species is the add-on in this 336-acre theme park, which has Moroccoan and African-style buildings and souk markets. There is the Serengeti Plain, Myombe Reserve for primates, and a skyride and monorail. The international flavor extends to the food, which includes tame versions of many foreign cuisines. Kids are chiefly interested in the thrill rides, such as Montu, the world's largest inverted roller coaster. You literally ride in cars underneath the tracks, which go underground after some big drops. *Busch Blvd., at McKinley Ave., Tampa, tel. 813/987–5082. Admission: $36.15 adults, $29.75 ages 3–9; parking $4. Open Sun.–Fri. 9–8:30, Sat. 8:45–9 PM.*

Ybor City. This national landmark district contains former and current cigar-making factories, old Latin restaurants, wrought-iron balconies on second-floor storefronts, cafes, bakeries, and an interesting State Museum (*1818 Ninth Ave., tel. 813/247–6323*). The museum catalogues the enterprises and residents of the area, which is named for Don Vicente Martinez Ybor, a cigar maker and Cuban exile, who arrived here in 1885. Ybor City, which has been called Tampa's Latin Quarter, has many shops, vintage clothing stores, and art galleries. Free guided walking tours are available through the Historic District from the Ybor City Chamber of Commerce (*1800 E. 9th Ave., Tampa, tel. 813/248–3712*). For a daily schedule of other free walking tours, contact the State Museum. *Bounded by 6th Ave., 12th Ave., 23rd Ave., and Nick Nuccio Pkwy., Tampa.*

St. Petersburg Devil Rays

League: Florida State League • **Major League Affiliation:** Tampa Bay Devil Rays • **Class:** A • **Stadium:** Al Lang Stadium • **Opened:** 1947 • **Capacity:** 7,004 • **Dimensions:** LF: 330, CF: 400, RF: 330 • **Surface:** grass • **Season:** Apr.–Labor Day

STADIUM LOCATION: 180 2nd Ave. SE, St. Petersburg, FL 33701

GETTING THERE: From I–275, exit 9 (First St.); First St. south 2 blocks to stadium.

TICKET INFORMATION: Box 12557, St. Petersburg, FL 33733, tel. 813/822–3384, fax 813/895–1556

PRICE RANGE: Field boxes $4; grandstand $3 adults, $2 children and senior citizens

GAME TIME: Mon.–Sat. 7:05 PM, Sun. 5 PM; gates open 75 min before game

TIPS ON SEATING: For best view of Tampa Bay beyond left-field wall, sit on first-base side high up in the stands; small roof shades some of upper grandstand seats.

SEATING FOR PEOPLE DISABILITIES: Behind field box sections 6 and 7

STADIUM FOOD: Florida ballparks may have ordinary menus, but at least there's usually good brown mustard—a legacy from the senior-citizen fans who grew up with good mustard in Philadelphia and New York. Use it here on a jumbo dog ($3) or a warm pretzel ($2.50). A grill on the outer concourse on the first-base side serves burgers and chicken sandwiches. Avoid the bad lemonade and go right to dessert. You have a choice of Italian ices or Haagen-Dazs ice cream or yogurt. The other offering is nachos.

SMOKING POLICY: No restrictions

PARKING: Parking near stadium operated by City of St. Petersburg; there may be a $2 charge.

VISITING TEAM HOTEL: Best Western Mirage (5005 34th St. N, St. Petersburg, FL 33714, tel. 803/525–1181 or 800/528–1234)

TOURISM INFORMATION: St. Petersburg, Clearwater, and Dunedin Convention & Visitors Bureau (Tropicana Field, 1 Stadium Dr., Suite A, St. Petersburg, FL 33705, tel. 813/464–7200 or 800/345–6710)

St. Petersburg: Al Lang Stadium

In 1911, Al Lang got sick. As a result, baseball changed forever. Stadium historian Michael Benson tells the story this way: Albert Fielding Lang, the 41-year-old owner of a successful Pittsburgh laundry business, fell ill and was told he had six months to live. He moved to St. Petersburg, Florida, and recovered. When he heard about the long stretch of bad weather that major-league teams were having in their spring training in Arkansas, Lang invited the St. Louis Browns to train in St. Petersburg in 1914 at Coffee Pot Park near the Coffee Pot Bayou. Many other teams followed. As Florida's ambassador to big-time baseball, Lang was the genius who brought spring training to the state. Lang's recovery was pretty solid. He lived to be 89.

The Boston Braves trained at Waterfront Park from 1921 to 1937. The St. Louis Cardinals have been training in St. Petersburg since 1938. In 1947, the city built a new $300,000 ballpark at the foot of First Avenue on the waterfront just south of Waterfront Park. The new field was dedicated in Lang's honor to express appreciation for his extraordinary devotion to baseball.

Al Lang Stadium is set comfortably at the base of the downtown. The cold, gray concrete exterior belies the warm, intimate interior. The field was shaped like the Polo Grounds until it was rebuilt in 1977 in a more conventional and symmetrical shape. Tall office buildings rise behind home plate, and a major hotel stretches down the right-field line. Palm trees blow in the breeze beyond the right-field wall. You can see Tampa Bay over the left-field wall.

There's a real organist performing the "Star Spangled Banner." There are lots of on-field contests. Emily won a Cardinals pennant for her prowess hitting water balloons tossed by Bruce.

Unfortunately, Al Lang Stadium is one of the few ballparks in the country that have absolutely no restrictions on smoking. To add insult to injury, we arrived on 50¢ beer night. We don't know which genius invented this horrible idea, but sure enough, two drunks squared off about 10 rows behind us.

In order to attract a major-league team, the community built the $138-million Florida Sun Coast Dome in 1990 and is spending an extra $30 million to make it baseball ready. It was renamed ThunderDome in 1993. They built it, and major-league baseball did come: In 1995 major-league owners voted to approve the Tampa Bay Devil Rays, a National League expansion team.

The St. Louis Cardinals used Al Lang Stadium for one last spring training in 1997. The new Tampa Bay Devil Rays will train here starting in 1998. A Florida State League Single A team affiliated with the Devil Rays plays in Lang Stadium in 1997 but may move in 1998 when the major league team begins play in the nearby dome.

The ThunderDome, now called Tropicana Field (1 Stadium Dr., St. Petersburg, FL 33705; Tampa Bay Devil Rays information, tel. 813/825–3174), is as hideous a piece of sports architecture as you can imagine. From the outside, it looks like a gigantic municipal water tank, a scar across an otherwise delightful city landscape. Inside, no amount of tinkering could add charm to this monstrosity, which is carpeted with artificial turf. The Tampa Bay Walk of Fame, in front of Tropicana Field, recognizes Tampa Bay sports figures from Al Lang to Wade Boggs. The stadium will be closed for much of 1997 so that it can be made ready for baseball in 1998.

Other Baseball Sites

Old-Timers Softball Game. St. Pete is famous for its Kids 'n Kubs senior-citizen league. You must be at least 75 years old to play, and the cheerleaders are the same age. The free games are played in a city park with bleachers at the foot of 8th Avenue Northeast. *Northshore Park, St. Petersburg, tel. 813/893–7108. Games played end Oct.–mid-Apr., Tues., Thurs., and Sat. at 1.*

Hurley Park. Colonel Frank T. Hurley Park is a full block along the water, with picnic tables, a tennis court, and basketball hoops. It's a crown jewel of a little-league diamond, fenced with a dugout and scoreboard. It's two blocks from Inn on the Beach (see below). *1201 Gulf Way, St. Pete Beach.*

Where to Stay

Inn on the Beach. The two-story wooden inn is worth the 20-minute drive from downtown to the gulf resort of Passe-a-Grille in St. Pete Beach. There are 12 homelike suites with kitchens. Ten of the rooms are doubles; two can sleep four. No two rooms are alike. Most have ceiling fans and window air conditioners. The inn is in a residential neighborhood and just steps from a swimming beach. *1401 Gulf Way, St. Pete Beach 33706, tel. 813/360–8844. 12 rooms. AE, D, DC, MC, V. $$*

Heritage Holiday Inn. This three-floor historic downtown hotel, built in the golden era of the 1920s, offers a free Continental breakfast on weekends. The medium-size rooms have high ceilings. *234 3rd Ave. N, St. Petersburg 33701, tel. 813/822–4814 or 800/283–7829, fax 813/823–1644. 75 rooms. Facilities: restaurant, pool, hot tub. AE, D, DC, MC, V. $$*

St. Petersburg Hilton Downtown. You can see into the ballpark from the top levels of this 15-floor high-rise hotel. Built next to the marina, it is convenient to all downtown attractions. *333 1st St. S, St. Petersburg 33701, tel. 813/894–5000 or 800/445–8667, fax 813/823–4797. 333 rooms. Facilities: 2 restaurants, pool, hot tub, exercise room. AE, D, DC, MC, V. $$*

Beach Park Motor Inn. This small, reasonably priced bay-front motel is across the street from the Museum of Fine Arts. Several of its rooms have kitchens. *300 Beach Dr. NE, St. Petersburg 33701, tel. 813/898–6325. 26 rooms. AE, D, MC, V. $*

Where to Eat

Tommy Lasorda's Dugout. Across the street from Al Lang Stadium is a franchise deli created by the legendary Los Angeles Dodgers manager. It's housed in a bank office building. The $2 Home Run egg, cheese, and ham subs are special. Try Mrs. Lasorda's hot sauce on the daily hot entrée ($3), and taste the fat-free cheesecake. *100 2nd Ave. S (Rte. N103), St. Petersburg, tel. 813/823–1305. MC, V. $*

Piccadilly Cafeteria. Fans come for the red velvet cake, but there are dozens of other desserts to consider. The salads may even tempt your children. The children's menu includes several meat-and-two-vegetable combinations. The cafeteria is on U.S. 19S in the Sun Coast Shopping Center, 4 miles from Al Lang Stadium.

1900 34th St. N, St. Petersburg, tel. 813/328–1501. AE, DC, MC, V. $

Ted Peters Famous Smoked Fish. All varieties of expertly smoked fish, especially the local favorite, mullet, are sold here. You may eat inside this small restaurant or at an outdoor picnic table. There also are burgers and a great homemade potato salad for people who don't eat fish. *1350 Pasadena Ave. S, St. Petersburg, tel. 813/381–7931. No credit cards. $*

Skyway Jack's. Early risers can choose from among four dozen different breakfasts, all of them bargains. The restaurant takes its name from the Sunshine Skyway Bridge, which is nearby. *6701 34th St. S, Exit 3 from I–275, St. Petersburg, tel. 813/866–3217. MC, V. No dinner. $*

Uncle Andy's at Don CeSar Beach Resort. It's too costly for most to stay here, but you can spring for an ice cream cone in Uncle Andy's ice cream parlor to see this gorgeous pink rococo landmark. Built on the beach in 1928, it was home to the vacationing Babe Ruth and Lou Gehrig. *3400 Gulf Blvd., St. Pete Beach, tel. 813/360–1881. AE, D, MC, V. $*

Entertainments

Great Explorations. There are six pavilions of a hands-on museum in the renovated five-story city pier. Younger children may not like the "Touch Tunnel," a dark maze. "Explore Galore" is a special section aimed at patrons under seven. The pier also contains an aquarium, miniature golf, restaurants, fishing, and shops. *1120 4th St. S, St. Petersburg, tel. 813/821–8885. Admission: $6 adults, $5.50 senior citizens, $5 ages 4–17. Open Mon.–Sat. 10–5, Sun. noon–5.*

Sunken Gardens. See the roller-skating macaws at this tropical paradise. There are bird and animal shows every two hours, plus alligator wrestling. At this amusement area there's a wax museum based on the life of Christ. *1825 4th St. N, Exit 12 from I–275 east at 22nd Ave., St. Petersburg, tel. 813/896–3186. Admission: $14 adults, $8 ages 3–11. Open daily 10–5.*

HISTORIC VIRGINIA
NORFOLK, RICHMOND, WOODBRIDGE

Three Virginia cities—Norfolk, Richmond, and Woodbridge in Prince William County—give you very different, but outstanding, baseball experiences. Norfolk's Harbor Park has an exciting backdrop of commercial boat traffic in the Elizabeth River. A new facility on the harbor, Nauticus, teaches children about oceans, boats, and marine animals. Williamsburg and the Jamestown Settlement are 25 miles northwest on Route 64, alongside the enticing Busch Gardens amusement park.

Another 30 miles west of Williamsburg on Route 64 brings you to The Diamond in Richmond, a 12,500-seat stadium in the same Triple AAA International League as Norfolk. The stadium was completely rebuilt in 1984 and radiates serious baseball, with no crazy contests or mascots. This is one of the few state capitols that you can view from a raft, as the James River runs through downtown.

Directly north 100 miles on Interstate 95 is Woodbridge, home of the Prince William Cannons, a member of the Single A Carolina League. Its county-run park is basic, but the spirit and games are fan-friendly. The bargain hunter in you will find an outlet at nearby Potomac Mills, the discount shopping megamall that is the state's biggest tourist attraction. The Manassas Battlefield and Paramount's Kings Dominion amusement park will keep you in the area, and you can easily add a trip to the nation's capital and to George Washington's home at Mt. Vernon.

NORFOLK TIDES

League: International League • **Major League Affiliation:** New York Mets • **Class:** AAA • **Stadium:** Harbor Park • **Opened:** 1993 • **Capacity:** 12,057 • **Dimensions:** LF: 333, CF: 410, RF: 338 • **Surface:** grass • **Season:** Apr.–Labor Day

STADIUM LOCATION: 150 Park Ave., Norfolk, VA 23510

WEB SITE: http://www.norfolktides.com

GETTING THERE: From I-264, exit 9 (Waterside Dr.), adjacent to Elizabeth River. At first traffic light, left onto Water St., which leads you to the ballpark.

TICKET INFORMATION: 150 Park Ave., Norfolk, VA 23510, tel. 804/622–2222, fax 804/624–9090

PRICE RANGE: Box seats $7; reserved seats $5.50 adults, $4.50 children, senior citizens, and military personnel.

GAME TIME: Mon.–Sat. 7:15 PM, Sun. 1:15 (Apr.–June) and 6:15 (July–Aug.); gates open 75 min before game.

TIPS ON SEATING: All seats reserved. Best harbor view is from third-base side. First few rows of upper reserved seats provide great view of water.

SEATING FOR PEOPLE WITH DISABILITIES: Available throughout park; stadium has elevators

STADIUM FOOD: In the concourse, try the smoky cheddar sausage ($2.50, sauerkraut 25¢ extra). It's from the grills on each side of the stadium. The chicken sandwich, Italian and Polish sausages, and BBQ

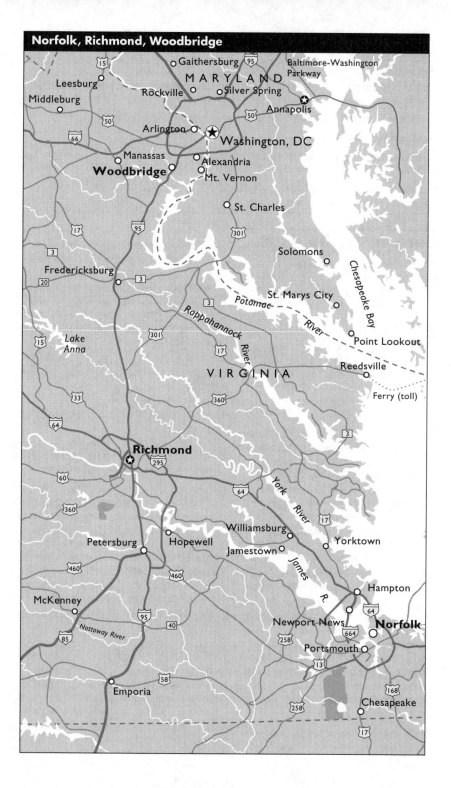

Norfolk, Richmond, Woodbridge

MARYLAND

Gaithersburg
Leesburg
Middleburg
Rockville
Silver Spring
Annapolis
Baltimore-Washington Parkway

Arlington
Washington, DC
Manassas
Woodbridge
Alexandria
Mt. Vernon

St. Charles

Solomons

Fredericksburg

Chesapeake Bay

St. Marys City

Potomac   River

Rappahannock River

VIRGINIA

Point Lookout

Reedsville

Ferry (toll)

Lake Anna

Richmond

York River

Williamsburg
Jamestown
Yorktown

Petersburg
Hopewell

McKenney

Nottoway River

Hampton

Newport News
Norfolk

Portsmouth

Emporia

Chesapeake

pork aren't special. There are Vinnie's hot pretzels from a grill, pan pizzas for $3, and fresh lemonade for $2.25. A picnic area is on the far wall behind second base. The three-tier restaurant on the first-base side opens 2 hrs before game time. The crab cakes dinner is excellent but pricey at $15.95. You can feed the kids from its four-item children's menu for less than the ballpark concessions.

SMOKING POLICY: Smoking prohibited throughout stadium with limited exceptions

PARKING: Ample parking available for $2

VISITING TEAM HOTEL: Omni Norfolk (777 Waterside Dr., Norfolk, VA 23510, tel. 804/622–6664 or 800/843–6664)

TOURISM INFORMATION: Norfolk Convention & Visitors Bureau (236 E. Plume St., Norfolk, VA 23510, tel. 804/441–1852 or 800/368–3097)

Norfolk: Harbor Park

What a difference a decade makes. The baseball in Richmond is first-rate. In Norfolk, the baseball and the stadium are both first-rate. Richmond's Diamond is built in the classic, imposing 1980s style that people expect at the Triple A level, where many of the players are on the road to the Show. It's a fine place to play and watch a game. Norfolk's new Harbor Park is a spectacular 1990s ballpark, ranked the best of minor-league ballparks by *Baseball America* in 1995. You can see trains, boats, and planes from your seat in the ballpark.

Designed by HOK and built for $15 million, the 12,057-seat Harbor Park sits on the bank of the Elizabeth River in Norfolk's revitalized downtown. Metropolitan Park, a 1970 stadium 6 miles from the downtown out near the airport, was showing its age when rival Virginia Beach began to make noises about building a stadium. Norfolk wasn't about to lose baseball to Virginia Beach. The Tidewater Tides, who had played in Met Park in Norfolk, became the Norfolk Tides, and Harbor Park opened in 1993.

The attractive brick entrance is colored in shades of beige. In Richmond, most of the seats are in the upper deck. In Norfolk, the majority of seats are on the first level. The best aspect of this beautiful new, fan-friendly stadium is the open concourse. You can go to the concession stands, buy what you need, and not miss a pitch. There are scoreboards in left and right, and you can get the scores of other International League games, a minor-league rarity.

The best view of the water is from the second deck on the third-base side in this waterfront park. Mostly what you see is industrial. Freight trains run behind left field. You cannot see the harbor well from many of the lower-level box seats. The Hits at Harbor Park restaurant out the first-base line is built on three levels, with lots of good views. There is an attractive multi-tier grass picnic area just beyond the left-field fence where kids can race around. It is reserved for private groups until 9 PM, when it opens to the public.

Arrive early and listen to the Tide Strolling Brass Band play for the hour before the game. Beware—the sound system is loud here and not friendly to the Tides' opponents. Rip Tide, the mascot, is giant, blue, fuzzy, lively, and friendly. You can get your child's face painted, and there is an excellent souvenir shop at the entrance. There are more contests and on-field antics than in most Triple AAA stadiums.

Norfolk baseball goes back almost 100 years, and it is worth the time to look at the Tidewater Baseball Shrine plaques along the concourse wall. Future Hall of Famer Pie Traynor, a Portsmouth star before being signed to play third base for the Pittsburgh Pirates, is here. Fastballer Bob Feller pitched for the Navy in Norfolk before going back to the Cleveland Indians. Philosopher and future Yankees great Yogi Berra drove in 23 runs in two games as a 17-year-old Norfolk Tar.

Where to Stay

Visiting Team Hotel: Omni Waterside. This impressive 10-story hotel is on the Elizabeth River, next to the Waterside festival marketplace and less than half a mile from the ballpark. Half the rooms have a harbor view. Guests may use a fitness center next door for $6 a day. *777 Waterside Dr., Norfolk 23510, tel. 804/622–*

6664 or 800/843–6664, fax 804/625–8271. 446 rooms. Facilities: restaurant, pool. AE, D, DC, MC, V. $$

Best Western–Center Inn. This quiet, attractive inn is in the southeast part of town, near the Military Circle shopping mall. The two-story inn, set back from the road in a country-club-style setting, is 10 minutes east of the ballpark. 235 N. Military Hwy., Norfolk 23502, tel. 804/461–6600 or 800/528–1234, fax 804/466–9093. 152 rooms. Facilities: restaurant, indoor and outdoor pools, hot tub, sauna, exercise room, coin laundry. AE, D, DC, MC, V. $$

Where to Eat

Doumar's Drive-In. This casual restaurant was founded by Abe Doumar, the creator of the ice cream cone at the 1904 St. Louis Exposition. Now run by his nephew, Albert Doumar, this is the place for fresh limeades, burgers, and sweet, freshly made ice cream cones. The cone press is within view, batter drippings and all. You can still get car service here. But with ice cream, you're likely to do better inside at the Formica booths. 19th and Monticello Sts., Norfolk, tel. 804/627–4163. No credit cards. $

Pierce's Pitt Bar-B-Que. Its Waterside festival marketplace stall is convenient for a stop before the ball game. This is a famed Virginia tomato-based sauce on lean, chewy pork. There also are Chinese, Greek, Mexican, Japanese, Cajun, and seafood fast-food restaurants in the Waterside mall food court, in the lower level. 333 Waterside Dr., Norfolk, tel. 804/622–0738. MC, V. $

Entertainments

Nauticus–National Maritime Center. This terrific learning museum is part science, part aquarium, and part amusement park. You can learn about the world's major shipwrecks in a fascinating audiovisual display. Visitors can ride in a submarine in Virtual Adventures and try out a naval battle simulator. There's a kid-friendly touch pool with (baby) sharks and starfish and squid in eye-level tanks. At an adjoining deep-water pier, working ships are docked. Its theater has a big-screen Living Sea film. You can park in city lots two blocks south. This attraction is less than a mile from Harbor Park baseball. 1 Waterside Dr., Norfolk, tel. 804/664–1000 or 800/

664–1080. Admission: $10.95 adults, $7.95 ages 6–17, under 6 free with paying companion. Open daily 10–7. MC, V.

Elizabeth River Ferry. If you don't have time or money for a cruise, this 5-minute paddle-wheel trip takes you across the harbor and back. It departs from the Waterside every 30 minutes on the quarter hour. The Waterside, Norfolk, tel. 804/640–6300. Admission: 75¢ adults, 50¢ children.

Carrie B. Norfolk Harbor Tour. This reproduction Mississippi paddle wheeler takes visitors past the Norfolk waterfront, the navy submarines, dry dock, and aircraft carriers. The noon tour is 90 minutes, the later tour 2½ hours. There also are sunset cruises from June through Labor Day. Phillips Waterside seafood restaurant offers lunch and dinner packages with the cruises. The Waterside, Norfolk, tel. 804/393–4735. Admission (90-min tour): $12 adults, $6 ages under 13. Open Apr.–Oct. noon and 2. AE, MC, V.

Children's Museum of Virginia. From Norfolk, you can take the five-minute ferry across the river and walk to this hands-on museum. Children use a working crane to haul (foam) I-beams in a construction exhibit. They also can climb walls, cover themselves in bubbles, learn about kaleidoscopes, and see constellations in the 64-seat planetarium. 221 High St., Portsmouth, tel. 804/393–8393 or 800/767–8782. Admission: $4. Open Sun.–Thurs. 10–5, Fri. 10–9.

Virginia Zoological Park. This small zoo, on the Lafayette River, has a superb tiger exhibit. The park is easily navigated by small children and is inexpensive. There also are elephants, monkeys, and snakes, among other animals. 3500 Granby St., Norfolk, tel. 804/441–5227. Admission: $2 adults, $1 children. Open daily 10–5.

Busch Gardens. This amusement park is based on four European countries during the 17th century—Germany, Italy, England, and France. Adults like this park for the superior food, and kids are delighted by the number and intensity of its rides. The "Escape from Pompeii" water ride is scary, and several other rides—"Loch Ness Monster" and "Drachen Fire" roller coasters, "Big Bad Wolf" free-fall—are best for teenagers. Beer is given out at the hospitality center. Discount coupons for the park and for Water

Country are available through the Norfolk Convention Center (tel. 800/368–3097). Parking is $4. *1 Busch Gardens Blvd. (U.S. 60), Exit 242A from I–64, Williamsburg, tel. 804/253–3350. Admission: $29.95 adults, $22.95 ages 3–6. Open mid-May–Labor Day, daily 10–7; Apr., weekends 10–7, early Sept.–end Oct., Fri.–Tues. 10–7.*

Water Country USA. This 40-acre water park has 30 rides, including "Rambling Water," a calming, lazy river ride. The park is decorated in a '60s surfing theme and is 3 miles from Busch Gardens, which owns it. *176 Water Country Pkwy., Williamsburg, tel. 804/229–9300. Admission: $21.95 adults, $15.95 ages 3–6. Open late May–Labor Day, daily 10–7; early Sept.–mid-Sept., weekends 10–dusk.*

Sites to See

Walking Tours of Historic Norfolk. A downtown walking tour should include the newly restored Wells Theatre (108 E. Tazewell St., tel. 804/627–6988) and the nearly intact 1890s-to-1930s commercial district. You can get a free brochure and map from the Norfolk Convention and Visitors Bureau. *236 E. Plume St., Norfolk, tel. 800/368–3097.*

Williamsburg. More than 500 buildings make up this living-history museum. Williamsburg was the state capital from 1699 to 1780, and this restoration returns you to those years, public stockades and all. In an ancient American tradition, the capitol building was surrounded by excellent taverns that still serve memorable meals. All the contradictions are shown—an 18th-century economy based on tobacco and slavery that produced some of the greatest leaders civilization has known. If your children don't have the patience to view historic interiors, you do not need to buy passes if you only walk the streets, browse the shops, or eat in the unique taverns. There is short-term parking in the Williamsburg shops area adjacent to the Historic District. *Rte. 132 and Francis St., Williamsburg, tel. 800/447–8679. Admission: $25 adults, $15 ages 6–12. Open daily 9–5.*

College of William & Mary. This beautiful college is second only to Harvard University in age in the U.S. Presidents Thomas Jefferson, James

Monroe, and John Tyler were graduates. Children may cringe at the hard chairs and severe atmosphere of the Wren Building, where classes have been held since 1695. Students act as tour guides. *Duke of Gloucester St., Williamsburg, tel. 804/221–3278. Open Sept.–May, Mon.–Sat. 9–5.*

Yorktown National Battlefield and Victory Center. The Revolutionary War comes alive here, at the site of the war's last major battle. You can explore Washington's headquarters site, Surrender Field, and the house where General Cornwallis discussed his surrender. It also is a good place to picnic. At the center, you can see a Colonial-era farm and an army camp. The battlefield is free and is open daily 8:30–5. Maps are available for a self-guided tour of the battlefield. *Old Rte. 238, Yorktown, tel. 804/887–1776. Admission: $6.75 adults, $3.25 ages 6–12. Open daily 9–5.*

Jamestown Settlement. The remains of the first permanent English settlement lie just west of Williamsburg. It is outdoor living history of the 1640s, with the original church tower, house foundations, three reconstructed ships, and a replica of a Powhatan Indian village. You can try on armor at a fort and play early versions of bowling and ring toss. A combination pass with the Yorktown Victory Center is available for $12.50 adults, $6 ages 6–12. *Rte. 31 S and Colonial Pkwy., Williamsburg, tel. 804/229–1607. Admission: $9 adults, $4.25 ages 6–12. Open daily 9–5.*

Unusual Shopping

The Tenth Inning. Baseball collectors and Cal Ripken, Jr. fans should be sure to stop at Don and Carolyn Harrison's excellent and extensive baseball-card shop in Hampton. The Harrisons are the authors of the *Cal Ripken, Jr. Checklist Book,* a comprehensive listing of more than 1,300 Ripken items, and devote 5 of their 50 showcases and much of their wall space to Ripken items for sale. Hampton is 15 miles southwest of Norfolk. *3324 W. Mercury Blvd., Hampton, tel. 804/827–1667.*

RICHMOND BRAVES

League: International League • **Major League Affiliation:** Atlanta Braves • **Class:** AAA • **Stadium:** The Diamond • **Opened:** 1954/85 • **Capacity:** 12,146 • **Dimensions:** LF: 330, CF: 402, RF: 330 • **Surface:** grass • **Season:** Apr.–Labor Day

STADIUM LOCATION: 3001 N. Blvd. Richmond, VA 23230

WEB SITE: http://www.rbraves.com

GETTING THERE: From I–95, take exit 78 (Blvd. exit) 2 blocks south to stadium. Traveling east or west, I–65 will merge with I–95.

TICKET INFORMATION: Box 6667, Richmond, VA 23230, tel. 804/359–4444, fax 804/359–0731

PRICE RANGE: Box seats $7; reserved seats $5; general admission $4 adults, $2 ages 3–12 and senior citizens, under 3 free.

GAME TIME: Mon.–Sat. 7 PM, Sun. 2 PM; gates open 1 hr before game time.

TIPS ON SEATING: Reserved seats in second deck are close to action, as there is little foul territory here. Roof provides shade on sunny Sunday afternoons.

SEATING FOR PEOPLE WITH DISABILITIES: On main concourse behind home plate with access by elevator; special parking is available on third-base side of stadium.

STADIUM FOOD: The **Diamond Room** restaurant, on the main concourse on the first-base side behind sections 101–104, is open to all fans starting 75 min before the game. There are children's prices— $6.95 for the turkey dinner that costs adults $12.95. Reserve one week to one month ahead for window seats. There's a no-smoking section. The concourse offerings are standard, but the hot dogs and corn dogs are not good. Fruit juices are available by the terraces, as are club sandwiches. There's a grilled Italian sausage on the third-base side by the entrance.

SMOKING POLICY: Smoking permitted anywhere in stadium.

PARKING: $2 at stadium and across street next to bus station.

VISITING TEAM HOTEL: Holiday Inn I–64 (6531 W. Broad St., Richmond, VA 23230, tel. 804/285– 9951 or 800/465–4329)

TOURISM INFORMATION: Metro Richmond Convention & Visitors Bureau (550 E. Marshall St., Richmond, VA 23219, tel. 804/782–2777 or 800/365–7272)

Richmond: The Diamond

The Diamond in Richmond got its name because of a letter from an anonymous fan, "a fan on the third-base side." The stadium could have been named for Dr. William H. Parker, the great supporter of amateur athletics in Richmond for whom the predecessor stadium had been named. Or it could have been named for former Richmond Brave Tommie Aaron, the younger brother of Hank Aaron who had died of leukemia in 1983. But the November 1984 letter won the day: "Richmond could use a healthy dose of hope and togetherness and the Diamond can be a special mix of our combined efforts in building the park along with the magic attraction of the game."

The catchy campaign slogan to replace the shabby Parker Field with a state-of-the-art stadium was "Diamonds Aren't Forever." The community rallied to the call with funds supplied by the city, and the suburbs matched by private contributions. "The Diamond" struck a chord with many as the perfect representation of that community partnership. The letter is reprinted on the Richmond Wall of Fame on the stadium's first-base side.

The Diamond sits just off I–95 not far outside town. A field was first built here on the Boulevard in 1934. The high-school football stadium was converted into a baseball stadium in 1954 and named Parker Field for Triple AAA International League baseball. After the 1984 season, the field was completely rebuilt in 226 days at a cost of $8 million. Amazingly, the double-decked, roofed stadium was ready for the 1985 season. Seven thousand of the 12,500 seats are in the upper deck. Foul territory is limited, and the steep-sloped upper-deck seats are surprisingly close to the action.

You are greeted on the concourse level by Chief Connecticut, a 10- by 20-foot fiberglass Native American acquired from a suburban Maryland shopping center. Next you will be struck by the wonderful smells from the grill at the third-base side of the entrance. The best food, however, is across the street at Bill's Barbecue. Stop there first.

The truth is that the view from the seats beyond the advertising signs on the stadium wall is uninspiring. Trucks and cars whiz by on I–95 beyond parking lots, hotels, factories, and an aging arena. But the Diamond isn't about beautiful views or on-the-field contests for fans. The Diamond is about baseball. And this is quality Triple AAA baseball. The Diamond is full of serious, well-informed fans. The crowd is in the game, egged on by the scoreboard flashing "Noise. Noise. Noise."

When the Braves moved south to Atlanta from Milwaukee, their Triple A Atlanta Crackers moved to Richmond. This three-decade affiliation has brought top talent to Richmond, from the brothers Niekro to David Justice and Tommy Glavine. Ted Turner, who owns both Braves teams, umpired a May 10, 1978, exhibition game between his two clubs here.

Where to Stay

If you don't have to plan ahead, you can save money and stay in one of the city's elegant hotels by using one of four visitor centers (1710 Robin Hood Rd., by the ballpark, Exit 78 from I–95 and I–64, Richmond, tel. 804/358–5511; 6th St. Marketplace, 2nd floor, 550 E. Marshall St., Richmond, tel. 804/782–2777; State Capitol grounds, bell tower, Capitol Sq., Richmond, tel. 804/648–3146; Richmond International Airport, Exit 197 from I–64, Richmond, tel. 804/

236–3260) to make same-day bookings. The centers offer walk-in customers the lowest prices at the elegant Berkeley Hotel, Linden Row Inn, and Jefferson Hotel, as well as moderately priced lodgings.

Visiting Team Hotel: Holiday Inn I–64. This hotel has a seven-story tower and a main five-story section. The ballpark is 3 miles away. The rooms are standard size, and kids eat free. *6531 W. Broad St., Exit 183 from I–64, Richmond 23230, tel. 804/285–9951 or 800/465–4329, fax 804/282–5642. 280 rooms. Facilities: restaurant, indoor pool, hot tub, exercise room. AE, D, DC, MC, V. $$*

The Jefferson Hotel. This gloriously renovated 1895 hotel has a majestic center stairway, an immense lobby, and high-ceiling rooms with tasteful reproduction antiques. The downtown landmark is on the National Register of Historic Places. Self-parking is $9.50 daily. Swimming is available free to guests across the street at the YMCA's indoor pool. *Franklin and Adams Sts., Richmond 23220, tel. 804/788–8000 or 800/424–8014, fax 804/225–0334. 275 rooms. Facilities: restaurant, grill, beauty salon, health club. AE, D, DC, MC, V. $$*

Omni Richmond Hotel. This downtown high-rise has 19 floors, with good views of the city. Rooms are slightly larger than usual. Underground parking is $9 per day. *100 S. 12th St., Richmond 23219, tel. 804/344–7000 or 800/843–6664, fax 804/648–6704. 361 rooms. Facilities: 2 restaurants, indoor pool. AE, D, DC, MC, V. $$*

Where to Eat

Bill's Barbecue. This has been a Richmond institution since 1930 and now has seven locations, including this one across from the ballpark. It serves wonderful fresh limeades, including one version with grape juice added. Its chopped pork sandwich is topped with dry coleslaw and wrapped in gray paper with a toothpick. There also are good onion rings and lemon chess pie. Its motto rings true: "A trial makes a customer at Bill's Barbecue." *3100 N. Boulevard, Richmond, tel. 804/358–8634. No credit cards. $*

Joe's Inn. This is the kind of warm, neighborhood place that Hollywood romanticizes. Service can be harried, because this wooden-booth spaghetti and pizza place is popular with families, students, and neighbors. There is a kid's menu. It is in the Victorian-era Fan District between Hanover and Grove streets. *205 N. Shields Ave., Richmond, tel. 804/355–2282. AE, MC, V. $*

John and Norman's. This casual spot near the Fan District is known for its breakfasts. There are jukeboxes on the tables and regulars in the chairs. *2525 Hanover Ave., Richmond, tel. 804/358–9731. D, MC, V. $*

Entertainments

Raft rides on the James River. You've probably never floated through a major city before. The Richmond Raft Co. will take you through downtown via class 3 and 4 white water for those 12 and older. Or the whole family can take the slower, flatwater run on Sunday at 2 and 4. Buy your tickets and embark at the foot of the former Tredegar Iron Works. *Tredegar St., Richmond, tel. 804/222–7238. Cost: $19.95–$45 per person. Times vary according to river conditions.*

Science Museum of Virginia. This hands-on museum with more than 250 exhibits is in the city's former Broad Street Railroad Station. An adjoining planetarium and space theater have planet and constellation shows and laser shows. The IMAX movie is $2 extra. *2500 W. Broad St., Richmond, tel. 804/367–0000 or 800/659–1727. Admission: $4.75 adults, $4.25 ages 4–12 and senior citizens. Open Mon.–Thurs. 9:30–5:30, Fri.–Sat. 9:30–7, Sun. 11:30–5.*

Sites to See

State Capitol. Richmond, as the capital of the South in the Civil War, is heaven for history buffs. The Thomas Jefferson–inspired Capitol houses the oldest English-speaking continuous lawmaking body in the Western Hemisphere. Jefferson selected the Maison Carrée, a Roman temple built in France, as the model and hand-picked the architect to assist him. The Classic Revival–style Capitol with Ionic columns has been in use since 1788 and was completed in 1800. It served as the Capitol of the Confederacy from 1861 to 1865. Side wings were added in 1904–06 to house the two legislative chambers. The Capitol Rotunda is adorned with one of America's most important pieces of sculpture—a life-size marble statue of George Washington executed from life by the French artist Jean-Antoine Houdon. *Capitol Sq., Richmond, tel. 804/786–4344. Open Apr.–Nov., daily 9–5; Dec.–Mar., Mon.–Sat. 9–5, Sun. 1–5.*

Executive Mansion. On an attractive park stands the 1813 Executive Mansion, the oldest governor's residence in the country. Nearby is an elegant equestrian statue of George Washington. *Governor's St., Richmond, tel. 804/371–2642. Open Tues. 2–4, Fri. 10–noon.*

White House of the Confederacy. As the president of the Confederacy, Jefferson Davis lived from 1861 to 1865 in the neoclassical John Brockenbrough House. The mansion contains an extraordinary number of original items, including a cast-iron cannon in the children's room that is capable of firing and the rosewood table where Jackson, Lee, and Davis worked out war strategy. The 35-minute tour may be too much for younger children. *1201 E. Clay St., Richmond, tel. 804/649–1861. Admission: $5.50 adults, $3.50 students. Open Mon.–Sat. 10–5, Sun. noon–5.*

Softball Hall of Fame Museum. There are four memento-crammed rooms, an eight-minute movie, and photos of some of the 100,000 teams in the U.S. Slo-Pitch Softball Association in this museum, 30 minutes south of Richmond. The industrial, church, Hispanic, men's, women's, mixed, and youth leagues cover every state. *3935 S. Crater Rd., Petersburg, Va, tel. 804/733–1005. Admission: $1.50 adults, $1 ages 12–18 and senior citizens, under 12 free. Open weekdays 9–4, Sat. 10–4, Sun. noon–4.*

Historic Richmond Tour. Guided walking tours of history, architecture, and specific Richmond sights, like the Hollywood Cemetery, are held weekly. The departure site varies depending on the topic. Reservations should be made a day in advance. *Historic Richmond Foundation, tel. 804/780–0107. Admission: $5 adults. Open Apr.–Oct., Sun. 2–4.*

St. John's Church. This is the site where Patrick Henry gave his "Give me liberty or give me death" speech to the Second Virginia Convention in March 1775. Tours of the church and yard are given. *2401 E. Broad St., Richmond, tel. 804/648–5015. Open Mon.–Sat. 10–3:30, Sun. 1–3:30.*

Richmond National Battlefield Park. View several Civil War forts and battle sites here. Start at the Chimborazo Visitor Center, once the site of a major Civil War hospital. There's a movie, exhibits, and several self-guided tours. *3215 E. Broad St., Richmond, tel.· 804/226–1981. Open daily 9–5.*

Shockoe Slip. Cobblestone streets, tobacco warehouses, new shops, and the elegant Berkeley Hotel mark this area. One of the city's three microbreweries, Richbrau, runs a pub here. *E. Cary St., between 12th and 15th Sts.*

Canal Walk. A pleasant walk borders the river from between 10th and Bank streets to the James River Plaza. The Kanawha Canal locks are at 12th and Byrd streets.

Monument Avenue. It is worth a drive down this broad 1887-era boulevard. Civil War monuments and a new statue of tennis star Arthur Ashe dot the wide median while mansions and churches line its sides.

Maggie L. Walker Home. In Jackson Ward, Richmond's historic black district, called "the birthplace of black capitalism," is the home of Maggie L. Walker, founder of the St. Luke Penny Savings Bank, the first bank founded by a woman. *110½ E. Leigh St., Richmond, tel. 804/780–1380. Open Wed.–Sun. 9–5.*

"Bojangles" Statue. Don't miss the monument to Bill "Bojangles" Robinson, the film star and tap dancer, at Leigh and Chamberlayne Parkway near his birthplace. The statue is where Robinson donated a stoplight to protect neighborhood children who followed the same route to school that he took as a child.

PRINCE WILLIAM CANNONS

League: Carolina League • **Major League Affiliation:** St. Louis Cardinals • **Class:** A • **Stadium:** G. Richard Pfitzner Stadium • **Opened:** 1984 • **Capacity:** 6,000 • **Dimensions:** LF: 315, CF: 400, RF: 315 • **Surface:** grass • **Season:** Apr.–Labor Day

STADIUM LOCATION: 7 County Complex Court, Woodbridge, VA 22193

WEB SITE: www.pwcweb.com/rec/sports/cannons

GETTING THERE: From Washington, I–95S to Exit 158B (Prince William Pkwy./Manassas). Continue on parkway 5 mi; right onto County Complex Court.

TICKET INFORMATION: Box 2148, Woodbridge, VA 22193, tel. 703/590–2311, fax 703/590–5716

PRICE RANGE: Field box seats $8.50; box seats $7.50; reserved $6.50; general admission $4.50 adults, $3.50 ages 6–14 and senior citizens; under 6 free

GAME TIME: Weeknights 7:30, Sat. 7 PM, Sun. 1:30 PM (Apr.–June) or 6 (July–Aug.); gates open 1 hr before game.

TIPS ON SEATING: General admission seats are metal grandstands down base lines.

SEATING FOR PEOPLE WITH DISABILITIES: Behind third base in general admission grandstand

STADIUM FOOD: The grilled chicken sandwich sold at the grills behind first and third bases is your best bet. Avoid the rib-b-que sandwich, which is pressed meat with heavy sauce. Also skip the grilled Italian sausage, which is sub-par. Pizza Hut pan pizzas are a hefty $4. There's not much choice for healthy eating.

SMOKING POLICY: Section 4 behind home plate is no-smoking.

PARKING: Ample $2 parking near stadium; as only one road leads out from stadium, expect delays leaving on nights with big crowds.

VISITING TEAM HOTEL: Days Inn–Potomac Mills (14619 Potomac Mills Rd., Woodbridge, VA 22192, tel. 703/494–4433 or 800/325–2525)

TOURISM INFORMATION: Prince William County Conference and Visitors Bureau (4349 Ridgewood Center Dr. Prince William, VA 22192, tel. 703/792–6680 or 800/334–9876)

Prince William County: Pfitzner Stadium

Pfitzner Stadium in Woodbridge, Virginia, is a clean, comfortable, suburban stadium of the mid-1980s. Set within a county government complex and surrounded by three lighted softball fields, the home of the Prince William Cannons represents the community spirit of a growing suburban area.

We first visited for a festive Fourth of July weekend game in 1992, and we loved it. There was plenty of action, both on-the-field playing and between-innings contests, to keep our entire family from grandmother to toddler happy. A thick stock of beautiful trees beyond the outfield wall sets the stadium off nicely. Our only complaint was the traffic jam at the end of the game, as the huge holiday crowd all had to leave by the same exit.

Now, we confess, this stadium seems ordinary. It does not compare to the fantastic minor-league stadiums of the 1990s. The uncovered metal grandstand lacks a feeling of permanence. The county added box seats in 1994 and made additional improvements in 1995, including a new souvenir store. The Prince William Cannons continue to put on a good show and draw solid crowds, but this is not the new Durham ballpark and no amount of tinkering will make it so.

A member of the Prince William County Board of Supervisors, G. Richard (Rick) Pfitzner, was the driving force behind the team's move from historic Alexandria to Prince William in 1984. As more and more young families moved farther from the central city, they needed the kind of inexpensive family entertainment that minor league baseball provides. Prince William County saw the market and took action. In 1994, the stadium was named after Pfitzner, a long-time supporter of youth sports.

Imagine the team the Cannons fielded in 1985, just a year after moving to Prince William County. A Pittsburgh Pirates franchise then, they had Barry Bonds and Bobby Bonilla. Well, imagine again. Hard as it is to believe, that team went 65–74.

Where to Stay

Visiting Team Motel: Days Inn–Potomac Mills. The shopping-mall surroundings lack atmosphere, but the rooms are clean, with no surprises. Guests get a free Continental breakfast. The hotel is 15 minutes from the ballpark. *14619 Potomac Mills Rd., Exit 156 from I–95, Woodbridge 22192, tel. 703/491–4433 or 800/325–2525, fax 703/385–2627. 176 rooms. Facilities: pool, coin laundry. AE, D, DC, MC, V. $$*

Where to Eat

Mike's Diner. The 1970s brick exterior resembles a pancake house on a commercial strip, but inside it's a family diner specializing in real turkey. Waitresses wear T-shirts saying EAT MORE MEAT-LOAF, and it's wise to take their advice. The good-value kid's meals include pudding or ice cream. The diner is 30 minutes from the ballpark. *8401 Digges Rd., Manassas, tel. 703/361–5248. AE, MC, V. $*

Red, Hot and Blue. This good local chain, in a commercial strip on Route 234, serves Memphis pit barbecue. It's a sit-down restaurant, but service is speedy. There is a children's menu. *8637 Sudley Rd., Manassas, tel. 703/330–4847. AE, MC, V. $*

Entertainments

Manassas Battlefield. The nickname Cannons was a no-brainer for Prince William County. Two of the most significant battles of the Civil War were fought just miles away. The first battle after the attack on Fort Sumter was fought on the plains of Manassas on July 21, 1861. Federal troops coming south from Washington expected to rout the Confederate Army easily on their way to take Richmond, the Confederate capital. The overconfident Northerners were beaten in what Southerners call the First Battle of Manassas and Northerners call Bull Run (after a nearby stream). The next year, Robert E. Lee took command of the Confederate Army and defeated the Union troops in the Second Battle of Manassas on August 28–30, 1862. The two Confederate victories made clear this would not be a short war. Climb on a cannon and walk the fields once red with blood.

The National Park Service runs a solid visitor center. There are a six-minute slide show, excellent walking-tour brochures, and a heroic statue of Confederate general Stonewall Jackson, who earned his nickname at the First Battle of Manassas, where he and his troops stood "like a stone wall." *12521 Lee Hwy. at S.R. 234, about 26 mi southwest of Washington between I–66 and U.S. 29, Manassas, tel. 703/754–1861. Admission: $2 adults, $4 family. Open: grounds 8:30–dusk; visitor center 8:30–6.*

Paramount's Kings Dominion. Experience the latest in thrill rides and the wild Hurricane Reef water park. There are 6 roller coasters and many other rides (the "Diamond Falls" boat plunge, the "Avalanche" bobsled, and the "Sky Pilot") too extreme for any but older teens. *Star Trek* figures wander the grounds. There is simulated white-water rafting and stock-car racing. The kiddie section is Hanna-Barbera Land, with cartoon characters in costume. Parking is $4. Discount coupons are available at Giant grocery stores. *S.R. 30, Exit 98 from I–95, Doswell, tel. 804/876–5000. Admission: $28.95 adults, $23.95 senior citizens, $19.95 ages 3–6. Open late Mar.–mid-Oct., 10:30–10; closing times vary. AE, MC, V.*

Sites to See

Old Town Alexandria. The Cannons left Alexandria more than a decade ago, but you can drive north on I–95 to the city George Washington and Robert E. Lee called home. Old Town has waterfront charm, historic buildings, fine restaurants, and superb neighborhoods. Visit the **Torpedo Factory Art Center** (105 N. Union St., between King and Cameron Sts., tel. 703/838–4565), a refurbished World Wars I and II factory where crafts have replaced torpedoes. The Alexandria Convention & Visitors Bureau has self-guided tour maps of the 18-block area and gives a free parking pass for up to 24 hours at street meters. *Alexandria Convention & Visitors Bureau, 221 King St., Alexandria, tel. 703/838–4200. 1-hr guided tours: $3 adults, $1.50 ages 6–17. Open 9–5.*

Mount Vernon. The home and burial place of George and Martha Washington is just south of Old Town Alexandria. The mansion has been beautifully restored to its appearance in the last year of President Washington's life. *George Washington Memorial Pkwy., Mount Vernon, tel. 703/780–2000. Admission: $7 adults, $3 ages 6–11. Open Apr.–Aug., daily 8–5; Mar. and Sept.–Oct. daily 9–5; Nov.–Feb. daily 9–4.*

STAR-SPANGLED BANNER WEEKEND   8
BALTIMORE, FREDERICK, HAGERSTOWN, DELMARVA

Maryland baseball is as varied as the state's topography, which is akin to a mini-America, containing mountains, ocean, plains, and cities. Visionary management is making it possible to see future Baltimore Orioles players at all levels of the minor leagues within Maryland. Start in Baltimore, where Camden Yards, our favorite new major league ballpark, is the epicenter. This dark green steel-and-brick classic ballpark has a restored Baltimore & Ohio warehouse running from right field to center. A city street was made part of the park, and it's become an outdoor concourse for some of the best food in baseball. Babe Ruth's birthplace and museum is two blocks northwest of the ballpark and just seven blocks from the city's Harborplace, a waterside mall that set the standard for downtown retail renovations. The National Aquarium is on the harbor, as is the Top of the World observation tower.

Two hours west of Baltimore on Interstate 70 is Frederick, the home of the Keys, a Single A Carolina League team. The stadium is the model for new, small minor-league parks, with a playground for kids, a carousel, and grass hills for restless young viewers. The Antietam National Battlefield is 25 miles west.

North 28 miles is Hagerstown, the home of the Single A Suns in the South Atlantic League. The blue-collar city's 1931 stadium has been renovated, keeping the charm of its covered grandstand but adding a new bullpen, a clubhouse, and picnic and play areas. This city has a spectacular small city park, with a vintage bandshell, ducks on its 50-acre lake, ball fields, and a fine small art museum.

Another Single A South Atlantic League team recently revived is in Salisbury, on Maryland's eastern shore. The Delmarva Shorebirds play two hours south of Baltimore, off Route 50. The brand-new stadium has a kid's playground, a carousel, and grassy berms for overflow crowds. This chicken-producing city has a fine museum of Wildfowl Art, along with a well-kept free-admission zoo.

BALTIMORE ORIOLES

League: American League • **Class:** Major • **Stadium:** Oriole Park at Camden Yards • **Opened:** 1992 • **Capacity:** 48,262 • **Dimensions:** LF: 335, CF: 400, RF: 318 • **Surface:** grass • **Season:** Apr.–early Oct.

STADIUM LOCATION: 333 West Camden St., Baltimore, MD 21201

WEB SITE: www.TheOrioles.com

GETTING THERE: From south, take I–95 exit 52 or 53. From north, take I–83 and follow St. Paul St. south to ballpark. From west, take I–70 to I–695 and U.S. 40. From east, take U.S. 40 or Eastern Ave. For

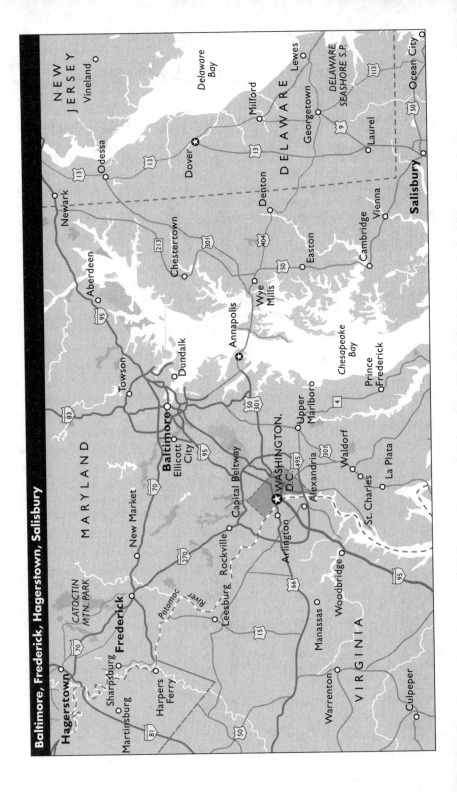

information about bus, light rail, and park-and-ride routes, call MTA (tel. 410/539–5000). Light rail trains run every 15 minutes. For information about MARC trains from Washington, call 800/325–7245.

Ticket Information: 333 West Camden St., Baltimore, MD 21201, tel. 410/685–9800, fax 410/547–6272.

Price Range: club box seats, $25; Box seats, $12–$20; reserved seats, $7–$9; bleachers, $5; and standing room, $3.

Game Time: Weekdays 7:35 PM, Sat. 7:05, Sun. 1:35 PM; gates open weekdays 90 min before game time and weekends 2 hr before.

Tips on Seating: Buy seats well in advance. Camden Yards is one of toughest tickets to get in baseball. We like seats on first-base side with view of historic Bromo Selzer Tower. At 5 PM before night games, 183 section-90 bleacher seats go on sale for $5. When a game is sold out in advance, 275 standing-room-only tickets go on sale for $3 two hours before game. Fans with SRO tickets may stand behind scoreboard wall in right field or bullpens in center.

Seating for People with Disabilities: More than 400 seats throughout ballpark are available. Call 410/685–9800 for information about special services. In lot A and lot B/C are 100 parking spaces for vehicles with permits.

Stadium Food: You'll smell **Boog's Bar-b-que** on the Eutaw St. walk before you see its lines. Go pre-game for good ribs, a great pit beef/pork/turkey platter ($7), and maybe Boog Powell's autograph. Don't miss **Uncle Teddy's** freshly made pretzels, doused in butter and cinnamon ($2.75). Good crab soup ($2.75) is sold in May, Sept., and Oct. at **Pastimes Cafe,** a cafeteria in the warehouse. It sells milk, yogurt, and salads and is quiet after the 2nd inning. Go to the third-base side for crab cakes; good, but they're $6.25 with a bad roll. Kosher hot dogs and knishes are sold Sun.–Thurs. at **Project Ezra** in the main concourse. Turkey-breast sandwiches ($5) and tropical fruit shakes ($2) are sold widely. Grilled chicken sandwiches ($5) and good coleslaw (75¢) are at **Bambino's Ribs** on Eutaw St.

Smoking Policy: Smoking prohibited in seating bowl, but allowed on lower and upper level concourses and other designated areas.

Parking: Parking at ballpark costs $5 in B/C/E lot (take exit 53 off I–95). Many garages nearby in business district.

Tourism Information: Baltimore Area Convention & Visitors Center (300 W. Pratt St., Baltimore, MD 21201, tel. 410/837–4636 or 800/282–6632).

Baltimore: Camden Yards

For a quarter of a century, America's cities built an unbroken string of horrid, sterile, concrete monstrosities for baseball's boys of summer. And there were those awful fields of plastic grass. All this changed dramatically in 1992 with the opening of Baltimore's Oriole Park at Camden Yards. Finally, somebody got it right—a fan-friendly baseball park right in the downtown.

How did it come about and how did it get that long name? Many in Baltimore feared that the Orioles might follow Baltimoreans' beloved NFL Colts, who were just about literally stolen in the middle of the night. The thought of it was too much for the strong-willed mayor of Baltimore,

William Donald Schaefer. When the mayor became governor, he devoted his considerable political skills to insisting that the state legislature approve a new stadium for Baltimore's downtown. Then came a new owner, this time a New York leveraged-buyout king named Eli Jacobs. The new owner, who had a long-standing interest in architecture, insisted on a ballpark, not a stadium.

Together, Schaefer and Jacobs set off a rush of superb downtown ballparks. But they disagreed on what to call their masterpiece. Jacobs, the champion of baseball-stadium architecture, wanted to name it Oriole Park after the long-time home of the International League Orioles that had burned to the ground in 1944. Schaefer, the champion of Baltimore's downtown, insisted that the ballpark be named Camden Yards to preserve the memory of the historic

1858 railroad station called Camden Station. After months of embarrassing stalemate, they agreed on Oriole Park at Camden Yards.

Red brick. Dark green steel. Real grass. This $105 million, 48,262-seat stadium has a classic ballpark look. HOK's baseball-only design and steel construction provide an intimacy never experienced in the monstrosities of the 1960s and '70s. The asymmetrical field is reminiscent of the old-time parks that were squeezed into neighborhoods. They brought home plate and the right-field foul pole from Memorial Stadium.

Truth be told, without the warehouse, this is merely a fine stadium. It is the redbrick eight-story B & O warehouse that makes Camden Yards the very best of the 1990s stadiums. The warehouse, the longest building on America's east coast, is 1,016 feet long, running from right field to beyond the huge scoreboard in straight-away center. The right-field lights hang from the warehouse roof, making the warehouse, 426 feet from home plate in right field, an integral part of the stadium. The dramatic Cal Ripken, Jr. streak countdown in 1995 took place here with 10-foot-high numbers being unfurled on the side of the warehouse night after night until the magic 2,131 was reached. The 1905 classic railroad warehouse might well have been bulldozed to open a vista toward Baltimore's Inner Harbor but for Eric Moss, a Syracuse University architecture student whose 1987 model featured the warehouse. Baseball fans everywhere owe Eric Moss our thanks.

Take a walk before the game and see if you don't agree that Eutaw Street is one of America's great urban spaces. First visit the 9-foot, 800-pound bronze Babe Ruth statue at the entrance near the north end of the warehouse. Look closely and you will see that the left-handed Ruth has a right-handed glove. Near the historic Camden Station and in front of the ticket windows are 4-foot-high aluminum figures honoring the retired Orioles uniform numbers—Jim Palmer (No. 22), Brooks Robinson (No. 5), Frank Robinson (No. 20), and Earl Weaver (No. 4). Eddie Murray's No. 33 will appear after he retires.

Once you've passed through the gates, look at the Orioles Hall of Fame plaques at the base of the scoreboard beyond center field. Stop in at the Orioles Baseball Store. Look for baseball-size markers embedded in the walkway that indicate where some of the longest homers hit in Camden Yards have landed. Buy a barbecue sandwich and get an autograph from big Boog Powell, a Baltimore favorite whose booming home runs won him an American League MVP Award in 1970. There is a bronze star on the warehouse next to Bambino's restaurant that marks the spot where Ken Griffey, Jr. hit a ball in the All-Star Workout Home Run Hitting Contest in 1993. Cal Ripken, Jr. fans will want to visit the left-field bleachers. The red seat in section 86 marks the spot where Cal's 278th home run—the highest number ever by a major-league shortstop—landed on July 15, 1993.

To visit the Orioles dugout, press box, scoreboard control room, and club-level suites, join a Camden Yards tour. These 90-minute tours are highly informative. Unfortunately, they don't take you into the locker rooms. *333 W. Camden St., Baltimore, tel. 410/547–6234. Admission: $5 adults; $4 senior citizens and children. Tours daily (except on days of afternoon games) Mar.–Nov., Mon.–Sat. at 11 and 2, Sun. at 12:30 and 2.*

More Baltimore Baseball

Memorial Stadium. Ironically, Baltimore's Memorial Stadium, the predecessor of Camden Yards, was a pretty fine stadium. When Oriole Park burned to the ground on July 4, 1944, the International League Orioles moved into Municipal Stadium on East 33rd Street. A new ballpark named Memorial Stadium was erected in its place beginning in 1950. Work was completed on the double-decked horseshoe in time for the St. Louis Browns' move to Baltimore in 1954. The Orioles won the World Championship once in each of the next three decades—1966, 1970, and 1983. Here Brooks Robinson put on a fielding clinic at third base for 23 seasons. Frank Robinson hit a home run entirely out of the stadium on May 8, 1966, on his way to a Triple Crown/MVP year. Jim Palmer won three Cy Young awards. Cal Ripken, Jr.'s incredible streak began here on May 30, 1982. Memorial Stadium still stands. From the downtown, drive 3 miles north on Charles Street and turn right on 33rd Street. The stadium is 1 mile farther on your left. Note the wonderful Art Deco lettering at Memorial Stadium's entrance. *1000 E. 33rd St., Baltimore, tel. 410/396–7113.*

The Babe Ruth Birthplace. When they were building the Camden Yards ballpark, they found some bricks and broken bottles in short center field. These were the remains of the George Herman Ruth Saloon. Midway along Eutaw Street, there is a plaque to memorialize the Ruth family saloon. Just blocks away on February 6, 1895, the Babe was born. Young George's mother had gone to her father's house to escape the noise and distractions of her life over the family saloon. This Baltimore brick row house is now the centerpiece of the Babe Ruth Birthplace, Baltimore Orioles Museum, and Maryland Baseball Hall of Fame.

On Friday, June 13, 1902, young George was dispatched to St. Mary's Industrial School for Boys of the City of Baltimore. At the birthplace museum, they explain his admission to the school by describing the seven-year-old Ruth as "too tough for his parents, too absent for the school system, and too incorrigible for everybody else."

Jack Dunn, the owner of the minor-league Baltimore Orioles, signed Ruth for $600 and at the same time signed papers making him the legal guardian of the 19-year-old. The Oriole veterans called Ruth Dunn's Babe, and the name stuck. Ten years later, with the minor-league Orioles struggling to compete at the box office with the Baltimore Terrapins of the Federal League, Dunn had to sell off his best players to stay in business. The Boston Red Sox picked up the Babe, Ernie Shore, and Ben Egan for $25,000 in 1914.

216 Emory St., off 600 West Pratt St., Baltimore, tel. 410/727–1539. Admission: $5 adults, $3 senior citizens, $2 ages 5–16. Open Apr.–Oct., daily 10–5 (until 7 when Orioles play at home); Nov.–Mar., daily 10–4.

Babe Ruth Baseball Center at Camden Station. Camden Station, the elegant building just beyond center field in Camden Yards, is being converted into the Babe Ruth Baseball Center, scheduled to open in 1998. A Baltimore Baseball Walk of Fame will connect Camden Station with the Birthplace Museum.

St. Mary's Industrial School. For a special treat, drive 2½ miles southwest from the museum to the site of the old St. Mary's Industrial School. The building is now occupied by Cardinal Gibbons School, a Catholic boys' school. The field where the Babe learned to play baseball is still here, in a valley behind the main school building. You can walk out to deep center field—Ruth's home plate—and imagine the left-handed Babe aiming at the gray stone school building. Babe Ruth made shirts in the white three-story stucco building behind the home plate of the early 1900s. There was a grandstand on the nearby hill where a sidewalk and stone fence are today. After a 1919 fire destroyed the main building, Babe Ruth and Cardinal Gibbons raised the money to rebuild it. Both the birthplace and the school can be seen from the third-base side of the upper deck of Camden Yards. *3225 Wilkens Ave., corner of Caton and Wilkens Aves., Baltimore, tel. 410/644–1770.*

Ripken Museum. This small but high-quality tribute to the Ripken baseball family opened in 1997 in Cal Jr.'s home town of Aberdeen, Maryland. *8 Ripken Plaza, at Bel Air Ave. and U.S. 40, Aberdeen, tel. 410/273–2525. Admission: $3 adults, $1 ages 6–18, under 6 free. Open Fri.–Sat. and Mon. 11–3, Sun. noon–3.*

Where to Stay

These first four are within walking distance of the ballpark:

Radisson Plaza Lord Baltimore. This older, refurbished downtown hotel is 23 stories high, with good views of the city, and ironing boards in each room. Guests may use an adjoining indoor pool for $5 per person. *20 W. Baltimore St., Baltimore 21201, tel. 410/539–8400 or 800/333–3333, fax 410/625–1060. 420 rooms. Facilities: 2 restaurants, health club, parking (fee). AE, D, DC, MC, V. $$*

Paramount Inner Harbor Hotel. This seven-story brick hotel is undergoing complete renovation in early 1997. It is three blocks from the ballpark. *8 N. Howard St., Baltimore 21201, tel. 410/539–1188, fax 410/539–6411. 90 rooms. Facilities: restaurant, parking (fee). AE, D, DC, MC, V. $$*

Holiday Inn-Inner Harbor. This is the hotel you see from the ballpark. Its 10-story exterior is from the 1970s, but the interior was renovated in 1995. The rooms are standard size with no special amenities. *301 W. Lombard St., Baltimore 21201, tel. 410/685–3500 or 800/465–4329, fax 410/727–6169. 375 rooms. Facilities: restaurant, indoor pool, parking (fee). AE, D, DC, MC, V. $$*

Days Inn Baltimore Inner Harbor. This nine-story hotel is three blocks from the ballpark. The rooms are small but nicely furnished. *100 Hopkins Pl., Baltimore 21201, tel. 410/576–1000 or 800/325–2525, fax 410/576–9437. 250 rooms. Facilities: restaurant, pool, coin laundry, parking (fee). AE, D, DC, MC, V. $$*

Baltimore Clarion Hotel. This elegant, 13-story hotel at Mt. Vernon Square is an older property that has been renovated with antiques and fresh flowers. A courtesy shuttle takes you the eight blocks to the Inner Harbor. *612 Cathedral St., Baltimore 21201, tel. 410/727–7101 or 800/252–7466, fax 410/789–3312. 104 rooms. Facilities: restaurant, parking (fee). AE, D, DC, MC, V. $$*

Where to Eat

Nates and Leons. Pick your choice of sandwiches at this modern 100-seat deli across the street from the ballpark. An $8 Bird Feeder Bag includes a sandwich, coleslaw, pickle, brownie, chips, and the baseball magazine *Outside Pitch.* The recipe for its formidable strawberry shortcake dates from the 1930s, when the family started in the deli business. *300 West Pratt St., at Howard St., Baltimore, tel. 410/234–8100. AE, MC, V. $*

Haussner's Restaurant. This one-of-a-kind emporium screams "It's Baltimore, hon." Artwork crowds the walls, the desserts are overpowering, and how can you choose from among 12 vegetable side dishes? The selection of German entrées seems endless, but the veteran waitresses are happy to bring children two side dishes and call it a day. *3242 Eastern Ave., Baltimore, tel. 410/327–8365. AE, D, DC, MC, V. $*

Sabatino's. In Little Italy, close to the park, this venerable family favorite is casual and cool and dim inside. There are eight dining rooms, including one shining with mirrors. Its Bookmaker salad, with shrimp, provolone, salami, and orange zest is original and good. It has a children's menu and great pasta dishes. *901 Fawn St., Baltimore, tel. 410/727–2667. AE, D, DC, MC, V. $$*

Maison Marconi's. Writer H. L. Mencken frequented this legendary small town-house restaurant. It offers a mix of Italian food with spectacular hot fudge sundaes for dessert. There is no children's menu, but half-orders of pasta dishes can be requested. *106 W. Saratoga St., Baltimore, tel. 410/727–9522. Reservations essential. MC, V. $$*

Lexington Market. The venerable **John W. Faidley Seafood** (tel. 410/727–4898; AE, D, MC, V; $) raw bar is also crab-cake heaven. Patrons eat the city's freshest fish at rough tables next to employees shucking oysters. You can amble a few stalls over to the **A.D. Konstant & Son Confectionery** (tel. 410/685–4422), and try the nut taffies and peanut brittle that Baltimoreans have been eating for a century. *Paca and Lexington Sts., Baltimore.*

Women's Industrial Exchange Restaurant. This longtime Baltimore institution serves comfort food from the 1930s and '40s—chicken croquettes, crab cakes, meringue pies, and real turkey sandwiches. Many of its waitresses are past 80 years old. There are knitted and sewn goods for sale, along with jars of preserves. This is tearoom eating. *333 N. Charles St., Baltimore, tel. 410/685–4388. No dinner. MC, V. $*

Entertainments

The B&O Railroad Museum. In 1825, Baltimore was the fourth-largest city and fourth-ranking port on the east coast. One hundred miles closer to the rivers and markets of the West than its rivals, Baltimore was the birthplace of the American railroad industry. As others built canals, Baltimore bet its economic future on the railroad. Much of America's early movement of people and goods westward was through Baltimore. The B&O Railroad Museum, just blocks from Babe Ruth's birthplace, captures this important contribution to America's history on a 37-acre site that includes five historic buildings and more than 120 full-size railroad locomotives, cars, and pieces of special-purpose equipment. The centerpiece is an 1884 roundhouse designed by Ephraim Francis Baldwin.

The 1851 Mt. Clare Station serves as the entrance to the displays of railroading memorabilia. America's first passenger trains headed west from this location in 1830. Here Peter Cooper operated the *Tom Thumb*, the first steam engine made in America. The shops that surrounded the station were the country's oldest and the birthplace of many of railroading's most important technologies. In 1844, Samuel F. B. Morse sent his famous "What hath God wrought?" telegraph from Washington, D.C., along the B&O right-of-way to Mt. Clare. Parking is free. *901 W. Pratt St., Baltimore 21223, tel. 410/752–2490. Admission: $6 adults, $5 senior citizens, $3 ages 5–12. Open daily 10–5.*

Maryland Science Center and Davis Planetarium. The fate of the Chesapeake Bay is a focus of this hands-on museum, located at the edge of the Inner Harbor, within walking distance of the ballpark. You can take a water taxi to get here, too. A five-screen IMAX theater can make some people feel queasy, as you are "on" a roller coaster and other adventures. Children 3–13 must have a parent in the theater. *601 Light St., at Key Hwy., Baltimore, tel. 410/685–5225. Admission: $8.50 adults, $6.50 senior citizens, military personnel, and ages 4–17. Open mid-May–Labor Day, Mon.–Thurs. 10–6, Fri.–Sun. 10–8; Sept.–mid-May, weekdays 10–5, weekends 10–6.*

National Aquarium. This is a huge, multipresentation aquarium with a Marine Mammal Pavilion, an Atlantic Coral Reef, an Open Ocean (sharks), and a South American rain forest. A large dolphin oceanarium has daily shows. There's a touch tank and other hands-on experiences in the Children's Cove. On summer weekend days, tickets to this hugely popular attraction can sell out. Try to go late in the day or call Ticketmaster ahead of time for tickets. *501 E. Pratt St., Baltimore, tel. 410/576–3800. Admission: $11.95 adults, $10.50 seniors citizens, $7.50 ages 3–11. Open July–Aug., Sat.–Thurs. 10–5, Fri. 10–8; Sept.–June, Sun.–Thurs. 9–6, Fri.–Sat. 9–8.*

Great Blacks in Wax Museum. This is the country's only wax museum dedicated to African-Americans. It portrays more than 100 leaders, musicians, writers, inventors, athletes, and other pioneering individuals. The museum uses animation, sound effects, and scenes from history.

1601 E. North Ave., 2 mi northeast of Camden Yards, Baltimore, tel. 410/563–3404. Admission: $5.50 adults, $3.50 ages 12–17, $3 ages 2–11. Open Tues.–Sat. 10–6, Sun. noon–6.

U.S. Frigate *Constellation*. Visitors can climb throughout the nation's oldest warship continuously afloat, which is moored at Constellation Dock in the Inner Harbor within walking distance of Camden Yards. This 1797 frigate carried soldiers to the shores of Tripoli and saw action in the Revolutionary and Civil wars and both world wars. *Pier 1, Pratt and Light Sts., Baltimore, tel. 410/539–1797. Admission: $2.50 adults, $1 ages 6–15. Open Memorial Day–Labor Day, daily 10–5; Sept.–May, daily 10–4.*

Sites to See

Fort McHenry National Monument and Historic Shrine. If you have ever wondered why "The Star-Spangled Banner" is such a difficult song to sing, consider that it was hastily written by a Washington lawyer who had just spent a long, anxious night. Francis Scott Key, who had gone to Baltimore to secure the freedom of a friend who had been seized by the British, watched the 25-hour British bombardment of Fort McHenry from a ship on the Patapsco River. The British had burned Washington. This battle for Baltimore was critical to the nation's future. At dawn on September 14, 1814, Key saw the large 42- by 30-foot American flag made by Mary Pickersgill still flying over the fort and was inspired to take the notes for the song that became the national anthem.

Fort McHenry has been restored to its pre–Civil War state. A 15-minute film is shown at the visitor center on the hour and the half hour. Regular tours are led by informative guides. A shuttle-boat service leaves Baltimore's Inner Harbor from Finger Pier opposite the Harbour Court Hotel every half hour daily from Memorial Day to Labor Day between 11 and 5:30. *Fort McHenry, Key Highway/Fort McHenry exit (Exit 55) from I-95, follow signs, Baltimore, tel. 410/962–4299. Admission: $2 adults. Open early June–Labor Day, daily 8–8; Labor Day–May, daily 8–5. Shuttle boat: Maryland Tours, Box 147, Royal Oak, MD 21662, tel. 410/685–4288. Round-trip fare: $5 adults, $3.75 ages 2–11.*

Mencken House. Visit his home to learn about the "Bard of Baltimore," writer H. L. Mencken. Children will be more interested in row-house living and the pony shed and grape arbor than the details of this American writer and newsman, but it's a good introduction to books and literature. See the couch where F. Scott Fitzgerald slept and look at a death mask of Ludwig van Beethoven. *1524 Hollins St., Baltimore, tel. 410/396–7997. Admission: $2 adults, $1.50 ages 4–18 and senior citizens. Open Apr.–Oct., Sat. 10–5, Sun. noon–5; Nov.–Mar., Sat. 10–4, Sun. noon–4.*

Top of World observation tower. If it's a clear day, take the elevator up 27 stories to see a city of brick row houses, old churches, factories, and docks stretch before you. You can see Camden Yards in a new light. *World Trade Tower, Inner Harbor, Baltimore, tel. 410/837–4515. Admission: $2 adults, $1 ages 5–15 and senior citizens. Open Memorial Day–Labor Day, weekdays 10–4:30, Sat. 10–6:30, Sun. 11–5:30; Sept.–May, Mon.–Sat. 10–4:30, Sun. noon–4:30.*

FREDERICK KEYS

League: Carolina League • **Major League Affiliation:** Baltimore Orioles • **Class:** A • **Stadium:** Harry Grove Stadium • **Opened:** 1990 • **Capacity:** 5,400 • **Dimensions:** LF: 325, CF: 400, RF: 325 • **Surface:** grass • **Season:** Apr.–Labor Day

STADIUM LOCATION: 6201 New Design Rd., Frederick, MD 21701

WEB SITE: keysinterpath.com

GETTING THERE: From I–270S, Market St./MD Rte. 355 exit and turn right. Pass I–70 exits, left at traffic light. From I–70, exit 31A/Market St., left at traffic light. Left on New Design Rd.

TICKET INFORMATION: Box 3169, Frederick, MD 21705, tel. 301/662–0013, fax 301/662–0018

PRICE RANGE: Box seats $7; general admission $5 adults, $3 ages 5–14, senior citizens, and military personnel, under 5 free; gates open 1 hr before game

GAME TIME: Mon.–Sat. 7:05 PM, Sun. 2:05 (Apr.–June) or 4:05 (July–Aug.)

TIPS ON SEATING: Smoking and alcohol prohibited in family section general admission seats on third-base side; these seats have no cover and can get hot on a sunny day. Berms in left and right field foul areas are great for kids to run around and try to snag foul balls.

SEATING FOR PEOPLE WITH DISABILITIES: Behind bleacher seats along concourse

STADIUM FOOD: A kids-only stand for children under 15 sells candy, ice cream, and cookies, for 75¢–$1. The best of regular concourse offerings is a $4.50 roast beef sandwich in the **O'Keys Corral** past third base. Grills are on both third- and first-base sides. Good french fries are boardwalk style, in $2.50 and $4 cups. There are onion rings ($2.75), chicken fingers ($3.50), personal pizzas ($3.75), and real roasted peanuts ($2 per bag). Reservations are required at the **Keys Cafe** on the second-level terrace overlooking home plate. A good six-item buffet dinner is $24.

SMOKING POLICY: No-smoking and no-alcohol section on third-base side

PARKING: Ample free parking adjacent to stadium

VISITING TEAM INFORMATION: Comfort Inn (420 Prospect Blvd., Frederick, MD 21701, tel. 301/695–6200 or 800/424–6423)

TOURISM INFORMATION: Tourism Council of Frederick County (19 E. Church St., Frederick, MD 21701, tel. 301/663–8687 or 800/999–3613)

Frederick:
Harry Grove Stadium

Peter Kirk is one of the handful of visionaries who have helped make minor-league baseball the great comeback success story it has been for the last decade. In the mid-1980s, Kirk bought into the Hagerstown Suns. In 1988, Kirk's Maryland Baseball Limited Partnership bought a Double AA Eastern League team and brought it to Hagerstown. They took the Single A Carolina League team just 28 miles south to Frederick, where Mayor Ron Young was eager to have baseball. Governor Schaefer and Mayor Young promised Kirk a new stadium.

One night after a game in the early 1990s, Kirk had two visions—first, "What if we could bring all the future Baltimore Orioles to play in Maryland near the parent team?" Piece by piece the dream is becoming reality. For Orioles fans, players don't appear seemingly out of nowhere as they do for most major-league fans. We watch them play in Frederick and then in Bowie. By the time they put on the Orioles uniform, we know them.

Kirk's other vision was of fan-friendly stadiums. We were amazed when we first visited Frederick's $5.5 million Harry Grove Stadium in 1990. It was brand new. It has plenty of free parking right near the stadium. The food in the concession stands is good and much less expensive than in the big leagues. You can buy a soda and a hot dog on the concourse and not miss a pitch. There are large grass hillsides beyond the seats on both first base and third for overflow crowds, restless kids, and even middle-aged parents trying to snag a foul ball. There is nonstop entertainment on and off the field, including a chance to jingle your car keys and sing along to "We're the Frederick Keys." Keyote, a 7-foot-tall coyote, is a kid favorite. This is family entertainment at its best.

In planning the stadium, Kirk wanted to make sure fans could walk down from the parking lot and entrance rather than hike up stairs to their seats. He wanted the concessions to be open so that parents could watch their kids without having to miss the game.

Frederick became the standard of comfort, efficiency, and family pleasure for Single A baseball.

The construction was simple—1,800 box seats, aluminum-bench general admission seats on concrete, an uncovered grandstand with an open concourse above the seats. The grass berms solve the problem of how many seats to build at minor-league parks. There are 5,400 actual seats at Grove Stadium, but 10,000 can pack in for fireworks.

Some of the easiest autographs in all of professional baseball are acquired here. The seats stop at the outfield grass, and the players have to walk up a hill from the field along the seats to their locker rooms. You can get them going back to their lockers after batting practice or on their way back to the field just before game time. The Keys' locker room is on the first-base side, and we have filled balls with autographs in as little as 30 minutes here. When we first saw Harry Grove Stadium in 1990, we couldn't imagine anyone doing it any better than this.

We were wrong, of course. Peter Kirk himself has done it bigger and fancier for his Double AA Eastern League team in Bowie. If you have an extra day in the Baltimore-Washington area, visit Prince George's Stadium (tel. 301/805–6000) to see the Bowie Baysox—it's Chesapeake Bay country—for a first-class baseball experience. In 1996, Kirk's Delmarva Shorebirds opened in a great new stadium in Salisbury on Maryland's Eastern Shore.

To our amazement, the modern, efficient stadiums of the late 1980s and early 1990s, of which Frederick is among the very best, have been far surpassed by such mid-1990s Single A beauties as Durham, North Carolina; Tampa, Florida; and Lake Elsinore and Rancho Cucamonga, California. Peter Kirk intends to try to keep up with the competition. In 1995, he added a full-size carousel and playground at Bowie and in 1996 did the same at Frederick. Also for 1996, there was a new tri-vision scoreboard above the left-field wall in Frederick.

A name-the-team contest honored Francis Scott Key, the author of the national anthem, who is buried in the cemetery directly across the street from the stadium. Harry Grove was an official of Frederick's first professional team in the Class D Blue Ridge League in 1915. The stadium was named in Grove's honor when his son helped finance it as a way of bringing professional baseball back to Frederick after a 59-year absence.

Where to Stay

Visiting Team Motel: Comfort Inn. This two-story hotel is in a quiet residential neighborhood 10 minutes from the ballpark. There is a free Continental breakfast. *4200 Prospect Blvd., Frederick 21701, tel. 301/695–6200 or 800/424–6423, fax 301/695–7895. Facilities: pool, exercise room, playground. AE, D, DC, MC, V. $$*

Masser's Motel. At this 1940s-era motor court you'll find economy lodging 5 miles west of the ballpark. The rooms are small, clean, and air-conditioned. *1505 W. Patrick St. (U.S. 40 W), ½ mi west of Frederick Towne Mall, Frederick 21702, tel. 301/663–3698. 30 rooms. Facilities: restaurant. MC, V. $*

Where to Eat

Barbara Fritchie Candystick Restaurant. Eating here is a walk back in time, from the dated but delectable menu items to the pink decor. You can choose meaty turkey pot pie with pepper slaw, a bargain oyster sandwich, hefty chipped beef on toast, or delicious apple dumplings. Other desserts include a homemade black walnut pound cake, caramel cake, and pies. The large counter has 33 stools, or you can have table or booth service. Decorative peppermint sticks adorn the facade, installed by the same family that's been running the place since 1920. *1513 W. Patrick St. (Rte. 40 W), Frederick, tel. 301/662–2500. No credit cards. $*

Dan-Dee Country Inn. Maryland fried chicken is the standout at this casual family restaurant that has long attracted the after-church crowd. Food is served family-style, except for the meat entrées. The children's menu is for those 10 and under. The restaurant, which has nicely landscaped grounds, is at the entrance to Gambrill State Park. *7817 Baltimore Pike (U.S. 40 W), Frederick, tel. 301/473–8282. AE, D, MC, V. $*

The Comus Inn. This pretty inn has an extraordinary view of Sugarloaf Mountain; you can call ahead to find out when the sun sets for the best view. Kids eat free, and babysitters are available on Tuesday nights. The extensive menu is supplemented by a large salad bar. There's a special brunch on Sunday. *23900 Old Hundred Rd. (Rte.*

109 and Comus Rd.), 12 mi south of Frederick, Comus, tel. 301/349–5100. AE, MC, V. $$

Entertainments

Antietam National Battlefield. Park rangers give 30-minute outdoor talks about the bloodiest battle in the Civil War here. A self-drive map directs you to several sites on the battlefield. The park is located northeast of Sharpsburg, about 25 miles from Frederick. *Maryland Rtes. 34 and 65, Antietam, tel. 301/432–5124. Admission: $2 adults, $4 family. Open 8:30–dusk.*

Rose Hill Manor and Children's Museum. Children can play with vintage toys and use historic kitchen utensils in this home of former Maryland governor Thomas Johnson. Look at the old ice house, the carriage museum, and the blacksmith shop. *1611 N. Market St. (Rte. 355), Frederick, tel. 301/694–1648. Admission: $3 adults, $2 senior citizens, $1 children. Open Mon.–Sat. 10–4, Sun. 1–4.*

Sites to See

Mt. Olivet Cemetery. Francis Scott Key, author of "The Star Spangled Banner" and namesake of the baseball team, and Barbara Fritchie (see below) are buried right next to the ballpark. The headstones are impressive in the old cemetery. *515 S. Market St., Frederick, tel. 301/662–1164.*

Barbara Fritchie House and Museum. Do you remember this heroine from Whittier's poem, "Shoot If You Must This Old Gray Head, but Spare Your Country's Flag"? This period home and small museum can help illuminate the moment in 1862 when Fritchie waved the Union flag as Confederate troops marched through Frederick. *154 W. Patrick St., Frederick, tel. 301/698–0630. Admission: $2 adults, $1.50 ages 2–12 and senior citizens. Open Apr.–Nov., Mon. and Thurs.–Sat. 10–4, Sun. 1–4.*

Frederick historic district. A six-block walking tour departs on the weekends from Frederick Visitor Center, led by experts in the history and architecture of the city. *19 E. Church St., Frederick, tel. 301/663–8687. Admission: $4.50 ages 12 and older. Open Apr.–Dec., weekends 1:30.*

Sugarloaf Mountain. Just 12 miles south of Frederick is a good challenge for young children not yet ready for a major mountain climb. Privately owned, this lovely conservation and recreation area provides the opportunity for hiking, picnicking, and nature study. At an elevation of 1,282 feet, the rugged cliffs on the summit stand 800 feet above the surrounding farmland. Drive 1½ miles up the mountain, park in the east-view lot, and take the orange trail up a steep slope for ¼ mile to the summit. The green trail down the west side of the mountain is aided by stone steps. It is then a short walk back to the east-view parking lot. *7901 Comus Rd. (Exit 22—Rte. 109—from I–270 south from Frederick, south 3 mi to Comus Rd., right on Comus Rd. 2½ mi), Dickerson, tel. 301/874–2024.*

HAGERSTOWN SUNS

League: South Atlantic League • **Major League Affiliation:** Toronto Blue Jays • **Class:** A • **Stadium:** Municipal Stadium • **Opened:** 1931 • **Capacity:** 4,600 • **Dimensions:** LF: 335, CF: 400, RF: 330 • **Surface:** grass • **Season:** Apr.–Labor Day

STADIUM LOCATION: 274 E. Memorial Blvd., Hagerstown, MD 21740

GETTING THERE: From I–70W, exit 32B (US 40) 2½ mi, left on Cleveland Ave. From I–81S, exit 6A through downtown, right on Cleveland Ave. From I–81N, exit 3E (I–70); follow it to exit 29N (MD 65), right at Memorial Blvd.

TICKET INFORMATION: Box 230, Hagerstown, MD 21741, tel. 301/791–6266, fax 301/791–6066

PRICE RANGE: Box seats $6; general admission $4 adults, $2 students, senior citizens, and military personnel

GAME TIME: Mon.–Sat. 7:05 PM, Sun. 2:05 PM; gates open 1 hr before game.

TIPS ON SEATING: General admission seats are right in action. Third-base side is best. Don't sit in first row of bleacher seats on first-base side or your view will be blocked by line of fans slowed by bottleneck.

SEATING FOR PEOPLE WITH DISABILITIES: About 50 places accessible by ramps: behind home plate, out third base, and near right field.

STADIUM FOOD: The place to eat is at the **Sunset Grille** on the third-base side of the ballpark. The first-rate barbecue chicken sandwich is $2.75. Its Super Dog ($2.25) is superior to most ballpark dogs, as is the Italian sausage ($2.50). Its Hot and Spicy hot dog will be too strong for most kids. A good hamburger is $2.25. There's a children's playground on a cushion of wood chips by the picnic area.

SMOKING POLICY: 400 no-smoking, no-alcohol seats in section 5 behind screen on third-base side

PARKING: Get here early. Only about 500 spaces near ballpark. If you see empty spaces near entrance, there's a reason. Locals know you can get a foul ball through your windshield there.

VISITING TEAM HOTEL: Ramada Inn Convention Center (901 Dual Hwy., Hagerstown, MD 21740, tel. 301/733–5100 or 800/228–2828)

TOURISM INFORMATION: Washington County Convention & Visitors Bureau (1826-C Dual Hwy., Hagerstown, MD 21740, tel. 301/791–3130 or 800/228–7829)

Hagerstown: Municipal Stadium

Hagerstown is one of those towns that almost got left behind in baseball's effort to upgrade minor-league stadiums. Built in 1931 for a team that did not last a full season in the depression-era economy, Municipal Stadium hosted amateur teams for the next decade. By 1947, the city's 16-year-old stadium was past its prime. In 1988, baseball owner Peter Kirk and his investors bought a Double AA Eastern League team and moved it to Hagerstown, replacing a Single A team. Because the economically depressed western Maryland city could not afford the stadium improvements required to maintain Double AA baseball, Kirk's Eastern League team moved out in 1993.

Happily for Maryland baseball fans and connoisseurs of vintage ballparks, Hagerstown didn't miss a season. Owner Winston Blenckstone moved a failing Single A South Atlantic League team here in 1993 from Myrtle Beach, South Carolina. The standards for Single A baseball required $500,000 in improvements. With support from the city and state, Blenckstone has installed a new bullpen, a new clubhouse and offices, and new rest rooms. Hundreds of old bleacher seats down the left-field line have been replaced with an attractive fan-oriented picnic, grill, and play area.

The improvements have made Hagerstown baseball a more enjoyable experience for fans and players alike, without destroying the feel of the 1931 Municipal Stadium. The fancy new box seats come complete with cup holders, but there are only 550 of them. A $4.50 general admission ticket still gets you a seat right near the action. The old-style covered grandstand is welcome on a sunny Sunday afternoon or when a late summer thundershower passes by.

Playing left field here still requires the skills of an acrobat. A large deposit of limestone causes a distinct grade in left center field up toward the left-field wall. The charitable way to describe this is that the players in left field have a unique warning track so they don't run into the outfield wall. The reality is that they have to run up the side of a ledge, a challenge major-league owners don't want for their high-priced future superstars.

Playing left field isn't the only challenge here. Getting to the game late, you might be tempted by some empty parking spaces near the entrance. Don't take them. Municipal Stadium is one of those ballparks where the foul balls fly out of the field throughout the night. According to the owner, "It's a neighborhood park. That's baseball-speak for 'It's best to get here early. We don't have enough parking spaces.'"

Hagerstown's Municipal Stadium oozes old-time baseball and small-town charm. Two recent art projects add to the nostalgic feelings evoked here. In 1987, students from nearby Williamsport High School painted a mural honoring the Owls, Braves, Packets, and Suns, who represented Hagerstown in professional baseball in the 1940s and '50s and, after a 26-year

sabbatical, again in the 1980s. The mural is near the souvenir stand on the third-base side. Babe Ruth's sister lived in Hagerstown, and the new owners in 1993 commissioned a huge 12- by 16-foot mural of the Babe down the right-field line. In 1995, they added a huge hot dog.

Not everyone is nostalgic about Hagerstown baseball. Willie Mays played his first game here on June 24, 1950, after breaking through baseball's color line to play for the Trenton Giants. In his biography, Mays blasted Hagerstown, where he wasn't allowed to stay in the same hotel with his new teammates. For those who think of Maryland as a northern state, remember that the Mason-Dixon line is only miles north of Hagerstown.

Where to Stay

Visiting Team Motel: Ramada Inn Convention Center. This sprawling hotel has a two-story main building and a five-story tower. The newer and brighter tower rooms are no-smoking. The hotel is along the main highway, about 2 miles from the ballpark. *901 Dual Hwy. (Rte. 40), Hagerstown 21740, tel. 301/733–5100 or 800/228–2828, fax 301/733–9192. 212 rooms. Facilities: restaurant, indoor pool, health club, track, coin laundry. AE, D, DC, MC, V. $*

Days Inn. This is an ordinary two-story highway motel, newly renovated, about 2 miles from the ballpark. *900 Dual Hwy. (Rte. 40), Hagerstown 21740, tel. 301/739–9050 or 800/329–7466, fax 301/739–8347. 140 rooms. Facilities: restaurant, pool, playground, coin laundry. AE, D, DC, MC, V. $*

Where to Eat

Chic's Seafood. Look for the 400-pound red crab on the roof across from the city park. Rolls of mill paper cover the wood tables for serious steamed crab eaters. The restaurant also serves mussels, great oysters, and clams. The apple crisp is homemade. *300 Summit Ave., Hagerstown, tel. 301/739–8220. MC, V. $*

Schmankerl Stube Bavarian Restaurant. The name means "cozy room," and this pretty, check-curtained restaurant is that. Don't miss the potato soup, the fried tomatoes, and the apple streusel. All meals come with a hearty German sunflower-seed rye bread. The waitresses and waiters wear Bavarian costumes. The back patio is cheerful, and the wood-floor dining rooms are hyperclean and attractive. *58 S. Potomac St., Hagerstown, tel. 301/797–3354. AE, MC, V. $*

Richardson's Family Restaurant. This casual highway restaurant is filled with mementos of the years since its opening in 1948. There is fine frozen custard, real milk shakes, and a larger-than-usual kid's menu. The buffet for kids under five is priced at 75¢ per year of their age. Adults can enjoy the crab cakes, clams, and Maryland oysters. *710 Dual Hwy. (Rte. 40), Hagerstown, tel. 301/733–3660. D, MC, V. $*

Hagerstown City Market. Gather breakfast and eat inside Maryland's oldest continuous farmer's market. Many Amish farmstands are among the 56 stalls here. You'll find superb fruits, vegetables, baked goods, meats, crafts, and flowers. Locals have been shopping here since 1875. *11 West Church St., Hagerstown, tel. 301/790–3200, ext. 112. Open year-round Sat. 5–11; June–Dec., Wed. 11–4 also. No credit cards. $*

Krumpe's Donuts. In an alley between Spruce and Maryland avenues, follow your nose for fresh-baked doughnuts. The Krumpes have been baking for 44 years, and their glazed, twisted, powdered, apple, chocolate, and cake doughnuts are heaven, especially warm. *912 Maryland Ave., Hagerstown, tel. 301/733–6103. No credit cards. $*

Entertainments

Hagerstown Park. This is one of America's best small-city parks. It has a historic bandshell, steam engines and cabooses for climbing, playgrounds, ball fields, and a multitude of swans and ducks on its 50-acre lake. In summer, there are Wednesday-night gospel concerts and Sunday-evening municipal band concerts. Its concession stand serves snow cones, hot dogs, and burgers,

plus 35¢ duck and goose feed. The city's excellent and compact art and history museums are also on the grounds. *501 Virginia Ave., Hagerstown, tel. 301/797–3088. Admission free. Open Mon.–Sat. 10–8, Sun. 10–9.*

Cal Ripken, Jr., Museum. This small museum, devoted to the Orioles' legendary shortstop, is on the second floor of the **Signature Shoppe** in the village of Thurmont, 15 miles east of Hagerstown. *106 Frederick Rd., Thurmont, tel. 301/662–5328. Admission free. Open Mon.–Tues. and Thurs. 11–5, Fri.–Sun. 11–7.*

Sites to See

Maryland Theatre. A fire wall saved this 80-year-old theater in 1974. Restored, the rococo theater offers a peek into America's theatrical past. Its facade is unimpressive, but the interior, with its 1,400 seats, is exquisite. *21 S. Potomac St., Hagerstown, tel. 301/790–2000 or 800/347–4697.*

Antietam National Battlefield. This 950-acre park, 30 minutes southwest of Hagerstown, is the site of the bloodiest day of the Civil War. More than 23,000 soldiers died when General George McClellans's Army met General Robert E. Lee's. Lee's withdrawal resulted in Lincoln's issuing the Emancipation Proclamation. Tour the small museum at the visitor center, view the 26-minute film, and walk the fields. *S.R. 34 and 65, Sharpsburg, tel. 301/432–5124. Admission: $2 ages 17 and up; $4 family. Open daily, dawn–dusk.*

Downtown walking tour. The 18 stops on the self-guided tour are marked by the town's Prussian soldier mascot, Little Heiskell. It covers the area where Jonathan Hager, the German-born founder, laid out the town in 1762. Obtain a map from the Washington County Tourism Bureau (1826 Dual Hwy., U.S. 40, tel. 301/791–3130 or 800/228–7829) or at City Hall (Potomac and Franklin Sts., tel. 301/790–3200).

DELMARVA SHOREBIRDS

League: South Atlantic • **Major League Affiliation:** Baltimore Orioles • **Class:** A • **Stadium:** Arthur W. Perdue Stadium • **Opened:** 1996 • **Capacity:** 5,200 • **Dimensions:** LF: 309, CF: 402, RF: 309 • **Surface:** grass • **Season:** Apr.–Labor Day

STADIUM LOCATION: Just off Rte. 50 and Rte. 13 Bypass.

GETTING THERE: From Salisbury on US 50E, pass Rte. 13 Bypass, exit to right onto Hobbs Rd. From US 50W, exit to left onto Hobbs Rd.

TICKET INFORMATION: Box 1557, Salisbury, MD 21802, tel. 410/219–3112, fax 410/219–9164

PRICE RANGE: Box seats $7; general admission $5 adults, $3 children and senior citizens, free for children in Little League uniforms and under 6.

GAME TIME: Mon.–Sat. 7 PM, Sun. 2 PM; gates open 90 min before game

TIPS ON SEATING: First rows of general admission are very close to action, but get there early. Even last rows of general admission are closer to action than best seats in many major league parks. General admission seats are aluminum benches with backs. There are 274 club-level second-deck seats. Alcohol prohibited in designated family areas (sections 119 and 209).

SEATING FOR PEOPLE WITH DISABILITIES: Seating for 90 people spread throughout stadium. Club level accessible by stadium elevator.

STADIUM FOOD: Chicken, not surprisingly, is the main attraction, with grilled chicken breast sandwiches and shredded chicken BBQ sandwiches for $4 each. One of the concession stands is called **The Hen House,** and nuggets and fried chicken may be served there in the future. A **Kid's Stand,** for those 12 and under, has fruit yogurt, hot dogs, and candy. All items are $1.

SMOKING POLICY: Smoking prohibited except in designated area on concourse on right field side

PARKING: Ample free parking

VISITING TEAM HOTEL: Holiday Inn (2625 N. Salisbury Blvd. Salisbury, MD 21801, tel. 410/742–7194 or 800/465–4329)

TOURISM INFORMATION: Wicomico County Convention & Visitors Bureau (Box 2333, Salisbury, MD 21802, tel. 410/548–4914 or 800/332–8687)

Delmarva: Arthur W. Perdue Stadium

Arthur W. Perdue founded an egg business in 1920. For most of the next three decades, baseball was big in Perdue's native region until the Eastern Shore League folded in 1949. Baseball returned in 1996 thanks in significant part to the success of Arthur Perdue's chicken company. The Perdue family donated the land and several million dollars for the construction of Arthur W. Perdue Stadium.

Where until recently were chicken houses and tenant farmers, there now sits a small jewel of a stadium. The exterior is red and beige cinderblock with the look of brick set off by a handsome dark green roof. Designed by the Design Exchange of Delaware, Perdue Stadium has seating for 5,200 and a state-of-the-art sound system. Trees and large outfield scoreboards frame the field beyond the fences.

The $10 million stadium has an attractive second deck with six skyboxes and 274 club-level seats. This unusual minor-league second level allows a compact design providing fans in all 5,200 seats extraordinary proximity to the baseball action. There are only nine rows of the dark green field and box seats, allowing for some of the best general admission seating in all of baseball.

Peter Kirk's trademark design—with the concession stands on a concourse immediately behind the seats—is a fan favorite, as you can follow the action while you stand in line for food. The grassy berms down each foul line allow for overflow crowds on big nights without destroying the intimacy that is the hallmark of minor-league-stadium design. Another Kirk winner is the carousel for kids. The 20-horse carousel, adding cheery music and lights, is on the third-base side. A mascot joins the team in May 1997.

On the first-base side of the stadium is the Eastern Shore Hall of Fame Museum. Highlighting the history of the Class D Eastern Shore League from 1922 to 1949, it includes the careers of such native sons as Hall of Famer Frank "Home Run" Baker. The Eastern Shore League drew teams from Delaware, Maryland, and Virginia, the three states that make up the DEL-MAR-VA region that is the home of the current team. The team's nickname—Shorebirds—reflects the wide variety of waterfowl in the Delmarva area.

The team plays in the South Atlantic League, the level above the rookie leagues. It's affiliated with the Baltimore Orioles franchise, allowing the fans to follow favorite players as they mature from A-level ball into full-fledged Birds in Baltimore.

Where to Stay

Sheraton Salisbury. This five-story downtown hotel overlooks a tributary of the Wicomico River. The restaurant has a view of the short Riverwalk. Ask for the sales department at extension 117 to get the $85 double-room Shorebirds promotion, which includes two adult general admission tickets. *300 S. Salisbury Blvd., Salisbury, MD 21801, tel. 410/546–4400 or 800/325–2525, fax 410/546–2528. 156 rooms. Facilities: restaurant, pool, free airport shuttle. AE, D, DC, MC, V. $$*

Super 8 Motel. North of town by the bypass, this no-frills motel is in a commercial strip next to a small field. The rooms are standard size and utilitarian. There's free toast, juice, and coffee in the mornings. *2615 N. Salisbury Blvd., Salisbury, MD 21801, tel. 410/749–5131 or 800/800–8000. 48 rooms. Facilities: refrigerators in suites, free cribs. AE, D, DC, MC, V. $$*

Where to Eat

English's Family Restaurant. This venerable chain has two locations, both serving its signature sweet-potato biscuits, Maryland fried chicken, Eastern-shore oysters, and apple dumplings with vanilla cinnamon sauce. There is an extensive kid's menu, and children six and under

eat free with a paying adult. The restaurants are built around old diners. *2525 N. Salisbury Blvd., Salisbury, tel. 410/742–8133; 735 S. Salisbury Blvd., Salisbury, tel. 410/742–8182. D, MC, V. $*

Zia's Pastaria. The Bubas family uses no microwave ovens in this casual Italian pasta house. Its homemade pesto sauce includes nuts and fresh basil. The children's menu includes ravioli, spaghetti, fettuccine, and chicken. *2408 N. Salisbury Blvd., Salisbury, tel. 410/543–9118. D, MC, V. $*

Old Mill Crab House. This casual, get-messy restaurant serves hard-shell crabs on brown paper. Make sure children don't rub their eyes with fingers filled with crab spice! The children's menu includes fried shrimp, crab, chicken, and pizza. *Rte. 54 and Waller Rd., 8 mi northeast of Salisbury, Delmar, DE, tel. 302/846–2808. AE, MC, V. $*

Entertainments

Salisbury Zoo. This 12-acre, beautifully landscaped free zoo is the perfect scale for smaller children. More than 400 animals live here, including long-eared rabbits, spider monkeys, two jaguars, a sloth, and a toucan. You can take as little as half an hour to walk the zoo or spend an afternoon at the playground at the west entrance. The adjacent city park has a lake and paddleboats. *755 South Park Dr., Salisbury, tel. 410/548–3188. Admission: donations. Open Memorial Day–Labor Day, daily 8–7:30; Labor Day–Memorial Day, daily 8–4:30.*

Ward Museum of Wildfowl Art. A gem of a museum, it is devoted to decoy carving and bird art. Its realistic re-creation of a duck blind gives the flavor of the Eastern Shore. Children like to see the workshop of Lem and Steve Ward, brothers who elevated decoys into art. The work of winning child carvers is featured. *900 S. Schumaker Dr., Salisbury, tel. 410/742-4988. Admission: $4 adults, $3 senior citizens, $2 kindergarten–12th grade. Open Mon.–Sat. 10–5, Sun. noon–5.*

PENNSYLVANIA DUTCH AND LITTLE LEAGUE WORLD SERIES

HARRISBURG, READING, WILLIAMSPORT, SCRANTON/WILKES-BARRE

Pennsylvania is filled with historic baseball stadiums, unique family-run amusement parks, and picturesque farms. In Harrisburg baseball is played in City Island Park, in the middle of the Susquehanna River, just a short walk across a bridge from downtown. Uncle Slam is the mascot of this Double AA Eastern League team.

By driving south of the city on Interstate 83 and picking up Route 422 east, you can go first to Hershey, with its chocolate museum and all-day amusement park, and through Pennsylvania Dutch country on your way to Reading, 35 miles east of Harrisburg. Reading's Memorial Municipal Stadium is a lesson in how to update a 1950 ballpark. The Double AA Reading Phillies park, in the Eastern League, has a landscaped plaza and real seats, no benches, for everyone. The city is best known for its acres of outlet malls, but there are also many antiques and collectibles markets and stores concentrating on Pennsylvania potato chips, pretzels, and chocolate. You'll also find one-of-a-kind roadside structures, like a pagoda overlooking Reading and the miniature villages in Roadside America in Shartlesville, 25 miles northwest of Reading.

Driving north on Route 61 to Route 81 north for 65 miles brings you to Scranton/Wilkes-Barre and its Lackawanna County Stadium. Even the AstroTurf surface cannot mar the beautiful mountain setting for these Triple AAA International League games. This is coal country; there's an anthracite mine to explore in the same cars miners used for more than 100 years. Railroads also built this area, and the train industry is shown in films, displays, and artifacts at the Steamtown National Historic Site in Scranton.

Heading south on Interstate 81, then west on the Pennsylvania Turnpike to Interstate 180 North, you'll reach Williamsport, one of America's baseball meccas, 70 miles from Scranton. Every young baseball fan holds central Pennsylvania in special regard, because Williamsport is where the Little League's World Series is played. The city also has its own 1926 minor-league stadium in the municipal park, where the New York–Penn League Cubs play short season A ball. About 35 miles southeast of Williamsport is one of America's most delightful vintage amusement parks, Knoebels Amusement Resort, in the midst of a cool pine forest.

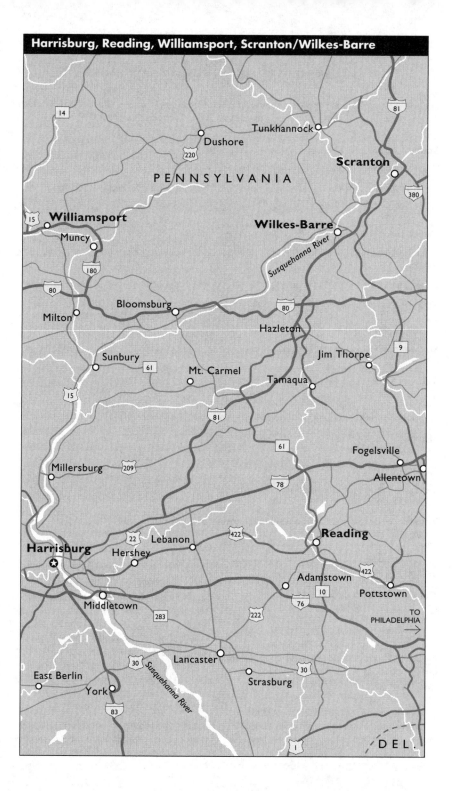

Harrisburg, Reading, Williamsport, Scranton/Wilkes-Barre

14

Dushore

Tunkhannock

220

Scranton

81

380

P E N N S Y L V A N I A

15

Williamsport

Muncy

Wilkes-Barre

Susquehanna River

180

80

Bloomsburg

80

Milton

Hazleton

9

Sunbury

61

Jim Thorpe

15

Mt. Carmel

Tamaqua

81

61

Fogelsville

Millersburg

209

78

Allentown

22

Lebanon

422

Reading

Harrisburg

Hershey

422

Adamstown

10

Pottstown

Middletown

283

222

76

TO
PHILADELPHIA
→

30

Susquehanna River

Lancaster

East Berlin

30

York

Strasburg

30

83

1

D E L.

HARRISBURG SENATORS

League: Eastern League • **Major League Affiliation:** Montreal Expos • **Class:** AA • **Stadium:** RiverSide Stadium • **Opened:** 1987 • **Capacity:** 6,300 • **Dimensions:** LF: 335, CF: 400, RF: 335 • **Surface:** grass • **Season:** Apr.–Labor Day

STADIUM LOCATION: City Island, Harrisburg, PA 17101

TEAM WEBSITE: http://www.fanlink.com/h-burg-senators

GETTING THERE: From I–83, 2nd St. exit (exit 23) to Market St; Market St. Bridge to City Island. Replica trolley buses go from downtown to City Island. Walking across bridge from downtown to City Island is recommended.

TICKET INFORMATION: Box 15757, Harrisburg, PA 17105, tel. 717/231–4444, fax 717/231–4445

PRICE RANGE: Box seats $7; reserved grandstand $6; general admission $5 adults, $3 ages under 13 and over 59.

GAME TIME: Mon.–Sat. 7:05 PM, Sun. 1:05 PM; gates open 90 min before game.

TIPS ON SEATING: General admission seats are on third-base side. Aluminum benches do not have backs and setting sun shines in your eyes in early innings. Reserved grandstand seats on first-base side have backs; some sections no-smoking.

SEATING FOR PEOPLE WITH DISABILITIES: On first-base side behind box seats with protective plastic screen

STADIUM FOOD: The food on City Island (ribs and chicken) just outside the park is better than the stadium food, but it cannot be brought in. At the grill under the grandstand on the first-base side, the meatball subs ($2.75) aren't bad, but are messy. Pizza is available, and there is a french fry stand. Small drinks are reasonable at $1. For adults, there are microbrewed beers.

SMOKING POLICY: Smoking permitted except in sections 201–204 of reserved grandstand on first-base side

PARKING: Parking at lot on island, $1.

VISITING TEAM HOTEL: Hilton Hotel and Towers (1 N. 2nd St., Harrisburg, PA 17101, tel. 717/233–6000 or 800/445–8667)

TOURISM INFORMATION: Capital Region Chamber of Commerce (114 Walnut St., Harrisburg, PA 17108, tel. 717/232–4121)

Harrisburg: RiverSide Stadium

Harrisburg's RiverSide Stadium is one of those places where the setting is so fine that it takes your mind off the fact that the ballpark is mediocre. RiverSide Stadium is the centerpiece of City Island Park, a 62-acre recreation complex on an island in the middle of the Susquehanna River. Here you can ride a miniature train around the island, take a boat ride on the river, play miniature golf, go for a swim, play volleyball, watch a soccer game, have a meal, or play at a children's playground. The view of the State Capitol and the Harrisburg skyline across the river is first-rate. It is hard to imagine a more delightful package of activities.

They have played professional baseball in Harrisburg since 1883. Minor-league and Negro League teams played on this very site for most of the first half of the century. In 1952, the Harrisburg Senators signed a 26-year-old stenographer named Eleanor Engle to play shortstop. Engle suited up for four games, but the professional baseball establishment voided her contract before she could get into the action.

Because of flooding on the island, no professional baseball was played there or anywhere else in Harrisburg from 1953 until 1987, when RiverSide Stadium was built for a new Double

AA Eastern League franchise. The city built the stadium using the same field layout of the wooden-bleachered Island Park, this time investing heavily in flood protection.

This stadium is still a work in progress. It opened in 1987 with a simple covered grandstand and wooden bleachers seating 4,000 at a cost of $1.9 million. In 1988, they added 808 box seats. Reserved aluminum bleachers with backs were built behind each dugout in 1990. In 1993, when Charlie Sheen and Tom Berenger were making the movie *Major League II* at Baltimore's Camden Yards, producers needed a nearby site for the early spring-training scenes. Harrisburg was the place. They filled the area down the first-base line with potted palm trees and put up ads for Florida companies on the outfield wall—an instant Florida in Pennsylvania. For the 1994 season, a new, no-smoking reserved section and picnic area went in where the moviemakers had had their palm trees. With general admission bleachers down the third-base line, the stadium now seats 6,300.

Harrisburg has one of baseball's best mascots, Uncle Slam, a giant in an Uncle Sam outfit. Slam is a friendly sort, hugging everyone in sight and always ready for a photo with your kids. The nickname Senators does not come from the legislature across the river but from a long-ago association with the Washington Senators.

The stands overlook the island's attractive grove of trees. Flags fly in left field, and a simple scoreboard fills right center. Unfortunately, you can't see the river or the Capitol from the stadium seats, but it is worth a walk to the top of the grandstand at midgame to view this wonderful setting. The bridge from the downtown to the island and all the major City Island attractions are lit up with strings of small lights.

They are serious about their baseball here in Harrisburg. In late August of 1995, they celebrated their 2 millionth fan from their first nine years of operation in RiverSide Stadium. Earlier that year, new owners had announced they were going to move the team to Massachusetts. The city leadership went ballistic, minor-league baseball stalled the move, and the city eventually purchased the team. This unusual arrangement should guarantee Senators baseball on City Island for a long time to come.

Where to Stay

Visiting Team Hotel: Hilton Hotel and Towers. This downtown high-rise hotel is within walking distance of the ballpark. The upper floors of the modern, 15-story hotel have great views of the city and the river. It has "Bounceback Weekend" rates of $95 per room, with kids free and free Continental breakfast for every guest. *1 N. 2nd St., Harrisburg 17101, tel. 717/233–6000 or 800/445–8667, fax 717/233–6271. 340 rooms. Facilities: restaurant, indoor pool. AE, D, DC, MC, V. $$*

Holiday Inn Express. This two-story motel at the edge of the Susquehanna River is in walking distance from the ballpark. Microwave ovens and refrigerators are available for $5 each per night, and there's a free breakfast bar. *525 S. Front St., Harrisburg 17104, tel. and fax 717/233–1611 or tel. 800/465–4329. 117 rooms. Facilities: health club. AE, D, DC, MC, V. $$*

Super 8 Motel–North. The surroundings are a traffic interchange, but this two-story motel is a direct 5 miles from the ballpark, right down Front Street along the Susquehanna River. *4125 N. Front St., Exit 22 from I–81, Harrisburg 17110, tel. and fax 717/233–5891 or tel. 800/848–8888. 57 rooms. Facilities: pool. AE, D, DC, MC, V. $*

Where to Eat

Broad Street Market. At this vintage farmer's market vendors sell prepared foods as well as produce. There is cluster seating throughout the two buildings, the Brick Market and Stone Market. Beiler's Poultry sells barbecue chicken, ribs, and cooked yams. There's Vietnamese noodle soup at Golden Gate, Jamaican jerk chicken at Auckland's Place, and Jamaican fish sandwiches at T. Oliver's. Jimmy's is a sit-down breakfast and lunch counter. There's also International Foods & Deli (Lebanese), Fisher's Deli (subs and pizza), and Yong's Kitchen (Chinese). Bradford's Bread has superb grab-and-go baked goods. Philadelphia-style pretzels are sold at Auntie Anne's Hot Pretzels. *1233 N. 3rd St., 3 blocks from Front St., Harrisburg, tel. 717/236–7923. $*

Gingerbread Man. You can watch the small marinas on the Susquehanna River from the glassed-in porch at this casual restaurant just across the Market Street Bridge, south of Harrisburg. The sandwiches and desserts are oversize. The portions on the children's menu are the right size. *313 S. Front St., Wormleysburg, tel. 717/737–1313. AE, D, DC, MC, V. $*

Entertainments

The Museum of Scientific Discovery. This building in downtown Strawberry Square offers marvelous experiments with light, temperature, sound, and static electricity. There is a Totspot for younger children. Children can get involved with science in the hands-on Discovery Bar. The good gift shop stocks many inexpensive science toys. Parking behind the Hilton Hotel can be validated by Strawberry Square merchants. *3rd and Walnuts Sts., Harrisburg, tel. 717/233–7969. Admission: $5 adults, $4 ages 3–17. Open: Tues.– Fri. 9–5, Sat. 10–5, Sun. noon–5.*

Pride of the Susquehanna. This 40-minute ride is relaxing, but you view the least interesting parts of City Island and Harrisburg. There's an on-board snack bar. *City Island Marina, Harrisburg, tel. 717/234–6500. Admission: $4.75 adults, $3 ages 2–12. Open June–Aug., Tues.–Fri. noon–4, weekends noon–8.*

Hershey's Chocolate World. You ride in an amusement park–style car while viewing equipment and vats of display chocolate. Up to 30-minute waits are common for this popular 10-minute tour. Everyone receives a free candy-bar souvenir before being discharged into a huge company store with several casual restaurants. *800 Park Blvd., Hershey, tel. 717/534–4900. Admission free. Open mid-June–Labor Day, daily 9–6:45; Labor Day–mid-Nov., daily 9–4:45; mid-Nov.–Dec., call for hrs; Jan.–Mar., Mon.–Sat. 9–4:45, Sun. noon–4:45; Apr.–mid-June, daily 9–4:45.*

HersheyPark. This well-planned amusement park has 50 rides, four roller coasters, 20 kiddie rides, and a walk-through zoo. Its new wooden roller coaster, the Wildcat, stretches over 2 acres. Nearly all Harrisburg and Hershey hotels offer money-saving HersheyPark discount packages or coupons. *300 Park Blvd., Hershey, tel. 717/534–3090 or 800/437–7439. Admission: $26.45 ages 9–54, $15.95 ages 3–8 and senior citizens; $13.95 after 5 PM. Open June–Aug., daily 10–10; mid-May and Sept., daily 10–8; closing times may vary.*

Sites to See

You can call for a copy of the excellent "City-wide Sights" brochure from the Office of the Mayor (Harrisburg, tel. 717/255–3040). It offers a detailed listing of the architecture, history, neighborhoods, and parking in downtown.

Peace Garden. The two blocks from Emerald Street to Maclay Street in the city's 5-mile **Riverfront Park** are dedicated to the pursuit of peace. The beautiful walk is adorned with inspiring quotes from world leaders. *Emerald and Maclay Sts., Harrisburg, tel. 717/255–3020.*

State Capitol and Museum. Pennsylvania has one of the most impressive of our nation's capitol buildings. "Commonwealth"—a gold-leaf statue nicknamed "Miss Penn"—stands atop the enormous Capitol dome that dominates the skyline of Harrisburg. The 52-million-pound dome, modeled after that of St. Peter's Basilica in Rome, rises 272 feet from the ground. There are two notable groups of statuary at the front of the Capitol done by Pennsylvania sculptor George Grey Barnard. Inside the Italian Renaissance building, the marble staircase is modeled on the grand stairway of the Opera House in Paris. Paintings by Pennsylvania artists Edwin Austin Abbey and Violet Oakley decorate the lobby and the other major chambers of the building. The beautifully restored and ornate Senate Chamber is most striking, dark rich green and gold with marble and mahogany and French gold drapes. The Pennsylvania General Assembly provides excellent free guided tours of the Capitol building. The rotunda is always open. For information, write the Pennsylvania General Assembly. *State Capitol, Harrisburg 17108, tel. 717/787–6810. Tours weekdays on the ½ hr, weekends on the hr except noon.*

State Museum of Pennsylvania. The 65-acre Capitol complex includes a free museum with exhibits that portray the commonwealth's cultural and natural heritage. The emphasis is on geology and industry rather than history and politics. There are rocks, cars, carriages, furniture, and a Conestoga wagon. The Curiosity Corner is a hands-on learning center for children. At the planetarium you can attend star shows. *3rd and North Sts., Box 1026, Harrisburg 17108-1026, tel. 717/787–4978. Admission:*

Curiosity Corner $1; planetarium $1.50 adults, $1 ages under 13 and senior citizens. Open: museum, Tues.–Sat. 9–5, Sun. noon–5; Curiosity Corner, *Tues., Thurs., and weekends 1–4; planetarium, weekends at 1 and 2:30.*

READING PHILLIES

League: Eastern League • **Major League Affiliation:** Philadelphia Phillies • **Class:** AA • **Stadium:** Memorial Municipal • **Opened:** 1950 • **Capacity:** 8,500 • **Dimensions:** LF: 330, CF: 400, RF: 330 • **Surface:** grass • **Season:** Apr.–Labor Day

STADIUM LOCATION: Rte. 61S/Centre Ave., Reading, PA 19605

TEAM WEBSITE: http://www.readingphillies.com

GETTING THERE: From Pennsylvania Turnpike, Rte. 222N to Rte. 422W to Rte. 61S. From I–78, Rte. 61S.

TICKET INFORMATION: Box 15050, Reading, PA 19612, tel. 610/478–8491, fax 610/373–5868

PRICE RANGE: Box seats $7; reserved seats $6; general admission $4 adult, $2.50 ages 5–14 and over 63.

GAME TIME: Mon.–Sat. 7:05 PM, Sun. 1:05 PM; gates usually open 90 min before game.

TIPS ON SEATING: Sit along the first-base side for easy access to the attractive patio area by the grill.

SEATING FOR PEOPLE WITH DISABILITIES: In right and left-field grandstands

STADIUM FOOD: The food is inexpensive and good. The best bet is the excellent pizza—cheese or pepperoni—for $1.50 a slice. Hot dogs are a bargain at $1 and have old-fashioned square-style buns. The **Food Grove** behind the right field bleachers does a good job on sandwiches—grilled chicken and sausage ($2.50), burgers ($2–$2.25). There are homemade pretzels and funnel cakes ($2) and heavy meatball sandwiches ($2.50). Wash down the BBQ peanuts ($2) with lemonade or spring water ($1). Other bargains are the hot fudge and butterscotch sundaes for $2.25. **The Deck,** a multi-tier bar with limited food selections behind the left-field wall, is open to all fans after the game begins. It features the local Yuengling beer.

SMOKING POLICY: Smoking prohibited in seating areas, but allowed in upper concourse directly behind general admission seats, in concourse, and in right-field food court

PARKING: Ample free parking

VISITING TEAM HOTEL: Wellesley Inn (910 Woodland Ave., Reading, PA 19610, tel. 610/374–1500 or 800/444–8888)

TOURISM INFORMATION: Reading-Berks Visitors Information Association (801 Hill Rd., VF Outlet Village, Wyomissing, PA 19610, tel. 610/375–4085 or 800/443–6610)

Reading: Memorial Municipal Stadium

Memorial Municipal Stadium in Reading, Pennsylvania, is a model of what can be done with an ordinary ballpark. Veteran Reading Phillies fans say the changes made in the last decade have dramatically improved this stadium. Before these renovations, box seats were folding chairs, the bleachers were wooden, and the grand-

stand had no roof. Today's stadium bears little resemblance to the ballpark built in 1950.

Owner Craig Stein bought the team in 1986 and immediately established a partnership with the city and the Reading Municipal Memorial Stadium Commission that has produced substantial improvements virtually every year. Investments of more than $2.5 million have transformed what was once a mediocre ballpark into a minor-league success story.

At the entrance, a landscaped plaza and new brick arches signal a commitment to excellence that continues inside. Just inside the entrance is a display case full of Reading baseball memorabilia. The concourse is red, white, and blue, wide and comfortable; a Reading-baseball Hall of Fame extends along the first-base side. The third-base-side concourse has a large, colorful mural of kids playing baseball.

The folding chairs and wooden bleachers have all been replaced by real seats—8,500 blue, green, yellow, and red plastic seats. This is an extraordinary commitment to the comfort of fans for a minor-league stadium. Flags fly from the new grandstand roof. Ironically, the one we looked for wasn't there. Just weeks after Mike Schmidt—the only player whose number has been retired by the Reading Phillies—was inducted into the Hall of Fame, the flag that flies from the grandstand roof with his number, 24, was shredded in a windstorm. Several replacement flags also tattered in the wind at that flag site. So Schmidt, who played for Reading in 1971, is honored in displays within the stadium.

We were especially impressed with the attractive picnic area behind the first-base bleachers. In many stadiums, this area under and behind aluminum bleachers looks like a trash dump. Here it is a beautifully treed patio-like area with small concession stands nearby. On the third-base side just past the grandstand, there is a picnic area for parties.

One distinctive feature from the original stadium remains—an attractive brick wall that surrounds the entire field. Wooden outfield fences stand inside it. The view beyond the wall is as eclectic as we saw anywhere: a mix of industrial plants and churches backed by mountains. The fire tower beyond right field on Mt. Penn is the most distinctive local landmark. Railroad tracks run close to the stadium, and planes from the nearby airport fly right over the grandstand roof.

The Phillies have an unusual mascot—a cross-eyed baseball on legs—and plenty of promotions. We attended one of the five fireworks nights in the season, even though there wasn't a holiday anywhere in sight. We particularly enjoyed Reading's practice of thrilling up to 10 birthday kids by inviting them to throw out a first ball.

Where to Stay

Visiting Team Hotel: Wellesley Inn. This four-story motel is 3 miles south of the ballpark. Guests are given Continental breakfast. The rooms are standard in size and furnishings. *910 Woodland Ave., Paper Mill Rd. exit off Rte. 422, Reading 19610, tel. 610/374–1500 or 800/ 444–8888, fax 610/374–2554. 105 rooms. Facilities: ironing boards provided. AE, D, DC, MC, V. $$*

Days Inn–Reading. Guests receive a free Continental breakfast at this well-kept motel, which is 8 miles north of the ballpark. Its rooms are freshly decorated. *15 Lancaster Pike, Exit 21, Hwy. 22 N, from Pennsylvania Turnpike, Reading 19607, tel. 610/777–7888 or 800/325–2525, fax 610/777–5138. 142 rooms. Facilities: pool, exercise room, game room. AE, D, DC, MC, V. $$*

Red Caboose Inn. It's an hour south of the ballpark, but here's your chance to sleep in a caboose in the middle of Amish country. Each of the 36 cabooses sleeps six (one double bed and four bunks). You'll need to reserve the cabooses four weeks in advance in summer. There also are seven rooms in an adjoining farmhouse. Meals are served in a dining car, and there's free country music in a barn on Wednesday and weekend nights in summer. *Rte. 741, Strasburg 17579, tel. 717/687–5000 or 888/687–5005, fax 717/ 687–5000. 43 rooms. Facilities: dining car, playground, caboose with video games. D, MC, V. $$*

Where to Eat

Arner's Family Restaurants. Children have many choices at this sunny, fast-service restaurant, including their own menu, half orders of any adult entrée, and a reduced price at the extensive salad bar. Arner's is known for its broiled crab cakes and its wide variety of vegetables. This site is eight blocks from the ballpark, the closest of its four Reading locations. There is a garden room in the rear. *9th and Exeter Sts., Reading, tel. 610/929–9795. AE, D, DC, MC, V. $*

The Crab Barn. Kids eat free from the children's menu here on Sunday with a paying adult. King crabs, blue crabs, softshells, and Dungeness are available, along with shrimp, chicken, and fishsticks for children. The dining room is on the second floor, and four tables are housed in a third-floor loft. There are crayons and special place mats for kids. The restaurant is just a couple of miles from the ballpark. *2613 Hampden Blvd., Reading, tel. 610/921–8922. AE, MC, V. $$*

The Peanut Bar and Restaurant. There are a multitude of sandwich choices at this noisy, popular restaurant, which encourages you to throw peanut shells on the floor. The children's menu includes spaghetti, grilled cheese sandwiches, and chicken tenders. Its signature dessert is frozen, chocolate-covered pretzel pie. *332 Penn St., Reading, tel. 610/376–8500 or 800/515–8500. AE, D, MC, V. $*

Entertainments

Roadside America. This one-of-a-kind attraction is 25 miles northwest of Reading and worth the drive. Picture a gigantic miniature village spanning history, with moving trains, trolleys, airplanes, animals, cars, and coal-mine equipment. This Cadillac of roadside tourist attractions was the life work of hobbyist Laurence Gieringer. You'll view the huge scene in light and "nighttime" darkness during the patriotic Evening Pageant. An employee told us it takes six years to dust the entire exhibit. *Rte. 22, Exit 8 from I-78, Shartlesville, tel. 215/488–6241. Admission: $3.75 adults, $1.25 ages 6–11. Open July–Labor Day, weekdays 9–6:30, weekends 9–7; Labor Day–June, weekdays 10–5, weekends 10–6.*

Strasburg Railroad. America's oldest short-line railroad takes you on a 45-minute ride through Amish farmland. As it's popular for school trips, advance reservations are a good idea. *Rte. 741, Strasburg, tel. 717/687–7522. Cost: $7.50 adults, $4 ages 3–11, under 3 free.*

Dorney Park. Pennsylvania has several amusement-park treasures and this is one, just 30 minutes from Reading. Open since the 1860s, it is both modern and vintage. A large water park adjoins it. There is a Care Bears show, miniature golf, bumper boats, two wooden coasters, a 90-foot Ferris wheel, and the sit-down Memories restaurant. A separate entry admission to either park is available. *3830 Dorney Park Rd., Rte. 222 (Pennsylvania Turnpike exit 16) east from Hwy. 309, Allentown, tel. 610/395–3724. Admission: mid-Apr.–June, $19.95 adults and children over 48″, $4.95 children under 48″, under 3 free, $10 discount after 5 PM; July–Labor Day, $24.95 adults and children over 48″, $4.95 children under 48″, under 3 free. Open mid-Apr.–Labor Day, daily 10–10.*

Sites to See

The Pagoda. This 72-foot-high Japanese structure overlooks the city and Schuylkill Valley. It was built in 1908 as a luxury resort hotel on Mt. Penn, but when it was denied a liquor license, it never opened. Visitors can walk into the pagoda, which was restored in 1992 and is now used for offices; the view is worth the drive up the mountain. *Skyline Dr., Mt. Penn, Reading. Open daily 11–5.*

Unusual Shopping

Wilbur Chocolate Factory Outlet. The home of the original chocolate chip, the Wilbur Bud, is 35 miles southwest of Reading. Chocolate has been made in this factory since 1884. Its Ideal Dutch Process Cocoa is used in Amish cakes. You can visit its free Candy Americana Museum, too. It is next to the city park and town square. *46 Broad St., Lititz, tel. 717/626–1131.*

Tom Sturgis Pretzel Outlet. You can buy big plastic bags of some of the region's best pretzels at bargain prices here. It's near the Shillington farmer's market. *325 Lancaster Pike W (Rte. 222), Shillington, tel. 610/775–0335.*

WILLIAMSPORT CUBS

League: New York–Penn League • **Major League Affiliation:** Chicago Cubs • **Class:** Short Season A • **Stadium:** Bowman Field • **Opened:** 1926 • **Capacity:** 4,200 • **Dimensions:** LF: 345, CF: 405, RF: 350 • **Surface:** grass • **Season:** mid-June–Labor Day

STADIUM LOCATION: 1700 W. 4th St., Williamsport, PA 17701

GETTING THERE: From south, Rte. 15 to Maynard St., right on Maynard, left on 4th St., 1 mi to stadium. From north, Rte. 15 to 4th St., left on 4th St., ballpark on left.

TICKET INFORMATION: Box 3173, Williamsport, PA 17701, tel. 717/326–3389, fax 717/326–3494

PRICE RANGE: Reserved box seats $4.50; general admission $3.25 adult, $2.50 under 12 and senior citizens.

GAME TIME: 7:05 PM; gates open 1 hr before game.

TIPS ON SEATING: General admission seats are fine. Only 900 blue box seats, so you're close to action. Except for bleacher seats beyond first base, general admission seats are aluminum benches with backs under a roof. Remember, this is a 1920s stadium; make sure you don't sit behind one of 8 poles that hold up grandstand roof.

SEATING FOR PEOPLE WITH DISABILITIES: On both first- and third-base sides

STADIUM FOOD: There is one large concession area under the stands offering normal and inexpensive baseball fare and a small stand past grandstand on the third-base side. The best items are the Italian sausage with onions and peppers, for $2.50, and the pan pizzas at $3. The hot dogs are made by the Hatfield Company in Philadelphia and are quite mild. Many eaters go for the chili topping, for an extra 25¢. An unusual dessert is the pie-shaped wedge of chocolate chip cookies, sold for $2 and decorated with frosting. Cracker Jack is a reasonable $1, and frozen lemonade is $1.50. The soft pretzels ($1.25) are kept warm and are chewy. Ice cream sundaes come in four varieties for $2.

SMOKING POLICY: No alcohol/no smoking section in bleachers directly behind home plate

PARKING: Ample free parking at stadium

VISITING TEAM HOTEL: Holiday Inn (1840 E. 3rd St., Williamsport, PA 17701, tel. 717/326–1981 or 800/465–4329)

TOURISM INFORMATION: Lycoming County Tourist Promotion Agency (454 Pine St., Williamsport, PA 17701, tel. 717/326–1971 or 800/358–9900)

Williamsport: Bowman Field

There's baseball to see in Williamsport even if you can't get here for the Little League World Series in late August. The Williamsport Cubs play in Bowman Field. Built in 1926, it is one of the oldest minor league parks still in use. A plain and simple New York–Penn League stadium, Bowman Field seats 4,200 with a partially covered grandstand. In 1929, they renamed the ballpark after businessman J. Walton Bowman, who had led the 1925 campaign to raise the $75,000 needed for construction. Lights were added in 1932. In 1934, the outfield walls were brought in (45 feet in center field), as only 10 home runs had been hit in the first eight seasons.

The field had deteriorated so much by the 1950s that Little League Baseball declined to take the ballpark from the city, saying that renovation costs to prepare it for the Little League World Series would be too great. From 1964 to 1987, Bowman Field was illuminated by lights originally used in New York's Polo Grounds. The ballpark was substantially upgraded in 1987. The wooden box seats were replaced and new lights installed without losing its old-time feel. The bleachers in left field were supplanted by a picnic area in 1988, reducing the capacity to 4,200. Further improvements were made in 1994 when the Cubs came to town.

The view from the grandstand is one of the most idyllic in all of baseball, with houses and a well-treed hillside beyond the outfield walls. There are non-stop contests and lucky numbers as well as good music in the intervals between baseball action. Kid Cub is the friendly bear mascot.

They have played professional baseball in Williamsport since 1907, starting with the Class B Tri-State League. In 1923 Williamsport joined the New York–Penn League, which became today's Class AA Eastern League in 1938. For the next 50-plus years, Williamsport was in and out of the Eastern League. The city returned to the New York–Penn League, now a short-season Class A league, in 1994.

Two of minor league baseball's most bizarre moments took place at historic Bowman Field.

In 1955, a young Reading outfielder named Roger Maris looked back over his shoulder while chasing a long fly ball and ran right through the outfield fence.

On August 31, 1987, with a Reading player on third base, Williamsport catcher Dave Bresnahan took a peeled round potato and threw it over the third baseman's head and into left field. When the runner tried to score from third, Bresnahan tagged him with the real ball. Bresnahan's professional playing career ended that night. But a year later, 4,000 fans showed up when Williamsport held Dave Bresnahan Day and retired his number 59. Admission that day was one dollar and one potato. Look on the concourse near the souvenir shop for the Bresnahan number 59 and pay tribute to a .149 hitter with a sense of humor.

Entertainments

Memorial Pool. This large, clean city pool, with a wading pool for children 5 and under, is just yards from the ballpark. After a long day of driving, you can cool off before the game. *Memorial Park, 1700 W. 4th St., Williamsport, tel. 717/322–4637. Admission: $2.50 adults, $2.25 ages 7–17, $1.50 ages 6 and under. Open Mon., Wed., Sat., Sun. 1–8, Tues., Thurs., Fri. 1–6.*

Williamsport: Lamade Field

"Oh, my gosh!" exclaimed our young son Hugh as he left the Little League Museum and turned the corner at the top of the hill overlooking Lamade Field. The Saturday in August when they play for the World Championship of Little League is an "Oh, my gosh!" experience. Down at the bottom of this hill sits a most beautiful green diamond, expertly manicured and ready for a big game. But it's different. It's smaller. It's not like the big-guy stadiums we had been in. It's the kind of stadium a little kid could imagine playing in. To a five-year-old, it's simply perfect.

On World Series Saturday, this 10,000-seat grandstand fills up early. And the families were filling the huge grassy hill beyond the outfield wall with blankets and beach towels. The festivities began two hours before game time.

It was like a carnival inside the stadium and out. Groups of people stood just behind the stadium frantically trading pins from their towns and teams, as these were the last hours of a busy week of meeting people from across the country and around the world. Little League Baseball began in Williamsport in 1939, and the first World Series was played in 1947. The final game, always played on a Saturday, marks the end of tournament play for 7,000 chartered Little League programs around the world. Three million children from 91 countries now participate in the Little League Baseball program. Tournament play begins in mid-July. One month later, eight regional champions come to Williamsport, representing four United States regions and four international regions.

The 44-acre complex includes the offices of Little League Baseball, a museum, the stadium, and other facilities. A huge American flag waves in right center field behind a very short, dark green fence with Dugout, the Little League mascot, painted on it. The offices and museum sit atop the hill. Most of the grassy hillside is filled with people. The view over the buildings is of more hills and trees behind. An open-air box full of television cameras hangs from the roof covering the grandstand.

Unless you are one of the lucky few in the VIP seating section directly behind home plate, you are sitting on a hard bench without a back. Bring a pillow, a blanket, or a seat cushion. The stadium was built in 1959 by Little League Baseball with a contribution from *Grit*, the national weekly newspaper published in Williamsport. The field was named for Howard J. Lamade, a *Grit* official and member of the Little League Board of Directors.

The sound system is spectacular, and the music—"Put Me In, Coach; I'm Ready to Play" seemed particularly appropriate—keeps the crowd energized before the game and during the too-long television commercial breaks between innings. The on-the-field entertainment includes a military marching band, a Mummers band, and the Phillie Phanatic, the mascot for the Philadelphia Phillies. It's a great show. The players enter the stadium with banners in English and Chinese. The Little League Pledge is recited in four languages. Dignitaries are introduced and "The Star-Spangled Banner" sung before we even realized two hours had gone by. The wait until 3:50 PM to accommodate national TV wasn't painful at all.

This is plenty professional for kids, and it might seem like too much pressure for a 12-year-old. But don't worry—this isn't exactly the big leagues. The teams from Taipei, who have dominated this tournament for years, completely overmatched the United States champion from Texas. Soon after the Taipei players hit two balls way over the 204-foot outfield fence, the United States manager made a pitching change. The pitcher went to left field. The catcher became the pitcher. The third baseman became the catcher. The left fielder went to first base, and the first baseman to third. What would Abbott and Costello have done with material like this?

When you are in Williamsport for the World Series, always have a pen ready for an autograph. There's no telling who you might run into. We saw Hall of Famer Stan Musial, and as we walked out of the stadium, there was New York Yankees pitching great Tommy John, whose young son had sung "The Star-Spangled Banner."

Other Baseball Sites

Peter J. McGovern Little League Baseball Museum. It tells the story of Little League Baseball from the first game in 1939 to the last pitch of the most recent World Series. Opened in 1982 and named in honor of Peter J. McGovern, the first president of Little League Baseball, the museum is fun for Little Leaguers and parents alike. In addition to housing extensive historic videos and memorabilia, the museum gives kids the opportunity to let off steam. The lobby is a reduced-size re-creation of Lamade Stadium, with a huge 110-foot-wide, 15-foot-high photograph from the 1982 World Series showing the fans in the stands. It took considerable coaxing to get our kids off the field and into the museum proper. After dutifully examining the cases full of Little League memorabilia, the kids were pleased to find the Play Ball Room on the lower level. Here you can bat and pitch and then watch yourself on an instant-feedback monitor. The Play It Safe Room on the lower level displays safety equipment and makes a strong antidrug pitch. The nutrition exhibit gives future stars the opportunity to choose between excel-

lent and poor meals. The decision to allow girls to compete in 1974 and the establishment of a Challenger Division for youngsters with disabilities in 1989 are not ignored in this tribute to athletic youngsters. There are displays showing how gloves and balls are made. Little League Baseball, the museum tells us, started in 1939 with a simple observation—"Kids love baseball." From that has grown an international movement that involves 3 million children and 1 million adult volunteers from more than 90 countries. This museum, on a hill just above Lamade Stadium, is a fitting tribute to an impressive institution. *Rte. 15, Box 3485, Williamsport 17701, tel. 717/326–3607. Admission: $5 adults, $3 senior citizens, $1.50 ages 5–13, $13 family. Open Memorial Day–Labor Day, Mon.–Sat. 9–7, Sun. noon–7; Labor Day–Memorial Day, Mon.–Sat. 9–5, Sun. noon–5.*

Memorial Park. This is where the very first Little League baseball game was played on June 6, 1939. Lundy Lumber defeated Lycoming Dairy 23–8. Local businesses put up $35 each to sponsor a team and provide uniforms and equipment. A statue of Carl Stotz with young ballplayers honors this spot. It sits beyond the right-field wall of Bowman Field on the other side of the community pool. The field across Third Street from Bowman Field is the **Original Field,** where the first Little League World Series game was played in 1947. *100 W. 4th St., Williamsport.*

Where to Stay

Lodging is at a premium during the Little League World Series; book a year in advance, if possible. Some of the more distant hotels on East Third Street, the so-called Golden Strip, a commercial area, may still have vacancies until January, seven months before the Series. Prices are significantly higher during the Little League World Series.

King's Inn. This '60s-era hotel, remodeled in 1993, is directly opposite the Little League Stadium. It consists of two one-story structures built into a hill. *Rte. 15, South Williamsport 17701, tel. 717/322–4707, fax 717/322–0946. 48 rooms. Facilities: restaurant. AE, D, DC, MC, V. $*

Genetti Hotel and Convention Center. This classic, 10-story downtown hotel was recently renovated. The older rooms have high ceilings; the newer ones don't. *200 W. 4th St., Williamsport 17701, tel. 717/326–6600, fax 717/326–5006. 166 rooms. Facilities: restaurant, pool, coin laundry. AE, D, DC, MC, V. $*

Sheraton Inn. This downtown inn overlooks the Susquehanna River and is a boarding point for the downtown trolley. You can ask for either a city- or river-view room in this 5-story brick box-style hotel that's surrounded by a parking lot. The rooms and halls are spacious and have modern furnishings. *100 Pine St., Williamsport 17701, tel. 717/327–8231 or 800/325–3535, fax 717/ 322–2957. 148 rooms. Facilities: restaurant, indoor pool. AE, D, DC, MC, V. $$*

Holiday Inn. This two-story hotel is a 15-minute drive from the Little League ballpark. It's in a commercial strip of restaurants and movie theaters, 5 miles from downtown. *1840 E. 3rd St., Faxon St. exit from I–80, Williamsport 17701, tel. 717/326–1981 or 800/465–4329, fax 717/323–9590. 160 rooms. Facilities: restaurant, pool. AE, D, DC, MC, V. $$*

Visiting Team Hotel: Econo Lodge. This two-story hotel is a 15-minute drive from the Little League ballpark and has been fully renovated. The rooms have cherry veneer furniture, comfort chairs, and new 25-inch televisions. It's in a commercial strip of restaurants and movie theaters, near both the Giant and Loyal shopping plazas, 5 miles from downtown. *2401 E. 3rd St., Faxon St. exit from I–80, Williamsport 17701, tel. 717/326–1501 or 800/424–6423, fax 717/326–9776. 98 rooms. Facilities: restaurant. AE, D, DC, MC, V. $*

Where to Eat

Triangle Tavern. Diners have been enjoying memorable family-style Italian meals here for four decades. The signature spaghetti sauce and homemade Italian salad dressing are the big draws. There are also pizza and individual deep-dish apple, cherry, and blueberry pies, as well as children-size portions of spaghetti and chicken fingers. It's 12 minutes north of the Little League ballpark. *308 Shiffler Ave., Williamsport, tel. 717/322–9945. MC, V. $*

Charlie's Caboose. You can eat in a caboose, two railcars, or a freight-station house at this downtown restaurant on rails. It's a tablecloth-dinner-only restaurant, with everything from chicken sandwiches to roast duck. The children's menu offers spaghetti, burgers, and chicken fingers. The vegetable platter, seafood, and pasta are good. If you want to sit in the two-table caboose, reserve ahead. *500 Pine St., Williamsport, tel. 717/327–9128. AE, MC, V. $$*

Entertainments

Clyde Peeling's Reptiland. Kids love holding and touching the nonpoisonous snakes, lizards, and tortoises. The many poisonous snakes are safely behind glass. The educational talks are geared to kids, with a wealth of living props and interesting audiovisual shows. This walk-through attraction 12 miles south of Williamsport contains a Subway restaurant. *Rte. 15, Allenwood, tel. 717/538–1869. Admission: $7 adults, $5 ages 4–11. Open May–Sept., daily 9–7; Oct.–Apr., daily 10–5.*

Herdic Trolley. Trolley passengers can see Memorial Park, where the first Little League baseball game was played. This trolley takes a one-hour trip through downtown Williamsport and Millionaire's Row. The motorized car is named for Peter Herdic, who started the Williamsport Passenger Railway Company. The regular trolley tour expands for Little League World Series Week. The Historic Little League Tour (Williamsport City Bus, tel. 717/326–2500) starts at the Little League Museum and Lamade Stadium. After a trip to the Lycoming County Museum to see the Carl Stotz collection and a ride down Millionaire's Row, the tour makes special stops at Point Park and Original Field. On Tuesday and Thursday, visitors can add a one-hour cruise on the *Hiawatha* Paddlewheeler on the Susquehanna River (tel. 717/321–1205 or 800/358–9900). *Trolley Gazebo, Sheraton Inn, Pine and Court Sts., Williamsport, tel. 717/326–2500 or 800/248–9287 in PA. Admission: $2. Open May–Sept., Tues. and Thurs. 10:45–3:15, Sat. 9–11.*

Knoebels Amusement Resort. This is one of the most delightful, noncommercial amusement parks in America. About 35 minutes southeast of Williamsport, it's nestled in a stream-crossed pine forest. The family-run park is cool on the hottest days. Step back in time with several hand-crafted rides, free admission, and free parking. Its new thrill rides delight older kids, and the boat, helicopter, and rocketship rides for younger children are better than the usual too-tame kiddie rides. All ages will scream on the wooden Phoenix roller coaster, resurrected from ruin in San Antonio. This park has great food—Cesari's pizza, pierogis, and addictive french fries. Its sit-down Alamo Restaurant specializes in coal-country food, including waffles with chicken sauce. The huge Crystal Pool has slides, a wading pool, and tube rides. The park takes pride in its brass-ring 1913 carousel and carousel museum. There are also a mining museum, a pioneer steam train, and two covered bridges. Many families stay at the adjacent campground. *Rte. 487, Rte. 15 S from Williamsport to Rte. 61 E to Rte. 487 N, Elysburg, tel. 717/672–2572 or 800/487–4386. Rides 50¢–$2; all-ride pass, weekdays, $16 adults, $11.75 under 48"; pass including roller coaster, $3 extra adults, $2 extra children; $5 discount on basic pass after 5 PM; pool admission weekends $4 adults,* $2.50 children under 12, weekdays $3.50 adults, $2 children. Open mid-June–early Sept., daily 11–10; Apr.–May, weekends noon–6 or 8.

Sites to See

Lycoming County Historical Society Museum. This facility has the personal collection of Carl Stotz, the founder of Little League Baseball. The first Little League uniforms are on display, as well as the very first home plate, hand-carved by Stotz in 1939. See a turn-of-the-century general store and learn about the variety of tools used in central Pennsylvania during the last two centuries. The museum is in the National Historic District just off Route 220 (Maynard Street exit) and Route 15. *858 W. 4th St., Williamsport, tel. 717/326–3326. Admission: $3.50 adults, $3 senior citizens, $1.50 children. Open May–Oct., Tues.–Fri. 9:30–4, Sat. 11–4, Sun. noon–4; Nov.–Apr., Tues.–Fri. 9:30–4, Sat. 11–4.*

SCRANTON/WILKES-BARRE RED BARONS

League: International League • **Major League Affiliation:** Philadelphia Phillies • **Class:** AAA • **Stadium:** Lackawanna County Stadium • **Opened:** 1989 • **Capacity:** 10,832 • **Dimensions:** LF: 330, CF: 408, RF: 330 • **Surface:** artificial turf • **Season:** Apr.–Labor Day

STADIUM LOCATION: 235 Montage Mountain Rd., Moosic, PA 18507

GETTING THERE: Stadium is just off I–81 between Scranton and Wilkes-Barre. From I–81, Montage Mountain Rd. exit (exit 51), stadium on east side of I–81.

TICKET INFORMATION: Box 3449, Scranton, PA 18505, tel. 717/969–2255, fax 717/963–6564

PRICE RANGE: Box seats $6.50; upper grandstand reserved $4.50; bleachers $3.50.

GAME TIME: Mon.–Sat. 7:30 PM; Sun. 6 PM; gates open 90 min before game time.

TIPS ON SEATING: Bleacher seats, at field level down first- and third-base lines, are a good buy. Upper grandstand reserved seats are as high above playing field as upper deck seats in major league stadiums. View beyond outfield walls is better from seats on third-base (visitors) side.

SEATING FOR PEOPLE WITH DISABILITIES: Behind box seats behind home plate

STADIUM FOOD: There is good regional food here—cheese steaks, potato pierogis, and thick-crust pizza. The deli on the ground floor, first-base side has hoagies. Adjacent is one of two grills with excellent steak-and-cheese hoagies. Across the aisle is a "kidcessions" stand. Its $2.75 Grumpy meal (named after the mascot) includes a hamburger, cheeseburger, or a good hot dog, with chips, fries, a drink, and a Barons key chain. Fresh-baked cookies are 3 for $1.50. Vendors sell juices for $1.75. Avoid the non-fresh peanuts. The pizza is baked on site. A glass-fronted **Stadium Club,** behind first base, is open to all ticket holders and has good chicken wings and fajitas. Its salad, sandwich, and kid's menus are extensive.

SMOKING POLICY: Smoking allowed throughout stadium

PARKING: Plenty of parking at stadium, $1

VISITING TEAM HOTEL: Radisson Lackawanna Station Hotel (700 Lackawanna Ave., Scranton, PA 18503, tel. 717/342-8300 or 800/333-3333)

TOURISM INFORMATION: Northeast Territory Visitors Bureau (Airport Aviation Center, 201 Hangar Rd., Suite 203, Avoca, PA 18641, tel. 717/457-1320 or 800/245-7711)

Scranton/Wilkes-Barre: Lackawanna County Stadium

The Philadelphia Phillies play in one of the very worst of all the major-league baseball stadiums. In 1989, when a new stadium was built for its Triple AAA International League franchise, it was designed to match the Phillies' horrid Veterans Stadium. To prepare future Phillies for their step into the big leagues, they duplicated the height of the outfield wall, the dimensions to the outfield fence, and, unfortunately, the fake grass.

Surprise—even the plastic that covers the field cannot ruin the experience at Lackawanna County Stadium. Set in a valley, the stadium has one of the finest natural settings in all of baseball. From inside the park, the view of the surrounding well-treed cliffs is one of the best of any East Coast ballpark we visited.

The baseball rivalry between Wilkes-Barre (pronounced "barry") and Scranton dates back to the 19th century, with both cities often fielding teams in the same minor leagues. In 1951, the Wilkes-Barre Barons folded, soon followed by the Scranton Red Sox in 1953.

To bring baseball back to this historic coal-mining region, Scranton and Wilkes-Barre combined forces, stitching together the nicknames of the former rivals into the Scranton/Wilkes-Barre Red Barons. (The nickname didn't come from the World War I flying ace.) Four seats from the old Scranton field are sitting now in the administrative office of the team just off the main concourse.

The 10,832 capacity Lackawanna County Stadium was built right at the base of Montage Mountain between the two cities. The nicely landscaped entrance is attractive, with tan blocks and a green roof with flags flying above. The double-decked grandstand presents a big league feel and provides fans throughout the stadium an excellent view of the action. There are 20 skyboxes, with two available for group rental on a game-by-game basis. The outfield wall is blue with a modest amount of orange lettering and numbers. The only ads are on billboards beyond the outfield fence. There are scoreboards in left-center and right-center of the batter's eye. The bullpens are tucked neatly behind the fences near the left and right field foul poles. There is a picnic deck above the bullpen in right field.

The Phillie Phanatic visited the night we were there. The local mascot, The Grump, is also a hairy, green thing. This one has a great big red mouth and a red gum ball–like nose. The Grump, according to local legend, was hatched when a prehistoric egg was found during stadium excavation. Grump is lovable and the food and the music are good, but not all is right yet. At present, there are absolutely no restrictions on smoking in the park or the restaurant and there are smokers everywhere.

From November through March, the right field area is converted to an NHL-size ice skating rink. The rink sits just under the stadium restaurant and is very popular with the locals.

The Stadium Club restaurant is open to the public Mon.–Fri. 11–2. It has a five-item children's menu and three pages of adult menu choices, from shrimp kebabs to cajun tuna salad. If no private party has claimed the adjoining 100-seat outside deck, patrons of the Stadium Club may sit there. Seating at the window tables is first-come, first-serve.

Fans of the wonderful movie *Field of Dreams* will want to know that the young ballplayer who only played in a single major league game and later became a doctor—Archibald "Moonlight" Graham—won the New York State League batting title hitting .336 for Scranton in 1906.

Where to Stay

Visiting team hotel: Radisson Lackawanna Station Hotel. This majestic six-story French

Renaissance hotel was the station for the Delaware, Lackawanna and Western railroad. Its lobby ceiling is Tiffany stained glass, the floor is terrazo tiles, and imposing marble columns are set off by tile panels of scenes along the rail route. Despite the elegance, the hotel and its restaurant, Carmen's, are affordable ($89 double) and child-friendly. The rooms have lovely antique reproduction furniture, expensive draperies, and modern baths. *700 Lackawanna Ave., Scranton 18503, tel. 717/342–8300 or 800/333–3333, fax 717/342–0380. 146 rooms. Facilities: whirlpool, exercise room, game room, restaurant. AE, D, DC, MC, V. $$*

Marriott Courtyard. This just-built hotel is adjacent to the ballpark complex and has a fine view of Montage Mountain. It is three stories, surrounded by a parking lot, and built around an interior courtyard. Rooms are modern, spacious, and have two double beds. *16 Glenmaura National Blvd., Scranton 18507, tel. 717/969–2100 or 800/228–9290, fax 717/969–2110. 120 rooms. Facilities: indoor pool. AE, D, DC, MC, V. $$*

Hampton Inn. Within one mile of the ballpark, this four-story motel is on a hill, with a view of the Montage Mountains. The rooms are attractive and basic. Refrigerators may be rented. Guests receive a free Continental breakfast. *22 Montage Mountain Rd., Scranton 18507, tel. 717/342–7002 or 800/426–7866, fax 717/342–7012. 129 rooms. Facilities: heated indoor pool, whirlpool, exercise room, restaurant. AE, D, DC, MC, V. $$*

Where to Eat

Cooper's Seafood House. You can't help but notice the larger-than-life octopus and pirates hanging on the roof of this ship-shaped restaurant. Inside is a cornucopia of marine artifacts, photos of historic Scranton and of Babe Ruth, and several whimsical and inviting dining rooms. Walking through the hallways, you can view the entire 20th century in frames. There's a vintage children's toy exhibit at the entry and a 40-foot whale is the ceiling ornament in the no-smoking room. Children's meals are served in a paper ship and desserts include the classic coconut ice cream ball in chocolate sauce. The fish soups and seafood dishes are nicely prepared, and unusual items, like alligator, mako shark, and blue marlin are served. *701 N. Washington Ave., Scranton, tel. 717/346–6883. Open Mon.–Thurs. 11–midnight, Fri.–Sat. 11–1 AM, Sun. 1–9. D, MC, V. $$*

The Original Coney Island. There are two Coney Island restaurants within 100 paces of each other, both with a two-sandwich menu—the Texas wieners and the Texas hamburger. The hot dogs are split, grilled, and topped with your choice of mustard, onions, and chili sauce. The hamburger and wieners are served in a soft, all-purpose bun that's several cuts above the usual cotton-like bun. Both sandwiches are very good, but children might want them without the spicy chili. Other than french fries, drinks, chips, and gum, there's nothing else sold. This locale opened in 1923 and most of it is below street level, with a 10-stool counter and six vintage wooden booths, with mirrors and glass globe lights. Look for the yellow and white checkerboard exterior near the downtown railroad bridge. You are stepping back in time here. *100 Cedar Ave., Scranton, tel. 717/961-8288. Open Mon.–Sat. 10–8. No credit cards. $*

Coney Island Lunch. This storefront restaurant is larger and newer than its competitor and serves a few more items, like bean soup, a good coconut cream pie, and homemade rice pudding. But the basic menu is the identical-tasting Texas wieners and Texas hamburgers, at the same bargain price of $1.30 each. There are photos of a young Babe Ruth and Shoeless Joe Jackson on the walls. The Karampilas family began the Coney Island tradition in Scranton and eaters are lucky to have two restaurants to indulge their passion for these spicy, satisfying sandwiches. *515 Lackawanna Ave., Scranton, tel. 717/961–9004. Open Mon.–Sat. 10–7, Sun. noon–7. No credit cards. $*

Preno's Italian Restaurant. This is the city's oldest restaurant, within steps of the former railroad station and the Coney Island lunch counters. Its mirrored and white plaster exterior is a result of past modernization. Inside, there's a dim bar on one side and two cozy dining rooms on the other. Each table has a tiny lamp whose shade matches the tablecloth. The third generation of the founding family now works here, serving reasonable and unusual Italian dishes, like rigatoni with chopped chicken, pasta with chicken livers, and many veal dishes. Children's portions are available. The desserts are home-made and special, particularly the apple walnut tart. *601 Lackawanna Ave., Scranton, tel. 717/346–2091. Open Tues.–Thurs. 11:30–2:30 and 4–10, Fri. 11:30–2:30 and 4–11, Sat. 4–11, Sun. 4–10. AE, D, MC, V. $$*

Smith's Family Restaurant. This cottage-style white frame restaurant has been part of this residential and warehouse neighborhood since 1934. This is plain, inexpensive food and its clientele are families and older neighbors. A counter and booth section gets heavy use at breakfast, and the two dining rooms, with its captain's chairs and wood paneling, are decorated with parish notables and the daily specials. There is a large offering of lighter menu items and sandwiches. Chicken and ribs are for heavier appetites. It's 3 miles northeast of the ballpark at Cherry Street, following Route 11 (Main Street), which turns into Cedar Avenue. *1402 Cedar Ave., Scranton, tel. 717/961–9192. Open weekdays 5:30–10, Sat. 5:30–8. No credit cards. $*

Entertainments

Lackawanna Coal Mine. Wear jackets to this fascinating attraction, as you will descend 1,350 feet via a mine cable car into the damp darkness of a huge anthracite mine. (There are jackets available if you forget yours.) This mine was first opened in 1860 and its underground world of child laborers, physical dangers, and miners who worked for 18¢ an hour, breathing coal dust for 12 hours, six days a week, is a scary and awesome spectacle. The guides are excellent, as they are all former miners. The last tour leaves at 4:30 and the adjoining anthracite museum closes at 5.

There is a gift shop with many small coal-related items and mood rings that are attractive to children. The restored mine, which closed in 1966, is in a park containing a swimming pool and children's fishing ponds. It is reached from I–81, exit 51 west to Davis Street, continuing on North Keyser Avenue for 5 miles. *N. Keyser Ave., McDade Park, Scranton, tel. 717/963–6463 or 800/238–7245. Admission: $5 adults, $3 children. Open April–Nov. daily 10–4:30.*

Steamtown National Historic Site and Trolley Museum. Steam railroading is described in films, displays, artifacts, and by exploring a huge 1902 working roundhouse and repair yard at the Scranton yard of the Delaware, Lackawanna & Western railroad. Visitors can climb on several rail cars and watch "Steel and Steam" an excellent 18-minute film created for the National Park Service, which runs this visitors center and museum complex. You can see how difficult railroad work is by viewing the repair troughs where mechanics work. An excursion train, powered by a steam locomotive, takes passengers to Moscow, PA. and back, a scenic tour through northeast Pennsylvania. A trolley museum adjoins Steamtown and shows the city's past, when it was known as "Electric City," for its many electric-powered trolleys. Trolley rides are offered on the former Laurel Line to the Lackawanna Visitors Center at Montage Mountain. There is an extra fee for the train and trolley excursions. *150 S. Washington Ave., entrance at Bridge St., at Lackawanna Ave., Scranton, tel. 717/340–5200. Admission: $6 adults, $5 senior citizens, $2 ages 5–15. Open daily 9–5. Closed Thanksgiving, Dec. 25, Jan. 1.*

BIG APPLE BASEBALL
TRENTON, NEW YORK, NEW HAVEN

Treats for baseball fans traveling in the New York City area include Trenton's new waterfront stadium, Yankee Stadium, and historic Yale Field in New Haven.

Begin in Trenton, which had been without professional baseball for 44 years until this handsome park on the Delaware River opened in 1994 for Double AA Eastern League ball. You can eat New Jersey diner food a few blocks from the ballpark, or in one of the Italian family establishments in the Chambersburg restaurant district, less than a mile from the park. The state capitol complex includes a free museum. Princeton University is 14 miles northeast, with its ivy-covered stone buildings. Two worthwhile amusement parks, Sesame Place and Six Flags Great Adventure, are each less than 20 miles from Trenton.

From Trenton, drive north on Interstate 95, crossing the Hudson River into the Bronx and onto the Major Deegan Expressway. Yankee Stadium is at exit 6, about an hour from Trenton. For many fans, the New York Yankees epitomize baseball, as the most prestigious ball club with the most memorable players in the history of the sport.

Taking the subway to Yankee Stadium is the preferred route; go early to explore Monument Park in center field. The subway is your ticket to most of Manhattan's attractions, as well as the must-see Botanic Gardens in Brooklyn, which makes you forget you are in a city. The gardens are just two blocks from the site of the now-demolished but long remembered Ebbets Field, home of the Brooklyn Dodgers. Be a tourist and go to the top of the Empire State Building, to the Statue of Liberty, and the petting zoo in Central Park. It's a long subway ride to Shea Stadium in Queens, but it's worth it to see the Panorama of New York, the world's largest architectural model, that is in the nearby Queens Museum of Art.

Taking the Cross-Bronx Expressway to Interstate 95 north, you'll reach New Haven in 65 miles. Here you'll find Double AA Eastern League ball in the 1927 stadium where George Bush played baseball for Yale. It was elegantly renovated in 1994, but its huge hand-operated scoreboard remains, along with a modern one. Yale University has spawned a number of quirky, superlative eateries. In nearby East Haven, there is a captivating trolley museum. Forty miles east is an all-day excursion site at Mystic Seaport.

TRENTON THUNDER

League: Eastern League • **Major League Affiliation:** Boston Red Sox • **Class:** AA • **Stadium:** Mercer County Waterfront Stadium • **Opened:** 1994 • **Capacity:** 6,439 • **Dimensions:** LF: 330, CF: 407, RF: 330 • **Surface:** grass • **Season:** Apr.–Labor Day

STADIUM LOCATION: 1 Thunder Rd., Trenton, NJ 08611

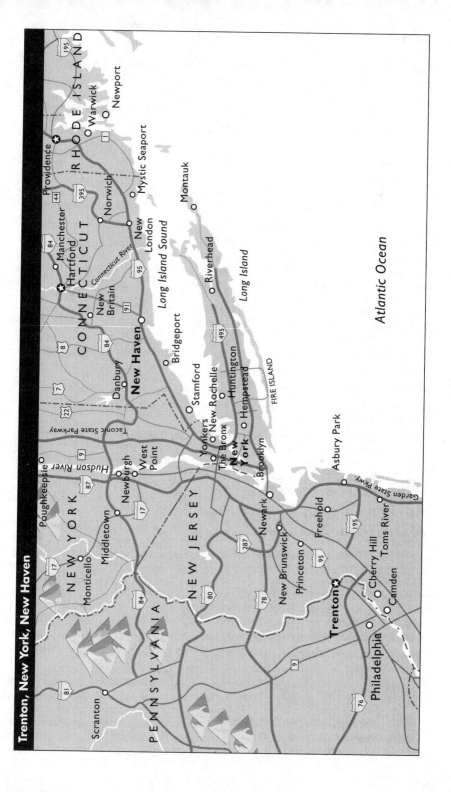

Trenton, New York, New Haven

GETTING THERE: From New Jersey Turnpike, Exit 7A to Rte. 195 W. Take Exit 2 at S. Broad St. This will merge with US 206. Continue on S. Broad St./US 206 for 2 mi. Left at Lalor St. to Rte. 29 and right at Delaware River.

TICKET INFORMATION: 1 Thunder Rd., Trenton, NJ 08611, tel. 609/394–3300, fax 609/394–9666

PRICE RANGE: Club level $7; pavilion $6.50; loge $5.50; terrace $5 adults, $3 ages 5–14 and senior citizens, under 5 free

GAME TIME: Mon.–Sat. 7:05 PM (May–Labor Day), Sat. (Apr.) and Sun. 1:35 PM; gates open 90 min before game.

TIPS ON SEATING: View of the Delaware River over right-field wall from seats on third-base side; it is windy off the river, so jackets are often needed.

SEATING FOR PEOPLE WITH DISABILITIES: Along concourse level, above pavilion and terrace seats, and behind club seats

STADIUM FOOD: Indulge in a great New Jersey pork-roll hero sandwich, with red sweet peppers, cheese, onions, and a fabulous chewy roll ($4.50). There are daily hero specials and big, crunchy Thunder (hot) Dogs for $2.50. French's bold and spicy mustard is the only kind in the park. A kid's meal of hot dog, chips, and baseball cards is $2.75. Healthier than the ice cream cones or chocolate-covered ice cream bars (both $3) are the Italian ices, hand-scooped in cups ($2). The hot french fries are better than ordinary, and a stand sells chicken nuggets. Giant chocolate chip cookies are $1.95. The glassed-in **Stadium Club Restaurant** offers a full buffet meal and a view from the top of the park.

SMOKING POLICY: Smoking prohibited throughout ballpark; permitted in designated area outside park down right-field line

PARKING: $1; on-street parking available

VISITING TEAM HOTEL: Palmer Inn–Best Western (3499 Rte. 1 S, Princeton, NJ 08540, tel. 609/452–2500 or 800/688–0500)

TOURISM INFORMATION: Trenton Convention & Visitors Bureau (Lafayette at Barrack St., Trenton, NJ 08608, tel. 609/777–1770)

Trenton, New Jersey: Mercer County Waterfront Stadium

In 1994, when Trenton opened its new waterfront stadium, New Jersey's capital city had not had a professional baseball team since 19-year-old Willie Mays hit .353 for the Trenton Giants in 1950. The Giants fell victim to television and the other amusement opportunities that helped kill minor-league baseball's short-lived postwar boom.

The arched redbrick entranceway to the new Mercer County Waterfront Stadium is especially handsome. Unfortunately, the rest of the building is faced in concrete. The Delaware River flows along the right-field side of the stadium. Over the center-field walls you'll see the Champale factory, a reminder of Trenton's manufacturing days. Our favorite Trenton monument is the huge lettered sign on a bridge as you enter the city: TRENTON MAKES—THE WORLD TAKES.

Although the concourse is covered, the seating area is not. The scoreboard is colorful in green and navy, and the seats are dark green, but, surprisingly, most of the rest of the interior lacks the elegance of the stadium entrance. If you hike up the steep steps to the main concourse, high above the stands, you can visit the concession stands and still see the action. The concessions, the bathrooms, and the souvenir stand, like everything else here, are clean, efficient, and functional.

Home runs over the right-field fence go into the river. You can walk down the concourse on the first-base side and watch the boaters on the Delaware River. It can be windy off the river, and you should take jackets for night games. Be sure to look for Boomer, the 6-foot, 4-inch blue Thunderbird mascot.

Where to Stay

Visiting Team Motel: Palmer Inn–Best Western. This busy two-story motel is set back from the highway. The rooms are comfortable, its lobby small, and guests are given a free, limited-menu breakfast. It offers a money-saving "Take Me Out to the Ballgame" package. The hotel is 15 minutes from the park and 3 miles from Princeton University. Children stay free. *3499 Rte. I S, Princeton, tel. 609/452–2500 or 800/688–0500, fax 609/ 452–1371. 105 rooms. Facilities: restaurant, pool, sauna, exercise room. AE, D, DC, MC, V. $$*

Nassau Inn. Campus visitors favor this nicely furnished five-story inn two blocks from Princeton University's Nassau Hall. *10 Palmer Sq., Princeton 08540, tel. 609/921–7500 or 800/862–7728, fax 609/921–9385. 215 rooms. Facilities: 3 restaurants. AE, DC, MC, V. $$$*

Where to Eat

Maneta's Diner. This well-worn diner dispenses comfort food of creamed chipped beef, crab cakes, beef goulash, and, to drink, brown cows. It offers an unusual kids' menu, with shrimp, veal cutlet, and roast sirloin. There are 22 flavors of ice cream and several fountain desserts. The diner is 3 miles from the ballpark. *2654 S. Broad St. (Rte. 206), Trenton, tel. 609/888–0208. AE, MC, V. $*

Ballpark Deli. Chewy hoagies are the ticket at this small corner restaurant, one block from the ballpark. The restaurant is filled with baseball memorabilia. It sells a variety of overstuffed sandwiches, as well as fruit juices and hot dogs. *Lamberton and Cass Sts., Trenton, tel. 609/695– 9400. No credit cards. Closed dinner except game nights. $*

Trionfetti's. Here you can eat a real tomato pie, which resembles pizza, but with the cheese layered underneath the tomato. There is pasta of many types, chicken dishes, mussels, and, for children, buffalo wings and spaghetti. Less than a mile from the ballpark, it's in the Chambersburg restaurant district. *598 Chestnut St., Trenton, tel. 609/777–9400. No credit cards. $*

Entertainments

Sesame Place. Bert, Ernie, and the gang roam this water-theme park run by Anheuser-Busch.

Guests walk the grounds in their bathing suits, as street wear is not permitted on most attractions. You can leave purses and clothes in pay lockers as you enter. There are imaginative sand playgrounds, a lazy-river raft ride, stage revues, and special computers that kids play with tokens. Very crowded on hot weekends, the park is much nicer during the week. The theme park is 9 miles from the Trenton ballpark. *U.S. I, Langhorne, PA, tel. 215/752–7070. Admission: $22.95, children under 2 free; after 4 PM $15.95; parking $4. Open mid-May–May 24, 10–5; May 25–June 21, weekdays 10–5, weekends 10–7; June 22–Aug. 25, daily 9–8; Aug. 26–Sept. 1, daily 10–7; Sept. 2–Oct. 12, weekends 10–5.*

Six Flags Great Adventure. This is an all-day destination, beginning with the drive-through animal safari on the edge of the New Jersey Pine Barrens, where some 1,500 animals live. The grounds also include a large theme amusement park with 70 rides, as well as a water park and young children's park. *Rte. 537, Jackson, NJ, tel. 908/928–1821. Admission to both parks: $35.85 adults, $25 those under 54″, $18 senior citizens, children under 3 free; $15 safari only; parking $5. Open mid-May–Labor Day, daily 10– 10; Sept.–May, Sat. 10–10, Sun. 10–8.*

Sites to See

New Jersey State House. First constructed as a modest building in 1790, the State House was rebuilt in 1885 when a fire destroyed the front wing. The result is a French Academic Classical Revival–style building faced with a double portico supported by Corinthian columns. A 1991 restoration refreshed the building. Take a tour to get the full feeling of the place. *W. State St., Trenton, tel. 609/633–2709. Open weekdays 7– 6; free tours by reservation (tel. 609/292–4661) Tues.–Wed. and Fri. 9–4.*

New Jersey State Museum. Adjacent to the State House you'll find four stories of interesting exhibit space and a 150-seat planetarium. The museum preserves the cultural, historic, artistic, and scientific resources of the state. There is a huge dinosaur model to examine. The planetarium's regular and laser shows are limited to those age six and older. *205 W. State St., Trenton, NJ, tel. 609/292–6308. Open Tues.–Sat. 9–4:45, Sun. noon–5. Closed state holidays.*

Trenton City Museum. A mansion named Ellarslie in the city's Cadwalader Park holds lively interactive exhibits. The Italianate villa was built in 1848 for summer use; the city bought it in 1888. Landscape designer Frederick Law Olmstead, the designer of New York's Central Park, was hired by the city to design the 100-acre Cadwalader Park around the building. *W. State St. and Parkside Ave., Trenton, NJ, tel. 609/989–3632. Admission: donations. Open Tues.–Sat. 11–3, Sun. 2–4.*

Washington Crossing State Park. At this park, you can see where George Washington crossed the Delaware River before the Battle of Trenton. Historic markers show where the Continental Army marched on Christmas Day, 1776. Its visitor center (open Wed.–Sun. 9–4:30) has descriptive exhibits. *355 Pennington Rd. Titusville, NJ, tel. 609/737–0623. Parking $3 weekends.*

Open Memorial Day–Labor Day, daily 8–8; Labor Day–Memorial Day, daily 8–sundown.

Princeton University. The fourth college established in North America, it was chartered in 1746 as the College of New Jersey. Ten years later, the college moved from its original site in Elizabeth to Princeton; Nassau Hall, then one of the largest buildings in the colonies, was built to house the school and served as home of the Continental Congress in 1783. The main campus of the university is one of the nation's most beautiful, with a broad range of architectural styles anchored by predominantly Gothic dormitories. The Orange Key Guide Service provides one-hour campus tours year-round (Mon.–Sat. 10, 11, 1:30, and 3:30; Sun. 1:30 and 3:30). *Maclean House, 73 Nassau St., Princeton, NJ, tel. 609/258–3603.*

NEW YORK YANKEES

League: American League • **Class:** Major League • **Stadium:** Yankee Stadium • **Opened:** 1923 • **Capacity:** 57,545 • **Dimensions:** LF: 318, CF: 408, RF: 314 • **Surface:** grass • **Season:** Apr.–Sept.

STADIUM LOCATION: 161st St. and River Ave., Bronx, NY 10451

WEBSITE: http://www.yankees.com

GETTING THERE: Take Subway 4, C, or D to 161st St. station. For additional transit information, call 718/330–1234. By car from Manhattan, take FDR Dr. north to Harlem River Dr. N. Continue to W. 155th St. Go east over Macombs Dam Bridge to Jerome Ave. From north, take I–87 south across Tappan Zee Bridge. Stadium is at Exit 6 from I–87.

TICKET INFORMATION: 161st St. and River Ave., Bronx, NY 10451, tel. 718/293–6000, fax 718/293–4331

PRICE RANGE: Club seats, field and loge, $27 (season only); main and loge box seats, $19; tier box, $16.50; main reserved, $16; tier reserved, $11.50; bleachers (day of game only), $6; senior citizens (day of game), $2

GAME TIME: 7:35 PM; weekday day games, 1:05 PM; weekend day games, 1:35 PM; gates open 90 min before weekday games, 2 hrs before weekend and holiday games.

TIPS ON SEATING: Except on Opening Day and Old Timers Day, plenty of seats available. Bleachers available on day-of-game basis, but pretty rowdy and not recommended for families. Main box seats just behind walking concourse and field box seats are excellent and reasonably priced. Main reserved seats just behind main box seats. You can often get much closer to home plate by buying main reserved rather than main box seats.

SEATING FOR PEOPLE WITH DISABILITIES: Five sections specifically designated: Sections 2, 7, 8, 10, Loge Section 8. Elevators at Sections 15, 22.

STADIUM FOOD: This park has basic ballpark fare, but at a higher quality and price than most. For all items except pasta and bakery sweets, it's wise to head first for the **Sidewalk Cafe,** on the field level at Section 15. It serves the park's notable sweet sausages with a great chewy roll. There are also good chicken fingers (real white meat, not pressed composite), crunchy french fries, and a real steak sandwich; it's the only place to get a kid's meal, which includes juice, Cracker Jack, and a hot dog for $4.50. Three dozen picnic tables under umbrellas fill its pleasant patio. A **Sbarro Express** sells baked ziti at $6 and personal pizzas for $6.50. There's also **TCBY** yogurt and a bakery with good cakes and so-so cookies and brownies.

SMOKING POLICY: Smoking prohibited throughout stadium except in limited designated smoking areas. Prohibition appears widely ignored outside seating bowl.

PARKING: Come by subway. If you must drive, arrive early. Stadium lots within walking distance charge $6–$12.

VISITING TEAM HOTEL: No designated hotel for visiting team.

TOURISM INFORMATION: New York Convention and Visitors Bureau (2 Columbus Circle, New York, NY 10019, tel. 212/397–8222)

New York City: Yankee Stadium

In 1913, the New York Giants invited the New York Yankees to share the Polo Grounds in upper Manhattan. The Giants handily outdrew the upstart Yankees until the Yankees acquired Babe Ruth for the 1920 season. Ruth hit 54 and 59 home runs in 1920 and 1921, respectively. Fans started to flock to Yankees games, and Giants owner John McGraw served an eviction notice on the Yankees.

"The House That Ruth Built"—Yankee Stadium—became the most famous baseball park ever built. Babe Ruth reinvented baseball here as a power game. In the Bronx, across the Harlem River from the Polo Grounds, Yankees owners Ruppert and Huston found a 10-acre plot that was served by the Lexington Avenue subway. More than 30 World Series—not games, series—have been played here, with the Yankees winning 23 world championships.

In the 1923 opening game, John Philip Sousa and the Seventh Regiment Band played, and Babe Ruth hit the game-winning home run. Ruth hit his 60th home run of the season here in 1927. Roger Maris broke Ruth's record with blast number 61 here in 1961. Baseball fans remember Yogi Berra's jumping into Don Larsen's arms after Larsen pitched a perfect game in the 1956 World Series, Reggie Jackson's hitting home runs on three straight pitches to win the final game of the 1977 World Series. This is where Babe Ruth and Lou Gehrig stood at home plate to say their good-byes. Joe DiMaggio, Yogi Berra, and Mickey Mantle each won three Most Valuable Player awards while playing here.

When you get off the subway, don't rush right into the stadium. The area is well lighted and well policed. Take in the sounds and sights and smells of the pregame stadium neighborhood. Walk along River Avenue and peek into a few of the souvenir shops outside the stadium. Follow the majestic, coliseum-like concrete exterior walls to the Gate 4 entrance to see a humongous Louisville Slugger baseball bat. Softball, basketball, and handball games are played at fields and courts all around the stadium.

The place to start inside Yankee Stadium is Monument Park. In this well-landscaped area, the legends of the game are honored. When first built, the area in center field, 490 feet from home plate, became known as Death Valley, as many mighty blasts became long fly-outs. In 1932, a stone monument honoring Miller Huggins, manager of the 1927 Yankees, arguably the greatest baseball team in history, was erected in Death Valley. Gehrig and Ruth monuments were added in 1941 and 1949, respectively. A monument to Mickey Mantle was added in 1996. These monuments were actually in fair territory at the time. Yankees manager Casey Stengel, frustrated with a center fielder who was having a hard time picking up a ball among the monuments, once yelled: "Ruth, Gehrig, Huggins, someone throw that darned ball in here NOW!" When Yankee Stadium was rebuilt in 1974–75, the monuments and the memorials were moved behind the center-field fence. To get a jump on the crowd and avoid a long wait in line, enter the stadium at Gate 2 and head for the staircase at the end of the aisles between the field- and main-level seats in Section 36. Monument Park closes 45 minutes prior to the start of the game.

On the inside, Yankee Stadium is every bit as formal and elegant as it seems from the outside: the sea of dark blue seats, the monuments, the classic white facade above the scoreboards beyond the outfield wall, the huge white Yankees insignia in the larger-than-normal area between home plate and the screen. This is impressive. The original triple-decked Yankee Stadium was built in 1923 at a cost of $2 million. The most striking feature was a copper Art Deco frieze facade that encircled the roof. Since the 1974–75 reconstruction of the stadium, this elegant feature remains on top of the outfield bleachers only. Death Valley was eliminated as left and center fields were brought in considerably.

Two gift shops are on the field level beyond left and right fields (Sections 21 and 24). Get a replica baseball card of yourself in the pinstripes from the booth on the main level, Section 4.

You may have decided you prefer the small, family-oriented ballparks of the minor leagues to the large stadiums of the major leagues. You may have decided New York is not for you. But make plans to go to Yankee Stadium. There is more baseball history per square foot here than you will see in a lifetime anywhere else. One day, it may be too late. The Bronx Bombers should stay in Yankee Stadium in the Bronx, but they may not. The lease on Yankee Stadium expires in 2002, and if you wait, you might be watching the Yankees playing in the New Jersey Meadowlands or on the West Side of Manhattan.

Other Baseball Sites in New York City

Polo Grounds. Perhaps the most famous offensive and defensive plays in baseball history took place in the Polo Grounds, across the Harlem River from Yankee Stadium. History does not record that anyone played polo here, but the land, a gift of the King of England, had been a 17th-century farm. In 1890, James J. Coogan built a ballpark here in a rectangular area between Coogan's Bluff and an adjacent ball field known as Manhattan Field. When the New York Giants moved here in 1891, it was named Polo Grounds after the Giants' field on 110th

Street where baseball had been played since 1880 on an actual polo grounds. A horseshoe-shape steel and concrete stadium was built after a 1911 fire destroyed the ballpark.

The "Shot Heard Round the World" was fired at 4:11 PM on October 3, 1951. The Giants had surged in the last six weeks of the season to tie the Dodgers atop the National League. In the bottom of the ninth of the playoff game, with the Giants trailing 4–2 and two men on base, Bobby Thomson hit a game-winning three-run home run. Just three years later, on September 29, 1954, Willie Mays made a sensational over-the-shoulder catch of Vic Wertz's 450-foot blast, spun, and threw a strike to second base to help the Giants beat the Cleveland Indians in the World Series. After the 1957 season, the Giants moved to San Francisco. The New York Mets played here in 1962 and 1963 while they waited for Shea Stadium to be completed. In 1964, the old stadium was leveled.

The Polo Ground Towers, four huge 30-story apartment buildings, now sit where Willie Mays once roamed. There is a bronze plaque on the building at 2999 8th Avenue (Frederick Douglass Boulevard) indicating the approximate location of home plate and noting that the New York Giants had been world champions six times when they played here from 1891 to 1957. The site is near the West 155th Street Station served by the "D" Line. It is across the river from Yankee Stadium via the Macombs Dam Bridge.

Ebbets Field. When Ebbets Field was built in 1913 by Dodgers owner Charles Ebbets, the stands were squeezed close to the field, creating an extraordinary intimacy between fans and players. It was here on opening day 1947 that the great Jackie Robinson began to break through baseball's greatest injustice, becoming the first African-American to play in the major leagues. And here was one of baseball's greatest signs—haberdasher Abe Stark's 3- by 30-foot HIT SIGN WIN SUIT ad on the right-field wall under the scoreboard. The pain and pleasure shared in rooting for the Dodgers brought Brooklyn's many ethnic groups together in a single community that would never have been possible without the ties of baseball. In 1958, the Dodgers moved to Los Angeles. Ebbets Field was demolished in 1960, ending one of baseball's most extraordinary eras.

From the Brooklyn Museum at the corner of Eastern Parkway and Washington Avenue, walk down Washington one block to the entrance of the Brooklyn Botanic Garden and three more blocks along the garden. Take a left on Montgomery Street and go two blocks. The huge 20-story-plus apartment complex, once called Jackie Robinson Apartments and now called Ebbets Field Apartments, stands where Ebbets Field once was. Ironically, there is a large sign on the McKeever Place entrance: PLEASE NO BALL PLAYING. Across McKeever is an urban playground devoted mostly to basketball and a large mural of Jackie Robinson's life on the wall of the middle school named in his honor. A 1962 cornerstone on the apartments at 1720 Bedford Avenue states simply: "This is the former site of Ebbets Field."

Shea Stadium. Shea Stadium is no Polo Grounds or Ebbets Field. William A. Shea was the man former mayor Robert Wagner put in charge of bringing National League baseball back to New York City after the stinging departure of New York's two National League teams, the Giants and the Dodgers. The stadium named after Shea opened in 1964 right next door to the New York World's Fair in Queens. Best known for the 1969 World Series victory of the "Miracle Mets," Shea Stadium hosted the New York Yankees in 1974 and '75 while Yankee Stadium was being rebuilt. To reach Shea Stadium by subway, take the No. 7 Flushing line to the Willets Point–Shea Stadium station. By car, take the Grand Central Parkway and exit at Shea Stadium.

Where to Stay

Several services, including the Hotel Reservations Network (tel. 800/964–6835), offer discounted rates. Weekend rates at most hotels are dramatically less than those on weekdays.

Quality Hotel Fifth Avenue. This convenient high-rise hotel is managed by the Canadian chain called Journey's End. Not just close to but right around the corner from the New York Public Library and Lord & Taylor, it draws guests with location and price. Rooms are small but serviceable. Coffee and muffins are served to guests in the small lobby on weekend mornings. Most views are of the back side of neighboring buildings. Parking is $18 daily at a garage two blocks away. Guests can swim and exercise at the nearby Vertical Club (335 Madison Ave.) for $15 daily. *3 E. 40th St., between 5th and Madison Aves., New York 10016, tel. 212/447–1500 or 800/668–4200, fax 212/685–5214. 189 rooms. Facilities: restaurant. AE, D, DC, MC, V. $$*

Excelsior Hotel. This quiet hotel, located behind the Museum of Natural History, offers bargain rates and large rooms. The two-room suites include kitchenettes. The standard double room includes a living room with a pull-out couch. All have dated Scandinavian-style furniture. *45 W. 81st St., New York 10024, tel. 212/362–9200 or 800/368–4575, fax 212/721–2994. 160 rooms, 103 suites. Facilities: coffeeshop. AE, D, MC, V. $$*

Gramercy Park Hotel. This 75-year-old hotel gives guests keys to Gramercy Park, which it overlooks, during their stay. Some rooms have kitchenettes, and single rooms have either double beds or a queen-size bed. The 18-story hotel is utilitarian, clean, and affordable. A nearby garage charges guests $17 daily. *2 Lexington Ave., between Gramercy Park N and 22nd St., New York 10010, tel. 212/475–4320 or 800/221–4083, fax 212/505–0535. 500 rooms. Facilities: restaurant, beauty salon. AE, D, DC, MC, V. $$*

Wyndham Hotel. This lovely small hotel is moderately priced for New York and has a great location. News of its value has spread, and advance reservations are a must. Its suites have refrigerators, and the rooms are freshly renovated. The garage next door charges $32 daily, but there is one at 58th Street between Broadway and 8th Avenue at $19 daily. The hotel is not part of the Wyndham chain. *42 W. 58th St., between 5th and 6th Aves., New York 10019, tel. 212/753–3500 or 800/257–1111, fax 212/754–5638. 150 rooms, 54 suites. Facilities: restaurant (winter only). AE, D, DC, MC, V. $$$*

Travel Inn. This tourist motel is in the rapidly improving West 42nd Street area and offers the bonus of free indoor parking. The seven-story motel looks as if it belongs at a freeway exchange, with balconies and pool deck chairs, but it works for families traveling to Manhattan. The rooms are large and utilitarian, and some have refrigerators. *515 W. 42nd St., between 10th and 11th Aves., New York 10036, tel. 212/ 695–7171 or 800/869–4630, fax 212/967– 5025. 160 rooms. Facilities: restaurant, pool, health club. AE, D, DC, MC, V. $$*

Where to Eat

Mickey Mantle's Restaurant and Sports Bar. This is not a boozy, smoky sports bar but a light, cheerful restaurant down Central Park South from the Plaza Hotel. There's a room for kids' birthday parties, and $7–$8 children's meals are offered from a Little League menu. The adult portions are generous, with pasta, seafood, and even several low-calorie items. The $13 chicken pot pie is exceptional. Mickey Mantle signed two photos over our table: "This is the 1927 Yankees the greatest team of all time. Except for the 1961 Yankees" and beneath it "The 1961 Yankees—The greatest team of all time." The restaurant is full of prints, photos, and other memorabilia of the players and great stadiums, much of it for sale. Some classic uniforms—including Satchel Paige's 1951 St. Louis Browns and Joe DiMaggio's 1948 Yankees jerseys—are definitely not for sale. Souvenir hats, T-shirts, and postcards are sold at the front. *42 Central Park S, New York, tel. 212/688–7777. AE, D, DC, MC, V. $$*

All-Star Cafe. There is so much visual excitement at this sports-theme restaurant that you'll find it hard to concentrate on eating. The celebrity owners have identified their menu favorites, like Andre Agassi's spaghetti pomodoro and Ken Griffey, Jr.'s chicken-fried steak and mashed potatoes. Other investors are Shaquille O'Neal, Wayne Gretzky, and Joe Montana. Four satellite dishes on the roof of this Times Square building feed into 17 big screens arranged in a circle, displaying all manner of sports events and celebrity interviews. The seats are oversize baseball gloves, with the tables resembling baseballs. Memorabilia from famous players are in glass cases throughout the two-story restaurant. You may be called upon to participate in a free-throw contest on the restaurant's basketball court. A big-league scoreboard hangs from the rafters. In one room devoted to the famous baseball collectibles owned by actor Charlie Sheen, you can see Babe Ruth's camel-hair coat, the legal papers that sent him to New York

from Boston, Ty Cobb's 1905 glove, a piece of cake from the wedding of Joe DiMaggio and Marilyn Monroe, and a rare and costly Honus Wagner baseball card, among other treasures. *1540 Broadway, New York, tel. 212/840–8326. D, MC, V. $$*

Jimmy's Bronx Cafe. This large, casual seafood and Caribbean restaurant is favored by Latino baseball players and baseball fans before and after the games. Its owner knows many ballplayers, and their photos line the walls. The restaurant holds a 250-seat main dining room, a 400-seat patio, a downstairs party room, and a sports bar. There is a children's menu. Paella and flan are the standouts here. *281 W. Fordham Rd., off the Major Deegan Expressway, Bronx, tel. 718/329–2000. AE, D, DC, MC, V. $$*

Motown Cafe. If your children love Little Anthony or the Imperials even more than you did, this is the place to rock out. Motor City music is the theme here, and you sit below a huge record on the ceiling. The desserts are over-the-top and the sandwiches are forgettable, but you come here to enjoy the atmosphere and to watch various groups sing. *104 W. 57th St., New York, tel. 212/581–8030. AE, D, MC, V. $$*

Stage Deli. Since 1937, this midtown deli has been turning out egg creams, smoked fish, baked apples, potato pancakes, and cheesecake. Yes, it's tourist heaven, but the corned beef sandwiches can't be beaten. They are so stuffed that a half is sufficient for most children. Here is where Joe DiMaggio sipped chicken soup before games, and other celebrities' photos line the wall. Sandwiches are named for New York notables; every table has good brown mustard and a bowl of huge pickles. *834 7th Ave., New York, tel. 212/245–7850. AE, D, MC, V. $$*

Grand Central Oyster Bar. The huge, domed tile ceiling gives you the illusion of eating inside a very large tunnel. Sit at the counter and watch the toque-hatted chefs custom-prepare your oyster stew and pan roasts; more than 90 different seafood dishes are offered. This bustling restaurant is open for lunch and dinner on weekdays. This is a treat for children, who can be counted on to like the chowders at least. *Grand Central Terminal, lower level, 42nd St. and*

Lexington Ave., New York, tel. 212/490–6650. AE, D, DC, MC, V. $$

Gray's Papaya. Hot dogs washed down with papaya drinks may be New York City's most ubiquitous regional food. You can find papaya drink stands in storefronts and mobile trucks throughout the city. This combination is the ultimate, inexpensive fast food, but these hot dogs are several cuts above the usual ballpark fare, and papaya juice is refreshing and healthful. Gray's is open 24 hours daily. 402 Avenue of the Americas, New York, tel. 212/260–3532. No credit cards. $

Tutta Pasta Ristorante. This inexpensive pasta restaurant, south of Washington Square Park, is part of a small chain of authentic Italian restaurants with charm and terrific pasta. There are grilled pizzas for $9 and 25 varieties of pasta from $7–$14. Half-orders are available for children. The wooden tables are pressed close to your neighbor's, making the atmosphere convivial and communal. There is another outlet in Little Italy (26 Carmine St., tel. 212/463–9653). 504 LaGuardia Pl., between Houston and Bleecker Sts., New York, tel. 212/420–0652. AE, DC, MC, V. $$

Entertainments

Brooklyn Botanic Garden. Who could have guessed that one of the most peaceful and relaxing afternoons of our entire tour of America would have come in New York City? The Brooklyn Botanic Garden is an urban jewel, just two blocks from the site of the former Ebbets Field. Founded in 1910 on a reclaimed waste dump, it is 52 acres of shaded beauty, with a sunny Japanese koi and turtle pond; a children's garden; a garden of the herbs, trees, and flowers mentioned in Shakespeare's works; a fragrance garden; and other specialized plots. There is a pleasant open-air restaurant on the grounds. In the basement of its Steinhardt Conservatory is a small children's museum devoted to the plants found in cities with interactive displays. In summer, the admission fees often include entry to the adjacent Brooklyn Museum (tel. 718/638–5000), which has an impressive mummy collection on the third floor. 1000 Washington Ave., Brooklyn, tel. 718/622–4433. Admission: $3 adults, $1.50 senior citizens, 50¢ ages 6–16. Open Apr.–Sept., Tues.–Fri. 8–6, weekends 10–6; Oct.–Mar., Tues.–Fri. 8–4:30, weekends 10–4:30.

Central Park. The 840 acres of this urban forest, designed in 1858 by Frederick Law Olmstead, are filled with diversions. There are baseball diamonds, playgrounds, boat ponds, a lake, and the Lehman children's petting zoo (admission: 10¢; open daily 10–5). There's also the Wildlife Conservation Center (5th Ave. and 64th St., tel. 212/360–3456; admission: $2.50 adults, $1.25 senior citizens, 50¢ ages 3–12; open weekdays 10–5, weekends 10:30–5:30), a zoo with 450 animals, including red pandas and lions, spread out on 5½ acres. Near 5th Avenue and 76th Street are characters from Alice in Wonderland crafted in bronze to climb on. The park's hand-carved carousel (90¢ per ride) is at the 65th Street transverse. Strawberry Fields is a 2½-acre garden and green memorializing John Lennon of the Beatles, who lived across the street on Central Park West at 72nd Street. 5th Ave. to Central Park West, from 59th to 110th Sts., New York, tel. 212/427–4040.

Empire State Building Observatory. Avoid the shills selling you tickets to travel movies as you wait in line for tickets to the observatory. The real show is just looking out over the city. You buy your tickets and take escalators and two high-speed elevators up to the 86th- and 102nd-floor observatories. Signs at the ticket booth tell you how many miles of visibility there are; on clear days, 25-mile views are possible. Take a map to pick out landmarks. Take jackets as well, as it's nearly always windy. The last tickets are sold at 11:30 PM. 5th Ave. at 34th St., New York, tel. 212/736–3100. Admission: $4.50 adults, $2.25 children under 12 and senior citizens. Open daily 9:30 AM–midnight.

American Museum of Natural History. At the world's largest museum of its type, you see one jaw-dropping dinosaur reconstruction after another. The five-story-tall Barosaurus in the entry of the main hall and the immense blue whale suspended overhead in the Hall of Ocean Life are hard to forget. Don't try to zip through this in an hour. Its Hall of Human Biology uses holograms and animation to teach anatomy and evolution. Admission for the shows in its Hayden Planetarium, including several for young children, and for the IMAX theater is extra; combination tickets are sold. Central Park W and 79th St., New York, tel. 212/769–5100. Sug-

gested admission: $7 adults, $5 senior citizens and students with ID, $4 children.

Staten Island Ferry. This is a shorter, cheaper alternative to the three-hour Circle Line (tel. 212/563–3200) boat tour of Manhattan. You join the commuters for the half-hour, 50¢ ferry ride from Battery Park to Staten Island, but be warned that the park is littered and the ferry terminal isn't in great shape either. Nevertheless, the views of the Statue of Liberty and lower Manhattan are worth it. Bring quarters to avoid the change-machine line, and try to visit after peak rush-hour times. The ferries leave every 20 minutes to half hour; call ahead for the exact schedule. *South Ferry, Battery Park at Whitehall St., New York, tel. 718/390–5253. Admission: 50¢ round-trip. Open all the time.*

Statue of Liberty National Monument & Ellis Island. If you feel up to it, climb the 151-foot statue's 300 steps for a great view. Younger children may not be happy devoting the time necessary to see Ellis Island immigration museum (tel. 212/363–8340), but older children are likely to be drawn into the gripping visual history depicted in its cavernous great hall, where 12 million immigrants were processed into America. Buy tickets for the ferry, which makes a loop to both sites, at the Castle Clinton National Monument in Battery Park, starting at 8:30 AM daily. Ferries leave Manhattan every 30 minutes, and return trips leave the statue every 90 minutes. *Liberty Island, Ellis Island, upper New York bay, New York, ferry tel. 212/269–5755. Monument and museum admissions: free. Ferry admission: $6 adults, $5 senior citizens, $3 ages 3–17. Open daily 9:30–3:30.*

Panorama at the Queens Museum of Art. Flushing Meadows–Corona Park in the New York City Borough of Queens was the site of the 1964–65 World's Fair. Robert Moses, the master builder of New York, had Lester Associates build the world's largest architectural model. The almost 10,000-square-foot $700,000 model of New York City now contains 895,000 individual structures at a scale of 1 inch to 100 feet. The Empire State Building is 15 inches tall, and Yankee Stadium is 2 inches tall.

The Panorama was one of the most popular exhibitions at the fair. In 1964, a visit to the New York City Pavilion included a simulated heli-

copter ride complete with a voice-over by the late Lowell Thomas, a famous NBC newscaster, extolling New York as the world's best-run city. After decades of neglect, the Panorama underwent a million-dollar restoration and update, reopening in 1994 without the helicopter ride or the well-known voice of Lowell Thomas.

By subway, take the No. 7 Flushing line to the Willets Point–Shea Stadium station. The museum is next to the Unisphere, the enormous steel globe from the World's Fair, about a 10-minute walk through the park from the station. By car, take the Grand Central Parkway, exit at Shea Stadium, and follow the signs to the museum. Parking is free. *Flushing Meadows–Corona Park, Queens, tel. 718/592–9700. Admission (suggested donation): $3 adults, $1.50 children and senior citizens. Open Wed.–Fri. 10–5, weekends noon–5.*

Manhattan Walking Trails. In 1995, Heritage Trails New York unveiled four walking trails connecting 50 historic sights in downtown Manhattan by a series of 2,376 colored dots on the city's sidewalks. Information and a colorful, informative $5 brochure are available by calling or visiting the Heritage Trails Hub & Visitor Information Center. *26 Wall St., at Broad St., New York, tel. 212/767–0637. Open daily 9–5.*

Unusual Shopping

There's no place like New York for specialty shopping. The city is known for its shopping districts—a few blocks dense with a particular kind of merchandise, such as the lighting district on The Bowery between Grand and Broome streets, the Garment District between 31st and 41st streets along 7th Avenue, or the theatrical music stores clustered between East 10th and 12th streets and 4th Avenue. Look for specialty stores in a telephone directory, or buy one of the many guidebooks on shopping in New York.

SportsWords, Ltd. You'll find one of the largest collections of sports books in America in this shop, which has well-known and obscure books, an out-of-print section, and a large selection of kids' sports books, from how-to to fiction to biography. There are nearly 3,000 titles, many from small presses that sports fans may not know. *1475 3rd Ave., at 83rd St., New York, tel. 212/772–8729.*

NEW HAVEN RAVENS

League: Eastern League • **Major League Affiliation:** Colorado Rockies • **Class:** AA • **Stadium:** Yale Field • **Opened:** 1927 • **Capacity:** 6,200 • **Dimensions:** LF 340, CF: 405, RF: 315 • **Surface:** grass • **Season:** Apr.–Labor Day

STADIUM LOCATION: 252 Derby Ave., West Haven, CT 06516

TEAM WEBSITE: http://www.ravens.com

GETTING THERE: From I–95, Exit 44 E or Exit 45 W to Rte. 10, follow Yale Bowl signs. From I–91, Exit 1 (downtown), follow Rte. 34 to ballpark. From Merritt and Wilbur Cross Pkwys., Exit 57 (Rte. 34 east) 4 mi to ballpark or Exit 59 (Whalley Ave.), and follow Yale Bowl signs. From downtown, north on Chapel St., left on Derby Ave. to ballpark.

TICKET INFORMATION: 63 Grove St., New Haven, CT 06510, tel. 203/782–3140 or 800/728–3671, fax 203/782–3150

PRICE RANGE: Luxury box seat $12.50; box seat $7; reserved seat $5; general admission $3 adults, $2 ages 6–12 and over 66, under 6 free

GAME TIME: Mon.–Sat. 7:05 PM, Sun. 2:05 PM; gates open 1 hr before game

TIPS ON SEATING: General admission seats in bleachers on third-base side are quite a bargain, especially for senior citizens and children. Best views outside stadium are from top rows of reserved seats in grandstand looking across to Yale Bowl football and track stadium.

SEATING FOR PEOPLE WITH DISABILITIES: Space on upper ring of reserved section accessed by ramp on right-field side of ballpark. Handicapped-accessible parking is available in Lot 1, adjacent to the ballpark, for $1.

STADIUM FOOD: The food stands, a bit dim and claustrophobic under the seats, offer good local food to sample. Hummel hot dogs (only $1), are made locally and are better than average. The New Haven Brewing Company developed a private label beer for the team, Black Bird Premium Ale, sold only at Yale Field. Prepackaged Italian ices are $1.50, and warm Otis Spelunker cookies are 50¢. Pizza is also available. A picnic area stretches down the right-field line and behind the right-field wall.

SMOKING POLICY: Smoking prohibited in seating area

PARKING: Available in Lot 2, at Marginal Dr. on Rte. 34, for $2. Other parking is available inside the Yale Bowl, on Yale Ave., for $1.

VISITING TEAM HOTEL: Days Inn Hotel (490 Saw Mill Rd., West Haven, CT 06516, tel. 203/933–0344 or 800/325–2525)

TOURISM INFORMATION: Greater New Haven Convention & Visitors Bureau (1 Long Wharf Dr., New Haven, CT 06511, tel. 203/777–8550 or 800/332–7829)

New Haven, Connecticut: Yale Field

You've seen the photograph—an aging Babe Ruth handing a manuscript of his autobiography for the university library to a lean, young captain of the Yale University baseball team. It happened here at Yale Field, and the young player became president of the United States. George Bush is not the only president to leave a mark at Yale Field. Former president and Yale law pro-

fessor William Howard Taft had a special double seat installed directly behind home plate to accommodate his extraordinary size. The seat remained for 65 years.

A president of Yale, who later got a *really* impressive job as Commissioner of Baseball, A. Bartlett Giamatti, watched many college games here. He once wrote of the game he loved: "None of us can go to a ball game without in some way being reminded of your best hopes, of your earlier times, some memory of your best memory. It's always nostalgic, even when it's most vital and present.... It's not paradise, but it's as close as you're going to get to it in America."

Yale defeated Wesleyan 39–13 on this spot in 1865. In 1927, a brand-new ballpark designed to resemble Yankee Stadium was constructed, complete with steel poles, concrete arches, and a covered grandstand. After World War II, steel from the war ships was used to build the monster 25-foot-high wall in center field, 405 feet from home plate.

Although the Yale team continued to play here, professional baseball left in 1932, not to return until a major stadium renovation for the 1994 season. Bart Giamatti would have loved this elegant restoration of his Yale Field. The $3.3 million renovation retains the character of the historic field while adding modern comforts, new bleachers, and party picnic areas down the foul lines. The huge hand-operated scoreboard in the outfield is still used alongside a modern, high-tech scoreboard.

As Giamatti warned, it's not quite paradise. To retain the character of the field, considerable compromises on comfort and efficiency had to be made. The bathrooms and concession stands are stuffed under the grandstand seating area without the space and openness of the concourses in modern stadiums. Although these compromises are noticeable, the wonderful restoration is full justification.

The classic 1920s stadium is not, however, used to justify a stodgy approach to the fans. The ownership of the New Haven Ravens puts on a great show full of on-field contests. Rally the Raven, who was hatched out of a 7-foot egg at a nearby shopping mall in February 1994, delights the fans at Yale Field. This place really explodes when the Ravens give the fans cause to stomp on the old-style metal floor.

Where to Stay

Visiting Team Motel: Days Inn Hotel. This seven-story motel has refrigerators and hot tubs in some rooms. Ask for the "Rock Bottom Rate," a program through Connecticut Days Inns. Guests who can book 29 days in advance are eligible for even lower "Super Saver" rates. *490 Saw Mill Rd., at Exit 42 from I–95, West Haven 06516, tel. 203/933–0344 or 800/325–*

2525, fax 203/937–1678. 102 rooms. Facilities: restaurant, indoor pool. AE, D, DC, MC, V. $

Super 8. This is an ordinary interchange motel behind a Taco Bell restaurant. Cribs are free here. It's 8 miles from Mystic Seaport (see below). *173 Rte. 12, at Exit 86 from I–95, Groton 06340, tel. 203/448–2818 or 800/848–8888, fax 203/446–0162. 99 rooms. AE, D, MC, V. $*

The Whaler's Inn. Three old, renovated inns have been joined as one property in downtown Mystic, adjacent to the drawbridge. The rooms are homey, with reproduction antiques and decorative touches. Guests can walk to the seaport museum and through the town's quaint shops and marina area. *20 E. Main St., Mystic 06355, tel. 203/536–1506 or 800/243–2588, fax 203/572–1250. 41 rooms. Facilities: restaurant. AE, MC, V. $$*

Where to Eat

Louis Lunch. There's room for about 30 customers in this dark wooden cottage, which is believed to be the birthplace of the hamburger. Various traditions reign—the bathroom is marked Room 363, some waiters refuse tips, and the limited menu has weird misspellings. Don't ask for ketchup or mustard—Louis doesn't do these condiments. You can get cheese, onion, or tomato slices. The incomparable burgers, which come on white toast, are cooked in ancient vertical cast-iron broilers. You usually can get root beer and Boston cream pie. While you sit in the high-backed booths, you can examine the table carvings of long-ago Yale undergraduates. *261 Crown St., New Haven, tel. 203/562–5507. No credit cards. Closed Sun. $*

Frank Pepe's Pizzeria. Believed by many to be the original home of pizza in the U.S., this is one of several superlative pizza shops on Wooster Street. The 150-seat shop is known for its wood-oven pizza covered with Rhode Island little-neck clams. You can watch the bakers work in the open kitchen. Also try its 50-seat annex restaurant, the Spot–Frank Pepe's (163 Wooster St., tel. 203/865–7602). *157 Wooster St., New Haven, tel. 203/865–5762. No credit cards. Closed Tues. $*

Yankee Doodle Sandwich Shop. In this tiny restaurant your children can see what the original fast-food shops looked like. The counterman and waitress work in a fast blur to satisfy the crowds at the counter's 12 stools. You can have a satisfying scrambled egg breakfast for $1.30. Breakfast ends at 11:30. *260 Elm St., New Haven, tel. 203/865–1074. No credit cards. $*

Bee Bee Dairy Restaurant. This cheery downtown restaurant is a local stop for breakfast, fast lunches, and ice cream. Its short-stack pancakes ($1.50) and half waffles are the right size for children. There is an extensive selection of ice cream, frozen yogurt, and sherbet, plus sinful hot fudge sundaes. *33 W. Main St., Mystic, tel. 203/536–4577. MC, V. $*

Sea Swirl. The great clams at this roadside drive-in are not cheap. An order is $5 for strips and $7 for the meatier bellies. There is also good corn chowder. Patrons have their choice of broth or milk in the clam chowder. You have a choice of hard or soft-serve ice cream. You can eat in your car or at the adjacent picnic tables. *Rtes. 1 and 27, Mystic, tel. 203/536–3452. MC, V. $*

Entertainments

Shore Line Trolley Museum. You can take unlimited rides in vintage trolleys at this special museum. There are more than 100 trolleys on the grounds, with dedicated volunteers eager to tell you their history. Children like switching the rattan seats to the opposite direction at the end of each short trip. The small gift shop has trolley-related toys. *17 River St., East Haven, tel. 203/467–6927. Admission: $5 adults, $2 children. Open Memorial Day–Labor Day, daily 11–5; May and Sept., weekends 11–5; Apr. and Nov., Sun. 11–5.*

Mystic Seaport Museum. Plan to spend a full day exploring the whaling ships and the restored 19th-century village in Mystic. You can climb through the tall ships, sign up for the crew via computer, and learn about geography and sea life through interactive displays. The exhibits are unusual—an oyster-sorting shop and a barrel factory have workers in costume who explain their jobs. The children's museum has many good hands-on activities. For additional fees you can ride on several of the ships. The grounds have several pleasant sit-down restaurants. Look for admission discount coupons in area stores. The museum admission ticket is good for two days. *Rte. 27, Mystic, tel. 203/572–0711. Admission: $16 adults, $8 ages 6–16. Grounds open daily 9–6, exhibits daily 9–5.*

Sites to See

Yale University. Hear the carillon in Harkness Tower and marvel at the Gothic look of this university, established in 1701. The Sterling Memorial Library (120 High St., tel. 203/432–1775) looks like a monastery. One-hour campus tours of the country's third-oldest university are available 10–4 from the Yale Information Office at Phelps Gateway, at the Green, the central square (among nine) in New Haven. The office also has maps for self-guided tours. Children may want to see the Brontosaurus skeleton in the Peabody Museum (170 Whitney Ave., tel. 203/436–0850; free weekdays 3–5; other times $2.50 adults, $1 ages 3–15; open Mon.–Sat. 10–5, Sun. noon–5). *Yale Information Office, 341 College St., New Haven, tel. 203/432–2302.*

SEAFOOD, SHIPS, AND FENWAY
PAWTUCKET, BOSTON, CAPE COD LEAGUE, PORTLAND

A four-to-five-day trip can cover a lot of baseball in the compact Northeast, even spanning the distance from Rhode Island to Cape Cod and Portland, Maine. You'll see one of the nation's finest classic parks, Fenway, in Boston, as well as its Triple AAA affiliate in Pawtucket. College stars play in the rustic ballparks of the Cape Cod League. Heading north, to Portland, you'll find a new stadium and a city with New England charm.

Pawtucket, Rhode Island, is the home of McCoy Stadium, an International League park. It's a 1942 Works Progress Administration stadium with winding staircases, no mascot, and no on-field hijinks. Here they play serious baseball like your parents used to watch. Diner fans will be in heaven in Pawtucket and nearby Providence, where dozens of originals still exist.

Boston, 50 miles north of Pawtucket, on Interstate 95, is the home of Fenway Park, one of baseball's cathedrals. The carnival atmosphere surrounding the park entrances is produced by fried clam vendors, souvenir stands, and cap salesmen all vying for your attention. This is a big-league park that's intimate, idiosyncratic, and beautiful. Park your car, buy a visitor's transport passport, and ride the T to the city's many attractions for children, including its computer museum, swan boats, aquarium, science museum, and children's museum.

Driving south on Route 3 after a night game, you'll reach Plymouth, home of the Rock, in an hour. Explore the waterfront in the morning, and then drive another hour southeast on Route 6A to Cape Cod to watch the premier college summer-league games. There are hundreds of beachfront motels throughout the Cape, and each village has its own clambakes, lobster suppers, and community band concerts. A restored railroad takes you through cranberry bogs and the Great Salt Marsh.

Portland, Maine, is 110 miles north of Boston on Interstate 95. Pro ball returned in 1994 after a 45-year absence. A Double AA Eastern League team plays in an attractive downtown park that sits behind a 1915 redbrick arena, a brick police-horse barn, and a football field. The city is beautifully situated on Casco Bay, where you can choose from dozens of boat excursions daily. The historic downtown area is fun to walk, and there's a classic, worn amusement park on a white sand beach 25 minutes south of Portland at Old Orchard Beach.

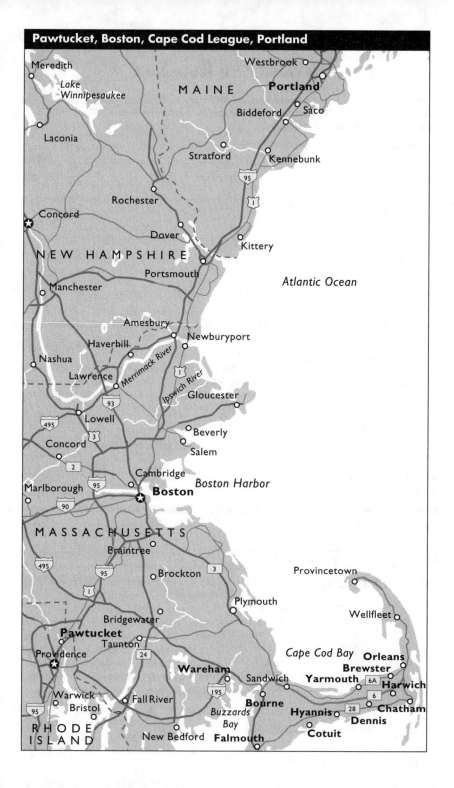

Pawtucket, Boston, Cape Cod League, Portland

Meredith

Lake Winnipesaukee

MAINE

Westbrook

Portland

Biddeford

Saco

Laconia

Stratford

Kennebunk

95

Concord

Rochester

1

NEW HAMPSHIRE

Dover

Kittery

Portsmouth

Atlantic Ocean

Manchester

Amesbury

Haverhill

Newburyport

Merrimack River

Nashua

Lawrence

Ipswich River

93

Gloucester

Lowell

495

3

Beverly

Concord

Salem

2

Cambridge

Marlborough

95

Boston Harbor

90

Boston

MASSACHUSETTS

Braintree

495

95

Brockton

3

Provincetown

1

Plymouth

Wellfleet

Bridgewater

Cape Cod Bay

Orleans

Pawtucket

Taunton

Brewster

Providence

24

Wareham

Sandwich

Yarmouth

6A

Harwich

6

Warwick

195

Bourne

28

Chatham

Bristol

Fall River

Hyannis

Dennis

95

Buzzards Bay

RHODE ISLAND

New Bedford

Falmouth

Cotuit

PAWTUCKET RED SOX

League: International League • **Major League Affiliation:** Boston Red Sox • **Class:** AAA • **Stadium:** McCoy Stadium • **Opened:** 1942 • **Capacity:** 7,002 • **Dimensions:** LF: 325, CF: 380, RF: 325 • **Surface:** grass • **Season:** Apr.–Labor Day

STADIUM LOCATION: 1 Columbus Ave., Pawtucket, RI 02860

GETTING THERE: From I–95N, Exit 28, School St. Bear right off exit, 2 blocks on School St. Left on Pond St. to Columbus Ave. Right on Columbus to stadium parking lot. From I–95S, Exit 2A, Newport Ave. Follow Newport Ave. 2 mi to Columbus Ave. Turn right, 1 mi on Columbus.

TICKET INFORMATION: Box 2365, Pawtucket, RI 02861, tel. 401/724–7300, fax 401/724–2140

PRICE RANGE: Box seats $5.50 adults, $4.50 under 13 and senior citizens; general admission $4 adults, $3 under 13 and senior citizens.

GAME TIME: Apr.–mid-May, weeknights 6, Sat. 7 PM, Sun. 1 PM; mid-May–Labor Day, Mon.–Sat. 7 PM, Sun. 1 PM; gates open 2 hrs before game.

TIPS ON SEATING: Call to order tickets in advance. PawSox sell out a number of games each year. Box seats are recommended.

SEATING FOR PEOPLE WITH DISABILITIES: Some of stadium's very few field-level seats reserved; vans may drive in on first-base side for direct access to seating area next to visitor's dugout.

STADIUM FOOD: Think Portuguese and Italian here. The PawSox even have an official coffee syrup— Silmo Milk Mate. The indulgence purchase is fried dough for $2; they are huge ovals that are cooked as you watch and are covered with cinnamon and confectioner's sugar. Italian sweet sausage is charbroiled with peppers and onions for $2.75, but may be too spicy for children. A $2 grilled hamburger is a bargain. But the pizza is undistinguished. The frozen lemonade ($1.50) helps in the heat.

SMOKING POLICY: Smoking prohibited in seating areas and allowed in concourse

PARKING: Parking limited; 650 free spaces at stadium, spill-over parking on streets and at school beyond outfield wall.

VISITING TEAM HOTEL: Comfort Inn (2 George St., Pawtucket, RI 02860, tel. 401/723–6700 or 800/424–6423)

TOURISM INFORMATION: Greater Providence Convention & Visitors Bureau (30 Exchange Terrace, Providence, RI 02903, tel. 401/274–1636 or 800/233–1636)

Pawtucket, Rhode Island: McCoy Stadium

Real baseball fans appreciate McCoy Stadium in Pawtucket, Rhode Island. Just 5 miles north of Providence, this is a gritty, blue-collar town with a gritty, no-nonsense stadium. Don't come here looking for fuzzy mascots or on-the-field contests. Somebody tried to start a wave the afternoon we were there, and it didn't last a minute. This is Triple AAA baseball in the International League. The players are headed for the big leagues, and everyone takes baseball seriously here.

The longest game in the history of professional baseball started at McCoy Stadium on April 18 and finished on June 23, 1981. Pawtucket beat Rochester 3–2 in 33 innings. In this early test of his Ironman legend, Cal Ripken, Jr. went 2 for 13. Wade Boggs was 4 for 12. A large collection of memorabilia from the longest game is on display just inside the main gate entrance. The perfect gift for baseball insomniacs—a cassette tape of the entire radio play-by-play—is on sale at the concession stand.

We love the winding staircases with 34 larger-than-life paintings of Pawtucket's baseball stars. The team has been a Red Sox franchise since 1973. As you work your way up the stairs to your seats, you see images of such Red Sox stars as Wade Boggs, Roger Clemens, and Jim Rice.

This is a 1942 WPA stadium named for Pawtucket mayor Thomas P. McCoy. Virtually all of the seating is under roof and far above the playing field. President Franklin Delano Roosevelt spoke here, and Louis Armstrong, Ella Fitzgerald, and Yogi Berra performed here. Substantial renovations were made for a 50th-anniversary rededication on July 4 weekend, 1992. Even with the renovations, the seats are tight and the bathrooms nothing to rave about.

This is a hitter's park, with the shortest center field in all of Triple AAA baseball, at 380 feet. The dugouts are built under the stands. Parking is limited here, so come early and watch the scene at the PawSox dugout. Just before a game, the dugout looks like a well-stocked fishing pond. The local kids bring large plastic containers with a side cut out. They put balls and pens into the container and fish from the top of the dugout for PawSox autographs below. It is quite a sight.

The locals like this baseball-purist experience and the chance to see the future stars of the neighboring Boston Red Sox. We were glad we called ahead and reserved tickets. Boston Red Sox superstar Roger Clemens was pitching on a rehabilitation assignment, and there wasn't an empty seat in the house.

Where to Stay

Visiting Team Motel: Comfort Inn. This five-floor brick hotel is newly decorated and clean. Its standard doubles are roomy but face the adjacent highway. Deluxe doubles are larger and away from traffic noise. Guests receive a free Continental breakfast. *2 George St., Exit 27 from I–95, Pawtucket 02860, tel. 401/723–6700 or 800/424–6423, fax 401/726–6380. 135 rooms. Facilities: restaurant, pool. AE, D, DC, MC, V. $$*

Where to Eat

Gregg's. This 180-seat restaurant, one of four in the state, is known for its rich chocolate layer cake, Reuben sandwiches, and real turkey sandwiches and dinners. Children can have half-orders of pasta, fish-and-chips, and 4-ounce hamburgers. The homemade apple pie, made with 5 pounds of apples, and the meat loaf are

toothsome. It's in a residential-commercial area 6 miles south of the ballpark. *1940 Pawtucket Ave., East Providence, tel. 401/438–5700. AE, D, DC, MC, V. $*

Modern Diner. Half of the delight of eating here is visual, as this is one of the nation's most remarkable diners. It's a vintage, maroon-and-buff Sterling streamliner diner with a bow end, set in the middle of a parking lot, looking nearly untouched since it was built in 1940. It's now on the National Register of Historic Places. Inside are wooden booths with large mirror panels. On Thursdays and Fridays, you can get all three meals here, but on most days it's just breakfast and lunch. Try to visit on a Friday for the excellent clam chowder. You can order beyond-the-norm items such as fried-egg sandwiches and frappes, a drink that also goes by the regional moniker "cabinets." Unusual and good pancakes—blueberry, plum, pumpkin, cranberry, apple, and banana—are on the breakfast menu, which is served all day. It's five minutes west of the ballpark. *364 East Ave., Pawtucket, tel. 401/726–8390. No credit cards. $*

Providence Cheese and Tavola Calda. The square pizza and focaccia are standouts at this premier take-out delicatessen. It's on Federal Hill, which is filled with good Italian bakeries and restaurants. Anything from the deli's cases would make a memorable pregame picnic. You can sit at one of the tables in the side courtyard in good weather. *407 Atwells Ave., Providence, tel. 401/421–5653. AE, MC, V. $*

Angelo's Civita Farnese. There are six community tables where guests are mixed and matched, if they wish, at the center of this inexpensive and cozy family restaurant on Federal Hill. Eight booths along the perimeter are for those who prefer not to mingle. Prices are low and no reservations are taken, but waits rarely exceed 15 minutes at dinner. The signature dish is stewed veal and sweet peppers, which is also sold as a sandwich. Half-orders of homemade macaroni and other pasta are available. Spaghetti accompanies nearly every dish, and a full plate of pasta costs as little as $3.10. *141 Atwells Ave., Providence, tel. 401/621–8171. No credit cards. $*

Diners began in Providence when horse-drawn canteens, devised by entrepreneur Walter Scott in 1892, served pies and coffee to mill workers.

It's a point of civic pride that this city has kept its vintage diners. Consider these survivors: At **Silver Top Diner** (13 Harris Ave., tel. 401/331–8247) don't miss the blueberry pancakes in a preserved Kullman diner, built in 1941. Try also the 1946 **Krystal's** (581 Atwells Ave., tel. 401/751–1650), the 1950s **Seaplane Diner** (307 Allens Ave., tel. 401/941–9547), the 1930s **Wampanaug Diner** (2800 Pawtucket Ave., East Providence, tel. 401/434–9880), and the upscale, '50s-furnished **Downcity Diner** (151 Weybosset St., tel. 401/331–9217).

Entertainments

Basketball Hall of Fame. This Cooperstown for basketball fans is 90 minutes west of Pawtucket in Springfield. You can walk through a tunnel decorated with the shoes of famous players, test your shooting ability at 15 baskets in the Spalding Shoot-Out, and play a one-on-one virtual game with Bill Walton. Check your hang time and jumping ability at the Wilson Imagymnation Theater. Watch past and present clips from famous games. Women players, wheelchair athletes, and the Olympic Games receive special notice. An Honors Court memorializes 207 great players. *1150 W. Columbus Ave., Springfield, MA, tel. 413/781–6500. Admission: $8 adults, $5 ages 7–15 and senior citizens. Open daily 9–5.*

Roger Williams Park and Zoo. This excellent city zoo has a good African-animals exhibit and a monkey house. You can see the polar bears underwater. *1000 Elmwood Ave., Providence, tel. 401/785–9450. Admission: $4 adults, $2.50 ages 3–12. Open Nov.–Apr., daily 9–5; May–Oct., weekdays 9–5, weekends and holidays 9–6.*

Children's Museum of Rhode Island. This small hands-on museum is in a renovated mansion, with its 1840s kitchen still intact. There are seven permanent exhibits, including areas on disabilities, construction, a shape lab, a sea aquarium, a small stage for making stories come alive, and a Revolutionary War sailing ship. *58 Walcott St., Pawtucket, tel. 401/726–2590. Admission: $3.50; free 1st Sun. of month. Open Tues.–Sat. 9:30–5, Sun. 1–5.*

Sites to See

State Capitol. The Rhode Island State Capitol is a massive white Georgian marble structure sitting high on Smith Hill. It overlooks but is physically removed from the city life of Providence. Begun in 1895 and completed in 1904, it was built on a design by the New York firm McKim, Mead & White, inspired by the U.S. Capitol, St. Paul's Cathedral in London, and New York's City Hall. The Capitol is 235 feet high from the terrace to the top of the statue on the marble dome, George Brewster's gilded "Independent Man." It is the second-largest unsupported marble dome in the world (the largest is atop St. Peter's Basilica in Rome). Gilbert Stuart's portrait of George Washington hangs in the State Room. *82 Smith St., bordered by Smith, Gaspee, and Francis Sts., Providence, tel. 401/277–2357. Open weekdays 8:30–4:30; free tours by appointment only (tel. 401/277–2357), weekdays at 10 and 11.*

Brown University. It is worth seeing University Hall, the center of this popular Ivy League school founded in 1764. The four-story brick building was copied from Princeton's Nassau Hall. A bust of John Jay, first chief justice of the U.S. Supreme Court in the library is supposed to bring students good luck if they rub its now-shiny nose. Tours of the campus begin at the admissions office in Corliss-Broekett House (45 Prospect St., at Angell St.). The university is on the city's east side. *College Hill, Providence, tel. 401/863–1000.*

BOSTON RED SOX

League: American League • **Class:** Major League • **Stadium:** Fenway Park • **Opened:** 1912 • **Capacity:** 33,871 • **Dimensions:** LF: 310, CF: 390, RF: 302 • **Surface:** grass • **Season:** Apr.–Sept.

STADIUM LOCATION: 4 Yawkey Way, Boston, MA 02215

TEAM WEBSITE: http://www.redsox.com

GETTING THERE: Take Green Line on T to Kenmore Square, 3 blocks north of Fenway. For transit information, call 617/722–3200 or 800/392–6100. By car from south, take Exit 20A/Rte. 9 east from I–95.

Go east on Rte. 9 about 10 mi. Turn left on Brookline Ave., right on Boylston St., and left on Yawkey Way. From north, take Rte. 93 south. Take Storrow Drive to Kenway/Kenmore Square exit and bear right on Boylston St. Take right on Ipswich St. and right on Yawkey.

TICKET INFORMATION: 4 Yawkey Way, Boston, MA 02215, tel. 617/267–1700, fax 617/236–6640

PRICE RANGE: Field box $23; infield roof box $20; upper box $18; right field roof box $18; grandstand $14; bleachers $9

GAME TIME: 7:05 PM; day games 1:05 PM. Gates open 90 min before game.

TIPS ON SEATING: Watch out for poles, which can obstruct views. Sections 32 and 33 near Green Monster prohibit alcohol. Bleachers can get rowdy and do not provide access to rest of ballpark.

SEATING FOR PEOPLE WITH DISABILITIES: In locations throughout ballpark. Listening devices for people with hearing impairments are available at Customer Service Booths.

STADIUM FOOD: The quality of food inside the park is uneven, but **Legal Seafoods** sells its terrific clam chowder here ($4), and you can bring in any food except items in cans. There are good take-out stands surrounding the park. You can bring in fresh scallops, clam rolls, or good pizza from the **Fenway Diner** (1 Yawkey Way). The biggest disappointment in the park is the Fenway Frank, which is mushy and bland. The steak and cheese sandwich has a chemical taste. There's average Chinese food at a ground-floor stand. The best bet is the chowder, plus real lemonade, which is sold in a large souvenir cup for $3. There are good packaged cranberry cookies, 2 for $1.50, and Boston's own Hood ice cream treats and Richie's Italian slushes are sold. A $2.75 kid's meal has a hot dog, chips, and apple juice.

PARKING: Expect to pay $10 for a lot that doesn't block your car. Prudential Center Garage ($5 if you show a Sox ticket stub) on Boylston St. between Dartmouth and Exeter offers easy access to Mass. Turnpike.

SMOKING POLICY: Seating area smoke-free; billboards announce, "Fenway Park should have a place in your heart. Not in your lungs."

TOURISM INFORMATION: Greater Boston Convention & Visitors Bureau (Prudential Plaza, Box 490, Boston, MA 02199, tel. 617/536–4100 or 800/888–5515)

Boston, Massachusetts: Fenway Park

"Ladies and gentlemen...boys and girls...welcome to Fenway Park" is the formal and familiar greeting of the public address announcer in one of baseball's classic ballparks.

The anticipation builds as you walk to the park. The streets are full of people darting in and out of the pubs and shops and around the food carts and souvenir tables that surround Fenway. You enter this small, redbrick arched building just as fans have before you for more than 85 years. You walk through a dark, dank area beneath the grandstand and then through a portal. There it is. It is truly breathtaking. Only here and at Chicago's Wrigley Field is there a feeling as pure and wonderful for the baseball fan.

As wonderful as Fenway Park is, baseball history has not been kind to the Fenway faithful. The whole story seems to be told on the roof above the right-field bleachers. Just below the sign for the Jimmy Fund—which has helped raise millions of dollars for the Dana–Farber Cancer Institute—are the numbers 9 4 1 8. These are the retired numbers of four great Red Sox players—Ted Williams, Joe Cronin, Bobby Doerr, and Carl Yastrzemski. They represent the numerical symbol of "the Curse of the Bambino." September 4, 1918 (9/4/18), was the eve of the World Series. Babe Ruth pitched and won the game the very next day, and the Red Sox won the World Series. Financially strapped Red Sox owner Harry Frazee sold Ruth to the Yankees for $100,000 cash and a $300,000 loan with a mortgage on Fenway Park. The Red Sox have not won a World Series since.

Fenway Park got its name when Red Sox owner General John I. Taylor decided to switch from Huntington Grounds in 1911 to a plot of marshy land nearby that was owned by the Fenway Realty Company. General Taylor was a major stockholder in the real estate company. The Fens was an area planned by Frederick Law Olmstead as part of a proposed ring of parks for the Boston area.

When the Red Sox were planning their new stadium, the era of the wooden ballpark was coming to a close. Pittsburgh and Philadelphia had built new concrete-and-steel ballparks, and Boston was not to be outdone. Osborne Engineering of Cleveland designed Fenway, and it was built in 1912 for $650,000 without public funds. The front was modeled on Philadelphia's 1909 Shibe Park; it was built without an upper deck. There's a lot of history here. President John F. Kennedy's grandfather, Boston mayor John F. "Honey Fitz" Fitzgerald, tossed out the first ball at the 1912 opener. President Franklin Delano Roosevelt gave the last campaign speech of his life here on November 4, 1944. Six months later he was dead.

The Green Monster, the huge green fence in left field, was not part of the 1912 ballpark. Lansdowne in left field was only 325 feet from home plate, and there was a railroad track just across the street. To remedy this, they built a wall in left field with an embankment just in front of it. This became known as Duffy's Cliff after Red Sox left fielder Duffy Lewis, who was the first to learn how to play it. In 1934, Duffy's Cliff was flattened and a 37-foot-high metal fence was installed. But even then it was not as we see it today. In the late 1930s and '40s, the wall was mostly covered with large advertisements. They were painted over in 1947 in Fenway green. In 1978, Yankee Bucky Dent popped a ball to left, and it somehow ended up in the net over the Monster for one of the shortest and most important home runs ever hit. Dent's pop-up enabled the Yankees to beat the Red Sox in a one-game playoff for the American League crown. Fenway's Green Monster and Wrigley's ivy are the two most distinctive features in any of America's ballparks.

We like to get to games early and watch batting practice, always hoping to snag a ball in the process. Nowhere is this experience as special as it is at Fenway. Stand as close to the field as you dare on the third-base side at the foot of the Green Monster, and watch the visiting-team batters slam the ball into and over the wall and right by your ear.

Your eyes can't miss the animated neon CITGO sign just over the Green Monster that mimics the triangular shape of the bleacher seats in center field. Before the fans fill the bleachers, look for the red seat in a sea of blue deep in the triangle. This is where a Ted Williams home run landed, 502 feet from home plate. They added bullpens in front of the bleachers in right and right center field in 1940. Contrary to what you might think, these bullpens weren't for the convenience of pitchers. The area is known as Williamsburg, as it was built to increase the output of the left-hand-hitting Ted Williams, who had hit .327 with 31 homers in his rookie season of 1939. The bullpens reduced the right-field home-run distance by 23 feet. Appropriately, Williams hit a home run in his very last at bat in the major leagues on September 28, 1960, into the right-field Red Sox bullpen. Not much else has changed in the 50-plus years since Ted Williams began playing here. A large scoreboard was constructed in 1976 and upgraded in 1988. In 1989, the enclosed "600 Club" seats behind home plate were added.

Okay, we won't kid you—there's not much legroom here. Someone is bound to spill some beer on you in such close quarters. Balls bounce wildly off the crazy angles in the outfield, and no lead is safe with the Green Monster so close to home. The concession area is dark. The food is mostly bad. You paid too much to park, and your car is blocked on every side. But believe us, you will love every minute of this.

Unfortunately, time is running out on this hopelessly and wonderfully outdated relic. The Red Sox are finding it difficult to compete financially for top players with the teams in Baltimore and Cleveland having fancy new stadiums that seem to be printing money. With all our hearts we say, "Save Fenway!" But the economic reality is that the Boston Red Sox will have a new ballpark soon after the turn of the century.

The carnival atmosphere outside Fenway includes the souvenir shops, sports pubs, and take-out food stands all vying for your business. The adjacent restaurants, such as Pizzeria Uno (645 Beacon St., at Brookline Ave., tel. 617/ 536–2337) and the Boston Beer Works (61 Brookline Ave., tel. 617/262–4911) often are too crowded for comfort, but there are dozens of other choices in the Kenmore Square area.

The Sausage Connection (Brookline Ave. and Lansdowne St.) has much better Italian sausage, onions, and peppers ($4) than the ballpark grill. If you show your ticket at RFA Amusements (under Fenway, 82 Lansdowne St., tel. 617/247–9252), you get a free game on one of its 20 candlepin bowling lanes. This is a worthy choice to make, a post-afternoon game to give the parking lots and crowded T trains a chance to empty.

There is a large souvenir shop, the Lansdowne Shop, inside Fenway on the left-field side; it can also be entered from Brookline Avenue. Twin Souvenirs (19 Yawkey Way, Boston, tel. 617/421–8686 or 800/336–9299 for retail catalog), a souvenir store across from Fenway's main entrance, bills itself as "the Supermarket of Sports Souvenirs" and appears to live up to its claim.

Tours of Fenway Park (Red Sox Service Gate D, corner of Yawkey Way and Van Ness St., tel. 617/236–6666. Admission: $5 adults, $4 senior citizens, $3 ages under 16) are conducted Monday through Friday at 10, 11, noon, and 1; on non-game days, there's also a tour at 2. Call in advance for a reservation.

Other Baseball Sites near Fenway Park

Huntington Avenue American League Baseball Grounds. A 1956 plaque on Northeastern University's Godfrey Lowell Cabot Physical Education Center (365 Huntington Ave.) explains that four games of the 1903 World Series were held on this site, with the Boston Americans defeating the Pittsburgh Nationals five games to three. The center houses a modest display of World Series memorabilia. The real treat is a small park behind the building. Go half a block down Forsyth Street and turn left at World Series Way to find a statue of the great Cy Young looking in toward home plate for a signal from the catcher. The home-plate-shape plaque, 60 feet away, explains that the games played here in 1903 were the first modern World Series. Let the kids pretend to catch and bat with the man who pitched the first perfect game of the 20th century here on May 5, 1904. The Boston Pilgrims (called the Americans for the World Series) played here from 1901 to 1911 before moving to Fenway Park as the Red Sox in 1912. Hunting-

ton Avenue was left field. The center-field fence was 530 feet from home in 1903 and moved back to 635 feet in 1908.

Braves Field. The Boston University football team plays at Nickerson Field, on the site where the Boston Braves played baseball from 1915 to 1952. Three World Series and the 1936 All-Star Game were played here. The Red Sox won the World Series here in 1915 and 1916 (played here because at the time Braves Field held more seats than Fenway), while the Braves lost to Cleveland in 1948. Babe Ruth pitched 13 straight innings of shut-out ball to help the Red Sox beat the Brooklyn Dodgers in the 1916 series. The Braves moved to Milwaukee in 1953 and Atlanta in 1966. In 1970, Boston University laid out its football carpet from the first-base dugout to right center field. The stands down the first-base line remain, along with much of the concrete outer wall in right field. The handsome, arched ticket office is now used as the Boston University Police Station. A 1988 plaque in a courtyard on the Commonwealth Avenue side of the ticket office pays tribute to Braves Field. *Nickerson Field, 1 block off Commonwealth Ave. at Harry Agganis Way.*

Where to Stay

Tremont House. This 15-floor hotel is in the theater district, two blocks from the Boston Common, and is one of the few nice downtown hotels where rooms are under $100. Built in 1924, the hotel has been fully renovated. Some rooms have refrigerators; all have free cable movies. The rooms and baths are small, but the bedrooms are nicely furnished in reproduction antiques. It is a half block from the Medical Center stop on the Orange Line of the T. A neighborhood pocket park with children's climbing equipment is next door. *275 Tremont St., Boston 02116, tel. 617/426–1400 or 800/331–9998, fax 617/482–6730. 288 rooms. Facilities: restaurant. AE, D, DC, MC. $$*

Hotel Buckminster. Built as a hotel in 1903, this impressive stone-front building saw use as a dorm for Boston University before being completely renovated in 1991 and reopened as a European-style hotel. Many of its spacious units are suites, and several have kitchens and dishwashers. The rooms are furnished in Chippendale reproductions, with forest-green draperies.

The two-bedroom suites, joined by a hallway and including a wet bar, cost between $100 and $140 per night. It is one block from Fenway Park and the Kenmore Square T station. It has no parking garage; you can use street meters or a private adjoining garage, which charges $17 daily. *645 Beacon St., Boston 02215, tel. 617/ 236–7050 or 800/727–2825, fax 617/262– 0068. 100 units. Facilities: restaurant. AE, D, DC, MC, V. $$*

Howard Johnson Lodge–Fenway. Parking is free at this two-story hotel, which backs up to Fenway Park. Guests receive a free cassette walking tour if they ask for the "AAA Freedom Trail Package," which lowers rates to $100 per night. The rooms are standard lodgings, and some have refrigerators and microwave ovens. *1271 Boylston St., Boston 02215, tel. 617/267– 8300 or 800/446–4656, fax 617/267–2763. 94 rooms. Facilities: restaurant, pool. AE, D, DC, MC, V. $$*

Howard Johnson Hotel–Kenmore. This well-used seven-story concrete hotel, built in the 1960s, overlooks the T tracks coming into Kenmore Square. It's a two-block walk from Fenway Park. Some rooms have refrigerators and microwave ovens. Most rooms are small, with contemporary furnishings. The "AAA Freedom Trail Package" lowers rates to $110 per night. *575 Commonwealth Ave., Boston 02215, tel. 617/267–3100 or 800/446–4656, fax 617/ 424–1045. 179 rooms. Facilities: restaurant, indoor pool. AE, D, DC, MC, V. $$*

Where to Eat

Fenway Diner. Huge yellow billboards leaning against the wall announce the menu of this fast-food takeout a few feet from Fenway's turnstiles. The counter help act as barkers, enticing the crowds to their windows to buy fried clam strips, buffalo wings, mozzarella sticks, and burgers. Eaters stand along the restaurant wall, chewing; those who have willpower to wait take their food into the park before digging in. *1 Yawkey Way, Boston, tel. 617/262–4228. No credit cards. $*

Jacob Wirth Company Restaurant. You creak on wooden floors in this charming, historic restaurant with round mahogany tables. It's the oldest German eatery in America. Since it was founded in 1868, the dark wood decor of the famous alehouse hasn't changed much. It serves exemplary clam chowder, red cabbage, Wiener schnitzel, scrod, and inexpensive sandwiches. Eight baseball Hall of Famers, including Cy Young and Tris Speaker, all of whom ate and drank here, have reproductions of their Baseball Hall of Fame plaques on a wall. A photo of Babe Ruth hangs over the bar. The children's meals are served with carrot and celery sticks; the selection includes turkey and mashed potatoes, grilled cheese, hamburgers, peanut butter and jelly sandwiches, and a salad. It's a 7-minute T ride from Fenway or a 20-minute walk. The restaurant validates an hour's parking in the next-door lot. *37–39 Stuart St., at Tremont St., Boston, tel. 617/338–8586. AE, D, MC, V. $$*

Durgin Park. You must experience the crusty waitresses, the noise, and the feeding-hall atmosphere because the food is exceptional in this second-floor restaurant. Regional specialties like Indian pudding, baked beans, and lobster are unequaled. A specialty is prime rib, but kids can opt for chicken fingers or fish off their own menu. Open for lunch and dinner, the restaurant has an oyster bar and long communal tables. *340 Faneuil Hall Marketplace, Boston, tel. 617/227–2038. AE, D, DC, MC, V. $$*

Emack & Bolio's. Indulge in calorie-laden refreshment at this local ice cream shop, which has several outlets in the area. Its cones are handmade and the ice cream flavors are imaginative. It's worth the 10-minute walk from the Swan Boats in the Public Garden (*see below*) for these cones, instead of settling for a frozen dessert from a concession truck. *290 Newbury St., at Gloucester St., Boston, tel. 617/247–8772. No credit cards. $*

Entertainments

Buy a Visitor's Passport, which gives you unlimited transport on all subway and bus lines for $5 per day. They are sold at the Boston Common Information Offices (Tremont St. in the Common) and at the Prudential Center (near Copley T station). These offices also give out pamphlets with valuable attraction coupons and restaurant discounts.

Swan Boats. Fans of Robert McClosky's classic book *Make Way for Ducklings* will remember the

Swan Boats. You wait in line to board these graceful antique boats on a sweep around the lagoon in the Public Garden. Athletic teens power the boats by pedaling, the same energy used when the boats debuted in 1877. Children will be amused by the antics of the ducks that fill the lagoon. After debarking, walk to the park gates at Beacon and Charles streets and find the statues of the book's Mrs. Mallard and her duck family. The Park Street stop on the Red Line is closest. *Boston Public Garden Lagoon, near Charleston and Boylston Sts., Boston. Admission: $1.50 adults, 95¢ ages under 13. Open Apr. 19–June 20, daily 10–4; June 21–Labor Day, daily 10–5.*

Freedom Trail. A faded red stripe marks 3 miles of sidewalk passing in front of the city's historic landmarks, including the Old North Church and Bunker Hill Monument. Maps are available from the National Park Service Vistor's Center (15 State St.) or the Boston Common Information Office (Tremont St.). The trail is too long to accomplish with young kids, but there's a shorter version for children 6–12 called "Boston by Little Feet," which covers several of the trail's highlights. This abbreviated tour leaves from the statue of Samuel Adams in Faneuil Hall Square. *Faneuil Hall Sq., Boston, tel. 617/367–2345. Admission: $6 adults, $5 ages 6–12. Tours May–Oct., Sat. at 10, Sun. at 2.*

Children's Museum of Boston. Here you'll find four floors of controlled mayhem, as children race from trying on costumes to flipping life-size photographs of children from other races and cultures. A big crowd-pleaser is the see-through toilet. A 40-foot wooden Hood Dairy milk bottle in front of the museum dispenses carry-out sandwiches, salads, and drinks. There is also a McDonald's outlet on the museum's first floor. *300 Congress St., Museum Wharf, Boston, tel. 617/426–8855. Admission: $7 adults, $6 ages 2–15 and senior citizens; $2 children age 1; $1 Fri. 5–9. Open Tues.–Thurs. and weekends 10–5, Fri. 10–9.*

Computer Museum. Next door to the Children's Museum you'll find two floors of computer simulations, games, and hands-on displays that delight older children. There's a walk-through computer that stretches the entire height of the museum and several stations that let visitors jump onto the information highway.

300 Congress St., Museum Wharf, Boston, tel. 617/426–2800. Admission: $7 adults, $5 ages 5–18 and senior citizens; ½-price Sun. 3–5. Open mid-June–Labor Day, daily 10–6; Labor Day–mid-June, Tues.–Sun. 10–5.

New England Aquarium. From woodland pools to oceans, this extensive aquarium presents all manner of fish and amphibians in various environments. Its centerpiece is a 190,000-gallon three-story cylindrical transparent tank containing a coral reef. Visitors walk a ramp around the tank, getting close to sea turtles and sharks. A penguin colony lives at its base, in a salt-water basin. Sea-lion shows are held every 90 minutes daily, beginning at 10:30, at Discovery, a floating auditorium. Nature films are shown throughout the day in the theater. There is an Aquarium stop on the Blue Line of the subway. *Center Wharf, Atlantic Ave. exit off Rte. 3 N, Boston, tel. 617/973–5200. Admission: $9.50 adults, $8.50 senior citizens, $5 ages 3–11. Open July–early Sept., Mon.–Tues. and Fri. 9–6; Wed. and Thurs. 9–8; weekends 9–7.*

Museum of Science. Learn about nature, medicine, and astronomy in this museum with hundreds of hands-on exhibits. Creative displays explain the laws of physics in an interesting fashion. There are separate fees to view the museum's four-story Omni theater; its laser shows, and the Charles Hayden planetarium. The T stop is Science Park on the Green Line. *Science Park, Boston, tel. 617/723–2500. Admission: $8 adults, $6 children and senior citizens, under 4 free. Open daily 9–7. Closed Thanksgiving, Dec. 25. AE, MC, V.*

Boston Tea Ship and Museum. It's corny and touristy, but our kids loved learning history by throwing canvas chests of "tea" over the rails of this reproduction of a Revolution-era ship. The costumed guides aim their history lessons at kids, and it works. A small museum, explaining the ship and the Revolution's origins, is below deck. There are photo ops with colonist cutouts. The closest T stop is South Station on the Red Line. The ship is anchored on the bridge approaching the Children's and Computer museums. *Congress St. Bridge, Boston, tel. 617/338–1773. Admission: $7 adults, $3.50 ages 6–12, $5.50 senior citizens and high school and college students. No credit cards.*

Sites to See

State House. The children's self-tour of this gold-domed building points out oddities like the sacred codfish that's on display in the Senate chambers. Charles Bulfinch designed the building's brick front, and the first African-American regiment to serve in the Civil War is memorialized by Augustus Saint-Gaudens in a bas-relief statue in front of the capitol. The T stop is Park Street. *Beacon St., at Park St., Boston, tel. 617/727–3676. Free tours weekdays 10–4. Open weekdays 10–5.*

John Fitzgerald Kennedy Presidential Library and Museum. This impressive museum has an excellent 17-minute documentary film, memorabilia, and videotapes. Kennedy's Oval Office desk is here, along with details of such groundbreaking initiatives of his as community mental-health centers. The Red Line T stop is JFK–University of Massachusetts. The library operates a free shuttle bus every 20 minutes to and from the T stop. *Morrissey Blvd., Exit 14 from I–93/Rte. 3, Boston, tel. 617/929–4523. Admission: $6 adults, $2 ages 6–16, $4 senior citizens and students. Open daily 9–5.*

On the Way to Cape Cod

If you have time, break up the drive from Boston to Cape Cod with a stop at Plymouth to see the famous Rock and enjoy the free Ocean Spray museum. If you attend a night game at Fenway, you can drive an hour south to Plymouth, stay overnight, walk its waterfront downtown, and still get to the Cape beaches in early afternoon.

Where to Stay

Pilgrim Sands Motel. Get a second-floor room in this hotel, where the lobby has a fireplace and there's a nice beach for walking. A public beach with lifeguards is a five-minute walk north from the motel. The rooms lack soundproofing, but they're very clean, have fresh ocean breezes, and are furnished simply. Ducks and swans congregate at the base of the rear patio for handouts. *150 Warren Ave., Plymouth 02360, tel. 508/747–0900 or 800/729–7263, fax 508/746–8066.*

Facilities: coffeeshop, outdoor and indoor pools, hot tub. AE, D, MC, V. $$

Where to Eat

Lobster Hut. Watch the fishing and pleasure boats from the large back deck of this 26-year-old fast-food restaurant. Every manner of fried seafood, from scallops to whole clams, is served. Crab and lobster rolls, stuffed quahogs, and steamed clams also are available. The service is speedy and the fish is undeniably fresh. *Town Wharf, at Water St., Plymouth, tel. 508/745–2270. MC, V. $$*

Sites to See

Plymouth Rock. This may be a 17th-century tourist fraud, as the historical evidence for establishing this as the original rock on which the Pilgrims first stepped ashore is shaky. But it's in a pretty bayside park, surrounded by a classic stone portico designed in 1921 by famed New York–based architects McKim, Mead & White, and there's no charge for looking. The rock has shrunk—visitors chipped off souvenirs in earlier years, when you could touch it, and bicentennial celebrants in 1820 carved that year on the rock. Erosion and several moves have also harmed it. But it's still a good visual way to explain the European discovery of the New World to children. As Alex de Tocqueville said, "Here is a stone which the feet of a few outcasts pressed for an instant, and the stone became famous. It is treasured by a great nation; its very dust is shared as a relic." A reproduction of the *Mayflower* is anchored a few yards away, and for a fee, you can explore it. *Water St., Plymouth.*

Cranberry World Visitors Center. This free museum in a former Ocean Spray packing house is a ten-minute walk north of Plymouth Rock. There are interesting videos, vintage equipment, and photographs of the immigrants and other workers who once hand-harvested this low-running vine on their knees. It's a quick and fascinating walk through this collection of cranberry knowledge, and there's an open kitchen on the ground floor that serves free samples of cranberry baked goods and drinks. *225 Water St., Plymouth, tel. 508/747–2350. Open May–Nov., daily 9:30–5.*

Cape Cod Baseball League

If you are a college freshman, sophomore, or junior baseball superstar, the Cape Cod Baseball League is where you want to spend your summer. Along with the Shenandoah Valley League and other NCAA-sanctioned summer leagues, the Cape Cod Baseball League attracts the most talented young college players. Major-league baseball makes a financial contribution to help support these summer leagues, and major-league scouts are ever present. The league is run by volunteers, who keep baseball going on the Cape for the sheer love of the game.

The league motto is "Where the stars of tomorrow shine tonight," and it is no exaggeration. Among former Cape Cod League stars, 144 are now in the major leagues, including 1995 American League MVP Mo Vaughn, Frank Thomas, and Chuck Knoblauch.

Organized baseball has been played on the Cape since 1885. It began as a semi-pro league, with such stars as Hall of Famers Pie Traynor and Mickey Cochrane. The NCAA has sanctioned the league since the late 1960s. Since 1985, players have been allowed to use wooden bats, adding to the glamour for college players used to that annoying ping of aluminum bats. The chance to watch future superstars swinging wooden bats has attracted many scouts, and the presence of so many scouts has attracted top-caliber players.

The longest trip in the 10-team league is 46 miles from Wareham on the west to Chatham on the east. Many of the "road trips" are less than 10 miles. Games start the second week in June, and the season ends in early August. Admission is free to all games. Most teams sell 50–50 tickets (raffle tickets whose proceeds are split between the club and the winning ticket holder) and pass the hat to keep the club financially sound.

The East Division teams include **Brewster Whitecaps** (Cape Cod Regional Technical High School, on Rte. 124 just north of Exit 10 off Rte. 6), **Chatham Athletics** (Veterans Field, just off Rte. 28 in Chatham Center), **Harwich Mariners** (Whitehouse Field, behind Harwich High School on Oak St.), **Orleans Cardinals** (Eldredge Park, on Rte. 28 near Exit 12 from Rte. 6), and the **Yarmouth-Dennis Red Sox** (Merrill "Red" Wilson Field at Dennis-Yarmouth High School, Station Ave., South Yarmouth).

The West Division teams are **Bourne Braves** (Coady School Field, across Trowbridge Rd. from Bourne High School in Bourne Village), **Cotuit Kettleers** (Elizabeth Lowell Park, 2 mi south of Rte. 28, Cotuit; turn right on Main St. and right again on Lowell Ave.), **Falmouth Commodores** (Guv Fuller Field, behind Gus Canty Community Center, 790 E. Main St., Falmouth), **Hyannis Mets** (McKeon Field, High School Rd., 2 blocks south of Main St. behind Barnstable Grade Five Building), and **Wareham Gatemen** (Clem Spillane Field, Wareham High School, 1 mi west of Wareham Center, Rte. 6). Most games start at 7 PM. The games in Bourne, Brewster, Cotuit, and Yarmouth-Dennis start at 5 because the ballparks do not have lights. The Hyannis home games also start at 5 PM.

The Chatham Athletics play at Veterans Field, where the fog rolled in and out the night we were there faster than at San Francisco's Candlestick Park. The U-shape wooden grandstand—five rows high—fits snugly into a hillside behind home plate. There are trees out left field. Fans bring blankets and picnic on the hillside beyond center and right field. There is a fabulous children's playground on the right-field side and an elegant historic train station on the hill beyond the playground. The Chatham coaches and players give clinics during the summer on the little-league ball field on the first-base side. Fans get a certificate for free ice cream for returning foul balls and are encouraged to volunteer to make sandwiches for the players.

When the Hyannis Mets play at McKeon Field, the school playing field behind home plate is full of kids racing around, playing catch, and stopping only to chase down a foul ball. There are small wooden bleachers on each side of the screen behind home plate. As with most other Cape Cod League parks, a two-story all-purpose cinderblock building houses the public address announcer on the second floor behind home plate. The one in Hyannis is dark baseball green and doubles as the concession stand at the back, where they sell home-made clam chowder. A larger, five-row wooden bleacher sits oddly on a scruffy hillside behind the third-base dugout. Small trees stand behind the outfield fence, and a hotel is well beyond the fence and scoreboard in right. Look on top of the light pole in right-center field to see if the osprey is still there. Ferries come into the town port every hour; you'll probably hear their horns.

The Chatham and Hyannis parks have the kind of raw, rustic charm that gives the Cape Cod League its authentic character. We visited several of the other fields and were especially charmed by Orleans's Eldredge Park and Cotuit's Elizabeth Lowell Park. The Orleans Cardinals play in an attractive ballpark with a four-tier grass grandstand cut out of a hill on the first-base side. Bring your own lawn chairs. Wooden steps help you maneuver the grass grandstand. The Cotuit Kettleers play in a gorgeous setting completely surrounded by trees. Wooden bleachers rise behind each dugout, but there are no lights. The "Kettleer Kitchen" building on the third-base side offers food and souvenirs.

Where to Stay

Many Cape Cod properties require a two- to three-night stay during the summer. The best bargains are along Route 28, a major commercial strip filled with motels of every vintage.

Tidewater Motor Inn. Some of the rooms overlook scenic Mill Pond in this Colonial-style motel, spread out across 4 acres. All rooms have a deck or balcony and contain refrigerators. *135 Main St., from Rte. 28, West Yarmouth 02673, tel. 508/775–6322 or 800/338–6322, fax 508/778–5105. 100 rooms. Facilities: coffeeshop, indoor and outdoor pools, sauna, playground, picnic area, game room. AE, D, MC, V. $$*

Park Beach Ocean Front Motel. The Falmouth Heights public beach on Vineyard Sound is across the street from this small motel. The rooms are quiet and ordinary. Minikitchen rooms, which have queen-size beds, refrigerators, and coffeemakers, cost $10 more. Standard rooms contain a double and a twin bed. Guests receive a free Continental breakfast. *241 Grand Ave. S, Falmouth Heights 02540, tel. 508/548–1010 or 800/341–5700. 50 rooms. Facilities: pool. AE, MC, V. $$*

Where to Eat

Kream & Kone. The two outlets of this fast-food fried-seafood restaurant serve standout chowder, clams, oysters, scrod, frappes, and onion rings, as well as Good Greek salads. You can eat at the Formica booths or order takeout. Its ice cream fountain is crowded in the evenings. *1653 Rte. 28, Chatham, tel. 508/945–3308; 528 Main St., Dennisport, tel. 508/394–0808. No credit cards. $*

The Breakfast Room. Terrific, inexpensive breakfasts and lunches have been served at this cozy cedar-shingled roadside restaurant for the last 26 years. Children's breakfasts are $1.99. The blueberry pancakes are very good, as are the French toast and eggs. The extra-large eggs translate into a huge serving of scrambled eggs—one is sufficient for most people. The two wood-paneled dining rooms are always busy, but the waitresses zip things along. You can get sandwiches, salads, and pizza for lunch. *675 Rte. 28, West Dennis, tel. 508/398–0581. MC, V. $*

Mildred's. This old-fashioned family restaurant near the Hyannis airport serves good lobster dinners for $14. Cape restaurants compete on price for lobster dinners, but many of the heavily advertised restaurants offer tiny crustaceans. Mildred's has dated decor but also keeps old values and recipes intact. Its chowder and Indian pudding are outstanding. *290 Iyanough Rd., Rte. 28, Hyannis, tel. 508/775–1045. AE, D, MC, V. $$*

Entertainments

Each of the seven villages on the Cape has its own town concerts, summer theaters, bird-watching expeditions, beaches, fishing piers, chowder suppers, lobster-roll lunches, clam bakes, art shows, antiques shops, whale-watching trips, and myriad other activities.

Ocean and Bay Beaches. There are many public-beach choices on the Cape. Most have a parking fee and include lifeguards (on duty 9–5), bathhouses, and a concession truck or stand.

CHATHAM. Ridgevale Beach (Ridgevale Rd. off Rte. 28), like all the beaches in Chatham, faces Nantucket Sound and so has little or no surf. This beach has a creek on its backside and 500 feet of waterfront facing the Sound. There are lifeguards, a concession stand, and portable toilets. There's freshwater swimming at Schoolhouse Pond (off Sam Ryder Rd., West Chatham). The secluded North and South beaches are reachable only by water shuttle (Outermost Harbor Marine, tel. 508/945–2030) or dune buggies. There are no lifeguards or concession stands here.

DENNIS. Corporation Beach (Corporation Rd.) has a play area, rest rooms, lifeguards, and a concession area on this placid half-mile-long beach on the bay. There's freshwater swimming at Scargo Lake (off Rte. 6A).

EASTHAM. Nauset Light Beach (off Oceanview Dr., tel. 508/349–3785) is a classic ocean-dune beach with a wooden walkway.

FALMOUTH. Surf Drive Beach (Elm Rd.) has a very shallow waters and is good for wading. Located on Nantucket Sound, this mile-long beach has a saltwater kiddie pool, lifeguards, and a concession stand.

ORLEANS. Skaket Beach (Skaket Beach Rd., off Main St.), with its beach extending nearly 2 miles at low tide, is a great place for children to explore hermit crabs and other sea life in a tidal pool. There are lifeguards, a bathhouse, and a snack shack. There's freshwater swimming at Pilgrim Lake (off Monument Rd.), with lifeguards, a bathhouse, and picnic areas.

WEST BARNSTABLE. Sandy Neck Beach (on Sandy Neck Beach Rd., off Rte. 6A, tel. 508/362–8300), on the north shore, is a 6-mile-long barrier beach.

YARMOUTH. Seagull Beach (off Rte. 28) faces Nantucket Sound and has dunes and about 600-feet of waterfront, with a concession stand, lifeguards, and a bathhouse.

Cape Cod Scenic Railroad. A two-hour ride on this vintage train is a relaxing, traffic-free way to see the cranberry bogs, the bay, the villages, the Cape Cod Canal, and the Great Salt Marsh. The trains go round-trip between Hyannis and Sagamore Bridge. There are stops in Sandwich and at the Cape Cod Canal. A reservation-only dinner train ($49 per person) departs daily at 6:30 in summer and fall and on weekends February through May. *Hyannis Train Station, 252 Main St., at Center St., Hyannis, tel. 508/771–3788 or 800/872–4508. Fare: $11.50 adults, $7.50 children, $10.50 senior citizens. Departures June–Oct., Tues.–Sun. at 10, 12:30, 3.*

Unusual Shopping

The Baseball Shop. This Orleans storefront shop has a wide variety of sports-related items. A good buy are the $2 magnets of the classic baseball stadiums. The store is next door to a good shoe outlet, Westies. *26 Main St., Orleans, tel. 508/240–1063.*

PORTLAND SEA DOGS

League: Eastern League • **Major League Affiliation:** Florida Marlins • **Class:** AA • **Stadium:** Hadlock Field • **Opened:** 1994 • **Capacity:** 6,500 • **Dimensions:** LF: 315, CF: 400, RF: 330 • **Surface:** grass • **Season:** Apr.–Labor Day

STADIUM LOCATION: 271 Park Ave., Portland, ME 04102

TEAM WEBSITE: http://www.mainelink.net/seadogs

GETTING THERE: From south, I–295 to Congress St. E (Exit 5), merge onto Congress St., left at St. John St., merge right onto Park Ave. (N. 1). From north, I–295 to Exit 6A (Forest Ave. S), right on Park Ave.; ballpark is just past Exposition Building on right.

TICKET INFORMATION: Box 636, Portland, ME 04104, tel. 207/874–9300, fax 207/780–0317

PRICE RANGE: Box seats (sold out) $6 adults, $5 ages under 17 and over 62; reserved $5 adults, $4 children and senior citizens; general admission $4 adults, $2 children and senior citizens

GAME TIME: 7 PM; some Sat. 1 PM; some Sun. 1 or 4 PM; gates open 90 min before game time

TIPS ON SEATING: Call ahead for tickets; some games each year are sold out in advance. General admission seats are fine if you get to stadium early enough to get good ones. Seats beyond third base are less than 20 rows from field and do not face late afternoon sun.

SEATING FOR PEOPLE WITH DISABILITIES: In last row of box seats; special free parking at stadium

STADIUM FOOD: Among unusual and inexpensive offerings here are the greasy but good fried pollack sandwich ($2) and the sweet Sea Dog ice cream biscuit ($1.50), which is two chocolate-chip cookies pressed onto a circle of vanilla ice cream. There is also broccoli-and-cheese stuffed bread ($2) and an average ice cream brownie. The grill on the first-base side serves good barbecue chicken, grilled sausage and peppers, and passable steak-and-cheese sandwiches, for $3.75 each. A sub shop in the concourse has minestrone, chicken noodle soup, chili, and three varieties of subs. Grape and apple juice are sold, and there's a milk and cookies stand.

SMOKING POLICY: Smoking prohibited except in designated area behind left-field stands

PARKING: Limited free parking near stadium; private lots nearby cost $4–$5. Free lot at University of Southern Maine is 10-minute walk. Shuttle buses (tel. 207/774–0351; $1) to stadium from downtown parking lots start 1 hr before game time.

VISITING TEAM HOTEL: Radisson Eastland Plaza (157 High St., Portland, ME 04101, tel. 207/775–5411 or 800/333–3333)

TOURISM INFORMATION: Convention & Visitors Bureau of Greater Portland (305 Commercial St., Portland, ME 04101, tel. 207/772–5800)

Portland, Maine: Hadlock Field

It was a long time coming, and the fans in Portland, Maine, responded. Professional baseball had not been played in Portland since 1949. So when Daniel Burke, a retired television executive, brought baseball back to Portland in 1994, the fans poured in, setting a new Eastern League annual attendance record of 375,187.

Hadlock Field seats 6,500 and you'd better call in advance to reserve a seat, as several games each year are sold out before the day of the game. This beautiful stadium was built by the city for the Class AA Eastern League franchise of the expansion Florida Marlins. Part of the Portland Sports Complex, the new ballpark was built on the site of the high school field already named in honor of Edson Hadlock, the man who coached baseball at Portland High School from 1950 to 1978.

On the southern edge of Portland's downtown, just below the Maine Medical Center, Hadlock Field has that just-right combination of old and new that has made Baltimore's Camden Yards so popular. The field sits just behind the handsome redbrick Portland Exposition Building, a 1915 classic arena. The Exposition Building, Portland's answer to the warehouse at Camden Yards, eliminates much of the seating that could be on the first-base side. The grandstand appears to be shaped like a fisherman's hook, with the long end down the third-base line. On the hillside beyond first base and behind the arena are a hockey rink, a brick police-horse barn, and a football field.

The front of the stadium is particularly attractive, with a significant part of the facade in brick and an oversize Sea Dog guarding the entrance. Flags fly above the skyboxes, but the main seating area has no roof. There is very little foul territory, as the seats are close to the field. The inside of the dugouts and a strip of wall down the third-base side are done in brick.

The fans in the general admission seats make quite a racket banging their feet on the aluminum grandstand floor to cheer on the home team. You'll want to hope a Sea Dog hits a home run or the Sea Dogs win the game so that you can see how inventive a retired television mogul can be with modern technology. A lighthouse pops up above the fence in center field, issuing a deep, loud whistle, shooting off fireworks, and spinning a bright light on top. The festive scoreboard in left center field sports flying flags and a clock on top.

Slugger the Sea Dog, a seal with a dog's head, quickly became a fan favorite. He's already gone flipper-to-hand with the likes of Barbara Bush, Frank Gifford, and Stephen King. In real life, he's not nearly so menacing as he looks in the team's logo. No one has figured out how to write with a flipper, so Slugger doesn't sign autographs. But each night a Sea Dog player does sign in the concourse about 45 minutes before the game. There is a photo display of "Mainers in the Majors" on the third-base concourse. Trash collectors dressed as orange and blue fish monsters encourage fans to fill their pouches to keep the stadium clean.

Portland is a walking city; we recommend that you pay a little more and stay in a downtown hotel. Portland was first established by the British as a fishing and trading settlement in 1632. The city has preserved much of its 19th-century Victorian feel from when it was completely rebuilt after the Great Fire of 1866.

Portland's Downtown District (tel. 207/772–6828) has an excellent visitor's guide, map, and suggestions for "a wandering tour" focused on the Old Port area. You can walk along Congress Street, the commercial and transportation spine of Portland, and see the boyhood home of poet Henry Wadsworth Longfellow (485 Congress St., tel. 207/772–1807), who dubbed Portland a "Jewel by the Sea." Turn down Exchange Street, now a lively shopping area, to see some of the best examples of the buildings constructed after the city's Great Fire of 1866. Continue walking to the wharfs along Commercial Street and watch the catch come in at the Portland Fish Pier.

The Visitor Information Center (305 Commercial St., tel. 207/772–5800) is well stocked with maps and brochures, including informative guides to Congress Street and Old Port Exchange prepared by Greater Portland Landmarks (tel. 207/774–5561) that will enhance your walking tours.

Where to Stay

Visiting Team Hotel: Radisson Eastland Hotel Portland. This imposing redbrick city landmark has harbor views from many of its rooms. The large, formal lobby has marble floors, Oriental carpets, and chandeliers. The rooms are pleasant, with wing-back chairs and flowered drapes.

You can walk to the Old Port area and to the ballpark shuttle. *157 High St., Portland 04101, tel. 207/775–5411 or 800/333–3333, fax 207/775–2872. 204 rooms. Facilities: 2 restaurants, lounge, exercise room, sauna, parking (fee). AE, D, DC, MC, V. $$*

Holiday Inn By the Bay. This convenient downtown hotel is not on the water, but many of its rooms have sweeping views of the harbor. The rooms and hallways have been tastefully remodeled, and the standard rooms are ample and light-filled. It is a two-block walk from the Children's Museum and the Old Port area. *88 Spring St., Portland 04101, tel. 207/775–2311 or 800/465–4329, fax 207/761–8224. 239 rooms. Facilities: restaurant, indoor pool, saunas, health club, parking (free). AE, D, DC, MC, V. $$*

Regency. This historic hotel, near the waterfront, is in an 1895 redbrick armory building, elegantly converted into comfortable rooms and a small, flower-filled lobby. The charming rooms, some with fireplaces, have reproduction antiques, elegant linens and drapes, and period wallpaper. It is on the National Register of Historic Places. *20 Milk St., Portland 04101, tel. 207/774–4200 or 800/727–3436, fax 207/775–2150. 95 rooms. Facilities: restaurant, hot tub, saunas, steam rooms, health club, parking (fee). AE, D, DC, MC, V. $$$*

Hotel Everett. This bargain hotel in the city's Arts District has a sweeping entry arch, high-ceiling rooms, and European character. It is not air-conditioned and has tubs, not showers; its '50s-era furnishings are slowly being upgraded from the residence hotel it once was. In part of the Old Port area, it is convenient to the waterfront and to ballpark shuttles. Its lobby is on the second floor. There is no extra charge for cots. A city parking lot (fee) is a block away. *51A Oak St., Portland 04101, tel. 207/773–7882. 49 rooms. MC, V. $*

Where to Eat

DiMillo's. The harbor views are spectacular from the side and, especially, the upper deck of this floating restaurant. You walk a gangplank to get aboard the former car ferry, which is festooned with such nautical artifacts as a diving suit and ship models. The huge wood reception desk has a live lobster tank. It may be too windy some days to sit up top, but make sure you look around and view the whale wall, a 450-foot-long waterfront mural on the Maine State Pier, by artist Robert Wyland. The seafood is excellent; its overfilled lobster roll is one of the best and most generous we've seen. There is a children's menu. Parking on Long Wharf is paid for by the restaurant. *25 Long Wharf, Portland, tel. 207/772–2216. AE, D, DC, MC, V. $$*

Benny's Famous Fried Clams. This roadside shack along Commercial Street adorned with fishing floats has 12 tables and umbrellas for outside eating. Many patrons take out their delicious, hand-cut french fries, fried clams, clam cakes, and clam burgers. The Maine potatoes really make a difference with these creamy french fries. The platter prices are low—$5.50 for two crab cakes, coleslaw, fries, and garlic rolls. Crisp clam cakes are $1 each. It's less than 2 miles from the ballpark, but you can't bring food into the stadium. *199 W. Commercial St., Portland, tel. 207/774–2084. No credit cards. $*

Keaney's Pancake Shoppe. This downtown storefront breakfast and lunch counter has cheery apple stencils and red-and-white oilcloth-covered tables throughout. The no-smoking room is separate. Silver-dollar pancakes and varieties as diverse as pineapple and banana are offered, along with creamed chipped beef on toast. A $2 breakfast special is served from 6 to 10:30 AM, and there is a children's menu. *617 Congress St., tel. 207/773–2785. No credit cards. $*

Port Bake House. Across the street from the docks, this is a good stopping place on your walking tour for morning muffins or light lunches of sandwiches and salads. Two varieties of homemade soup and 11 types of substantial bread are cooked daily. There is limited outdoor seating. *205 Commercial St., Portland, tel. 207/773–2217. MC, V. $*

Entertainments

Children's Museum of Maine. This clever, two-story museum has a computer room, space-shuttle cockpits that children can operate, a play firehouse with pole and rescue equipment, a

bank, and many hands-on exhibits involving insects and the environment. There is a café on its lower level. *142 Free St., Portland, tel. 207/828–1234. Admission: $5 ages 2 and up. Open June–Aug., Mon.–Sat. 10–5, Sun. noon–5; Sept.–May, Wed.–Sat. 10–5, Sun. noon–5.*

Casco Bay Harbor Cruises. More than 50 boat excursions from the docks of Portland set out daily. Three major boat companies offer a range of times and activities, including whale watches, deep-sea fishing, dinner cruises, harbor sea-lion cruises, and trips to Nova Scotia. They include **Olde Port Mariner Fleet** (Long Wharf, 170 Commercial St., Portland, tel. 207/775–0727 or 800/437–3270 outside Maine); **Casco Bay Lines** (Casco Bay Ferry Terminal, Commercial and Franklin Sts., Portland, tel. 207/774–7871), the mail, school, and supply lines for Maine islands; and **Bay View Cruises** (Fisherman's Wharf, 184 Commercial St., Portland, tel. 207/761–0496).

Palace Playland at Old Orchard Beach. This vintage amusement park is on a 7-mile-long white-sand swimming beach 25 minutes south of Portland. Its Galaxy roller coaster is tame enough for preteens, and its large, vintage Dodgem cars are in good condition. There's an 11-ride kiddieland, a 56-foot-high triple water slide, a 1910 Philadelphia Toboggan carousel with a calliope, and a 75-foot Sunwheel Ferris wheel. There's no entry fee, but rides are $1–$2 each. *1 Old Orchard St., Exit 5 off Maine Turnpike, Old Orchard Beach, tel. 207/934–2001. Admission: free; rides $1–$2 each; all-day pass $16.50, $11 kids' rides only. Open weekdays noon–10, weekends 11–10. MC, V.*

Unusual Shopping

L.L. Bean. The Freeport home of this famed Maine sporting-goods and clothing retailer is 20 minutes from Portland. Mr. Bean developed a simple scoring system for baseball that never caught on, but he remained a lifelong fan. Babe Ruth was a grateful customer of his, using Bean's outdoor gear on hunting trips. *Depot St., Freeport, tel. 207/865–4761.*

COOPERSTOWN AND THE HUDSON VALLEY
COOPERSTOWN, FISHKILL, ONEONTA, ELMIRA

Every baseball fan should make a pilgrimage to Cooperstown, New York, home of the Baseball Hall of Fame. While you're there, plan on attending several New York–Penn League games, too. This league is one of our favorites because of its history-steeped cities and stadiums.

Start with the Hudson Valley Renegades. They play in Fishkill, New York, in a brand-new stadium just 18 miles south of Hyde Park. Visit Franklin and Eleanor Roosevelt's separate homes and the "other" CIA, the Culinary Institute of America, which trains many of the country's best chefs. The Renegades play Single A ball in this small park where the bouncy spirit and funny mascots mean frequent sell-outs. The U.S. Military Academy at West Point is 20 miles southwest; the views of the Hudson River there are lovely.

From Fishkill, drive west on Interstate 84 and pick up the New York Thruway, Interstate 87, north to Albany. From here you head west on Route 20 and south on two-lane Route 166 into Cooperstown. It's a 135-mile trip. You can spend a full day in the picture-perfect town of Cooperstown, at minimum. Reserve as far in advance as possible. The town's Main Street is filled with baseball memorabilia shops. A few blocks from the Hall of Fame, you can go boating and swimming in the crystal-clear Otsego Lake. At the Cooperstown Bat Company, 2 miles north of town, you can watch baseball bats being made.

From Cooperstown, continue south on Route 166, then south on Route 28 to reach Oneonta, 23 miles away. Damaschke Field is in the same Single A league, but this endearing, primitive park has none of the flash and hoopla of new parks. The grandstand looks as it did in 1939, when it was built. The National Soccer Hall of Fame and Museum is in Oneonta.

Take Interstate 88 southwest to Route 17 north into Elmira, 105 miles from Oneonta. This home of the Pioneers is part of the independent Northeast Baseball League. The current stadium was built in 1939 by the Works Progress Administration. The lovely setting includes a dike beyond left field holding back the Chemung River. This is Mark Twain country; you can see his summer writing gazebo on the grounds of Elmira College. The National Women's Hall of Fame is 70 miles north of Elmira and worth seeing.

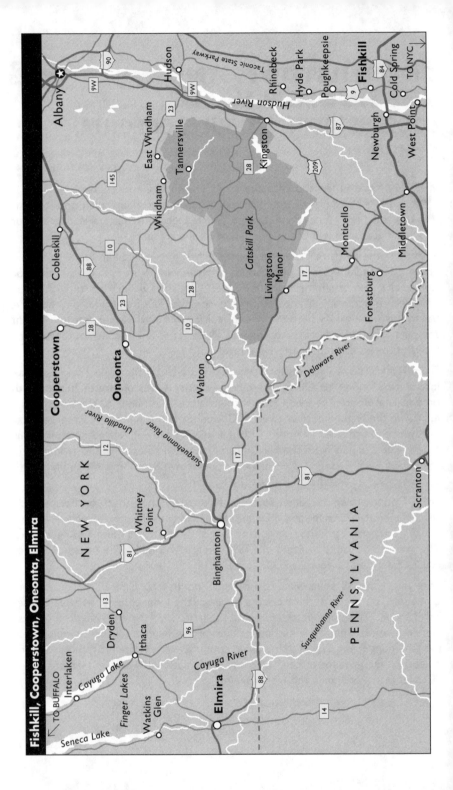

Fishkill, Cooperstown, Oneonta, Elmira

HUDSON VALLEY RENEGADES

League: New York–Penn League • **Major League Affiliation:** Tampa Bay • **Class:** Short Season A • **Stadium:** Dutchess Stadium • **Opened:** 1994 • **Capacity:** 4,320 • **Dimensions:** LF: 325, CF: 400, RF: 325 • **Surface:** grass • **Season:** mid-June–early Sept.

STADIUM LOCATION: 1090 Rte. 9D, Wappingers Falls, NY 12590

GETTING THERE: From north or south on New York State Throughway, Exit 17 in Newburgh to I–84 E, across Newburgh-Beacon Bridge to Exit 11 immediately after toll booth, Rte. 9D north 1 mi to stadium, on right. From east or west, I–84 to Exit 11, Rte. 9D north 1 mi to stadium, on right.

TICKET INFORMATION: Box 661, Fishkill, NY 12524, tel. 914/838–0094, fax 914/838–0014

PRICE RANGE: Box seats $7.50; reserved seats $6.50; general admission $4.50; $3 Mon.–Thurs. ages 2–14 and over 60

GAME TIME: Mon.–Sat. 7:15 PM, Sun. 2:35 PM; gates open 75 min before night games and 1 hr before day games.

TIPS ON SEATING: Call ahead and buy reserved or box seats early. Many games sold out in advance, especially in Aug.

SEATING FOR PEOPLE WITH DISABILITIES: On internal concourse just behind box seats in Sections 101, 105, 106, 107, and 111.

STADIUM FOOD: Food is not a highlight. The best treat is the frozen orangeade and lemonade, which you scrape out of cups ($2). Quite ordinary grilled sausages, hamburgers, and chicken are available from grills near the tents down each foul line. The park also offers soft-serve ice cream.

SMOKING POLICY: Smoking prohibited in seating area but allowed in outer concourse

PARKING: Limited to first 1,200 cars at $2. Shuttle bus service from parking lot ¼ mi from stadium.

VISITING TEAM HOTEL: Ramada Inn–West Point (1055 Union Ave., Newburgh, NY 12550, tel. 914/564–4500 or 800/228–2828)

TOURISM INFORMATION: Greater Southern Dutchess Chamber of Commerce (300 Westage Business Center, Suite 100, Fishkill, NY 12524, tel. 914/897–2067)

Hudson Valley: Dutchess Stadium

The 4,320-capacity Dutchess Stadium in Fishkill was built in what must be a record time of 71 days. Construction began on April 8, 1994, and they were still painting it on opening night, June 18. Dutchess County, New York State, and private funders shared in the $5.2 million cost. A quick walk through the park reveals Dutchess Stadium as a model of architectural simplicity. The uncovered grandstand is small, with 1,462 dark green box seats, 812 purple reserved seats above the internal concourse, and 8 skyboxes and a press box under a green roof. There are aluminum bleachers without backs past the dugouts and behind box seats on each side.

Small picnic areas with grills extend down each baseline.

Dutchess Stadium provides the fans with an attractive view of trees beyond the outfield fence. The view past the right-field foul line includes a highway, a mountain, and an elegant redbrick building that, surprisingly, is a jail. The animated scoreboard in left center is far above the New York–Penn League norm. The entranceway is an attractive outline of a baseball diamond in green, gray, and beige concrete. Parking is limited and on an unfinished surface. There are plans to improve the parking and landscape. But no amount of landscaping will make up for the inadequate access to and egress from the stadium. If you have to get out of the parking lot and on the road in a hurry, leave early.

Whatever the limitations of this stadium, they are more than overcome by the fan-friendly atmosphere provided by the Renegades. The team bonded with its community almost instantly, with sellouts more often than not in its inaugural year of 1994. The team colors—dark green and purple— are attractively reflected in the box and reserved seats. There are two mascots: Rookie, a 6-foot, 7-inch raccoon, does a great job of entertaining the fans when he is not flirting with his girlfriend, Renée.

The music and sound effects join with the animated scoreboard and energetic public address announcer to make for a loud and lively time at the ballpark. When fans want the Renegade pitcher to blaze a fastball past an opposing batter, the scoreboard flashes "Renegade Express," while the public address system blares the sounds of a roaring train, and the fans in the aluminum bleacher seats stamp their feet. A local kid leads the crowd in singing "Take Me Out to the Ballgame" at the seventh-inning stretch each game.

Where to Stay

Fishkill Holiday Inn. This three-story hotel is part of a hotel row on Route 9. The rooms are standard and newly redone. The hotel is five minutes east of the ballpark. *511 Rte. 9, Exit 13 from I-84, Fishkill 12525, tel. 914/896-6281 or 800/465-4329, fax 914/896-5410. 156 rooms. Facilities: restaurant, pool, health club. AE, D, DC, MC, V. $$*

Holiday Inn Express. This new four-floor hotel has inside corridors and a Continental breakfast bar. It is 6 miles south of Hyde Park. *341 South Rd. (Rte. 9), Poughkeepsie 12601, tel. 914/473-1151 or 800/465-4329, fax 914/473-8127. 123 rooms. Facilities: pool, coin laundry. AE, D, DC, MC, V. $$*

Super 8 Motel. The two-story Tudor-style motel, built in 1988, offers a free Continental breakfast. Children 12 and under stay free. It costs $5 to rent a crib. *528 Albany Post Rd. (Rte. 9), Hyde Park, 12538, tel. 914/229-0088 or 800/848-8888, fax 914/229-8088. 61 rooms. AE, D, MC, V. $*

Where to Eat

The American Bounty and **St. Andrew's Café—Culinary Institute of America.** These

fine restaurants are on the campus of America's "other CIA," the country's premier cooking college. Students prepare and serve your meals under the guidance of their professors. The café gives the nutrition rankings of all its foods. There are two even more formal restaurants, Caterina di Medici (Italian) and the Escoffier (French). All four have formally set tables with cloths and china. Children's appetites will be best served at the casual St. Andrew's Café, a contemporary restaurant with wood-oven pizzas, grilled specialties, and an outdoor terrace. The American Bounty focuses on regional food, particularly Hudson Valley produce and American wines. *433 Albany Post Rd., Hyde Park, tel. 914/471-6608. Reservations essential. AE, DC, MC, V. Closed 3 wks in July. $$*

Brass Anchor. Diners can watch the water at this rustic seafood restaurant on the Hudson River. There are plastic patio chairs outside and wooden, nautical-theme tables inside. Lobster and shrimp are the standouts here; the children's menu includes fried shrimp, chicken, and hamburgers. *31 River Point Rd., Poughkeepsie, tel. 914/452-3232. AE, D, DC, MC, V. Closed Nov.–Feb. $*

Hudson's Ribs & Fish. This quaint, Cape Cod–style seafood and steak restaurant specializes in live lobsters and hot popovers with strawberry butter. Children have their own menu. It's 10 miles east of the ballpark. *Rte. 9, 3 mi north of I-84, Fishkill, tel. 914/297-5002. AE, MC, V. $$*

Entertainments

Splash Down. There are raining mushrooms, water cannons, and a pirate ship named *Shipwreck Island* to climb on at this small water park, which also has a miniature golf course and an activity pool with balls. Toddlers and crawlers can use a cushioned pollywog pond. *2200 Rte. 9 N, 2 mi north of Exit 13 from I-84, Fishkill, tel. 914/896-6606. Admission: $15 adults and children 46" and taller, $11 children 34–42", $8 children under 34"; $4, 3–7 PM. Open daily 10–7. AE, MC, V.*

Sites to See

Franklin Roosevelt Birthplace and Library. Franklin Delano Roosevelt was born in Hyde Park on January 30, 1882. Children are given an informative brochure on FDR's childhood at the house they called Springwood. In "The Snuggery" next door to the family room, there is a television—the 34th RCA console television made, a gift to the president in 1939 from David Sarnoff. Fala, Roosevelt's most famous dog, is buried in the rose garden near FDR and Eleanor between the house and the museum. There are stables, an ice house, and much for children to explore on the grounds.

A June 17, 1935, letter from Harry Hopkins, director of the Works Progress Administration, spelled out the concept behind the WPA program that was responsible for the construction of many baseball stadiums in communities across America: "The real objective is to take three and a half million unemployed from the relief rolls and put them to work on useful projects." A wing of the museum is devoted to the contributions of FDR's much-admired wife, Eleanor. *519 Albany Post Rd. (Rte. 9), Hyde Park, tel. 800/337–8474. Admission: $5 adults, $4 senior citizens. Home open daily 9–5; museum daily 9–6.*

Eleanor Roosevelt National Historic Site. Val-Kill was Eleanor Roosevelt's home. Known as the First Lady of the World, Mrs. Roosevelt pressed her husband to face the plight of the disadvantaged and played a leading role in comforting Americans wounded in World War II. As chair of the United Nations Human Rights Commission years after FDR's death, Eleanor Roosevelt was the catalyst for the adoption of the Declaration of Human Rights. She used Val-Kill as a retreat for decades and moved here after FDR's death. The home was almost lost to bulldozers

in 1984 and now is run by the National Park Service. There is a 19-minute video and a 15-minute tour of the cottage. You can take a 2½-mile walking trail from FDR's Springwood to Eleanor's Val-Kill. *Rte. 9G, ½ mi north of St. Andrews Rd., Hyde Park, tel. 914/229–9115 (National Park Service). Open May–Oct., daily 9–5; Mar.–Apr. and Nov.–Dec., weekends.*

Vanderbilt Mansion. Two miles up the road from the FDR home is a riverfront product of the gilded age. This three-story Italian Renaissance–style mansion was designed for Frederick W. Vanderbilt by McKim, Meade & White. Finished in 1898 at a cost of $660,000, it looks more like a grand city library than a country home. Vanderbilt died in 1938, and FDR himself talked Vanderbilt's niece into donating the mansion to the federal government as a historic property. *Rte. 9, Hyde Park, tel. 914/229–9115. Admission: $2 adults. Open May–Oct. and Christmas wk, daily 9–5; Nov.–Apr., Thurs.–Mon. 9–5.*

United States Military Academy. Twenty miles southwest of Fishkill is the Army's famed college. You can drive or walk sections of the grounds, and guided tours are given through the visitor center in Building 2107, outside South Post's Thayer Gate. The chapels are impressive, especially the huge pipe organ in the Cadet Chapel. A free museum, in Olmstead Hall at Pershing Center, will only interest older children. Standard tours last 55 minutes. *Rte. 9 W, West Point, NY, tel. 914/938–2638. Tour admission: $5 adults, $2 ages under 13. Grounds open daily 9–4:45; tours Mon.–Sat. 10–3:30, Sun. 11–3:30.*

ONEONTA YANKEES

League: New York–Penn League • **Major League Affiliation:** New York Yankees • **Class:** Short Season A • **Stadium:** Damaschke Field • **Opened:** 1905 / 39 • **Capacity:** 4,200 • **Dimensions:** LF: 333, CF: 401, RF: 335 • **Surface:** grass • **Season:** mid-June–Aug.

STADIUM LOCATION: 95 River St., Oneonta, NY 13820

GETTING THERE: From I–88, Exit 15 toward town on NY 23W ½ mi, left as NY 23W becomes Main St., take immediate left on Grand St., which winds around and becomes Prospect St., left on Market St., and immediate left on Gas Ave. to stadium. From Cooperstown, take NY 28 south 17 mi to I–88. Take I–88 mi 5 more mi to Exit 15.

TICKET INFORMATION: 95 River St., Oneonta, NY 13820, tel. 607/432–6326, fax 607/432–1965

PRICE RANGE: $3.50 adults, $2.50 under 16, free under 6

GAME TIME: Mon.–Sat. 7:15 PM, Sun. 6 PM; gates open 75 min before game except Sun., when they open 1 hr early

TIPS ON SEATING: Everything is general admission. Sit in bleachers down left-field line, and you can talk with players in visiting team bullpen.

SEATING FOR PEOPLE WITH DISABILITIES: At field level on each side of grandstand

STADIUM FOOD: The food is a bargain. A good grilled sausage with peppers is $1.75. Ice cream bars and sodas are bargains at 75¢. Alcohol is not sold or allowed in the stadium.

SMOKING POLICY: No restrictions

PARKING: Ample free parking

VISITING TEAM HOTEL: Town House Motor Inn (318 Main St., Oneonta, NY 13820, tel. 607/432–1313)

TOURISM INFORMATION: Otsego County Chamber of Commerce (12 Carbon St., Oneonta, NY 13820, tel. 607/432–4500)

Oneonta: Damaschke Field

Damaschke Field is about baseball, not hoopla. This is baseball the way Sam Nader likes it. No mascot. No beer. No fancy logo or trendy nickname. Just baseball. "This is family entertainment. A pleasant night, as inexpensive as possible. I don't want to change the atmosphere. I don't need any skyboxes. It's not fair to the taxpayers," explains Nader, a former two-term mayor of Oneonta who brought professional baseball to town and has kept it here for 30 years. Nader's Oneonta team has been a New York Yankees farm club since 1967. Since that time, George Steinbrenner has fired dozens of Yankees managers. "Who says there's no longevity with George?" says Nader with a broad, wry smile.

If you have never fully appreciated the power of the Yankees' pinstripes, come to Oneonta. In this raw, almost primitive setting, these uniforms are awesome. You won't have to spend five minutes with a clerk, a computer, and a seating chart to figure out if you want a field box seat or a club-level seat or a reserved grandstand seat or a whatever. Just go up to the blue-and-white cinderblock ticket office, pay your $3.50, and walk through the chain-link-fence gate.

But watch out that you don't get run over by a player. The main concourse is crawling with them as the game approaches. Your kids want

autographs of future Yankees stars? No problem. Our children sat on the bench at the locker-room door, just yards from the front gate on the first-base side. They filled two New York–Penn League balls with signatures in about 15 minutes. These are players fresh out of college and some talented teenagers, all just starting their professional careers. Most won't make the big leagues, but there are future stars among them. Don Mattingly began his career here, hitting .349 in 1979 as an 18-year-old. Football star John Elway hit .318 in 1982 while debating between a career in football and one in baseball.

They have played baseball on this field since 1905. And, yes, Babe Ruth played here, too. In October of 1920, just two weeks after eight Chicago White Sox players were indicted for throwing the 1919 World Series, the mighty Babe and his All-Stars barnstormed through town. The local newspaper called on the Merchants Association and school authorities to end business early so everyone could see Ruth smack a home run. Three thousand people showed up, and Ruth knocked one over the left-center-field fence, which was about 30 feet farther back than it is today.

The small, covered blue-and-white grandstand seating 750 fans was built in 1939 and has hardly changed a bit. The fans sit on blue wooden benches without backs. A rickety navy blue wooden press box perches on the roof. A huge net protects people on the small concourse behind the grandstand. The bleachers down the first-base line are wooden benches, while the third-base bleachers are aluminum. There are tiny box-seat areas divided by metal poles down each line. Each has a sign with the owner's name—Sam Nader's is the second box on the first-base side; drop by and say "hi"—and the box holders sit on blue metal folding chairs.

The ballpark lies in the middle of a city park, where the view is first rate, with the foothills of the Catskills beyond the outfield wall. The scoreboard in center field, donated in 1977, is blessedly free of ads. It is wonderfully simple: green with just the basics, not even an inning-by-inning recap, and a clock painted with the Yankees logo. Nader—he makes all the decisions here—had the field renamed in 1968 to honor Ernest C. "Dutch" Damaschke, who served as chairman of the city's Parks and Recreation Commission for 35 years.

No beer is sold or allowed in the park. To Sam Nader, beer is inconsistent with a pleasant family night at the ballpark. Smoking, unfortunately, is allowed everywhere.

A tiny, old stadium like Damaschke Field provides the best opportunities to talk with the players. In addition to the benches near the locker rooms before the game, the best place is by the visiting-team bullpen, down the third-base line.

Where to Stay

Visiting Team Motel: Town House Motor Inn. You will have no problem walking the five minutes to the ballpark from this two-story motel. Oneonta is a college town (State University of New York at Oneonta); its Main Street is safe and filled with pedestrians through early evening. This frame hotel offers a free Continental breakfast and standard double rooms. *318 Main St., Oneonta 13822, tel. 607/432-1313, fax 607/ 432-3887. 40 rooms. AE, D, MC, V. $$*

Super 8 Motel. From this nine-year-old two-story frame motel beside the Susquehanna River you can see the ballpark a little over a mile in the distance. The motel is behind the Southside Shopping Mall. The rooms are clean and conventional. Guests receive free doughnuts and beverages in the morning, and children 12 and under stay free. *Rte. 23, Southside (Oneonta) 13820, tel.* 607/432-9505 or 800/848-8888, fax 607/ 432-9505. 60 rooms. Facilities: coin laundry. AE, D, DC, MC, V. $$

Where to Eat

Scorchy's Metropolitan Diner. You can get breakfast—including New York Yankees blueberry pancakes—anytime at this hangout on the corner of Main Street. You may sit at its 14-stool counter or in one of the well-used booths. The meat loaf is everything a blue-plate special should be. There's also fish-and-chips, homemade slaw, burgers, and kids' meals. *139 Main St., Oneonta, tel. 607/432-2154. No credit cards. $*

Brooks House of Bar-B-Q. Meat lovers drive out of their way for Brooks's pit-barbecue chicken, beef, and pork, especially its ribs. There is a children's menu, and you can eat outside or inside this casual restaurant. *Rte. 7, ¼ mi west of Exit 16 from I-88, Oneonta, tel. 607/432-1782. MC, V. $*

Neptune Diner. This 10-year-old prefabricated restaurant offers everything from pancakes to surf and turf, with an emphasis on exceptional Greek food, including gyros, souvlakia, and rice and bread puddings. It stands across the street from the Southside Mall, a mile southwest of the ballpark. *Rte. 23, Southside (Oneonta), tel. 607/432-8820. AE, MC, V. $*

Cooperstown

National Soccer Hall of Fame and Museum. Just minutes from Damaschke Field, you'll find America's oldest soccer ball, a relic from an 1863 game on Boston Common. There are World Cup uniforms, trophies, and a video room. The ultimate plan is to build a 61-acre soccer campus complete with a major stadium. The museum will become part of that complex. *5–11 Ford Ave., Oneonta, tel. 607/432-3351. Admission: $4 adults, $2 ages 5–16. Open June–mid-Sept., Mon.–Sat. 9–7, Sun. noon–7.*

Baseball Hall of Fame–Cooperstown. Baseball's mecca is 23 miles from Oneonta. It's a charming village to visit, made more so by the magnetic attraction of baseball. In 1907, the Mills Commission concluded: "The first scheme for playing baseball, according to the best evidence obtainable to date, was devised by Abner

Doubleday at Cooperstown, New York, in 1839." It's a great story, but it is not accurate. Doubleday, a distinguished Civil War soldier, was at West Point that summer, not Cooperstown. Nonetheless, the National Baseball Library and Museum was established in Cooperstown and the first greats of baseball were enshrined in the Hall of Fame on August 27, 1939. Cooperstown is a wonderful place to be with your kids and your memories as the summer ends and the baseball season comes to a close.

The **Hall of Fame Museum**'s strength is its depth of material—the "General History of Baseball" walks you right through from the earliest game of town ball to modern times. Many of the items that are part of baseball's lore are here—the bat Babe Ruth used to hit his 60th home run in 1927, Ty Cobb's 1926 glove, Walter Johnson's locker, Jackie Robinson's warm-up jacket, Hank Aaron's uniform the night he hit his 715th career home run in 1974, and on and on.

There are plenty of treats in the specialty exhibits as well, but none of these exhibits live up to their potential. We were pleased to see a special display called "Women in Baseball" and a Rockford Peaches uniform but disappointed in the exhibit's lack of depth. "It's so small," complained our eight-year-old daughter, Emily. The display on "Black Baseball" is equally disappointing.

On the third floor, the section on baseball cards has the most prized of all baseball cards—the 1909 Honus Wagner tobacco-company card. It is so rare because it was recalled when Wagner objected to being associated with a tobacco product.

In the library wing sits famed sports writer Grantland Rice's typewriter, with a date and a simple byline typed on an otherwise empty page from the day he retired. "Baseball at the Movies" is also in the library wing. Here you can see Geena Davis's Rockford Peaches uniform from *A League of Their Own* and Robert Redford's New York Knights uniform from *The Natural*, as well as clips from a number of other baseball movies.

The Hall of Fame gallery isn't flashy, but it is impressive. There are two rows of bronze plaques—228 in all—in order of induction date,

hung on the natural wood-paneled walls of a rectangular room with alcoves marked by marble pillars. A glass-roofed rotunda is at one end, with nine alcoves that will not begin to be filled until the year 2000. Visitors are quiet as they read the career capsules of the players, umpires, managers, and baseball executives who have been voted into the hall since 1936. There is a discreet note that the facts described on the plaques are as they were known at the time the plaques were made, so you may find some exaggerations as you walk along these hallowed walls.

If your schedule permits, start your visit after dinner. If you buy your ticket after 7 PM, it is good for the next day as well. Watch the movie, find your favorite players' plaques, and begin the tour of the general history exhibit. Return the next day for the specialty exhibits.

Before arriving, you might want to join the Friends of the Hall of Fame for $25 and receive an individual season pass to the museum, a T-shirt, a yearbook, and a quarterly newsletter. You can also buy combination tickets with the nearby Farmers' and Fenimore House museums. *25 Main St., Box 590, Cooperstown 13326, tel. 607/547–7200. Admission: $9.50 adults, $8 senior citizens, $4 ages 7–12. Open early May–late Sept., daily 9–9; Oct.–Apr., daily 9–5. AE, D, MC, V.*

Doubleday Field. Before you become immersed in the memorabilia shops that line both sides of Cooperstown's Main Street, visit Doubleday Field, just down the street from the Hall of Fame. Legend has it that this is where the mythical Doubleday game was played. The ballpark was rebuilt for the 100th anniversary in 1939 with funds from WPA. The entrance is picture-perfect, with a redbrick facade and white wooden trim, a fine setting for the obligatory family-vacation photo. The capacity of the old brick and wood grandstand has been expanded with aluminum bleachers down each baseline to accommodate the annual July Hall of Fame game between two major-league teams. Major leaguers must not enjoy pitching here, as left field is only 296 feet from home. *Village of Cooperstown, 22 Main St., Box 346, Cooperstown, tel. 607/547–2411.*

Where to Stay

Try to make your reservations in February or March for your summer visit. The motels in this small town (2,200 people) can fit you in with two to three weeks' notice in summer, but you'll pay top price. Motels are expensive during the summer—$100 and up for a double—and the rates drop dramatically in the off-seasons. The Hall of Fame Weekend (end of July–beginning of August) boosts rates even higher. To save money, call the county Chamber of Commerce (tel. 607/432–4500) early, get its travel guide, and book one of the many guest houses.

Tunnicliffe Inn. Half a block from the Hall of Fame is this three-story brick, Federal-style building, which allows children to use sleeping bags in their parents' room. Parking is limited to seven vehicles in the rear, so nearby overflow lots are used. *34–36 Pioneer St., Cooperstown 13326, tel. 607/547–9611. 17 rooms. Facilities: 2 restaurants. AE, D, MC, V. $$*

Cooperstown Best Western Inn. This new motel, behind a McDonald's and overlooking a field and hills, offers guests a free Continental breakfast and clean, well-lit rooms. It is 3 miles southwest of town. Ask for a room facing east, overlooking the pretty farmland. The clerks wear baseball jerseys and sell discount combination passes to the Hall of Fame, the Farmer's Museum, and the Fenimore House. *Rte. 28, Cooperstown 13326, tel. 607/547–9439 or 800/528–1234, fax 607/547–7082. 62 rooms. Facilities: indoor pool, game room, coin laundry. AE, D, DC, MC, V. $$*

The Lake Front Motel. This late-1950s-era motel is on the waterfront, with some rooms overlooking Otsego Lake. The two-story motel is 1½ blocks from the Hall of Fame and offers free parking. There is lake swimming at the adjacent public beach. *10 Fair St., Cooperstown 13326, tel. 607/547–9511. 44 rooms. Facilities: restaurant. MC, V. $$*

Hotel Otsego. Built in 1909, this five-story hotel is the grande dame of the lake, with a sweeping view from its veranda. It looks like a small college, with an imposing, white-columned entry. Half of the rooms, which are decorated handsomely, have a lake view. A full breakfast and dinner are included. Parking is free. *60 Lake St.,*
Cooperstown 13326, tel. 607/547–9931 or 800/348–6222, fax 607/547–9675. 137 rooms. Facilities: restaurant, pool. AE, MC, V. $$$

The Cooper Inn. The original part of the two-story brick Georgian mansion, built in 1812, has four guest rooms and three sitting parlors. A wing built in 1936 contains five two-bedroom suites, and there is a manicured, shaded lawn. The inn is two blocks from the Hall of Fame. Guests have access to the golf, tennis, and swimming pool at the affiliated Hotel Otsego. Continental breakfast is served in the breakfast room of the main house. *Main and Chestnut Sts., Cooperstown 13326, tel. 607/547–2567 or 800/348–6222, fax 607/547–1271. 15 rooms. Facilities: breakfast room. AE, MC, V. $$$*

Where to Eat

TJ's Place. The service is speedy, but your children may be distracted by the sports videos being screened while you eat. This is a combination restaurant and baseball memorabilia and merchandise store. It offers a wide selection of baseball-motif sandwiches, plus Italian entrées, salads, and soups. The portions and drinks are huge. *124 Main St., Cooperstown, tel. 607/547–4040. AE, D, DC, MC, V. $*

Doubleday Cafe. At this upscale diner on Main Street the specials are posted on a chalkboard. Its basics are hamburgers, sandwiches, and chicken, plus Mexican food on the weekends. The breakfast muffins are particularly good. *93 Main St., Cooperstown, tel. 607/547–5468. D, MC, V. $*

Tunnicliffe Tap Room. Patrons are allowed to carve their names into the wooden tables of this vintage restaurant; you can even find Mickey Mantle's. It serves sandwiches, burgers, steaks, and pasta dishes in a casual setting downstairs. Children under 10 eat for $3.95, including a beverage. More formal dining is offered upstairs ($$). *34 Pioneer St., Cooperstown, tel. 607/547–9611. AE, D, MC, V. $*

Entertainments

Classic Boat Tours. You can tour the crystal-clear Otsego Lake on a classic mahogany launch. The one-hour trip is a good way to learn about James Fenimore Cooper and this amazing lake.

Fair St. Dock, Cooperstown, tel. 607/547–5295. Admission: $8.50 adults, $5 ages 3–12. Runs mid-May–mid-Oct., daily at 10, 11, 1, 2, 3, 4, 6. MC, V.

The Farmer's Museum and Town Ball. You can time-travel in this living-history museum, with its restored buildings where craftspeople blow glass, shoe horses, and weave baskets. A combination ticket is available with the Baseball Hall of Fame and Fenimore House Museum. The town trolley stops here. If your schedule permits, time your visit to the Farmer's Museum to allow you to take in a game of Town Ball, demonstrated by the Leatherstocking Base Ball Club in conjunction with the museum. They play an early 1800s game by rules with a distinctly sandlot feel. Play is with a soft leather ball and the players do not have gloves. *Lake Rd., Cooperstown, tel. 607/547–1400. Admission: $9 adults, $4 ages 7–12. Open June–Labor Day, daily 9–5; May and Sept.–Oct., daily 10–4; Apr. and Nov., Tues.–Sun. 10–4; Dec., weekends 10–4.*

Unusual Shopping

Cooperstown's Main Street. Browse through the excellent store in the Hall of Fame Museum and a few other stores before you buy. Our impression is that the baseball stores here are growing rapidly and improving their products.

If your time is limited, try a few of the following, recognizing that this is not a definitive list of quality stores. Our favorite is **Gallery 53 Artworks** (118 Main St., Cooperstown, 13326, tel. 607/547–5655), dedicated to original baseball art. We particularly like **National Pastime** (81 Main St., tel. 607/547–2524 or 800/462–9391) and **Mickey's Place** (74 Main St., tel. 607/547–5775 or 800/528–5775). For cards, we like **Pioneer Sports Cards** (106 Main St., tel. 607/547–2323) and **Baseball Nostalgia** (Doubleday Plaza, next to Doubleday Field, tel. 607/547–6051). The **Doubleday Batting Range** (Doubleday Court, tel. 607/547–5168) also adjoins the Field. Take a few swings in the batting cage, then send home a phony newspaper for $5 telling how you were a big hit in Cooperstown. The **American Baseball Archives** (99 Main St., tel. 607/547–1273) features a baseball wax museum and a superb collection of Mickey Mantle memorabilia. The virtual-reality exhibit lets you feel the impact of a Roger Clemens fastball. *Admission: $5.95 adults, $2.95 ages under 13, $3.95 senior citizens. Open Memorial Day–Labor Day, daily 9–9. AE, D, MC, V.*

Cooperstown Bat Company. The retail store is in Cooperstown, but you should go to the factory just 2 miles north of town. Here pieces of white ashwood are shaved into beautiful bats. Extraordinary care goes into applying the gorgeous color decals that go on the Cooperstown Bat Company's modern-era bats. Many of the greatest names in baseball have sat in this factory and signed bats for hours at a time. There are items available in everyone's price range. *Retail store: 66 Main St., Box 41, Cooperstown, tel. 607/547–1090. Factory: Rte. 28, Fly Creek, tel. 607/547–2415. Open Apr.–Oct., Mon.–Sat. 11–7 (retail), 8:30–5 (factory); Nov.–March weekdays 9–5. AE, MC, D, V.*

Elmira Pioneers

League: Northeast Baseball League • **Major League Affiliation:** None • **Class:** Independent • **Stadium:** Dunn Field • **Opened:** 1939 • **Capacity:** 4,200 • **Dimensions:** LF: 386, CF: 325, RF 546 • **Surface:** grass • **Season:** June–Aug.

Stadium Location: Luce St., Elmira, NY 14904

Getting There: From Rte. 17, Church St. exit (NY 352W), left on Judson St. and right on Water St. ½ mi (past Huck Finn Little League ballpark); left on Madison St., cross river, left on Maple Ave., go ½ mi left on Luce St. to stadium. From Rte. 14 N, take a right on Miller St., then a left on Maple Ave. and a right onto Luce St.

Ticket Information: Box 238, Elmira, NY 14902, tel. 607/732–2228, fax 607/732–1985

Price Range: Box seats $5; reserved seats $4; general admission $3 adults, $2 children and senior citizens, under 6 free.

GAME TIME: Mon.–Sat. 7 PM, Sun. 5 PM; gates open 1 hr before game.

TIPS ON SEATING: Among least expensive seats in professional baseball; some general admission seats have obstructed views. Buy a reserved seat; there are only 320 box seats, so the reserved seats are quite close.

SEATING FOR PEOPLE WITH DISABILITIES: Behind box seats on walking concourse

STADIUM FOOD: The prices are low, and juices and pretzels (50¢) are available for healthy snacks. There are also $1.25 hot dogs, Italian sausage sandwiches for $2.50, chicken breast sandwiches for $2, and hamburgers for $1.75. Burgers, chicken and sausages are available from the grill on the first-base side. This is ordinary baseball fare, but cheaper. There's also soft ice cream, nachos, popcorn, and cookies.

SMOKING POLICY: Smoking permitted throughout ballpark

PARKING: Ample free parking

VISITING TEAM HOTEL: Holiday Inn (760 E. Water St., Elmira, NY 14901, tel. 607/734–4211 or 800/465–4329)

TOURISM INFORMATION: Chemung County Chamber of Commerce (215 E. Church St., Elmira, NY 14901, tel. 607/734–5137 or 800/627–5892)

Elmira: Dunn Field

They have been playing professional baseball in Elmira for a very long time. It started with the Elmira Babies in 1888 and continues today with the Pioneers, a team in one of the new independent leagues, the Northeast Baseball League. Dunn Field was built in 1939 with home plate not far from where it was in Monument Park, a wooden grandstand stadium that had burned the previous year.

We talked with retired New York State judge Dan Donahoe, who has been watching baseball in Elmira for 70 years. He told us why baseball has been such an important part of his life: "Baseball is how I kept my sanity. No matter how bad a day I had in the courtroom, I left my troubles at the turnstile." Judge Donahoe was in Dunn Field in the inaugural year of 1939 to see a barnstorming game between teams led by Babe Ruth and Lou Gehrig. The Babe clobbered one that hit the tall white house over the right-field wall. The judge was here when future major-league manager Don Zimmer, then a .273 hitter for the Pioneers, was married on the field. From the Baltimore Orioles years here with a Double AA team in the Eastern League in the 1960s, Judge Donahoe says he watched Earl Weaver perfect his habit of turning his hat around so he could get just a little closer to the umpire's face in a heated argument. And he remembers a young kid and future Hall of

Famer who was bat boy in the late 1960s when his father, Cal Ripken, Sr., managed the team.

Dunn Field was built with federal Works Progress Administration (WPA) money. The grand yellow-brick, three-story entrance has a distinctive 1930s style. Before you go inside, look at the concrete pedestal carefully ringed with flowers in front of the stadium. You might notice that something is missing. It's the bronze bust of Edward Joseph Dunn, the local industrialist who donated the land for the stadium. Someone stole it one night after a game in the late 1980s. The plaque explaining his contribution is also missing.

If you sit anywhere other than in the general admission seats, you are probably sitting on a chair paid for by President Franklin Roosevelt's government. These wooden seats were repainted and repaired for the 1996 season. Six rows of new plastic blue reserved seats were added in 1996 behind the box seats. The simple covered grandstand sits between the dugouts.

When major-league baseball demanded that the minor-league stadiums be improved, the focus was on improving conditions for the players. In cities that could not afford a complete upgrade or a new stadium, the tradeoff was clear. There is no place in minor-league baseball where the consequences are more pronounced than at Dunn Field. When the team was a Florida Marlins franchise in the New York–Penn League, brand-new clubhouses with attractive

Marlins-green roofs were built attached to the dugouts at each side of the grandstand. The seats the fans sit in were falling apart. The New York–Penn League team left for a new stadium in Lowell, Massachusetts, after the 1995 season.

The attractive view from the grandstand spans a lovely collection of white and gray houses with gray and green roofs just beyond the right-field wall. The tallest house is the one Ruth is said to have hit. The scoreboard is in center field surrounded by tall trees. An embankment beyond the left-field fence serves as a dike to hold back the floods from the Chemung River just behind it. Hurricane Agnes in 1972 flooded the ballpark and contributed to Elmira's losing its Double AA Eastern League team. High hills finish this appealing scene. We saw several clusters of fans standing on the dike, which provides an excellent vantage point for games.

Where to Stay

Visiting Team Hotel: Holiday Inn–Riverview. The rooms and hallways are large in this quiet, two-floor motel beside the Chemung River. It is a mile from downtown. *760 E. Water St., Elmira 14901, tel. 607/734–4211 or 800/465–4329, fax 607/734–3549. 150 rooms. Facilities: restaurant, indoor pool, outdoor pool. AE, D, DC, MC, V. $$*

Econo Lodge. Its proximity to chain restaurants and shops is the attraction at this two-story chain motel. Arnot Mall and Consumer's Square shopping center, which includes a 24-hour supermarket, are within walking distance. The rooms are standard size, with refrigerators and microwave ovens in each. Guests receive free movies and a free Continental breakfast. *1339 Rte. 64, Exit 51 from Rte. 17, Elmira, tel. 607/739–2000 or 800/424–6423, fax 607/739–3552. 48 rooms. Facilities: in-room refrigerators and microwave ovens, coin laundry. AE, D, DC, MC, V. $*

Where to Eat

Moretti's Restaurant. The same family has owned this large Italian restaurant for the past 85 years, and its walls are filled with family pictures and photos of the softball teams it has sponsored. Dress here ranges from shorts to business suits. Filet mignon is the specialty, and all types of veal, pasta, and chicken dishes are served. The children's menu includes very good ravioli with a salad, chicken fingers, and spaghetti. The restaurant is two blocks east of Elmira College and 5 miles north of the ballpark. *800 Hatch St., Elmira, tel. 607/734–1535. AE, D, MC, V. No lunch. $$*

Manos Diner. Superlative rice pudding and souvlakia salads are the biggest draws at this Greek-owned restaurant and pizza parlor–lounge, which is 8 miles north of the ballpark. Its pastries and bread are homemade. Children can order small portions of gyros, among other offerings. *118 College Ave., Elmira, tel. 607/733–2366. AE, MC, V. $*

Maple Lawn Dairy Family Restaurant. This casual, place-mats-on-wood-table restaurant grew from an ice cream store operated by a dairy. Homemade ice cream remains its biggest attraction, with flavors such as praline cashew, almond joy, and white chocolate cherry. Every Friday, there's a haddock fry. The children's menu includes ham, spaghetti, and grilled cheese sandwiches. The restaurant is just outside the city limits, 4½ miles west of the ballpark. *3162 Lower Maple Ave., Elmira, tel. 607/733–0519. No credit cards. $*

Entertainments

Trolley Tour. A motorized trolley takes passengers in summer on a 90-minute tour of Chemung County, emphasizing the area's ties to Mark Twain. (Twain had a local home, and is buried in town.) The reproduction trolleys depart from the Chamber of Commerce building, where free parking is available in the rear. *215 E. Church St., Elmira, tel. 607/734–5137 or 800/627–5892. Admission: $2 adults, ages under 13 free with adult. Runs end of June–Labor Day, Tues.–Sat. at 10, 11:30, 1, and 2:30.*

National Soaring Museum. The air currents around Elmira are optimal for gliding, and contests have been held on Harris Hill since 1930. This museum teaches you about early forms of aircraft and their pilots. Children particularly like climbing into a hydraulically equipped sailplane cockpit and controlling its movements. On the computer simulator, you can see if you're capable of landing a plane. You can also arrange a sailplane ride for a fee. *Harris Hill, 51 Soaring Hill*

Dr., Elmira, tel. 607/734–3128. Admission: $3 adults, $2 ages 7–18. Open daily 10–5.

Sites to See

Mark Twain Exhibit in Hamilton Hall. Elmira College has assembled photographs of Samuel Clemens and his family, as well as artifacts from their local home and Quarry Farm. Clemens's father-in-law, Jervis Langdon, helped found the college. There's a short video. Clemens is buried at a well-marked grave in **Woodlawn Cemetery** (Walnut St.) that has a 12-foot MARK TWAIN stone. *Washington and College Aves., Elmira, tel. 607/735–1941. Admission: donations. Open mid-June–early Sept., Mon.–Sat. 9–4, Sun. 11–4.*

Mark Twain Study. Visitors can walk into the remarkable octagonal gazebo, now on the grounds of Elmira College, where Twain wrote *The Adventures of Huckleberry Finn,* the first half of *The Adventures of Tom Sawyer,* and much of his other best work. Small but magical, it was built for him by his sister-in-law to resemble a Mississippi riverboat pilothouse. It originally stood on East Hill at Quarry Farm, his family's summer home in Elmira, which now holds the Elmira College Center for Mark Twain Studies. A musical dramatizing Twain's life is performed throughout the summer in the **Murray Center Domes** (tel. 800/395–6275). *N. Main St., Elmira, tel. 607/735–1941. Admission: donations. Open mid-June–early Sept., Mon.–Sat. 9–4, Sun. 11–4.*

National Women's Hall of Fame. Seventy miles north of Elmira is Seneca Falls, the birthplace of women's rights. Elizabeth Cady Stanton, leader of the first Women's Rights Convention, lived here. The hall contains photographs and descriptions of 108 women who have won induction because of the greatness of their achievements. *76 Fall St., Seneca Falls, tel. 315/568–8060. Admission: donations. Open May–Sept., Mon.–Sat. 9:30–5, Sun. noon–4; Oct.–Apr., Wed.–Sat. 10–4.*

CHAUTAUQUA, BUFFALO   **13**
WINGS, AND NIAGARA FALLS
BUFFALO, ST. CATHARINES, JAMESTOWN

Western New York has serious baseball amidst its loganberry fields, Lake Chautauqua, and the wondrous natural beauty of Niagara Falls and Lakes Ontario and Erie. In Jamestown, on Route 17, you'll find another of the small stadiums in the New York–Penn League. Less than a mile from the park is the Roger Tory Peterson Institute, a celebration of birds. The Chautauqua Institution, 18 miles northwest, has a full schedule of cultural events, and there are boat rides on the lake on a historic paddle wheeler. Twenty miles from Jamestown is a century-old amusement park that overlooks Lake Chautauqua.

Head north on scenic Route 62 for 51 miles to Buffalo, where you can go directly downtown to look at the nation's premier minor-league park. In hopes of getting a major-league team, Buffalo built a serious stadium with a view of the city skyline. The city didn't get a major-league team, but fans enjoy many of the amenities, such as some of the best food in baseball, anyway. The Bisons, a Triple AAA team, part of the American Association, are affiliated with the Cleveland Indians. The city has a venerable zoo and a children's science center.

Driving north on Interstate 190 for 30 miles, you'll enter the Niagara Falls park system, a beautiful emerald necklace of parkways and roadside attractions. Don a plastic poncho and see the American and Canadian Falls from the deck of the *Maid of the Mist,* and consider riding across Niagara Gorge on a cable car. The beauty of the falls and the adjacent parks is memorable; the commercialism is less apparent than we expected.

You can cross into Canada at the Rainbow Bridge and continue on Queen Elizabeth Way to St. Catharines, Ontario, where the Stompers baseball team is part of the New York–Penn League. Its unassuming stadium is part of a community park. It has added a children's play area and a new purple-masked mascot. Old Port Dalhousie on Lake Ontario has a scenic park, with a 5-cent carousel. St. Catharines also has a thriving downtown farmers' market.

BUFFALO BISONS

League: American Association • **Major League Affiliation:** Cleveland Indians • **Class:** AAA • **Stadium:** North AmeriCare Park • **Opened:** 1988 • **Capacity:** 20,900 • **Dimensions:** LF: 325, CF: 404, RF: 325 • **Surface:** grass • **Season:** Apr.–Labor Day

STADIUM LOCATION: 275 Washington St., Buffalo, NY 14203

GETTING THERE: From I–190, Elm St. exit, left on Swan St. For information about public transit, call Niagara Frontier Transportation Authority (tel. 716/855–7300).

TICKET INFORMATION: Box 450, Buffalo, NY 14205-0450, tel. 716/846–2000 or 800/283–0114, fax 716/852–6530

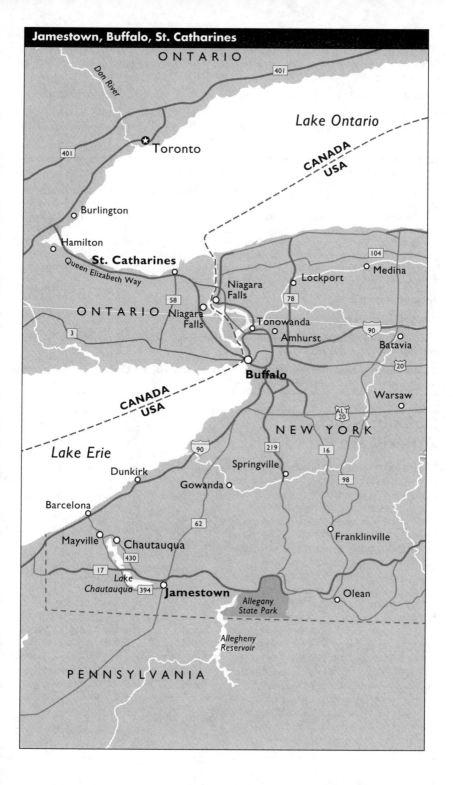

ONTARIO

401

Don River

Lake Ontario

401

★ Toronto

CANADA
USA

Burlington

Hamilton

104

St. Catharines

Medina

Queen Elizabeth Way

Niagara
Falls

Lockport

58

78

ONTARIO

Niagara
Falls

Tonowanda

90

3

Amhurst

Batavia

20

Buffalo

Warsaw

CANADA
USA

ALT
20

NEW YORK

Lake Erie

90

219

16

Dunkirk

Springville

98

Gowanda

Barcelona

62

Mayville

Chautauqua

Franklinville

430

17

Lake
Chautauqua

394

Jamestown

Allegany
State Park

Olean

Allegheny
Reservoir

PENNSYLVANIA

PRICE RANGE: Field- and club-level special reserved seats $8.25; field-and club-level reserved seats $6.75; bleacher seats $4.25 adults, $3.25 under 15 and senior citizens

GAME TIME: Mon.–Thurs. 7:05 PM, Fri. 7:35 PM, Sun. 2:05 PM; gates open 1 hr before game.

TIPS ON SEATING: Best seats taken by season ticket holders. Call well in advance and order reserved seats. Top rows of last two sections down left-field line—sections 123 and 125—are no-alcohol family sections.

SEATING FOR PEOPLE WITH DISABILITIES: On walking concourse level just above special reserved seating area in Sections 100–114, 123, and 125; parking spaces in Exchange St. parking lot.

STADIUM FOOD: The food is outstanding. The star: roast beef on weck, fragrant meat on a chewy salt-topped roll ($3.75). Try Buffalo chicken wings, plus celery (or carrots) and bleu cheese. The veggies are great for kids. There are bins of fresh-roasted peanuts, good coleslaw at the **Sub Shop,** and tossed salads. Kids may like the (fried) onion chips, but avoid the greasy fried bologna sandwich. The **Kid's Corner** at the Oak Street exit serves loganberry juice, milk, and popcorn for 75¢. Kid's pizza, hot dogs, grilled cheese, and pb&j sandwiches are $1.25 each. Italian ices are $1.50; a good custard cone is $2. Upstairs, **Pettibone's Restaurant** has toasted ravioli ($4.75), a kid's menu and 40 no-smoking seats by the windows. It's open weekdays from 11:30 to 3 and opens at 4 on game days.

SMOKING POLICY: Smoking prohibited in seating areas

PARKING: Ample parking in private downtown lots, $4

VISITING TEAM HOTEL: Buffalo Downtown Holiday Inn (620 Delaware Ave., Buffalo, NY 14202, tel. 716/886–2121 or 800/465–4329)

TOURISM INFORMATION: Greater Buffalo Convention and Visitors Bureau (107 Delaware Ave., Buffalo, NY 14202, tel. 716/852–0511 or 800/283–3256)

Buffalo: North AmeriCare Park

Buffalo's ballpark—built with major-league ambitions—is the nation's premier minor-league stadium. The city longed for major-league baseball and, to overcome its cold spring climate, made major investments. The city hired the premier baseball-stadium architects—HOK Sport of Kansas City—and spent nearly $42 million. Buffalo built the bottom half of a modern major-league stadium—a street level complete with 17 concession booths, souvenir shops, and modern facilities with a club level above. Had Buffalo been successful in getting a major-league team, an upper deck would have been added where the bluish green roof is today. As it is, the club-level seats give the Buffalo ballpark a second level that is rare in minor-league baseball. Buffalo has a major-league 40- by 50-foot scoreboard in straightaway center field. The outfield fence was reconfigured for the 1996 season to resemble the parent club Cleveland's Jacobs Field and to produce more home runs.

Best of all, the city built the stadium right downtown, a daring move in the late 1980s. The feel from the street level is major league all the way. Past the attractive street-level arches at the Swan Street entrance, inside the stadium, you can see some of the city's skyline, including the top of the historic Post Office building over third base.

Beyond the right-field fence, there is an ordinary parking garage. Beyond left field is a huge net to stop balls from hitting cars on the ramp to the interstate highway. The seats in right field are benches without backs.

Unfortunately, the name of this fine stadium is for sale. Whatever happened to the dignified practice of naming a stadium after a leading citizen, a baseball person, or as a war memorial? After a short period in 1995 as the Downtown Ballpark in Buffalo, it was renamed North AmeriCare Park. Who knows what it will be called when you go.

Bison is an obvious nickname for a city named Buffalo. The baseball-green outfield walls have the outfield dimensions outlined with a white bison.

The Bisons have one of baseball's best mascots— Buster T. Bison. Buster has a little cousin named Chip. And these aren't the only strange creatures that inhabit this stadium. We saw the Earl of Bud dancing on the dugout in the fourth inning. Other vendors here are dressed as Conehead and Zorro.

A Buffalo-baseball Hall of Fame stands on the first-base side of the concourse. Two players sign autographs near it for about 20 minutes starting an hour before every game. There are fireworks every Friday night. Every Sunday at the park is Kid's Day. Below the right-field bleachers a children's playground and picnic area provide a field-level view of the game.

Other Baseball Sites

War Memorial Stadium. Buffalo's War Memorial Stadium—built for football and track and field in 1936–37 with Works Progress Administration (WPA) funds—was the site of that spectacular closing scene when the clinching home run explodes off the lights in *The Natural*, Robert Redford's 1984 bouquet to baseball. The stadium was not used for baseball until 1961. Nicknamed the Rockpile, the stadium deteriorated along with the neighborhood in the 1960s. Summer riots in 1967 led to a curfew that forced the Bisons to play night games in Niagara Falls. A gang invaded the clubhouse during batting practice in 1969. Buffalo lost its Triple A franchise in 1970. The American Football League Buffalo Bills played here from 1960 to 1972. Baseball returned in 1979 and gained popularity after the team was purchased by Rich Products in 1983.

The site looks like a modern-day Stonehenge, as the Buffalo Urban Renewal Agency saved two massive concrete corner structures in its redevelopment of the stadium complex into a community center. At the top of the structures, two sculpted bison face off. Today, the complex includes a small baseball field, a football field, and other community facilities. To see the remains of War Memorial Stadium, go north on Main Street from the downtown. Take a right on Best Street to Jefferson Street. Home plate was near Dodge Street, with right field at Best Street. The monument at Best and Jefferson was behind center field.

Where to Stay

Downtown Buffalo has very few hotels; this is a city where you'll need reservations. If you don't have them, you'll stay out by the airport, a 30-minute drive from the ballpark.

Visiting Team Motel: Holiday Inn–Downtown. This busy eight-story hotel is only five minutes from the park and offers guests a free full breakfast. The rooms are on the small side, but the upper floors have a nice view of the city. It is recessed from the busy street it faces and is next door to a drugstore. *620 Delaware Ave., Buffalo 14202, tel. 716/886–2121 or 800/465-4329, fax 716/886–7942. 168 rooms. Facilities: restaurant, pool, coin laundry. AE, D, DC, MC, V. $$*

Others to consider downtown: The **Radisson Suite Hotel** (601 Main St., Buffalo 14203, tel. 716/854–5500, $$$); **Buffalo Hilton** (120 Church St., Buffalo 14202, tel. 716/845–5100, $$); **Best Western Inn-Downtown** (510 Delaware Ave., Buffalo 14202, tel. 716/886–8333, $$).

Where to Eat

Parkside Candy. This faded beauty is a dimly lit Art Deco relic, with unforgettable sundaes (known here as frappés) and homemade chocolates. The molasses paddles (50¢), sponge candy, and bittersweet hot fudge are stars. Desserts are the attraction, but there are also sandwiches. The interior has secluded wooden booths around the perimeter, stained glass, and torch lamps that add up to the genuine atmosphere of a 1930s-era soda parlor. *3208 Main St., Buffalo, tel. 716/833–7540. No credit cards. $*

Ted's Red Hots. Children may find Ted's hot sauce too sharp, but they'll be happy with the charcoal-grilled hot dogs and crisp onion rings. Red hots (thin, red-colored hot dogs with a very thin casing) are a regional specialty, and they're served here with another Buffalo standby, loganberry juice. There are seven Ted's locations in the area; this site has indoor booths and outdoor seating in good weather. *2312 Sheridan Dr., Tonawanda (north Buffalo), tel. 716/836–8986. No credit cards. $*

Eckl's Beef and Weck. Near Rich Stadium, home of the Buffalo Bills football team, it is an authentic place to eat Buffalo's best sandwich, made of fragrant sliced beef piled on a chewy salt roll. *4936 Ellicott Rd., Orchard Park (southeast Buffalo), tel. 716/662–2262. No credit cards. $*

Entertainments

Buffalo Zoo. This zoo is aging, but the various animal compounds are compact, which makes it easy to walk. Kids and adults can get a thrill from the white tiger, the gorilla rain forest, and the children's zoo. There are carousel, train, and camel rides for $2 each. The Zootique gift shop has terrific and cheap animal masks. Free, very professional magic shows are given indoors from July to Labor Day at 1 and 3 PM. A restaurant is on the grounds, and strollers can be rented for $2. Parking is $3. *300 Parkside Ave., Buffalo, tel. 716/837–3900. Admission: $6 adults, $3 ages 4–16 and senior citizens. Open Memorial Day–Labor Day, daily 10–5:30; Labor Day–Memorial Day, daily 10–4:30. MC, V.*

Buffalo Museum of Science. This towering turn-of-the-century building has several sections that appeal to children, featuring a climbing wall and an inventive Pretend Play area with a beaver lodge, two boats, nature puppets, and a dinosaur nest. There are more traditional exhibits behind glass, including an impressive collection of stuffed animals, including several who once lived in the Buffalo Zoo. *1020 Humboldt Pkwy., Buffalo, tel. 716/896–5200. Admission: $5.25 adults, $3.25 ages 2–18, $12.50 family (except during special exhibits). Open Tues.–Sun. 10–5. AE, MC, V.*

Sites to See

Buffalo and Erie County Historical Society. It's the only remaining building from the 1901 Pan-American Exposition. It was then the New York State Building. Now a statue of Lincoln sits behind the building overlooking a small lake in Delaware Park. Its exhibits tell the economic and social history of the Buffalo region. *25 Nottingham Ct., Buffalo, tel. 716/873–9644. Admission: $3.50 adults, $1.50 ages 7–15. Open Tues.–Sat. 10–5, Sun. noon–5. MC, V.*

McKinley Assassination Site. The 1901 Exposition is remembered as the site of the shooting on September 6, 1901, of President William McKinley, who had come to speak at the Exposition. The exact site where McKinley was assassinated—the Exposition's Temple of Music—is marked only with a small plaque set into a rock in a median strip in a residential neighborhood. *Fordham Dr., not far from Lincoln Pkwy., 3 blocks north of Historical Society, Buffalo.*

Niagara Square. A more appropriate memorial to President McKinley—a large obelisk—stands in Niagara Square in the downtown just blocks from the new ballpark. The magnificent Art Deco City Hall dominates one side of the square, flanked by statues of the two Buffalo residents who became president—Millard Fillmore and Grover Cleveland. *Bordered by Jeroe, Perkins, Nasara, and Court Sts.*

Theodore Roosevelt Inaugural National Historic Site. If you're staying at the hotel used by the visiting baseball teams, you'll notice the handsome Greek Revival mansion across the street. The longtime home of a prominent Buffalo family, the Wilcox Mansion was saved from bulldozers because Theodore Roosevelt took the oath of office here. He became the 26th president of the United States on September 14, 1901, just hours after President McKinley died. *641 Delaware Ave., Buffalo, tel. 716/884–0095. Admission: $3 adults, $1 ages 6–12, $6.50 family. Open weekdays 9–5, weekends noon–5.*

St. Catharines Stompers

League: New York–Penn League • **Major League Affiliation:** Toronto Blue Jays • **Class:** Short Season A • **Stadium:** Community Park • **Opened:** 1987 • **Capacity:** 2,500 • **Dimensions:** LF: 320, CF: 400, RF: 320 • **Surface:** grass • **Season:** mid-June–Aug.

STADIUM LOCATION: 2 Seymour Ave., St. Catharines, Ontario L2P 1P3

TEAM WEB SITE: http://vaxxine.com/stompers

GETTING THERE: From east (Niagara Falls/Buffalo), Queen Elizabeth Expwy to Glendale exit, left on Glendale, right on Merritt St., and right on Seymour Ave. From west (Toronto/Hamilton), Queen Elizabeth Expwy to 406 cutoff, Hwy. 406 to Glendale Ave. ramp, left at Glendale Ave, left on Merritt St. and right on Seymour Ave.

TICKET INFORMATION: 426 Merritt St., St. Catharines, Ontario L2P 1P3, tel. 905/641–5297, fax 905/641–3007

PRICE RANGE: Reserved chairs $7.50 adults, $6.50 children and senior citizens; reserved bench with backs $6 adults, $5 children and senior citizens; general admission $5 adults, $4 children and senior citizens; family pack $25 (2 adults, 2 children, 4 hot dogs, 4 soft drinks, 1 large bag popcorn)

GAME TIME: Mon.–Sat. 7:05 PM, Sun. 2:05 PM

TIPS ON SEATING: Reserved chairs are behind 8-foot-high chain link fence. View from general admission seats at top of grandstand is better, but benches have no backs. 3 rows of reserved aluminum benches behind reserved chairs have backs. Setting sun shines in eyes of people on third-base side. Visiting team hotel has free general admission tickets. All Avondale Dairy Bar and McDonalds area restaurants give Junior Stompers cards to children under 13, which entitle them to $1.99 general admission.

SEATING FOR PEOPLE WITH DISABILITIES: Directly behind home plate in front of reserved chairs; concourse is extra wide here.

STADIUM FOOD: The fare is ordinary baseball food. A grill on the third-base side near a patio picnic deck serves hamburgers and sausages. There are also nachos, drinks, and popcorn.

SMOKING POLICY: Smoking not allowed in grandstand

PARKING: Ample free parking

VISITING TEAM HOTEL: Howard Johnson (89 Meadowvale Dr., St. Catharines, Ontario L2N 3Z8, tel. 905/934–5400 or 800/446–4656)

TOURISM INFORMATION: Niagara Falls Convention & Visitors Bureau (310 4th St., Niagara Falls, NY 14303, tel. 716/285–2400); **Niagara Falls Information Center** (tel. 800/421–5223)

St. Catharines: Community Park

Community Park in St. Catharines, Ontario, is just that—a true community park. While the professionals play in the big park, there are three ball fields beyond the outfield wall in constant use by little leagues and women's softball teams. Past the left field outfield wall is a public swimming pool. You enter the park walking between the local high school, which sits behind the grandstand on the third-base side, and a lawn bowling green. Train tracks run alongside the park's first-base line. Beyond the right-field wall are trees, trains, and a church.

The stadium is as simple as it gets. Minor-league baseball returned to St. Catharines in 1986, and the games were played on an old field with a wooden grandstand where baseball had been played since the 1930s. For the 1987 season, home plate was shifted and a new grandstand of steel and aluminum installed. The Community Park grandstand seats 2,000, with 308 in blue plastic seats behind an 8-foot-high chain-link fence that rings the entire grandstand between the dugouts from first to third. Three rows of aluminum benches with backs stand behind the real seats. The rest of the grandstand benches have no backs. Down the left-field line stretches a conventional aluminum bleacher. A blue, wooden press box with flags flying above it sits at the top of the uncovered grandstand behind home plate.

Past the lawn bowling green is one of the least pretentious entrances to any stadium we saw—your basic chain-link fence and gravel entryway with a modest concession area and souvenir shop on your left before you enter the seating area. The scoreboard is in left center.

Baseball's roots in St. Catharines are shallow. There was a team in 1930 in a league that went bust the same year. In 1986, the Toronto Blue Jays, seeing the value of having a farm team nearby, put a New York–Penn League team here. Early in 1994, a group of business leaders bought the St. Catharines Blue Jays with the intention of moving the team west to London. The New York–Penn League blocked the deal. Local business leaders, former Toronto Blue Jay catcher Ernie Whitt, and the Sorbara Group from Toronto bought the team, ushering in a new era, with greater focus on the local community.

In 1995, the new owners selected a new name—the Stompers—to reflect the wine-making industry in the Niagara region. The clever Stomper logo has an old-time baseball player with purple feet in mid-stomp. Stomper purple, green, and white has replaced Blue Jay blue, light blue, and white. Its new mascot is the Grape Crusader, a fuzzy, cream-colored character with a purple mask across his eyes and a purple cape. The new owners added a children's playground protected by netting behind the grandstand on the first-base side, the new blue box seats, and a patio picnic deck down the first-base line. The picnic area is open to all fans once the game begins.

Where to Stay

Visiting Team Motel: Howard Johnson's. There are big savings here, as guests get free tickets to the Stompers games. The rooms are ordinary, but the pool is outstanding. The motel is off the Queen Elizabeth Way (Lake Street exit) in the midst of car dealerships and shopping malls. *89 Meadowvale Dr., St. Catharines L2N 3Z8, tel. 905/ 934–5400 or 800/446–4656, fax 905/646– 8700. 96 rooms. Facilities: restaurant, indoor pool, sauna, batting cage, volleyball. AE, D, DC, MC, V. $$*

Ramada Parkway Inn. This five-story brick hotel includes a 40-lane bowling alley and is 5 miles from the ballpark on the edge of a shopping mall. Visiting teams also stay here on occasion. The hotel is off Queen Elizabeth Way (Ontario Street exit). *327 Ontario St., St. Catharines L2R 5L3, tel. 905/688–2324 or 800/272–6232, fax 905/684–6432. 124 rooms. Facilities: restaurant, indoor pool, hot tub, sauna, bowling. AE, DC, MC, V. $$*

Skyline Brock. There are good views of Niagara Falls from this 12-story hotel, especially from the 10th-floor restaurant, the Rainbow Room. Built in 1929, the hotel has small rooms with antique mahogany beds. You'll need to reserve early for less expensive, city-side rooms. Half of

the rooms have falls views. Parking is $6 (Canadian) daily. It is one block from the falls, near the Rainbow Bridge. *5685 Falls Ave., Niagara Falls, Ontario L2E 6W7, tel. 905/374–4444 or 800/ 263–7135, fax 905/358–0443. 238 rooms. Facilities: restaurant, pool. AE, D, DC, MC, V. $$*

Comfort Inn on the River. Some of the rooms in this quiet, two-story hotel have Niagara River views. It has pretty landscaping and is adjacent to the Niagara Parkway, between the Spanish Aero Cars and the Canadian Falls. *4009 River Rd., Niagara Falls, Ontario L2E 3E9, tel. 905/356–0131 or 800/424–6423, fax 905/356–3306. 67 rooms. Facilities: pool. AE, D, DC, MC, V. $$*

Quality Inn Fallsview. This quiet, nicely land-scaped hotel has a golf course on one side, hotels on the other, and is directly across from the Minolta Tower. You cannot see the falls from any of its 3 floors, but they are only a five-minute walk away. The rooms are small. *6663 Stanley Ave., Niagara Falls, Ontario L2G 3Y9, tel. 905/ 354–2322 or 800/424–6423, fax 905/354– 4955. 58 rooms. Facilities: restaurant, pool. AE, D, DC, MC, V. $$*

Where to Eat

Keystone Kelly's. This cheery family restaurant with funky signs and musical instruments on the walls is part of a small restaurant chain with unusual items, such as pierogis and dry cider. The large salads are fine for a meal. Kids have their own menu and gravitate toward the fried ice cream for dessert. It's a half mile from the ballpark in an area of small shops and a firehouse. *338 Merritt St., St. Catharines, tel. 905/227–2788. AE, MC, V. $*

Astoria Restaurant. This small, ultraclean Greek-owned restaurant is across the street from the downtown Market Square. You can eat at the Formica booths or take away its sandwiches. All meals have hearty portions and low prices. Even egg-avoiders will want to try its truly farm-fresh eggs at breakfast. *104 King St., St. Catharines, tel. 905/684–2206. V. $*

Top of the Falls. This restaurant on Goat Island is at Terrapin Point, at the side of Horsehoe Falls. It's only two stories high but still has a good view. Most tables are behind large plate-glass windows that face the water. There are large platters of pasta and generous, refreshing salads, as well as a children's menu with burgers, chicken fingers, and grilled cheese sandwiches. *Goat Island, Niagara Falls, NY, tel. 716/278–0340. AE, D, MC, V. $*

Entertainments

Lakeside Park. This lakeside community park at Old Port Dalhousie on Lake Ontario has a 5¢ carousel. You can use the picnic tables by Lake Ontario after visiting the nearby **Avondale Dairy Bar** (tel. 905/646–8263) for provisions. At one end of the park, you can see the course where the Royal Canadian Henley Regatta is held. *Lock and Main Sts., St. Catharines. Carousel runs mid-June–Labor Day, daily noon–4:30 and 5:30–8; mid-May–mid-June, weekends noon–4:30 and 5:30–8.*

Maid of the Mist. It's fun to shimmy into disposable blue raincoats and get sprayed in this exciting cruise to the base of the falls. You should hold on to children during the moments of heaviest spray if you're standing. There also are bench seats, and more cautious passengers can sit below deck. To get to the boats, you pay a 50¢ fee (children under six free) to enter the observation tower–elevator. Boats leave from either Prospect Point (U.S. side) or Clifton Hill Street (Canadian) every 15 to 30 minutes. You can park for $3 in a lot adjacent to Prospect Point. *Prospect Point, Niagara Falls, NY, tel. 716/284–8897. Admission: $7.75 adults, $4.25 ages 6–12. Open mid-May–late Oct., daily 9:15–8.*

Niagara Spanish Aero Car. This 12-minute ride on red cars suspended on strong cables across Niagara Gorge and over Whirlpool Basin is thrilling for everyone. It traverses beautiful scenery that only you, birds, and airplane passengers can see. *3850 Niagara Pkwy., Niagara Falls, Ontario, tel. 905/356–2241. Admission: $4.75 (Canadian) adults, $2.40 (Canadian) ages 6–12. Open mid-May–late Oct., daily 9–dusk. AE, MC, V.*

Maple Leaf Village. Admission to this amusements area is free. The midway and arcades are forgettable, but it's worth seeing the falls from the giant Ferris wheel. *5705 Falls Ave., Niagara Falls, Ontario, tel. 416/374–0711. Rides $1–$2. Open Apr.–Labor Day, weekdays 10–10, weekends 10–midnight.*

Sites to See

Black History Sites. Canada was the last stop—freedom—on the underground railroad. **Salem Chapel** (92 Geneva St., tel. 905/682–0993) was where Harriet Tubman worshiped between more than a dozen forays to the U.S. to rescue slaves. She lived here during the years the Fugitive Slave Act was in force. **Niagara Falls Tours** (tel. 800/263–5701) leads a Niagara Freedom Trail tour to Ontario black history sites.

Niagara Reservation State Park. If your vision of Niagara Falls is of tacky wedding hotels, you'll be amazed that the area is first and foremost a beautiful park system. On the Canadian side, make sure to see the Floral Clock and drive the Niagara Parkway. You can park at Table Rock and buy passes on the (Canadian) Niagara Parks People Mover (tel. 905/356–2241; fare, $4 (Canadian) adults, $2 (Canadian) ages 6–12; passes available at any site; open daily 9 AM–11 PM) bus to go to 22 sites. On the U.S. side, you can take the Viewmobile to six major sites, including the visitor center at Prospect Park (tel. 716/278–1770; fare $4.50 adults, $3.50 ages 6–12; open daily 9 AM–11 PM).

Unusual Shopping

Market Square. This St. Catharines city market has varieties of apples, pears, and potatoes rarely seen in the U.S. There are fresh figs, flowers, meats, eggs, and berries of all types. *King St., St. Catharines, no phone. Open Tues., Thurs., and Sat. 6:30–3:30. No credit cards.*

DiCamillo Bakery. This is one of the nation's best bakeries. Customers line up at each of the three stores at any time of day. You'll find a family-run cornucopia of Italian breads, biscotti, cookies, pastas, and focaccia. Its products are found in fancy gourmet shops nationwide, but they're the daily fare here. *811 Linwood Ave., Niagara Falls, NY, tel. 716/282–2341; 7927 Pine Ave., tel. 716/236–0111; 1700 Pine Ave., tel. 716/284–8131.*

JAMESTOWN JAMMERS

League: New York–Penn League • **Major League Affiliation:** Detroit Tigers • **Class:** Short Season A • **Stadium:** College Stadium • **Opened:** 1941 • **Capacity:** 3,324 • **Dimensions:** LF: 335, CF: 410, RF: 353 • **Surface:** grass • **Season:** mid-June–Aug.

STADIUM LOCATION: 485 Falconer St., Jamestown, NY 14702

GETTING THERE: From Rte. 17S, exit 12; go ¾ mi, right on Rte. 60, left on Buffalo St. (Rte. 460) for 1 mi, then left on Falconer St., 5 blocks to stadium.

TICKET INFORMATION: Box 638, Jamestown, NY 14702, tel. 716/664–0915, fax 716/664–4175

PRICE RANGE: Box seats $4.50; grandstand seats $3.50; bleacher seats $2.50; senior citizens receive 50¢ off all tickets.

GAME TIME: 7:05 PM; gates open 1 hr before game

TIPS ON SEATING: General admission bleacher seats begin directly behind dugouts. Setting sun shines in your eyes on first-base side.

SEATING FOR PEOPLE WITH DISABILITIES: In both grandstand and general admission areas

STADIUM FOOD: The unexpected item worth trying here is loganberry juice, a pleasant locally produced favorite. For $1.25, it makes the ordinary hot dogs and popcorn bearable.

SMOKING POLICY: Smoking prohibited in grandstand

PARKING: Ample free parking

VISITING TEAM HOTEL: Jamestown Holiday Inn (150 W. 4th St., Jamestown, NY 14701, tel. 716/664–3400 or 800/465–4329)

TOURISM INFORMATION: Chamber of Commerce (101 W. 5th St., Jamestown, NY 14701, tel. 716/484–1101); **Chautauqua County Visitors Bureau** (tel. 800/242–4569)

Jamestown: College Stadium

College Stadium in Jamestown, New York, is pretty standard fare for the New York–Penn League. It's nothing flashy, just a good place to be on a summer night. The stadium was built in 1941 by the city of Jamestown for a team that had joined the new league the year before. In the mid-1980s, the city spent $3 million to rebuild the brick front and redo the concrete. The entrance, concessions, offices, and lockers that now sit in front of the grandstand were part of this renovation. Before the short season begins in mid-June, high school, college, and senior-league teams share the stadium.

The covered grandstand seats 1,056, with just 121 real box seats. The rest are aluminum benches with backs. The bleachers are weathered gray wooden benches that begin just behind each dugout and extend down the lines

beyond the bases. The wooden press box sits atop the grandstand roof and has the weathered gray look that shows this stadium's age. The scoreboard in right field gives just the very basics. The team's wish list includes brighter lights and stronger, safer bleacher seats. Both are needed. Often these rookie-league parks have failing sound systems. Not here. In Jamestown, the nonstop patter and music and goofy sounds designed to rattle opponents come through loud and clear.

The view from the stands is picturebook western New York in the summertime—rolling, green, and treed. Jamestown Community College buildings cluster behind the wall in center, but they are largely hidden by the scoreboard and the ads on the fence. A picnic area complete with a horseshoe pit and volleyball sand pit—two facilities we had not seen in our travels—stretch down the right-field foul area. A new children's playground opened in 1996.

Fans helped select the team nickname, the Jammers, the meaning of which is left to each fan's imagination. The Chautauqua region is noted for its grapes, so maybe that's a partial answer for people who insist on some kind of nickname logic. The mascot—a very strange-looking animal with long teeth, whiskers, and tail—is friendly with children but said to be an aggressive irritant to opponents. Whatever the mascot is and whatever Jammers means, the local fans seem happy with them. We were disappointed that the Jammers didn't repeat the Lucille Ball look-alike contest from 1994 to honor Jamestown's most famous citizen. They did have a spectacular "Sky Jam" night with 18 hot-air balloons rising up from the field one at one time.

Jamestown has been in and out of baseball since 1939. Russ Diethrick, a former city recreation director, has been a leader in keeping baseball in Jamestown. Diethrick helped bring professional baseball back to Jamestown in the early 1970s. His vision led to the creation of the Chautauqua Sports Hall of Fame, and he helped bring the Babe Ruth League World Series to Jamestown's College Stadium. The Rich-family baseball organization came to Jamestown in 1994 when the Montréal Expos left town. The Rich family—which also owns the Buffalo team—signed the Jamestown team on as an affiliate of the Detroit Tigers.

We were lucky many times on this trip, finding treats we never expected. We got to watch the Olympic tryouts for women's soccer in Denver's Mile High Stadium and men's baseball at the Air Force Academy. But our biggest piece of sports luck was finding the Babe Ruth World Series for 16-year-olds in Jamestown after a lovely morning at the nearby Chautauqua Institution. This turned out to be the most exciting of the 67 games we saw that summer. Since 1980, Jamestown has hosted eight Babe Ruth World Series. The community has recruited hundreds of volunteers and will likely continue to serve as a regular host. For information, contact the Babe Ruth League, Inc. (1770 Brunswick Pike, Box 5000, Trenton, NJ 08638, tel. 609/695-1434).

Where to Stay

Visiting Team Hotel: Holiday Inn Jamestown. The rooms are large in this convenient, eight-story downtown hotel and have big windows that look out on the city. It's Jamestown's largest hotel and is used chiefly for conventions. There is free, adjacent parking. *150 W. 4th St., Jamestown 14701, tel. 716/664-3400 or 800/465-4329, fax 716/484-3304. 148 rooms. Facilities: restaurant, indoor pool. AE, D, DC, V. $$*

Hotel Lenhart. This vintage, four-story yellow clapboard hotel fronting onto Chautauqua Lake is open only in summer. Highback rockers in primary colors populate the front porch, and a huge American flag hangs between a maple tree and the hotel. The cozy, well-worn hotel first opened in 1880. A bathing beach adjoins the property, and muskie fishing trips cam be arranged. There's a smorgasbord on Sunday. *20 Lakeside Dr. (Rte. 17), Bemus Point, NY 14712, tel. 716/386-2715. 18 rooms. Facilities: restaurant, boating, sandy bathing beach. MC, V. Closed mid-Sept.–Memorial Day. $$*

Athenaeum Hotel. This majestic lakefront beauty, part of the Chautauqua Institution, a summer educational retreat, was built in 1881 and has been recently restored. On the huge, picture-perfect veranda are rows of rockers. The rooms have wooden floors and antique furniture. Breakfast and lunch are informal, but there is a dress code for dinner. Guests must buy a Chautauqua gate ticket and a parking pass. Only a few of the double rooms, which have twin beds, can hold roll-aways for children. The Chautauqua Institution also runs an accommodations referral service (tel. 716/357-6204) for the many homes, rooming houses, inns, and condos in the area, most of which are on the Institution's grounds, but most require a seven-day stay in summer. *James Ave. and Promenade, Chautauqua Institution, Rte. 394, Chautauqua 14722, tel. 716/357-4444 or 800/821-1881, fax 716/357-2833. 157 rooms. Facilities: restaurant. $12 per person service charge added daily. MC, V. $$$*

Where to Eat

Athenaeum Hotel Dining Room. Reserve here weeks in advance for weekend meals, especially Sundays, when there is no fee for the Chautauqua gate tickets or for parking. You dine in airy, Victorian splendor, on American cuisine with an emphasis on prime rib, fresh fish, and local vegetables. The dress code for dinner includes jacket and tie for men. There are five other restaurants on the Chautauqua Institution's grounds, including the pleasant **Rhapsody Cafe** (tel. 716/357–2844), at Bowman and Palestine streets, in the ground floor of a Victorian home. It serves sandwiches, salads, and light meals in a cozy dining room with sheet music menus. *James Ave. and Promenade, Chautauqua Institution, Chautauqua, tel. 716/357–4444 or 800/821–1881. MC, V. $$*

Dick's Harbor House Restaurant. This restaurant, across the street from the Chautauqua marina, has been serving food since the 1940s. It is known for fish fry, the huge salad bar, genuine turkey dinners on Sundays, and the pot roast. There is a children's menu and an extensive selection of homemade pies. Breakfast is served until 1 PM, but no alcohol is served. *95 W. Lake Rd., 15 mi west of ballpark, Mayville, tel. 716/753–2707. No credit cards. $*

Erickson's Family Restaurant. This casual restaurant, which offers hearty cooking, has been known since 1968 for daily Cuban sandwiches and fish fries on Wednesday through Saturday nights. Booths and tables seat 150 patrons, and children can order small spaghetti or fish platters. *144 W. Fairmount Ave., 7 mi west of ballpark, Lakewood, tel. 716/763–1421. No credit cards. $*

Friendly's. This chain restaurant is one of the few family restaurants in downtown Jamestown. It serves a wide variety of sandwiches, soups, and ice cream concoctions in a brightly lit fast-food setting. *10 S. Main St., 2½ mi west of ballpark, Jamestown, tel. 716/483–0081. AE, D, MC, V. $*

Entertainments

Boat ride on Chautauqua Lake. A two-hour ride on this steam-engine paddle wheeler offers a painless history lesson of the area. Operated by Chautauqua Lake Historic Vessels, the craft has original parts from the 1880s. It departs from Lakeside Park, and snacks are sold on board. *Lakeside Park, Rte. 394, Maysville, tel. 716/753–2403 or 800/753–2506. Fare: $12 adults, $6 ages under 13, $25 family (with additional charge for more than 1 child). Open May–*

June and Sept.–Oct., weekends at 11, 1:15, and 3; July–Aug., daily at 11, 1:15, and 3.

Midway Park. This century-old amusement park is terrific for kids 10 and under. There are a gentle roller coaster and 15 other rides, including a 50-year-old Herschell carousel, as well as a vintage second-story wooden roller rink that overlooks Lake Chautauqua. The small swimming beach has lifeguards, and you can visit an amusement-park museum, use picnicking pavilions, and rent paddleboats. Take Route 17 across the lake bridge to Exit 9 to Bemus Point. *Rte. 430, Maple Springs, tel. 716/386–3165. Admission: free gate; individual tickets 65¢ (1–2 tickets per ride); unlimited ride tickets $6.50 (Fri. 1–5 PM), $7.50 (weekends 1–3 or 3–7), or $9 (weekends 1–7). Open late May–late June, weekends, 1–sunset; late June–early Sept., Tues.–Sun. 1–sunset. D, MC, V.*

Sites to See

Roger Tory Peterson Institute. This celebration of ornithology comes from the collection of America's most famous bird-watcher. Peterson was a native of Jamestown, and the institute was opened in 1993 on his 85th birthday. The walls are filled with nature photography and art exhibits. *311 Curtis St., Jamestown, tel. 716/665–2473. Admission: $3 adults, $2 senior citizens, $1 students. Open Mon.–Sat. 10–4, Sun. 1–5.*

Unusual Shopping

Webb's Candies. You can buy creamy goat-milk fudge—once a staple of roadside America—and molasses sponge candy. This enterprise, which now includes an attractive lakeview motel, began in 1946 in a barn. Goat-milk fudge used to be sold from New York farmhouses in the 1930s–'50s, but it's rarely made today. *125 W. Lake Rd. (Rte. 394), Mayville, tel. 716/753–2161.*

Jones Tasty Baking. This is an exemplary Swedish bakery, with outstanding bread, particularly the loaves of Swedish limpa. The family-run operation, in business downtown since 1909, also turns out terrific hamburger and hot dog rolls. *209 Pine St., Jamestown, tel. 716/484–1988.*

BUCKEYE BASEBALL
CLEVELAND, TOLEDO

14

B aseball is big in northern Ohio. It helped revive Cleveland's downtown, and it put Toledo on the nation's sports map with the clever Mudhens logo. In addition to Cleveland's glorious new Jacobs Field stadium, there is the world-famous Rock and Roll Hall of Fame and its lakefront neighbor, the new Great Lakes Science Center. A short walk up the lakefront brings you to Municipal Stadium, the former home of the Indians and the Cleveland Browns. The flats area along the Cuyahoga River has been revitalized with dozens of restaurants, a light rail stop, and an outdoor amphitheater. If you can't get a ticket to a sold-out Indians game, take a guided tour through the stadium's stunning modern architecture.

West 115 miles, along the Ohio Turnpike, is Toledo, a glass-making center with a comfortable ballpark in what was once a horse track. Children will beg to stop at Cedar Point, an amusement park on Sandusky Bay, halfway between Cleveland and Toledo. It's worth it, and your entry fee includes the use of its clean beach. Toledo is a city with surprises, including the finest small zoo in the country. It is imaginative, with beautiful restoration of its clever Depression-era animal houses. The ballpark has a Triple AAA team. You can swim before the game at one of the adjacent city pools.

CLEVELAND INDIANS

League: American League • **Class:** Major League • **Stadium:** Jacobs Field • **Opened:** 1994 • **Capacity:** 42,800 • **Dimensions:** LF: 325, CF: 405, RF: 325 • **Surface:** grass • **Season:** Apr.–Sept.

STADIUM LOCATION: 2401 Ontario St., Cleveland, OH 44115

TEAM WEB SITE: http://www.indians.com

GETTING THERE: Jacobs Field is 10-minute walk from Tower City Center, where all RTA trains go. For additional transit information, call Regional Transit Authority (tel. 216/621–9500). By car from south, take I–77 north to E. 9th St. exit to Ontario St. From east, take I–90/Rte. 2 west to downtown. Stay on Rte. 2 to E. 9th St. Turn left to stadium.

TICKET INFORMATION: 2401 Ontario St., Cleveland, OH 44115, tel. 216/420–4200, fax 216/420–4396

PRICE RANGE: Field box, view box, and club seats, season tickets only; lower box $17; lower reserved, mezzanine, and upper box $14; upper reserved $10; bleachers $8; reserved general admission, standing room $6.

GAME TIME: 7:05 PM; day games 1:05 PM; gates open 90 min before game.

TIPS ON SEATING: Don't be picky here. If you can get a ticket for an Indians game at Jacobs Field, be happy.

SEATING FOR PEOPLE WITH DISABILITIES: Throughout stadium. Parking spaces available in on-site garage directly beyond left field. Call 216/420–4200 for brochure for Indians fans with disabilities.

STADIUM FOOD: Egg rolls, ribs, chili bowls, salads, fajitas, and cheesecake make up the diverse menu here. The bakery at Section 129 is a good first stop, for a fruit cup or a cinnamon roll. The delis have

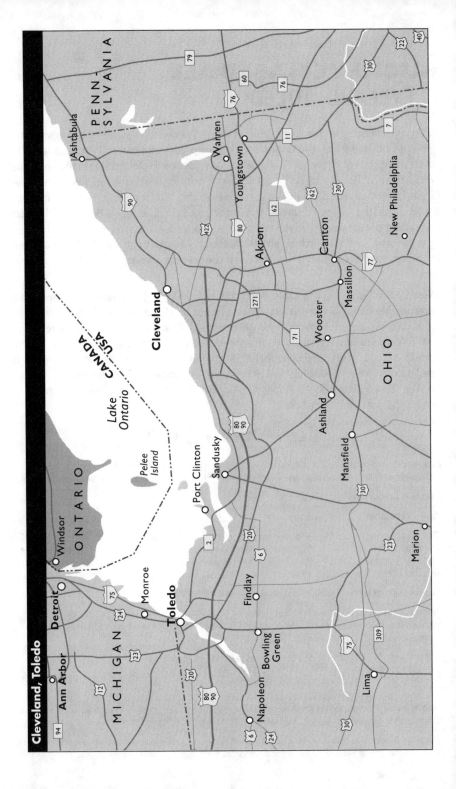

good chicken Caesar salads and so-so corned beef sandwiches. The best bargain is the $2 soft taco with sour cream at Section 154. Five pierogis are $2.75 and come loaded with buttery onions. Cleveland's excellent Pierre's ice cream gives you two large scoops for $2.25. Bertman's spicy brown Ballpark Mustard, another great Cleveland item, is the only mustard served. **KidsLand,** at Section 116, has lower prices than other concession stands for everything but red licorice (50¢ more) and sells milk and peanut butter and jelly sandwiches. There's a picnic area in KidsLand, plus picnic plazas throughout the stadium, with the largest in center field.

SMOKING POLICY: Non-smoking facility with designated smoking areas. Not allowed in seating bowl.

PARKING: Plenty of parking in downtown within walking distance of Jacobs Field; $10 at stadium, less farther away.

TOURISM INFORMATION: Cleveland Convention & Visitors Bureau (Terminal Tower, Suite 3100, 50 Public Sq., Cleveland, OH 44113, tel. 216/621–4110 or 800/321–1004)

Cleveland: Jacobs Field

Only a few years ago, you could walk up to the ticket booth in Cleveland and buy tickets right behind the Indians dugout. It was one of the weirdest sights we have ever seen in sports— 2,000 people in a stadium built to hold 80,000. In Cleveland's Municipal Stadium, a depression-era ball field hard by Lake Erie, the most exciting thing a fan could do during the 1980s was to visit with the fan beating the huge drum in the stands down the right-field line.

The faded, usually almost empty Municipal Stadium was a perfect symbol of Cleveland's down-and-out era of the 1960s and '70s, when the city was known as "the Mistake by the Lake." In the 1970s, Cleveland went into bankruptcy and the Cuyahoga River actually caught fire.

It's different in Cleveland now. They have a beautiful new ballpark and a winning team. Sports fans in Cleveland have rediscovered baseball. If you are planning a trip to Jacobs Field, plan ahead. In 1996, every ticket to every game was sold before the first pitch was thrown on opening day.

They did it right in Cleveland this time—no concrete doughnut in a sea of asphalt here. Following the lead of Baltimore and using the same architects, HOK Sport of Kansas City, they fit a huge sports complex neatly into the fabric of the city. With a landscape team led by Sasaki Associates, the Gateway Sports Complex has been a key element of the astonishing revitalization of downtown Cleveland.

The 28-acre Gateway Sports Complex includes, in addition to Jacobs Field, Gund Arena, the home of the Cleveland Cavaliers of the NBA. Built on the edge of the downtown on the site of a decaying market, the complex has considerable tree-lined public space and a million dollars' worth of public art.

At the main entrance on East 9th Street (Gate C) stands a statue of Cleveland's great Hall of Fame pitcher Bob Feller, about to deliver one of his awe-inspiring fastballs. Nearby, a set of granite benches, the work of artist Nancy Dwyer, spells out WHO'S ON FIRST? Another set of Dwyer benches spells out MEET ME HERE in front of the adjacent Gund Arena, at Ontario and Huron streets. Inside the park are several large baseball paintings and scores of banners celebrating Indians stars and great moments in Cleveland baseball history.

Opened in 1994 and called the Jake by the locals, the field is named after the Jacobs family, who bought the Indians in 1986. The ballpark's playing field is 18 feet below street level, helping to keep the 42,400-capacity stadium on a reasonable downtown scale. In 1920s slang, "It's jake" meant everything was fine. In 1990s baseball, this park is jake with us.

In contrast to the traditional redbrick exterior of Baltimore's Camden Yards, Cleveland opted for a sleek, modern look. With its white exterior, exposed steel beams, and vertical light towers, Jacobs Field is making a strong architectural statement—you are in steeltown.

Walk up to the upper deck on the third-base side to see the boats on the Cuyahoga River's Collision Bend. From the first-base side at the upper level, you can see the skyscrapers of the downtown and the elegant stone-gated Erie

Street Cemetery and church on East 9th Street below.

A huge American flag flutters in the lake breezes in center field. A 19-foot-high mini–Green Monster stands in left field, complete with the scores of all major-league games being played that day. A gigantic three-screen, 120- by 220-foot scoreboard, unfortunately littered with too much advertising, hangs above the bleachers. From behind home plate, you can see Cleveland's downtown office buildings over the standing-room-only porch above the left-field mini-Monster and past the flag in center. Three decks of seats rise beyond right field.

The Indians Team Shop, on the third-base side, is well worth a visit even if you have to wait in line. The shop includes an excellent display of Cleveland baseball memorabilia, along with replica Cleveland uniforms and hats back to 1908. It also has a display of photos of the members of the Indians Hall of Fame.

KidsLand, on the lower level down the right-field line, has a kid-oriented souvenir shop, a food stand, a picnic area, and a playground with a dozen (made-in-Ohio) Little Tike houses, slides, and cars for young children. We ran into Slider, the Indians' colorful purple-and-yellow mascot, here. Kids especially like Homer Zone, an interactive video game behind home plate near Gate D, where batters can experience what it feels like to hit one into the bleachers at Jacobs Field (eight pitches for $2). In a sensible and unusual twist on a shoe-shine, you can get your sneakers washed and polished here. Two sisters, Jennifer Gutauckas and Nadine Macasek, of Broadview Heights, Ohio, have been cleaning up fans' favorite shoes for the last three years at Section 134. Washes are $2, shines are $3, and you can get new laces, too.

Inclusion is the byword of the stadium's food choices. From meatball heroes to fried chicken, churros, tossed salads, and brownies, there's going to be something to tempt you. The pizza, fresh turkey breast sandwiches, and soft tacos are the best choices. The fancy, glass-fronted multilevel Terrace Restaurant, past the club-level seating down the third-base line, is open to season ticket holders only.

With Jacobs Field seemingly sold out for the rest of the century, your best bet for a visit might be

to take the official tour. Tours leave from the Indians Team Shop on Ontario Street and last about 45 minutes. Proceeds from the tours benefit Cleveland Indians Charities. *Tickets, tel. 216/241–8888 at least 11 days in advance; information, tel. 216/420–4400. Admission: $5 adults, $2.50 ages under 15 and over 59. Tours May–Sept., Mon.–Sat. every ½ hr 10–2, excluding day games, special events, and holidays.*

Gund Arena, which hosts the Cleveland Cavaliers basketball team, is down the left-field line across Ontario Street from Gate A. Hour-long public tours leave from the Arcade entrance. *Huron Ave. at E. 6th St., tel. 216/420–2010. Admission: $4 adults, $2 ages under 13 and senior citizens. Tours Fri. at 1 PM.*

Other Cleveland Baseball Sites

League Park. The Indians began playing baseball at Municipal Stadium in 1932, but mostly only on Sunday and holidays until 1947. The legendary League Park at East 66th Street and Lexington Avenue opened in 1891 and closed for good in 1947. This was a wonderfully quirky ballpark of another era, with an oddly shaped outfield configuration and no lights. The right-field fence was only 290 feet from home plate, and in 1929 Babe Ruth hit his 500th home run over the 40-foot-high chicken-wire fence there. The field where Hall of Famers Tris Speaker and Bob Feller played is now a neighborhood recreation center. Most of the ballpark was demolished in 1951, but the field has been preserved, and Cleveland Indians home-run slugger Larry Doby's RBI Program (Reviving Baseball in Inner Cities) plays its games here. Now called League Park Center, the two-story ticket booth built in 1909 still stands, along with the redbrick exterior wall along East 66th Street, a portion of the grandstand, and the remains of what appears to have been the dugout on the first-base side. A historical marker notes that Cy Young pitched the very first game played here, on May 1, 1891, for the Cleveland Spiders, and that the Cleveland Buckeyes won the 1945 Negro World Series here. The site has been on the National Register of Historic Places since 1979. To get here, drive east from the downtown on Lake Superior for approximately 3 miles. Take a right on 66th Street. In six blocks, you will find League Park between Lexington and Linwood avenues.

Municipal Stadium. Completed in 1931 at a cost of nearly $3 million, Municipal Stadium was the first city-owned major-league baseball stadium in the United States. It was also the largest baseball stadium ever built, as Cleveland was bidding to host the 1932 Olympics, an honor that went instead to Los Angeles. Originally, the outfield wall in center field was 470 feet from home plate, with the power alleys 463 feet. Babe Ruth said, "You'd have to have a horse to play outfield there." In 1947, after more than a decade when the Indians played here only on Sunday and holidays, new owner Bill Veeck moved the Indians to Municipal Stadium full-time. An inner fence was built with center field 410 feet from home. Veeck hired Larry Doby, the first African-American in the American League, and won the World Series in 1948. When you visit the Rock & Roll Hall of Fame and the Great Lakes Science Center, take a look left down the lake at the site where monumental Municipal Stadium stood. It was demolished in late 1996.

Where to Stay

Holiday Inn Lakeside City Center. If you get a room facing the lake in this convenient, 18-story hotel, you can watch the ships and pleasure boats on Lake Erie and the small-plane traffic at adjacent Burke Lakefront Airport. This 23-year-old hotel is well used; the rooms are standard in size and decor. But you are only two blocks from the Rock & Roll Hall of Fame and nine blocks from the ballpark. It's wise to leave the car here and walk to the park. *1111 Lakeside Ave., Cleveland 44114, tel. 216/241–5100 or 800/465–4329, fax 216/241–7437. 370 rooms. Facilities: restaurant, indoor pool, sauna, exercise machines, coin laundry, parking (fee). AE, D, DC, MC, V. $$*

Embassy Suites. Near Playhouse Square and within walking distance of all downtown attractions, this modern hotel has 11 floors of nicely decorated two-room suites. Guests receive a full breakfast and an afternoon reception. Each room has a microwave oven, an iron, and an ironing board. *1701 E. 12th St., Cleveland 44114, tel. 216/523–8000 or 800/362–2779, fax 216/*

523–1698. 288 suites. Facilities: restaurant, indoor pool, parking (fee). AE, D, DC, MC, V. $$

Sheraton Cleveland City Centre. Half of the rooms in this 22-story hotel have views of the lake and the Rock & Roll Hall of Fame; the others face the city. All rooms were renovated with contemporary furnishings in 1996 and contain irons, ironing boards, and hair dryers. Guests can pay $8 daily for access to the nearby Athletic Club (1326 E. 9th St.), which has an indoor pool, a sauna, a hot tub, indoor and outdoor tracks, and racquetball courts. The hotel is across from the convention center and a four-block walk from Jacobs Field. *777 St. Clair Ave., at E. 6th St., Cleveland 44114, tel. 216/771–7600 or 800/321–1090, fax 216/566–0736. 470 rooms. Facilities: restaurant, hair salon, health center, parking (fee). AE, D, DC, MC, V. $$*

Where to Eat

New York Spaghetti House. An unassuming Tudor cottage across the street from the ballpark houses the city's oldest downtown restaurant. Its bustling, veteran waiters are characters, and its delicious, thick spaghetti sauce is legendary. Downstairs, candles, table lights, carnations, red-checked tablecloths, and warm-toned murals give the main dining room a dim, cozy feel for families and a romantic look for others. Lunch is a bargain—one spaghetti special is $3.99. You can order a half-portion of spaghetti for children, as the servings are generous. Patricia Brigotti, a granddaughter of the founders, operates a gallery of local and regional artists in the upstairs dining rooms. *2173 E. 9th St., Cleveland, tel. 216/696–6624. AE, D, MC, V. No lunch Sun. $$*

Ninth Street Grill. This bright, modern restaurant is on the second floor of a block-long enclosed shopping mall just two blocks from the Rock & Roll Hall of Fame and nine blocks from the ballpark. It serves upscale versions of pizza, chicken sandwiches, various pastas, and salads. Through the glass back wall you have a good view of the city's 70,000-pound Claes Oldenburg FREE red rubber-stamp sculpture. On the mall's first floor is a food court with nine even more casual restaurants. The **French Bakery & Bistro** sells cookies resembling baseballs. While you wait for your food, your kids can run across the mall to the **Cleveland Indians Company Team Shop,** packed with great Indians memorabilia. *Galleria, E. 9th St. and Sinclair Ave., Cleveland, tel. 216/579–9919. AE, D, MC, V. $$*

Entertainments

The Rock and Roll Hall of Fame and Museum. The '70s outrage acts like Alice Cooper's seem to get the biggest play in this unusual I. M. Pei building with huge open spaces and walls of flashy graphics. The steel-and-glass triangle has seven floors and a guitar-shape wing. You begin touring on the ground floor, with two excellent short films, which can take 15 minutes of waiting time to enter on busy weekend days. Stars' costumes, instruments, hand-written songs, and other fine memorabilia are well displayed. The film on the fourth floor is not suitable for younger children. Wonderful displays throughout allow you to wear headsets and choose songs you'd like to hear. There's a good memorial to Cleveland's Alan Freed, radio's tireless promoter of rock and roll, with vintage radio sets tuned to influential music broadcasters, arranged by decade and city. The actual Hall of Fame room at the very top of the building is pitch black, crowded, and unenlightening, as it is simply the signatures of honorees etched on black panels. The cafeteria-style café inside the Hall has rich desserts, some sandwiches, and photos of stars eating. *One Key Plaza, Cleveland, tel. 216/781–7625 or 800/493–7625. Admission: $12.95 adults, $9.50 ages 4–11 and senior citizens. Open Memorial Day–Labor Day, Sun.–Tues. 10–5:30, Wed.–Sat. 10–9; Labor Day–Memorial Day, Thurs.–Tues. 10–5:30, Wed. 10–9.*

Great Lakes Science Center. Next door to the Rock & Roll Hall is the lakefront's latest attraction, an impressive science center with more than 350 displays and hands-on exhibits. The bountiful and shipwreck-filled Great Lakes are the emphasis here. An IMAX theater has a separate admission at the same rate as that of the museum. *601 Erieside Ave., Cleveland, tel. 216/694–2000. Admission: $6.75 adults, $4.50 ages 3–17, $6 senior citizens; combination ticket $9.95 adults, $7 children, $9 senior citizens. Open Fri.–Tues. 9:30–5:30, Wed.–Thurs. 9:30–9.*

Crawford Auto-Aviation Museum. Operated by the Western Reserve Historical Society, this museum contains early bicycles, an 1897 gaso-line-powered car, vintage cars from the turn of the century, a Sears catalog car, and a street of old-time shops. Cleveland once led the country in carmaking, and this collection has touring and racing cars. Admission also gives you entry to the two mansions that make up the society's History Museum. *10825 East Blvd., Cleveland, tel. 216/721–5722. Admission: $6 adults, $4 ages 6–12, $5 senior citizens; free Tues. 3–5. Open Tues.–Sat. 10–5, Sun. noon–5.*

The Flats. Restaurants line each side of the Cuyahoga River in this former industrial section, which now offers tour boats, Jet Ski rentals, a bandshell, and a power plant that's been renovated into more restaurants and a comedy club. The river still is used by working tugboats and barges. As you sit at waterside, you are surrounded by some of the city's 50 impressive bridges, a busy rail line, and the skyline of the city. (The Cleveland Children's Museum, tel. 216/791–7114, will send you a copy of its "Bridge Hunt" if you want to track the bridges that connect the city's east and west sides.) A shuttle to Indians games leaves from Nautica boat lines, and a water taxi takes you from the east to the west bank of the flats. A light-rail stop has been added on the east side of the flats. *Foot of Saint Clair and Superior Aves., Cleveland, tel. 216/566–1046.*

Sites to See

Terminal Tower Observation Deck. See the city's skyline, the Lake Erie shoreline, steel mills, Cleveland's bridges, and the Cuyahoga River from the top of what was for decades the city's tallest building, the 52-story Terminal Tower. Erected on Public Square, the Gothic tower took 11 years to build before it opened in 1930. Across Public Square is the Old Stone Church, a stopping place on the Underground Railroad. The Soldiers and Sailors Monument in the square is topped with a Statue of Liberty. Ticket sales stop 30 minutes before the enclosed deck closes. *50 Public Sq., Cleveland, tel. 216/621–7981. Admission: $2 adults, $1 ages 6–16. Open Memorial Day–Labor Day, daily 11–5; Labor Day–Memorial Day, daily 11–4.*

The Arcade. This 1890s structure on the National Register of Historic Places once hosted the Republican National Convention. Shops and restaurants fill many of its floors. Inside, beautiful brass balconies and a soaring atrium make this a one-of-a-kind urban shopping mall from the last century. *401 Euclid Ave., Cleveland, tel. 216/621–8500. Open weekdays 7–7, Sat. 7–6.*

Playhouse Square. Cleveland has renovated three grand movie palaces, all within steps of each other on Euclid Avenue. Free guided tours of the theaters for kids are given one weekend each month. There is also a children's and a Broadway theater series for children ages three and up. *Playhouse Square Center, 1501 Euclid Ave., Cleveland, tel. 216/771–4444.*

Unusual Shopping

The Cleveland Indians Team Shop. There are two shops downtown, one inside Jacobs Field (tel. 216/420–4444) and one at the Galleria Mall. The merchandise is varied: umbrellas, books, CDs, even Wahoo perfume. These stores are several cuts above the usual jerseys-and-caps merchants. You'll find a wide selection of Indians watches, rhinestone pins spelling out "Go Tribe," and many balls and photos signed by Indians stars. *Galleria Mall, 1301 E. 9th St., Cleveland, tel. 216/420–4443.*

West Side Market. Food mavens have long done their shopping at this fresh-food heaven. There are more than 180 stalls of fresh fruit, vegetables, baked goods, live poultry, and ethnic meats, spices, and prepared foods from a host of European and Asian countries. The low prices and high quality will make you cry over your supermarket's offerings. Come early in the day with a large carry-all bag. *W. 25th St., at Lorain Ave., Cleveland, tel. 216/ 664–3386. Closed Sun., Thurs.*

TOLEDO MUD HENS

League: International League • **Major League Affiliation:** Detroit Tigers • **Class:** AAA • **Stadium:** Ned Skeldon Stadium • **Opened:** 1965 • **Capacity:** 10,025 • **Dimensions:** LF: 325, CF: 410, RF: 325 • **Surface:** grass • **Season:** Apr.–Labor Day

STADIUM LOCATION: 2901 Key St., Maumee, OH 43537

GETTING THERE: From Ohio Turnpike, exit 4 north to Toledo onto Reynolds Rd, right onto Heatherdowns, and right onto Key St. From Detroit, I–75S to exit 201A (Rte. 25), right on Key St. From Dayton, I–75 via Rte. 475 to Maumee exit (Rte. 24), left on Key St.

TICKET INFORMATION: Box 6212, Toledo, OH 43614, tel. 419/893–9483, fax 419/893–5847

PRICE RANGE: Box seats $6; reserved seats $5; general admission $3; $1 off all tickets for under 15 and senior citizens

GAME TIME: Mon.–Sat. 7 PM, Sun. 2 PM; gates open 1 hr before game

TIPS ON SEATING: It's worth it to buy box seats here. Kids and senior citizens get $1 off even on box seats. In sections K and L, right near home plate, smoking and alcohol are prohibited. If you buy reserved seats, ask for first-base side, where they are real seats. On third-base side (visitor's dugout), they are benches with backs. General admission seats are aluminum benches without backs and beyond bases.

SEATING FOR PEOPLE WITH DISABILITIES: In front of box seats on first-base side on home plate side of dugout

STADIUM FOOD: The pizza, bratwurst, deli sandwiches, and salads are the best bets here. The pizza is baked on-site and has a thick crust and less grease than most. **The Grillery** behind home plate has exceptional bratwurst ($3) and natural-casing hot dogs ($2.75). Kiddie drinks are $1.50, and you and your children can sit in booths inside the cavernous concession stand area to eat. You can get garden salads, Caesar salads, fruit cups, and just-sliced corned beef, ham, or turkey sandwiches at the deli. Homemade, frosted brownies are $1.25 at the deli. There are also burgers, grilled chicken sandwiches, and good french fries available. Frozen Lemon Chill is $3 per cup and the hand-scooped ice cream is Pierre's, a fine regional brand.

SMOKING POLICY: No smoking/no alcohol in sections K and L near home plate on first-base side

PARKING: Plenty of free parking at stadium

VISITING TEAM HOTEL: Ramada Inn (2429 S. Reynolds Rd., Toledo, OH 43614, tel. 419/381–8765 or 800/272–6232)

TOURISM INFORMATION: Greater Toledo Convention and Visitors Bureau (401 Jefferson Ave., Toledo, OH 43604, tel. 419/321–6404 or 800/243–4667)

Toledo, Ohio: Ned Skeldon Stadium

In Toledo, the baseball team is called the Mud Hens, and you are probably thinking that this clever nickname is a product of the minor-league logo-and-name-changing mania of the '90s. Correct, but it was the 1890s. A mud hen is a bird with short wings and long legs that inhabits swamps or marshes. In 1896, the Toledo baseball team played at Bay View Park and there were plenty of mud hens in the marshland outside the ballpark. Team mascot Muddy the Mud Hen, a large, pinstriped yellow bird, carries on the tradition today.

Teams have been playing professional baseball in Toledo since 1883, and for almost all of that time they have been called the Mud Hens. Ned Skeldon Stadium is the 11th ballpark of Toledo's professional teams. Swayne Field, built in 1909 and considered the best minor-league park of its era, was torn down and replaced by a shopping center in 1955 when the team moved to Wichita. In 1965, baseball returned to Toledo thanks largely to the efforts of Lucas County Commissioner Ned Skeldon, who led the charge to establish the community nonprofit group that owns the team. A former Thoroughbred racetrack was converted into a 10,025-capacity baseball park when Toledo was awarded its Class AAA International League franchise. The Lucas County Recreation Center baseball stadium was renamed for Skeldon in 1988. The ballpark sits in a sports complex that includes softball fields, three swimming pools, and the county fairgrounds.

This is a typical, gritty 1960s Triple AAA International League stadium, but with contests on and off the field more like what you find in Single A baseball. This converted horse-racing track—the stretch to the finish line was in front of the third-base grandstand—has a large roof on both sides, covering much of the seating area

and extending well past first and third bases. General admission seating is on aluminum benches not covered by the roof.

In most International League stadiums, it's all baseball with few of the on-field contests and antics of the lower minor leagues. But the Mud Hens are different, with a fan-friendly booth at the gate to sign up for contests. Several lucky fans get to sit in the couch-potato skybox, a couch just on the third-base side of the press box.

The old-style concourse under the grandstand is brightly spruced up with colorful concessions signs for the deli and the Dog Hut.

Many celebrities have played in Toledo, but the most interesting person to have played ball here is perhaps the least known. In Toledo, they will tell you that Jackie Robinson was not the first African-American to play baseball in the major leagues. Sixty-three years before, Moses Fleetwood Walker, the son of an Ohio clergyman, played for the 1884 Toledo Blue Stockings in the American Association, then considered a major league. Walker immediately ran into a wall of bigotry. Toledo pitcher Tony Mullane ignored catcher Walker's signals, saying he would not take orders from a black man.

Native American Jim Thorpe, the hero of the 1912 Olympics, hit three home runs in one game for the Hens in 1921. Casey Stengel managed at Toledo from 1926 to 1931, winning the Junior World Series in 1927 before going on to a Hall of Fame career as the skipper of the New York Yankees. Pete Gray, the great one-armed pitcher, played here. Jamie Farr, the actor who brought the Mud Hens national attention as Corporal Klinger's favorite team on *M*A*S*H*, has made many special appearances at the ballpark.

Where to Stay

Visiting Team Hotel: Ramada Inn. Between a Bob Evans restaurant and a Toys R Us on a busy commercial street, this hotel has a free shuttle to the ballpark. The rooms in the eight-floor tower cost $10 more than the main-floor and wing rooms because of the countryside views and distance from road noise. The center of the hotel is an indoor pool with brightly colored banners overhead. *2429 S. Reynolds Rd., Toledo 43614, tel. 419/381–8765 or 800/272–6232, fax 419/ 381–0129. 264 rooms. Facilities: restaurant, indoor pool, coin laundry. AE, D, DC, MC, V. $$*

Cross Country Inn. This well-kept nine-year-old budget hotel, part of a regional chain, is 2 miles from the ballpark, at the edge of Toledo and suburban Maumee. It adjoins a field next to a freeway exit. The long, rectangular rooms are modern and plain. Patrons check in at a drive-through window resembling one at a suburban bank. *1704 Tollgate Dr., Exit 4 from Ohio Turnpike, Maumee 43537, tel. 419/891–0880 or 800/621–1429, fax 419/891–1017. Facilities: pool. AE, D, DC, MC, V. $*

Holiday Inn West. The ballpark is a half mile from this newer 11-story hotel, which is on a busy commercial strip adjacent to Southwyck Mall. It is 7 miles from downtown and 1 mile from the ballpark. The rooms are larger than ordinary, with contemporary furnishings. *2340 S. Reynolds Rd., Exit 4 from Ohio Turnpike, Toledo 43614, tel. 419/865–1361 or 800/465–4329, fax 419/865–6177. 217 rooms. Facilities: restaurant, indoor pool, beauty salon, exercise room, coin laundry. AE, D, DC, MC, V. $$*

Where to Eat

Tony Packo's Cafe. This may be the only restaurant decorated with celebrity-signed hot dog buns, shellacked and mounted on walls. There are signatures from Esther Williams, Nancy Reagan, Charlton Heston, Patti LaBelle, Ray Charles, and Burt Reynolds. Customers order from a counter and sit at tables with red-checked vinyl cloths. The eatery serves extraordinary hot dill pickles and sells an entire line of condiments, such as spoonable ketchup and chunky hot peppers. Its sausages, macaroni and cheese, mashed potatoes, strudels, and fruit dumplings are exemplary. On Saturday and Sunday afternoons, a magician entertains, and on Friday and Saturday nights, a Dixieland jazz band prompts crowds to dance around the restaurant to "When the Saints Go Marchin' In." *1902

Front St., at Consaul St., Toledo, tel. 419/691– 6054. AE, D, MC, V. $*

Maumee Bay Brewing Company. This impressive brewery and wood-fired brick pizza-oven restaurant is housed in what was Toledo's premier hotel, circa 1859. Beautifully renovated, this Greek Revival palace is listed on the National Register of Historic Places. It has light ash floors, exposed-brick walls, views of the Maumee River, and huge copper kettles and serving tanks behind glass. The spacious restaurant, with a pub section downstairs, has excellent sandwiches, pizzas, pastas, and salads. An entire dining room is no-smoking. Its steak soup and cheddar beer soup are appealing and unusual. The Mud Hen pie consists of coffee ice cream with a cookie-crumb crust. For adults, there are varieties of ales, lagers, and specialty brews. *27 Broadway, off Summit St. at Oliver St., Toledo, tel. 419/243–1302. AE, MC, V. $$*

Linck's Too Cafeteria. This 150-seat cafeteria downstairs in the National City Bank Building serves breakfast and lunch during the week, with a different cake and cream pie daily. The Linck family operates two other full-service restaurants in the area and is known for great versions of such American favorites as meat loaf, turkey and dressing, and pineapple upside-down cake. *405 Madison Ave., at Saint Clair St., Toledo, tel. 419/242–8701. No credit cards. $*

Entertainments

Toledo Zoo. This is our favorite small zoo in the country, and it has plenty of good competition. First built in the depression, by WPA artists, its gorgeous and fanciful vintage buildings have been beautifully renovated. The high-ceilinged former carnivore house is a riot of blue, purple, and mauve inside, with two cafeterias. You can eat in the former lion cages at bright blue tables behind bright blue iron bars. The aquarium has dozens of windows looking in to sharks, stingrays, and snapping turtles. The zoo's two Nile hippos can be viewed from an underwater tank, and there's a good petting zoo. For $1, you can ride a carousel; a ride in a bright red train is $1.25. A playground is imaginatively done, as are all the graphics in this zoo. There's a South African rain forest, with sloths and iguanas, plus giraffes, cougars, and monkeys. Currently, visitors must use a dim tunnel with stairs to enter the zoo from the parking lot. A new bridge will open in 1998, making it much easier for strollers and wheelchairs. Polar-bear and African-predators exhibits are part of its 9-acre expansion. The zoo belongs to the 100-member American Zoological Association, which gives free entry to members of other zoos. It's 3 miles south of Toledo. *2700 Broadway; Exit 201A off I–75, follow Collinwood Ave. (Rte. 25) south; Toledo, tel. 419/385–4040. Admission: $5 adults, $2.50 children; parking $2. Open Apr.–Sept., daily 10–5; Oct.–Mar., daily 10–4.*

Toledo Firefighters Museum. This free museum is housed in Fire House 18, built in 1920 and replaced in 1975. It shows how the city's fire protection evolved from volunteer bucket brigades to the computer-directed system of today. The city's first fire pumper, an 1837 hand-pulled tanker, is on display. In the model child's bedroom on the second floor, kids can act out fire emergencies and plan escape routes. *918 Sylvania Ave., Toledo, tel. 419/478–3473. Open June–Aug., Sat. noon–4; Sept.–May, weekends noon–4.*

Cedar Point. This all-day amusement park, perched on Lake Erie's Sandusky Bay since 1870, has a nice beach and picnic areas for patrons. It's roller-coaster heaven, with five coasters, including Magnum XL-200 and the inverted Raptor, two of the most thrilling in the country. Both are too frightening for preteens, as is the 15-story plunge ride, the RipCord. The Wildcat is a good roller coaster–like ride for children ages 6–12. Several vintage rides were rescued from Cleveland's late, lamented Euclid Beach Park, including Cedar Downs (a racing carousel), and the wooden Blue Streak coaster. In Berenstain Bears Bear Country, a clever indoor science center–playground leads to an outdoor funland of swings, sandboxes, a train, and treehouses. Children also love driving the Turnpike Cars and going on the sports-car rides. At Aunt Em's restaurant, you can get pepperoni rolls, a regional favorite. There are two hotels and a campground on the Cedar Point grounds. The park is an hour west of Cleveland and 45 minutes east of Toledo. *U.S. 6, Sandusky, 10 mi north of Ohio Turnpike Exit 7, tel. 419/626–0830. Admission: $28.95 adults, $26.95 children 48"–54", $6.95 children 48"–age 3, $15.95 senior citizens; $18.95 after 5 PM; parking $5.*

Unusual Shopping

Libbey Factory Outlet. Toledo is a glass-producing city; the already low prices of this outlet and its bargain room really drop for the items in its tent sale, held each June through August. These are first-quality glasses, canisters, platters, dinnerware, mugs, candleholders, and gift sets. *1205 Buckeye St., near I–75 and I–280, North Toledo, tel. 419/727–2374.*

Mud Hens Souvenir Store. This is the main store of eight Mud Hens stores in the area, a testament to the popularity of its terrific logo. Located under the third-base stands, it contains many items under $1 for young fans, as well as former uniforms for $250. *2901 Key St., Maumee, tel. 419/891–9520 or 800/736–9520.*

STABLES AND THE SPEEDWAY
LOUISVILLE, INDIANAPOLIS, CHICAGO, GENEVA

15

A baseball trip covering Louisville, Indianapolis, and Chicago can be as short as three days or as long as a week, depending on how many other appealing diversions, from the Louisville Slugger factory to the Indianapolis Speedway, you want to add. The Louisville stadium feels friendly even though it is the largest stadium in the minor leagues, with room for 33,500. You'll find a real organist, a carnival midway–style concourse, and family-size banana splits to eat at your seat. Its fairgrounds include the Kentucky Kingdom amusement park, with its Hurricane Bay wave pool. The Louisville Slugger factory is downtown, instantly recognizable with a 120-foot bat as exterior art. You can stay at the glorious Seelbach Hotel, affordable on weekends, walk the downtown area with its restored movie palaces, and see the exciting Kentucky Derby Museum at Churchill Downs.

North 98 miles, on Interstate 65, is Indianapolis, with its just-finished $18-million ballpark, which has a picnic berm and seating bowls above the recessed field. The team, the Indianapolis Indians, is in the Triple AAA American Association. The stadium is the latest addition to an impressive renovation of downtown Indianapolis. The city has the world's largest children's museum, a spectacular cageless zoo, and the RCA sports dome. You can be driven around the actual track of the Indianapolis Speedway and have your picture taken in a racecar at its Hall of Fame museum.

Northward on Interstate 65, it's 182 miles to Chicago, where you can take in the classical splendor of Wrigley Field, as pure a baseball experience as it gets. From the ivy on its brick back wall to the hand-recorded scoreboard for all major league games, there is tradition at every corner. The children's attractions in this city add up to an illuminating summer vacation, with the Field Museum of Natural History, the Shedd Aquarium, the Chicago Children's Museum, and the free Lincoln Park Zoo. The Navy Pier's 150-foot Ferris wheel and the Sears Tower Skydeck offer superb views of the sparkling city.

Forty miles west of Chicago, off Interstate 90, is Geneva, home of the Kane County Cougars, one of baseball's biggest suburban success stories. Opened in 1991, the stadium continues to have sell-out after sell-out despite its proximity to Chicago's two major-league teams. Antiques stores cluster downtown, and you can cycle and rollerblade along the Fox River.

Louisville, Indianapolis, Chicago, Geneva

WISCONSIN

Waukesha

Madison

Milwaukee

Racine

Kenosha

Rockford

Arlington Heights

Geneva

Aurora

Waukegan

Evanston

Chicago

Joliet

La Salle

Kankakee

Normal

Bloomington

Champaign

Danville

Decatur

MICHIGAN

Muskegan

Grand Rapids

Lansing

Lake Michigan

Battle Creek

Kalamazoo

Michigan City

Hammond

La Porte

South Bend

Angola

Auburn

Gary

INDIANA

Ft. Wayne

Huntington

Logansport

Wabash River

Kokomo

Muncie

Lafayette

Anderson

Indianapolis

ILLINOIS

Effingham

Terre Haute

Columbus

Greensburg

Bloomington

Bedford

Centralia

Wabash River

Vincennes

New Albany

Corydon

Mount Vernon

Gentryville

Louisville

Evansville

Ohio R.

Carbondale

KENTUCKY

LOUISVILLE REDBIRDS

League: American Association • **Major League Affiliation:** St. Louis Cardinals • **Class:** AAA • **Stadium:** Cardinal Stadium • **Opened:** 1959 • **Capacity:** 33,500 • **Dimensions:** LF: 360, CF: 405, RF: 312 • **Surface:** Artificial turf • **Season:** Apr.–Labor Day

STADIUM LOCATION: Phillips Lane and Freedom Way, Louisville, KY 40213

GETTING THERE: Stadium at intersection of I–65 and I–264, at Kentucky Fair and Expo Center. From I–65, take Crittenden Dr./Fairgrounds exit. From I–264, take Airport/Fairgrounds exit.

TICKET INFORMATION: Box 36407, Louisville, KY 40233, tel. 502/367–9121, fax 502/368–5120

PRICE RANGE: Sun.–Thurs.: reserved seats, $5 and $3.50 adults, $3 and $1 children and senior citizens; general admission, $3.50 adults, $3 senior citizens, $1 children. Prices higher Fri., Sat., and fireworks nights.

GAME TIME: Mon.–Sat. 7:05 PM, Sun. 1:30 PM; gates open 80 min before games.

TIPS ON SEATING: Seats on first-base side face the sun

SEATING FOR PEOPLE WITH DISABILITIES: 56 seats in reserved seating

STADIUM FOOD: Try the mettwurst or brats ($2), BBQ pork platter ($3.50), BBQ sandwich ($2.50), or grilled chicken breast sandwich ($3). The barbecue is Owensboro-style, with lots of meat in a tomato-based sauce. Tortilla chips are made in Louisville, and they're served hot and fresh here. Pickles go for 75¢ and good lemonade for $1.25. There are family-sized banana splits with ice cream by Ehrler's, a local dairy, for $3. There are also made-to-order milk shakes at the Ehrler's stand.

SMOKING POLICY: Sections 206 and 306 smoke-free

PARKING: Ample parking for $1 at Fair and Expo Center

VISITING TEAM HOTEL: Executive Inn (978 Phillips La., Louisville, KY 40209, tel. 502/367–6161 or 800/626–2706)

TOURISM INFORMATION: Louisville & Jefferson County Visitors Bureau (400 S. 1st St., Louisville, KY 40202, tel. 502/584–2121 or 800/626–5646)

Louisville: Cardinal Stadium

If we had known that Cardinal Stadium had artificial turf, we probably would have skipped Louisville. Who would have imagined they play baseball on green plastic in the blue-grass state? If we had skipped Louisville, it would have been our loss. Louisville is a terrific town, and despite the dreaded fake grass, we had a blast at Cardinal Stadium.

Professional baseball was born in Louisville in 1876 when the key meetings to form the National League were held in a Louisville saloon. Louisville was a charter member of the league. In 1902, Louisville joined the American Association and stayed there for 61 years. After a stint in the International League, Louisville has been back in the American Association since 1982, when the St. Louis Cardinals Triple AAA franchise moved here from Springfield, Illinois. The Redbirds became the first minor-league team to draw more than 1 million fans.

Unlike many other popular teams, Louisville has no capacity limitations that might hold down attendance. Cardinal Stadium, built in 1957 on the Kentucky State Fairgrounds, has the largest seating capacity in minor-league baseball, at 33,500. The right-field bleachers are more for football—the University of Louisville Cardinals football team plays here—than for baseball and create the shortest right-field home-run porch in Triple AAA.

For a family used to minor-league stadiums that seat 5,000, Cardinal Stadium seems cavernous. The huge grandstand is completely covered by a roof. But this is a fan-friendly place. The grandstand seats are an array of colors—red, yellow, blue, and green. An organist plays from a platform in the seating area behind home plate. The festive red concourse area under the seats is lit up like a carnival midway. The mascot—Billy Bird—flies over the center-field wall in the seventh inning and then signs autographs for the kids.

Picnic in the Park is a picnic area complete with grilled chicken and burgers on the first-base side of the concourse. Right next door is the Strike Zone, with video games and a basketball net. Walk along the concourse wall to learn the rich history of baseball in Louisville back to 1876 from a dozen excellently designed display panels.

More Louisville Baseball

Louisville Slugger Factory. For 20 years the famous Louisville Slugger bats were made across the Ohio River in southern Indiana. No more. Hillerich & Bradsby moved its corporate headquarters, museum, factory, and warehouse back to Louisville in 1996. A 120-foot metal Louisville Slugger bat rises above the Main Street entrance. The new redbrick facilities are at Eighth Street, just two blocks up from the river and a half block from the Louisville Science Center on the nicely revitalized Main Street. H&B turns out PowerBilt golf clubs and more than a million wooden baseball bats a year.

It all began in 1884, when Pete Browning broke a bat at a Louisville game attended by John Andrew Hillerich. Hillerich took Browning back to his father's woodworking shop and turned a bat for the ballplayer. Browning got three hits with it the next day. The Hillerichs decided there was money in making baseball bats. On September 1, 1905, Honus Wagner became the first ballplayer to have his signature on a Louisville Slugger bat. Today, a majority of major leaguers have bat contracts with the company. The H&B museum has a collection of bats from many of the most famous players who ever played the game. After you tour the plant and museum, drop by the souvenir store to order a personalized 35-inch white-ash bat for $36 to memorialize your baseball trip to Louisville. *800 W. Main St., Louisville 40202, tel. 502/585–5226. Admission: $4 adults, $3.50 senior citizens, $3 children ages 6–12, children under 6 free. Open mid-July–June, Mon.–Sat. 9–5; tours every 30 min.*

Where to Stay

Seelbach Hotel. This glorious 1905 hotel has an unusual lobby of fine woods, marble, and brown-hued murals. Charles Dickens, Ernest Hemingway, and F. Scott Fitzgerald slept here. Even the modest rooms have lovely antique beds, armoires, and high ceilings. *500 4th St., Louisville 40202, tel. 502/585–3200 or 800/333–3399, fax 502/585–3200. 321 rooms. Facilities: 2 restaurants, parking (fee). AE, D, DC, MC, V. $$*

Visiting Team Hotel: Executive Inn Hotel. Guests can walk to the ballpark from this dark wood, English Tudor–style hotel, which is across the street from the fairgrounds. Bargain packages that include free Kentucky Kingdom admission are available. *978 Phillips La., Watterson Expressway at fairgrounds, Louisville 40209, tel. 502/367–6161 or 800/626–2706, fax 502/363–1880. 478 rooms. Facilities: 2 restaurants, indoor and outdoor pools, health club. AE, D, DC, MC, V. $$*

Where to Eat

Lynn's Paradise Cafe. It's impossible to resist the huge, unusual meals served in this kitsch-filled room of imagination. The decor includes cowboy items, old toys, kitchen appliances, and lava lamps. None of the tables match, and the waitresses wear vintage 1950s aprons. The chefs in this former laundromat turn out terrific French toast, fresh juices, and waffles for breakfast and new American classics for dinner. Children are given crayons, toys, and their own menu. Plastic kitties often adorn each plate as a take-home prize. *984 Barrett Ave., Louisville, tel. 502/583–3447. AE, MC, V. $*

Paul Clark's BBQ. Eaters can get Owensboro-style barbecue here, with its distinctive tangy vinegar taste. This casual restaurant, which is five minutes from the ballpark, also serves a good vegetable casserole, homemade coleslaw, and southern green beans. *2912 Crittenden Dr., Louisville, tel. 502/637–9532. No credit cards. $*

Blue Boar Cafeteria. "A bundle of food, but not a bundle of money" is the slogan of this 1950s-era cafeteria. Kentucky's basic dish, turkey hot brown, is featured, along with German favorites such as sauerkraut and bratwurst. The apple crisp is notable, as are the fried chicken and kale.

There are children's portions and prices. The decor is burnt-orange Naugahyde chairs, Formica tables, and early '60s furnishings. *802 Eastern Pkwy., Louisville, tel. 502/634–1052. D, MC, V. $*

Entertainments

Kentucky Kingdom Amusement Park. More than 60 rides and the huge Hurricane Bay wave pool fill this park, which is adjacent to the ballpark and fairgrounds. Avoid the wooden roller coaster—the violent head-jerking causes discomfort for adults and children. There are dozens of other, calmer ride choices, but watch your beginning swimmers carefully in the wave pool, which can be too rough for the inexperienced. Inner tubes are included in the park admission. Teenagers like the new free-fall ride, Hellavator, and the Top Eliminators dragster race, which has an extra fee. *Kentucky State Fairgrounds, Crittenden Dr. exit from I–264 or I–65. Louisville, tel. 502/366–2231. Admission: $23.95 adults and children 54" and taller, $13.95 children ages 2–54" and senior citizens; $9.95 Fri. after 6 PM. Open Sun.–Thurs. 11–9, Fri.–Sat. 11–11; Hurricane Bay closes weekdays at 6, weekends at 7. D, MC, V.*

Belle of Louisville. Listen to a calliope on a paddle-wheel ride on the Ohio River aboard the oldest operating Mississippi-style stern-wheel steamboat. This 1914 beauty, a National Historic Landmark, makes several two-hour cruises. A second boat, the *Spirit of Jefferson,* leaves from the Greenwood Road pier on Friday and Saturday only, 1:30–3:30 and 7–9. *Belle: Wharf at 4th Ave. and River Rd., Louisville, tel. 502/574–2355. Fares: $8 adults, $7 senior citizens, $4 ages 3–12. Open Memorial Day–Labor Day, Tues.–Sun. 1–2 boarding for a 2–4 cruise, 6–7 boarding for a 7–9 sunset cruise. MC, V. Spirit: Greenwood Rd. pier. Fares: same as for Belle. Open Memorial Day–Labor Day, Fri.–Sat. 1:30–3:30 and 7–9.*

Kentucky Derby Museum at Churchill Downs. A 360-degree screen shows an exciting film of Derby day every half hour, with vibrant color and sound. You can climb onto a full-size horse figure in a paddock, view the famous racetrack, and pet a live former champion horse. *704 Central Ave., Louisville, tel. 502/637–7097. Admission: $5 adults, $4 senior citizens, $2 ages 5–12. Open daily 9–5. MC, V.*

Sites to See

Louisville Walking Tour. The Main Street Association (tel. 502/562–0723) has an elegant brochure describing Louisville's nine-block "Time Machine" walk. You can follow Fourth Street, which was the dominant commercial and social avenue of the city in the early 1900s. Presidents Teddy Roosevelt and Franklin Roosevelt both paraded here. It's car-free for several blocks. The Galleria shopping mall (Fourth Avenue between Muhammad Ali Blvd. and Liberty St.) has 80 stores and a dozen restaurants. Don't miss three beautiful old theaters on Fourth Avenue, especially the **Palace,** a John Eberson-designed Atmospheric Theatre, which creates the impression of being outdoors, with stars on the ceiling, alfresco statues, and marble staircases. Only 23 of his Atmospheric Theatres exist, and this is one of the largest. Adjoining are the vintage **Ohio** and **Kentucky** theaters. Tours of the Palace are offered. *Palace Theatre, 625 4th Ave., Louisville, tel. 502/583–4555. Admission: $2 adults, children under 6 free.*

INDIANAPOLIS INDIANS

League: American Association • **Major League Affiliation:** Cincinnati Reds • **Class:** AAA • **Stadium:** Victory Field • **Opened:** 1996 • **Capacity:** 13,000 • **Dimensions:** LF: 320, CF: 402, RF: 320 • **Surface:** grass • **Season:** Apr.–Labor Day

STADIUM LOCATION: Maryland and West Sts., Indianapolis, IN 46225

GETTING THERE: From I–70, exit 79A (West St.), follow it north for 3 min to ballpark, across street from RCA Dome. From I–65N, exit 114 to Martin Luther King Blvd., follow it south to ballpark.

TICKET INFORMATION: 1501 W. 16th St., Indianapolis, IN 46202, tel. 317/269–3545, fax 317/269–3541

PRICE RANGE: General admission $5; reserved grandstand $7; field box or view box (first four rows of upper and lower levels) $8; $1 off ages under 15

GAME TIME: Mon.–Sat. 7 PM, Sun. 2 PM; gates open 5:30 PM regular games, 5 PM double-headers, 12:30 PM Sun.

TIPS ON SEATING: General admission lawn berm seats have good views of city and action.

SEATING FOR PEOPLE WITH DISABILITIES: 131 seats distributed in every price level; stadium has elevators.

STADIUM FOOD: The specialty here is Tribe fries—spicy wedges of potatoes. The rest of the menu includes Italian sausages, hamburgers, hot dogs, pizza, popcorn, slush puppies, and popcorn. You can continue to watch the games from the concession concourse level.

SMOKING POLICY: Smoking prohibited throughout stadium

PARKING: $2 on-site parking; parking garage across street also charges $2

VISITING TEAM HOTEL: Ramada Inn East (7701 E. 42nd St., Indianapolis, IN 46226, tel. 317/897–4000 or 800/272–6232)

TOURISM INFORMATION: Indianapolis City Center (Pan American Plaza, 201 S. Capitol Ave., Indianapolis, IN 46225-1022, tel. 317/237–5206 or 800/323–4639)

Indianapolis: Victory Field

Our strong preference is almost always to try to preserve the old ballparks. Nevertheless, after watching a game at 64-year-old Bush Stadium in Indianapolis, it is hard to second-guess the city's decision to build a brand-new stadium downtown. When built in 1931 by then-Indians owner Norman A. Perry, the 13,000-seat, roofed, single-deck Bush Stadium was state-of-the-art concrete and steel. Its distinctive ivy-covered redbrick walls remind fans of Chicago's Wrigley Field. In fact the stadium is a virtual clone of Wrigley Field before Wrigley's upper deck was built in 1928. For that reason, Bush Stadium was used in the filming of *Eight Men Out*, the 1988 film about the 1919 baseball scandal that rocked the nation.

Once a decision is made to build a new stadium, the extensive maintenance needed to preserve these classic ballparks stops, and they can go downhill fast. That is what had happened at Bush Stadium by the time we visited in the summer of 1995. It is, however, still well worth a visit for fans of historic stadiums. Much baseball history has been made at this ballpark. Indianapolis won 12 championships here while hosting teams in all three existing Triple AAA leagues—the American Association, the International

League, and the Pacific Coast League. Hank Aaron played for the Indianapolis Clowns. In 1954, 20-year-old Herb Score struck out 330 on the way to winning 22 games. In 1956, Roger Maris drove in 75 runs with 17 home runs for the Indians.

The city bought the stadium in 1967 and renamed it in 1968 in honor of the Indians' president, Owen J. Bush, a Detroit Tiger teammate of Ty Cobb. There are 15 wonderful life-size color paintings of some of the greats who have played here on the inner concourse wall, making a trip to the old stadium well worth the effort. Beyond the fence in right center field is a teepee, apparently the home of an Indian mascot. Bush Stadium is just 10 minutes from downtown Indianapolis. From the Circle in the downtown, go north on Meridian Street and take a left on 16th Street to 1501 West 16th Street. The city has not yet announced plans for the old ballpark.

The new $18 million, 13,000-seat downtown ballpark was designed by HOK, the premier baseball-stadium architects, to maintain the intimate feel of Bush Stadium. The city and the Indians split the cost of the new stadium, which opened July 11, 1996. It takes its name from Victory Gardens, the former name of Bush Stadium. The playing field is 20 feet below street level and has lower and upper seating bowls

The main entrance is behind center field, and fans travel around a walkway to their seats. The exterior is blond and sandy-brown brick, and the seats are forest green. An electronic scoreboard set in the right-field wall is protected by a plastic shroud. Fans can sit on a picnic berm beyond the outfield wall, where they can see a set of train tracks and smoke stacks from a power plant south of the ballpark.

Where to Stay

Visiting Team Motel: Ramada Inn East. This two-story motel is in a field off an Interstate exchange, 10 minutes northeast of the ballpark. There are standard rooms and business-class rooms, which have desks and refrigerators. Both styles have been remodeled recently. The hotel has a pleasant atrium and indoor pool. *7701 E. 42nd St., at I–465, Pendleton Pike exit, Indianapolis 46226, tel. 317/897–4000 or 800/272–6232, fax 317/897–8100. 192 rooms. Facilities: restaurant, indoor and outdoor pools, exercise room, game room. AE, D, DC, MC, V. $*

Courtyard by Marriott Downtown. Guests can watch the game from the upper floors of this eight-story 1966 hotel, which is across the street from the new stadium. Half the rooms are doubles; the rest have king-size beds. The furnishings are contemporary. *501 W. Washington St., Indianapolis 46204, tel. 317/635–4443 or 800/321–2211, fax 317/687–0029. 233 rooms. Facilities: restaurant, pool, playground, coin laundry. AE, D, DC, MC, V. $$*

Crowne Plaza Union Station. Imagine building a hotel around 13 Pullman train cars. The cars, which have been gutted and fitted with two double beds and private baths, are on the second floor of this three-story downtown hotel, which is adjacent to the city's convention center and six blocks from the ballpark. This is a splurge hotel. *123 W. Louisiana St., Indianapolis 46225, tel. 317/631–2221 or 800/227–6963, fax 317/236–7474. 276 rooms. Facilities: restaurant, indoor pool, exercise room. AE, D, DC, MC, V. $$$*

Where to Eat

Shapiro's. This traditional Jewish deli has great corned beef, puddings, and home-canned peaches. Patrons walk through a cafeteria line and try not to get too much. You may order half-sandwiches, which are more than enough for children. The Formica tables are seat-yourself, and there's a take-out section. *808 S. Meridian St., Indianapolis, tel. 317/631–4041. No credit cards. $*

Hollyhock Hill. The decor has stayed loyal to the 1928 hollyhock theme, and, luckily, the fried chicken has maintained its quality, too. Lazy Susans serve hearty meals family-style. Brownies and peppermint ice cream are the customary desserts. *8110 N. College Ave., Indianapolis, tel. 317/251–2294. MC, V. $*

Dodd's Town House. You'll need reservations for this family favorite for special dinners. Its panfried steaks and chicken compete with the pies, particularly the buttermilk pie, for fans. *5694 N. Meridian St., Indianapolis, tel. 317/257–1872. AE, D, DC, MC, V. $*

Entertainments

Indianapolis Motor Speedway and Speedway Hall of Fame. It's thrilling to be able to drive around this historic track, even though you're going 35 mph in a 15-minute bus tour, not the 230 mph that racecars reach. The track is nicknamed the Brickyard because initially the 2½-mile oval was paved with 3 million bricks. Just a yard of bricks remains at the start-finish line. The museum holds ornate Art Deco trophies, laughable early safety helmets made of leather, and other racing memorabilia, plus a film. The bus tour is an extra $2. *4790 W. 16th St., Indianapolis, tel. 317/481–8500. Admission: $2 adults. Open daily 9–5.*

Indianapolis Zoo. This downtown, cageless zoo has several habitats and several daily demonstrations of animal behavior. A good place to cool off is at the large aquarium, which has a water-show extravaganza with whales and dolphins. Be prepared for many extra-admission items, like rides on camels, elephants, ponies, and a 1920 Parker carousel. There is a Subway restaurant on the premises, along with several outdoor cafés. The zoo is 1 mile west of downtown, 600 yards past the White River Bridge. The grounds stay open an hour after the admission office closes at 5. *1200 W. Washington St., Indianapolis, tel. 317/630–2001. Admission: $9 adults, $5.50 ages 3–12, $6.50 senior citizens; $3 parking. Open daily 9–5. D, MC, V.*

Children's Museum. You'll need several hours to cover the five floors of the largest children's museum in the world. There's a planetarium (shows, $2), an extensive computer area, and a hands-on center for younger children. Kids can explore an Indiana limestone cave, view a lifesize *Tyrannosaurus rex*, and check out a mummy. A carousel offers rides (50¢). The large-screen Cinedome Theater ($4.50 adults, $3.50 ages 2–17) shows two films. The museum, just north of downtown, houses a restaurant. *3000 N. Meridian St., Indianapolis, tel. 317/924–5431. Admission: $6 adults, $5 senior citizens, $3 ages 2–17; free 1st Thurs. of mo. Open daily 10–5; 1st Thurs. of mo., 10–8. MC, V.*

Sites to See

Indianapolis City Center. This excellent one-stop resource center is near the Indiana Convention Center and the RCA Dome. You'll find a three-dimensional scale model of the city to orient you and a multimedia slide show. *Pan American Plaza, 201 S. Capitol Ave., Indianapolis, tel. 317/237–5206 or 800/323–4639. Open weekdays 10–5:30, Sat. 10–4.*

RCA Dome. Formerly known as the Hoosier Dome, this air-supported domed stadium has a self-cleaning roof. Tours last 45 minutes and leave from the Indianapolis City Center. Visitors also see a movie about the myriad sports and entertainment activities in this 60,500-seat stadium. *100 S. Capitol Ave., Indianapolis, tel. 317/262–3410. Admission: $5 adults, $4 ages 5–17. Tours Mon.–Sat. at 11, 1, and 3; Sun. at 1 and 3.*

Indiana State Capitol Building. Completed in 1878, this Renaissance–style capitol building was constructed mostly with Indiana limestone, granite, and marble. The Capitol is topped by a 234-foot copper-covered stone dome. There are self-guided tours of the building, which is in the center of downtown. Free guided sessions are by appointment. *Capitol Ave. and Washington St., Indianapolis, tel. 317/233–5293. Open weekdays 9–3.*

National Art Museum of Sport. This museum is a good way to introduce sports-fiends to art. On the campus of Purdue–Indiana University–Indianapolis, it shows paintings and sculptures chiefly of male athletes. *University Place Hotel Conference Center, 850 W. Michigan St., Indianapolis, tel. 317/274–2700. Donations appreciated. Open weekdays 8–5.*

CHICAGO CUBS

League: National League • **Class:** Major • **Stadium:** Wrigley Field • **Opened:** 1914 • **Capacity:** 38,710 • **Dimensions:** LF: 355, CF: 400, RF: 353 • **Surface:** grass • **Season:** Apr.–early Oct.

STADIUM LOCATION: 1060 West Addison St., Chicago, IL 60613

TEAM WEB SITE: www.cubs.com

GETTING THERE: Wrigley Field, on north side of Chicago, is bounded east and west by Sheffield Ave and Clark St. and north and south by Waveland Ave. and Addison St. From I–90/I–94, take Addison St. exit east 5 mi to stadium. Call 312/836–7000 for information about rail and shuttle bus information.

TICKET INFORMATION: 1060 West Addison St., Chicago, IL 60613, tel. 312/404–2827 or 800/347–2827, fax 312/404–4014

PRICE RANGE: Prices higher weekends, holidays, nights, and summer weekdays. Field box seats $15–$19 bleacher seats $6–$10.

GAME TIME: 1:20 PM except Fri., 2:20 and 18 games 7:05 PM; gates open 2 hrs before game.

TIPS ON SEATING: Seats on lower level farther back under upper deck have obstructed views. Upper deck seats are better than obstructed-view seats. Small section in left-field bleachers reserved for families.

SEATING FOR PEOPLE WITH DISABILITIES: Arrange for seating and parking for people with disabilities in advance: call 312/404–4107.

STADIUM FOOD: There's is a 25% early bird discount on food and non-alcoholic beverages for the first hour after the gate opens. On the main concourse, are the **Italian Market, Bullpen Barbecue,** and **Chili Peppers Mexican Fair,** along with standard hot dog booths. Avoid Diamond's Grill, where mushrooms and ketchup are added to the grilled pork chop sandwich, and the walleye pike and BBQ chicken sandwiches contain cheese. Warning to parents: most of the "Tropical Delights" frozen drinks have alcohol. The fruit bar popsicle is good ($1.75).

SMOKING POLICY: Smoking prohibited in seating areas.

PARKING: Parking is limited and expensive ($10–$15). Call to order parking passes for Cubs lot (1126 West Grace St., tel. 800/347–2827; $12.50).

TOURISM INFORMATION: Chicago Office of Tourism (78 E. Washington St. Chicago, IL 60602, tel. 312/744–2400 or 800/822–0292, IL Office of Tourism–Sears Tower).

Chicago: Wrigley Field

Former baseball commissioner A. Bartlett Giamatti has written of the thrill of walking into a ballpark and first seeing the field: "... after we ascend the ramp or go through the tunnel and enter the inner core of the little city, we often are struck, at least I am, by the suddenness and fullness of the vision there presented: a green expanse, complete and coherent, shimmering, carefully tended, a garden." To our minds, there is no place closer to this ideal of the garden in the city than Chicago's Wrigley Field. For a pure baseball fan, it simply doesn't get any better than a sunny afternoon at Wrigley.

Wrigley Field was built right into the fabric of a city neighborhood. Enter from the main gate at North Clark Street. The swarm of people standing in front of the red "Welcome to Wrigley Field" sign lets you know you are about to enter a very special place. Most approaches to Wrigley have all the charm of the back side of an aging resort hotel. Its what's inside that counts.

Unlike the megamillion-dollar parks of today, this baseball jewel evolved over decades. Designed by Zachary Taylor Davis and built for $250,000 in four weeks in 1914 as Weeghman Park, the single-decked ballpark was the home of the Chicago ChiFeds of the Federal League.

When the Federal League, an upstart association that had attempted to be a third major league, folded after two years, Weeghman and his associates bought the National League Cubs and moved them from their West Side Grounds to the Addison Street site, renaming it Cubs Park. Joa, a live bear cub, lived in a cage outside

the ballpark during the 1916 season. Weeghman in 1916 first allowed fans to keep balls that went into the stands. This would not become a common practice until a judge in 1923 ruled that keeping baseballs was not stealing.

In 1921, chewing-gum executive William Wrigley bought the team. The ballpark was renamed Wrigley Field in 1927, the year the upper deck was added to double capacity to 40,000. Wrigley was the site of Babe Ruth's famous "called shot" home run off Cubs pitcher Charlie Root in game three of the 1932 World Series. Legend has it that in the fifth inning of a tie game, the great Bambino let two strikes go by, pointed to right-center field, and hit a massive home run exactly where he had pointed. "I'd play for half my salary if I could bat in this dump all the time," Ruth commented after the series.

The bleachers as we know them today—the home of Chicago's "Bleacher Bums" and undoubtedly the most famous bleachers in all of baseball—were added in 1937. Architects Holabird & Root carefully designed the new bleachers so that houses on Waveland and Sheffield avenues beyond the outfield walls could continue to watch the games for free from their rooftops as they still do today. At first, the bleachers were solid across the outfield. After complaints by batters who lost pitches against the background of white shirts, a section of seats was blocked off to give the hitters a solid background against which to hit—the batter's eye you see in all ballparks today.

A young Cub executive and future Hall of Famer named Bill Veeck had a huge 27-foot-high, 75-foot-wide green-and-white scoreboard built on the top of the center-field bleachers. Here the scores of all major-league baseball games are recorded by hand. After games, a flag is flown from a center-field pole—a blue flag with a white W indicates a Cubs win; a white flag with a blue L indicates a loss. The only ball ever to hit the scoreboard was hit by Sam Snead in 1951, and it was a golf ball. Roberto Clemente once barely missed it. Veeck is also responsible for planting the ivy on Wrigley's brick outfield walls, perhaps the most distinctive and charming aspect of this wonderful ballpark. Balls that disappear into the ivy are ground-rule doubles.

Philip K. Wrigley bought lights for Wrigley Field in the winter of 1941 but donated them to a shipyard to help with the World War II effort the day after the attack on Pearl Harbor. After a decades-long controversy, lights were installed 47 years later in August of 1988. Eighteen night games are now played at Wrigley Field each year. Much to the relief of many, the lights have not destroyed Wrigley's greatness. In the 1950s, the grandstand seats in right field were rebuilt to improve visibility. During the late 1960s and early 1970s, the upper deck was rebuilt in sections.

An attractive brick wall circles the playing field. The breezes from Lake Michigan can change the nature of the game at Wrigley. With its short power alleys and the wind blowing out, Wrigley can be a home-run hitter's dream. But with a cool wind blowing off the lake into the batters' faces, home runs become scarce. Number 14 flies on a flag on the left-field foul pole to honor Ernie Banks, the shortstop Hall of Famer they call "Mr. Cub." Number 26 flies on a flag in right in honor of Hall of Famer Billy Williams. From the picnic deck behind home plate at the upper level, there is a wonderful view of the city and of the neighborhood bars and souvenir shops that surround Wrigley Field.

The top of the visitors dugout on the first-base side says "Welcome to the Friendly Confines of Wrigley Field." And it is friendly, warm, and intimate. The seats are right near the field, unlike those at many of the concrete doughnut monstrosities built in the 1960s with their huge foul territories. The atmosphere is as much that of a party as of a baseball game. No crowd any-

where in baseball gets into the seventh-inning stretch like a Wrigley crowd. No hyped-up exploding video scoreboard is needed to get fans into the game here. Led by Hall of Fame announcer Harry Caray, the crowd sings a boisterous rendition of "Take Me Out to the Ballgame." The rowdiest of all Cubs fans—the shirtless "Bleacher Bums"—sit in the bleachers in right-center field. A home-run ball into any bleachers by an opposing player is certain to be rejected by the fans and tossed back onto the field.

For information on 90-minute tours of Wrigley Field that are held several Saturdays each summer, call 312/831–2827. A $10 donation to a Cubs charity is the price of admission. There is a Cubs Walk of Fame with stars in the sidewalk in front of the ticket windows.

Where to Stay

Best Western River North. This redbrick high-rise was built pre–World War II but was completely remodeled inside and out in 1994. The seven-floor hotel is convenient—the Hard Rock Cafe and Michael Jordan's Restaurant are one block away, and the Miracle Mile is a four-block walk. You get free coffee and a paper in the morning. 125 W. Ohio St., Chicago 60610, tel. 312/467–0800 or 800/528–1234, fax 312/467–1665. 148 rooms. Facilities: restaurant, indoor pool, health club. AE, D, DC, MC, V. $$

Ohio House. This popular, small 1950s-era motel is in the bustling River North area, with Michael Jordan's Restaurant one block away. The rooms are freshly painted and standard-size, and the price is right. There's an all-night drugstore and an all-night McDonald's within walking distance. It's a 15-minute elevated train (El) ride to Wrigley from here. 600 N. La Salle St., Chicago 60610, tel. 312/943–6000, fax 312/943–6063. 50 rooms. Facilities: coffeeshop. AE, D, DC, MC, V. $$

Comfort Inn of Lincoln Park. This four-story motel is 1 mile from Wrigley Field and offers a free Continental breakfast. 601 W. Diversey Pkwy., Chicago 60614, tel. 312/348–2810 or 800/424–6423, fax 312/348–1912. 74 rooms. Facilities: outdoor whirlpool, indoor hot tub, parking (fee). AE, D, DC, MC, V. $$

Days Inn–Gold Coast. This property is known here as the former Hotel Lincoln. Across the street from the Chicago Zoo, it is 2 miles south of Wrigley. Most rooms have twin or queen beds, and only suites have two double beds. It offers guests a free Continental breakfast. *1816 N. Clark St., Chicago 60614, tel. 312/664–3040 or 800/325–2525, fax 312/664–3045. 243 rooms. Facilities: restaurant, parking (fee weekends). AE, D, DC, MC, V. $$*

Neighborhood Inns of Chicago. These three small hotels are close to Wrigley Field. A fourth, the **Lake** (3434 N. Broadway, tel. 312/404–3401), is slated to open in 1997.

The Surf. The rooms in this small hotel are done in country French style. It's close to the Lincoln Park Zoo, in a quiet residential neighborhood that's 10 blocks from Wrigley Field. There is a free Continental breakfast. *555 W. Surf St., Chicago 60657, tel. 312/528–8400 or 800/787–3108, fax 312/528–8483. 55 rooms. Facilities: coin laundry, parking (fee). AE, D, DC, MC, V. $$*

City Suites Hotel. The rooms have European styling in a Deco theme here. The hotel was built in the 1920s and once served the vaudeville and gangster set. It is five blocks from Wrigley. There is a free Continental breakfast. *933 W. Belmont Ave., Chicago 60657, tel. 312/404–3400 or 800/248–9108, fax 312/404–3405. 45 rooms. Facilities: coin laundry, parking (fee). AE, D, DC, MC, V. $$*

Park Brompton. English country is the decorating theme in this small hotel, which is across from the lakefront and from Lincoln Park. It's a 10-minute drive from Wrigley Field. Guests receive a free Continental breakfast. *528 W. Brompton Ave., Chicago 60657, tel. 312/404–3499 or 800/727–5108, fax 312/404–3495. 52 rooms. Facilities: coin laundry. AE, D, DC, MC, V. $$*

Where to Eat

The Busy Bee. This busy Polish restaurant offers good, inexpensive food, including a hearty meat loaf, sandwiches, and steaks, served either at the counter or at tables. It is a traditional hand-shaking stop for decades of politicians. In a Wicker Park neighborhood of art galleries and bookstores, it is close to the El, at the Damen Street stop. *1540 N. Damen St., at North Ave., Chicago, tel. 312/772–4433. MC, V. $*

Lou Mitchell's. Women are handed a tiny box of Milk Duds or a doughnut hole as they walk in, setting the tone here. There are awe-inspiring pecan rolls, fresh orange juice, malt waffles, stewed fruits, and omelettes of every type. *560 W. Jackson St., Chicago, tel. 312/939–3111. No credit cards. $*

Manny's Coffee Shop. You can pick up blintzes, fragrant corned beef, chopped liver, chicken pot pies, and great potato pancakes at this quintessential Jewish deli. It is cafeteria-style. *1141 S. Jefferson St., Chicago, tel. 312/939–2855. No credit cards. $*

Ed Debevic's. This is the granddaddy of the new '50s diners, with lots of neon reflecting on real mashed potatoes, chicken pot pie, burgers, sodas, and pies. The waitresses have their wisecracks down pat. *640 N. Wells St., Chicago, tel. 312/664–1707. AE, D, DC, MC, V. $*

Michael Jordan's Restaurant. Your kids will drag you here. It's crowded, with a sports-bar atmosphere, but the food isn't bad. It shares a neighborhood with a musical-themed McDonald's, a Hard Rock Cafe, and Planet Hollywood, so it's tourist heaven. There are $8 hamburgers, $10 calamari and Caesar salads, plus ribs, pasta, and, yes, Gatorade. *500 N. La Salle, St. at Illinois St., Chicago, tel. 312/644–3865. AE, D, MC, V. $$*

The Berghoff. This dim, clubby restaurant serves great German food and root beer floats. It's old-style Chicago, with murals of the city's origins surrounding the dining rooms on each of its two levels. It's in the downtown Loop and has been "on Adams and State since 1898." *17 W. Adams St., tel. 312/427–3170. AE, MC, V. Closed Sun. $$*

Pizzeria Uno and Due. The cornmeal crust is outstanding in this pair of restaurants. Diners get a history of pizza with their meal. The two restaurants are within steps of each other and are far superior to any of their nationwide chain extensions. Due is larger and has a terrace. Uno, the original creator of deep-dish pizza, has been baking it since 1943. *Uno: 29 E. Ohio St., Chicago, tel. 312/321–1000. Due: 619 N. Wabash, Chicago, tel. 312/943–2400. AE, D, DC, MC, V. $*

Giordano's Pizza (730 N. Rush St., tel. 312/951–0747) and Gino's (930 N. Rush St., tel. 312/337–7726) are other good pizza sources.

Entertainments

Field Museum of Natural History. The world's largest reconstructed dinosaur, a four-story Brachiosaurus, is at the door of this museum. You can learn about Egypt by viewing 23 mummies and by participating in hands-on stone building and Nile River navigation. There's too much to see in one visit, so pick a few sections and avoid overload. *1200 S. Lake Shore Dr., at Roosevelt Rd., Chicago, tel. 312/922–9410. Admission: $5 adults, $3 ages 3–17. Open daily 9–5.*

Shedd Aquarium and Oceanarium. You can see two Beluga whales, electric eels, penguins, and sharks in this huge facility, which is adjacent to the Field Museum. It's wise to bring a sweater for the Oceanarium. You can buy passes to just the aquarium and its coral-reef exhibit. There's a restaurant and snack bar in the building. *1200 S. Lake Shore Dr., Chicago, tel. 312/939–2426. Admission: $10 adults, $8 ages 3–11 and senior citizens; aquarium only, $4 adults, $3 children, free Thurs.; Oceanarium Thurs., $4 adults, $3 children. Open daily 9–6.*

Museum of Science and Industry. Ride a train through a coal-mine shaft, see a captured German U-boat, and walk through a 16-foot pulsating heart. If you want to avoid lines, be aware that the coal mine is busiest midday. The Omnimax theater is extra. *57th St. and Lake Shore Dr., Chicago, tel. 312/684–1414. Admission: $6 adults, $2.50 ages 5–12; free Thurs. Open daily 9:30–5:30.*

Navy Pier. Fun is the sole activity on this 50-acre complex on Lake Michigan, but most of it will cost you. You can rent in-line skates or ride a 150-foot Ferris wheel or a carousel. There are arcades and shops, including a store called Oh Yes Chicago, which sells city street signs and other memorabilia. You can also ride the free trolley. Parking is costly ($6 for two hours and up), so consider a bus. (Bus 29 Northbound State Street is among those stopping at the pier.) *600 E. Grand Ave., between Illinois St. and Grand Ave., Chicago, tel. 800/595–7437.*

Chicago Children's Museum. At the entrance to the Navy Pier stands this new, three-floor museum. Children love crawling through its landfill exhibit, "The Stinking Truth About Garbage." They can also create rubbish art and Lego masterpieces. There's a "Touchy Business" sensory exhibit for kids under six with a machine to manipulate that's part airplane, part boat, and part tractor. A special lab lets older children be inventors. *700 E. Grand Ave., Chicago, tel. 312/527–1000. Admission: $5. Open Tues.–Sun. 10–5.*

Lincoln Park Zoo. This world-class zoo contains a 5-acre farm, a children's zoo and nursery, a great ape house, and a penguin and seabird house. There are giant Clydesdales, trees full of koalas, and a large collection of big mammals. Children's-zoo demonstrations are weekdays 10–2, weekends 10–4. There is pay parking in summer and a restaurant on the premises. *2200 N. Cannon Dr., Chicago, tel. 312/742–2000. Admission free. Open daily 9–5.*

Sites to See

Thomas Hughes Children's Library. On the second floor of the stunning, metal-trimmed Harold Washington Library Center is the world's largest children's library space. There's a Story Stairs area, where parents can read to preschoolers; a Learning Center, with Macintosh computers; and a huge selection of books and audiovisual materials. *400 S. State St., Chicago, tel. 312/747–4300. Open Mon., Wed., and Fri.–Sat. 9–5; Tues. and Thurs. 11–7; Sun. 1–5.*

Sears Tower Skydeck. A speedy elevator takes you up 103 floors to marvel at the view. You can see Comiskey and Wrigley fields, the orange Calder "Universe" mobile, Adler Planetarium, and other landmarks. Mornings are less crowded here than nights. *233 S. Wacker Dr., Chicago, tel. 312/875–9696. Admission: $6.50 adults, $4 ages 5–17, $4.75 senior citizens, $18.50 family. Open Mar.–Sept., daily 9 AM–11 PM; Oct.–Feb., daily 10–10.*

KANE COUNTY COUGARS

League: Midwest League • **Major League Affiliation:** Florida Marlins • **Class:** A • **Stadium:** Philip B. Elfstrom Stadium • **Opened:** 1991 • **Capacity:** 5,900 • **Dimensions:** LF: 335, CF: 400, RF: 335 • **Surface:** grass • **Season:** early Apr.–Labor Day

STADIUM LOCATION: 34W002 Cherry Ln., Geneva, IL 60134

GETTING THERE: From I-88, take the Farnsworth Rd. North exit (which becomes Kirk Rd). Travel north on Kirk for 5½ mi to Cherry Ln. (½ mi north of Fabyan Pkwy.). From I-90 take Rte. 59 south to Rte. 64 (North Ave.). Take Rte. 64 west to Kirk Rd. Travel south on Kirk Rd. 3 mi to Cherry Ln. (first stoplight south of Rte. 38). Go right on Cherry Ln. to the stadium.

TICKET INFORMATION: 34W002 Cherry Ln., Geneva, IL 60134, tel. 630/232–8811, fax 630/232–8815

PRICE RANGE: Box seat $7; reserved seat $6; bleacher seat $5; lawn seat $4

GAME TIME: Weekdays 7 PM, Sat. 6 PM (Apr.–May) or 5 PM (June–Aug.), Sun. 2 PM. Gates open 2 hours before games.

TIPS ON SEATING: There are only seven rows of box seats, so the reserved seats are quite close. The box seats are real seats, and the reserved seats are aluminum benches with backs. The lawn seating begins just past the dugouts, but the hills are quite steep and were in bad shape when we visited. The bleacher seats beyond right center field are a family fun section. For $100, you can take seven of your friends to watch the game from a hot tub on the right-field deck; the fee includes soda, beer, and service by a waiter.

SEATING FOR PEOPLE WITH DISABILITIES: There is seating for people with disabilities on the concourse and behind screen on the first- and third-base sides. Parking is free for people with disabilities along the first-base (south) side of the stadium.

STADIUM FOOD: The pork chop sandwich ($4.75) is the specialty here and is quite good. The brats ($2.75) also are excellent. There is variety here with fajitas ($3.50) and tacos ($2.75), which are sold at the end of the concourse on the first-base side. The grills are located in both the first- and third-base sides just beyond the concourse. Try the funnel cakes ($2.50) at the ice cream stand on the third-base side beyond the concourse.

SMOKING POLICY: Smoking is prohibited in the seating area but allowed on the concourse.

PARKING: Parking at the stadium is free. The main lot is unpaved, and there is only one exit.

VISITING TEAM HOTEL: Travelodge Naperville (Naperville Rd. at East-West Tollway, Naperville, IL 60563, tel. 630/505–0200 or 800/578–7878)

TOURISM INFORMATION: Geneva Chamber of Commerce (8 S. 3rd St., Geneva, IL 60135, tel. 630/232–6060)

Geneva, IL: Philip B. Elfstrom Stadium

The Kane County Cougars were the right team in the right place at the right time. They weren't the first team to locate in a fast-growing suburb of a major metropolis. They didn't build the finest stadium. They weren't the only team to feature non-stop family entertainment with contest after contest between the baseball innings. But the Cougars put it all together as well as anyone.

A Baltimore Orioles franchise moved here from Wausau, Wisconsin, for the 1991 season and drew an astonishing 240,290 fans. The conventional wisdom was that a minor league team couldn't make it just 40 miles from not one but two major league teams. The conventional wisdom underestimated the number of young families in the emerging suburbs thirsting for affordable family entertainment.

Philip B. Elfstrom Stadium was built in 1991 by the Kane County Forest Preserve District and named for one of its long-time leaders. Geneva, Illinois, 40 miles west of Chicago, is a 19th-century Victorian town now largely populated by Chicago commuters and antiques shops. The Cougars quickly became the area's number-one family entertainment stop.

The main grandstand is fairly standard for a 1990s Single A stadium. The field is below the concourse so fans can watch the action from all concession stands. There is lawn seating on grassy hills down both the third- and first-base lines. The capacity has been expanded from 4,800 to 5,900 by adding seating down the first-base line and bleachers beyond the right-field wall, an unusual touch for Single A baseball. In most ballparks, the bleachers are for rowdy, boozy guys and families are wise to avoid them. Not here in family-friendly Kane County, where the bleachers are the designated family fun section. There is a large scoreboard beyond the left field fence. From the grandstand, fans see a well-treed area beyond the outfield fence in left center and right fields. There is a huge solid-waste landfill behind the stadium, but fans neither see it nor smell it.

Ozzie T. Cougar, a huge friendly brown cougar with a long tail and a baseball jersey and hat, quickly established himself as one of minor league baseball's most popular mascots. The Cougars have been pioneers in the minor league efforts to entertain fans between the innings. They do it all here—from the dizzy bat contests and mascot races to the Goose Is Loose Race and a human bowling ball competition. In 1994, they added a hot tub out beyond right field for eight fans willing to put up $100.

This is a park with plenty of attractions. Jake the Diamond Dog is a real golden retriever who lives in a dog house right near the ball boy on the first base side. Jake takes a basket with water bottles to the umpires between innings. The Million Dollar Mitt is an enormous inflatable mitt beyond the outfield wall in right center field. If a player hits a home run in the advertiser's sign in the mitt, the player gets $100,000, a fan gets $450,000, and a charity gets $450,000. On Sundays, kids are allowed on the field to chase player autographs 30 minutes before the game.

On Saturdays, kids are allowed to run the bases after the game, and there are fireworks every Saturday night.

There isn't much baseball history here. The Orioles farm team left after two seasons and were replaced by future Florida Marlins stars. There were occasionally teams in the Kane County/Fox Valley area back as far as the 1890s, but the best story of the limited pre-Cougar era involves a league that folded at mid-season in 1910. The Kankakee team in the Class C Northern Association owed 19-year-old center fielder Casey Stengel $67 in back pay when it withdrew from the league in July. The ever-inventive Stengel, a wily future Hall of Fame manager, confiscated the team's uniforms as his payment. In 1911, Stengel hit .352 for Aurora to lead the Class C Wisconsin-Illinois League in batting.

Where to Stay

Super 8. This small hotel is just 3½ miles south of the ballfield. The nine-year-old three-story motel has the beige and dark brown Tudoresque exterior that is standard in this chain. The rooms are clean and plain, with double and single bed combinations. There is a Continental breakfast bar, and the suites have microwave ovens and refrigerators. Rollaways are $6. *1520 E. Main St., St. Charles, IL 60174, tel. 630/377–8388 or 800/ 800–8000, fax 630/377–1340. 66 rooms, 2 suites. AE, D, MC, V. $*

Visiting Team Hotel: Travelodge Naperville. The 12-year-old three-story motel was renovated in 1993. It stands in a commercial strip of fast-food and family restaurants. Guests receive a free Continental breakfast. The utilitarian rooms' only extra is a loveseat. It's a 15-minute drive east from the ballpark. *1617 Naperville Rd. at I–88, the East–West Tollway, Naperville, IL 60563, tel. 630/505–0200 or 800/255–3050, fax 630/505–0501. 103 rooms. Facilities: coin laundry. AE, D, MC, V. $*

The Herrington Inn. Geneva's Rock Springs Creamery has been restored into this elegant riverfront inn. In the late 19th century on the homesite of the town's first permanent settler, James Herrington, the Creamery began processing butter and milk for the fast-growing community. The attractive limestone building on the river's edge now houses 40 guest rooms and a restaurant. Guests receive a Continental breakfast, and each room has a mini-bar, a whirlpool, a fireplace, and a balcony. Chilled milk and warm cookies are part of its turndown service. *15 S. River Lane, on the west side of Fox River Bridge, Geneva, IL 60134, tel. 630/208–7433 or 800/216–2466, fax 630/208–8930. 40 rooms. Facilities: restaurant, whirlpool spa. AE, D, DC, MC, V. $$$*

Where to Eat

The Country Inn at Mill Race Inn. This complex, on the Fox River at the entrance to Herrington Island Park, houses five distinctive restaurants. The Country Inn includes part of a stone blacksmith shop built in 1842 on the east side of the Fox River. In 1933, Ann and Marjorie Forsythe opened the former blacksmith shop as a tea room for people shopping at the local antiques shops. It's grown into the inn complex. The menu is classic American and Swedish cuisine. The Swedish meatballs are served on black-pepper fettucine with lingonberries and a sour cream sauce. There's also prime rib and good salmon. *4 E. State St.,* *east side of Fox River Bridge, Geneva, tel. 630/ 232–2030. AE, MC, V. $$*

Entertainments

Mill Race Cyclery. You can pick up a trail guide and rent bicycles or Rollerblades here to take on the Fox River Trail. After passing under a bridge you're in the glorious Herrington Island Park in the Fox River. *11 E. State St., at Water St. at the Geneva Dam, Geneva, tel. 630/232–2833. Bike rentals: $6/hr, $26.25 daily. Rollerblade rentals: $6/hr with protective gear. Open weekdays 10–8, Sat. 10–5, Sun. 11–5.*

Fabyan Forest Preserve. One mile south of Geneva is this forest preserve, a public park with no entrance fee that preserves several buildings from a magnificent turn-of-the-century estate. These include the Fabyan Villa, a giant shingled windmill at the gate on the Route 25 side, and a lighthouse on an island that is accessible by a bridge. The villa, designed in 1907 by Frank Lloyd Wright and now a museum, is on the west side of the river, along Route 31. *Rte. 31, Geneva, tel. 630/232–4811. Villa open mid-May–mid-Oct., Wed. 1–4 and weekends 1–4:30.*

FIELD OF DREAMS   16
CEDAR RAPIDS, DES MOINES, DAVENPORT

Iowa baseball includes a magical site, the Dyersville farm where the movie, *A Field of Dreams* was set. Visitors have been playing on the field, for free, every day in good weather since the movie crew built a ball diamond in the cornfield.

Start your Iowa vacation in Davenport to watch the Quad Cities River Bandits play in John O'Donnell Stadium beside the Mississippi River. Paddleboats meander behind the stadium and the beautiful 1939 Centennial Bridge hangs at roof level along the first-base side. This 66-year-old stadium has been modernized and survived a flood; its scoreboard explodes after runs and victories. Cross the river to watch the barges float through Lock and Dam 15 and continue on to Moline's excellent children's museum. Lunch should be at Lagomarcino's, a vintage candy store and ice cream parlor.

Herbert Hoover's birthplace and presidential museum is 50 miles west of Davenport on Interstate 80, in West Branch. After passing Iowa City, head north on Route 380, first turning west and stopping for a farm-style meal at the Amana Colonies. A half-hour northeast is Cedar Rapids, home of Quaker Oats. Watching a game in the city's Veterans Memorial Stadium is like traveling back in time. The design, prices, and food all are reminiscent of 1949, when the park was built. The Kernels are a Single A, Midwest League team.

You'll find baseball magic 60 miles northwest of Cedar Rapids, where 60,000 visitors a year play pick-up games on the *Field of Dreams* cornfield diamond. The town is also home to the Ertl Toy Company, where you can take a free factory tour and visit an outlet shop for miniature tractors and farm toys. Continue west on Route 20 until you reach Interstate 35, the major north–south route that will speed you to Des Moines, which is 155 miles from Dyersville. Sec Taylor Stadium is a 10,500-seat gem at the junction of the Des Moines and Racoon rivers, with a great view of the golden state capitol dome. There is an engaging Living History Farm just north of town, in Urbandale, and a family-oriented theme park, Adventureland, on the city's east side. Big leaguer Bob Feller rates his own museum in his hometown of Van Meter, 12 miles west of Des Moines.

CEDAR RAPIDS KERNELS

League: Midwest League • **Major League Affiliation:** California Angels • **Class:** A • **Stadium:** Veterans Memorial Stadium • **Opened:** 1949 • **Capacity:** 6,000 • **Dimensions:** LF: 325, CF: 385, RF: 325 • **Surface:** grass • **Season:** Apr.–Labor Day

STADIUM LOCATION: 950 Rockford Rd., SW, Cedar Rapids, IA 52404

GETTING THERE: From I-380, Wilson Ave. exit (exit 18), west 1½ mi to Rockford Rd. Right on Rockford, 1 mi to stadium, corner of 8th Ave. and 15th St. SW.

TICKET INFORMATION: Box 2001, Cedar Rapids, IA 52406, tel. 319/363–3887, fax 319/363–5631

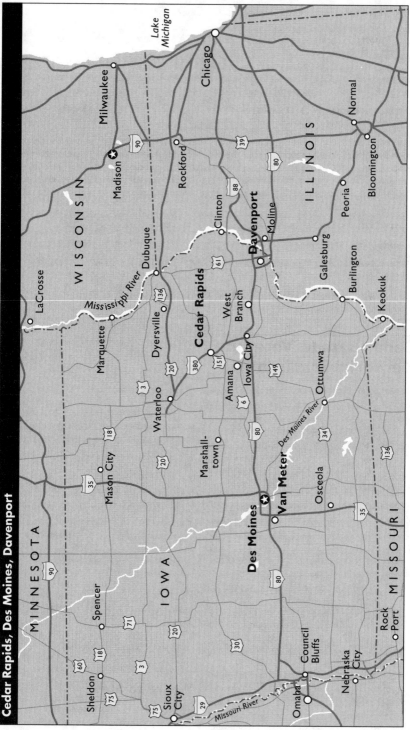

Cedar Rapids, Des Moines, Davenport

PRICE RANGE: Box seats $4; general admission $3 adults, $2 children and senior citizens

GAME TIME: Mon.–Sat. 7 PM, Sun. and other afternoon games 2 PM; gates open 1 hr before game.

TIPS ON SEATING: Only 4 rows of box seats; general admission seats under grandstand excellent. Grandstand is designated no-smoking area.

SEATING FOR PEOPLE WITH DISABILITIES: Just beyond dugout on first-base side between grandstand and right-field bleachers

STADIUM FOOD: Don't miss the pork chop sandwich for $2.50 from the grill on the first-base side behind the bleacher seats. Another bargain is the creamy hand-dipped ice cream in the concourse on the third-base side. It's $1 a scoop and the scoops are huge. The large candy stand has 50 varieties of candy. A picnic area with six green-and-white striped umbrellas is by the grill. Hot dogs and chili dogs are served behind the grandstand on the third-base side. The big condiment table includes great mustard, sauerkraut in a crock pot, jalapeños, relish, and onions.

SMOKING POLICY: Smoking prohibited in box seats and in any seats under grandstand

PARKING: Ample free parking

VISITING TEAM HOTEL: Village Inn (100 F Ave. NW, Cedar Rapids, IA 52405, tel. 319/366–5323 or 800/858–5511)

TOURISM INFORMATION: Cedar Rapids Area Convention & Visitors Bureau (119 1st Ave. SE, Cedar Rapids, IA 52406-5339, tel. 319/398–5009)

Cedar Rapids: Veterans Memorial Stadium

Watching a ball game from the packed grandstand of Veterans Memorial Stadium in Cedar Rapids, Iowa, on a steamy summer night is about as close as you'll ever get to going back in time. With a ballplayer at the plate showing a lot of sock like the players did when we were kids, it was an eerie experience. It felt like 1949, the year this fine old stadium was built.

As the stadium sits up on a hill, fans have a bit of a climb to their seats. The elevated location provides a fine view of the Cedar Rapids skyline beyond center field. Veterans Memorial Park, dedicated in 1992, includes an Air Force plane that can be seen beyond the center-field wall from the grandstand, as well as two tanks and an anchor. Out beyond right field are several of the grain-processing plants that are the backbone of the Cedar Rapids economy. Kingston Stadium, a 13,000-seat high school football stadium, is near the ballpark on the third-base side.

The stadium design is simple. There are four rows of box seats, only 500 in all. The general-admission seats are just behind the box seats and are covered by a roof. But you have to watch where you sit, as the 10 dark-green poles

holding up the grandstand roof can obstruct your view. Remember, this is the 1940s. There are aluminum bleachers down each baseline, with a picnic area beyond the bleachers on the third-base side.

As much as we enjoyed this almost 50-year-old stadium, it has one serious design flaw. The concourse area under the grandstand is too small and crowded. It does not allow the fans to get from the first-base side to the third-base side without climbing the ramp and walking through the grandstand seating area. On nights with large crowds pedestrian traffic jams block the first few rows of the general-admission seating in the grandstand. The two team locker rooms are below the center of the grandstand, breaking the concourse into two halves.

They have been playing professional baseball in Cedar Rapids since 1891. The Kernels wore replica uniforms of the 1938 Cedar Rapids Raiders for "Turn Back the Clock" Days every Sunday in 1995 and hope to include a museum tribute to Cedar Rapids baseball history in their next renovation.

Where to Stay

Visiting Team Hotel: Village Inn. This utilitarian four-story hotel is on an isolated and quiet downtown block, overlooking the Cedar River. The rooms are small and clean, with contemporary furniture. *100 F Ave. NW, Cedar Rapids 52405, tel. 319/366–5323 or 800/585–5511, fax 319/366–5323. 86 rooms. Facilities: restaurant. AE, D, MC, V. $*

Visiting Team Hotel: Wyndham Five Seasons Hotel. This is Cedar Rapids' downtown convention hotel, and its 16 stories look out over the city. The rooms are spacious and traditionally furnished. The 18-year-old hotel was refurbished in 1993. *350 1st Ave. NE, Cedar Rapids 52401, tel. 319/363–8161 or 800/996–3426, fax 319/363–3935. 275 rooms. Facilities: restaurant, indoor pool, sauna, exercise room. AE, D, DC, MC, V. $$*

Where to Eat

Metro Grill. Neon and funky artwork fill the walls of this casual family restaurant that specializes in wood-oven pizzas, pastas, and grilled meats. There are healthy menu choices, sandwiches, and a children's menu available. The restaurant, which has booth and table service, is 15 minutes northeast of the ballpark. *4407 1st Ave. SE, Cedar Rapids, tel. 319/393–9727. AE, D, DC, MC, V. $*

Sports Page Family Restaurant. The owner, Jim Googler, cooks the steaks, and the seafood is fresh, a rarity in Iowa. This Formica-booth restaurant is very casual, with a sports theme and memorabilia on the walls. The children's menu offers spaghetti and burgers. The restaurant is about 8 miles northeast of the ballpark. *38th St. and 1st Ave., Cedar Rapids, tel. 319/362–3350. MC, V. $*

Zio Johno's Spaghetti House. This small, inexpensive Italian restaurant is 15 minutes northwest of the ballpark. It has a children's menu and a good, basic meat sauce. *355 Edgewood Rd. NW, Cedar Rapids, tel. 319/396–1700. No credit cards. Closed Sun. $*

Skyora Bakery. Visitors to Czech Village can stop for incomparable breakfast kolaches and huge cinnamon rolls here. There are six tables in front of the counter, next to shelves selling gooseberries, cherries, sauerkraut, popcorn, and bread. The bakery is down the street from the **Czech Museum** (10 16th Ave. SW, tel. 319/362–8500). *73 16th Ave. SW, Cedar Rapids, tel. 319/364–5271. No credit cards. Closed Sun. $*

Country Junction. This ordinary country-style family restaurant has three dining rooms, plus a coffeeshop. The local dairy ice cream is very good, and its sandwiches and dinners are fine but nothing special. It is convenient to the Ertl toy factory and Field of Dreams. *Hwys. 136 and 20, Dyersville, tel. 319/875–7055. AE, D, MC, V. $*

Entertainments

Dyersville National Farm Toy Museum. A half-hour drive north of Cedar Rapids brings you to the home of Ertl Toys, the world's largest producer of farm toys. Display cases show metal toys through the ages. The museum includes a film and a huge miniature circus made with meticulous detail. *1110 16th Ave. SE, at Hwys. 20 and 136, Dyersville, tel. 319/875–2727. Admission: $3, children under 12 free. Open daily 8–7.*

Ertl Toy Company. This toymaker offers a serious 45-minute factory tour that is open to children. Everyone wears goggles and sees the spray painting, the metal manufacturing, and the decal sticking that go into the production of miniature trucks, tractors, and toy banks. The tour is too long for some preschoolers. Reservations are necessary, particularly in summer. *Dyersville, tel. 319/875–2000. Tours May–Sept., weekdays at 10, 11, 1, and 2; Oct.–Apr., weekdays at 10 and 1.*

Sites to See

Amana Colonies. The colonies are settlements that specialize in farming, crafts, and food. The original settlers were members of the Community of True Inspiration, who were persecuted heavily in Germany. They first moved to Buffalo in 1840s, outgrew their land, and then found 26,000 acres along the Iowa River. The church society continues, but in 1932 the residents voted to end the communal meals and other aspects of their successful socialist experiment. Visitors may tour a furniture shop, a wool mill, and several wineries for free and are asked to pay small admission fees to view a barn museum, a communal kitchen, and a history museum. A self-guided tour map is available at the colonies' Visitors Bureau (Rtes. 151 and 220, tel. 319/622–7622 or 800/245–5465).

Bill Zuber's Homestead Restaurant. Children's games were allowed in the Amana villages, but such organized games as baseball were forbidden by the church elders. Nonetheless, word of an exceptional young athlete spread. One day in 1930, C. C. (Cy) Slapnicka, a scout for the Cleveland Indians, came to the villages and found 17-year-old Bill Zuber doing his assigned chore helping with the onion harvest in the community-kitchen gardens. The scout found a baseball-size onion and asked young Zuber if he could hit a faraway barn. The kid threw the onion over the barn roof and 10 years later was pitching in Yankee Stadium. Zuber was noted more for his speed than his control, once putting Red Sox star Ted Williams in the hospital. His greatest thrill was a 1–0 victory over a Yankee lineup that included Joe DiMaggio. After a 10-year career was cut short by an arm injury, Zuber and his wife, Connie, bought a two-story brick hotel built in 1862 in the Amana village of Homestead. Zuber died in 1982, but his baseball legacy lives on here. Inside is a display of baseball memorabilia, including signed balls and a Babe Ruth–autographed photo. The dining-room walls are covered with photos of sports and other celebrities. There's a hearty, German-American menu served family-style. All meats are Amana-raised, and pork is never as good outside this state. *V St., Homestead, tel. 319/622–3911. AE, D, MC, V. $*

Field of Dreams. Dyersville, Iowa, where they filmed the 1989 baseball classic, *Field of Dreams*, is 60 miles northeast of Cedar Rapids. Don't miss this. This is every bit as fabulous as it looked on the big screen. We all know that the sites of many movies are substantially enhanced by the moviemakers. Not here. The field and farmhouse are as they were in the movie. More than 60,000 visitors come each year. There were at least 50 people playing pickup baseball on the field and sitting in the bleachers the entire time we were there. Bring your glove, take your turn in the outfield, and stand in line to take a few cuts at the ball. If you want to be here when the corn is high, come some time after mid-June. The Field of Dreams Ghost Players appear from the corn field, as in the movie, from June through September on the second to last Sunday of each month from 12 to 2. *Hwys. 20 and 136, 25 mi west of Dubuque and 95 mi northwest of Davenport. Admission free.*

Unusual Shopping

Ertl Toy Outlet Store. A quarter of a mile north of the factory, you may buy the closeouts and specials on farm sets, cars, trucks, dolls, and sports-hero replicas. *Hwy. 136, Dyersville, tel. 319/875–5613.*

Two farms were used in filming *Field of Dreams* and, you guessed it, there are two souvenir stands.

The Field of Dreams Movie Site. This shop, to the side of the farmhouse, has the widest choice of souvenirs. *28963 Lansing Rd., Dyersville, tel. 319/875–8404.*

Left & Center Field of Dreams. This stand has souvenirs plus snacks. As part of the generous spirit that surrounds this site, if you don't have baseball equipment, you can use its balls, bats, and gloves for free. *29227 Lansing Rd., Dyersville, tel. 319/875–7985.*

IOWA CUBS

League: American Association • **Major League Affiliation:** Chicago Cubs • **Class:** AAA • **Stadium:** Sec Taylor Stadium • **Opened:** 1947 / 92 • **Capacity:** 10,500 • **Dimensions:** LF: 335, CF: 400, RF: 335 • **Surface:** grass • **Season:** Apr.–Labor Day

STADIUM LOCATION: 350 S.W. 1st St., Des Moines, IA 50309

TEAM WEB SITE: http://www.dsmnet.com/Icub/icub

GETTING THERE: From I-235, 3rd St. exit; follow 3rd St. south through downtown to Court Ave. Left on Court and right on 2nd Ave. From south side of Des Moines, 7th or 9th St. to Cherry St., right on Cherry to 5th St., take 5th St. to Elm St., turn left then right on 2nd Ave.

TICKET INFORMATION: 350 S.W. 1st St., Des Moines, IA 50309, tel. 515/243–6111, fax 515/243–5152

PRICE RANGE: Club box seats $8; field box seats $6.50; reserved grandstand $6.50 adults, $4.50 under 14; general admission $4.50 adult, $3 under 14, under 4 free in lap

GAME TIME: Mon.–Sat. 7:15 PM, Sun. 2:05 (Apr.–May) or 6:05 (June–Sept.); gates open 90 min before game.

TIPS ON SEATING: Club box seats sold to season ticket holders. Reserved grandstand seats behind home plate provide great view of Capitol beyond center field. Section X down first-base line is only no-smoking, no-alcohol section, but setting sun shines in your eyes in early innings of night games.

SEATING FOR PEOPLE WITH DISABILITIES: Available throughout stadium; parking adjacent to stadium in west lot

STADIUM FOOD: There is a wonderful variety of food. The grilled Iowa Chop, which can be found behind the seats out the first-base line, is heaven for $5. Split one for two children. Add fresh-squeezed orangeade or lemonade for $2. Meaty ribs ($3) are smoked in the concourse, along with potato spuds ($2). Good brats and tasty boneless rib sandwiches are $3 and are available from the grills on the first- and third-base sides. Healthy fare includes chef salads, veggie and turkey breast sandwiches. A hot sliced caramel apple is $1.75. There is both good ice cream and frozen yogurt. There are picnic areas down the left-field line and on the mezzanine level behind home plate. Both are open to all fans after pregame parties are over.

SMOKING POLICY: In section X in general admission area down first-base line, smoking and alcohol are prohibited.

PARKING: Stadium parking $3; limited, as ballpark is on edge of downtown. Parking on street and in private lots within walking range of stadium.

VISITING TEAM HOTEL: Hotel Savery and Spa (401 Locust St., Des Moines, IA 50309, tel. 515/244–2151 or 800/798–2151)

TOURISM INFORMATION: Division of Tourism, Iowa Department of Economic Development (200 E. Grand Ave., Des Moines, IA 50309, tel. 515/242–4705 or 800/345–4692)

Des Moines: Sec Taylor Stadium

Sometimes it's best to start over. Sec Taylor Stadium in Des Moines, Iowa, was built in 1947 and was clearly below the standard expected for Triple AAA baseball in the 1990s. With the potential of losing the top franchise of the Chicago Cubs, the city leveled the entire stadium. It built a $12 million, state-of-the-art 10,500-capacity minor-league stadium for the 1992 season.

Wisely, city officials built it on the exact site of the old stadium. It would be hard to find a finer place. Named since 1959 for Garner W. ("Sec") Taylor, for 50 years the sports editor of the *Des Moines Register and Tribune*, the stadium sits at the junction of the Raccoon River, which runs behind the stadium on the first-base side, and the Des Moines River, which flows behind the outfield wall. Unfortunately, you can see only the Raccoon River and that only from the picnic area on the mezzanine level looking behind home plate. There is, however, a spectacular view of the impressive gold-domed state capitol building beyond the flag flying in center field.

The entranceway is attractively landscaped, and the wide concourse has a full supply of concession stands, an excellent souvenir store, and plenty of bathrooms. Designed by HOK with a mezzanine level of skyboxes and press box, the stadium provides cover to only a few rows of the otherwise open grandstand. Everything about this stadium is modern and first-rate; all but 1,000 of the seats are individual stadium chairs.

The wall in left field also serves as the Cub Club, a members-only restaurant overlooking the field. Balls that hit the restaurant wall are in play. Players must hit the ball over the wall to get a home run. In 1995, a dozen skyboxes were built in left field with a sports ticker scoreboard 4½ feet tall and 39 feet long along the roof line of the skyboxes.

Perhaps Des Moines's greatest claim to baseball fame came before the first Sec Taylor Stadium was built. The city hosted the first minor-league game under permanent lights in 1930.

Where to Stay

Visiting Team Hotel: Hotel Savery. This venerable downtown hotel, built in 1919, has an 11-story redbrick exterior and a remodeled interior. The lobby has historic charm and a stenciled ceiling, but other areas are more contemporary. Room sizes vary. The hotel is within walking distance of the ballpark. *401 Locust St., Des Moines 50309, tel. 515/244–2151 or 800/798–2151, fax 515/244–1408. 221 rooms. Facilities: 3 restaurants, hot tubs, health club (fee), pool, sauna, indoor track. AE, D, DC, MC, V. $$*

Kirkwood Civic Center Hotel. Built in 1929, this 12-story downtown hotel is an Art Deco treasure. Room furnishings are an eclectic mixture of old and new, and public spaces are enlivened by hand-painted murals of old Des Moines. The hotel is in the city's Court Avenue district, with several restaurants and a coffee house nearby. The ballpark is a quarter-mile walk. *400 Walnut St., Des Moines 50309, tel. 515/244–9191 or 800/798–9191, fax 515/282–7004. 160 rooms. Facilities: 3 restaurants. AE, D, DC, MC, V. $$*

Comfort Suites. This two-story hotel in a northwest suburb was built in 1993. White narrow-wood siding, a green roof, and decorative eaves give it a nostalgic, homey look. Inside, the decorating is pure country, in hunter green and burgundy. Rooms have painted wood armoires and tables, and beds with quilted comforters and gathered bedskirts. Each room has an undercounter refrigerator. *11167 Hickman Rd., Urbandale, tel. 515/276–1126 or 800/395–7675, fax 515/276–1126. 101 rooms. Facilities: indoor pool, hot tub. AE, D, DC, MC, V. $$*

Where to Eat

Stella's Blue Sky Diner. For a dose of 1950s nostalgia and great malts, head to the skywalks that criss-cross downtown Des Moines. On the skywalk level of the Capitol Square building, which is near the ballpark, Stella's Blue Sky Diner is a hit with youngsters, who delight in having waiters and waitresses pour malts into glasses perched on customers' foreheads. There are jukeboxes on each table, so bring quarters. The decor runs to lava lamps, vintage working televisions, and bowling trophies. The menu is heavy on American blue-plate specials. *400 Locust St., Des Moines, tel. 515/246–1953. AE, MC, V. Closed Sun. $*

Spaghetti Works. This antiques-filled, exposed-brick former warehouse is a safe bet for children. Pasta of all descriptions is on the menu, and the service is generally speedy. There are good salads and a children's menu for small eaters. The high-backed wood booths fill up first. *310 Court Ave., Des Moines, tel. 515/243–2195. AE, D, MC, V. $*

King Ying Low. The decor has changed little since this Chinese restaurant, the city's oldest, opened in 1907. In the Court Avenue district, the restaurant has a narrow storefront and is easy to miss. The color scheme is red and green, and the ambience is comfortable and familiar, not elegant. Its moo shu pork is a standout. *233 4th St., Des Moines, tel. 515/243–7049. AE, MC, V. $*

Java Joes. This large popular coffee house is near the ballpark. It's smoke-free and has a thoughtful children's play alcove. Late-night offerings include folksingers, classical music, poetry- and play-readings, and jazz. Eaters like its hearty sandwiches, homemade soups, pastries, and coffee drinks. The high-ceilinged space is enlivened with vintage neon signs and billboards, recycled from an old sign company. *214 4th St., Des Moines, tel. 515/288–5282. AE, D, MC, V. $*

The Waterfront. This excellent locally owned seafood restaurant has fresh fish flown in daily from East Coast contract fishing rigs. There's a chowder and oyster bar, a seafood market, and live lobster in tanks. There is a children's menu, as well as items other than fish, such as chicken fingers. *2900 University Ave., West Des Moines, tel. 515/223–5106. AE, D, MC, V. Closed Sun. $$*

Drake Diner. There are three diners in this local chain: This one is adjacent to the Drake University campus, the West End Diner (13731 University Ave., tel. 515/222–3131) is in the suburb of Clive, and the North End Diner (5055 Merle Hay Rd., Johnston, tel. 515/276–5151) is just north of I–80 at the Merle Hay exit. All have sleek chrome and neon exteriors and a classy, updated 1950s look inside. You can sit at the counter, in booths, or at tables. All three serve an exceptional meat loaf, real mashed potatoes, and large salads. The ample menu also has healthy choices and a wide selection of breakfast items. *1111 25th St., Des Moines, tel. 515/ 277–1111. AE, D, MC, V. $*

Entertainments

Des Moines Botanical Center. This large geodesic dome filled with unusual plants dominates the riverfront near the freeway in downtown Des Moines. Inside, you take an escalator to an African rain-forest environment and see midwestern oddities, such as a producing banana tree. Exotic birds fly inside the dome, giving visitors close-up views when they alight. Exhibits of annual and perennial plants change regularly, and there are frequent lectures and hands-on plant demonstrations. *909 E. River Dr., Des Moines, tel. 515/242–2934. Admission: $1 adults, 50¢ ages 6–17. Open Mon.–Thurs. 10–6, Fri. 10–9, weekends 10–5.*

Living History Farms. This 600-acre outdoor museum of farming shows visitors how agriculture was practiced from Native American times through the present. The farmsteads' buildings, crops, and furnishings are true to their era. These include a Native American settlement from 1700; an 1850 pioneer farm; a replica of an 1875 town with 17 shops, a school, homes, and a turn-of-the-century farm. Employees in authentic costumes demonstrate farming practices and crafts. You should plan to spend at least three hours. There are seasonal special events, such as baseball games with historic costumes and rules, and nostalgic celebrations on the Fourth of July, Labor Day, and Memorial Day. *2600 N.W. 111th St., Urbandale, tel. 515/278–2400. Admission: $7 adults, $4 ages 4–16. Open May–Oct., Mon.–Sat. 9–5, Sun. 11–6. MC, V.*

Adventureland. This clean, nicely landscaped theme park is a manageable size for children, with thrill rides, Wild West and magic shows, and two water rides, including a white-water raft ride. There are three large roller coasters and a new "slow coaster," "the Underground," which takes visitors down into an Old West mining camp. Benches and shady spots are available near the rides for parents to perch. *I–80, Exit 142A, at U.S. 65, Des Moines, tel. 515/266–*

2121. Admission: $17.50 adults, $16 ages 4–9. Open Memorial Day–late Sept., weekends 10–8. Closing times vary. AE, D, MC, V.

Science Center of Iowa. Heat, light, electricity, and earth and physical sciences are covered in hands-on exhibits at this museum 45 blocks west of downtown in Greenwood Park, which also houses the Des Moines Art Center. The Science Center has a planetarium, which presents laser shows daily for an additional $1.50. There are family laser shows on weekends at 1 and 3. In the evening, it presents laser rock shows, which charge $5 admission. The Science Center often has traveling exhibits on topics such as space travel or dinosaurs and has a full schedule of demonstrations. *4500 Grand Ave., Des Moines, tel. 515/274–4138. Admission: $5 adults, $3 ages 3–12. Open Mon.–Sat. 10–5, Sun. noon–5. AE, MC, V.*

Kate Goldman Children's Theatre. This new 250-seat theater is in the Des Moines Playhouse, one of the nation's oldest community theaters. It presents a full season of children's and family entertainment throughout the school year, and the Playhouse usually offers a family musical during the summer. *831 42nd St., just north of I–235 at 42nd St. exit, Des Moines, tel. 515/277–6261. Ticket prices vary.*

Blank Park Zoo. This small, accessible zoo is in southwest Des Moines, not far from the airport. The monkey section is tops, and children also are fascinated by the prairie-dog settlement. The only indoor exhibits are in the Discovery Center, where you can see snakes and fish. There are walk-through habitats that show landscapes and wildlife common to Africa and Australia. Train and camel rides are available at an extra fee, as is food to feed the goats and fish. *7401 S.W. 9th St., Des Moines, tel. 515/285–4722. Admission: $3.50 adults, $2.75 senior citizens, $2 ages 2–11. Open May–mid-Oct., daily 10–5.*

Sites to See

Bob Feller Hometown Exhibit. Van Meter, Iowa, didn't settle for the obligatory "Home of" sign for its hometown hero. This tiny Iowa town, 12 miles west of Des Moines, has created a wonderful monument to baseball's greatest living right-handed pitcher. We expected a few pieces of memorabilia displayed in the front window of a loyal fan's business office. We were surprised by an attractive new building designed by Feller's architect son on land donated by the local bank. There is a first-rate brick relief sculpture by Jay Tschetter on the parking-lot side of the museum that depicts Feller's Hall of Fame career. The museum, which opened in 1995, includes two well-conceived exhibit rooms full of Feller memorabilia. Our favorite item is the catcher's mitt used by Feller's father, William, to catch for young Bob on their Van Meter farm. The museum is free; signed photos, balls, and other memorabilia are for sale. *310 Mill St., Van Meter 50261, tel. 515/996–2806. Open Mon.–Sat. 10–5, Sun. noon–4.*

State Capitol. The Iowa Capitol building, in Des Moines, is among the most ornate in the nation. Begun in 1871 and completed in 1886, this neo-Romanesque building has a large gilded central dome with four smaller, equally ornate domes on its corners. The most striking view is from one flight up the Grand Staircase on the floor containing the House and Senate chambers. From here you can best see the statues and half-moon-shape paintings around the base of the dome. You can't enter the door marked "THIS WAY TO DOME" unless you are on a tour. *E. 9th St. and University Ave., Des Moines, tel. 515/281–5591. Free tours by reservation, weekdays 9–3:30, Sat. 9:30–3.*

State of Iowa Historical Building. Just down the hill from the Capitol is this modern museum containing creative displays on early Native American life, settlers' lives, and Iowa geology, history, and transportation. *600 E. Locust St., Des Moines, tel. 515/281–6412. Donations appreciated. Open Tues.–Sat. 9–4:30, Sun. noon–4:30.*

QUAD CITY RIVER BANDITS

League: Midwest League • **Major League Affiliation:** Houston Astros • **Class:** A • **Stadium:** John O'Donnell Stadium • **Opened:** 1931 • **Capacity:** 5,500 • **Dimensions:** LF: 340, CF: 390, RF: 340 • **Surface:** grass • **Season:** Apr.–Labor Day

STADIUM LOCATION: 209 S. Gaines St., Davenport, IA 52802

GETTING THERE: From I–74, State St. exit, to River Dr, right on River Dr., 3 mi to stadium at corner of S. Gaines St. and River Dr. From I–80, Harriston St. exit, to River Dr, right on River Dr., 3 blocks to S. Gaines St.

TICKET INFORMATION: Box 3496, Davenport, IA 52808, tel. 319/324–2032, fax 319/324–3109

PRICE RANGE: Box seats $6; reserved $5; general admission $4 adults, $3 ages 5–14 and over 64, under 5 free

GAME TIME: Mon.–Tues. and Thurs.–Sat. 7 PM, Wed. 12:30 PM, Sun. 2 PM (Apr.–May) or 6 PM (June–Sept.); gates open 1 hr before game.

TIPS ON SEATING: Sit on third-base side for best view of riverboats and spectacular Centennial Bridge. Only 8–10 rows of box seats and 3 rows of reserved, so general admission seats in grandstand are fine. But look before you sit, as poles holding up grandstand roof could obstruct your view.

SEATING FOR PEOPLE WITH DISABILITIES: Just past dugout on first-base side between grandstand and bleachers.

STADIUM FOOD: Treat yourself to a great brat ($2.50) or cheddar wurst ($2.75) at the grills on the first- and third-base side. There's also a good local brown mustard, Boetje's, from Rock Island. The sausages are better than the pork sandwich, which is $3.50. Small sodas are a bargain for 50¢. Unusual offerings include caramel apple chips for $2, bandit pie (Frito chips with chili and cheese) for $2, and root beer floats for $3. Corn dog mininuggets are $2.25. A pizza slice is $2.50.

SMOKING POLICY: Smoking prohibited in section 200 in general admission area under grandstand and directly behind home plate—family section

PARKING: Ample free parking

VISITING TEAM HOTEL: Best Western Riverview Inn (227 LeClaire St., Davenport, IA 52801, tel. 319/324–1921 or 800/528–1234)

TOURISM INFORMATION: Quad Cities Convention & Visitors Bureau (1900 3rd Ave., Rock Island, IL 61204-3097, tel. 309/788–7800 or 800/747–7800)

Davenport/Quad Cities: O'Donnell Stadium

You remember John O'Donnell Stadium. You saw a picture of it in the newspaper. The classic photograph from the extraordinary Midwest floods of the summer of 1993 was of John O'Donnell Stadium under water. It's dry now, and it is a jewel of a park. This is an old-time ballpark like Cedar Rapids', with exactly the right amount of modernization.

Davenport's Levee Improvement Commission decided in 1930 that it was time to turn the garbage dump along the Mississippi River waterfront into a city landmark to honor those who had served in the military. Municipal Stadium was dedicated in 1931 with a 25-piece band playing. The stadium was a modest-size covered grandstand with the curve of the outfield fence in contour with the river.

We found 83-year-old Bill Montgomery, a retired tavern owner, in his seat near the home-team third-base dugout. As an 18-year-old, he attended the first game in 1931 and has been a loyal fan and a community baseball advocate ever since. Montgomery claims to have gotten the very first flat tire on the gorgeous 1939 Centennial Bridge to Rock Island that hangs at roof level along the first-base side. The view at night of this bridge, with its five arches illuminated with large light bulbs, is spectacular. In 1970, the name was changed to John O'Donnell Stadium to honor a longtime sports editor of the *Davenport Times-Democrat*.

One of the community leaders who helped keep professional baseball in Davenport along with Bill Montgomery was George Majerkurth. According to Montgomery, Majerkurth was the umpire when Babe Ruth was alleged to have called his shot in the most famous home run ever hit at Chicago's Wrigley Field, on October 1, 1932. Years later, Majerkurth told Montgomery that Babe was actually gesturing to the pitcher that he had one strike left.

For the 1989 season, the city invested more than $4.5 million in one of the very best restorations of an old ballpark that we have seen. The exterior is an elegant series of brick archways leading to a completely covered grandstand.

The stadium sits in a city park complete with a handsome bandstand. Gambling riverboats cruise by on the Mississippi River. Bleacher seats extend beyond the grandstand on both the first- and third-base sides, and picnic and play areas stretch down each baseline.

Davenport has been a leader in bringing excitement to minor-league baseball. After decades of using the nickname of their major-league affiliate, they became the Quad Cities River Bandits in 1991. The notion of tying the team name to the local community and designing a distinctive logo—in this case a baseball with a red bandanna—helped launch minor-league logo mania across the nation. In 1991, they added an exploding scoreboard that shoots off firecrackers for River Bandit home runs and wins. The design of the exploding scoreboard in left-center field echoes the lighted arches of Centennial Bridge and has the team logo on top.

Where to Stay

Visiting Team Hotel: Best Western Riverview Inn. There are great views of the Mississippi River from this six-story riverfront hotel within walking distance of the ballpark. The rooms are contemporary and well used. *227 LeClaire St., at River Dr., Davenport 52801, tel. 319/324–1921 or 800/528–1234, fax 319/324–9621. 150 rooms. Facilities: restaurant, indoor and outdoor pools, hot tub, sauna, coin laundry. AE, D, DC, MC, V. $$*

Blackhawk Hotel. This classic brick 11-story downtown hotel has been renovated into a convention center. The standard rooms are small, with older, small bathrooms, many with the original tile from 1914 suites. The lobby is majestic, with some shops on the ground floor. Guests are repeatedly encouraged to patronize the city's gambling riverboat. The hotel is less than a mile from the ballpark. *3rd and Perry Sts., Davenport, 52801, tel. 319/328–6000 or 800/553–1173, fax 319/322–4778. 152 rooms, 36 suites. Facilities: restaurant, sauna, exercise room, coin laundry. AE, D, DC, MC, V. $$*

Where to Eat

Lagomarcino's. This storefront restaurant is a not-to-be-missed jump back in time in downtown Moline. The candy store–lunch counter has been dispensing its own ice cream, homemade rye bread, and fountain drinks since 1918. Its ceiling is white tin, the booths are mahogany, and the lamps are Tiffany-style. You can order real turkey sandwiches, phosphates (an old-fashioned, fruit-flavored carbonated drink), strawberry shortcake, and memorable hot fudge. *1422 5th Ave., Moline, IL, tel. 309/764–1814. No credit cards. Closed Sun. $*

Iowa Machine Shed Restaurant. Apple dumplings and roast pork attract families to this rustic, barn-style restaurant. The portions are huge and the atmosphere cheery, with a multitude of farm antiques on the walls and checkered napkins at the table. There is a children's menu as well as a large salad bar here. Breakfasts are hearty. The restaurant is 15 minutes north of the ballpark. *7250 Northwest Blvd., Exit 292 south from I–80, Davenport, tel. 319/391–2427. AE, D, DC, MC, V. $*

Entertainments

Quad Cities Kids and Co. At this children's museum kids don't become overwhelmed or run from attraction to attraction but actually play with the equipment. There are lots of dress-up costumes, a doctor's and a dentist's office, a beauty parlor with wigs, a big grocery store, a post office, a bubble machine, a rain forest, and a TV station. There are some small animals in cages and terrariums. *1723 2nd Ave., District of Rock Island, IL, tel. 309/788–9599. Admission: $2 adults, $2.50 children, under 2 free. Open weekdays 10–4:30, Sat. 10–4, Sun. 12:30–4.*

Sites to See

Mississippi River Visitors Center. You can watch barges, tugboats, and sailboats go through Lock and Dam 15. Park rangers explain the process, and displays illustrate the mechanics. There is a great visual explanation of the Mississippi's stairway of water. *Rodman Ave., Rock Island, IL, tel. 309/794–5338. Open mid–May–Labor Day, daily 9–9; Labor Day–early May, daily 9–5.*

Herbert Hoover Presidential Library and Birthplace. Herbert Hoover was born in 1874 in West Branch, Iowa, just 50 miles west of Davenport. His parents and grandparents had come to Iowa in covered wagons. The small 14-by-20-foot birthplace cottage is the centerpiece of a National Historic Site managed by the National Park Service. It includes a blacksmith shop similar to the one Hoover's father operated in the 1870s, an 1853 Quaker schoolhouse, an 1857 meetinghouse, and the Hoover gravesite. In the Presidential Library-Museum, a short film and excellent display recount Hoover's five decades of public service, painting him as a great man and a flawed politician. As a former president, Hoover proposed a set of reforms to improve American life, including an end to political ghostwriters and adding a fourth strike to baseball. We're glad that one wasn't adopted, as the games are long enough, thank you, Mr. President. *Herbert Hoover National Historic Site, ½ mi north of Exit 254 from I–80, West Branch, tel. 319/643–2541. Admission: $2 adults, $1 senior citizens, children under 16 free. Open daily 9–5.*

THE NORTHERN LEAGUE
ST. PAUL, SIOUX CITY

17

Minneapolis–St. Paul has both major- and minor-league teams, but the choice is clear. Bigger is not better. Head for St. Paul, in the independent Northern League, for the most fun you can have in a ballpark. The stadium is scruffy and located by the railyards. There are wacky on-field contests, the announcing is hilarious, and the fan-first philosophy shows. St. Paul has a lovely city park, Como Park, with a free-admission kiddie amusement land and a small zoo. It also has an outstanding children's museum and science center. More commercial amusements are found at Camp Snoopy at the Mall of America, in Bloomington, 12 miles southwest of St. Paul, where 375 stores compete for your wallet, or Valleyfair, a huge amusement park and waterpark in Shakopee, 31 miles southwest of St. Paul.

The Northern League has a more conventional team in Sioux City, Iowa, where the Explorers play in Lewis and Clark Park. It's a 272-mile drive from St. Paul to Sioux City, south on Interstate 35 to Albert Lea, west on Interstate 90 to Luverne, Minnesota, then south on Route 75 to Sioux City. This family-oriented park has real seats, not benches, as well as expansive picnic areas. This is the ballpark that put David Letterman's souvenir-selling pal, Mujibur Rahman, in uniform as a pitcher as a crowd-pleasing joke. The riverfront offers most of the city's other activities for visitors, from Missouri River cruises to a bike path to a free riverboat museum.

ST. PAUL SAINTS

League: Northern League • **Affiliation:** Independent • **Class:** Independent/Short Season • **Stadium:** Midway Stadium • **Opened:** 1982 • **Capacity:** 6,311 • **Dimensions:** LF: 320, CF: 400, RF: 320 • **Surface:** grass • **Season:** June–Labor Day

STADIUM LOCATION: 1771 Energy Park, St. Paul, MN 55108

GETTING THERE: From west, I–94 to Hwy. 280 to Kasota/Energy Park Dr. exit. East on Energy Park Dr. 1 mi to stadium. From east, I–94 to Snelling Ave. N to Energy Park Dr. exit. West ¼ mi on Energy Park Dr.

TICKET INFORMATION: 1771 Energy Park, St. Paul, MN 55108, tel. 612/644–6659, fax 612/644–1627

PRICE RANGE: Reserved $6 adult, $5 youth/seniors; general admission $4 adult, $3 children and senior citizens

GAME TIME: Mon.–Sat. 7:05 PM, Sun. 2:05 PM; stadium opens 1 hr before game.

TIPS ON SEATING: Most games sell out. 200 general admission seats go on sale 2 hrs before game. Best seat in house is in barber's chair behind home plate. Haircuts are $10. A 20-minute massage in the stands is $7.

SEATING FOR PEOPLE WITH DISABILITIES: 50 seats on main aisle

STADIUM FOOD: Hot and addictive mini-donuts are sold from a truck outside the park. Once inside, make a beeline for one of the two field-level concession stands and order the fantastic Walleye sandwich

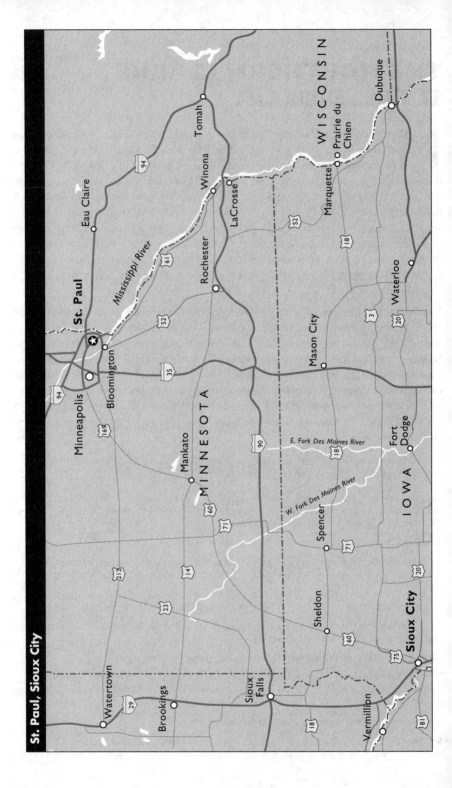

for $3.50. They sell out before game time. Good brats are $3. The Kool Jerk Calypso Chicken, sold from a stand beyond the third-base bleachers, is worth the $3.75. The official beer, Pig's Eye, is dispensed by vendors with backpacks. Iced mocha is $3. As you leave the park, vendors often sell smoked fish, like Northern goldeneye, at give-away prices.

SMOKING POLICY: Smoke- and alcohol-free seats in bleachers along right-field fence

PARKING: Lot opens 3 hrs before game for tailgate parties. Parking $3.

VISITING TEAM HOTEL: Holiday Inn Express (1010 Bandana Blvd. W., St. Paul, MN 55108, tel. 612/647–8711 or 800/465–4329)

TOURISM INFORMATION: St. Paul Convention and Visitors Bureau (102 Norwest Center, 55 E. 5th St., St. Paul, MN 55101, tel. 612/297–6985 or 800/627–6101)

St. Paul: Midway Stadium

"Fun is good," says Mike Veeck, the president of the St. Paul Saints. And we had more fun in St. Paul than in any of the other cities we visited. Veeck can't help himself. It's in his genes. His father was Bill Veeck, the zaniest, most fan-conscious owner in the history of baseball. Veeck Senior got into the Hall of Fame despite a career as a baseball iconoclast. He was the owner of the Cleveland Indians, the Chicago White Sox, and the St. Louis Browns. Veeck Senior is the guy who planted the ivy at Wrigley Field. He's the one who sent 3-foot, 7-inch Eddie Gaedel to bat against the Detroit Tigers on August 19, 1951. In a crouch, Gaedel's strike zone was about 1½ inches. He walked on four pitches.

If you want to understand why major-league baseball is losing fans while minor-league baseball is gaining them, visit the Twin Cities of Minneapolis–St. Paul. These twins have long had a sibling rivalry over everything from baseball to economic development. For six decades, they were opponents in the American Association. Then St. Paul lost its minor-league team in 1961 when the Washington Senators moved to Minneapolis. Minor-league baseball returned to St. Paul in 1993 with the start-up of the audacious Northern League, a renegade group of investors and baseball people fed up with the arrogance and greed of today's major-league baseball.

Nowhere is the minors' supremacy over the majors more apparent than in the Twin Cities. The Minnesota Twins play on plastic grass under a roof in the sterile and ugly Metrodome. The fans—and there aren't many anymore—seem somnolent. In Minneapolis baseball, there's a sense of complacency. In St. Paul, there's excitement, community, and a waiting list for season tickets.

For "REAL GRASS AND REAL BEER," as the sign in center field in Midway Stadium says, go across the river from the Metrodome. The St. Paul Saints are playing to sellouts in the funky, geranium-filled ballpark, where fans can get haircuts and massages during games and a pot-bellied pig delivers new balls to the umpire. Saint, the "prince of pork, the sultan of swine, the Buddha of bacon," is a real live pig who rests under the grandstand between assignments.

In St. Paul, they play in a scruffy concrete and aluminum municipal stadium that seats only 6,311 people. In 1957, St. Paul built $2 million, 10,000-seat Midway Stadium for its longtime Triple AAA American Association team. But after just four seasons, the team was history when a major-league team moved in across the river and the stadium was leveled. The new Midway Stadium, built in 1982, sits in an industrial park with a train track just feet from the left-field wall and a six-story fire-department practice building beyond right field. Veeck calls Midway "the ugliest ballpark in the country." But it has a sense of fun and community that's absolutely irresistible.

The fans come first with the Saints owners, who help run the turnstiles and roam the park for fan-friendly ideas. In contrast to the pretentiousness of the major-league owners, the owners here watch the game on folding chairs behind a chain-link fence right next to where the pig rests. "The corporate money sucked the life out of baseball," laments Saints president Veeck. "Our club offers the fan hope, in our players and in their world." Veeck is now sharing his time and philosophy of fan-driven baseball with the Charleston RiverDogs as well.

If you think the snail should be the mascot of major-league baseball, you'll find the pace a lot faster in the Northern League. There's a 20-second clock in center field, and a horn goes off when pitchers exceed the time per pitch that the major leagues require but never enforce.

The Saints' endearing off-field nuttiness with contests, imaginative music, and comedic announcing is joined by exciting action on the field. The night we were at Midway Stadium, the hometown Saints blew a lead in the top of the eighth and regained it in the bottom of the inning. With two outs in the top of the ninth and the Saints' 6,311 fans on their feet and screaming for the final out, a train passed and blew its whistle. The fans turned and waved and screamed to the train. The flustered umpire called time-out. Play resumed for the final pitch and the final out. Then Veeck blew up the night's profits with a spectacular fireworks show that kept the sellout crowd entranced and cheering late into the night. Really. That's the way it is here in St. Paul, where they work hard to live up to the team's motto, "Wild and Outside."

Where to Stay

Make sure you get the coupon book from the St. Paul Convention & Visitors Bureau (tel. 612/297–6985). It offers genuine savings for lodgings, restaurants, museums, and shopping.

Visiting Team Motel: Holiday Inn Express. This unusual hotel in a renovated train repair shop is a half-mile from the ballpark. The comfortably furnished rooms are built around a spacious courtyard that holds a pool, a sauna, and a breakfast area. There are a free Continental breakfast and evening snacks. The walls contain photos of the structure in its earlier life as a repair and paint yard. *1010 Bandana Blvd. W, St. Paul 55108, tel. 612/647–1637 or 800/465–4329, fax 612/647–0244. 109 rooms. Facilities: indoor pool, wading pool, sauna. AE, D, DC, MC, V. $$*

Embassy Suites St. Paul. This downtown, all-suite hotel is near the museums. Each suite has two rooms, including a living room with a couch that folds out to a double bed. Guests can choose a king bed or two double beds in the bedroom. There is a microwave in each room, and all guests receive a free breakfast. *175 E. 10th St., St. Paul 55101, tel. 612/224–5400 or 800/362–2779, fax 612/224–0957. 210 suites. Facilities: restaurant, indoor pool, hot tub, sauna, coin laundry, free parking. AE, D, DC, MC, V. $$*

Days Inn Civic Center. This newly remodeled, eight-story hotel has good views of the Cathedral of St. Paul. It is downtown and convenient to the museums. Guests receive a free Continental breakfast. *175 W. 7th St., St. Paul 55102, tel. 612/292–8929 or 800/325–2525, fax 612/292–1749. 203 rooms. Facilities: restaurant, free parking. AE, D, DC, MC, V. $$*

Where to Eat

Cafe Latté. This great soup, salad, and sandwich place is in the midst of a row of small, attractive shops a mile west of downtown. Its fresh American food is served cafeteria-style. Its high quality and low prices fill this 150-seat restaurant with customers all day long. *850 Grand Ave., St. Paul, tel. 612/224–5687. AE, DC, MC, V. $*

Downtowner Cafe. You can get inexpensive breakfasts at this storefront restaurant two blocks west of the Civic Center. Cajun eggs and sausage are a specialty. The tables are Formica and the cooking is short-order. *253 W. 7th St., St. Paul, tel. 612/228–1221. No credit cards. No dinner. $*

Rain Forest Cafe. This wildly popular special-effects restaurant is on the first floor of the Mall of America, next to Bloomingdale's. The sound of thunder, flashes of lightning, and large aquariums give you the feel of eating in a jungle. There are oversize drinks and huge portions of food. You can expect at least a 90-minute wait on weekends. There are no reservations, so check in early and see the mall while you wait. The restaurant is smoke-free. *Mall of America, Bloomington, tel. 612/854–7500. AE, D, DC, MC, V. $$*

Twin City Grill. You can get old-fashioned favorites in this check-tablecloth restaurant, which resembles a 1940s diner. Especially good are the meat loaf, Northern Lakes fish, and several varieties of rich milk shakes. There is a children's menu. *Mall of America, North Garden*

Entrance, Bloomington, tel. 612/854–0200. AE, D, DC, MC, V. $$

Entertainments

Como Park. The entry is free to this charming kiddie-land amusement park, which contains 15 rides, a small zoo, and a beautiful greenhouse. You can feed the seals for 50¢. Sparky the sea lion performs while you sit in a concrete amphitheater. The gorillas and the pelicans usually draw crowds. The conservatory, a glass Victorian beauty, is filled with flowers and runs an admirable Summer Garden Program in which youth volunteers design, plant, and maintain plantings in the park. *Lexington Ave. and Kaufman Dr., St. Paul, tel. 612/487–8200. Open Apr.– Sept. daily 8–8, Oct.–Mar. daily 8–5. Conservatory: 50¢ adults, 25¢ children; open April–Sept. 10–6, Oct.–March 10–4.*

Capital City Trolley. Old-fashioned rubber-wheeled trolleys run throughout the city and pick up passengers at red and green stop signs. *55 E. 5th St., St. Paul, tel. 612/223–5600. Fare: 25¢; children under 6 free; Sun., children under 13 free with paying adult. Capital route, every 15 min, Mon.–Sat. 11–5; After Hours route, every 10 min, Mon.–Sat. 5–11; Lunch Express route (links Space Center area with downtown, World Trade Center, Town Square, and Lowertown areas), every 13 min, weekdays 11–2.*

Minnesota Children's Museum. The museum's new downtown installation has dozens of hands-on exhibits in six galleries. Children can work with tools, cranes, and an indoor waterworks and explore an anthill maze and a re-creation of a Twin Cities ethnic neighborhood. Toddlers and infants have a special exhibit, Minnesota Habitat, scaled to their sizes and interests. *10 W. 7th St., St. Paul, tel. 612/225–6000. Admission: $5.95 adults and children over 2, $3.95 children under 3 and senior citizens. Open Mon.–Wed. and Fri.–Sun. 9–5, Thurs. 9–8.*

Science Museum of Minnesota. You need to schedule four hours to do this downtown museum top to bottom, with its anthropology hall, dinosaur lab, hands-on experiments gallery, and Green Street environmental display. The museum has the world's largest film projector and it puts visitors into the picture by simulcasting photos with its existing film. The large-screen theater shows exciting nature, weather, and exploration films. *30 E. 10th St., St. Paul, tel. 612/221–9444. Admission: Exhibits and Omnitheater, $8 adults, $6 ages 4–12; museum only, $5 adults, $4 ages 4–12; Omnitheater only, $6 adults, $5 ages 4–12. Open Mon.–Sat. 9:30–9, Sun. 10– 9. D, MC, V.*

Minnesota History Center. This museum has family-focused shows and several interactive exhibits. Visitors can examine a 24-ton boxcar and a voyageur canoe and climb on a 24-foot mock-up of a grain elevator. There is an on-site cafeteria and pay parking. *345 Kellogg Blvd. W, St. Paul, tel. 612/296–6126. Admission free. Open Tues.–Wed. and Fri.–Sat. 10–5, Thurs. 10–9, Sun. noon–5.*

Padelford Packet Riverboats. Five paddleboats tour the Mississippi River from Harriet Island, offering exciting views of the Twin Cities. These stern-wheel cruises have historic narration that younger children may not follow closely. *Harriet Island, St. Paul, tel. 612/227–1100. Admission: $8.50 adults, $5.50 ages under 13. Open Memorial Day–Labor Day; departures daily at noon and 2; Labor Day–Memorial Day, departures weekends at 2.*

Valleyfair. This huge amusement park is 30 miles southwest of downtown and includes an adjacent waterpark, White Water Country, in its admission. The amusement park has a well-preserved 1915 Philadelphia Toboggan Company carousel. IMAX films are shown on a six-story screen. The booming sound may be too intense for younger children. There are good river-raft rides and six heart-stopping roller coasters. The water park has slides, a splash station for younger children, and a lazy river ride. *1 Valleyfair Dr., Rte. 101, 9 mi west of I–335 and Rte. 13, Shakopee, tel. 612/445–7600. Admission: $22.95 persons over 48″, $4.95 children age 4–48″ and senior citizens. Open late May–Labor Day, daily 10–10 or midnight on occasion. D, MC, V.*

Sites to See

Take a look at the streamlined Mickey's Diner (36 W. 7th St., tel. 612/222–5633), a vintage hash house that's on the National Register of Historic Places. Its appeal is visual. Inside, it's cramped and the food isn't worth the second-hand smoke.

Fitzgerald Theater. Formerly known as the World Theater, this is the elegant playhouse from which Garrison Keillor now broadcasts "A Prairie Home Companion" on Saturday-afternoon live shows, starting at 4:45 when he's in Minnesota. This 916-seat theater also hosts local and traveling shows. *10 E. Exchange St., at Wabasha St., St. Paul, tel. 612/290–1221. Admission: $17.50–$23; tickets to all attractions available through Ticketmaster (Dayton's Department Store, downtown, tel. 612/989–5151); box office open on Prairie Home Companion broadcast days, Sat. 11–6. AE, D, MC, V.*

State Capitol. Local architect Cass Gilbert, who did the Woolworth Building in New York, created this U.S. Capitol look-alike in 1905. The House and Senate chambers have been restored. Free 45-minute tours are given regularly, and special tours focusing on women in government, art, and architecture can be arranged. *Aurora Ave., between Cedar and Park Sts., St. Paul, tel. 612/296–2881. Open weekdays 8:30–5, Sat. 10–4, Sun. 1–4; tours weekdays 9–5, Sat. 10–3, Sun. 1–3. Closed holidays.*

Unusual Shopping

Dome Souvenirs Plus. If you do go near the Dome in Minneapolis, there is a sports mavens' emporium across the street from gate A. It's as funky as the Dome is stiff. There's a free baseball museum, souvenirs for sale, and a modest food counter with ballpark comestibles at lower prices than the Dome's. The walls are full of old uniforms, bats, and autographed photos of the owner with some of baseball's greats. *406 Chicago Ave. S, Minneapolis, tel. 612/375–9707.*

Mall of America. Near the entrance to the "Mystery Mine Ride" in the Camp Snoopy amusement park here is a home plate; the mall is on the former site of Metropolitan Stadium. Built in 1955 to attract a major-league team, it finally got one in 1961. In 1965, the All-Star Game and the World Series were both played here. The Twins moved to the Metrodome in 1982. The biggest hit in Metropolitan Stadium history was a 520-foot home run by Hall of Famer Harmon Killebrew in 1961. Stand at home plate and look all the way across Camp Snoopy for the red-chair replica hanging on the wall above the Log Chute. That's where Killebrew's blast landed. *Cedar Ave. and Killebrew Dr., Bloomington, tel. 612/883–8800.*

SIOUX CITY EXPLORERS

League: Northern League • **Affiliation:** Independent • **Class:** Independent • **Stadium:** Lewis & Clark Park • **Opened:** 1993 • **Capacity:** 3,800 • **Dimensions:** LF: 330, CF: 400, RF: 330 • **Surface:** grass • **Season:** June–Labor Day

STADIUM LOCATION: 3400 Line Dr. Sioux City, IA 51106

GETTING THERE: From I–29, exit 143 east 4 blocks. Left at U.S. 75 to stadium.

TICKET INFORMATION: 3400 Line Dr. Sioux City, IA 51106, tel. 712/277–9467, fax 712/277–9406

PRICE RANGE: Box seats $6; reserved seats $5; reserved bench seating $4 adults, $3 ages under 13 and over 61

GAME TIME: Mon.–Sat. 7:05 PM, Sun. 2:05 PM; gates open 2 hrs before game.

TIPS ON SEATING: Reserved seats are worth extra dollar

SEATING FOR PEOPLE WITH DISABILITIES: Call 712/277–9467 to arrange for seating and parking.

STADIUM FOOD: The food is uninspired. The standout is the $2.75 pork sandwich, which is generous and has a good flavor. Grilled hamburgers are available under the blue-and-white striped tent on the third-base side. For $2, you get a large slice of pizza. There are also frozen malt cups.

SMOKING POLICY: Smoking prohibited in seating area

PARKING: Ample parking for $1

VISITING TEAM HOTEL: Best Western (130 Nebraska St., Sioux City, IA 51101, tel. 712/277–1550 or 800/528–1234)

TOURISM INFORMATION: Sioux City Convention Center/Tourism Bureau (801 4th St., Box 3183, Sioux City, IA 51102, tel. 712/279–4800 or 800/593–2228)

Sioux City: Lewis & Clark Park

Five hours southwest from St. Paul you can see the Sioux City Explorers, who play in Lewis & Clark Park. The nickname of the team and the name of the park honor Meriwether Lewis and William Clark, the leaders of an 1803–06 expedition initiated by President Jefferson to explore the territory from the upper reaches of the Missouri River to the Pacific Ocean. The team nickname was controversial, as many locals favored "Soos," the name used when Sioux City last had a team in 1960. After protests from Native Americans, the team wisely opted for Explorers. The park, built in 1993 for the revival of the Northern League, is so well designed that it was featured on the cover of the 1995 *Baseball America* calendar.

This is the basics—a comfortable family night at the ballpark, well done but simple. Designed by Dana Larson Roubal & Associates of Omaha, the exterior is an attractive gray stone. Inside are blue and red plastic seats—real seats, not the rows of benches in most other Northern League parks—on a concrete and steel foundation with a press box and four skyboxes on top. There are large picnic areas and places for the kids to race around beyond the aluminum grandstands down both foul lines.

We were here for fireworks night in Sioux City, and that means a big crowd. Lewis & Clark Park seats 3,800. About five times a season, the crowds here overflow the seating and the Explorers sell standing-room-only tickets for $3. This may sound unattractive, but it's really quite fun. The locals know to bring lawn chairs because S.R.O. customers are allowed to sit down each foul line within a foot or two of fair play. Seating fans in the outfield or near the baselines was a practice common in minor-league baseball in the early decades of this century.

Fireworks and the Famous Chicken draw overflow crowds to Lewis & Clark Park, and so does Mujibur Rahman. When David Letterman made the switch to CBS, virtually every local CBS affiliate picked him up. Not Sioux City. So Letterman made Sioux City the "home office" for his nightly "Top 10 List." St. Paul isn't the only Northern League team with a sense of humor. The Explorers signed Mujibur, the Broadway souvenir-store owner who appears regularly on Letterman's *Late Show*, put him in a uniform, and had him start a game as the official pitcher of record. After one pitch reported to be 20 feet over the catcher's head, they pulled him out. But Mujibur is a big crowd favorite when he returns to Lewis & Clark Park.

Frankly, there isn't that much for families to do in Sioux City beyond visiting the new riverfront parks system. That's one of the reasons Lewis & Clark Park was built. For $4 million the city built this stadium in a cornfield 5 miles from downtown in eight months, on budget and on time for the start of the inaugural Northern League 1993 season.

As much as we enjoyed our night at Lewis & Clark Park, we need to warn you of a serious problem. Beyond the right-field fence is an attractive woods. Beyond left field, a highway. Unfortunately, that's not all. Beyond the road is a sewage treatment plant. The night we were there, the smell was noticeable for the first six innings. Mayor Scott told us this is unusual. Other residents note that Sioux City commonly has similar odors from factories, like a meat-packing plant and soybean processor, but that they're considered "the smell of money," so no one complains.

Where to Stay

Visiting Team Hotel: Best Western City Centre. The rooms are large and furnished in hotel contemporary in this two-floor facility four blocks from the river. Guests receive a free full breakfast. *130 Nebraska St., off Exit 147B from I–29, Sioux City 51101, tel. 712/277–1550 or 800/528–1234, fax 712/277–1120. 114 rooms.*

Facilities: pool, health center, coin laundry. AE, D, DC, MC, V. $

Fairfield Inn by Marriott. The rooms are small and clean in this three-story hotel, which is five minutes from the ballpark. It's in a commercial area. *4716 Southern Hills Dr., at U.S. 20 and Lakeport St., Sioux City 51106, tel. 712/276-5600 or 800/228-9290, fax 712/276-5600. 62 rooms. Facilities: indoor pool, hot tub. AE, D, DC, MC, V. $*

Where to Eat

Bishop's Buffet. This is an outlet of a great Iowa cafeteria chain where locals go for their Sunday meals. The groaning-board selections include roast beef, a multitude of vegetables, and a wide choice of baked goods. The chocolate ambrosia pie is hard to resist. There is a separate kid's buffet line on weekends. Waitresses carry your tray if asked in this cheery, casual, and busy restaurant. It's in the Southern Hills Mall. *4400 Sergeant Rd., at I-29 and U.S. 20 (Exit 144A), Sioux City, tel. 712/276-0551. AE, D, DC, MC, V. $*

Green Gables. This is an old-fashioned family restaurant known for its matzo-ball soup. It also specializes in ice cream parlor desserts, particularly hot fudge sundaes. There is a children's menu with soup and sandwiches, along with fish, chicken, and roast beef platters. It's 3½ miles northwest of the ballpark. *1800 Pierce St., Sioux City, tel. 712/258-4246. AE, D, MC, V. $*

Garfield's. This chain restaurant in Southern Hills Mall offers inexpensive American food. The tables are covered with butcher paper for kids to crayon on. There are kid's meals, and waiters make a fuss over children, with special drinks and treats. *4400 Sergeant Rd., Sioux City, tel. 712/276-6505. AE, D, DC, MC, V. $*

Entertainments

Belle of Sioux City Riverboat. You can ride this gambling boat for free on the top deck 10 AM– noon as it cruises the Missouri River. Children cannot enter the casino below, but there are refreshments and rest rooms on the top deck. The two-hour cruise down the Missouri reaches

Dakota City before turning back. *100 Larsen Park Rd., Sioux City, tel. 712/255-0552. Cruises late May–early Sept. depart 10 AM.*

Riverfront Walk. In Chris Larsen Park, along the Missouri River, you can walk the bike path from the city marina past the Riverboat Museum and the memorial to the passengers on the United Airlines jet that crashed in Sioux City in 1989. There's a dance pavilion, an exceptional playground, and picnic areas for public use. *Chris Larsen Park Rd., Sioux City, tel. 712/279-6126.*

Riverside Family Aquatic Center. This large public pool has a waterslide. The pool starts at zero depth for toddlers and has a maximum depth of 5 feet. *1301 Riverside Blvd., Exit 149 off I-29, Sioux City, tel. 712/279-6903. Admission: $1.50 adults, $1 ages under 18. Open late May–Labor Day, daily 1–5:30 and 6:30–8.*

Sergeant Floyd Museum. This free riverboat museum on the Missouri River is dedicated to the river's history. It is named for the only member of the Louis and Clark expedition to die (of appendicitis) during the three-year trip. A 100-foot obelisk marks his burial site at Floyd's Bluff, U.S. 75 South. *South Larsen Park Rd., Sioux City, tel. 712/279-4840. Open May–Sept., daily 8–6; Oct.–Apr., daily 9–5.*

Sites to See

Stone State Park. See three states—South Dakota, Nebraska, and Iowa—from **Dakota Point Lookout.** There are hiking trails, picnic areas, and the new **Loess Ridge Nature Center** (4500 Sioux River Rd., tel. 712/258-0838) within the park. The center features wildlife specimens, aquariums, and a working beehive. The park is on the west edge of town. *Riverside Blvd. (Hwy. 12 N), via Exit 151 from I-29, Sioux City, tel. 712/255-4698. Park open dawn–dusk; Loess Ridge Nature Center open Tues.–Fri. 9–4, weekends 1–4.*

Fourth Street Historic District. There are antiques shops, a bookstore, and two restaurants in this three-block district of unusual and renovated storefronts. Take Exit 147B off I-29.

BIG SKY BASEBALL
HELENA, BUTTE, IDAHO FALLS

18

H itters like mountain baseball because the thinner air allows the ball to travel farther. We like it for the scenery, which makes even an ordinary game special. Helena and Butte both have breathtaking views, and Idaho Falls, while not near mountains, has a charming neighborhood feel. These are unusual rookie-league parks.

Helena has a cozy wooden grandstand, with Mount Helena beyond right center field and the Capitol dome and the spires of St. Helena Cathedral behind the outfield. This is rookie ball for the Milwaukee Brewers in the Pioneer League. The city has many remnants of its gold-mining past. Twenty miles north of Helena you can take an unforgettable flatboat canyon tour of the Missouri River at Gates of the Mountains Recreation Area.

South 55 miles from Helena off Interstate 15 is Butte, home of the Copper Kings rookie-league team and the Berkeley Pit, an immense open pit copper mine. The baseball stadium, Alumni Coliseum, is rudimentary, but has a spectacular view of the Rocky Mountains. It's an impressive backdrop for this team, affiliated with the Tampa Bay Devil Rays. The city of Butte is unlike any other in America, with its rough mining edges visible in the former bordellos and mines, and current gambling joints, all on display.

Idaho Falls is directly south, 143 miles away on Interstate 15, along the Snake River. It has a modest concrete stadium, but a colorful history of good rookie-league ball. There are lots of fan contests and a fancy scoreboard salvaged from another stadium. The city boasts a lovely greenbelt adjoining its natural and man-made falls. Another popular park complex has a zoo, a kiddie land, a playground, and an indoor ice rink.

HELENA BREWERS

League: Pioneer League • **Major League Affiliation:** Milwaukee Brewers • **Class:** Rookie/Short Season • **Stadium:** Kindrick Field • **Opened:** 1943 • **Capacity:** 1,800 • **Dimensions:** LF: 328, CF: 390, RF: 315 • **Surface:** grass • **Season:** mid-June–Labor Day

STADIUM LOCATION: Warren and Memorial Sts., Helena, MT 59601

GETTING THERE: From I–15, Cedar St. exit west. This turns into Main St. Left at Memorial St. just past city swimming pool and park.

TICKET INFORMATION: Box 4606, Helena, MT 59604, tel. 406/449–7616, fax 406/449–6979

PRICE RANGE: Box seats $6.25; dugout reserved $5.25; general admission $4.25 adults, $3.25 ages under 13 and senior citizens

GAME TIME: Mon.–Sat. 7:05 PM, Sun. 5:05 PM; gates open 1 hr before games.

TIPS ON SEATING: Best view of mountains, Capitol dome, and St. Helena Cathedral is from top of general admission bleacher seats on first-base side. Setting sun shines in eyes of fans on third-base side.

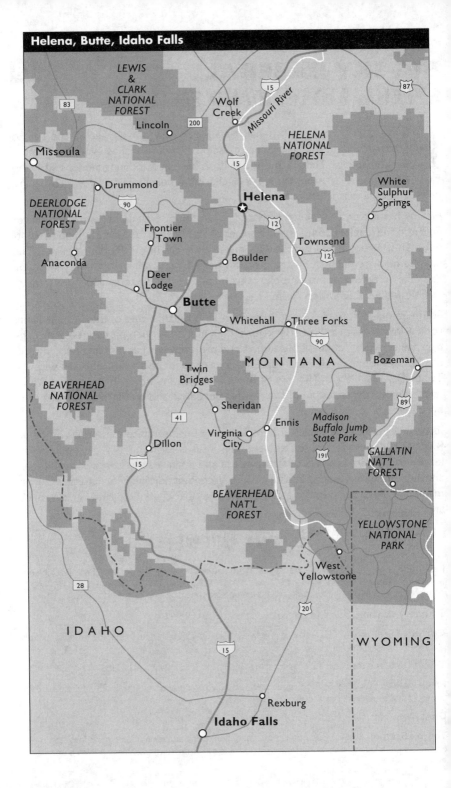

Helena, Butte, Idaho Falls

SEATING FOR PEOPLE WITH DISABILITIES: Box seat area behind home plate accessible by ramps

STADIUM FOOD: The grill on the first-base side serves burgers, Polish dogs, BBQ roast beef, and broiled chicken sandwiches ($3.25). Iced tea is available, and small soft drinks are $1.25. A generous slice of better-than-average pizza costs $2.25. Special beers and wine coolers are available at the concession stand near the bullpen down the first-base line.

SMOKING POLICY: Smoking prohibited in seating areas

PARKING: Free but limited; overflow parking available at adjacent city pool and park.

VISITING TEAM HOTEL: Shilo Inn of Helena (2020 Prospect Ave., Helena, MT 59601, tel. 406/442–0320 or 800/222–2244)

TOURISM INFORMATION: Helena Area Chamber of Commerce (225 Cruse Ave., Suite A, Helena, MT 59601, tel. 406/442–4120 or 800/743–5362)

Helena: Kindrick Field

It is hard to imagine a finer place to watch a ball game than atop the right-field bleachers at Kindrick Field in Helena, Montana. Mount Helena is just 2 miles beyond right center field. The Capitol dome and the spires of St. Helena Cathedral are visible just beyond the outfield walls, with the snow-capped Rocky Mountains in the far distance. Stand up between innings, turn around, and try to find the sleeping giant of the mountains. Hint: First look for the nose.

When the stadium was laid out in 1943, the assumption was that all games would be played during the day. Now, night games are the rule and right-handed batters and fans on the third-base side have a tough time seeing the ball because of the setting sun shining in their eyes.

The Montana State League began play in 1892, and Helena had professional teams in several leagues off and on until 1914. The city has been a member of the short-season, rookie-league Pioneer League since pro ball returned here in 1978. Kindrick Field is named for a local businessman who financed the construction of the field in the mid-1940s. The grandstand is wooden and the roof sags. But Helena, unlike Butte, isn't content to coast on its great vistas. In 1995, the city government fronted the money for a $500,000 renovation of the aging park. A new fence and scoreboard as well as almost 2,000 new blue box seats and modern bathrooms and a clubhouse are key aspects of the upgrading effort. The entranceway is substantially upgraded, with a new ticket booth and a souvenir stand.

We were constantly amazed by the people we would run into on our trip through the minor leagues. The biggest surprise came in Helena. There he was—Calvin Griffith—the man who took major-league baseball from us. Bruce grew up a Washington Senators fan, and we have two seats from the old Griffith Stadium in our living room. Calvin Griffith, whose uncle Clark Griffith played for the 1892 Missoula club before his Hall of Fame career as manager-owner of the Senators, was the man who moved the Washington team to Minnesota. But there were no hard feelings that night. We got a few autographs, reminisced for an hour, and drove off to the next city bemused by our chance encounter with our baseball past.

Where to Stay

Park Plaza. This attractive seven-floor downtown hotel has a modern small lobby and contemporary rooms. It is next to the Gaslight Cinemas in the downtown walking mall. Children 12 and under stay free; the cost for children 13–18 is $6 each per night. *22 N. Last Chance Gulch, Helena 59601, tel. 406/443–2200, 800/332–2290 in MT, fax 406/442–4030. Facilities: restaurant, free parking. AE, D, DC, MC, V. $*

Super 8 Motel. This three-story hotel is in a historic area, 10 blocks from the state capitol buildings. Its double rooms have two queen beds. Cribs are free. *2200 11th Ave., Helena 59601, tel. 406/443–2450 or 800/848–8888, fax 406/443–2450. 110 rooms. Facilities: free parking. AE, D, MC, V. $*

The Sanders Bed and Breakfast. The attractive 1875 mansion has its original Queen Anne antiques and furnishings. Each room has a private bath, and guests are given homemade cookies and lemonade at 4. It is three blocks from downtown, eight blocks from the Capitol, and directly down Ewing Street 15 blocks from the ballpark. Children are welcome. *328 N. Ewing St., Helena 59601, tel. 406/442–3309, fax 406/443–2361. 7 rooms. AE, D, MC, V. $$*

Where to Eat

Rialto Bar & Grill. This hole-in-the-wall restaurant is on the city's walking mall, amid several bookstores. It serves great burgers, fries, chicken wings, and barbecue beef sandwiches in Formica booths. Sundaes are a bargain $1.25. Gambling machines are in the back. *52 N. Last Chance Gulch, Helena, tel. 406/442–1890. No credit cards. Closed Sun. $*

Yat Son. This well-loved family restaurant has been in business for a century. In updated quarters just yards away from its original site, it serves a wide variety of Cantonese and American food. You can get shrimp with snow peas or steaks, fried chicken, or burgers. There are several children-size entrées. *2 S. Last Chance Gulch, at Main St. and Broadway, Helena, tel. 406/442–5405. AE, D, MC, V. $*

Stonehouse Restaurant. The decor is a bygone-mine theme in this upscale seafood and pasta restaurant. It's in historic Reeder's Alley, now a quaint shopping area but once the living quarters for gold-rush miners. Built as a private home in the 1890s, it now has several dining rooms. *120 Reeder's Alley, Helena, tel. 406/449–2552. AE, D, MC, V. Closed Sun. $$*

Entertainments

Last Chance Gulch Tour. In 1864, four out-of-luck prospectors declared a gulch in Helena to be their "last chance." They struck gold and the gulch became Helena's Main Street, now largely a pretty walking mall. You can take an interesting one-hour tour in a train of bumpy, open-sided cars through the city. You can learn about the gold collection in the Norwest Banks building on Lawrence Street and see where actress Myrna Loy grew up. The car-train leaves from the side of the State Historical Museum, at 6th and Roberts streets. *Prospect Ave., Helena, tel. 406/442–1023. Fare: $4.50 adults, $4 senior citizens, $3.50 ages under 13. Departs daily at 9, 10, 11, 1, 2, 3, and 4; June–Sept., also at 6.*

State Historical Museum. The biggest hit for children is trying out the various saddles on three horse replicas in the entry. The museum's stuffed white buffalo is unusual. Several artifacts describe the accomplishments of the state's African-American cowboys and soldiers. *225 N. Roberts St., Helena, tel. 406/444–2694. Donations appreciated. Open weekdays 8–6, weekends 9–5.*

Gates of the Mountains Recreation Area. Sunscreen is a must for an awe-inspiring boat tour of this spectacular canyon, formed by the Missouri River 20 miles north of Helena. You are likely to see bald eagles and mountain goats, pointed out by knowledgeable guides who also show you the sites of major forest fires. There is one stop for a brief exploration of a canyon park. *Gates of the Mountains Landing, Helena National Forest, Exit 209 from I–15, tel. 406/458–5241. Admission: $7.50 adults, $6.50 senior citizens, $4.50 ages 4–17. Tours weekdays at 11, 1, and 3; Sat. at 10, noon, 2, and 4; Sun. and holidays, on the hr 9–5.*

Sites to See

State Capitol. The dome of this Greek neoclassical sandstone capitol is copper. The House of Representatives displays Charles M. Russell's largest painting, *Lewis and Clark Meeting the Flathead Indians at Ross' Hole*, now valued for insurance purposes at $16 million. Look for Russell's trademark buffalo-head signature and note that Russell put the Native Americans, not Lewis and Clark, at the center of his painting. Make sure you visit the statue of Jeannette Rankin behind the grand staircase in the Capitol Rotunda. Rankin, the first woman elected to the Congress of the United States, was one of our country's leaders in the fight for women's right to vote. *6th and Montana Sts., Helena, tel. 406/444–4789. Open daily 8–5; 45-min tours hourly Mon.–Sat. 9–4, Sun. 9–3.*

BUTTE COPPER KINGS

League: Pioneer League • **Affiliation:** Tampa Bay Devil Rays • **Class:** Rookie/Short Season • **Stadium:** Alumni Coliseum • **Opened:** 1962 • **Capacity:** 1,750 • **Dimensions:** LF: 345, CF: 475, 360 • **Surface:** grass • **Season:** mid-June–Labor Day

STADIUM LOCATION: Montana Tech Campus, West Park St., Butte, MT

GETTING THERE: From I–90, Montana St. exit north to Park St. West to stadium on Montana Tech campus.

TICKET INFORMATION: Box 186, Butte, MT 59703, tel. 406/723–8206, fax 406/723–3376

PRICE RANGE: Reserved $5; general admission $4 adult, $3 children, senior citizens, and military personnel; under 6 free

GAME TIME: Mon.–Sat. 7 PM, Sun. 6 PM; gates open 1 hr before game

TIPS ON SEATING: All seats have extraordinary view of Rocky Mountain highlands. Seats in top right corner of general admission grandstand on first-base side have best view of mountains and less sun in your eyes.

SEATING FOR PEOPLE WITH DISABILITIES: Along first- or third-base foul line

STADIUM FOOD: The offerings are inexpensive and better than you'd expect. A grill on the first-base side serves hamburgers, bratwurst, Polish sausage, and chicken sandwiches. There is also corn-on-the-cob, and the team's own brand of beer, Copper Kings Ale.

SMOKING POLICY: No-smoking section in general admission area above first-base dugout

PARKING: Free parking available next to stadium; overflow parking available on campus.

VISITING TEAM HOTEL: WAR BONNET INN (2100 Cornell Ave., Butte, MT 59701, tel. 406/494–7800 or 800/443–1806)

TOURISM INFORMATION: BUTTE-SILVER BOW CHAMBER OF COMMERCE (2950 Harrison Ave., Butte, MT 59701, tel. 406/494–5595 or 800/735–6814)

Butte: Alumni Coliseum

For raw physical beauty, it is hard to imagine a finer setting for baseball than Alumni Coliseum in Butte, Montana. From the covered hilltop grandstand, you have an almost unobstructed scenic view of the Rocky Mountains over the center- and right-field fences.

The Berkeley Pit, not far from the stadium, was once the largest truck-operated open-pit copper mine in the United States. As a result, the Butte team is called the Copper Kings and has one of the best logos in baseball—a smiling bearded miner wearing a crown and holding a bat.

This stadium is rudimentary. The covered, cinderblock grandstand has fixed reserved seats and general admission seats along the foul lines.

Picnic tables, a speedpitch, and a playground also are at the field. The press box is a small wooden cage in the back row of the grandstand. Because the Copper Kings share this field with the Montana Tech University football team, there are 3,000 seats out beyond left field in the football bleachers.

The play is uneven here in the Pioneer League. In Idaho Falls, we saw three runners score on a Copper King wild pitch. In Butte, we saw a fabulous running catch by Butte's center fielder against the fence in left center.

We had fun in this mountain park. The weather on a July night was almost perfect, and it didn't grow dark until the very last innings of the game. (Bring a jacket because of the westerly winds and high elevation.) The Copper Kings have a full array of contests and give-aways.

Where to Stay

The Capri Motel. This inexpensive '50s-era motel is next door to the now abandoned Orphan Girl mine in downtown Butte. The rooms have sliding glass doors that overlook the central parking lot. Some of the rooms have a second bedroom with twin beds in an alcove. There are free morning coffee and doughnuts. *220 N. Wyoming St., Butte 59701, tel. 406/723–4391 or 800/342–2774, fax 406/723–4391. 64 rooms. Facilities: coin laundry. AE, D, MC, V.* $

Finlen Hotel and Motor Inn. Built in 1923, this venerable but inexpensive downtown hotel is a monument to the faded glory of the Copper Kings. Once a grand hotel, it is now a clean and unusual alternative to interstate lodging. The marble-floored lobby is a step backward in time. The rooms have high ceilings and vintage 1960s furnishings. *100 E. Broadway, Butte 59701, tel. 406/723–4121 or 800/729–5461. 50 rooms. Facilities: free parking. AE, D, MC, V.* $

Comfort Inn of Butte. This three-story motel is near Butte Plaza Mall, behind a restaurant. The rooms were renovated in 1996, and a free Continental breakfast is served. *2777 Harrison Ave., at Exit 127 off I–90, Butte 59701, tel. 406/494–8850 or 800/424–6423, fax 406/494–2801. 150 rooms. Facilities: restaurant, hot tub, sauna, coin laundry, casino. AE, D, DC, MC, V.* $$

Where to Eat

M & M Cafe. This one-of-a-kind establishment is an 1890s saloon, eatery, and gambling house. There's a bar on one side, a food counter on the other, and Texas hold-em poker games in the back room. A historic remnant of the mining era it's a gritty place, with keno machines in plain view of the kids. Jack Kerouac and other devotees of the open road ate here. Its oyster stew is a bargain. *9 N. Main St., Butte, tel. 406/723–7612. No credit cards.* $

Matts's Place. This family-run soda fountain, opened in 1931 and now the oldest drive-in in Montana, has homemade ice cream, terrific burgers and fries, and tons of atmosphere. The Cokes are served in old-fashioned bottles, at the counter or with table service. You can get a hamburger with egg, a sardine sandwich, or a glass of cold buttermilk. It is 1½ miles north of the ballpark. *2339 Placer St., Butte, tel. 406/782–8049. No credit cards. Closed Sun.–Mon.* $

Pekin Noodle Parlor. In the Tam family since 1916, this downtown restaurant is famous as a noodle parlor for the immigrant copper workers. The high-backed booths are private, and the atmosphere is old Chinatown. Noodle dishes of every description are served, along with western standbys like steak sandwiches. The prices are reduced for children's portions. *117 Main St., Butte, tel. 406/782–2217. MC, V. Closed Tues.* $

Entertainments

Old No. 1 Streetcar Ride. You can see the Berkeley Open Pit Mine, immigrants' living quarters, the bordellos, and the Copper King Mansion in this 90-minute tour. Make sure you look at three enormous copper doors to the now closed Central High School. There are sights in this Old West town that are never seen in eastern cities and that are remade each decade. The 1880s town hospital is still standing and is now an apartment building. The gift shop at the Berkeley Pit has many intriguing kid's items fashioned from copper. *2950 Harrison Ave., Butte, tel. 406/494–5595 or 800/735–6814. Admission: $4 adults, $2.50 ages 4–12. Tours daily at 10:30, 1:30, 3:30, and 7.*

Mining Camp and Museum. This re-creation of an 1899 mining camp includes a Chinese laundry, an herb store, an assay office, a sauerkraut factory, a print shop, a bank, and a dozen other shops. Built around an inactive silver and zinc mine, the original Orphan Girl, this cobblestone history museum allows kids to see what mining life was like. The buildings are spread campus-style, allowing you to stroll throughout and stop at whatever catches your eye. *W. Park and Granite Sts., Butte, tel. 406/723–7211. Admission: donations ages 12 and up. Open mid-June–Labor Day, daily 9–9; Labor Day–late Nov. and Apr.–mid-June, Tues.–Sun. 10–5.*

Sites to See

Our Lady of the Rockies. This 90-foot concrete statue of the Virgin Mary was put in place on the edge of the Continental Divide in 1985 by the Nevada Air National Guard, the Montana National Guard, and the U.S. Army Reserve

from Butte. It's intended as a tribute to mother-
hood. Two-hour bus tours depart twice daily
from the Butte Plaza Mall. *3100 Harrison Ave.,*

*Butte, tel. 406/782–1221 or 800/800–5239.
Admission: $10 adults, $5 ages 5–12. Tours June–
Oct. at 10 and 2. D, MC, V.*

IDAHO FALLS BRAVES

League: Pioneer League • **Major League Affiliation:** San Diego Padres • **Class:** Rookie/Short Season • **Stadium:** McDermott Field • **Opened:** 1940/76 • **Capacity:** 2,800 • **Dimensions:** LF: 350,
CF: 400, RF: 340 • **Surface:** grass • **Season:** mid-June–Labor Day

STADIUM LOCATION: 568 W. Elva, Idaho Falls, ID 83402

GETTING THERE: From I–15, take Broadway exit. East across Snake River. Immediate left onto Memorial Dr., right on Mound Ave. to stadium.

TICKET INFORMATION: Box 2183, Idaho Falls, ID 83403, tel. 208/522–8363, fax 208/522–9858

PRICE RANGE: Reserved $5.25; general admission $3.75 adults, $2.75 ages under 13 and senior citizens

GAME TIME: Mon.–Sat. 7:15 PM, Sun. 5 PM

TIPS ON SEATING: General admission seats directly behind home plate are close to action and in a no-
smoking section. Two fans are selected to sit in "Horizon Air IST CLASS" seats for each game.

SEATING FOR PEOPLE WITH DISABILITIES: Row behind reserved seats on first-base side of home accessible by ramp

STADIUM FOOD: Grilled cheeseburgers and hot dogs are available from a stand on the third-base side.
A picnic area is down the left field line. Microbrewed regional ales are sold from a stand on the first-base
side.

SMOKING POLICY: Section directly behind home plate is no-smoking.

PARKING: Limited free parking at stadium. This is a small park; try to park as far from entrance as possible to avoid foul balls.

VISITING TEAM HOTEL: Motel West (1540 W. Broadway, Idaho Falls, ID 83402, tel. 208/522–1112 or
800/582–1063)

TOURISM INFORMATION: Greater Idaho Falls Chamber of Commerce (505 Lindsay Blvd. Idaho
Falls, ID 83405, tel. 208/523–1010)

Idaho Falls: McDermott Field

McDermott Field in Idaho Falls, Idaho, is just what
Central Casting would order for a movie on
rookie-league baseball. The surroundings don't
match the physical beauty of Idaho Falls' Pioneer
League rivals, but it is a simple, cozy, and unpre-
tentious place. McDermott is a compact neighborhood park where everyone is close to the
action and foul balls are constantly flying into the
adjacent children's park and stadium parking lot.

They have been playing Pioneer League baseball
games in Idaho Falls since 1940, longer than anywhere else. The veteran Idaho Falls baseball fans

we sat with bemoaned the loss of the 5,000-
seat wooden Highland Park that was on this
site until burned down by arsonists in the mid-
1970s. Highland Park, built in 1940 by the
Works Progress Administration, they told us,
was more spacious, with more comfortable
seats and a roof. Future New York Yankees
player and coach Billy Martin began his professional career at Highland Park in 1946, playing
for the Idaho Falls Russets, a team named for
Idaho's famous potato.

The insurance money from the fire allowed the
city to build a modest concrete stadium without
a roof and with seat backs only for the reserved
seats. The rebuilt stadium was named for E. F.
McDermott, general manager of the *Post Regis-*

ter of Idaho Falls and known as Mr. Baseball of the Pioneer League. The billboards are only one row high on the outfield wall. Billboards along the dark green walls behind the seating areas add to the stadium's cozy feel. The surprise here is the large scoreboard beyond the left-field fence, which has up-to-date player stats like those in the more advanced minor leagues. Idaho Falls bought the scoreboard from a Salt Lake City AAA Pacific Coast League team that was about to scrap it when it tore down an old stadium.

Other than the fancy scoreboard, there are few frills here. McDermott Field doesn't even have a tarp to protect against rain.

Not having much money doesn't stop the Idaho Falls team from providing the 1,000 or so fans who come each night with a good time. There are plenty of contests and an imaginative game of baseball bingo about once a week. In Idaho Falls, fans who buy programs get contest coupons.

Remember, this is rookie-league ball. Even some future stars are struggling at this critical early time in their careers. The night we visited, the home team scored three runs on a bases-loaded wild pitch. Even the umpire had to share a laugh with the first-base coach on this one.

Where to Stay

Holiday Inn Westbank. If you want to see the Snake River Falls, ask for a room in the eight-story section. The low-rise section along the riverfront does not have a falls view, but is along the outdoor pool. The rooms are standard size and have been recently renovated. *475 River Pkwy., Idaho Falls 83402, tel. 208/523–8000 or 800/465–4329, fax 208/529–9610. 141 rooms. Facilities: pool, hot tub, sauna. AE, D, DC, MC, V. $$*

Best Western Driftwood. Some of the rooms in this two-story, remodeled hotel have views of the falls. The 2.7 mile greenbelt around the falls and the falls themselves are just steps away. There is a refrigerator and a microwave oven in each room. *575 River Pkwy., Idaho Falls 83402, tel. 208/523–2242 or 800/528–1234, fax 208/ 523–0316. 74 rooms. Facilities: pool, coin laundry. AE, D, DC, MC, V. $$*

Where to Eat

Le Baron's Lounge. This 1950s-style coffeeshop is popular with many locals because of its low

prices. You can get homemade biscuits and a full breakfast for under $2. There's a children's menu for breakfast. Roasted chicken, breaded veal, and liver and onions are dinner favorites. *1700 Yellowstone Ave., Idaho Falls, tel. 208/523– 1564. MC, V. $*

Jake's Steak and Fish House. This bright, contemporary fish restaurant has a good salad bar and a varied children's menu. Locally caught trout is a specialty. Both booths and tables are available in the hunter-green and dark-wood dining room. *851 Lindsay Blvd., Idaho Falls, tel. 208/524–5240. AE, D, MC, V. Closed Sun. $$*

Bubba's Bar B Que. This extremely casual restaurant is in a former Bonanza Steakhouse building with pig ornaments throughout. It's known for its ribs, salad bar, and buttermilk pie. There's an all-you-can-eat rib special every Monday night for $8.95. The children's menu includes turkey, kid ribs, pork, and chicken. The restaurant is 10 miles south of the ballpark. *888 E. 17th St., Idaho Falls, tel. 208/523–2822. D, MC, V. $*

Entertainments

Tautphaus Park Zoo. This well-maintained park complex has a small zoo, an ice rink, the Funland amusement park, a playground, and several tennis courts. You can rent a stroller for $2. Funland has miniature golf, a merry-go-round, a train, a Ferris wheel, little airplane rides, and an octopus ride. The zoo and park are ¾ mile off 17th Street, which is a main road. *South Blvd. and Rogers St., Idaho Falls, tel. 208/529–1470 or 208/525–9814 (Funland). Zoo admission: $2 adults, $1.25 senior citizens, $1 ages 13–17, 75¢ ages 4–12. Funland coupon books: 15 tickets for $7.85; 25 tickets for $12.30; most rides cost 2–5 tickets. Zoo open daily 9–7:30; Funland open Mon.–Sat. noon–7:30, Sun. 12:30–7:30.*

Sites to See

Idaho Falls. A 2½-mile greenbelt adjoins the falls, half of which are natural and half man-made. In a landscaped picnic area along the Snake River, you can watch ducks, joggers, and walkers. This is a cool retreat on a summer afternoon. *River Pkwy., ½ mi east of I–15, Broadway exit, Idaho Falls.*

PACIFIC NORTHWEST
VANCOUVER, EVERETT, PORTLAND

19

S tartling beauty is a constant in Pacific Coast League baseball. A trip that combines Vancouver and two Northwest League teams, in Bellingham and Everett, Washington, will convince you that cool nights and forests are the essential backdrops for baseball.

Vancouver's Nat Bailey Stadium is in Queen Elizabeth Park, where majestic evergreens provide the backdrop for batters. This is Triple AAA baseball; the Canadians are affiliated with the California Angels. The old-time grandstand has a wide concourse with a variety of foods you don't find in U.S. stadiums, such as hot mini-doughnuts and cider. You can spend much of your time in parks during your visit in Vancouver, as they hold many attractions, such as the indoor/outdoor aquarium in Stanley Park, the Capilano suspension bridge in a North Vancouver park, and Bloedel Conservatory in Queen Elizabeth Park. An urban park holds Vancouver Playland, an amusement park especially appealing to pre-teens. There are water taxis to take to Granville Island, in the city's center, with an exceptional public market.

Leaving British Columbia on Route 99 south and following Interstate 5 south to Bellingham will bring you to Everett in just over two hours. The city's gem of a park has been completely upgraded to give 3,700 fans a view of Seattle Mariners minor-league Single A play set between the Cascade and Olympic mountains. Management advises you to wear warm clothes and if you forget, will rent you blankets in July. The park is irresistible to kids because of its endearing logo, the AquaSox frog and its hip-hop fashions. The adjoining football field is open for children to play their own games on. Nature cruises from the Everett marina to the San Juan Islands bring you back before game time. Forest Park in the city has a children's zoo, a heated pool, and a large playground.

Portland is another three hours south on Interstate 5. It's the city of roses, public art, beautiful bridges over the Willamette River, and a wealth of family activities, from exploring Washington Park to an exceptional science center to the nation's oldest amusement park. The girls' Little League Softball World Series is played here at Alpenrose Stadium. Portland's ballpark, with the largest capacity in Single A or Double AA baseball, has the fan-friendly Rocky Raccoon to keep the action going.

VANCOUVER CANADIANS

League: Pacific Coast League • **Major League Affiliation:** California Angels • **Class:** AAA • **Stadium:** Nat Bailey Stadium • **Opened:** 1951 • **Capacity:** 6,500 • **Dimensions:** LF: 335, CF: 395, RF: 335 • **Surface:** grass • **Season:** Apr.–Labor Day

STADIUM LOCATION: 4601 Ontario St., Vancouver, BC V5V 3H4

GETTING THERE: From downtown, Cambie St. Bridge. Left on E. 33rd St., left on Clancy Loringer Way, and right to stadium. From south, Hwy. 99 to Oak St. Right on 41st Ave. and left on Ontario.

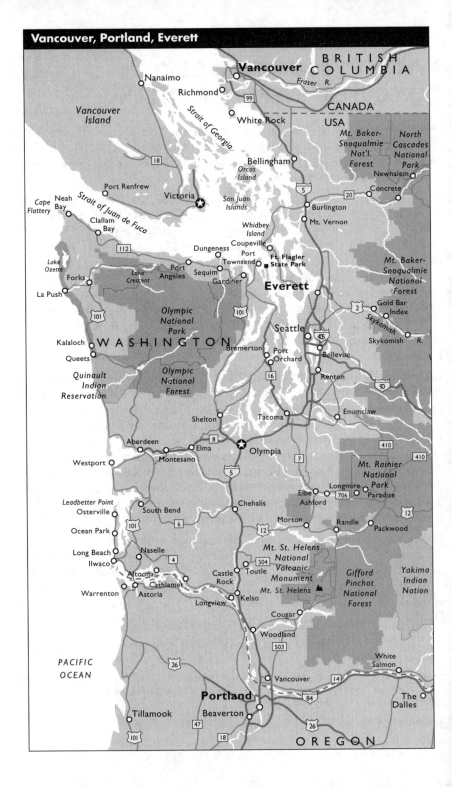

Vancouver, Portland, Everett

Vancouver

B R I T I S H
C O L U M B I A

Fraser R.

Nanaimo

Richmond

White Rock

99

CANADA
USA

*Vancouver
Island*

Strait of Georgia

Bellingham

*Orcas
Island*

*Mt. Baker-
Snoqualmie
Nat'l.
Forest*

*North
Cascades
National
Park*

Newhalem

18

Port Renfrew

Victoria

*San Juan
Islands*

5

20

Concrete

Burlington

Mt. Vernon

*Cape
Flattery*

Neah
Bay

Strait of Juan de Fuca

Clallam
Bay

*Whidbey
Island*

Coupeville
Port
Townsend

Dungeness

*Ft. Flagler
State Park*

*Mt. Baker-
Snoqualmie
National
Forest*

112

*Lake
Ozette*

*Lake
Crescent*

Port
Angeles

Sequim

Gardiner

Everett

Forks

101

La Push

101

Kalaloch

W A S H I N G T O N

*Olympic
National
Park*

Bremerton

Seattle

405

Gold Bar
Index

2

Skykomish

Skykomish R.

Queets

Port
Orchard

Bellevue

*Quinault
Indian
Reservation*

*Olympic
National
Forest*

16

Renton

90

Shelton

Tacoma

Enumclaw

Aberdeen

Elma

8

Olympia

410

410

Westport

Montesano

5

7

*Mt. Rainier
National
Park*

Leadbetter Point

Osterville

South Bend

101

6

Chehalis

Elbe
Ashford

Longmire

706

Paradise

12

Morton

Randle

Packwood

Ocean Park

Long Beach

Ilwaco

Naselle

4

12

*Mt. St. Helens
National
Volcanic
Monument*

504

Toutle

*Gifford
Pinchot
National
Forest*

*Yakima
Indian
Nation*

Altoona

Cathlamet

Castle
Rock

Warrenton

Astoria

Mt. St. Helens ▲

Longview

Kelso

Cougar

Woodland

503

*PACIFIC
OCEAN*

26

Vancouver

14

White
Salmon

Portland

84

The
Dalles

Tillamook

Beaverton

47

18

O R E G O N

26

101

TICKET INFORMATION: 4601 Ontario St., Vancouver, BC V5V 3H4, tel. 604/872–5232, fax 604/872–1714

PRICE RANGE: Box seat $7.50 Canadian; lower reserved $6.50; upper reserved $5.50 adults, $3.25 children and senior citizens; general admission $2 at Safeway

GAME TIME: Mon.–Tues., Thurs.–Sat. 7:05 PM; Wed. 12:15 PM; Sun. 1:30 PM; gates open 1 hr before game

TIPS ON SEATING: Upper reserved seats are close to action

SEATING FOR PEOPLE WITH DISABILITIES: Special seating area down left-field line

STADIUM FOOD: Warm and unusual foods are found here. The homemade mini-doughnuts and the espresso stand are standouts. There are biscotti for $1.50, or gourmet hot chocolate for $3. Pizza slices have a ham and pineapple topping for $4, and chicken and turkey burgers are $4.50. Onion rings are $2. Root beer, ale, and cider are on draft. Fans are allowed to bring their own food to grill in a picnic and playground area down the left-field line. Two grills are available for early bird picnickers.

SMOKING POLICY: Smoking prohibited in seats under grandstand roof.

PARKING: Ample parking, $2

VISITING TEAM HOTEL: Coast Vancouver Airport Hotel (1041 SW Marine Dr., Vancouver, BC V6P 6L6, tel. 604/263–1555 or 800/663–1144)

TOURISM INFORMATION: Tourism Vancouver (200 Burrard St., Plaza Level, Vancouver, BC V6C 3L6, tel. 604/683–2000)

Vancouver: Nat Bailey Stadium

Vancouver's Nat Bailey Stadium combines the three things we like best in a ballpark—quality facilities, an old-time feel, and a gorgeous view beyond the outfield walls. The bold red, white, and blue paint—the colors of prime sponsor and former owner Molson's Ale—gives the stadium a distinct 1950s look. The wide concourse beneath the seats reminds us of Louisville's cheerful Cardinal Stadium, a real people place. But Nat Bailey Stadium seats only 6,500 people and puts the fans really close to the action.

The view beyond the outfield walls is of the heavily treed Queen Elizabeth Park, the highest point in the city. Few large-city sport facilities can rival this. The trees not only provide a great background for hitters, but they rate along with the majestic views of the more rural, small-city stadiums of the Pioneer League. The contrast between the colorfully painted, almost gaudy stadium and the gorgeous stock of evergreen trees is striking and appealing.

Vancouver, which has had professional baseball off and on since 1905, fielded a team called the Capilanos in the Western International League during much of the 1930s through the early '50s. When a new stadium was built in 1951, it was named Capilano Stadium after the brewery that owned it. The new stadium was modeled after the much-admired 1938 Sick's Seattle Stadium. Unfortunately, they bulldozed Sick's Stadium and Seattle now plays baseball under an ugly dome.

In 1956, Vancouver moved up to the prestigious Triple AAA Pacific Coast League with a team called the Mounties. Future Hall of Fame third baseman Brooks Robinson, a mainstay of the World Champion Baltimore Orioles in the 1960s and early '70s, hit .331 for the Mounties in 1956. Vancouver dropped out of the Pacific Coast League twice but came back for good as the Canadians in 1978. The refurbished stadium was renamed for Nat Bailey, a local restaurateur who was a leader in bringing baseball back to Vancouver. Bailey began his business career as a teenager selling peanuts at Vancouver's Denman Arena and Athletic Park.

Nat Bailey Stadium is a family-friendly place. Most of the seats are under roof, where smoking is prohibited. There is a playground for children down the first-base line alongside a picnic area.

Okay, we've seen that combination before. But in Vancouver there are two grills for fans who want to cook their own meals, available on a first-come, first-served basis. Most parks prohibit you from bringing your own food, raw or cooked.

Where to Stay

Vancouver hotels typically offer a 30%–35% exchange rate from U.S. to Canadian dollars. Any rates listed for lodging and attractions are in Canadian dollars.

Visiting Team Hotel: Coast Vancouver Airport Hotel. This three-story hotel, 10 minutes from Vancouver International Airport and 20 minutes from the ballpark, is located just before the Arthur Lang Bridge. The rooms in the newer rear section are larger and cost $10 more than the standard rooms. Airport noise is not a problem, but the front rooms are affected by noise from the Oak Street Bridge traffic. *1041 S.W. Marine Dr., Vancouver V6P 6LP, tel. 604/ 263–1555 or 800/663–1144, fax 604/263– 0245. 132 rooms. Facilities: restaurant, hot tub, sauna, free parking. AE, DC, MC, V. $$*

Plaza 500 Hotel. This medium-rise hotel is down the street from City Hall on a busy commercial corner three minutes from downtown. It is an efficient, business-oriented hotel with a good location and pleasant rooms. Guests have free access to a fitness club across the street. *500 W. 12th Ave., Vancouver V5Z 1MZ, tel. 604/ 873–1811 or 800/473–1811, fax 604/873– 5103. 153 rooms. Facilities: restaurant, parking (fee). AE, DC, MC, V. $$*

Sylvia Hotel. Early reservations are a must for this ivy-covered hotel, as its relatively low cost and choice location next to English Bay make it very popular in summer. There's a new addition to handle the overflow, but the nicer rooms are in the original eight-story brick building. Rooms facing the bay have the most charm. The doubles are small, but there are several one-bedroom suites with kitchens. *1154 Gilford St., at Beach Dr., Vancouver V6G 2PG, tel. 604/681– 9321. 116 rooms, 15 suites. Facilities: restaurant. AE, MC, V. $$*

Where to Eat

White Spot. This is a fast, no-surprises family restaurant chain started by the man for whom the baseball stadium is named. Founder Nat Bailey sold concessions at the stadium that preceded this one and started Canada's first drive-in restaurant. The offerings include soup, salads, and burgers with healthy accompaniments, as well as good barbecue and macaroni. Children 12 and under can order Pirate Paks, with a choice of carrots and celery instead of fries, and the food comes in a paper take-home ship. There are 10 locations in Vancouver. This one is 10 minutes from the ballpark and across the street from the Plaza 500 Hotel. The site closest to the ballpark is at the Oakridge Mall (41st and Cambie Sts., tel. 604/261–2820). *13th and Cambie Sts., tel. 604/873–1252. MC, V. $*

The Fish House in Stanley Park. This beautiful seafood restaurant at the Beach Drive entrance to Stanley Park resembles a country clubhouse on a well-manicured lawn. It is a splurge restaurant for lunch in a lovely setting overlooking English Bay. There are unusual but not too exotic choices, such as grilled prawns, calamari, fisherman's pot pie, and clam and corn chowder. Among its noteworthy vegetables are spaghetti squash and buttermilk mashed potatoes. *8910 Stanley Park Dr., Vancouver, tel. 604/681–7275. AE, DC, MC, V. $$*

Blue Parrot. This casual bakery café is within the public market. Patrons place their orders for muffins, pastries, and unusual coffees and fruit drinks before grabbing a table near the water. You can watch the harbor while drinking real hot chocolate and eating crumpets. *1689 Johnstone St., Granville Island, Vancouver, tel. 604/ 688–5127. No credit cards. $*

The Bread Garden. You'll find nine of these café-bakeries throughout Vancouver, offering very good light breakfasts, lunches, and dinners. In addition to the excellent breads and beverages, you'll find shepherd's pie, lasagna, and, for children, Rice Krispie treats. *1880 W. 1st Ave., between Burrard and Cypress Sts., Vancouver, tel. 604/738–6684. MC, V. $*

Entertainments

Vancouver Playland. This small 1960s-era amusement park within the city limits has a history dating from the 1920s. It is an urban park, with few trees, but the rides, not the landscaping, attract children. There is a good wooden roller coaster that people age six and up can ride. The midway is extensive. There's an appealing 12-ride kiddieland and a putt-putt golf course on the grounds. Each entry includes 10 tokens for the noisy arcade. The only food available is at concession stands specializing in hot dogs and cotton candy. From the third week in June until early September, adults pay $5 on Sunday and Monday when they are accompanied by a child older than three. In spring and early June, this offer is good on Sunday only. Parking is $3. *Renfrew, E. Hastings, and Cassiar Sts., Vancouver, tel. 604/255–5161. Admission: $16.95 adults, $13.95 children 48″ or less. Open mid-June–Aug., Sun.–Thurs. 11–10, Fri.–Sat. 11–11; Sept.–mid-June, some weekends, 11–10. MC, V.*

Vancouver Aquarium. More than 8,000 animals, including many sharks, sea lions, and a huge octopus, make their home in Stanley Park. The interior tanks are at eye level for children. You can see outdoor and indoor whale tanks and sit in a concrete amphitheater to watch a beluga whale show. There are several hands-on geography and anatomy displays. The exhibits are clever; several are interactive, and unusual species are displayed in a huge freshwater tank in an Amazon rain-forest environment. While you're in Stanley Park, you can visit its famous collection of totem poles, near Hallelujah Point, and its beaches. If you're here at night, listen for the 1816 cannon rigged to fire a blank charge at 9. Bring coins, as the pay parking in the park requires quarters. *Stanley Park, Vancouver, tel. 604/682–1118. Aquarium admission: $11.50 adults, $10 ages 13–18 and senior citizens, $8 ages 4–12, $39 family (2 adults, 3 children). Open July–Labor Day, daily 9:30–8; Sept.–June, daily 10–5:30.*

Sites to See

Capilano Suspension Bridge and Park. You may feel like Indiana Jones as you walk 450 feet across the Capilano River on a swaying wooden-plank bridge. This attraction is only for those without a fear of heights, as you're 230 feet up. No strollers are allowed. It is not dangerous—the sides are mesh, the bridge is reinforced with steel, and no one has tumbled off since the original hemp-and-rope bridge was strung in 1889. The current bridge was built in 1956. The scenery is awe inspiring; you can hike on forest trails, watch local craftspeople at work, and visit nature displays. There is a restaurant on the grounds, and native Canadian goods are sold at a trading post. *3735 Capilano Rd., North Vancouver, tel. 604/985–7474. Admission: $8.25 adults, $5.75 students, $2.75 ages 6–12. Open May–Oct., daily 8:30–dusk; Nov.–Mar., daily 9–5.*

Granville Island. This spectacular downtown public market has several casual breakfast and lunch restaurants, a sail-making factory and ship outfitters, and clothing, book, and toy shops. You can watch canvas being cut and fitted at the sail factory. This is a working marina, with many ships under restoration. The city's Aquabus ferries serve the island. At the indoor market, you can buy raspberries and cherries at give-away prices. The island is under the Granville Street Bridge near West 4th Street. *Granville Island, Vancouver, tel. 604/666–5784. Market open Tues.–Sun. 9–6.*

Bloedel Conservatory. This domed conservatory in Queen Elizabeth Park gives visitors a 360-degree view of the city. Tropical parrots and 50 other varieties of birds live in this climate-controlled greenery. Children enjoy the brightly colored fish in its koi pool. *33rd Ave. and Cambie St., Vancouver, tel. 604/257–8570. Admission: $3.25 adults, $1.60 ages 6–18 and senior citizens. Open early Apr.–late Sept., weekdays 9–8, weekends 10–9; Oct.–May, daily 9–5.*

Everett Aquasox

League: Northwest League • **Major League Affiliation:** Seattle Mariners • **Class:** Short Season A • **Stadium:** Everett Memorial Stadium • **Opened:** 1984 • **Capacity:** 3,700 • **Dimensions:** LF: 330, CF: 395, RF: 335 • **Surface:** grass • **Season:** mid-June–Labor Day

Stadium Location: 39th and Broadway, Everett, WA 98201

GETTING THERE: From I–5, take exit 192, which immediately becomes Broadway. Be prepared for quick left turn at sign for Memorial Stadium at 39th St.

TICKET INFORMATION: Box 7893, Everett, WA 98201, tel. 206/258–3673, fax 206/258–3675

PRICE RANGE: Pavilion chairs $7 adult, $5 ages under 15; general admission $5 adult, $4 ages under 15, under 2 free

GAME TIME: Weekdays 7:05 PM, weekends 6:05 PM; gates open 1 hr before game.

TIPS ON SEATING: Seats high up on third-base side have best views and do not have glare from sun.

SEATING FOR PEOPLE WITH DISABILITIES: Fully accessible

STADIUM FOOD: For cold nights, there are a good vegetable soup ($2.25) and chili ($3). There's a veggie tray for $2, fruit drinks, and pasta salad. The $5 meal deals include a big hot dog, peanuts, and a large soda. Kid's meals have a hot dog, chips, small soda, and a prize. A good local pizza is $2.50 per slice. An espresso and dessert stand includes wonderful It's It ice cream bars from California ($1.50). The bars are two superlative oatmeal cookies filled with ice cream. You also can buy gourmet chocolate cake, cookies, and cafe latte. The popcorn is particularly good ($2–$3).

SMOKING POLICY: Smoking prohibited in seating areas

PARKING: Ample free parking at 39th St. entrance

VISITING TEAM HOTEL: Howard Johnson's (3105 Pine Ave., Everett, WA 98201, tel. 206/339–3333 or 800/654–2000)

TOURISM INFORMATION: Everett/Snohomish County Convention & Visitor Bureau (Box 1086, 1710 W. Marine View Dr., Everett, WA 98206, tel. 206/252–5181)

Everett: Memorial Stadium

Seattle is a wonderful city, with an exciting public market and a truly awful stadium, the Kingdome, where the Mariners now play. Wait and visit there in 1999, when a new stadium will be built. In the meantime, we prefer the Northwest League, where the play is erratic but you can breathe real air and see beautiful sights and just maybe bump into a future American hero.

Everett, Washington, is known for Boeing, not baseball. With the exception of a year—1905— in the Northwest League, Everett had no history in professional baseball until 1984. But the current Everett baseball ownership has a gene pool hard to match. You get a hint of this by looking at the scoreboard in right center field. It's different. There aren't many that are still hand-operated. And to the fan with a sense of baseball, it looks familiar. The tip-off is the bank advertisement at the bottom of the black-and-white scoreboard: "HIT THE SIGN—WIN A SUIT!"

On the 40th anniversary of Jackie Robinson's gallant 1947 breaking of baseball's odious color line, Bob and Margaret Bavasi, the co-owners of the Everett team, wanted to do something special. They had the Ebbets Field scoreboard re-created for Everett Memorial Stadium. Memorial Stadium is no Ebbets Field—although ironically it does have an asymmetrical outfield wall—but it has one of the great scoreboards in the minor leagues. When the banker asked Bob Bavasi how many suits he would have to spring for, Bavasi said he didn't know, but he could put the former general manager of the Brooklyn Dodgers on the line to answer. He called his dad, Buzzie Bavasi, to seal the deal.

The baseball gene pool in Everett doesn't stop with the Bavasis. Our daughter, Emily, raced the head groundskeeper, Jim Averill, around the bases between the sixth and seventh innings. Averill's grandfather Earl, a left-handed home-run slugger for the Cleveland Indians in the 1930s, is in baseball's Hall of Fame. Emily got a ball for her efforts and had it signed by Buzzie Bavasi himself.

Bob and Margaret Bavasi are cautious managers. "What we do we want to do well," Bob Bavasi told us. "Our goal is fan comfort." The stadium we visited in 1995 held 2,285 with room for spillover into grassy areas down the baselines. Built in 1984 next to a football stadium in an athletic complex owned by the Everett School District, the baseball stadium was just the basics—an uncovered grandstand with wooden bleachers down each baseline. The grandstand had real seats of generous proportion and cup holders for every seat.

But Snohomish County and the city of Everett pooled resources to fund a $4.2 million upgrade of the existing stadium. By the time you visit Everett, expect to see new stands, with room for 3,700, that do not compromise on comfort and are fully accessible to people with disabilities. The upgrade includes new lighting, dugouts, concessions, rest rooms, and press boxes.

This park has lively music—an eclectic mix of oldies, country, the classics, and Disney. The Cascade Mountains are visible over the outfield wall, and the Olympic range is behind the stadium. Beware: When the sun goes down, it can get cold here. "DRESS WARMLY!" the pocket schedule says in bold letters, and they mean it, even in July. This is Puget Sound country, not a shorts and T-shirt place. They rent blankets for $3. Wear long pants, and visit the souvenir stand famous for its "Hip Hop Fashions." The Bavasis worked hard on the logo and came up with a winner—the Everett AquaSox is a cross between a Pacific Tree Frog, a Central American Red-Eyed Tree Frog, and superstar fielder Brooks Robinson.

Our son, Hugh, rated this stadium one of his favorites. His number one criterion is a place to run and play ball. Kids love the well-kept and well-supervised football practice field immediately behind the first-base stands.

Tacoma's Cheney Stadium is another good baseball alternative to the Kingdome. The Tacoma Rainiers play just 30 miles south of Seattle in a fading but fine 1960 stadium with a large covered grandstand. The light towers are from San Francisco's famed Seals Stadium. The Rainiers, who represent the Seattle Mariners in the Triple AAA Pacific Coast League, promise "off the wall fun" and they deliver. There is a reindeer mascot named Rhubarb, mountain bacon burgers, and a view of the imposing Mount Rainier, which lies 60 miles beyond first base. For information, call 206/752–7707.

Where to Stay

Best Western Cascadia Inn. This modern, three-story white stucco motel is just over a mile north of the ballpark at a freeway interchange. Its contemporary rooms were remodeled in 1994. There is a free Continental breakfast buffet. *2800 Pacific Ave., off I–5, Exit 193 (north) or 194 (south), Everett 98201, tel. 206/258–4141 or 800/448–5544, fax 206/258–4755. 133 rooms. Facilities: pool, hot tub, coin laundry. AE, DC, MC, V. $$*

Marina Village Inn. This luxurious small hotel provides beautiful views of Port Gardner Bay on the Everett waterfront. Several of the rooms on the harbor side have telescopes for guests to zero in on sea lions, ships, and sunsets. It is five minutes from the ballpark in an upscale shopping village. There is a free Continental breakfast. The contemporary rooms have couches, wet bars, and refrigerators; many have hot tubs. *1728 W. Marine View Dr., Everett 98201, tel. 206/259–4040 or 800/281–7087, fax 206/252–8419. 26 rooms. AE, DC, MC, V. $$*

Travelodge of Everett. This small, newly remodeled downtown motel has outdoor corridors and wooden staircases. The rooms are small and basic. *3030 Broadway, Everett 98201, tel. 206/259–6141 or 800/578–7878, fax 206/339–5150. 29 rooms. AE, D, DC, MC, V. $*

Where to Eat

Ray's Drive-In. Great fish-and-chips have been dispensed at this take-out spot since 1962. It offers milk shakes in many flavors; the best is fresh strawberry. The kid's menu includes fish, burgers, egg salad sandwiches, and corn dogs. There are four picnic tables for inside seating. Ray's is 4 miles north of the ballpark. *1401 Broadway, Everett, tel. 206/252–3411. No credit cards. $*

Totem Family Dining. This family restaurant, open since 1940, is known for its breakfasts and cinnamon rolls. It has counter service and booths. There are hearty homemade soups and a Light Eater menu for children and senior citizens. It is less than a mile southwest of the ballpark. *4410 Rucker Ave., Everett, tel. 206/252–3277. D, MC, V. No dinner Sun. $*

Ivar's Mukilteo Landing. Diners have a lovely view of Port Gardner Bay at this waterfront establishment next to the ferry dock in Mukilteo, a historic district 10 miles south of Everett. In addition to sampling fare at the outdoor raw bar, you can feast on fish smoked over alderwood. Prawns, clam strips, fish-and-chips, tuna fish, and salmon are included on the children's menu. *710 Front St., Mukilteo, tel. 206/347–3648. AE, MC, V. $$*

Mitzel's American Kitchen. You can get real turkey, meat loaf, and homemade pies at this family restaurant, where there genuinely is a Mama Mitzel involved in the operations. *303 128th St. SW, just off I–5, Everett, tel. 206/355–3383. AE, D, MC, V. $*

The Village Restaurant. This casual family restaurant was founded in 1939 and is famous for its meringue and apple-raisin pies. The prawns also are exceptional here, and the extensive kids' menu covers all meals. The restaurant is 10 minutes north of the ballpark. *220 Ash Ave., at Exit 199 from I–5, Marysville, tel. 360/659–2305. AE, D, DC, MC, V. $*

Entertainments

Forest Park. A modest children's zoo and a large playground share space in this pretty park with a heated pool and several jogging tracks. *802 Mukilteo Blvd., 1 mi west of Exit 192 from I–5, Everett, tel. 206/259–0300. Pool admission: $2 adults, $1.50 ages under 18. Open daily 9–6.*

San Juan Islands Nature Cruises. Orca whale sightings are frequent on this full-day whale-watching cruise around the San Juan Islands. Minke whales, seals, eagles, and sea lions also make appearances. The 9½-hour cruise is narrated by a naturalist. There is a stop in Friday Harbor, where passengers can either debark to shop and explore its whale museum or remain on board for the whale-watching portion of the trip. Passengers are returned to the Everett marina by 6 PM. *Mosquito Fleet, 1724-F W. Marine View Dr., Everett, tel. 206/787–6400 or 800/325–6722. Admission: $69 adults, $59 senior citizens, $49 ages 3–17. Open May–mid-Sept., daily; mid-Sept.–Oct., weekends; boarding at 8 AM, departure at 8:30 AM. AE, D, MC, V.*

Jetty Island Days. Jetty Island, a 2-mile-long man-made island, is just off the Everett waterfront. From July through September, a free ferry takes visitors to see beaches, dunes, birds, and sea lions here. There are free weekly children's programs, including crafts and environmental puppet shows. Everett Parks Department rangers give 45-minute walks introducing plant and animal life on the island. The ferry, the *Spirit of Saratoga Passage,* leaves from behind Anthony's Homeport restaurant. *Marina Village Visitor's Dock, Everett, tel. 206/259–0304. Open Wed.–Sat. 10–5:30, Sun. 11:30–5:30; departures on ½ hr.*

PORTLAND ROCKIES

League: Northwest League • **Major League Affiliation:** Colorado Rockies • **Class:** Short Season A • **Stadium:** Civic Stadium • **Opened:** 1926 • **Capacity:** 23,105 • **Dimensions:** LF: 309, CF: 407, RF: 325 • **Surface:** artificial • **Season:** mid-June–Labor Day

STADIUM LOCATION: 1844 Morrison St., Portland, OR 97207

GETTING THERE: From downtown, take Jefferson St. to N.W. 18th Ave. and turn right to Morrison St. From I–84, take I–5 N, then I–405 across Fremont Bridge; follow I–405 S in right lane to Everett St. exit; turn right on Couch St., left on N.W. 19th Ave., cross Burnside St., go one block to Morrison St., and turn right to N.W. 20th Ave. For public transit, call Tri-Met (tel. 503/238–7433).

TICKET INFORMATION: Box 998, Portland OR 97207, tel. 503/223–2837, fax 503/223–2948

PRICE RANGE: VIP boxes on season basis only. Reserved $6.50; general admission $5.50 adults, $4.50 children and senior citizens; left-field bleacher seats day of game only, $2.50 adults, $1 ages under 13.

GAME TIME: Mon.–Sat. 7:05 PM, Sun. 2 PM; gates open 1 hr before game

TIPS ON SEATING: Reserved seats on first-base side behind Rockies dugout are worth the extra dollar or two. Bargain-price tickets ($2.50 adults, $1 ages under 13) are sold for left-field bleachers, known as Rockpile, only on day of game from ticket booth at N.W. 18th St. and Morrison St.

SEATING FOR PEOPLE WITH DISABILITIES: Tickets sold at booth at N.W. 20th Ave. and Morrison St. Designated parking spaces for people with disabilities permits on N.W. 18th and 20th avenues at Morrison St. and in 30-minute-and-over zones and meters.

STADIUM FOOD: Vegetarians get a break with gardenburgers, grilled along with hamburgers, hot dogs, and sausages. You can sit in the Bullpen Barbecue next to the pitcher's bullpen along the right-field line for $4 per person. A kid's meal includes hot dog, chips, soft drink, and red licorice for $3.

SMOKING POLICY: Smoking permitted only in plaza of main stadium and above bleachers in Rockpile; prohibited in all seating areas.

PARKING: 4,000 parking spaces on street within 5-block radius of stadium. Nearest public lot is 8 blocks east of stadium at S.W. 10th and Yamhill; walk to Washington St. and take Bus 15 to and from stadium.

VISITING TEAM HOTEL: Red Lion Coliseum (1225 N. Thunderbird Way, Portland, OR 97227)

TOURISM INFORMATION: Portland Oregon Visitors Association, 26 S.W. Salmon St., Portland, OR 97204, tel. 503/222–2223 or 800/345–3214

Portland: Civic Stadium

Why is a team in the short season Northwest League, just one step up from rookie ball, playing in a 23,105-seat stadium? Opened in 1926 for football, the stadium did not host baseball until 1956 when the Triple AAA Portland Beavers were forced to move from the wooden 1901 Lucky Beavers Stadium at the fire marshal's strong suggestion.

Portland became a charter member of the prestigious Triple AAA Pacific Coast League in 1903. The Portland team played in the PCL all but six years until it lost its Triple AAA franchise to Salt Lake City in 1994. In 1995, the Colorado Rockies moved its Northwest League franchise to Portland's Civic Stadium and immediately shattered the attendance record for the short season league, averaging 6,571 fans.

Just west of Portland's vital downtown, in a residential neighborhood, the stadium is surrounded by apartments and shops. The Multnomah Athletic Club, which first built a 1,000-seat stadium here in 1885, towers over the stadium beyond right field. The main grandstand used today was built by the club in 1926. In 1967, the Athletic Club sold the stadium to the City of Portland, which was the first owner to install artificial turf for an outdoor baseball and football stadium. The new owners, Jack and Mary Cain, are fan-friendly baseball people who provide good times and top entertainment. Rocky Raccoon, the local mascot, is a hit. There is space to roam, with a walkway the full length of the J-shape covered grandstand. The long stem of the J is on the first-base side. The Rockpile bleachers sit above left field and a 25-foot-high wall.

Other Portland Baseball Sites

Alpenrose Stadium and Dairy. Home of the Little League Softball World Series, the stadium is one of the nation's sweetest ball fields. Although this girls' championship, held each June during the city's Rose Festival, is less famous than the boys' championship played each August in Williamsport, PA, the experience is every bit as exciting. From the flower-bedecked hilltop grandstand, a great view stretches beyond the rose-strewn green scoreboard in center field. The dairy farm also holds a bicycle track, a miniature western village, a 600-seat opera house, and a museum of musical instruments and dolls. *6149 S.W. Shattuck Rd., Multnomah exit off I-5 S, Portland, tel. 503/244–1133. Admission free (fee for bike track). Grounds open June–Aug., Sun. 1:30–4:30.*

Where to Stay

Visiting Team Motel: Red Lion Coliseum. This two- and three-story brick motel has a variety of room sizes, and nearly all have nice views of the Willamette River. *1225 N. Thunderbird Way, Portland 97227, tel. 503/235–8311 or 800/547–8010, fax 503/232–2670. 211 rooms. Facilities: restaurant, outdoor pool, free airport shuttle, game room. AE, D, DC, MC, V. $$*

Mallory Hotel. The eight-story, turn-of-the-century hotel is two blocks from the ballpark.

Several of the smaller rooms have bargain rates. *729 S.W. 15th St., Portland 97205, tel. 503/223–6311 or 800/228–8657, fax 503/223–0522. 122 rooms, 20 suites. Facilities: restaurant, free parking. AE, D, DC, MC, V. $$*

Imperial Hotel. The rooms are large in this bargain downtown hotel. The 1908 redbrick beauty is 12 blocks from the ballpark. It has a large lobby, European-style rooms, and small bathrooms. *400 S.W. Broadway, Portland 97205, tel. 503/228–7221 or 800/452–2323, fax 503/223–4551. 136 rooms. Facilities: restaurant, free airport shuttle. AE, D, DC, MC, V. $$*

Where to Eat

Dan and Louis Oyster Bar. This Portland standout since 1907 now resembles a nautical museum that serves lunch and dinner. Young children can eat for as little as $1.99. Adults may want the more costly panfried oysters or shrimp or the crab and oyster stews. *208 S.W. Ankeny St., Portland, tel. 503/227–5906. AE, D, MC, V. $$*

B. Moloch/Heathman Bakery & Pub. A brew pub of Widmer, the state's largest microbrewer, it adjoins the elegant Heathman Hotel. The wood-fired ovens cook pizza and chicken. Children are welcome in the casual, art-filled restaurant, which also serves breakfast. *901 S.W. Salmon St., Portland, tel. 503/227–5700. AE, D, DC, MC, V. $$*

Lorn and Dottie's Luncheonette. This center-city diner serves huge breakfasts and lunches. Sit at the counter for blue-plate cuisine, and don't miss the crisp waffles. *322 S.W. 2nd Ave., Portland, tel. 503/221–2473. MC, V. $*

Sites to See

Portland is ideally located. Pacific Ocean beaches are just over an hour west. Mt. Hood is an hour east and visible from the city. The Columbia and Willamette rivers meet here, and the fertile Willamette Valley is just to the south. Call ahead for a free "City Kids Fun Book" from the Association for Portland Progress (tel. 503/224–8684).

Washington Park. Designed by the Olmsted brothers, this 145-acre park sits high above the city's west side. Look for the International Rose Garden's Children's Park. Kids enjoy the zoo's African Rain Forest, Asian elephants, and zoo railway. *4001 S.W. Canyon Rd., tel. 503/226–7627. Zoo admission $5.50 adults, $4 senior citizens, $3.50 ages 3–11; free 2nd Tues. of the month after 3. Open Memorial–Labor Day, daily 9:30–6; Labor Day–Memorial Day, 9:30–5.*

Oregon Museum of Science and Industry (OMSI). Six exhibit halls make up this extensive hands-on science center. Visitors "travel" through outer space, make electricity, and view an exceptional astronomy show. *1945 S.E. Water Ave., Portland, tel. 503/797–4000. Admission: $6 adults, $4.50 senior citizens and ages 4–13; 2-for-1 admission Thurs. 3–7. Open Tues.–Wed. and Fri.–Sun. 9:30–5:30, Thurs. 9:30–8.*

Oaks Amusement Park. This is the oldest U.S. amusement park still in operation. Created in 1905 for the Lewis and Clark Exposition, it has 25 rides, miniature golf, a 1924 carousel, and a year-round roller rink with a Wurlitzer organ. *S.E. Oaks Pkwy., tel. 503/233–5777. Admission free. Open Memorial–Labor Day, daily 1–10; closed nonholiday Mon.*

Unusual Shopping

Powell's City of Books. One of the largest and best book stores in the United States, it covers two full city blocks and includes a coffee shop. *1005 W. Burnside St., Portland, tel. 503/228–4651 or 800/878–7323.*

Saturday Market. This outdoor market of 200 food and art vendors opens each weekend under the west end of the Burnside Bridge. *S.W. Ankeny at 1st Ave., between Front St. and the MAX tracks, Portland, tel. 503/222–6072.*

JOLTIN' JOE AND MIGHTY CASEY
STOCKTON, SAN FRANCISCO, SAN JOSE

I f you are in San Francisco to see the Giants play, make it a triple play with visits to two California League Single A teams, in Stockton and in San Jose.

If you're driving down from northern California, you can stop in Sacramento to see the sprawling, and beautifully landscaped, state capitol grounds. Stockton, 40 miles to the south, is a port city, despite being 48 miles east of San Francisco. Baseball has a long tradition here. The Ports' mascot, Mighty Casey, helps orchestrate the exceptional number of contests and giveaways at this older stadium in the city's Oak Park. Stockton is a gritty city, whose charms are not obvious, but they exist. One of the country's sweetest children's parks, Pixie Woods, with a boat ride, a train, a carousel, and a wading pool, is found at Louis Park. There's also a good children's museum and an extraordinary World Wildlife Museum, with more than 3,000 preserved animals, from giraffes to an orca whale, displayed extremely close to visitors and not behind glass.

Driving west to San Francisco, you'll have a chance to weather a game at 3COM/Candlestick Park, but only until the end of the century. A new downtown park in China Basin is being readied to replace the wind tunnel of Candlestick. You'll be chilled if you didn't bring warm clothes, but you'll eat better in Candlestick than in any ballpark in the country. The food choices and quality are staggering. The City by the Bay will never be accused of cookie-cutter sameness. Delight in its abundance of small, neighborhood hotels, its thriving coffee houses and ethnic eateries, and its singular experiences, like the ferry to Alcatraz, the Japanese Tea Garden, and the fortune cookie factory in Chinatown. More than a day can be spent simply sampling the attractions in Golden Gate Park, from Steinhart Aquarium and the California Academy of Sciences to the Children's Playground.

Forty miles south of San Francisco in San Jose is a well-kept Works Progress Administration ballpark, featuring the Santa Cruz Mountains in the distance. The San Jose park is decorated with hand-painted baseball murals and serves unusual food—grilled turkey legs and abalone steaks—in a large picnic area. The city has the most imaginative children's museum in the country, and two all-day amusement parks, Raging Waters and Paramount's Great America (in nearby Santa Clara), to entice you as well. As you drive down the coast, you can stop in Santa Cruz for its beach boardwalk with the 1924 Giant Dipper roller coaster. Another worthwhile stop is Monterey, for its extraordinary, ever-expanding aquarium and the charming, free-admission Dennis the Menace playground, donated by the comic strip's creator, Hank Ketchum.

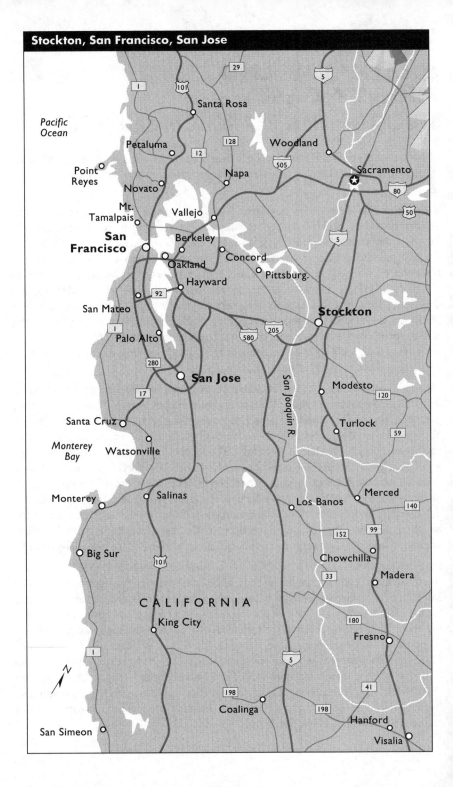

Pacific
Ocean

29

1

101

Santa Rosa

5

Petaluma

128

Woodland

Point
Reyes

12

505

Sacramento

Novato

Napa

80

Mt.
Tamalpais

Vallejo

50

San
Francisco

Berkeley

5

Oakland

Concord

Hayward

Pittsburg.

92

San Mateo

Stockton

1

Palo Alto

580

205

280

San Jose

San Joaquin R.

17

Modesto

120

Santa Cruz

Turlock

59

Monterey
Bay

Watsonville

Monterey

Salinas

Los Banos

Merced

140

Big Sur

101

152

99

Chowchilla

33

Madera

CALIFORNIA

180

King City

Fresno

1

41

N

5

198

Coalinga

198

Hanford

San Simeon

Visalia

STOCKTON PORTS

League: California League • **Major League Affiliation:** Milwaukee Brewers • **Class:** A • **Stadium:** Billy Hebert Field • **Opened:** 1950s • **Capacity:** 3,500 • **Dimensions:** LF: 325, CF: 392, RF: 335 • **Surface:** grass • **Season:** Apr.–Labor Day

STADIUM LOCATION: Oak Park, Sutter St., and Alpine Ave., Stockton, CA 95204

GETTING THERE: From I–5, March Lane exit east for just over 2 mi. Right on El Dorado St. for 1 mi. Left on Alpine St. Stadium is in Oak Park on left. From State Hwy. 99, take Wilson Way exit. Right on Alpine Ave. Stadium is in Oak Park on left.

TICKET INFORMATION: Box 8550, Stockton, CA 95208, tel. 209/944–5943, fax 209/463–4937

PRICE RANGE: Reserved $6; general admission $5 adults, $2.50 ages under 13 and over 65, under 3 free

GAME TIME: Mon.–Sat. 7:05 PM, Sun. 5 PM; gates open 1 hr before game.

TIPS ON SEATING: General admission seats excellent; less than 500 reserved seats. Sit on third-base side behind home-team dugout to avoid sun and smokers on first-base side.

SEATING FOR PEOPLE WITH DISABILITIES: In first row of bleachers just past dugouts on each side; access by ramps

STADIUM FOOD: The **Casey Barbecue Area** down the third-base line has BBQ chicken and burger dinners, with watermelon wedges and a choice of beans or potato salad, for $7.50. Plain, grilled hamburgers are $4. Smaller appetites will be happy with the Junior Ports menu of hot dog, chips, and a soda for $3.75. Hot churros are $1.75.

SMOKING POLICY: Smoking prohibited except in bleachers on first-base side and concourse.

PARKING: Ample free parking

VISITING TEAM HOTEL: **Best Western Stockton Inn** (4219 E. Waterloo Rd., Stockton, CA 95215, tel. 209/931–3131 or 800/528–1234)

TOURISM INFORMATION: Stockton/San Joaquin Convention & Visitors Bureau (46 W. Fremont St., Stockton, CA 95202, tel. 209/943–1987 or 800/350–1987)

Stockton: Billy Hebert Field

They've been playing baseball in Stockton, California, since the 1870s. The current team's excellent mascot is the Mighty Casey of baseball lore. This, according to local Stockton boosters, is the Mudville in the famous poem "Casey at the Bat," by Ernest Thayer. The best baseball in Stockton in the late 1800s was played at a field on Banner Island nicknamed Mudville. The local team had players named Flynn, Blake, and Cooney, as in Thayer's poem.

In 1890, the center of Stockton's baseball activity shifted to the Oak Park Baseball Field, where Billy Hebert learned to play baseball in Stockton's Recreation Department boys' league. He played Junior Legion ball and became a professional in the California League. He was the first player in all of organized baseball to give his life for his country when he was killed in action in the South Pacific in World War II. In 1950, the City Council renamed the Oak Park field Billy Hebert Field. In the 1950s, the wooden grandstand burned and was replaced with the stadium that now sits among the oak trees and softball fields of Oak Park.

Billy Hebert Field is a traditional-looking stadium with seating for 3,500 fans, mostly on aluminum benches with backs. There are fewer than 500 individual reserved seats. In the hot California sun, the absence of a roof is noticeable. But after the sun goes down, it can grow cool quickly. Stockton is California's most inland port—the team is called the Ports in tribute to the importance of the shipping industry here. A stiff breeze from the San Joaquin Delta blows into home plate from left field, making it tough on hitters and providing a delightfully cool night for spectators.

When a pitcher is pulled out of a game, keep an eye on him. More likely than not, you'll see him slip through a gate in left center field at a break between innings. That's where the showers are at Hebert Field. The locker rooms were rebuilt for the 1995 season at a cost of $250,000, but they remain in center field. It's a tradition here and one of the most unusual arrangements in professional baseball. There aren't any further plans for upgrading Hebert Field as the city and the team are considering a new field as part of a downtown revitalization plan.

This is an exciting, fan-friendly place. There is a souvenir stand and a fan information booth at the main entrance. We have never seen so many contests, lucky numbers, and giveaways. The best treat at Stockton came during the seventh-inning stretch, with the traveling mascot BirdZerk hip-hop dancing with the home-plate umpire.

Where to Stay

Days Inn. On the water, the three-story brick downtown hotel overlooks the Stockton Channel. The rooms are standard size and furnished plainly. Guests receive a free Continental breakfast. *33 N. Center St., Stockton 95202, tel. 209/ 948–6151 or 800/325–2525, fax 209/948– 1220. 96 rooms. Facilities: indoor pool. AE, D, DC, MC, V. $*

Plaza Inn. This motor inn off I–5 has three stories of standard rooms 1½ miles north of the ballpark. It is part of a commercial strip, next to a grocery store. *111 E. March La., Stockton 95207, tel. 209/474–3301, fax 209/474–7612. 204 rooms. Facilities: coffeeshop, pool, hot tub. AE, D, DC, MC, V. $$*

Where to Eat

On Lock Sam. A family-run restaurant, it has dispensed Cantonese cuisine since founder Wong Sai Chun arrived from Kwangtung Province in 1898. Don't miss the asparagus with chicken. (Stockton is known for its asparagus festival each April.) The restaurant specializes in family-style meals; its booths even have drapes for privacy. *333 S. Sutter St., Stockton, tel. 209/466– 4561. AE, MC, V. $$*

Pacific Baking Company. This is a very California country restaurant, with great pastries, pasta, and wine. The tables are wooden, tiles adorn the walls, and the mood is casual. Half-orders of pasta, ample for light eaters and children, and good polenta and salads are available. *3236 Pacific Ave., at Alpine St., Stockton, tel. 209/462–7939. MC, V. $*

Ye Old Hoosier Inn. A former Hoosier turned this truck stop into a warm family restaurant filled with antiques, stained-glass windows, and marble-topped tables. The midwestern yeast rolls and homemade sausage are especially good. *1537 N. Wilson Way, at Harding Way, Stockton, tel. 209/463–0271. MC, V. $*

Entertainments

World Wildlife Museum. This former warehouse holds an incredible collection of 3,000 stuffed animals—thousands of bears, tigers, and wolves shot by hunters worldwide over the last century. Black jaguars, giraffes, orca whales, great white sharks, and every species of sheep in the world are arranged by species. This is a mecca of fine taxidermy, with such tableaux as a 16-foot African crocodile lunging for a sable antelope. Many endangered or extinct species are preserved in death. Children can get very close to these animals, which are not behind glass. Some scenes, like one of a zebra and a lion fighting, are intense. *1245 W. Weber St., Stockton, tel. 209/465–2834. Admission: $5 adults, $3 children. Open Wed.–Sun. 9–5. MC, V.*

Children's Museum of Stockton. This is a bright, airy warehouse of make-believe. Kids get to act out many professional fantasies—working in a hospital, a bank, a grocery store, a pet shop, a fast-food restaurant, a TV station, or a factory. The police cruiser, with working lights and alarm, and the ambulance are especially popular. *402 W. Weber St., Stockton, tel. 209/465–4386. Admission: $4. Open weekdays 9–2, Sat. 10–4.*

Pixie Woods at Louis Park. This sweet, small park run by the city has a boat ride, a train ride, a carousel, and a wading pool. Rides are 60¢ each. Opened in 1956, it is built around a lake. Good for younger children, it has live rabbits and goats and a play town, a toadstool theater, and an *Alice in Wonderland* playground. There's also a concession stand and a picnic area. *Occi-*

dental and Monte Diablo Aves., in Louis Park, Stockton, tel. 209/937–7366. Admission: $1.50 adults, $1 children. Open Feb.–May and Sept.–Oct., weekends noon–5; June–Labor Day, Wed.–Fri. 11–5, weekends 11–6.

Sites to See

State Capitol. Sacramento is only 40 miles north of Stockton and well worth a visit. The State Capitol building was handsomely restored and structurally enhanced to withstand earthquakes in the late 1970s and early 1980s. Originally opened in 1869, the building is a model of how modern technology can help preserve the past. Highlights include the magnificent copper dome with a gold-leafed ball on top, the eight Corinthian columns on the front portico, the 1871 marble statue of Columbus and Queen Isabella, and the bizarre portrait of former governor Jerry Brown on the third floor. A pamphlet is available for self-guided tours. In the basement, a large, inexpensive cafeteria for state workers is open to the public. *State Capitol, at 10th and L Sts., Sacramento, tel. 916/324–0333. Open daily 9–5; free tours every hr 9–4.*

SAN FRANCISCO GIANTS

League: National • **Class:** Major • **Stadium:** 3COM/Candlestick Park• **Opened:** 1960 • **Capacity:** 58,000 • **Dimensions:** LF: 335, CF: 400, RF: 335 • **Surface:** grass • **Season:** Apr.–early Oct.

STADIUM LOCATION: 3COM Park (formerly known as Candlestick), San Francisco, CA 94124

TEAM WEB SITE: http://www.sfgiants.com

GETTING THERE: From San Francisco and north, take Cow Palace/Brisbane exit from U.S. 101 (not Candlestick exit). Go to 3rd St. and turn left over freeway. Turn right on Jamestown Ave. to main lot. From south, take 3rd St. exit from U.S. 101 and continue as above. For information about transit to stadium, call 415/673–6864 or 800/660–4287.

TICKET INFORMATION: 3COM Park, San Francisco, CA 94124, tel. 415/467–8000, fax 415/467–3803

PRICE RANGE: Lower box $15.50; upper box and lower reserved $12.50; upper reserved $7.50; pavilion $6.50; reserved bleachers $5.50. Ask for lower prices for children under 15 and senior citizens.

GAME TIME: Night games, 7:05, 7:35, 8:05 PM; day games, 12:35, 1:05 PM; gates open 90 min before game.

TIPS ON SEATING: For a rowdy time, join "The Bonds Squad" in left-field bleachers. The 1,800 field bleacher seats are sold only on day of game. The Pavilion behind the right-field fence is popular with families; alcohol is prohibited there. Bring several layers of clothes no matter where your tickets are.

SEATING FOR PEOPLE WITH DISABILITIES: Call 415/467–8000 to arrange for seating; wheelchair accessible entrance near Players' Lot between Gates A and F. Parking near Gates E and F.

STADIUM FOOD: This is the nation's best ballpark for food. Don't even consider eating first. Don't miss the guacamole, steak taco salad, and fresh nachos at **Compadres.** Also try the **Hot Dog Lovers** stand with a dozen great varieties and the **Bay Seafood Shop.** Garlic from the 40-clove garlic chicken sandwich ($5.25) wafts through the park. There is outstanding ravioli and tortellini ($5.25), onion straws, biscotti, and espresso. Caramelized nuts are sold on days when turnout exceeds 32,000. There's Ben & Jerry's ice cream, tofu dogs for $2, a micro-brewery with 16 varieties, and terrific pizza from Ruby's at $3.50 a slice. Vendors carry paddles announcing their wares. Others wear backpacks that dispense cafe mocha.

SMOKING POLICY: No smoking in seating areas.

PARKING: Ample parking available, $7. Shuttle service available.

TOURISM INFORMATION: San Francisco Visitor Information Center (900 Market St., lower level, San Francisco, CA 94102, tel. 415/391–2000).

San Francisco: 3COM Park/Candlestick Park

The California gold rush brought baseball to the West Coast, and organized ball playing has been here ever since. The California League was organized in 1885 with three teams from San Francisco. In 1903, San Francisco became a charter member of the Pacific Coast League and finished first in the league 12 times in the next 55 years, six times between 1915 and 1928. Many major-league-caliber ballplayers opted to stay in the Pacific Coast League during its heyday in the 1920s and 1930s because its longer, 200-plus-game schedule allowed them to make more money than major-league players. Joe DiMaggio hit in 61 consecutive games for the Seals in 1933 and led the league in runs batted in in 1933 and 1934 before going east to the Yankees.

Seals owner Paul I. Fagan was a major advocate of the league's plans to be recognized as a third major league. It was a campaign that greatly changed baseball, as it brought major leagues to the West Coast. He invested heavily in turning Seals Stadium—built in 1931 and nicknamed "The Queen in Concrete"—into a first-class facility. The 1946 PCL champion Seals drew 670,563 fans, a minor league single season record. In 1957, the New York Giants announced that they would move from the Polo Grounds to San Francisco for the 1958 season. The Giants played in Seals Stadium in 1958 and 1959. When Candlestick Park opened in 1960, Seals Stadium was leveled.

San Francisco's Candlestick Park, which was renamed 3COM Park in 1996 to honor a sponsor, is the stadium local fans love to hate. But as a place to visit once every few years, it definitely belongs in your travel plans. The first major-league stadium built exclusively of reinforced concrete, it was called "a dazzling diamond palace." But the fans knew Candlestick Park was a mistake almost from day one. The reviews turned nasty soon after the initial flurry of positive comments. In the top of the ninth at the 1961 All-Star Game played at Candlestick, Giants relief pitcher Stu Miller was blown off the mound by a wind gust. The umpire called a balk, and Candlestick's reputation as baseball's wind tunnel was firmly established.

3COM Park stands on Candlestick Point, overlooking San Francisco Bay on a landfill. The main criterion, apparently, was to find a cheap site near a highway and on the way to the suburbs. If Camden Yards marked the return of baseball to the downtowns, Candlestick Park in 1960 was the beginning of the unfortunate era of turning one's back on the downtowns.

An inexperienced architect, a grand-jury investigation into the stadium financing, and a teamsters strike are all part of the story of the birth of Candlestick. Half the seats were to be heated, but the contractors installed the heating pipes 5 inches deep in the concrete floor, rendering them useless. Lawyer Melvin Belli won a lawsuit against the city in 1962 to recover the cost of his season tickets on the argument that they had come with a temperature guarantee.

In 1971, the city spent $16 million putting a double deck of seats in the stadium, which had been open in the center field section. This accommodated the San Francisco 49ers football team but did little to reduce the chilling impact of the winds for baseball fans.

On August 29, 1966, Candlestick hosted a Beatles' concert, and on May 8, 1977, the Great Wallendas walked across the stadium on a tightrope. An earthquake just before game three of the 1989 World Series with the Giants' cross-bay rival Oakland Athletics did only limited damage to the stadium. The 1962 Giants, led by Willie Mays, Willie McCovey, Juan Marichal, and Orlando Cepeda, took the Yankees to the very last out of the ninth inning of the seventh game of the World Series.

The most rabid fans sit in temporary aluminum bleachers just over the left-field wall. The self-proclaimed "Bonds Squad" stomps and cheers especially when local hero Barry Bonds is in the spotlight. Before it gets dark, walk to the upper deck on the first-base side and take a look at spectacular San Francisco Bay.

One vital precaution: No matter how warm it is during the day, you must take along three layers of clothes. After a night here, you'll understand why Mark Twain said that the coldest winter he ever spent was a summer in San Francisco.

Where else in professional baseball can you see a cloud roll in, all but envelop the center fielder, and then roll out with equal speed?

After years of failure at the polls, advocates of a new baseball stadium finally received approval from the voters of San Francisco in March 1996. The new, $255 million downtown park will be financed privately and is scheduled to open in the year 2000 on 13 acres by the bay in the China Basin district. The 42,000-capacity Pacific Bell Park will be designed by the architects of HOK Sport of Kansas City. Left-handed power hitters will be able to blast home runs over a right-field fence only 309 feet from home plate and into the bay beyond.

Where to Stay

As with most major-league teams, no one hotel is used by the visiting team. Players frequently stay at the pricey Parc 55 and the Hilton in the Union Square area. If you're going to pay top dollar, consider the new Marriott at 4th and Mission streets, which overlooks the beautiful Yerba Buena Gardens. But we advise you to take advantage of San Francisco's abundance of small hotels, many of them bargains. The San Francisco Lodging Guide, mailed from the Convention & Visitors Bureau (tel. 415/391–2000), includes 11 hotels with bargain package rates. Two reservation firms also offer discount lodgings: Preferred Hotel Rates (tel. 800/964–6835) and California Reservations (tel. 800/576–0003).

The Grant Plaza. This clean, compact hotel is a longtime Chinatown bargain, so you'll need to reserve two months in advance for summer weekends. Its Super Saver Package includes free parking, breakfast, and a passport to the shop-filled arcades of Pier 39. The lobby is tiny and the rooms are standard-size, with updated furniture, two double beds, and private baths. It's near the gate to Chinatown, but away from much of the street noise. 465 Grant St., San Francisco 94108, tel. 415/434–3883 or 800/472–6899, fax 415/434–3886. 72 rooms. Facilities: parking (fee). AE, D, MC, V. $

Britton Hotel. This pleasant bargain hotel is owned jointly with its three neighboring hotels (Best Western's Americania, Carriage House, and Flamingo Motor Inn; see below), and all are good deals for visiting families. The five-story brick Britton is the oldest and most expensive. Guests at any of the four hotels can use the large, tiled outdoor heated pool at the adjacent Americania Motor Lodge Best Western. The Britton has a free shuttle to the convention centers and Amtrak stations for out-of-city excursions. 112 7th St., at Mission St., San Francisco 94103, tel. 415/621–7001 or 800/444–5819, fax 415/626–3974. 79 rooms. Facilities: coffeeshop, coin laundry, parking (fee). AE, D, DC, MC, V. $$

Americania Motor Lodge Best Western. This white, salmon, and green hotel is built over the parking lot and outdoor pool. The lobby is cool, with California greenery. Most of the quiet rooms face an interior courtyard filled with hanging plants. The hotel offers a free shuttle to Union Square, where you can get the 9X express bus to 3COM/Candlestick Park. 121 7th St., San Francisco 94103, tel. 415/626–0200 or 800/444–5816, fax 415/626–3974. 142 rooms. Facilities: restaurant, pool, sauna, exercise room, coin laundry, parking (free). AE, DC, MC, V. $$

Best Western Carriage House. This is the quietest of the quartet and includes a Continental breakfast delivered to your room. The rooms are standard size and newly renovated in an English-inn theme. Parking is $6 daily. 140 7th St., San Francisco 94103, tel. 415/552–8600 or 800/444–5817, fax 415/863–2529. 48 rooms. Facilities: parking (fee). AE, DC, MC, V. $$

Best Western Flamingo Motor Inn. Everything in this Spanish-style motor lodge is small-scale. Its lobby, shared with the Britton, leads to an inner parking courtyard and two floors of rooms. Fresh flowers are put in rooms daily; the furnishings are contemporary. Guests have access to the pool and shuttle services of the Americania, across the street. The Flamingo shares the Britton's restaurant. 114 7th St., San Francisco 94103, tel. 415/621–0701 or 800/444–5818, fax 415/863–2529. 38 rooms. Facilities: parking (free). AE, DC, MC, V. $$

Essex Hotel. This European-style hotel has many foreign guests, attracted by its low prices and convenient civic-center location, near several Vietnamese restaurants. The tasteful lobby has marble floors, chandeliers, and fresh flowers. The rooms are small, but nicely furnished in reproduction antiques. *684 Ellis St., San Francisco 94109, tel. 415/474–4664 or 800/453–7739, fax 415/441–1800. 100 rooms. Facilities: parking (fee). AE, MC. V. $$*

Columbus Motor Inn. This 1970s-style motor lodge is along a bus route but away from the bustle of the city. Located between Fisherman's Wharf and North Beach, it has clean rooms with updated furnishings. *1075 Columbus Ave., at Francisco St., San Francisco 94133, tel. 415/885–1492, fax 415/928–2174. 45 rooms. Facilities: parking (free). AE, D, MC, V. $$*

Where to Eat

Lefty O'Douls. You get a flavor of old, bohemian San Francisco in this Irish cafeteria-restaurant. Lefty played for the New York Giants, Dodgers, and Yankees, and much Joe DiMaggio, Stan Musial, and Babe Ruth memorabilia, including Marilyn Monroe DiMaggio's driver's license, adorns the walls. There are old carved wooden booths and tables, and its cafeteria line includes such Irish favorites as corned beef and lamb shanks. A kid's plate for those 10 and under is $3.99. *333 Geary St., tel. 415/982–8900. MC, V. $*

Sears Fine Foods. This character-laden restaurant typifies old San Francisco. Waiters serve its signature silver-dollar Swedish pancakes, sourdough French toast, and baked apples in a storefront restaurant with a faded tearoom atmosphere. *439 Powell St., San Francisco, tel. 415/986–1160. No credit cards. Closed dinner. $*

Boudin Fisherman's Wharf Bakery. Boudin is one of the oldest bakeries in the country, and it turns out a terrific French sourdough bread. You can try its bread solo or as a foundation for sandwiches or an accompaniment to thick New England clam chowder. These fast-food restaurants also serve salads, pizza bread, and a few desserts. This site has outdoor seating only. Boudin's is also at tourist spots on Pier 39, Ghirardelli Square, and Macy's Cellar, all with indoor seating. *156 Jefferson St., between Mason and Taylor Sts., San Francisco, tel. 415/928–1849. AE, D, MC, V. $*

California Culinary Academy. You can eat at the source of the city's great chefs, in the Carême Room, a cavernous dining room where you watch the students work behind glass, or the more casual Sonoma Grill downstairs, in a dark-wood-boothed pub-style room. Both serve excellent, unusual fare, with the grill concentrating on American themes and the dining room covering Continental cuisine. Reservations are suggested for the Carême Room, which accommodates bus tours. You'll have student waiters, and you'll see scores of students in their customary checked pants and white-coat uniform throughout the building. There's a take-out carrying beautiful salads, sandwiches, and desserts. *625 Polk St., San Francisco, tel. 415/771–3536 or 800/229–2433. AE, D, DC, MC, V. Closed weekends. $$*

Sheraton Palace Hotel's Garden Court Restaurant. Breakfast or tea at this hotel's glorious glass-domed restaurant is a rare treat and affordable. Families won't feel as comfortable at dinner. The room is massive, with crystal chandeliers, stained glass, and potted palms. Built in 1909, it is one of the lightest, prettiest places to eat in the city. The orange juice is fresh and the hot chocolate is genuine, not a water-based mix. *2 New Montgomery St., at Market St., San Francisco, tel. 415/392–8600. AE, DC, MC, V. $$*

Entertainments

Get an official San Francisco transit guide ($2) from the San Francisco Municipal Railway. It's also a good street map. You'll save money by buying one-day ($6) or three-day ($10) transit passes, good on all MUNI vehicles, including cable cars. The pass reduces your bus fare to 3COM/Candlestick Park. It may save time to buy it by mail ahead of time, as most MUNI offices do not open until 9. The passes also give you discounts at various tourist destinations and museums. You can buy them at the San Francisco Visitor's Information Center (below street level at Powell and Market Sts.). Write or call MUNI (949 Presidio Ave., San Francisco 94115, tel. 415/673–6864). The map is sold at bookstores as well. San Francisco has 20 attractive green-and-gold public bathrooms throughout the city. The fee is 25¢, there's room for strollers inside, and the toilet and floor are scrubbed automatically after each use.

Cable Cars. Your children will be thrilled to use this exciting and noisy mode of transport. Don't wait in line forever with the tourists at the obvious turnarounds. Pick an intermediate stop, get collected, and help your children navigate onto the cars. The Powell-Hyde line has the best curves and hills. The cars require a token, which is available at major stops. No transfers are given. If you reach Nob Hill, you can see videos about the cars and view their operations underground at the free **Cable Car Museum** (1201 Mason St., tel. 415/474–1887; open Apr.–Oct. daily 10–6, Nov.–Mar. daily 10–5). Cable-car fare is $2, and they operate 7 AM–1 AM.

Ferry to Alcatraz. There are wonderful views from this island of misery. The harshness of life in the prison, which held the country's toughest federal prisoners from 1934 to 1963, can awe children. Robert (the Birdman) Stroud, Al Capone, and "Machine Gun" Kelly slept here. It's a steep quarter-mile walk to the cellblocks on the self-guided tour. Those in wheelchairs or pushing strollers may want to use interactive computers to see the cellblocks by video through the Alcatraz Easy Access Program. National Park Service rangers give short talks, and you can rent audiocassette tours ($3 adults, $1 ages 5–11). You'll need to reserve ferry tickets to the island at least a day in advance, as space often sells out. It's a 12-minute cruise each way. Boats depart every 45 minutes weekdays, every 30 minutes weekends. The time of the last departure to the island varies considerably during the year; call ahead to check. *Pier 41, San Francisco, tel. 415/546–2896 or 800/445–8880 (in CA). Admission: $7.50 adults, $4 children. Open daily 9:15–4:15. AE, MC, V.*

Golden Gate Ferry to Sausalito. This 30-minute ride is a great introduction to bay living. After debarking, choose one of several restaurants with decks for a lunch overlooking Richardson Bay along Bridgeway, the city's main street. Children 12 and under ride free with a paying adult. The Red and White Fleet (tel. 415/546–2896; $5.50 adults, $2.75 children) also leaves from Pier 43½ on Fisherman's Wharf. *Ferry Bldg., foot of Market St., Embarcadero, San Francisco, tel. 415/332–6600. Fare: $4.25 adults, $3.20 children. Weekend family fares available; up to 2 children under age 13 are free, with adults paying full fare. MC, V.*

Exploratorium. This wacky, imaginative hall of wondrous science experiments is in the impos-

ing Palace of Fine Arts, at Marina Boulevard. The science center is extremely well used, to the point that many exhibits are under repair. There are bold, live demonstrations, including the dissection of cows' eyes. Major sections on sound, motion, heat, color, weather, electricity, and light are arranged throughout. Many children will not want to crawl through the Tactile Dome, which is pitch black and requires an extra fee. Much of the main floor is dim, but Angel's Cafe is cheery under the skylights. There is a great kid- and knowledge-oriented gift shop. You'll probably want to drive here or telephone for a cab, as it's not particularly convenient by public transport. Admission is free on the first Wednesday of the month. *3601 Lyon St., at Bay St., San Francisco, tel. 415/561–0360. Admission: $8.50 adults, $6.50 senior citizens and students, $4 ages 6–17. Open Labor Day–Memorial Day, Thurs.–Tues. 10–5, Wed. 10–9:30; Memorial Day–Labor Day Tues.–Sun. 10–5, Wed. 10–9:30. MC, V.*

Golden Gate Park. This huge expanse of green space has dozens of attractions. Children are likely to enjoy visiting the historic **Children's Playground,** with its 1912 Herschel Spillman carousel, and watching the koi fish and drinking tea (or juice and soda) at the **Japanese Tea Garden** ($2 adults, $1 ages 6–12). Six varieties of tea are served at wooden tables from 10:30 to 5, and guests walk across bridges and enjoy the serene waterfalls, ponds, koi pools, and pagodas. The most convenient park entry points are at 8th and Fulton streets (north side) and 9th and Lincoln streets (south). Parking at meters is free on weekdays, $1 per hour on weekends and holidays. *Stanyan and Fulton Sts., San Francisco. tel. 415/221–1311.*

Steinhart Aquarium and California Academy of Sciences. These Golden Gate attractions are across an open amphitheater lot from the Japanese Tea Garden. The well-designed exhibition covers three wings. Fish swim around you in the peaceful blue Fish Roundabout tank, and there's a touch pool at its base, stocked with starfish. The alligator pool is fascinating. You can be on hand to watch the penguins, the seals, or the dolphins being fed. The aquarium admission also includes entry to the two buildings that make up the **Natural History Museum,** which contains a Safequake artificial earthquake.

Guests stand on a floor plate that simulates the motion of a quake while viewing films and photographs of destruction caused by past quakes of similar intensity. There's also a large blow-up of a Pacific beach in the Wild California exhibit; an open, walk-through planetarium; and dinosaur reproductions. Admission is free on the first Wednesday of the month. A money-saving consideration is the $12.50 Explorer Pass to all Golden Gate Park attractions. *Golden Gate Park, San Francisco, tel. 415/221–5100. Admission to aquarium and museum: $7 adults, $4 ages 12–17, $1.50 ages 6–11. Open daily June–Aug. 10–6, daily Sept.–May 10–5.*

Strybing Arboretum. Children can enjoy walking through its Garden of Fragrance, testing their powers of smell. As the garden is aimed at people who are blind, visitors are permitted to touch the plants. Admission is free on the first Wednesday of the month. *Lincoln Way, at 9th Ave., San Francisco, tel. 415/661–1316. Donations appreciated. Open weekdays 8:30–4:30, weekends 10–5.*

San Francisco Zoo. This impressive, large, and handsomely designed zoo is at the south end of Ocean Beach. It has a smaller feel because of its self-contained sections, such as Penguin Island, Koala Crossing, and Gorilla World. The white tiger and pygmy hippopotami are the zoo's stars. You can watch the lions eat Tuesday through Sunday at 2. A separate **Children's Zoo** ($1; open daily June–Aug. 10:30–4:30, Sept.–May weekdays 11–4, weekends 10:30–4:30) for younger kids includes a petting park and an insect zoo. The entire zoo is free on the first Wednesday of the month. *Sloat Blvd., at Great Hwy., San Francisco, tel. 415/753–7083. Admission: $7 adults, $3.50 ages 12–15, $1.50 ages 6–11. Open daily 10–5.*

Cartoon Art Museum. This visual delight is on the second floor of what was the *San Francisco Bulletin,* the city's oldest daily—now part of the *Examiner.* Teenagers with a love of *Mad* magazine tend to be particularly attracted to this collection, which has art from magazines, ads, comics books, and videos displayed in one large room, with a gift shop. Admission is free on the first Wednesday of the month. *814 Mission St., between 4th and 5th Sts., San Francisco, tel. 415/227–8666. Admission: $3.50 adults, $2.50 senior citizens and students, $1.50 ages 6 and up. Open Wed.–Fri. 11–5, Sat. 10–5, Sun. 1–5.*

Sites to See

Golden Gate Cookie Company. If you're in crowded, bustling Chinatown, find this alley 30 steps in from Jackson Street and step into this small storefront to watch fortune cookies being shaped by hand by two workers. (Ignore the hot-pink "FRENCH ADULT FORTUNE COOKIE" sign outside.) Most companies use automatic cookie folders, but this authentic shop does it the old-fashioned way on Rube Goldberg–like iron contraptions. Samples are given freely, and you can buy bargain bags of fortune and almond cookies for $3. *56 Ross Alley, between Jackson and Washington Sts., west of Grant Ave., San Francisco, tel. 415/781–3956. Open daily 10 AM–midnight.*

San Francisco Public Library. This new main library is a beauty, with more than a million books and dozens of computers for your free use. Kids will find a special electronic discovery center and an expansive children's room. *Larkin and McAllister Sts., San Francisco, tel. 415/557–4400. Open Mon. 10–6, Tues.–Thurs. 9–8, Fri. 11–5, Sat. 9–5, Sun. noon–5.*

Pier 39. More than 100 shops, two amusement arcades, sea lions, and a Victorian double-deck carousel ($2 per ride) attract families here. The most fun is ignoring the commercial activity and walking outside to the actual pier to watch the multitude of sea lions that have made this home since the 1989 earthquake. These huge lumps of mammal lie on wood platforms in the bay, barking and yawning. Many of the 600 sea lions migrate to the Channel Islands from June through August, but there always are some on hand. An underwater world takes visitors (for a fee) on a simulated dive through a fish-filled tank. Pier 39 is at the end of Fisherman's Wharf, which is filled with tourist shops. Adjacent parking lots are expensive—four hours for $25. If you eat at one of the pier's full-service restaurants, your waterfront parking tab is cut one hour for lunch, two hours for dinner. Pier 39 also contains a farmer's market (Friday 8–1), with California's great produce, especially its apricots and pistachios. *The Embarcadero and Beach St., San Francisco, tel. 415/981–7437.*

Open late June–early Sept., Mon.–Wed. 10:30–9:30, Thurs.–Sat. 10:30–10, Sun. 10:30–8:30; mid-Sept.–mid-June, Sun.–Thurs. 11–7, Fri.–Sat. 10:30–8:30.

Golden Gate Bridge Walkway. You won't want to walk the entire 8,980-foot span to Marin County, but it can be exhilarating to stand over the bay. The hike across the bridge is on a pedestrian walkway that's about 1½ miles each way. It's blustery unless you get a rare, mild day. Free parking lots are at either end of the bridge, off Route 101. On the San Francisco side, take the last exit on the right (Vista Point) before the toll plaza. *Rte. 101, San Francisco, tel. 415/457–3110. Open daily 5 AM–9 PM.*

Muir Woods National Monument. You'll see the world's tallest trees in this Marin County redwood forest, with some exceeding 250 feet in height and 3,000 years in age. There are 6 miles of hiking trails here, but no picnicking. It's 17 miles northwest of San Francisco, reached by car across the Golden Gate Bridge and continuing north on S.R. 1. The Red and White ferry fleet, at Pier 41, also has boat-bus trips to Muir Woods. A free visitor center is open Memorial Day–Labor Day, daily 9–6, and Labor Day–Memorial Day, daily 9–5. *Muir Woods, tel. 415/388–2595. Open daily 8–dusk.*

SAN JOSE GIANTS

League: California League • **Major League Affiliation:** San Francisco Giants • **Class:** A • **Stadium:** Municipal Stadium • **Opened:** 1942 • **Capacity:** 5,000 • **Dimensions:** LF: 340, CF: 400, RF: 340 • **Surface:** grass • **Season:** Apr.–Labor Day

STADIUM LOCATION: 588 E. Alma Ave., San Jose, CA 95112

GETTING THERE: From I–280, 10th St. exit to Alma Ave. Left on Alma, stadium is on left. Going north on Hwy. 101, take Tully Rd. exit east. Right on Senter Rd. and left on Alma Ave. Going south on 101, take Story Rd. exit east. Left on Senter Rd. and right on Alma Ave.

TICKET INFORMATION: Box 21727, San Francisco, CA 95151, tel. 408/297–1435, fax 408/297–1453

PRICE RANGE: Box seats $7; general admission $5 adult, $3 ages 4–10 and over 64, under 4 free

GAME TIME: Weekdays 7:15 PM, Sat. 5 PM, Sun. 1:30 PM (Apr.–June) or 5 PM (July–Aug.); gates open 1½ hrs before game

TIPS ON SEATING: 882 box seats; general admission seats excellent. Sit on first-base side to avoid sun in your eyes.

SEATING FOR PEOPLE WITH DISABILITIES: At field level between grandstand and bleachers on both first- and third-base sides

STADIUM FOOD: Follow the white painted footprints out to **Turkey Mike's Baseball and BBQ** beyond third base. Here you'll find huge roast turkey drumsticks for $3 and a grilled abalone steak sandwich for $4. Pay $2 more for a dinner and add fruit, pasta, or potato salad. You can sit at the long picnic tables here and watch the game. There is chili for $1.75 and clam chowder for $3; if you want them in hollowed-out sourdough bowls, add $1.50. If you have any room left, there are ice cream bars at $2 each.

SMOKING POLICY: Smoking prohibited in seating areas and on main concourse; allowed behind bleachers down first- and third-base lines

PARKING: Ample parking, $2

VISITING TEAM HOTEL: Gateway Inn Best Western (2585 Seaboard Ave., San Jose, CA 95131, tel. 408/435–8800 or 800/528–1234)

TOURISM INFORMATION: San Jose Convention & Visitors Bureau (333 W. San Carlos St., San Jose, CA 95110, tel. 408/295–9600)

San Jose: Municipal Stadium

The art's the thing at San Jose's Municipal Stadium. Fans are greeted at the entrance by larger-than-life paintings of Babe Ruth, Brooks Robinson, and Roberto Clemente. For even more fun and a history of professional baseball in San Jose, follow the painted white footprints under the grandstand on the third-base side. As you walk the concourse, you will see the faded, painted pennants from minor-league teams of long ago. Once out from under the grandstand, you will find a huge, colorful mural with the logos of every current professional team, organized by league. A wonderful mural timeline beginning in 1891, when San Jose won the California State League, includes a list of San Jose Bees, the team nickname in the 1960s and '70s, who made it to the majors, including George Brett.

The food is as good as the art at Municipal Stadium. Just beyond the murals on the third-base side is Turkey Mike's Baseball & BBQ. "Turkey Mike" Donlin got his start in professional baseball in San Jose in the 1890s and hit .351 in 1903 for the New York Yankees before leaving baseball for Hollywood. His distinctive, turkeylike strut onto the field has been memorialized into a great new item of ballpark food, huge barbecued turkey drumsticks.

San Jose's 1942 Municipal Stadium is a fine example of the contribution the Works Progress Administration (WPA) made to baseball and municipal architecture. Municipal Stadium is typical of California League ballparks before the construction spree of the late 1980s and '90s. This is a solid, simple, WPA-era grandstand with excellent general admission seating. The dark green benches have backs, providing comfort but limiting legroom. There are only 882 individual box seats. A modest press box sits at the top of the grandstand, with two pennants flying above. Bleacher seats stretch down both left- and right-field lines. As young families have streamed into this, the heart of the Silicon Valley, the city has upgraded Municipal Stadium to provide modern amenities to go along with the tradition this stadium represents. In recent years, the murals have been added, the parking lot paved, and the bathrooms renovated. The stadium is uncovered, but a small orange canvas shades the grandstand seats on the first-base side.

There is plenty of fun here between innings as at most other minor-league ballparks. But we have never seen anything quite like the "Smash for Cash" contest at San Jose. Three players, each representing fans, throw balls and try to break the headlights of an old bread truck. Winners—both players and fans—get cash.

The setting is better than average, with a well-treed city park across the street and behind the stadium entrance. The Santa Cruz Mountains dominate the landscape out beyond the outfield wall in center and right fields. Over the left-field fence is a huge, long-closed factory where Beechnut used to manufacture Lifesavers and baby food.

Where to Stay

Visiting Team Motel: Best Western Gateway Inn. This spacious motel offers guests free baseball tickets and Continental breakfast. The rooms are generous in size and contain refrigerators, and many face the large outdoor courtyard, which holds a large pool. The inn is a mile from the airport, but jet noise isn't a problem. Guests are shuttled free to Paramount's Great America amusement park. *2585 Seaboard Ave., San Jose 95131, tel. 408/435–8800 or 800/ 528–1234, fax 408/435–8879. 146 rooms. Facilities: pool, hot tub. AE, D, DC, MC, V. $$*

Airport Inn. This standard, two-story brick motel is quiet, although only a half mile from San Jose International Airport. The rooms have been newly renovated, and most have two double beds. *1355 N. 4th St., San Jose 95112, tel. 408/453–5340, fax 408/453–5208. 194 rooms. Facilities: pool, coin laundry. AE, D, MC, V. $$*

Fairmont Hotel. This elegant downtown hotel has bargain weekend rates of $89 per double room. Otherwise, the 20-story deluxe high-rise is too pricey. The rooms are beautifully decorated, with thick carpets, prime city views, and refrigerators and free cable movies. *170 S. Market St., San Jose 95113, tel. 408/998–1900, fax 408/287–1648. 541 rooms. Facilities: 4 restaurants, pool, sauna, exercise room. AE, D, DC, MC, V. $$$*

Where to Eat

Rock 'N Tacos. Fish tacos sound weird but taste great. Healthy Mexican food is the draw at this brightly colored fast-food storefront—chicken burritos, "health-Mex" salads, and quesadillas. The tortillas and black beans are made without lard. You can get free refills on soft drinks, and the homemade chips are free. You perch on stools in the neon-decorated, green-Formica room. There's a sister restaurant (tel. 408/246–4500) across the street from the Winchester Mystery House at Town & Country Mall. *131 W. Santa Clara St., San Jose, tel. 408/993–8230. No credit cards. $*

The Old Spaghetti Factory. Part of a chain that renovates old buildings into engaging eateries, it serves typical American fare. Kids enjoy the pasta and the casual clutter of old signs and machinery in this former textile factory. There is a separate kids' menu. *51 N. San Pedro St., San Jose, tel. 408/288–7488. D, DC, MC, V. $*

Entertainments

Children's Discovery Museum of San Jose. This is among the best children's museums in the country. The bright, airy purple building has an imaginative array of hands-on games, all of which work. Children can climb on a fire truck, a Wells Fargo wagon, or a Model T, and sort mail in a post office. At the huge waterworks, children are the engineers, and they can run a Rube Goldberg contraption with tennis balls. You should plan on closing the museum, because you'll never get the kids to leave early. Parking is $2, and you should have singles or change for the automatic tellers. The museum is at the Technology Center stop of San Jose's light-rail system. *Woz Way and Auzerais St., San Jose, tel. 408/298–5437. Admission: $6 adults, $5 senior citizens, $4 ages 2–18. Open July–Aug., Mon.–Sat. 10–5, Sun. noon–5; Sept.–June, Tues.–Sat. 10–5, Sun. noon–5.*

Winchester Mystery House. This is overpriced but memorable. It's not wise to go on a hot day, as it's stuffy and kids will complain about the hour-long trek. This weird house and gardens, designed by haunted Sarah Winchester to ward off the spirits killed by Winchester rifles, can be fascinating. Guides take you through 110 of the house's 160 rooms. There is a Victorian garden, too. The tour arrangements make the gift shop and pricey concessions hard to avoid. The house is reached by Highway 280 south to Winchester Boulevard. *525 S. Winchester Blvd., San Jose, tel. 408/247–2101. Admission: $12.50 adults, $6.50 ages 6–12. Open daily 9–5:30.*

Raging Waters. This water park has 32 activities, with a good assortment for young children, including a lazy river. The toboggan rides, flume rides, and wave-machine "beach" require bathing suits. Cutoffs and long pants are forbidden. Nearby Lake Cunningham has windsurfing rentals, fishing, and boating. *2333 E. Tully Rd., Lake Cunningham Regional Park, San Jose, tel. 408/270–8000. Admission: $18.95 those taller than 42", $14.95 under 42", $9.95 senior citizens, $12.95 after 3 PM. Open daily 10–7. AE, D, MC, V.*

Paramount's Great America. This movie-theme amusement park has five major areas, which feature five roller coasters, a *Days of Thunder* stockcar race, kiddie rides, and *Star Trek* characters roaming the grounds. You'll want to ride the 100-foot-tall double-decker Carousel Columbia, with its 106 enameled, fiberglass replicas of classic carousel animals. You can choose a sea horse, an ostrich, a cat, or another rare carousel animal and watch scenes of American history as you whirl by. The Drop Zone 22-story free-fall ride and the 110-foot Ferris wheel are too intense for most children. There are casual restaurants, concerts, an IMAX theater, and an ice show in the park. *2401 Agnew Rd., Santa Clara, tel. 408/986–5845. Admission: $28.95 ages 7 and up, $18.95 senior citizens, $15.95 ages 3–6. Open Sun.–Fri. 10–9, Sat. 10 AM–11 PM. AE, MC, V.*

Up the Coast

Stanford University. One of the nation's finest and most attractive universities lies midway between San Francisco and San Jose in Palo Alto, about 20 miles north of San Jose. Founded in 1885 on the site of a world-famous horse-breeding ranch, the university is arranged on a master plan that was done by Frederick Law Olmstead, the designer of New York's Central Park. Mission-style sandstone buildings with red-clay roof tiles dominate. The Rodin sculpture garden and the 285-foot landmark Hoover Tower are special treats. Free one-hour walking tours of the campus leave from the Fountain in front of Memorial

Auditorium daily at 11 and 3:15. *Palm Dr., Palo Alto 94305, tel. 415/723–2560.*

Down the Coast

As you leave San Jose and drive down the coast toward Monterey, drive first to Santa Cruz (30 miles southwest) and then another 18 miles south to Castroville, which is artichoke country. Stop at a fruit stand for delicious, inexpensive strawberries and pistachio nuts. Monterey is another 15 miles south.

Santa Cruz Beach Boardwalk. Its 1924 roller coaster, Giant Dipper, is worth the ride. The boardwalk also contains a 1911 Charles I.D. Looff Carousel with expressive horses, a working brass-ring dispenser, and an 1894 pipe band organ. You can try to win a free ride by throwing a brass ring into a clown's mouth. Lot parking is $5; try for one of the quarters-only 10-hour meters on the street. After five on Monday and Tuesday in summer, "1907 Night" prices kick in, and rides are 50¢ each. *400 Beach St., Santa Cruz, tel. 408/423–5590. Admission free; rides $1.50–$3 each; all-day pass $17.95. Open daily 11–10. D, MC, V.*

Santa Cruz Mystery Spot. The attraction is hokey, but kids love it. This spot of woods appears to favor mind over matter, as odd gravity occurs here. Guides take you on a short walk into a redwood forest where you stand in a rustic cabin and feel a gravitational pull that appears to alter your ability to stand straight. Despite the signs, it can be difficult to find. *Branciforte Dr., 2½ mi north on Market St. off Rte. 17, Santa Cruz, tel. 408/423–8897. Admission: $4 adults, $2 children. Open June–Aug., daily 9:30–8; Sept.–May, daily 9:30–5.*

Monterey Bay Aquarium. This is the largest aquarium in the nation, with a three-story underwater kelp forest. A new wing showcases sharks and barracuda in a Monterey Bay environment behind a 13-inch-thick window the size of a drive-in movie screen. You can view sea snakes, eels, and others poisonous creatures up close and personal. At the touch pool you can handle starfish, bat rays, and crabs. A jellyfish display is one of nearly 100 galleries displaying the world's sea life. Special tanks allow you to watch sea otters, and daily feeding shows are held for many creatures. On weekends, you may have to wait in line for tickets, which can be bought in advance from Monterey Bay hotels, for no service fee, or with a service fee from Bass ticket outlets or by calling the aquarium (in California) at 800/756–3737. The last tickets are sold at 5 daily. From the end of May through early September, WAVE shuttle buses ($1 daily) link the aquarium with parking garages and waterfront attractions. *886 Cannery Row, Monterey, tel. 408/648–4888. Admission: $13.75 adults, $11.75 senior citizens and ages 13–17, $6 ages 3–12. Open June 15–Sept. 2 and weekends year-round daily 9–6; Sept. 3–June 14 weekdays 10–6.*

Monterey Bay Sports Museum. Visitors enter this interesting museum through a 1909 turnstile from Pittsburgh's Forbes Field. You will find memorabilia from college football, boxing, and baseball well presented throughout its three rooms. The glory days of the Pacific Coast League are among the treats. *883 Lighthouse Ave., 2 blocks from aquarium, Monterey, tel. 408/655–2363. Admission: $2.50 adults, $1.50 ages under 16. Open weekdays noon–5, Sat. 10–6, Sun. 11–5.*

Dennis the Menace Playground. Cartoonist Hank Ketchum donated the money for this wonderful free playground, just off Route 1. It has great slides, imaginative bridges, and a cushion of sand. An adjacent lake has paddleboats for rent. *El Estero, Monterey, tel. 408/646–3866. Open daily 10–dusk.*

DISNEYLAND AND HOLLYWOOD
LOS ANGELES, RANCHO CUCAMONGA, SAN BERNARDINO, LAKE ELSINORE

21

When you make the pilgrimage to Dodger Stadium in Los Angeles, don't neglect three sparkling new Single A California League parks in the outer suburbs of Rancho Cucamonga, Lake Elsinore, and San Bernardino. You may want to base yourself east of Los Angeles, in Anaheim, home of Disneyland, to take advantage of the lodging and park discounts.

Start with a Dodgers game in Chavez Ravine, where you see palm trees, the Elysian hills, and the San Gabriel Mountains in the distance. This 1962 ballpark has produced a winning franchise, packing in fans and championships ever since the Dodgers left Brooklyn's Ebbets Field for California sunshine. You'll battle traffic here, so come early. Universal Studios and Disneyland are fun, exhausting, and expensive. You can drive to Griffith Park Observatory for a close-up view of the famed HOLLYWOOD sign, or to the La Brea Tar Pits for free tours of the grounds. A stroll down Santa Monica's Municipal Pier provides endless people-watching amusement at no charge.

East 38 miles from Los Angeles on Interstate 10 is the emerging city of Rancho Cucamonga and its spectacular mini-version of Baltimore's Camden Yards stadium. This is a gorgeous tree-lined park, with handsome seating and concourse. The Quakes' mascots are clever. The fans pack this stadium in record numbers, so you'll need to buy tickets in advance.

San Bernardino is 20 miles east of Rancho Cucamonga. Proud of its Western roots, the city has adopted that theme for its new stadium, the Ranch. The team is the Stampede and the park is true to its heritage, with adobe walls adorned by red tiles. The management of this club has reached out to all cultures in this city, drawing a mix of fans that is the most diverse we've seen in baseball, a healthy sign.

Forty miles south of Rancho Cucamonga is Lake Elsinore, a city of 25,000 that built a $15 million stadium in the foothills of the Ortega Mountains to meet the needs of the new families moving here from Los Angeles and San Diego. The lake provides good recreaton.

LOS ANGELES DODGERS

League: National League • **Class:** Major • **Stadium:** Dodger Stadium • **Opened:** 1962 • **Capacity:** 56,000 • **Dimensions:** LF: 330, CF: 400, RF: 330 • **Surface:** grass • **Season:** Apr.-early Oct.

STADIUM LOCATION: 1000 Elysian Park Ave., Los Angeles, CA 90012

TEAM WEB SITE: http://www.dodgers.com

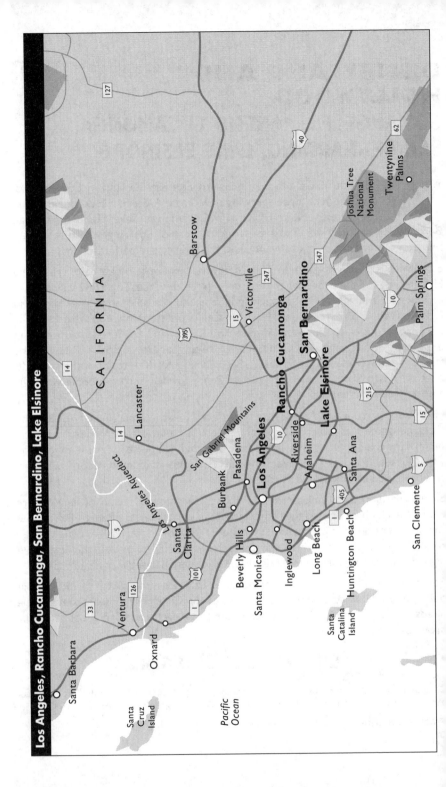

Los Angeles, Rancho Cucamonga, San Bernardino, Lake Elsinore

GETTING THERE: From I–5 southbound, take Stadium Way exit. Go left on Stadium Way. Take quick left onto Academy Rd. and equally quick left back onto Stadium Way. Turn left on Elysian Park Ave. From Rte. 101 northbound, take Alvarado exit and turn right. Take right on Sunset and go 2 mi. Turn left on Elysian Park Ave. and go 1 mi. From Rte. 110 northbound, take Dodger Stadium exit. Turn left on Stadium Way. Turn right on Elysian Park Ave. Call 800/266–6883 for bus information.

TICKET INFORMATION: Box 51100, Los Angeles, CA 90051-0100, tel. 213/224–1471, fax 213/224–1269.

PRICE RANGE: Field (yellow) and loge (orange) box seats $14 and $12; blue level reserved seats $9 and $8; red level top deck $6; pavilion (bleachers) $6.

GAME TIME: Mon., Tues., Thurs.–Sun. 7:05 PM; Wed. 7:35 PM; day games 1:05 PM; gates open 90 min before game.

TIPS ON SEATING: In pavilion bleacher seats, no alcohol allowed. Loge seats are equivalent of club level seats at newer stadiums at half the price.

SEATING FOR PEOPLE WITH DISABILITIES: Available on top deck (red), loge (orange), and reserved (blue) levels. Special parking in lots 2, 3, and 4.

STADIUM FOOD: The healthiest meal—the teriyaki chicken bowl at **Yoshinoya**—is the best: rice, vegetables and chicken for $4. (There is a beef bowl and a vegetable bowl too). Garden salads and antipasto salads are available and Buffalo wings are $4.50. There are several **Carl Jrs.** within the park for the usual fast-food fare, as well as TCBY Yogurt and Pizza Hut. The famed Dodger Dog sticks out beyond the bun by several inches on each end but isn't otherwise notable ($2.50). A good buy is the kid's meal at the **Dodger Dog** stands. The hot dog is full-sized and is accompanied by chips, a drink, and an activity book.

SMOKING POLICY: Smoking prohibited except in several small designated smoking areas on concourse.

PARKING: Ample parking, $5. Color of number on baseball-shape light stand in lot should match color of level on which you sit.

TOURISM INFORMATION: Los Angeles Convention & Visitors Bureau (633 West 5th St., Suite 6000, Los Angeles, CA 90071, tel. 213/624–7300 or 800/228–2452).

Los Angeles: Dodger Stadium

When the Dodgers arrived in Los Angeles from Brooklyn in 1958, they began what has become one of the most successful franchises in baseball history. In 1978, the Dodgers were the first team to draw more than 3 million fans in a single season. Nine times the World Series has been played here, with the Dodgers' becoming World Champions five times since arriving in Los Angeles.

From the very start of the Pacific Coast League, Los Angeles had one and sometimes two top teams. In 1921, William K. Wrigley, Jr., the chewing gum executive, bought the Los Angeles Angels and built a new stadium. The $1 million-dollar double-decked Wrigley Field was opened in 1927 with capacity for 22,000 fans.

After the 1956 season, the Chicago Cubs traded the Angels and Wrigley Field to Walter O'Malley, the owner of the Brooklyn Dodgers, for the Dodgers' Ft. Worth, Texas, ball club. When the Dodgers moved to California, they played in the Los Angeles Coliseum rather than Wrigley Field. Before being leveled, Wrigley Field hosted the Los Angeles Angels, the American League expansion team.

The Los Angeles Coliseum was completed in 1923 and enlarged for the 1932 Olympics. It was more suited for football and track and field than baseball. With a baseball seating capacity of 93,600, it was a shock to the Dodgers, coming from the intimate 31,497-seat Ebbets Field. Dodgers pitcher Clem Labine pretty much summed up the sentiments of his teammates: "Nobody understood those freeways, and nobody could deal with that ballpark." But almost 2 million people came to watch the

Dodgers play in 1958, twice the previous year's attendance at Ebbets Field.

The Dodgers were forced to play four seasons in the Coliseum as landslides and the law stalled construction of their new stadium. This was the first major-league park built by private funds since Yankee Stadium in 1923. The massive parking lot seemed appropriate for car-crazy California, holding 16,000 cars on 21 terraced lots at five different levels. Seating levels and parking levels were color-coordinated for fan convenience.

Architect Emil Praeger designed the ballpark to seat 56,000, with the ability to enclose the outfield and raise capacity to more than 80,000. Dodger management deserves enormous credit for not succumbing to greed and turning Dodger Stadium into just another concrete doughnut.

The huge screen in left field produces a picture of spectacular quality. There is an older, more traditional scoreboard in right field. The view beyond the stadium is impressive, including palm trees and the Elysian Hills, with the San Gabriel Mountains in the distance. In memory of Ebbets Field, Dodger Stadium is located on Elysian Park Avenue.

Unlike at most major-league stadiums, especially of this era, you can get a hot dog and a drink on the concourse and still see the game.

In southern California, it's traffic, not rain, that is the major concern about whether or not you are going to see a game. The Dodgers haven't had a rain-out in Los Angeles since April 21, 1988. You'll notice many of the locals come into the park a few innings late and leave early, a practice baffling to East Coast baseball fans. Maybe it's to beat the traffic.

Where to Stay

Best Western Dragon Gate Inn. This small three-floor hotel is in Chinatown, just a mile from Dodger Stadium. There is a free Continental breakfast and a refrigerator in every room. *818 N. Hill St., Los Angeles 90012, tel. 213/617–3077 or 800/528–1234, fax 213/680–3753. 50 rooms. Facilities: 2 restaurants, parking (free). AE, D, DC, MC, V. $$*

Metro Plaza Hotel. This popular four-story Chinatown hotel is a mile from Dodger Stadium. Because of its low prices, summer bookings go fast. Most rooms are standard doubles, but a few singles are available. *711 N. Main St., Los Angeles 90012, tel. 213/680–0200 or 800/223–2223, fax 213/620–0200. 82 rooms. Facilities: restaurant. AE, D, DC, MC, V. $$*

Westin Bonaventure. City travel and tourist buses frequent this huge downtown convention hotel, which is 35 stories tall. The corporate tower suites, with a king-size bed and a queen-size sofa bed, are the best for families. It's worth visiting the revolving lounge for the terrific view of the city. The hotel is 2 miles from the ballpark. *404 S. Figueroa St., Los Angeles 90071, tel. 213/624–1000 or 800/228–3000, fax 213/612–4800. 1,462 rooms. Facilities: 5 restaurants, pool, parking (fee). AE, D, DC, MC, V. $$$*

Anaheim Marriott. This fresh, California-look hotel is two blocks from Disney, with a free continuous shuttle. Its "Special to Disneyland" package is a good buy, including two adult tickets to Disneyland and free breakfast for two people. The offer is good for two adults and three children under 18. *700 W. Convention Way, Anaheim 92802, tel. 714/750–8000 or 800/228–9290, fax 714/750–9100. 1,033 rooms. Facilities: 3 restaurants, indoor and outdoor pools, hot tubs, saunas, coin laundry. AE, D, DC, MC, V. $$*

Where to Eat

Carney's. This former railroad dining car dishes out superlative hot dogs, hamburgers, and chocolate-dipped frozen bananas. There are sandwiches and tacos, but walk through the grill line and go for the $1.65 Chicagoan hot dog or a $1.75 hamburger. The small frozen banana (90¢) is more than enough dessert. *12601 Ventura Blvd., Studio City, tel. 818/761–8300; 8351 Sunset Blvd., Hollywood, tel. 213/654–8300. No credit cards. $*

Philippe's Original. An unbeatable French-dip sandwich with its own terrific mustard is the bedrock of this longtime eatery. The sliced beef sandwich is served alongside a bowl of salty beef broth for dipping. Sit at a wooden booth or table, or buy sandwiches to take out. There also are French-dip lamb, pork, and ham sandwiches and great baked apples. *1001 N. Alameda St., Los Angeles, tel. 213/628–3781. No credit cards. $*

Pink's Famous Chili Dogs. Chili dog and hamburger heaven has been found here since 1939, first from a pushcart and now in a restaurant under a flashing pink neon sign. There are 25 varieties of hot dogs, plus tamales, burritos, and a pastrami Reuben dog. For vegetarians, there's a guacamole dog. The all-beef hot dogs have bite and a crunchy casing. Also sold are strong, non-alcoholic brewed sodas, in strawberry, black cherry, raspberry, and peach. Check out its Wall of Fame, with photos of Pink's customers such as Jay Leno and Diana Ross. *709 N. La Brea Ave., at Melrose Ave., Hollywood, tel. 213/931–4223. No credit cards. $*

The Farmer's Market. More than 100 ethnic food stands, from Cajun to Bolivian, are sprinkled throughout Los Angeles's famed produce market. You can sample while you walk or eat at the outdoor cafés. *6333 W. 3rd St., Los Angeles, tel. 213/933–9211. $*

Clifton's Brookdale Cafeteria. This is one of five Clifton's cafeterias in the city, all dispensing nostalgia food and good value. The huge facility, seating 500 eaters on three floors, is decorated with a California redwood theme. Many items served today, like the coconut, raisin, and walnut "millionaire pie," were on its original menu in 1935. *648 S. Broadway, Los Angeles, tel. 213/627–1673. MC, V. $*

Nate 'n Al's. The bustling deli, decorated in 1972-era earth tones, has four rows of booths, plus table service. The blintzes, lox, and bagels are the best in their class. The corned beef sandwiches are overstuffed, and halves are available. Children like the hot dogs with baked beans and the potato pancakes. *414 N. Beverly Dr., Beverly Hills, tel. 310/274–0101. AE, MC, V. $*

Entertainments

Disneyland. Children can have a splendid day of fun if the park is done in moderation. To save time and money, prepurchase your discount tickets at AAA. Get to the park early and head first for Fantasyland, Critter Country, and Pirates of the Caribbean. Skip Toontown—the attractions can't handle crowds. The train around the park is a restful interlude. Eat lunch early, around 11, to avoid lines. It's hard to pull the children

away, but take an afternoon break, return to your hotel for the pool and, for younger children, a nap. Go back to the park around four, finish the essential rides, and reserve a table at an outdoor restaurant on the night parade route. This gives you comfortable seating and a slight elevation. It's good to rent a stroller, even for five-year-olds. *1313 Harbor Blvd., Anaheim, tel. 714/999–4565. Admission: $34 adults, $26 ages 3–11, $30 senior citizens. Open daily 9 AM–about 10 PM; closing times vary.*

Universal Studios. This park is a visual and entertainment delight, with movie characters and props throughout. Be warned that children five and under may be frightened by the earthquake, King Kong, floods, avalanche, and great white shark that threaten you on the back-lot tram tour. The tram tours end at 4:15. Be prepared to bail out before boarding other rides, such as "Back to the Future" and "Jurassic Park," which may be too scary for younger children. The theme shows are popular, so study the daily schedule and arrive at five minutes early so you won't be turned away. It's fun to have lunch with Laurel and Hardy and other costumed stars at the Studio Commissary. A warning—you can't use credit cards at 14 of the 16 restaurants. *Lankershim Blvd. and Hollywood Freeway (U.S. 101), Universal City, tel. 818/508–9600. Admission: $34 adults, $26 ages 3–11, $29 senior citizens; parking $5. Open May 25–June 14, 9–8; June 15–June 28, 8 AM–10 PM; June 29–Aug. 18, 7 AM–11 PM; Aug. 19–May 24, 9–7. AE, D, MC, V.*

Los Angeles Zoo. This older, sprawling zoo in Griffith Park emphasizes African animals. In the large aviary you can see a World of Birds show. The Zoo Safari Train is an extra $3 for adults and $1 for children. Throughout the park are six small restaurants, several of which offer shade. Ticket sales stop at 4 PM, and the animals are taken from view starting at 4:30. *5333 Zoo Dr., Golden Gate (I–5) and Ventura Freeways (Rte. 134), Los Angeles, tel. 213/666–4090. Admission: $8.25 adults, $3.25 ages 2–12, $5.25 senior citizens. Open daily 10–5.*

Gene Autry Western Heritage Museum. Children can dress in Western garb and ride play horses in this celebration of things Western. There are cowboy movies, photos of real pioneers, and artifacts of Americans' western trek. A children's section has saddles to play on. It's across from the zoo in Griffith Park. *4700 Western Heritage Way, Los Angeles, tel. 213/667–2000. Admission: $7 adults, $3 ages 2–12. Open Tues.–Sun. 10–5.*

TV Tapings. If you want to spend your time cheering at a game show or watching a live sit-com, plan ahead. You must call at least three weeks in advance to get tickets mailed to you. Some shows require audience members to be at least 12 to 18 years old. Ticket holders should arrive an hour early to the tapings, as seats are distributed on a first-come, first-served basis. Call CBS (tel. 213/852–2458), ABC (tel. 818/506–0067), NBC (tel. 818/840–3537), Fox (tel. 818/506–0067), and Paramount Television (tel. 213/956–5575) for tickets. Audiences Unlimited (tel. 818/506–0067) has a limited number of same-day tickets available at the Fox TV Center (5746 Sunset Blvd., Hollywood; open weekdays 8:30–6). The center is one block west of the 101 Freeway.

La Brea Tar Pits. More than 600 species of Pleistocene animals and plants have been uncovered in this section of Hancock Park. Kids are fascinated to see how the animals were caught when they tried to drink water. *Wilshire Blvd. and Curson Ave., Los Angeles, tel. 213/857–6311. Observation pit open weekends 11–2; free guided tours Wed.–Sun. at 1.*

George C. Page Museum of La Brea Discoveries. You can watch fossils from the pits being cleaned and identified and a 15-minute film that explains the ice-age finds. *5801 Wilshire Blvd., Los Angeles, tel. 213/936–2230. Admission: $6 adults, $2 ages 5–10; free 1st Tues. of month; parking (fee). Open Tues.–Sat. 10–5.*

Sites to See

Griffith Park Observatory and Planetarium. To get a great view of the city and to see the 50-foot HOLLYWOOD sign on Mt. Cahuenga; drive up a hill and park in front of this observatory. You'll recognize the Art Deco building from dozens of movies. You can use the planetarium's telescope or view its array of stars every summer night from dusk to 9:45. The Hall of Science and the observatory are free; the planetarium has daily star and laser shows for a fee. *Los Feliz Ave., Los Angeles, tel. 213/664–1191. Admission: planetarium $4 adults, $2 ages 5–12; laser shows $7 adults, $6 ages 5–12. Open Tues.–Fri. 2–10, weekends 12:30–10.*

Santa Monica Municipal Pier. Its restored carousel is worth a weekend visit, but some of the other games and rides are shabby. Renovation is under way, however. The city's Main Street and Third Street Promenade offer nice bookstores, street art, and coffeehouses. The pier is about 20 miles southwest of downtown Los Angeles. *200 Santa Monica Pier, at Colorado Ave., Santa Monica, tel. 310/458–8900. Carousel: 50¢ adults, 25¢ children; open weekends 10–5.*

Richard M. Nixon Presidential Library and Birthplace. Skip the Ronald Reagan museum in Simi Valley (tel. 805/522–8444), which is cold and unappealing. Instead, come to Yorba Linda for an admirably honest portrayal—warts and all—of a complex and difficult man. Children respond to the birthplace cottage and the grounds. The Nixon museum has a gift shop with a sense of humor—it sells a birthplace birdhouse—and offers baseball memorabilia. Richard and Patricia Nixon are buried between the museum and the cottage. *18001 Yorba Linda Blvd., Yorba Linda, tel. 714/993–3393. Admission: $4.95 adults, $1 ages 8–11. Open Mon.–Sat. 10–5, Sun. 11–5.*

RANCHO CUCAMONGA QUAKES

League: California League • **Major League Affiliation:** San Diego Padres • **Class:** A • **Stadium:** The Epicenter • **Opened:** 1993 • **Capacity:** 6,631 • **Dimensions:** LF: 330, CF: 400, RF: 330 • **Surface:** grass • **Season:** Apr.–Labor Day

STADIUM LOCATION: 8408 Rochester Ave., Rancho Cucamonga, CA 91730

GETTING THERE: From Los Angeles, take I–10E to I–15N to Foothill Blvd., exit left for less than 1 mi. Take left on Rochester Ave. to parking lot. Epicenter is in Rancho Cucamonga Sports Complex.

TICKET INFORMATION: Box 4139, Rancho Cucamonga, CA 91729, tel. 909/481–5252, fax 909/481–5005.

PRICE RANGE: Superbox $7.50; field box $7; box $6; view $4.50; terrace $3; café $5; club $5.

GAME TIME: Mon.–Sat. 7:15 PM, Sun. 1:15 (Apr.–mid-June) or 5:15 (mid-June–Sept.); gates open 75 min before game

TIPS ON SEATING: Call ahead and order reserved tickets; most games sold out. $4.50 view seats are fine. $5 café seating is good.

SEATING FOR PEOPLE WITH DISABILITIES: In two superbox sections just behind dugouts and in cafés

STADIUM FOOD: Fruit and vegetable trays are the best tickets here. For $3, your children can snack on a variety of good California fruits. For $2.75, try the vegetables. The chicken burrito, at $3.50, is worth it. The french fries actually are potato wedges, at $2. It's most pleasant to sit at one of the **outdoor cafés,** along each base line. Concession stands on the main concourse include an **espresso shop** with nine concoctions, including good hot chocolate. For bigger appetites, there's the **Sausage House** with spicy hot dogs, brats, burgers, a meatball grinder, and a sub sandwich. A chicken sandwich is relatively pricey at $4.50.

SMOKING POLICY: Smoking prohibited in seating areas; permitted only in main concourse behind both cafés

PARKING: Available throughout Sports Complex, $2

VISITING TEAM HOTEL: Best Western Heritage Inn (8179 Spruce Ave., Rancho Cucamonga, CA 91730, tel. 909/466–1111 or 800/528–1234)

TOURISM INFORMATION: Ontario Convention & Visitors Bureau (421 N. Euclid Ave., Ontario, CA 91762, tel. 909/984–2450 or 800/455–5755)

Rancho Cucamonga: The Epicenter

Drive due east from Los Angeles on I–10 for about an hour. Head north on I–15 for a bit and turn off at the emerging suburban city of Rancho Cucamonga. Cucamonga is the "land of many waters" in the language of the native people who first settled here. These waters later fed some of the largest vineyards in the world. They now feed mostly suburban sprawl, but Rancho Cucamonga isn't all ticky-tacky. Here lies the Epicenter, one of the finest little baseball parks in all of America. It's a miniature of Baltimore's Camden Yards, deep green elegance and all. Trees—palm and others—line your walk from the nicely landscaped parking lot. Beautiful softball fields with brand-new aluminum bench seating surround the Epicenter.

This is California-style architecture at its best, with a handsome white stucco exterior. Designed by Grillias-Pirc-Rosier-Alves of Irvine, six large glass and dark green tile arches flank a larger center arched entryway. As we passed through the turnstiles, we were greeted by a life-size statue of Jack Benny complete with violin.

The Quakes, who play at the Epicenter in Cucamonga, have a huge green dinosaur mascot named Tremor, the Rallysaurus. When it turned out the 6-foot, 7-inch Tremor was too scary for some of the youngest Quake fans, the club added a smaller little brother named Aftershock. According to the coloring book sold in the excellent gift shop at the entrance to the stadium, Tremor was a baseball-playing Rallysaurus who was swallowed up during an earthquake 2 million years ago and awoke in a recent earthquake in time to be named mascot for the Quakes' inaugural season. These folks aren't afraid to have a little fun with California's number one threat.

The city-owned stadium sits in the valley with a stunning view of the towering San Gabriel Mountains in the background. The interior is every bit as good as the exterior, with dark green tiles, fence, and hand rails nicely setting off the white stucco. The seats are all wide and close to the Class A California League action.

While the concourse access to food and bathroom facilities is wide and attractive, it is under the seating area and requires fans to miss the action when they go for food and drinks. There is a wonderful "Quakes Fun Zone" on the concourse that has games only for little kids but no large grassy area to really let off steam on. In a new twist, the scoreboard measures the speed of each pitch.

The main problem with the Epicenter is that this $20 million stadium was too small from the day it opened on April 8, 1993, with room for only 4,648 fans. In 1994, they added two not completely satisfactory bleacher areas out past each café. In 1995, they very successfully added almost 500 superbox seats near home plate. There are now 6,500 seats. More than 446,000 fans attended in 1995. The lesson here is clear—if you build a stadium as fine as the Epicenter, plan on the fact that people will come in big numbers.

Where to Stay

Visiting Team Motel: Best Western Heritage Inn. This attractive adobe hotel, built in 1992, has a red tile roof and good views of the San Gabriel Mountains. The grounds are nicely landscaped, and most of the fresh, airy rooms have two queen-size beds. Guests receive a free Continental breakfast. *8719 Spruce Ave. (Rte. 66), Rancho Cucamonga 91730, tel. 909/466–1111 or 800/682–7829, fax 909/466–3876. 117 rooms. Facilities: pool, exercise room, spa, coin laundry. AE, D, DC, MC, V. $$*

Where to Eat

Knollwood Roadhouse Cafe. This family restaurant is on the original Cucamonga Rancho in the former Thomas Winery, California's oldest vineyard. Winery artifacts, such as a waterwheel-powered conveyor belt, remain. The portions are huge here—the salads are served in colanders. Try the fish-and-chips or whole batter-dipped onion. Burgers are a specialty. The children's menu includes chicken strips and corn dogs. *8916 Foothill Blvd. (Rte. 66), at Vineyard Blvd., Rancho Cucamonga, tel. 909/941–8793. AE, D, MC, V. $*

Entertainments

Scandia Family Fun Center. There are rides, 16 baseball pitching machines, miniature golf, and a speedway at this roadside amusement park. You can see the blue-and-white roller coaster from I–15. The bumper boats are fun, but the Scandia Screamer coaster is too jolting for kids under 10. The kiddie rides are more creative than usual, and the Little Dipper roller coaster is fun. You can buy individual tickets for $1 each or an unlimited pass for $11.95 for visitors under 54 inches or $15.95 for guests over 54 inches. *1155 S. Wanamaker Ave., 1 mi south of I–10, at I–15, Ontario, tel. 909/390–3092. Admission: $15.95 persons 54" tall and taller, $11.95 children under 54". Open Sun.–Thurs. 10 AM–11 PM, Fri.–Sat. and holidays 10 AM–1 AM.*

SAN BERNARDINO STAMPEDE

League: California League • **Major League Affiliation:** Los Angeles Dodgers • **Class:** A • **Stadium:** The Ranch • **Opened:** 1996 • **Capacity:** 5,000 • **Dimensions:** LF: 330, CF: 410, RF: 330 • **Surface:** grass • **Season:** Apr.–Labor Day

STADIUM LOCATION: Between Mill St. and Rialto Ave. and between E and G Sts.

GETTING THERE: From Los Angeles, take I–10 east to I–215 north, right on 2nd St. to G St., then right to stadium.

TICKET INFORMATION: Box 1806, San Bernardino, CA 92402, tel. 909/888–9922, fax 909/888–5251

PRICE RANGE: Superbox $7; field box $6; upper box $5; general admission $4 adults, $3 children and senior citizens

GAME TIME: Mon.–Sat. 7:05 PM, Sun. 2:05 PM (Apr.–mid-June) and 5:05 PM (mid-June–Sept.); gates open 1 hr before game.

TIPS ON SEATING: Best bargain seats are in upper boxes. From first-base side, you can see downtown. On third-base side (home team dugout), you have sun at your back. **Boot Hill** is a grass area beyond left-field outfield fence.

SEATING FOR PEOPLE WITH DISABILITIES: Throughout stadium

STADIUM FOOD: The roasted ears of corn are particularly great. Other best bets are the $5–$8 meals from the grill that include either a chicken or rib sandwich or hamburger, plus potato salad and baked beans. There are also pork chop sandwiches. Don't miss the homebaked extra-large chocolate chip and peanut butter cookies, for $1.25. Sunday is 2-for-1 hot dog day, and Wednesday nights are "buck-beverage" nights with all 12-ounce drinks priced at $1.

PARKING: Ample parking, $2

SMOKING POLICY: No restrictions

VISITING TEAM HOTEL: Radisson Hotel & Convention Center (295 N. E St., San Bernardino, CA 92401, tel. 909/381–6181 or 800/333–3333)

TOURISM INFORMATION: San Bernardino Convention & Visitors Bureau (201 N. E St., San Bernardino, CA 92401, tel. 909/889–3980 or 800/867–8366)

San Bernardino: The Ranch

Just 20 miles east of Rancho Cucamonga and in the same county is San Bernardino, a very different place. San Bernardino has roots. It has an older, more culturally and economically diverse population than the new suburban cities nearby.

You wouldn't expect to see a fancy 1990s HOK Sport–designed stadium here. And we didn't. In 1935, the federal Works Progress Administration (WPA) built a fine ballpark—Perris Hill Park—on the edge of town. In 1941 San Bernardino fielded a team in the California League. The San Bernardino team did not finish the 1941 season, and the California League did not go back to San Bernardino until 1987. The returning San Bernardino Spirit found a remodeled aluminum-bench and blue-plastic-seat stadium renamed Fiscalini Field on the site of Perris Hill Park. Ken Griffey, Jr. tore through here in 1988, batting an impressive .338 in 58 games before moving up to Double AA baseball. The stadium is a standard 1980s Single A stadium, but the view is terrific, with the building surrounded by tall trees and taller hills. This was the only stadium we found with a violet neon ELKS lodge sign set against a mountain over the left-field fence.

We enjoyed Fiscalini Field, but now only local and college baseball is played on the Highland Avenue site. In 1995, San Bernardino signed on as a Los Angeles Dodgers farm team and followed the lead of several of its California League rivals, bringing in HOK Sport of Kansas City, the architects who designed Camden Yards. The $13 million state-of-the-art stadium you visit opened August 12, 1996. It was designed to look like the 18th-century Spanish missions that were instrumental in the settlement of this region, with the outside walls made of adobe and red tiles.

The theme is now Western. The team nickname has been changed to Stampede, and the stadium is called the Ranch. A grassy area beyond the outfield fence in left field is called Boot Hill. The mascot is a giant bug with a baseball head—the Stampede Bug.

In most places, unfortunately, baseball as a spectator sport has become largely a white person's game. We don't know what they are doing in San Bernardino, but major-league baseball should find out. The lively crowd at Fiscalini Field the night we attended was the most culturally diverse we saw anywhere on our travels.

Where to Stay

Radisson Hotel & Convention Center. This imposing 12-story downtown hotel is near City Hall and across the street from the grand Harris Department Store. Parking is free, and the hotel offers family packages that include four full breakfasts for $89 in a standard-size room. *295*

N. E St., San Bernardino 92401, tel. 909/381–6181 or 800/333–3333, fax 909/381–5288. 231 rooms. Facilities: restaurant, hot tub, health club. AE, D, DC, MC, V. $

Comfort Inn. This two-story peach stucco motel is in a commercial strip of hotels and restaurants. All of its freshly renovated rooms have refrigerators, microwave ovens, and hair dryers. Guests receive a free Continental breakfast. The inn is 8 minutes south of the ballpark. 1909 S. Business Center Dr., at the Waterman Ave. exit (north) off I–10. San Bernardino 92408, tel. 909/889–0090 or 800/424–6423, fax 909/889–0090. 50 rooms. Facilities: pool. AE, D, DC, MC, V. $

Super 8 Motel–Downtown. This ordinary beige concrete hotel is convenient to the ballpark and offers guests free use of its laundry machines. The rooms for four have two double beds. Extra rollaways are $4 each. 777 W. 6th St., San Bernardino 92410, tel. 909/889–3561 or 800/800–8000, fax 909/884–7127. 58 rooms. Facilities: outdoor hot tub, sauna, laundry service. AE, D, DC, MC, V. $

Where to Eat

Buffalo Ranch. The decor is Old West here, with attractive cowboy artifacts, such as chaps, antlers, and saddles for children to sit on. The food is exceptional, with fresh salads, imaginative combinations, and overgenerous portions. The buffalo stew and mashed potatoes are standouts. There are also good buffalo burgers

and lake trout. On the kids' menu you'll find shrimp, ribs, and steak. The entire restaurant is no-smoking. 970 S. E St., San Bernardino, tel. 909/884–3819. AE, D, MC, V. $

El Torito. This busy Mexican restaurant has pleasant ethnic decor, with hanging flowers and stucco walls, and an extensive menu. 118 E. Hospitality La., 2 blocks northwest of I–10 from Waterman exit, San Bernardino, tel. 909/381–2316. AE, MC, V. $

Entertainments

Santa's Village. You'll find two dozen rides, a children's theater, and a large gingerbread house in this amusement center in the San Bernardino Mountains. You can ride a donkey, try out a bobsled, watch live reindeer, or hike a nature trail within the park. The village is 30 minutes north of the ballpark. S.R. 18, Skyforest, tel. 909/337–2481. Admission: $11. Open mid-June–early Sept. and mid-Nov.–early Jan., daily 10–5; mid-Jan.–early June, weekends 10–5.

Sites to See

Rim of the World Drive. This winding, 40-mile drive leads to the Lake Arrowhead resort. You can see Big Bear Lake and Bear Canyon from Lakeview Point. Elevations on the drive range from 1,100 to 7,000 feet. There are adjacent picnic areas within the San Bernardino National Forest. S.R. 18, San Bernardino, tel. 909/383–5588.

LAKE ELSINORE STORM

League: California League • **Major League Affiliation:** California Angels • **Class:** A • **Stadium:** The Diamond • **Opened:** 1994 • **Capacity:** 8,066 • **Dimensions:** LF: 330, CF: 400, RF: 310 • **Surface:** grass • **Season:** Apr.–Labor Day

STADIUM LOCATION: 500 Diamond Dr., Lake Elsinore, CA 92530

GETTING THERE: From San Diego, I–15 north, Diamond Dr. exit, west ½ mi to stadium. From Los Angeles, I–10 or Freeway 60 east to I–15 south, Diamond Dr. exit, west to stadium. From Orange County, Freeway 91 east to I–15 south, Diamond Dr. exit west.

TICKET INFORMATION: Box 535, Lake Elsinore, CA 92531, tel. 909/245–4487, fax 909/245–0305

PRICE RANGE: Super box seats $6.50; box seats $5.50; reserved seats $4.50; general admission $3.50 adults, $3 ages under 15 and over 66

GAME TIME: Mon.–Sat. 7:05 PM, Sun. 2:05 (Apr.–early June) or 5:05 (early June–Sept.); gates open 90 min before game.

TIPS ON SEATING: General admission tickets allow you to sit on a grassy berm beyond first base. If you want a real seat, buy a reserved seat ticket.

SEATING FOR PEOPLE WITH DISABILITIES: Available on concourse in both box and reserved seating areas. Special food line at each concession stand.

STADIUM FOOD: The offerings are ordinary and overpriced. A small soda is $2.25 and a pizza slice is $2.50. Avoid the BBQ beef sandwich. You'll find a latte stand and microbrews. A better bet is the **Diamond Club,** a 400-seat sports bar and restaurant open to anyone in the stadium. Outdoor tables on two levels provide an excellent view of the game, and the menu has better choices.

SMOKING POLICY: Smoking prohibited in stadium except small designated area in general admission area beyond first base.

PARKING: Ample parking, $2; lot opens 2½ hrs before game.

VISITING TEAM HOTEL: Lakeview Inn (31808 Casino Dr., Lake Elsinore, CA 92530, tel. 909/674–9694)

TOURISM INFORMATION: Lake Elsinore Valley Chamber of Commerce (132 W. Graham Ave., Lake Elsinore, CA 92530, tel. 909/245–8848)

Lake Elsinore: The Diamond

When we first visited Rancho Cucamonga in its inaugural season of 1993, we thought it wasn't possible that a Single A baseball team could play in such a wonderful facility. Now, just 40 miles south on I–15 in Lake Elsinore, we found an equally spectacular stadium. What will it be like for the players who spend a summer playing baseball in these miniature Camden Yards and Jacobs Fields in Rancho Cucamonga and Lake Elsinore and then graduate to far inferior Double AA stadiums the next year?

The Lake Elsinore Diamond, opened in 1994, has all the modern comfort of the Epicenter in Rancho Cucamonga, with even more character. After a couple of weeks of watching ball games in the Pioneer, Northwest, and Northern leagues, we found it literally breathtaking to approach the Diamond. As you walk up the tree-lined pathway from the parking lot, you see the marvelous pointed entryway of brick and Camden Yards green. There are nine large concrete baseballs in a circle around a wire sculpture of a baseball pitcher and an impressive clock tower. You know immediately that this is the work of people who care about baseball tradition. The architects were HNTB of Kansas City.

Once inside, you are not disappointed. The outfield wall is an irregular shape with left center

425 feet from home and right field only 310 but with a Fenway Park–type 36-foot-high wall. Since this is minor-league baseball, the wall is covered with 17 large ads as well as a scoreboard. Behind home plate is a 90-foot-high clock tower reminiscent of the one in the famed minor-league Wrigley Field in Los Angeles.

No benches without backs here—all 6,066 seats are real seats, maroon with plenty of legroom. The field was dug out amphitheater-style so the concourse is directly behind the seats and you don't have to miss the action to get your hot dog and soda. The concourse and the dozen skyboxes are covered with a dark green roof. General-admission ticket holders sit on a grassy berm down the first-base line just below an arcade of speed pitch and other games. Pity the smokers here. They stand in a small fenced area above the general-admission area that evokes memories of 17th-century stocks.

There is a huge, almost major-league-quality scoreboard beyond the left-field wall. Down the third-base line is the Diamond Club, a 400-seat restaurant and bar open to all fans. Three outside levels rise above left field. To see Lake Elsinore, southern California's largest natural inland lake, walk through the restaurant to the grill area before the game starts.

The excellent souvenir shop at the entrance has plenty of items celebrating the Diamond's biggest celebrity—Hamlet, the 8-foot, 4-inch sea serpent who ranges all over the stadium throughout the game urging the fans to cheer on the home team. Hamlet—a coloring book in the souvenir shop tells the story of how he traveled from Shakespeare's Castle Elsinore in the 16th century to 20th-century California—shoots the visiting-team players with a water gun after the game and then signs autographs and poses for pictures at the entranceway.

Where to Stay

Visiting Team Motel: Lakeview Inn. Ask for a room on the second floor, stadium side. Postgame, you'll see a spectacular view of the illuminated, empty stadium. Morning views include Lake Elsinore and the Ortega Mountains. The hotel is near the I-15 freeway but is quiet. A small heated pool is suited to children, with a maximum depth of 4½ feet. *31808 Casino Dr., Lake Elsinore 92530, tel. 909/674–9694, fax 909/245–9249. 56 rooms. Facilities: pool, hot tub, coin laundry. AE, D, DC, MC, V. $*

Where to Eat

Park Plaza Family Restaurant. This casual, family-run enterprise offers ostrich and buffalo burgers. Both taste like slightly gamier versions of beef but are much lower in fat. There are also salads, fajitas, pot pies, and cobblers, served at the counter or at tables. The children's menu includes burritos and spaghetti. The restaurant is 10 minutes north of the ballpark by Lake Elsinore State Park. *31731 Riverside Dr., Lake Elsinore, tel. 909/674–5744. DC, MC, V. $*

The Family Basket. This corner restaurant has Mexican and American favorites at bargain prices. Its kids' breakfast, for $1.59, comes with two pancakes, one egg, sausage, and a drink. Likewise, the chorizo-and-eggs platter is more than you can eat. The atmosphere is fast-food,

but you'll find much more than burgers, including pork chops and fresh pies. *202 N. Main St., Lake Elsinore, tel. 909/674–8577. MC, V. $*

Entertainments

The town has a surprisingly long and interesting history. The lake was called Entengvo Wumoma—Hot Springs by the Little Sea—by its first inhabitants, the Pai-ah-che Indians. In 1797, Father Juan Santiago of the Mission San Juan Capistrano found it while searching for a new mission site. In the 1850s, it was on the stagecoach mail route between San Francisco and St. Louis, and in the 1880s, it became a link in the transcontinental railroad. Developers came in the 1880s and changed the name to Lake Elsinore to celebrate Shakespeare's castle. People flocked here for the hot mineral waters. The Crescent Bath House, a historic landmark built in 1887 and visited by such notables as Grover Cleveland and Buffalo Bill, still stands in the downtown albeit in quite bad shape. In the 1920s, Lake Elsinore's baths and recreation opportunities attracted Hollywood's elite. But the boom crashed with the depression, not to revive again until the 1980s. At night, Main Street, which is lined with assortment of antiques stores and a Mexican bakery, is illuminated by small white lights.

Lake Elsinore Recreation Area. Rent pedal boats and aquacycles by the half hour ($8) for a closer look at Lake Elsinore. When water conditions permit, Jet Skis are available. Rowboats and fishing tackle can be rented at the adjacent West Marina. Fishing licenses are required for those 16 or older. There are swimming areas on both sides of the lake. *32040 Riverside Dr. (Hwy. 74), Lake Elsinore, tel. 909/674–3177. Open daily 7–dusk.*

BASEBALL IN THE DESERT
PHOENIX, TUCSON

Phoenix and Tucson are in the Valley of the Sun. Take the name seriously! With 300 days of sunshine, there is baseball from March through November in Arizona. We recommend the warm glow of spring training in March, rather than the oppressive heat of summer. Eight major-league teams train here in the Cactus League each spring, all within 90 miles of each other, much closer together than the teams in Florida's Grapefruit League.

There are Pacific Coast League Triple AAA teams in Tucson and Phoenix. In 1998, an expansion major-league team will begin play in a new downtown Phoenix stadium with a retractable roof and real grass. In October and November each year, six teams square off in the Arizona Fall League.

The San Francisco Giants have a sparkling new stadium in Scottsdale, outside Phoenix, for their spring training and for summer play by the Phoenix Firebirds. The Colorado Rockies train at Hi Corbett Field in Tucson, built in 1937.

The big sports attraction outside of baseball here is golf, with dozens of courses throughout the Valley. Both Phoenix and Tucson have exceptional zoos, and Phoenix has the downtown Heard Museum, which highlights Native American cultures with intriguing exhibits, many aimed at children. Tucson's zoo is in the same park complex at its ballpark, and has an imaginative children's museum in a renovated downtown library. There's a vivid display of Mexican masks in the free state museum on the campus of the University of Arizona. To see life on an Indian reservation, it is worth a drive to the Mission at San Xavier south of the city, where wall paintings are undergoing restoration.

SAN FRANCISCO GIANTS SPRING TRAINING/PHOENIX FIREBIRDS

League: Cactus League • **Class:** Major League Spring Training • **Stadium:** Scottsdale Stadium • **Opened:** 1992 • **Capacity:** 8,250 • **Dimensions:** LF: 360, CF: 430, RF: 340 • **Surface:** grass • **Season:** March spring training

STADIUM LOCATION: 7408 E. Osborn Rd., Scottsdale, AZ 85251

GETTING THERE: From I–10, Broadway Rd., exit to Rural Rd.; north on Rural Rd., which becomes Scottsdale Rd., 4½ mi to Osborn Rd.; right on Osborn, stadium on left. From 202 Fwy E, right at McDowell exit, north on Osborn to stadium. For information about spring training express shuttle, Ollie the Trolley, call 602/994–7696.

TICKET INFORMATION: 7408 E. Osborn Rd., Scottsdale, AZ 85251, tel. 602/784-4444; Firebirds: tel. 602/275–0500, fax 602/990–8987

PRICE RANGE: Spring training, lower/upper box seats $13; line box seats $12; reserved grandstand $11; reserved bleachers $9; lawn seating $6; Firebirds, field and terrace boxes $7; reserved $6; general admission $4; children and senior citizens $1 off reserved and general admission

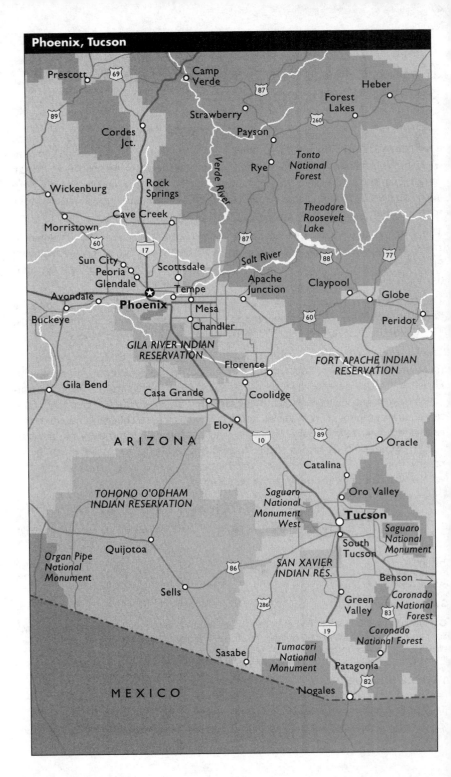

Phoenix, Tucson

GAME TIME: Most spring training games 1:05 PM; gates open 2 hrs before game. Firebirds, Mon.–Sat. 7:05 PM, Sun. 1:05 PM (Apr.–May) and 6:05 PM (June–Sept.)

TIPS ON SEATING: Many seats behind walking concourse between first and third base are shaded during afternoon games. For especially hot summer games, a spray from underside of stadium roof cools off fans seated in misting area.

SEATING FOR PEOPLE WITH DISABILITIES: Just behind field box seats behind home plate and past first and third bases

STADIUM FOOD: There is a grill behind the bleachers on the third-base side that serves BBQ chicken sandwiches, locally-made Italian sausages, hamburgers, and jumbo hot dogs. To give a California flavor, iced lattes and Anchor Steam beer are served. The most refreshing drinks are lemon and strawberry frozen fruit concoctions. Fresh lemonade with grenadine is also sold. Children gravitate toward the pizza, cookies, and yogurt waffle cones. Dippin' Dots, the odd ice cream that comes in a mound of bits, is here, too. A nice picnic area behind home plate is shaded by palm trees.

SMOKING POLICY: No-smoking ballpark with designated smoking areas

PARKING: Free around stadium on city streets and in public parking garages north of stadium.

VISITING TEAM HOTEL: Days Inn-Scottsdale (4710 N. Scottsdale Rd., Scottsdale, AZ 85251, tel. 602/947–9511 or 800/325–2525)

TOURISM INFORMATION: Phoenix & Valley of the Sun Convention & Visitors Bureau (1 Arizona Center, 400 E. Van Buren St., Suite 600, Phoenix, AZ 85004-2290, tel. 602/252–5588)

Phoenix: Scottsdale Stadium

New York's loss was Phoenix's gain. The 1957 National League decision to allow the Dodgers and Giants to move from New York to California catapulted Phoenix several steps closer to its place in baseball's major leagues. The Giants' Triple AAA Pacific Coast League team, the San Francisco Seals, moved to Phoenix, replacing a Class C team in the Arizona-Mexico League.

As early as the 1940s, the Giants trained in Phoenix. In 1982, they moved to Scottsdale, the fancy tourist magnet next door to Phoenix. Scottsdale had hosted spring-training baseball off and on since 1956. Designed by HOK Sport of Kansas City, the new stadium was built in 12 months for $7 million and opened in 1992. They tore out the green wooden stands of the old Scottsdale Field to build this baseball beauty. Owned and operated by the city of Scottsdale, the new stadium seats 8,250, with room for 2,500 more fans in the general admission grass-berm area beyond the outfield fence.

In the attractive and inviting new stadium, all seats are close to the action. Eight rows of comfortable, dark green field box seats line the first-and third-base lines. The food and souvenir concourse is wide and customer-friendly, but as it's behind the seats, you can't see the game and grab a hot dog and drink. The grass berm in the outfield is often wall-to-wall beach blankets packed with tanners. An attractive rust-color roof with flags flying above provides some shade between first and third.

As is often the case to avoid excessive sun in the players' eyes, the stadium layout is turned so that fans in the stands miss the best natural vistas. Walk to the top of the seating area on the third-base side for the best view of Phoenix-area mountains.

Sunscreen is a must at this ballpark, as is plenty of water. Savvy fans bring water bottles and refill them at the stadium. There are also good fruit drinks, both frozen and fresh-squeezed, to keep you hydrated.

Scottsdale Stadium will remain the spring-training home of the San Francisco Giants at least through 2007, but in 1998 the Phoenix Firebirds of the Pacific Coast League will move to Fresno, California, to make way for one of the two new major-league expansion teams. The Arizona Diamondbacks will bring big-league baseball to Arizona beyond the short Cactus League spring schedule.

The new stadium in downtown Phoenix—the Bank One Ballpark (BOB), designed by Ellerbe Becket, Inc.—with a retractable roof and a natural-grass playing field, will seat 48,569. There will be an outdoor swimming pool just beyond the fence in right center field. For information about the Diamondbacks, call 602/514–8500 or write Box 2095, Phoenix, AZ 85001.

Michael Jordan played in Scottsdale Stadium in the 1994 Arizona Fall League as a member of the Scottsdale Scorpions. The six teams of the Arizona League, founded in 1992, play 51-game schedules each October and November. Players with less than one year of major-league service are eligible to play. For information about the Arizona Fall League, write 10201 S. 51st St., Suite 230, Phoenix, AZ 85044, or call 602/496–6700.

Where to Stay

Holiday Inn Old Town Scottsdale. This campus-style low-rise hotel complex is convenient for walks into the Old Town area, which is filled with tourist shops and restaurants. It's just one block from the San Francisco Giants' spring-training facility. The hotel rooms are decorated in cool Southwest colors and have full-length windows fronting interior courtyards. *7353 E. Indian School Rd., Scottsdale 85251, tel. 602/944–9203 or 800/465–4329, fax 602/941–2567. 206 rooms. Facilities: restaurant, pool, tennis court. AE, D, DC, MC, V. $$*

Ambassador Inn. This two-story Spanish-motif motel on a busy street doesn't have great curb appeal, but it does have a pleasant interior courtyard built around a lovely pool and hot tub. Prices are lowest for streetside rooms, slightly higher for courtyard and poolside rooms. The large, clean rooms have 1970s-era furnishings and galley kitchens. *4727 E. Thomas Rd., Phoenix 85018, tel. 602/840–7500 or 800/624–6759, fax 602/840–5078. 170 rooms. Facilities: restaurant, pool, hot tub, exercise room, airport shuttle. AE, D, DC, MC, V. $*

San Carlos Hotel. Built in 1928, this affordable Italian Renaissance–style downtown hotel is on the National Register of Historic Places. Its lobby is small but elegant, and the rooms have updated plumbing, lovely city views, and expensive furnishings. Summer rates can be low. *202 N. Central Ave., at Monroe St., Phoenix 85004, tel. 602/253–4121 or 800/528–5446, fax 602/253–6668. 107 rooms, 9 suites. Facilities: 2 restaurants, pool, exercise room, parking (fee). AE, DC, MC, V. $$*

Where to Eat

Don & Charlie's. This busy, casual rib and steak house is popular with ballplayers. It serves huge entrée-size salads, frogs' legs, garlic cheese toast, creamed spinach, and steaks of all varieties. The children's menu is more expensive than most—$5 to $8—and the portions are large. *7501 E. Camelback Rd., Scottsdale, tel. 602/990–0900. AE, D, DC, MC, V. $$*

Landry's Pacific Fish Company. The maritime atmosphere and the open center kitchen are the stars in this friendly two-story restaurant. Climb to the balcony to get the best views of the cooks, sea relics on display, and the boats and shellacked trophy fish that hang overhead. The seafood is fine, the portions distressingly large, and the children's menu all fried food. *4321 N. Scottsdale Rd., south of Camelback Rd., Scottsdale, tel. 602/941–0602 or 800/394–3839. AE, D, MC, V. $$*

The Oyster Grill. Shark tacos are an attraction in this contemporary, casual restaurant in the Arizona Center, a downtown mall. A colorful marble wall, inspired by Caribbean colors, is a focal point. The children's menu includes pasta, grilled cheese sandwiches, and fish-and-chips. *455 N. 3rd St., at Van Buren St., Phoenix, tel. 602/252–6767. AE, D, MC, V. $$*

Yoshi's. This three-outlet Chinese restaurant chain resembles a burger palace, with Formica tables and bright lighting, but is a welcome departure from fried food. Chicken teriyaki, cold noodle salads, sushi, and potstickers are the mainstays here. Half-orders of teriyaki are available. This branch is closest to the ballpark. *18 W. Adams St., at Central Ave., Phoenix, tel. 602/254–7174; 24th St. and E. Indian School Rd., tel. 602/468–9737; 4060 N. Central Ave., at E. Indian School Rd., tel. 602/274–6470. No credit cards. $*

Entertainments

Phoenix Zoo. You enter this lovely, 125-acre zoo by a bridge walkway, framed by palm trees.

The zoo is arranged around separate trails—covering Arizona wildlife, desert creatures, the tropics, Africa, and a children's trail with a barnyard petting zoo and a prairie-dog village. A 35-minute safari-zoo train ride with good narration is $2 and worth it. The zoo's desert terrain makes this a very different zoo experience. You hear and see uncaged birds throughout the grounds and can get very close to bobcats and mountain lions. There are uncommon specimens, like roadrunners, piglike javelinas, and gazelles. You'll find a shaded area for lunch, camel rides ($2), and areas where you can pan for gold and look for gems (50¢ each). *455 N. Galvin Pkwy., Papago Park, Phoenix, tel. 602/273–1341. Admission: $7 adults, $3.50 ages 4–12, $6 senior citizens. Open May–Labor Day, daily 7–4, Labor Day–Apr., daily 9–5.*

Telephone Pioneers of America Park. In the far northern part of the city is the nation's first barrier-free park and playground, created in 1988 by engineers and employees of the Bell Telephone system. Most of the equipment is wheelchair-accessible and the overall design is aimed at those with reduced coordination. Beep baseball, which uses balls that emit noises for low-vision or sightless players, is played here. This is a wonderful climbing playground, good for children of all abilities. *1946 W. Morningside Dr., Phoenix, tel. 602/262–4543. Open daily, dawn–dusk.*

Sites to See

The Heard Museum. This beautiful downtown museum was founded in 1929 to showcase the cultural heritage of the country's native people. The permanent exhibit presents a journey through time and across the landscape of the Southwest. At the museum entrance, your kids can use mano and metate stones—lava rock and sandstone grinding tools traditionally used by Native Americans—to make meal. There is a sidewalk café and a superb gift shop with Native American–handcrafted art. *22 E. Monte Vista Rd., 1 block east of Central Ave., Phoenix, tel. 602/252–8848. Admission: $5 adults, $4 senior citizens and students, $3 ages 13–18, $2 ages 4–12. Open Mon., Tues., and Thurs.–Sat. 9:30–5, Wed. 9:30–9, Sun. noon–5.*

State Capitol. Arizona's Capitol building has been restored to its condition in 1912, the year of Arizona's statehood. Now serving as Arizona's State Capitol Museum, the building was constructed of native Arizona stone between 1898 and 1901 to serve as the territorial capitol. The highlight of the building is the 16-foot-high "Winged Victory" crowning the copper dome. Sculpted as a weather vane, the lady has a few bullet nicks in her from turn-of-the-century marksmen. *1700 W. Washington St., Phoenix, tel. 602/542–4581. Open weekdays 8–5.*

COLORADO ROCKIES SPRING TRAINING/TUCSON TOROS

League: Cactus League • **Class:** Major League Spring Training • **Stadium:** Hi Corbett Field • **Opened:** 1937 • **Capacity:** 8,000 • **Dimensions:** LF: 366, CF: 392, RF: 348 • **Surface:** grass • **Season:** March Spring Training

STADIUM LOCATION: 3400 E. Camino Campestre, Tucson, AZ 85716

GETTING THERE: Field is in Randolph Park. From I–10, east on Broadway Blvd., right on Randolph Way; or go east on 22nd St., left on Randolph Way to E. Camino Campestre. For information about bus system, call 520/792–9222.

TICKET INFORMATION: Colorado Rockies Spring Training, Box 28830, Tucson, AZ 85775, tel. 800/388–7625; Toros, tel. 520/325–2621, fax 520/327–2371

PRICE RANGE: Spring training, home-plate grandstand $9; reserved grandstand $8; pavilion $7; midfield bleachers $5; outfield bleachers $4. Toros, box seat $6; reserved $5; general admission $4 adults, $3 children, senior citizens, and military personnel; under 6 free.

GAME TIME: Most spring training games, 1:05 PM; gates open 2 hrs before game. Toros games, Mon.–Sat. 7:30 PM, Sun. 6 or 7 PM

TIPS ON SEATING: To avoid Tucson's ever-present sun, sit under small grandstand roof in yellow seats directly behind home plate. Bright red seats between first and third base are bench seats with rounded backs, far preferable to aluminum bleacher seats beyond bases.

SEATING FOR PEOPLE WITH DISABILITIES: Directly behind home team dugout on first-base side; protected from foul balls by small chain link fence

STADIUM FOOD: The longest lines for the Rockies' concessions are at the water fountain, with fans filling bottles to drink under the Arizona sun. Eegee's $3 frozen fruit drinks are a sweet alternative, in lemon and strawberry. There's also fresh lemonade here, also for $3. At the Eegee stand on the first-base side are veggie subs and turkey grinders for $4. Personal pan pizzas are $3.75. A grill serves burgers, Polish dogs, and hot dogs. One warning: some of the soft pretzels contain jalapeño peppers that are too hot for children. At the Toros games, you'll find pizza, grilled chicken, bratwurst, ice cream in helmets, pretzels, and hot dogs. The grill is on the third-base side.

SMOKING POLICY: Smoking prohibited in seating area.

PARKING: Free parking at ballpark and a shuttle from El Con Mall

VISITING TEAM HOTEL: Viscount Suite Hotel (4855 E. Broadway Blvd., Tucson 85711, tel. 520/745–6500 or 800/527–9666)

TOURISM INFORMATION: Metropolitan Tucson Convention & Visitors Bureau (130 S. Scott Ave., Tucson, AZ 85701, tel. 520/624–1817 or 800/638–8350)

Tucson: Hi Corbett Field

Hi Corbett Field isn't a fancy 1990s ballpark like Scottsdale Stadium. After six decades of baseball history and several restorations, Hi Corbett Field is a splendid combination of old and new—efficient enough to please most 1990s fans while authentic enough for central casting. This prototype of an old-style spring-training stadium was featured in the 1989 movie *Major League*.

Hi Corbett played for a local railroad team in some of Tucson's first intracity games on Elysian Grove Field in 1907. Forty years later, his friendship with Cleveland Indians owner Bill Veeck led the Indians to establish their 1947 spring-training camp in Tucson. Corbett served for many years as the president of the Tucson Baseball Commission, and in 1951, the stadium was named for him.

A 1972 remodeling gave the ballpark a distinct Southwestern style, with a white stucco exterior wall. The current grandstand is a product of the 1972 renovation. The park was further improved in 1989 by new owner Rick Holtzman. A new press box, new right-field bleachers, a new clubhouse, and larger dugouts were added in 1993 to lure the Colorado Rockies to replace the departed Indians.

The Catalina Mountains lie behind the ballpark, but the Rincon Mountains can be seen beyond the palm trees past left field. The ballpark is in Reid Park near a golf course. The city zoo lies just beyond the right-field fence. Center field is only 392 feet from home plate, but the dark green outfield fence is monster-high, and the power alleys are deep, at 410 and 405 feet. The Southwestern stucco style predominates in the wide concourse behind the grandstand where the concessions, souvenirs, and bathrooms are located.

The Tucson Toros have played here in the Pacific Coast League since 1969. Tuffy, the Toros' mascot, is an unthreatening, child-friendly bull.

Where to Stay

Visiting Team Hotel: Viscount Suite Hotel. This striking stucco hotel has a large central courtyard with a fountain, potted palms, and seating for breakfasts and casual lunches. Local radio shows regularly host mixers and broadcast from the sports bar that adjoins the courtyard. The spacious rooms include a refrigerator and a dressing table. *4855 E. Broadway Blvd., Tucson 85711, tel. 520/745–6500 or 800/527–9666, fax 520/790–5114. 215 2-room suites. Facilities:*

2 restaurants, pool, hot tub, exercise room. D, DC, MC, V. $$

Where to Eat

Carlos Murphy's. This imposing restaurant is in the former El Paso and Southwestern Railroad depot. Built in classical style in 1913, it has a stained glass dome and a large rotunda. The restaurant is casual, serving American versions of Mexican favorites, including fish tacos and nachos. Terrific fajitas are the specialty here; you can get them made with shrimp, vegetables, shark, chicken, or beef. The full children's menu includes burritos, quesadillas, burgers, and chicken fingers. *419 W. Congress St., Tucson, tel. 520/628–1956. AE, D, MC, V. $$*

Cocina. You can eat inside this wooden, mission-style restaurant in the Old Town Historic District or in its beautifully shaded courtyard. The courtyard is part of an 1850s adobe marketplace, with hanging baskets, crafts stalls, and Native American art. The simple and inexpensive food includes Southwestern pasta salads, roasted poblano chiles, sandwiches, and mesquite-grilled fish. *201 N. Court Ave., at Meyer St., Tucson, tel. 520/622–0351. AE, D, MC, V. $$*

The Good Earth Restaurant and Bakery. This lovely, casual restaurant has an atrium filled with cacti. It serves homemade soups, pasta, beef, seafood, and several types of fruit crepes. An irresistible dessert is the mangoes with crème anglaise. *6366 E. Broadway Blvd., at Wilmot St. (El Mercado), Tucson, tel. 520/745–6600. No credit cards. $*

Entertainments

Tucson Zoo and Reid Park. A two-minute walk from the ballpark brings you to this cool, shaded zoo, threaded with streams. There are only about 300 animals, but their habitats are attractive, and visitors can get as close as 8 feet to macaws, lions, and anteaters. It's a stroller-friendly zoo, but watch for the ducks that cross your path. You may want to eat here before the ball game at the inexpensive snack bar. Reid Park also has a man-made lake with half-hour paddleboat rentals (tel. 520/791–4088; $10 deposit; four-person boats, $4.50; two-person boats, $3.75). *22nd St. and Country Club Rd., at Randolph Way, Tucson, tel. 520/791–4022. Admission: $3.50 adults, $2.50 senior citizens, 75¢ ages 5–14. Open daily 9–4.*

Tucson Children's Museum. This 1901 former Carnegie library has been transformed into a colorful, imaginative children's museum. You are welcomed by a large iron dinosaur in pink and green on the front lawn. The museum contains hands-on exhibits focusing on health and nature. *200 S. 6th Ave., Tucson, tel. 520/884–7511. Admission: $5 adults, $4 senior citizens, $3 ages 3–16. Open Tues.–Sat. 10–5, Sun. noon–5.*

Arizona State Museum. Children enjoy this free museum's display of some 20 dozen colorful Mexican masks. Located just inside the main gate of the University of Arizona, the two-story museum includes Hopi pottery, with good questions put to visitors on each display. Across the campus roadway is the Arizona Historical Society (tel. 520/628–5774), with a children's history exhibit. *949 E. 2nd St., at Park Ave., Tucson, tel. 520/628–5774. Open Mon.–Sat. 10–5, Sun. noon–5.*

Sites to See

Mission at San Xavier. Approach this Spanish mission by the slower Mission Road to see life on the Indian reservation that surrounds it. There's a rural Hispanic cemetery near the mission church, which was founded in 1692. Its vivid wall paintings are under renovation by some of the same curators who did the Sistine Chapel cleaning. Rows of prayer candles are joined by sonograms, hospital bracelets, and driver's licenses pinned to religious icons by those seeking miracles or other good fortune. Residents of the Tohonó O'odham Reservation frequently make and sell Indian fry bread outside the mission. *1950 W. San Xavier Rd., Tucson, tel. 520/294–2624. Donations appreciated. Open daily 8–6.*

ROCKY MOUNTAIN BASEBALL
DENVER, COLORADO SPRINGS, ALBUQUERQUE

Colorado's mile-high baseball provides many glorious views and lots of home runs flying through the thin mountain air. Start with the Colorado Rockies' Coors Field, a $215-million HOK-designed beauty in Denver's historic lower downtown district. While exploring the downtown near the ballpark, make sure you find baseball's best art, a funky arched sculpture titled "The Evolution of the Ball." Visit the U.S. Mint to see where 38 million coins are minted every day. The Elich Gardens amusement park, the Denver Zoo, and the State Capitol are three of Denver's other treasures.

Colorado Springs, 75 miles south of Denver on Interstate 25, is the home of the Rockies' Triple AAA franchise in the famed Pacific Coast League, the Colorado Springs Sky Sox. When you ride the Cog Railway to the top of Pikes Peak, you will be twice as high above sea level as Sky Sox Stadium. The Air Force Academy, the Pro Rodeo Hall of Fame, and the stately Broadmoor Hotel are among our favorites here.

Albuquerque, New Mexico, lies 280 miles south of Colorado Springs, but is worth the long haul. For the real experience of New Mexico's Native American culture, stop in Santa Fe, 60 miles north of Albuquerque. Nearly every building is adobe-style in Santa Fe, including one of the most unusual state capitol buildings you will ever visit.

The Albuquerque Dukes are the Los Angeles Dodgers' entry in the Pacific Coast League. The Dukes play in the Albuquerque Sports Stadium with its unique drive-in baseball, where 100 cars can park atop a wall of black lava beyond left field, 30 to 40 feet above the playing surface. The Indian Pueblo Cultural Center on the edge of Old Town lets children grind corn, weave baskets, and make jewelry in old-fashioned ways.

COLORADO ROCKIES

League: National League • **Class:** Major • **Stadium:** Coors Field • **Opened:** 1995 • **Capacity:** 50,000 • **Dimensions:** LF: 347, CF: 415, RF: 350 • **Surface:** grass • **Season:** Apr.–early Oct.

STADIUM LOCATION: 2001 Blake St., Denver, CO 80205-2000

GETTING THERE: From north, take I–25 south to exit 213/Park Ave. From east and west, take I–70 to I–25 south. Take exit 213/Park Ave. From south, take I–25 north to exit 207A/Broadway/Lincoln. Follow downtown signs. Call 303/299–6000 for information about RockiesRide—express routes from free park-n-ride lots—and other transit alternatives. A free Mall Shuttle runs along 16th St. to Market St. Station.

TICKET INFORMATION: Box 120, Denver, CO 80201-0120, tel. 303/762–5437 or 800/388–7625, fax 303/312–2219.

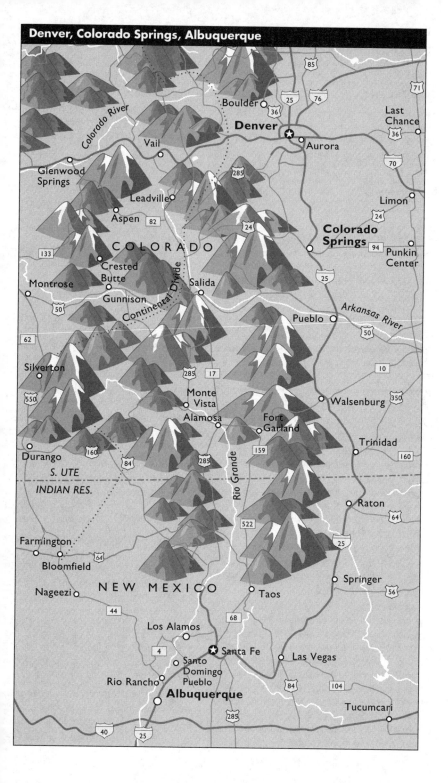

Denver, Colorado Springs, Albuquerque

PRICE RANGE: Box seats $16–$20; club level $26; reserved $6–$12; pavilion $5; Rockpile $4 (limit 4), $1 (limit 2; ages under 13 and over 54).

GAME TIME: Sun.–Fri. 7:05 PM, Sat. 6:05 PM, day games 1:05.

TIPS ON SEATING: Order tickets in advance; ballpark usually sold out. 2,300 seats in bleacher section on top of batter's eye in deep center field—called the Rockpile—go on sale 2½ hours before each game at ticket window near gate A; line forms early. To see mountains past left-field foul pole, sit on first-base side.

SEATING FOR PEOPLE WITH DISABILITIES: Available throughout stadium. Parking behind right field, accessible from Wazee and Park Ave.

STADIUM FOOD: If you have a club-level ticket, you can get a plate of Mt. Ranch pasta ($4) or a sliced turkey sandwich on a decent roll ($5.25). Otherwise, there are endless repeats of the same two pizza and hot-dog stands throughout the park. The Chicago dog at $3.50 is passable, and Itza Pizza at $3.75 tastes fine but is overpriced. You can get Rocky Mountain oysters, which are deep-fried bull testicles, but you won't want to; they're gamey and greasy. At **Madeline's,** behind center field, there are Green River drinks for $2.75 and six flavors of Dreyer's ice cream. There are also Columbo frozen yogurt, squishy frozen lemonade ($3), and beers of the world. A deli behind section 136 has chef salads, potato and pasta salad, and sandwiches. But surprisingly for Colorado, there's no Mexican food.

SMOKING POLICY: Smoking not allowed in seating areas; designated smoking areas in stadium.

PARKING: Stadium lots ($5) have entrances on Blake St. at 23rd, 27th, and 33rd Sts.; open 3 hrs before game. At private lots within blocks of stadium, $9 is about average for 6-block walk.

TOURISM INFORMATION: Denver Metro Convention & Visitors Bureau (225 W. Colfax Ave., Denver, CO 80202, tel. 303/892–1112 or 800/645–3446)

Denver: Coors Field

When Denver won a major-league baseball franchise, the Colorado Rockies played two seasons in aging Mile High Stadium, home of the Denver Broncos of the National Football League. The baseball-starved fans of the Rocky Mountain region flocked to Mile High Stadium. They were richly rewarded for their patience in 1995 with the inaugural season of a magnificent new ballpark in Denver's downtown.

Designed by HOK of Kansas City, Coors Field was built at a cost of $215.5 million. Originally designed for 43,500 fans, it was reconfigured for 45,000 and then 50,249 because of the amazing fan support of the Rockies at Mile High Stadium. The ballpark fits neatly into the historic lower downtown area known as LoDo to locals. It is on the former site of the Denver Pacific Depot, Denver's first railroad station. The exterior red brick matches the warehouses and office buildings that surround it. A huge clock sits high atop the entranceway under the American flag and between the large silver letters spelling out Coors Field. Musical groups often welcome you into the park, and official greeters help you find your way.

The field is 21 feet below street level, providing for a 350-yard main concourse encircling the field. Workers dug up a 66-million-year-old dinosaur rib bone near home plate while building the stadium.

This is a hitter's park; the ball goes 9 percent farther at Denver's mile-high altitude, and the thin air is said to flatten out pitchers' curveballs. With a small foul territory, a ball that is an out in most parks often goes home with a fan here.

There is an old-fashioned hand-operated scoreboard in right field and a huge video screen above left center field. The field is circled by deep-reddish-colored crushed lava rock that serves as the outfield warming track. The lower-deck seats at first and third bases are as close to the action as major-league baseball will allow. Seats in the front rows of the upper deck have an excellent view of the field. The Rockpile is a horseshoe-shape, 2,300-seat bleacher section high up above the batter's eye in center field.

This is a kid-friendly park with a small playground for children out past the left-field wall. Dinger, the Rockies' purple dinosaur mascot, is a friendly reminder of the stadium site's prehistoric times.

Our favorite piece of Denver baseball art is "The Evolution of the Ball" by Lonnie Hanzon. You will find this funky arched sculpture on the Wynkoop Street pedestrian way across the street from deep left field. Its 108 balls include a matzo ball, a spitball, Lucille Ball, and a mothball. Don't miss the 40 lovely terra-cotta tiles of the state flower—the columbine—designed by Barry Rose that appear at the top of the stadium's exterior columns. Walk around the front of the stadium on Blake Street to the opposite corner of the stadium complex at 22nd Street to see "The Bottom of the Ninth" by Erick Johnson. This neon and aluminum piece depicts a runner sliding into home with an umpire making a call.

Plan to take a walk inside the park. One of the best features of Coors Field is the concourse open to the field. You can get a hot dog or a drink without missing a pitch. For the best art inside the stadium, make sure you see the 100-foot-long mural out beyond center field. "The West, the Worker, and the Ballfield" by Matt O'Neill and Jeff Starr hits a few of the highlights of the history of this site from the buffalo to baseball.

The very best views in Coors Field are from the upper deck on the third-base side looking away from the field to the downtown and the mountains beyond. From way down the left-field side, you can see Mile High Stadium. Hike up to the top of the stadium and sit in one of the purple seats six rows from the top of the upper deck, 1 mile high at 5,280 feet above sea level. You'll need to bring windbreakers or plastic ponchos, as Denver frequently has short rainstorms.

Take a pregame tour of the park. The walking tours of Coors Field take about 60 minutes, cover 1 mile, and are excellent. Call 303/762–5437 for information on times.

Where to Stay

Holiday Inn–North/Coliseum. This four-story, mid-city hotel offers a game plan that may be the easiest way to get a ticket to the sold-out Rockies: $50.50 per person includes double-occupancy lodging, transportation to the game, a "premium" seat, and a full breakfast. Kids eat free with an adult. *4849 Bannock St., Exit 215 from I–25 N, Denver 80216, tel. 303/292–9500 or 800/465–4329, fax 303/295–3521. 218*

rooms. Facilities: pool, health center. AE, D, DC, MC, V. $$

Wyndham Garden Hotel. Ask for an upper mountain-view room in this high-rise hotel in a busy restaurant and hotel area in midtown Denver. The rooms are standard size. *1475 S. Colorado Blvd., Denver 80222, tel. 303/757–8797 or 800/996–3426, fax 303/758–0704. 240 rooms. Facilities: restaurant, indoor pool, coin laundry. AE, D, DC, MC, V. $$*

Best Western Landmark Inn. The upper floors in the west tower of this nine-story high-rise have mountain views. The rooms are modern and have queen-size beds. *455 S. Colorado Blvd., Exit 240 from I–25 N, Denver 80222, tel. 303/388–5561 or 800/528–1234, fax 303/388–7936. 280 rooms. Facilities: restaurant, indoor pool, hot tub, sauna, exercise room, coin laundry. AE, D, DC, MC, V. $$*

Holiday Chalet Hotel Apartments. This three-story renovated brownstone has large bedrooms with private baths, queen-size beds, kitchens, and some studio couches for children. It does not have an elevator; an advance deposit or credit-card hold is required. *1820 E. Colfax Ave., Denver 80218, tel. 303/321–9975 or 800/626–4497, fax 303/377–6556. 10 rooms. Facilities: parking (fee). AE, D, DC, MC, V. $$*

Where to Eat

Rounders at the Sandlot. You must have a ticket to the ball game to eat here. You enter through a turnstile and then step inside Rounders to see the only beer-brewing operation in a baseball stadium. The restaurant is named after a 17th-century British game that preceded baseball. Rounders offers good American café food, including salads, sandwiches, burritos, pizza, and, of course, beer. *2151 Blake St., Denver, tel. 303/312–2553. AE, D, MC, V. $$*

Rocky Mountain Diner. There is a rustic cowboy theme and healthy food at this cheerful downtown restaurant. You can get a children's menu and fresh limeade and lemonade. Do you dare try the Rocky Mountain Oysters? The sandwiches are overstuffed, and the venison chili is unusual and hot. The kids will want to try sitting in the bar's saddle barstools. *800 18th St., Denver, tel. 303/293–8383. AE, D, MC, V. $$*

Wynkoop Brewing Company. This brewpub occupies a renovated warehouse in downtown Denver, near Union Station. There's a children's menu, healthy food choices, and a very good shepherd's pie. Upstairs is a busy billiard room. *1634 18th St., Denver, tel. 303/297–2700. AE, D, MC, V. $$*

Gunther Toody's. This bright diner is spacious enough to hold a Corvette, a motorcycle, and dozens of booths. Named after one of the hapless cops on *Car 54, Where Are You?*, the restaurant dishes out slapstick in addition to good salads, phosphates, wet fries, and lumpy mashed potatoes. There are old pinball machines, joking waitresses, and funny signs throughout. *4500 E. Alameda Ave., exit on Colorado Blvd. from I–25, Denver, tel. 303/399–1959. AE, MC, V. $*

Furr's Cafeteria. This chain of inexpensive, high-quality cafeterias is a regional institution. Decorated in a Southwest theme, the western Denver branch has a kiddie buffet bar. Families fill the booths and tables, especially after church, for its chicken and dumplings, pecan surprise pie, and tapioca pudding. *4900 Kipling St., Denver, tel. 303/423–4602. AE, D, MC, V. $*

Entertainments

Elitch Gardens. This attraction relocated in 1995 to become America's only downtown amusement park. You can ride the huge 1926 Philadelphia Toboggan carousel and an old wooden coaster and see the lights of the city. There's an extensive kiddieland, but it's very strict on heights. The kiddie-roller-coaster attendants check after the first turn and ask if all riders want to continue. The pirate diving show is thrilling; the many juggling and magic shows are also good. *4620 W. 38th St, at I–25 and Speer Blvd., Denver, tel. 303/629–7712. Admission: $19.95 ages 8–54, $9.95 ages 3–7, $14 senior citizens 55–69, under 3 and over 69 free. Open mid-Apr.–Labor Day, Mon.–Thurs. 10–10, Fri.–Sat. 10–11.*

Children's Museum of Denver. This is an extensive hands-on center, with science experiments and visual games. Reserve ahead to try skiing without snow on Kidslope, where instructors give 90-minute lessons for a $6 fee. In-line skating lessons also are given to children five and older, for $8 a session. A separate theater in the

museum has a $1 entry fee. The museum is just east of the Mile High Stadium. *2121 Children's Museum Dr., I–25 at 23rd Ave. exit, Denver, tel. 303/433–7444. Admission: $4 ages 2–59, $1.50 senior citizens; free Fri. 5:30–8. Open late May–Labor Day, daily 10–5; Labor Day–late May, Mon.–Thurs. 10–5, Fri. 10–5 and 5:30–8, Sat. 10–5, Sun. noon–5.*

Denver Museum of Natural History. The emphasis is on Botswana, Egyptian mummies, dinosaurs, bears, and sea mammals at this extensive museum. Its Hall of Life health-education center is popular, with the heart's function explained in clever graphics. The Gates Planetarium and IMAX shows require extra fees. *2001 Colorado Blvd., Denver, tel. 303/370–6357. Admission: $4.50 adults, $2.50 ages 4–12. Open Labor Day–Memorial Day, daily 9–5; Memorial Day–Labor Day, Sat.–Thurs. 9–5, Fri. 9–8.*

Denver Zoo. This nicely landscaped zoo in City Park has Primate Panorama, a 5-acre primate habitat. There's an endearing nursery for baby animals. You can watch polar bears swim underwater and attend free-flight bird shows daily in summer at 11:30, 1, or 3 in the Event Meadow. The gates close an hour before closing time. *2300 Steele St., between Colorado Ave. and York St., Denver, tel. 303/331–4100. Admission: $6 adults, $3 ages 4–12 and senior citizens. Open Apr.–Sept., daily 9–6; Oct.–Mar., daily 10–5.*

Tiny Town. Built in 1915, this vintage miniature village is a hit with younger children. It includes homes, shops, church, a newspaper office, and a toy store, all constructed at one-sixth scale and in the style of the late 1800s. Guests can ride a small steam train on a mile journey throughout the 100 buildings for $1. *6249 S. Turkey Creek Rd., exit on S. Turkey Creek Rd. from Hwy. 285 S, Denver, tel. 303/697–6829. Admission: $2.50 adults, $1.50 ages 3–12. Open daily 10–5.*

Sites to See

U.S. Mint. Here 38 million coins are manufactured daily. The guides show you the stamping machines and recite some big financial numbers. Until the 1970s, many of these mounds of pennies were counted by hand. There's an old-time security guard's nest and a gift shop. Tours start every 15 minutes. Go early in the day to avoid lines for this free downtown attraction. *320 W.*

Colfax Ave., Denver, tel. 303/837–3582. Open weekdays 8–2:45.

Denver Art Museum. At this kid-friendly museum, a Kids Corner on the first floor has hands-on art activities. On each floor you'll find an Eye Spy detective game, with match-up cards at the elevators, and kids' videos and books relating to the gallery's collections. On Saturdays, families make art in the Creative Center after visiting galleries with guides at 11, 12:30, and 2. The 28-sided glass building, at the south end of the Civic Center, is an eye-opening start to the visual treasures within. *100 W. 14th Ave. Pkwy., at 14th Ave. and Bannock St., Denver, tel. 303/640–7577. Admission: $3 adults, $1.50 ages 6–18; free Sat. Open Mon.–Sat. 10–5, Sun. noon–5.*

Lower Downtown Walking Tour. Don't just drive in, see the game, and leave. Coors Field has sparked an impressive revival of Denver's lower downtown, with its warehouses and ethnic neighborhoods. For a "Lower Downtown Walking Tour" brochure and information about events, call the Lower Downtown District, Inc. (tel. 303/628–5428).

The Capitol. The Colorado Capitol is based on the classic Corinthian design of the nation's Capitol in Washington. Construction began in 1886 but was not completed for 22 years, in part because of a strong commitment to using state materials. The exterior walls are Gunnison granite, the foundation is sandstone from Fort Collins, and the floors and stairs are marble from a town called Marble. Be sure to see the stained-glass windows in the old Supreme Court chambers and "Women's Gold," a hand-stitched wallhanging that tells the stories of Colorado's most prominent women. For a fabulous view of the Rocky Mountains, visit the observation deck in the 272-foot gold dome, up 93 winding steps from the third floor. Denver is known as the Mile High City, and there is a granite step on the west side of the Capitol identified as "ONE MILE ABOVE SEA LEVEL." In 1969, engineering students from Colorado State University found the designation inaccurate. A geodetic survey marker three steps above the original one indicates the real mile-high point. *Colfax Ave. and Lincoln St., Denver, tel. 303/829–2604. Open weekdays 7:30–5:30; tours and observation deck, weekdays 9–3:30 and Sat. June–Aug. 9:30–2:30*

The Colorado History Museum. Run by the Colorado Historical Society, it's just blocks from the Capitol. You can see an authentic sod house, a gold rush-era log cabin, and displays on early Colorado settlers and achievers. *13th Ave. and Broadway, Denver, tel. 303/866–3682. Admission: $3 adults, $1.50 ages 6–16. Open Mon.–Sat. 10–4:30, Sun. noon–4:30.*

Unusual Shopping

Colorado Rockies Dugout Store. This souvenir store is open year-round, with merchandise and autographed memorabilia. *1730 Sherman St., 2½ blocks north of Capitol, Denver, tel. 303/832–8326.*

The Show. Major League teamwear, sports collectibles, pennants, and cards are sold at this first-rate sports specialty shop near Coors Field. *1925 Blake St., Denver, tel. 303/293–3698.*

COLORADO SPRINGS SKY SOX

League: Pacific Coast League • **Major League Affiliation:** Colorado Rockies • **Class:** AAA • **Stadium:** Sky Sox Stadium • **Opened:** 1989 • **Capacity:** 6,200 • **Dimensions:** LF: 350, CF: 410, RF: 350 • **Surface:** grass • **Season:** Apr.–Labor Day

STADIUM LOCATION: 4385 Tutt Blvd., Colorado Springs, CO 80922

GETTING THERE: From Denver, I–25 S. to Woodmen Rd. exit. Turn left, east on Woodmen 5 mi. Right on Powers Blvd., go 3 mi, left on Barnes Rd.

TICKET INFORMATION: tel. 719/597–3000, fax 719/597–2491

PRICE RANGE: Box seats $6 adults, $5 ages over 59 and under 13; general admission $4 adults, $3 ages under 13 and over 59

GAME TIME: Apr.–mid-June, weekdays 6:35 PM, Sat. 1:35 PM; mid-June–Labor Day, Mon.–Sat. 7:05 PM, Sun. 1:35 PM; gates open 1 hr early.

TIPS ON SEATING: Seats on third-base side have view of Pikes Peak (behind first base) but face sun during early innings of night games.

SEATING FOR PEOPLE WITH DISABILITIES: On main concourse under canopy

STADIUM FOOD: Mexican food is the standout here, with excellent beef and chicken burritos at the **Casa Llenas** stand for $2.50. The hottest food in baseball has to be the jala bumpers, deep fried jalapeño peppers with cheese (50¢). Also on the menu are chicken wings, brats, and espresso. Because the manager is from Philadelphia, you can buy Tastykake cupcakes here. Also from Pennsylvania are huge, toothsome funnel cakes for $2.50. Once the game starts, anyone is welcome in the **Hall of Fame Bar and Restaurant**; it's worth a trip to get the chicken Caesar salad with crackers for $5.

SMOKING POLICY: General-admission section behind home plate and box seats section (section 100) near third base are no-smoking.

PARKING: At stadium, $3

VISITING TEAM HOTEL: Best Western Le Baron Hotel (314 W. Bijou St., Colorado Springs, CO 80905, tel. 719/471–8680 or 800/528–1234)

TOURISM INFORMATION: Colorado Springs Convention & Visitors Bureau (104 S. Cascade Ave., Colorado Springs, CO 80901, tel. 719/635–1632 or 800/888–4747)

Colorado Springs: Sky Sox Stadium

The state-of-the-art in stadium design improved so dramatically in the early 1990s that it bypassed Sky Sox Stadium, built in 1988. The design is one used by several stadiums in the late 1980s. It has three great attributes for fans: The food is on the concourse above the seats so you don't have to miss the action; the players have to walk up stairs just beyond the seating areas at third and first bases after batting practice, so even the shyest child can bring home a ball full of autographs; and just past these stairs on each side are grassy berms for kids to roam and chase foul balls. At Sky Sox Stadium, they have 2,200 box seats and room for 4,000 in general admission bench seating with backs. Eighteen skyboxes are built over the roof above the concourse.

The night we attended, more than 7,000 fans poured into Sky Sox Stadium to see their local heroes win their 14th straight game and take over first place in the competitive Pacific Coast League in a game televised nationally by ESPN. It was about 1,500 fans more than the stadium handles comfortably. The food lines packed the concourse above the seating while hundreds of general-admission fans sat on the grass berms beyond first and third.

Sky Sox Stadium claims to be the highest ballpark in North America; it is a full 1,000 feet above Denver's Coors Field, and there were plenty of home runs flying through the thin mountain air—six by the Sky Sox—when we were there. Fireworks go off beyond the left center scoreboard after the National Anthem, at the seventh-inning stretch, and after every Sox home run and victory—nine times the night we visited.

In 1901, the Colorado Springs baseball team was called the Millionaires in tribute to the local residents who had made their fortunes mining nearby hills and mountains. The current Sky Sox draw their name from the high altitude and a long association with the Chicago White Sox in the 1950s when Colorado Springs was in the now-defunct Western League.

From the seats on the third-base side, fans can see the front range of the Rocky Mountains. Pikes Peak—14,110 feet above sea level and twice as high as Sky Sox Stadium—is visible. At night, look over first base and way beyond for a light—it's at the Summit House at the top of the peak.

We were here on a gorgeous day in late July, and it was chilly. Wear long pants and take a sweater or coat. When the sun drops behind the mountains, the air cools off quickly.

We found Colorado Springs—both the city and the ballpark—an odd combination of trendy and backward. There is a hot tub near the right-field foul pole. Eight fans pay big bucks for dinner, champagne, and baseball. You have to wonder what the attraction is on a cool Colorado Springs night.

Where to Stay

Visiting Team Motel: Best Western Le Baron Hotel. The back of this three-story downtown hotel is built around a courtyard, with a large pool and gazebo. Most of its rooms are standard doubles, with contemporary furnishings. *314 W. Bijou St., at Exit 142 off I–25, Colorado Springs 80905, tel. 719/471–8680 or 800/528–1234, fax 719/471–0894. 206 rooms. Facilities: restaurant, pool, coin laundry. AE, D, DC, MC, V. $$*

Mel Haven Lodge. Reserve in advance for this small, clean facility, which is set up for families as summer weekends sell out. Some rooms on the second floor have nice views of Pikes Peak or the Garden of the Gods. Equipped kitchens are available for an extra fee. *3715 W. Colorado Ave., Colorado Springs 80904, tel. 719/633–9435 or 800/762–5832, fax 719/633–9435. 21 rooms. Facilities: grills, pool, hot tub, playground, coin laundry. AE, D, MC, V. $*

Dale Motel. This old-fashioned two-story bargain motel has a pool and is convenient to the freeway, downtown, and attractions. The rooms are clean, with dated furnishings, and have writing alcoves. Kitchens are available in six rooms for an extra fee. *620 W. Colorado Ave., Exit 142 off I–25, Colorado Springs 80905, tel. 719/636–3721 or 800/456–3204. 29 rooms. Facilities: pool. AE, D, DC, MC, V. $*

Where to Eat

Conway's Red Top. All three Red Tops in the city serve huge (dinner-plate-size) hamburgers, fine fries, and a good beef stew. Children should get the half-burgers. These casual restaurants with Formica booths concentrate on a few items done well. *1520 S. Nevada St., at Navaho St., Colorado Springs, tel. 719/633–2444. MC, V. $*

The Mason Jar. This antiques-filled family restaurant has a peaceful atmosphere. You can have chicken-fried steak, real mashed potatoes, and excellent home-style fruit cobblers. There is a children's menu. Drinks are served in mason jars. *2925 W. Colorado Ave., Colorado Springs, tel. 719/632–4820. Open daily 11–10. D, MC, V. $*

The Broadmoor. It's too pricey for most to stay in this sprawling Italian Renaissance–style hotel, built in 1918, in the foothills of the Rockies. You can eat lunch at the casual Grill Room (in the main golf club) or Julie's (at Broadmoor West, across the lake) or have pastries at Espresso Broadmoor (in the main lobby) and view the resort. Afternoon tea is served in the mezzanine daily from May through October from 4 to 5 and November through April on Fridays and Saturdays. There are ducks on a man-made lake and paddleboats for hire. Non-guests may pay to swim here. *Lake Ave. and Circle Dr., 2 mi west of I–25, Colorado Springs, tel. 719/634–7711 or 800/634–7711. AE, D, DC, MC, V. $$*

Entertainments

The Colorado Springs Visitors Bureau will give you $100 worth of discount coupons for many attractions if you stop in at the visitor center (104 S. Cascade Ave., Suite 104, Colorado Springs, tel. 800/368–4748; open weekdays 8:30–5).

Pro Rodeo Hall of Fame and Museum of the American Cowboy. Watch a clever movie with an audiovisual cowboy and climb on models of rodeo horses. This handsome museum lets you gawk at the intricate saddles and achievements of the men and women who are and were daredevils on horseback. The informative and classy Hall of Fame includes movie cowboy Gene Autry, owner of the California Angels and former semipro ballplayer. It contains a great gift shop with many imaginative and inexpensive items. *101 Pro Rodeo Dr., Colorado Springs, tel. 719/528–4764. Admission: $6 adults, $3 ages 5–12, $5 senior citizens. Open daily 9–5.*

Cheyenne Mountain Zoo. A wolf exhibit, 500 animals, and a merry-go-round are what you'll find here. Visitors can drive up the Tutt Scenic Highway to the Shrine of the Sun, a monument to Will Rogers. The zoo is at the base of Cheyenne Mountain. Entry gates close one hour before closing time. *4250 Cheyenne Mountain Zoo Rd., Exit 128 from I–25, Colorado Springs, tel. 719/475–9555. Admission: $6.50* adults, $3.50 ages 3–11, $5.50 senior citizens. Open Memorial Day–Labor Day, daily 9–6; Labor Day–Memorial Day, daily 9–5.

Pikes Peak Cog Railway. You'll need to dress warmly for this three-hour journey to the 14,110-foot top of Pike's Peak. You can see the Garden of the Gods below you as well as Denver, which is 75 miles to the north. Passengers have a half hour to explore the peak before returning. There is a café at the depot. Train reservations are advised; passengers should arrive 30 minutes before departure. Trains depart every 80 minutes. *515 Ruxton Ave., Manitou Springs, tel. 719/685–5401. Admission: $21 adults, $9.50 ages 5–11; under 5 free if held on adult's lap. Open daily 8–5:20.*

Sites to See

U.S. Air Force Academy. The architecture is striking and the feeling of isolation is strong at this impressive service academy. Visitors are permitted in the chapel, the field house, the planetarium, and the cadet social center. The chapel is open for services Sunday mornings at 9 and 11. Jewish services that are open to the public are held Friday at 8 PM. On Monday through Friday, visitors may watch the cadets line up in the Noon Meal Formation. The visitor center contains a theater, a gift shop, and a snack bar. *I–25, Exit 156B, Colorado Springs, tel. 719/333–2025. Open daily 9–6.*

Garden of the Gods. This free city park has magnificent red sandstone formations that are more than 300 million years old. Shaped by erosion, the rocks cover 1,350 acres. Visitors may hike or picnic among the unusual geology and plant life. Entry is free, but the visitor center requests donations. Take I–25 west at Garden of the Gods Road to 30th Street. *Garden of the Gods Rd., Colorado Springs, tel. 719/578–6939. Open May–Oct., daily 5 AM–11 PM; Nov.–Apr., daily 5 AM–9 PM.*

U.S. Olympic Complex. Take a free guided tour of the Olympic Training Facility that serves 15,000 athletes yearly. The 90-minute tour includes a film and access to the gym, aquatic, and training centers. *1750 E. Boulder St., Colorado Springs, tel. 719/578–4644. Open Mon.–Sat. 9–5, Sun. 10–4.*

World Figure Skating Hall of Fame. Nancy Kerrigan, Sonja Henie, Dick Button, and Dorothy Hamill are among those honored in this free museum, which adjoins the headquarters of the U.S. Figure Skating Association. Costumes, videos of various choreographed works, skates, and medals are on display. There is a library and archives downstairs and a small gift shop. The museum is a half mile northeast of the Broadmoor Resort. *20 1st St., Colorado Springs, tel. 719/635–5200. Open Mon.–Sat. 10–4.*

ALBUQUERQUE DUKES

League: Pacific Coast League • **Major League Affiliation:** Los Angeles Dodgers • **Class:** AAA • **Stadium:** Albuquerque Sports Stadium • **Opened:** 1969 • **Capacity:** 10,510 • **Dimensions:** LF: 360, CF: 410, RF: 340 • **Surface:** grass • **Season:** Apr.–Labor Day

STADIUM LOCATION: 1601 Stadium Blvd. SE, Albuquerque, NM 87106

TEAM WEB SITE: http://www.fanlink.com/albq_dukes

GETTING THERE: I–25 to Stadium Blvd. exit. East several blocks on Stadium Blvd.

TICKET INFORMATION: 1601 Stadium Blvd. SE, Albuquerque, NM 87106, tel. 505/243–1791, fax 505/842–0561

PRICE RANGE: Box seats $5; general admission $4 adults, $3.50 students and senior citizens, $2 ages 6–12; drive-in $3.50 adults, $2 children

GAME TIME: Mon.–Sat. 7 PM; Sun. 1 PM; gates open 1 hr before game.

TIPS ON SEATING: General admission seats in grandstand are fine. Sit on third-base side to avoid sun in your eyes and to get a better view of mountains.

SEATING FOR PEOPLE WITH DISABILITIES: On concourse just behind box seats

STADIUM FOOD: In this park, the servings are large, prices are low, and the selections limited. The souvenir cups are huge—$2.50 for a huge lemonade, non-alcoholic piña colada, or soda. Regular-size drinks are $1, including an orange whippee (like an Orange Julius). Hamburgers are a bargain at $1.75, hot dogs at $1.50, and burritos at $2. The always refreshing lemon chill is $2.50. Churros and popcorn are $1 each.

SMOKING POLICY: Smoking prohibited in seating areas. Designated areas in lower concourse near rest rooms, behind left-field bleachers, and in drive-in area.

PARKING: $1 at stadium lots and free across street in parking lot of University of New Mexico football stadium

VISITING TEAM HOTEL: Plaza Inn Albuquerque (900 Medical Arts NE, Albuquerque, NM 87106, tel. 505/243–5693 or 800/237–1307)

TOURISM INFORMATION: Albuquerque Convention & Visitors Bureau (Box 26866, Albuquerque, NM 87125, tel. 505/842–9918 or 800/733–9918)

Albuquerque: Sports Stadium

In 1705, the Viceroy of New Spain, Francisco Fernández de la Cueva Enríquez, the Duque de Albuquerque, sent a temporary acting governor to Santa Fe. The next year, the agent founded what is now Albuquerque, New Mexico. In 1915, the Albuquerque Dukes competed in the Class D Rio Grande Association. Albuquerque began a long association with the Los Angeles Dodgers in 1963, first as a Double AA Texas League team. In 1972, under the direction of manager Tommy Lasorda, the Dukes became the Dodgers' Triple AA team in the Pacific Coast League.

"We're not into nuttiness. We're into baseball," Pat McKernan, the longtime Dukes president and general manager says. That pretty much sums up what you get at the Albuquerque Sports Stadium. No dizzy bat contests or mascots here. The Dukes play some of the very best baseball in the minor leagues, winning the Triple AAA Pacific Coast League championship six times since McKernan took over in 1980.

The Albuquerque Sports Stadium was a state-of-the-art stadium when it was built in 1969 to replace the WPA-era Tingley Field. It is showing its age. Sports Stadium—a city-owned stadium across the street from the athletic complex of the University of New Mexico—seats more than 10,000. This is a formidable baseball place in the tradition of Richmond's Diamond and Pawtucket's McCoy Stadium. The large grandstand has 2,528 box seats and 3,714 general admission seats. There is a live organist, but there aren't any skyboxes. The gray roof covers many of the general admission seats in the grandstand. Down the third-base side, there is a huge football-like bleacher area—aluminum benches without backs—with seating for 4,254 fans. The grassy area down the first-base line is not open to fans unless the crowd exceeds 10,000. The Sandia Mountains rise beyond right center field.

The bathrooms and concession stands are in the dark, not very fan-friendly concourse under the grandstand. There isn't anything fancy or innovative here—just traditional baseball food. We did find the largest souvenir cups with the best prices for beverages anywhere in baseball.

The Albuquerque Sports Stadium offers the only drive-in baseball in the professional ranks. They dug 320,000 cubic yards of earth in 10 days to create a stadium bowl, so that the stands sit above the field, especially beyond the outfield fences. There is room for more than 100 cars to pay and park just beyond the outfield fences. People come early for tailgating and barbecue, bringing blankets, lawn chairs, and grills. No alcohol is allowed in the drive-in area. Home runs into or over the drive-in area are frequent. The 30- to 40-foot drop from the car level to the field level is a wall of black lava rock quarried from volcanoes near the city.

Another special treat is the general manager's office on the lower concourse, directly across from the main food stand. In the program, Pat

McKernan invites fans to drop by to talk. And he means it. You might have to wait a few minutes—a Los Angeles Dodgers executive was arranging to bring a Duke to the majors when we knocked on McKernan's door. You will find a true baseball man in a comfortable and cluttered office with walls covered with family photos, fish, and baseball memorabilia.

Where to Stay

Visiting Team Motel: Plaza Inn Albuquerque. Children stay free at this five-story, white-brick former Howard Johnson's motel, which sits on a hilltop overlooking the West Valley. The standard-size rooms, which have small balconies, were remodeled in 1993. At night the motel is aglow in twinkling white lights. There's a restaurant next door. *900 Medical Arts Ave. NE, at I-25 and Lomas Blvd., Albuquerque 87102, tel. 505/243–5693 or 800/237–1307, fax 505/843–6229. 120 rooms. Facilities: pool, exercise room, coin laundry. AE, D, MC, V. $*

Traveler's Inn. This bargain four-story hotel is in a quiet industrial neighborhood downtown. The beds are queen-size and the rooms freshly furnished. The surroundings aren't scenic, but the price is right for this pleasant hotel. *411 McKnight Ave. NW; exit I-40 at 4th or 2nd Sts.; Albuquerque 87102, tel. 505/242–5228 or 800/633–8300, fax 505/766–9218. 100 rooms. Facilities: pool, hot tub. AE, D, DC, MC, V. $*

Where to Eat

M & J Restaurant. This city favorite has a kids' menu and great burritos, sopapillas, and warm corn chips. The tortillas are wonderfully fresh, as the Sanitary Tortilla Factory is part of this smoke-free restaurant. *403 2nd St. SW, Central Ave. exit from I-25, Albuquerque, tel. 505/242–4890. No credit cards. Closed Sun. $*

Frontier. Across the street from the University of New Mexico, this busy student standby is known for its butter-drenched pale sweet rolls. Come for breakfast and get fresh orange juice and breakfast burritos. The food is cheap, the Formica-tabled restaurant is open 24 hours, and the clients are loyal. *2400 Central Ave. SE, at Cornell St., Albuquerque, tel. 505/266–0550. MC, V. $*

Powdrell's Barbeque. A former home has been renovated into a restaurant with very good barbecue slathered with a sauce handed down in the Powdrell family since 1870. You can enjoy smoked meats of all kinds—beef, pork, chicken, ribs, and sausages. Miniplates are available for children with one meat, one side dish, and Texas toast. The cobblers are a bit too sweet, but you'll be too full to try them or the sweet-potato pie anyway. *5209 4th St. NW, Albuquerque, tel. 505/345–8086. MC, V. $*

Entertainments

Indian Pueblo Cultural Center. This museum, gallery, gift shop, and restaurant is owned by the 19 Pueblo tribes of New Mexico. Youngsters can grind corn, weave baskets, and dress in shawls, bandoliers, bells, and fox tails in the hands-on children's center. Try your hand at making heishi jewelry the pre-electric way and learn to use an Indian bow and arrow. Native dancers perform on Saturday and Sunday at 11 and 2. You can also get directions here on how to tour the existing pueblos in the area. *2401 12th St. NW, 1 block north of I-40, Albuquerque, tel. 505/843–7270 or 800/766–4405. Admission: $3 adults, $2 senior citizens, $1 students; under 6 free. Museum open daily 9–5:30; children's center, Tues. and Thurs.–Fri. 9–4, Wed. 9–12:30, occasional Sat. 10–2.*

New Mexico Museum of Natural History. This small museum in Old Town allows you to walk through a volcano, stand on a pretend earthquake, and marvel at real-size dinosaurs. Children skip through it quickly, learning about the geology of the region. Films on the hour are an extra $4 for adults, $2 for children. Cheaper combination tickets are available. *Mountain Rd. NW, at 18th St. NW, Albuquerque, tel. 505/841–8837. Admission: $4 adults, $1 ages 3–11. Open daily 9–5.*

Sandia Peak Tramway. Travel nearly 3 miles on the world's longest aerial tramway to Sandia Peak in Cibola National Forest. Trams leave every 20 to 30 minutes; count on a round-trip time of 1½ hours. There are mountain-bike trails and rental bikes and skiing in the winter. Tramway passengers often see hang-gliders and hot-air balloonists. If you have reservations to eat at the High Finance Restaurant (tel. 505/243–9742), at the peak, or the Firehouse restaurant (tel. 505/856–3473), at the base, the adult tram fees drop to $10. There's also a sandwich shop, Yogi's, at the lower tramway terminal. *Tramway Blvd., Exit 234 off I–25, Albuquerque, tel. 505/856–7325. Admission: $13.50 adults, $10 ages 5–12 and senior citizens; earlybird discount fare (9–11 AM) $10 adults, $8.50 ages 5–12 and senior citizens. Open Memorial–Labor Day, daily 9 AM–10 PM.*

Rio Grande Zoo. View an extraordinarily large number of species, from white tigers to gorillas, in one of the country's least expensive zoos. The reptiles and rain-forest animals are particularly good. From April through September, a bird show is presented. *903 10th St. SW, Albuquerque, tel. 505/843–7413. Admission: $4.25 adults, $2.25 ages 3–15 and senior citizens. Open weekdays 9–5, weekends 9–6.*

Sites to See

Route 66. Central Avenue is one section of famous Route 66. There are Art Deco storefronts, decorative metal signposts, and the 66 Diner (1405 Central Ave. NE, Albuquerque, tel. 505/247–1421), in a former Phillips 66 gas station, with a jukebox and vintage Route 66 photographs on the walls. It's worth driving through this section of Albuquerque to learn about the Mother Road. At night, look for the El Vado Motel's (2500 Central Ave. SW, near Old Town Plaza) neon Indian sign. It dates from 1937 and is a beauty.

Santa Fe. The state capital, just 60 miles north of Albuquerque, is well worth a visit. New Mexico's Native American culture dates back centuries. The area was a Spanish colony for more than 250 years until 1821, when Mexico declared its independence and New Mexico became a province of Mexico. It became a United States Territory in 1850, soon after the Mexican-American War, and our 47th state in 1912.

The Palace of Governors, built in 1610, was the center of Spanish, Mexican, and American governments for several centuries. The Palace, which contains the State History Museum, stands in Santa Fe's downtown on the north side of the Plaza. *Palace Ave., Santa Fe, tel. 515/827–6483.*

The New Mexico State Capitol. Completed in 1967 and renovated in 1992, this is one of the most modern capitols in the nation. As with most other buildings in Santa Fe, the building's exterior is a tan stucco in the adobe style. The round structure is patterned after the Zia Indian Sun Symbol, with four entrances representing the four rays of the symbol. The only accommodation to more traditional, Greek Revival capitol architecture is the columns around the building. Look for the Great Seal of the State of New Mexico, inlaid in turquoise and brass, in the floor of the rotunda. *Old Santa Fe Terr. and Paseo de Peralta, Santa Fe, tel. 505/827–3050. Open weekdays 8–5; free tours weekdays at 10 and 3.*

Loretto Chapel. The Sisters of Loretto dedicated their chapel in 1878, but it lacked space for a staircase to the choir loft. A gray-haired carpenter arrived, built a staircase with two complete 360-degree turns, and left without being paid. See his wood masterpiece and wonder. *207 Old Santa Fe Trail, Santa Fe, tel. 505/982–0092. Admission: $1. Open Mon.–Sat. 8–6, Sun. 10:30–5.*

COWBOYS AND OIL WELLS
SAN ANTONIO, ARLINGTON, OKLAHOMA CITY

24

Texas baseball goes back to the 1880s, when some fans packed six-shooters at the games. The best of Texas baseball now is played in brand-new ballparks that reflect the local cultures. San Antonio's Wolff Stadium is as modern as they come, but in an attractive Spanish Mission style, complete with twin bell towers at the entrance. Whether you eat a catcher's mitt pita sandwich or a beef fajita, make sure you leave room for roasted corn-on-the cob, one of baseball's best food treats. The Missions are the Dodgers' entry in the Double AA Texas League.

There is too much for families to explore in a single day in spectacular San Antonio, with its signature Riverwalk and historic missions. Your children will learn history on your visit to the Alamo, the oldest and most famous of the missions, later turned into a fort, where 187 men died fighting for Texas independence from Mexico. On your 190-mile drive north on Interstate 35 to the Fort Worth-Dallas area, stop in Austin, a booming college and state-government town full of energy and history.

Arlington, Texas, is a stop on the turnpike between Dallas and Fort Worth where builders put the airport, the theme parks, and the ballpark. In 1994, The Ballpark in Arlington opened here. Lacking the downtown location that has made the new Baltimore, Cleveland, and Denver ballparks so successful didn't seem a problem to Texans. They simply built a steel and glass office building right in the stadium. On the state fairgrounds in Dallas, you'll find activities for children, including a comprehensive science museum and a small aquarium.

Oklahoma City is 160 miles north of Dallas on Interstate 35. The Oklahoma City 89ers got their name from the land rush that first settled this city in 1889. The 89ers, who represent the Texas Rangers in the Triple AAA American Association, play in the aging All Sports Stadium at the state fairgrounds, but will move to a new stadium in the historic downtown in 1998. Residents aren't bashful about their allegiance to oil; the State Capitol is surrounded by working oil wells. Don't miss the wonderful National Softball Hall of Fame during your visit here.

SAN ANTONIO MISSIONS

League: Texas League • **Major League Affiliation:** Los Angeles Dodgers • **Class:** AA • **Stadium:** Wolff Stadium • **Opened:** 1994 • **Capacity:** 6,300 • **Dimensions:** LF: 310, CF: 402, RF: 340 • **Surface:** grass • **Season:** Apr.–Labor Day

STADIUM LOCATION: 5757 Hwy. 90 W., San Antonio, TX 78227

GETTING THERE: From downtown, I–35 south to Hwy. 90 west. 6 mi to Callaghan Rd. exit. Stadium at intersection of I–90 and Callaghan.

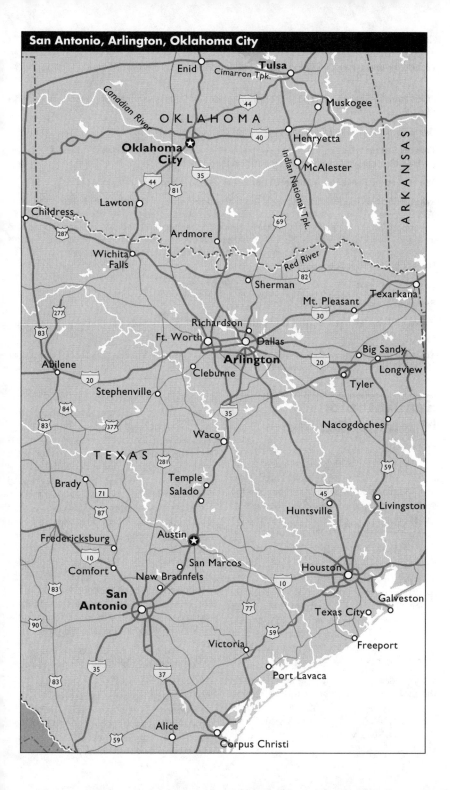

TICKET INFORMATION: 5757 Hwy. 90 W., San Antonio, TX 78227, tel. 210/675–7275, fax 210/670–0001

PRICE RANGE: Executive box $8; box seats $7; upper box $6; reserved seats $5; general admission $4 adults, $2 ages under 13

GAME TIME: Mon.–Sat. 7:05 PM, Sun. 6:05 PM; gates open 1 hr before game.

TIPS ON SEATING: Upper box seat preferable, as reserved seating uncomfortable. Arrive early and get general-admission seats near field down first- and third-base lines.

SEATING FOR PEOPLE WITH DISABILITIES: In many sections throughout stadium

STADIUM FOOD: There is a wide array of foods here, from excellent marinated beef and chicken fajitas ($2.75) to roasted corn on the cob ($2.25) and huge, fabulous pickles ($1). Roasted turkey legs are $4 and are too large for a young child to finish. A pita filled with ground beef and chili and topped with cheese is called a Catcher's Mitt ($3.50). It's messy, as is the Frito Pie, which has the same ingredients minus the pita ($2.25). There are also gyros ($3.25), which are easy for children to eat, and pizza ($1.75). The grill is on the third-base side.

SMOKING POLICY: One no-smoking, no-alcohol family section

PARKING: Available, $2

VISITING TEAM HOTEL: Thrifty Inn–Northwest (I–10 at Wurzbach, San Antonio, Tx 78230, tel. 210/696–0810 or 800/325–8300)

TOURISM INFORMATION: San Antonio Convention & Visitors Bureau (Box 2277, San Antonio, TX 78298, tel. 210/270–8700 or 800/447–3372)

San Antonio: Municipal Stadium

The Texas League was a wild and woolly affair right from its start in 1888, with teams in Austin, Dallas, Fort Worth, Galveston, Houston, and San Antonio. Wild Bill Setley, an umpire in 1910, said: "I've seen them wear six-shooters to games in the Texas League, and when a fan pulled one out in Fort Worth and took a shot at a fly ball, I was ready to check out."

Fans in the Dallas, Fort Worth, and Houston areas now cheer for major-league teams. Of the six charter members, only San Antonio remains in the Texas League. The team has gone by many different nicknames in its long history, but the one they use now—Missions—has the longest tradition and best represents San Antonio's rich history.

Wolff Stadium, opened in 1994 and named for the mayor who helped get it built, is reminiscent of the old Mission Stadium used from 1947 to 1964. This gorgeous new stadium is in the mission style, with twin bell towers at the entrance.

Designed by Ford, Carson & Powell of San Antonio, Wolff Stadium now has 6,300 permanent seats, but more than 8,000 showed up the night we were there and were plenty comfortable. The stadium—built in 194 days for $10.5 million—has a grassy berm down the left-field line. In San Antonio, the berm also goes beyond the fence in left field, serving as grass bleachers. These areas have room for 3,000 fans, but are likely to be replaced with seats within the next few years, given the popularity of the Missions. There is a large, state-of-the art, almost-Alamo-shape scoreboard in right field. The reserved seats at the back of the grandstand, covered by a roof, are aluminum benches with backs but not enough leg room. The general-admission seats down the baselines are really close to the action but are taken soon after the gates open.

You would pay to be a pitcher here. A stiff breeze from the Gulf blows from right center field toward home plate.

Wolff Stadium has a spectacular sound system and wonderful, eclectic taste in music. The crowd—mixed almost equally Anglos and Hispanics—was really into the music and the game as the music switched rapidly from country to

Sinatra to Motown to salsa. Puffy Taco—with a tomato head and jalapeño feet—is a perfect mascot. Puffy comes out in the sixth inning and races around the bases, always letting a young fan tackle him just before home plate.

Don't miss the Wall of Fame near the Mission's souvenir shop. Hall of Famers Brooks Robinson and Joe Morgan both played their Texas League ball here. San Antonio has been a Los Angeles Dodgers farm team since 1977.

Where to Stay

This is one of the few cities with a multitude of historic hotels in a concentrated downtown area.

Visiting Team Hotel: Thrifty Inn—Northwest. This 25-year-old motel was fully renovated in 1991. Its large rooms are well kept and furnished with contemporary drapes and spreads. Guests receive a free Continental breakfast. *9806 I–10 W., at Wurzbach Rd., San Antonio, TX 78230, tel. 210/696–0810 or 800/325–8300, fax 210/696–0810. 93 rooms. Facilities: outdoor pool, wading pool. AE, D, MC, V. $$*

Menger Hotel. This beautiful, historic hotel is opposite The Alamo. Built in 1859, it has five floors of luxurious rooms, many with refrigerators. *204 Alamo Plaza, San Antonio, TX 78205, tel. 210/223–4361 or 800/345–9285, fax 210/228–0022. 320 rooms. Facilities: restaurant, heated pool, sauna, whirlpool, parking (fee). AE, D, DC, MC, V. $$$*

Ramada Emily Morgan Hotel. This grand older hotel is across from The Alamo. Its 12 stories offer fine views of the city. Most of the rooms have Jacuzzi tubs and refrigerators. *705 E. Houston, San Antonio, TX 78205, tel. 210/225–8486 or 800/228–2828, fax 210/225–7227. 177 rooms. Facilities: outdoor pool, saunas, whirlpool, exercise room. AE, D, DC, MC, V. $$*

Best Western Historic Crockett Hotel. This is yet another grand, classic hotel within feet of The Alamo. Its huge atrium lobby has a waterfall. The spacious rooms have reproduction antique furniture. The grounds are nicely landscaped, and there's a seventh-floor sundeck with a Jacuzzi. *320 Bonham, San Antonio, TX 78205, tel. 210/225–6500 or 800/292–1050, fax 210/225–6251. 206 rooms. Facilities: restaurant, pool,*

whirlpool, coin laundry, parking (fee). AE, D, DC, MC, V. $$

Where to Eat

The Pig Stand. This is the start of America's first drive-in restaurant chain. It's the originator of Texas toast, onion rings, and car hops. You can get burgers, chicken fried steak, Western omelets, black cows, and frosted root beer here. Table jukeboxes and vintage neon signs serve as wall art. *1508 Broadway, San Antonio, tel. 210/222–2794; 801 S. Presa St., tel. 210/227–1691; 3054 Rigsby Ave., tel. 210/333–8231. AE, D, MC, V. $*

Earl Abels. A city institution for 64 years, Abels's slogan is "Is Everything All Right?" This is American comfort food. You can sit at its long counter or have table service. There is a children's menu. *4200 Broadway, at Hildebrand Ave., San Antonio, tel. 210/822–3358. AE, D, DC, MC, V. $$*

Boudro's on the Riverwalk. Imaginative Southwestern food is served at this restaurant, one of dozens lining the city's Riverwalk. You can eat at a sidewalk table or inside in one of the two dining rooms. *421 E. Commerce St., San Antonio, tel. 210/224–8484. AE, D, MC, V. $$*

Landry's Seafood House. The fish is fresh and cooked any way you can imagine it at this cheery family restaurant. There is a children's menu, and you get free downtown parking when you eat here. *600 E. Market St., San Antonio, tel. 210/229–1010. AE, D, MC, V. $$*

Entertainments

Call or visit the **Visitor's Center** (317 Alamo Plaza, San Antonio, TX 78205, tel. 800/447–3372; open 8:30–6), to get valuable discounts to area attractions.

Riverwalk/Paseo del Rio. This system of walkways is romantic at night, bustling by day. Dozens of sidewalk restaurants and shops line the river. On sunny days you can walk, ducking under shade, rather than ride in the open river barges. Two walking-tour brochures are offered by the San Antonio Conservation Society (tel. 210/224–6163).

Kiddie Park. This small amusement park in Brackenridge Park contains a 1918 Hershell Spillman carousel and nine other rides. On the edge of Brackenridge Park at Broadway and Mulberry Sts., also is **Kiddieland,** which is careworn but only 50¢ a ride. It is good for small children and has a Little Dipper roller coaster and a small carousel. *Brackenridge Park, 3015 Broadway, San Antonio, tel. 210/824–4351. Open 10–10.*

San Antonio Children's Museum. There is a gravity wall, a child-sized tour trolley, a pretend bank, a toddler play center, and a build-a-building area in this small, imaginative museum. Conservation, anatomy, and computers are emphasized in its displays. *305 E. Houston, San Antonio. tel. 210/212–4453. Admission: $3; under 3 free. Open Tues.–Sat. 9–6, Sun. 12–5.*

San Antonio Zoo. This sprawling zoo is within Brackenridge Park. An aerial ride takes you from the zoo to the park's sunken gardens. Of special note are the outdoor hippo pool and Monkey Island. There also is a petting zoo. The grounds remain open until 8 each day. Single and double strollers, wagons, and wheelchairs can be rented to cover the spacious grounds. *3903 N. St. Mary's St., San Antonio, tel. 210/734–7183. Admission: $6 adults, $4 children 3–11 and senior citizens. Open daily 9–6:30.*

Six Flags Fiesta Texas Theme Park. This amusement and water park is 20 minutes from downtown. There is ice skating, miniature golf, a kiddie ride area, mariachi bands and a nightly fireworks and laser show. Its tall wooden roller coaster, the Rattler, is suitable for older children. Parking is $5. *17000 I–10W, exit 555 off Loop 1604, San Antonio, tel. 210/697–5050 or 800/473–4378. Admission: $31 those over 48″, $21 those under 48″ and senior citizens; $15 people with disabilities; ages 2 and under free. Open late May–Aug. 31, daily 10–10; Apr.–May and Sept.–Oct. weekends 10–10. Closing hrs vary. AE, D, MC, V.*

Natural Bridge Wildlife Ranch. This is a drive-through safari, where you can see and feed zebras, ostriches, and antelopes that approach your car. There is a petting zoo and caged section for less-tame animals. The ranch is 17 miles northeast of downtown, between San Antonio and New Braunfels. *Natural Bridge Caverns Rd., exit 175 off I–35, San Antonio, tel. 210/438–7400. Admission: $6.55 adults, $4.20 ages 3–11, $5.85 senior citizens. Open Memorial Day–Labor Day 9–6:30, Labor Day–Memorial Day 9–5.*

Sea World of Texas. There are killer whales, sharks, and touch pools in this busy water world 16 miles northwest of the city. Admission includes entry to a water park with wave pool and slides. *10500 Sea World Dr., off Loop 1604, San Antonio, tel. 210/523–3611 or 800/722–2762. Admission: $26.95 adults, $18.95 ages 3–11, $24.25 senior citizens. Open Memorial Day–mid-Aug. 10–10, mid-Mar.–Memorial Day and mid-Aug.–late Oct. weekends 10–6. D, MC, V.*

Sites to See

The Alamo. This is the oldest and most famous of the city's missions. San Antonio de Valero was established in 1718 as part of an effort to convert the Native Americans and extend Spain's frontier. In 1836, the former mission site was the scene for one of the great dramas in American history. It was here—known popularly as The Alamo—that 189 men died in the cause of Texas independence. The names Travis, Bowie, and Crockett are immortalized for their efforts in slowing the advance of Santa Anna's Mexican Army. *100 Alamo Plaza, San Antonio, tel. 210/225–1391. Donations appreciated. Open Mon.–Sat. 9–5:30, Sun. and holidays 10–5:30.*

Tower of the Americas. A few blocks from the Alamo is a tall reminder of Texas's 1968 World's Fair. The observation level—579 feet high—provides a spectacular view and is reached by a glass-walled elevator. *HemisFair Plaza, Commerce and Market Sts., San Antonio, tel. 210/207–8615. Admission: $2.50 adults, $1 children 4–11. Open 8 AM–11 PM.*

Institute of Texan Cultures. This exhibit, in HemisFair Park, tells of Texas's 27 different cultural groups. It is more appropriate for older children who can look for the life-sized buffalo, a buffalo-hide tepee, and stuffed Texas longhorn cattle. There is a silk Chinese dragon and a two-room sharecropper's house of the 1910s on display. The African-American section pays tribute to Hall of Fame slugger Frank Robinson, born in Beaumont, Texas in 1936. Parking is $2. *801 S. Bowie St., San Antonio 78205, tel. 210/558–2300. Donations appreciated. Open Tues.–Sun. 9–5 PM.*

San Antonio Mission National Historical Park. This site includes four Spanish Colonial missions that cover 835 acres. The National Park Service has preserved these missions to remember the Spanish empire's effort to colonize North America. You should begin with the Mission Concepcion, where Park Service Rangers give information and suggest driving routes along the Mission Trail. *2202 Roosevelt Ave., exit I–10 at Probandt Dr., San Antonio 78210-4919, tel. 512/229–5701. Open summer 9–6, winter 8–5.*

Austin. Don't just pass by Austin on I–35 from Dallas to San Antonio. Stop for a meal and at least an hour to sample this fine town.

Texas State Capitol. This was built in 1888 in the classic style of the United States Capitol but is 7 feet higher for Texas superiority. The Goddess of Liberty stands 16 feet high and holds the Lone Star in her raised hand. The exterior walls are pink granite quarried at Marble Falls.

A magnificent restoration and renovation was completed in 1995 to re-create the interiors as they were between 1888 and 1915. The original 1835 San Jacinto silk battle flag hangs behind the Speaker's desk in the House of Representatives chamber. Free tours are given every 15 minutes: weekdays 8:30–4:30, Saturday 9:15–4:30, Sunday 12:30–4:30. Also visit the Capitol Complex Visitors Center (112 E. 11th St., Austin, tel. 512/305–8400; open Tues.–Fri. 9–5, Sat. 10–5), in the 1856 General Land Office Building on the Capitol grounds. *Congress Ave., Austin*

78710, tel. 512/463–0063. Open weekdays 7 AM–10 PM, Sat. 9–5, Sun. noon–5.

Lyndon Baines Johnson Library. This is a superb presidential museum with films, artifacts, and a reconstruction of the Oval Office. Kids will like the weird and artistic homemade presents that Americans sent LBJ. There is a one-hour film on Lady Bird Johnson and a 20-minute video about the president. Both are shown several times daily. *2313 Red River St., Austin, tel. 512/482–5137. Open daily 9–5.*

Where to Eat

Joe's Bakery and Coffee Shop. This is a casual roadside restaurant that serves traditional Mexican breakfasts and bakes Mexican sweets in its bakery. It's a busy local hangout and resembles an expanded diner. For breakfast try a miga, which is scrambled eggs, crushed corn tortillas, and sausage. *2305 E. 7th St., Austin, tel. 512/472–0017. Open Tues.–Sun. 7–5. MC, V. $*

Hut's Hamburgers. Milk shakes made with real ice cream and oversized burgers are the draw to this 1939 Moderne-style restaurant in downtown Austin. The onion rings, chicken fried steak, daily 2-for-1 specials, and the Beachboy burger (with pineapple and jack cheese) are good reasons to visit. *807 W. 6th St., between Congress St. and Lamar Blvd., Austin, tel. 512/472–0693. Open daily 11 AM–10 PM. AE, MC, V. $*

TEXAS RANGERS

League: American League • **Class:** Major • **Stadium:** The Ballpark in Arlington • **Opened:** 1994 • **Capacity:** 49,178 • **Dimensions:** LF: 332, CF: 400, RF: 325 • **Surface:** grass • **Season:** Apr.–early Oct.

STADIUM LOCATION: 1000 Ballpark Way, Arlington, TX 76011

TEAM WEB SITE: http://www.texasrangers.com

GETTING THERE: From Dallas, take I–30 west 16 mi to Ballpark Way exit. Go south off exit and follow Ballpark Way to stadium. From Ft. Worth, take I–30 east 13 mi to Nolan Ryan Expressway exit. Turn right off exit and follow Ryan Expressway to stadium.

TICKET INFORMATION: Box 90111, Arlington, TX 76004, tel. 817/273–5100, fax 817/273–5190.

PRICE RANGE: Club box $20; field box $16; upper reserved $9; home run porch $8; grandstand reserved $6 ($3 ages under 14); bleachers $4 ($2 ages under 14). Half-price tickets available Tues. at Tom Thumb grocery stores.

GAME TIME: 7:05, 7:35, 2:05 PM; gates at first and third bases open 3 hrs before night games, 90 min before day games.

TIPS ON SEATING: Home-run porch seats in right field sound like fun and have fans, but Texas hot is too hot under that roof.

SEATING FOR PEOPLE WITH DISABILITIES: Call Fan Relations Office (tel. 817/273–5128).

STADIUM FOOD: Most of the large assortment of food is very good. The **Hall of Flame BBQ** and **Red River BBQ** have competing forms of smoked meats. Be sure to ask for mild versions for the children. The **Tex Mex Express** has great soft tacos ($2) and nachos ($3.50). The customary heat makes lemon and lime chills essential ($3). For healthy eating, try the turkey club ($5) and a bagel on a stick ($2). A park **bakery** carries average brownies ($1.75) and cookies ($1.25). **The Grill** serves good bratwurst for $4, ordinary hot dogs for $1.75, burgers for $3.50, and a good chicken sandwich for $4.25.

SMOKING POLICY: Smoking prohibited in seating areas but allowed in designated areas on outer concourse.

PARKING: Stadium complex has 9 parking lots ($5) surrounding ballpark.

VISITING TEAM HOTEL: No hotel designated for visiting team.

TOURISM INFORMATION: Arlington Visitors Center (921 Six Flags Dr., Arlington, TX 76011, tel. 817/640–0252 or 800/342–4305).

Arlington: The Ballpark in Arlington

Dallas and Fort Worth were two of the original six teams when the Texas League began in 1888, and both continued in the league until the late 1950s. During much of the 1960s, they fielded combined Dallas–Fort Worth teams in several different leagues. In 1965, the appropriately named Turnpike Stadium was built in Arlington, midway between the two cities, and the Dallas–Forth Worth Spurs rejoined the Texas League. Built with seating for 10,000, it was doubled in capacity in 1970. It was doubled again after the 1971 season to accommodate major-league baseball as the Washington Senators moved to Texas. The park's name was changed to Arlington Stadium when the Texas Rangers played their 1972 inaugural season.

The Rangers played in this former minor-league stadium for 22 seasons until 1994, when they moved nearby to the Ballpark in Arlington. Rangers pitcher Kenny Rogers highlighted the inaugural season with a perfect game on July 28, 1994. The All-Star Game was played here in 1995. The new stadium is part of a $189 million entertainment complex.

The Ballpark is a huge beauty designed in the manner of the new stadiums in Baltimore, Cleveland, and Denver, but lacking a downtown location. It sits in the middle of a parking lot. Its neighbor is the Six Flags over Texas amusement park. Plans call for a Little League stadium, an amphitheater, and a public park with lakes and trails.

To get here, you drive on the Nolan Ryan Expressway—named in honor of the future Hall of Famer who ended his extraordinary strikeout career here in Arlington. Designed by architect David Schwarz, the stadium's neo-Romanesque exterior is sunset-red granite topped by red brick and punctuated by four handsome brick corner towers. Tall brick arches stand on a base of granite arches to give the stadium an open appearance from the outside. Cast-stone carvings of 35 longhorn-steer heads and 21 Lone Star emblems adorn the spaces between the tops of the upper arches. A brick Texas Rangers Walk of Fame rings the entire stadium with a historical record of the club going back to 1972.

The almost completely enclosed interior does not match the spectacular exterior. There are enough concession stands and memorabilia shops to empty your wallet. A picnic area lies beyond the center-field wall. An art gallery and an exceptional souvenir shop sit behind that. What does not work here for us is the four-story, 138,000-square-foot office building beyond the shops. It adds too much bulk for too little architectural advantage.

There is an old-style Wrigley Field scoreboard in left field and a modern version of Detroit's Tiger Stadium home-run porch in right. The ceiling fans were hard at work on the late July night we visited, but it was 105° outside and surely hotter under the second deck. Next to the television screen is a sign inspired by Brooklyn's Ebbets Field: HIT IT HERE & WIN A FREE SUIT. 501 FEET. Fifty-minute tours of the Ballpark in Arlington are given year-round. *Tel. 817/273-5098. Admission: $5 adults, $4 senior citizens, $3 ages under 14. Tours on the hr, weekdays 9–4, Sat. 10–4, Sun. noon–4 on nongame days; on game days, tours end at noon, none on Sun.*

Where to Stay

Arlington imposes a 90¢-per-night tax per hotel room in its entertainment district to finance no-fee trolleys and shuttle buses that take guests at the following hotels, among others, to the ballpark, Six Flags over Texas amusement park, and Wet 'N' Wild water park. The trolleys (tel. 800/824–2024) run every 30 minutes daily 9:30 AM–11:30 PM or later if the ball game runs late. They're worth taking to avoid the $5–$6 parking fees at the attractions.

Courtyard by Marriott. You can walk to the ballpark from this new three-story hotel, which is in an office-park setting. The rooms are modern and standard size, with dark wood and burgundy furnishings. *1500 Pennant Dr., Arlington 76011, tel. 817/277–2774 or 800/321–2211, fax 817/277–3103. 147 rooms. Facilities: restaurant, indoor and outdoor pools, hot tub, exercise room, game room, coin laundry. AE, D, DC, MC, V. $$*

La Quinta Inn and Conference Center. This two-story stucco motel is in a commercial area, with several chain restaurants nearby. The rooms are standard size, with contemporary furnishings. *825 N. Watson Rd., at S.R. 360 and I–30, Arlington 76011, tel. 817/640–4142 or 800/551–5900, fax 817/649–7864. 340 rooms. Facilities: pool, wading pool, hot tub, coin laundry. AE, D, DC, MC, V. $$*

Best Western Great Southwest Inn. Less than 2 miles from the ballpark, this two-story stucco motel is close to the Six Flags amusement park. Its standard rooms have extra-long double beds. *3501 E. Division St., Arlington 76011, tel. 817/640–7722 or 800/346–2378, fax 817/640–7043. 122 rooms. Facilities: restaurant, pool, hot tub, playground. AE, D, DC, MC, V. $$*

Where to Eat

Landry's Seafood House. This casual neon-marquee chain restaurant is in the same office park as the baseball stadium. It's an eight-minute walk from the park, and restaurant patrons may park free in its rear lot for baseball games. You can sit at tables, in booths, or on the patio and order all manner of broiled or fried fish. All is fresh, except the catfish, which is frozen. The dessert favorite is bananas Foster, made with Texas's incomparable Blue Bell ice cream. The children's menu includes fried shrimp, a good pizza, and macaroni and cheese. *1520 Nolan Ryan Expressway, Arlington, tel. 817/261–4696. AE, D, MC, V. $$*

Luby's Cafeteria. This outstanding Southern chain cafeteria is open for lunch and dinner, serving regional favorites, an array of salads, and hard-to-resist pies, especially its coconut and egg custard varieties. It is less than a mile from the ballpark. *701 N. Watson Rd., Arlington, tel. 817/649–5090. D, MC, V. $*

Paris Coffee Shop. Fifteen minutes west of Arlington is a classic Texas lunch counter. Since 1926, happy eaters have debated among the each day's specials. A *light* lunch includes two vegetables, a regular lunch includes three. There are great mashed potatoes, fried chicken, and pies, especially cherry and custard. Baseball memorabilia fill the walls. *704 W. Magnolia, Fort Worth, tel. 817/335–2041. AE, D, MC, V. No dinner Sat. Closed Sun.*

Entertainments

Legends of the Game Baseball Museum & Learning Center. This is a fascinating children's museum within the ballpark. Learn about the sweet spot and ball construction, and feel the speed and intensity of a Roger Clemens or Nolan Ryan pitch through a glove. The Dugout, for younger fans, lets you put magnetic clothes on players and sign balls. The lower floors house an impressive collection of memorabilia. *The Ballpark in Arlington, I–30 at Hwy. 157, Arlington, tel. 817/273–5600. Admission: $6 adults, $4 ages 6–13, $5 senior citizens. Open Mar.–Oct., Mon.–Sat. 9–6:30, Sun. noon–4.*

The Science Place. This imaginative center has many unusual features, including an area where you pay $1 and get made up with special effects, like bruises, scrapes, or gruesome cuts. A crowd-pleaser is a huge dinosaur that kids ride while watching themselves on TV. Kids seven and under can build water canals and dams; they can also play on an inflatable raft on a water bed. There's also a 79-foot domed-screen IMAX theater with separate admission that shows nature and adventure films. The center is in Dallas Fair Park, 2 miles from downtown. *Fair Park, 1st St. exit off I–30 W, Dallas, tel. 214/428–5555. Admission: $6 adults, $3 ages 3–12 and senior citizens. Open Mon.–Sat. 9:30–5:30, Sun. noon–5:30.*

Dallas Aquarium. Just in front of the huge Ferris wheel at Fair Park is this small, approachable aquarium stocked with species found in local rivers, plus some tropical fish. Visitors can watch the piranhas being fed at 2:30 on Tuesday, Thursday, and Saturday and the sharks being fed at 2:30 on Wednesday, Friday, and Sunday. *1st St. and Martin Luther King Blvd., Dallas, tel. 214/670–8443. Admission: $2 adults, $1 ages 3–11. Open daily 9–4:30.*

Dallas World Aquarium. This large aquarium is located in the city's West End District and displays both fresh- and saltwater species. There's a walk-through tunnel surrounded by fish tanks, as well as displays housing penguins and coral reefs. The world's various aquatic habitats are featured. *1801 N. Griffin St., Dallas, tel. 214/720–1801. Admission: $5 adults, $3 ages 4–12. Open daily 10–6.*

Dallas Zoo. Three miles south of downtown is a large natural-habitat zoo with many rare species. There are six African habitats, including one with lowland gorillas, and a free-flight aviary. A monorail ($1.50 for visitors ages three and up) takes you for a 1-mile ride through the Wilds of Africa exhibit. Several sit-down casual restaurants are sprinkled throughout the grounds. *621 E. Clarendon Dr., Ewing Ave. exit off I–35 E, Dallas, tel. 214/670–5656. Admission: $5 adults, $2.50 ages 3–11, $4 senior citizens; parking $2. Open daily 9–5.*

Six Flags over Texas. Yosemite Sam and other Looney Tunes characters have joined this theme park. Teens can try many extreme thrill rides, including Flashback, a coaster that turns you upside down six times each ride. There are more than 100 attractions here, including a 1926 Dentzel carousel and the Texas Giant wooden coaster. *I–30 at Hwy. 360, Dallas, tel. 817/640–8900. Admission: $30.95 adults, $24.92 those 48" or shorter and senior citizens, parking $6. Open May–Aug. daily 10–10, Apr. and Sept.–Oct., weekends 10–10.*

Wet 'N' Wild. This huge water park has slides, rides, and five swimming pools. There are 48 different attractions, including a separate section with huge water guns for smaller children. The park also has 22 picnic areas, snack bars, and locker rooms. *1800 E. Lamar Blvd., Ballpark Way exit off I–30 E, Arlington, tel. 817/265–3356. Admission: $23.75 adults, $19.25 ages 3–9, $13.75 senior citizens; parking $5. Open mid-May–mid-Sept., daily 10 AM–11 PM.*

Sites to See

Fair Park. This 277-acre national historic landmark, with a large collection of Art Deco exposition buildings, was constructed for the 1936 Texas Centennial. Fair Park is still the home of the State Fair of Texas and boasts, in Texan style, that the Texas Star is the tallest Ferris wheel in North America. This aging Texas treasure is a welcome relief from the steel and glass of downtown Dallas. Start with the visitor center near the 1st Avenue entrance to the park.

Perhaps the most impressive building at Fair Park is the **Hall of State,** with its magnificent entrance. Tejas Warrior, a tribute in gold leaf honoring the Native Americans of Texas, set off by blue tiles representing the bluebonnet, the state flower, stands above the bronze doors. Admission is free.

The site of the annual **Cotton Bowl** football classic, on January 1 since 1936, sits just behind the Hall of State. To arrange a tour of the 72,000-capacity stadium, call the Fair Park administrative office (tel. 214/670–8400) in advance. *Fair Park, 1st or 2nd Ave. exit off I–30, tel. 214/421–4500 or 214/890–2911, or write Dallas Historical Society, Box 26038, Dallas, TX 75226. Open Tues.–Sat. 9–5, Sun. 1–5.*

Fort Worth. Fort Worth—like St. Paul, Minnesota—is the underrated twin to a powerhouse sibling. And, like St. Paul, it has a charm and style that are worthy of a visit.

OKLAHOMA CITY 89ERS

League: American Association • **Major League Affiliation:** Texas Rangers • **Class:** AAA • **Stadium:** All Sports Stadium • **Opened:** 1961 • **Capacity:** 12,000 • **Dimensions:** LF: 340, CF: 415, RF: 340 • **Surface:** grass • **Season:** Apr.–Labor Day

STADIUM LOCATION: State Fairgrounds, Oklahoma City, OK 73107

GETTING THERE: I–44 west to NW 10th St. East to 89th Dr. to State Fairgrounds

TICKET INFORMATION: Box 75089, Oklahoma City, OK 73147, tel. 405/946–8989, fax 405/942–4198

PRICE RANGE: Lower box $6; upper box $5; reserved $3; general admission $2; $1 off box seats for senior citizens and ages under 13

GAME TIME: Mon.–Thurs. 6:35 PM (Apr.–May), 7:05 PM (June–Aug.); Fri.–Sat. 7:30 PM; Sun. 1:35 PM; gates open 75 min before game.

TIPS ON SEATING: Seats along third-base line are away from sun and on the side of 89ers' dugout. General admission hillside seating on third-base side where kids can play at bottom of hill.

SEATING FOR PEOPLE WITH DISABILITIES: Behind home plate and along third-base line

STADIUM FOOD: The best booth is **Taco Mayo** with soft chicken tacos for $1.25 and regular tacos for 75¢. A good bean burrito is $1. Roasted corn on the cob is $2 and tastes great with frozen fruit drinks in strawberry, peach, and lemon ($2). Turkey subs are $4, and a good BBQ beef sandwich is $3. Frito chili pies are $2. Pizza slices are $2.25; a whole pie is $8. At the grill, chicken breast, Italian sausage, and Polish sausage are each $3.50.

SMOKING POLICY: Smoking prohibited in stands; allowed in concourse

PARKING: Ample free parking at fairgrounds. Parking at stadium, $2.

VISITING TEAM HOTEL: Ramada Inn Airport Northwest (3535 N.W. 39th Expressway, Oklahoma City, OK 73147, tel. 405/947–2351 or 800/272–6232)

TOURISM INFORMATION: Oklahoma City Convention & Visitors Bureau (123 Park Ave., Oklahoma City, OK 73102, tel. 405/297–8910 or 800/225–5652)

Oklahoma City: All Sports Stadium

The land that is now Oklahoma was long a Native American territory. When a strip of land was opened in 1889, white settlers flocked here. Oklahoma City sprang up virtually overnight in the land rush of 1889, and baseball fields were built east and west of Oklahoma City that summer. Professional baseball has been played here since 1904.

It was seven decades before an Oklahoma City professional baseball team took the nickname to honor these 1889 pioneers. In 1958, Oklahoma City built a new ballpark—called All Sports Stadium—on the State Fairgrounds west of downtown. In 1961, the city got a Triple AAA franchise in the American Association and held a contest to name the team. Velma Petree, a grade-school teacher, submitted the winning entry: "The name 89ers stands for pioneers starting from nothing to build a future."

Between 1963 and 1968, Oklahoma City switched to the Pacific Coast League, only to switch back to the American Association. In 1977, Oklahoma City nearly lost its team. Allie Reynolds, a Native American New York Yankees pitcher in the late 1940s and '50s, stepped forward and helped put together an ownership group to keep the team from leaving.

Allie Reynolds isn't the only big-league name associated with Oklahoma City baseball. Carl "the Meal Ticket" Hubbell began his Hall of Fame career as an Oklahoma City Indian in 1924 and 1925. Hall of Famer Roger Hornsby managed the team in 1940 and for a while in 1941.

Curt Gowdy began his broadcast career as the voice of the Oklahoma City Indians in 1947.

When we visited in 1995, the 89ers were still playing in the aging All Sports Stadium, with the engines of motorcycles from the State Fair Speedway roaring in the background. Generally, we prefer old ballparks to new ones, but it is time to retire All Sports Stadium. It has a '50s feel, with an uncovered grandstand between first and third and aluminum bleacher benches without backs down the right-field line.

The voters of Oklahoma City approved a $238 million downtown revitalization plan that includes a new baseball stadium, a 20,000-seat sports arena, a riverwalk, and a library. The 12,000-seat baseball stadium is expected to open for the 1998 season. City planners and politicians chose the historic Bricktown area on the edge of downtown as the place to focus the revitalization effort. The $21 million stadium is expected to be a hitter's park, with an irregular outfield wall configuration. They are calling the street behind left field Power Alley and wishing Juan Gonzalez were back in an 89ers uniform.

Where to Stay

Visiting Team Hotel: Ramada Inn Airport Northwest. This two-story motel is adjacent to several jogging trails. The rooms are slightly larger than average and have contemporary furnishings. *3535 N.W. 39th Expressway, Oklahoma City 73112, tel. 405/947–2351 or 800/272–6232, fax 405/948–7752. 158 rooms. Facilities: restaurant, pool, wading pool, playground, game room. AE, D, DC, MC, V. $$*

Quality Inn West. This well-maintained two-story brick hotel offers guests a free Continental breakfast. Some rooms have love seats or recliners. It's in a commercial strip with several other hotels. *720 S. MacArthur Blvd., Oklahoma City 73128, tel. 405/943–2393 or 800/424–6423, fax 405/943–9860. 65 rooms. Facilities: pool. AE, D, DC, MC, V. $*

Where to Eat

Coit's Root Beer. Sweet root beer in frosty mugs is the draw at this casual hangout. It's summertime heaven, with floats, whips, malts, limeades, and fried pies. There also are chicken sandwiches, burgers, hot dogs, and great onion rings. *5001 N. Portland Ave., Oklahoma City, tel. 405/946–8778. No credit cards. $*

Leo's. You can watch the pit men working at this dimly lit authentic rib joint. Skip the barbecued bologna and stick to the ribs and beef, especially the generous chopped beef dinner. There is a children's menu. You'll smell the smoke from its smoking pits before you see this converted gas station. The tables are Formica-covered; photos of local residents who have made good line the walls. *3631 N. Kelley, Oklahoma City, tel. 405/427–3254. AE, D, MC, V. $*

Bricktown Brewery. The brewing kettles are on view in this two-floor restaurant in a renovated warehouse in historic Bricktown, an area bounded by Sheridan and California streets. The menu covers Mexican favorites, steak, ribs, and salads. It's a noisy place, as there are pool tables and video games upstairs. (No children are allowed upstairs after 8 PM.) Its kids' menu, with $2.95 entrées, includes a good pot pie, pasta, and grilled cheese sandwiches. A bubbling cherry cobbler is the dessert standout. *1 N. Oklahoma Ave., Oklahoma City, tel. 405/232–2739. AE, D, MC, V. $$*

Spaghetti Warehouse. This former furniture store has filled up with antiques, old enamel gas-station signs, and plants and turned into a family restaurant with American cuisine. You can get an express lunch on the upper floor. The children's menu is a bargain, with spaghetti, pizza, cheese sticks, or ravioli dinners for $2.99. *101 E. Sheridan St., Oklahoma City, tel. 405/235–0402. AE, D, DC, MC, V. Closed Sun. $$*

Entertainments

Kirkpatrick Center and Omniplex Science Museum. You can spend a full day or two at this complex of museums, gardens, and a planetarium. Your admission gives entry to museums exploring science, air and space, photography, art, history, and Indian culture. The science center has 320 hands-on exhibits, including a crystal molecule that children enjoy crawling through. The planetarium's daily shows are free. *2100 N.E. 52nd St. and Martin Luther King Jr. Ave., Oklahoma City, tel. 405/427–5461. Admission: $6.50 adults, $4 ages 3–12, $4.50 senior citizens. Open Memorial Day–Labor Day, Mon.–Sat. 9–6, Sun.*

noon–6; Labor Day–Memorial Day, weekdays 9:30–5, Sat. 9–6, Sun. noon–6.

Oklahoma City Zoo. This sprawling zoo houses 2,000 animals, a children's zoo, and a Great EscApe primate center. Marine life from around the world is presented in Aquaticus, which offers dolphin and sea-lion shows several times daily ($2 fee). There's also a free-flight aviary and a herpetarium. You can make use of the sky safari overhead tram and the zoo train ($1 fee) to cover its 110 acres. *Remington Pl. and Martin Luther King Jr. Ave., Oklahoma City, tel. 405/424–3344. Admission: $4 adults, $2 ages 3–11 and senior citizens. Open Apr.–Oct., daily 9–6; Nov.–Mar., daily 9–5.*

Frontier City Western Theme Park. There are staged gunfights and magic shows in addition to the 32 rides here, including 8 kiddie rides. Teens gravitate to the three roller coasters, the sky-coaster bungee jump, and the go-carts. *11601 N.E. Expressway, 122nd St., exit off I–35, Oklahoma City, tel. 405/478–2412. Admission: $19.99 adults, $14.99 those 48" or shorter; under 3 free; parking $4. Open June–Aug., Mon.–Thurs. 10:30–10, Fri.–Sat. 10:30–midnight, Sun. noon–10; Apr.–May and Sept.–Oct., various weekend hrs. AE, MC, V.*

Lazy E Arena. This arena, on a 300-acre working ranch 30 miles north of Oklahoma City, holds exciting rodeos and horse shows throughout the year. *Rte. 5, I–35 north, Seward Rd. East exit, Guthrie, tel. 405/282–3004 or 800/234–3393.*

National Cowboy Hall of Fame and Western Heritage Center. Children may want to skip the art galleries and see the basement exhibits, depicting saloons, chuck wagons, and a general store. A children's hands-on section is under way. The good gift shop has western wear. *1700 N.E. 63rd St., Oklahoma City, tel. 405/478–2250. Admission: $6.50 adults, $3.25 ages 6–12. Open June–Labor Day, daily 8:30–6, Labor Day–May, daily 9–5.*

Sites to See

National Softball Hall of Fame. This terrific small museum focuses equally on the women and men involved in softball across the country. There are films of winning teams and star athletes, current and vintage uniforms, and other memorabilia. Seeing the community and company teams that compete gives you a picture of how basic this sport is to small-town America. A 2,000-seat stadium behind the museum hosts national tournaments. The gift shop contains a variety of jerseys and equipment. *2801 N.E. 50th St., tel. 405/424–5266. Admission: $1 adults, 50¢ ages 6–12. Open weekdays 8–5, weekends 10–4.*

State Capitol. Even if you don't share our enthusiasm for state capitols, take a few minutes to drive by Oklahoma's. Oklahoma is famous for oil and not bashful about it. The Capitol is surrounded by working oil wells. Petunia One, set in a petunia bed near the front of the Capitol, produced up to 600 barrels of oil a day from 1941 until it ran dry in 1986.

The building itself is a quite handsome Greco-Roman building done in white Indiana limestone on a foundation of Oklahoma pink and black granite. Completed in 1917, the Oklahoma Capitol is one of only a dozen in the nation without a dome. In the rotunda there are portraits of four great Oklahomans, including humorist Will Rogers and Jim Thorpe, one of the greatest athletes in history. Information is available at the Oklahoma Tourism and Recreation Department (Box 60789, Oklahoma City, OK 73146). *2300 Lincoln Blvd., Oklahoma City, tel. 405/521–2409 or 800/652–6552. Free guided tours. Tours weekdays on the hr. 8–3.*

State Museum of History. This free museum is just southeast of the Capitol. Operated by the Oklahoma Historical Society, it details the "Trail of Tears," the road created by displaced Native American during their forced removal from their territories. *2100 N. Lincoln Blvd., at N.E. 20th St., Oklahoma City 73105, tel. 405/521–2491. Open Mon.–Sat. 8–5.*

Baseball Teams in the United States and Canada

To access Minor League Baseball websites, use this format: http://www.minorleaguebaseball.com/teams/NAME OF TEAM CITY/

Teams with names in **bold face** below are major league.

Alabama

Birmingham Barons (Hoover Metropolitan Stadium; AA; Southern League), 100 Ben Chapman Dr., Birmingham, AL 35244, tel. 205/988–3200, fax 205/988–9698

Huntsville Stars (Joe W. Davis Municipal Stadium; AA; Southern League), 3125 Leeman Ferry Rd., Huntsville, AL 35801, tel. 205/882–2562, fax 205/880–0801

Arizona

Phoenix Firebirds (Scottsdale Stadium; AAA; Pacific Coast League), 7503 E. Osborn Rd., Scottsdale, AZ 85251, tel. 602/275–0500, fax 602/990–8987

Tucson Toros (Hi Corbett Field; AAA; Pacific Coast League), 3400 E. Camino Campestre, Tucson, AZ 85716, tel. 520/325–2621, fax 520/327–2371

Arkansas

Arkansas Travelers (Ray Winder Field; AA; Texas League), War Memorial Park, Little Rock, AR 72205, tel. 501/664–1555, fax 501/664–1834

California

Bakersfield Blaze (Sam Lynn Ballpark; A; California League), 4009 Chester Ave., Bakersfield, CA 93301, tel. 805/322–1363, fax 805/322–6199

California Angels (Anaheim Stadium; American League), 2000 Gene Autry Way, Anaheim, CA 92806, tel. 714/937–7200, fax 714/937–7277

High Desert Mavericks (Mavericks Stadium; A; California League), 12000 Stadium Way, Adelanto, CA 92301, tel. 619/246–6287, fax 619/246–3197

Lake Elsinore Storm (Lake Elsinore Diamond; A; California League), 500 Diamond Dr., Lake Elsinore, CA 92530, tel. 909/245–4487, fax 909/245–0305

Lancaster Jethawks (The Hangar; A; California League), Ave. I and Hwy. 14, Lancaster, CA 93536, tel. 805/726–5400, fax 805/726–5406

Long Beach Riptide (Blair Field; Independent; Western League), 1119 Queens Hwy., Long Beach, CA 90802, tel. 310/499–1772, fax 310/499–1786

Los Angeles Dodgers (Dodger Stadium, National League), 1000 Elysian Park Ave., Los Angeles, CA 90012, tel. 213/224–1500, fax 213/224–1269

Modesto A's (John Thurman Stadium; A; California League), 4707 Greenleaf Cir., Modesto, CA 95356, tel. 209/529–7368, fax 209/529–7213

Oakland Athletics (Oakland-Alameda County Coliseum; American League), 7000 Coliseum Way, Oakland, CA 94621, tel. 510/638–4900, fax 510/562–1633

Palm Springs Suns (Suns Stadium; Independent; Western League), 1901 E. Baristo, Palm Springs, CA 92262, tel. 619/323–7867, fax 619/323–8649

Rancho Cucamonga Quakes (The Epicenter; A; California League), 8408 Rochester Ave., Rancho Cucamonga, CA 91730, tel. 909/481–5000, fax 909/481–5005

Salinas Peppers (Salinas Municipal Stadium; Independent; Western League), 1398 Northridge Mall, Salinas, CA 93906, tel. 408/449–9100, fax 408/449–4610

Sonoma County Crushers (Rohnert Park Stadium; Independent; Western League), 5900 Labath Ave., Rohnert Park, CA 95404, tel. 707/588–8300, fax 707/588–8721

San Bernardino Stampede (The Ranch; A; California League), 208 S. East St., San Bernardino, CA 92401, tel. 909/888–9922, fax 909/888–5251

San Diego Padres (Jack Murphy Stadium; National League), 9449 Friars Rd., San Diego, CA 92108, tel. 619/283–4494, fax 619/282–2228

San Francisco Giants (3COM Park; National League; Candlestick Park, San Francisco, CA 94124, tel. 415/468–3700, fax 415/467–0485

San Jose Giants (Municipal Stadium; A; California League), 588 E. Alma Ave., San Jose, CA 95112, tel. 408/297–1435, fax 408/297–1453

Stockton Ports (Billy Hebert Field; A; California League), Alpine and Sutter Sts., Stockton, CA 95204, tel. 209/944–5943, fax 209/463–4937

Visalia Oaks (Recreation Park; A; California League), 440 N. Giddings Ave., Visalia, CA 93291, tel. 209/625–0480, fax 209/739–7732

Colorado

Colorado Rockies (Coors Field; National League), 2001 Blake St., Denver, CO 80205, tel. 303/292–0200, fax 303/312–2319

Colorado Springs Sky Sox (Sky Sox Stadium; AAA; Pacific Coast League), 4385 Tutt Blvd., Colorado Springs, CO 80922, tel. 719/597–1449, fax 719/597–2491

Connecticut

Hardware City Rock Cats (Beehive Field; AA; Eastern League), S. Main St., New Britain, CT 06051, tel. 860/224–8383, fax 860/225–6267

New Haven Ravens (Yale Field; AA; Eastern League), 252 Derby Ave., West Haven, CT 06515, tel. 203/782–3140, fax 203/782–3150

Norwich Navigators (Sen. Thomas J. Dodd Stadium; AA; Eastern League), 14 Stott Rd., Norwich, CT 06360, tel. 860/887–7962, fax 860/886–5996

Delaware

Wilmington Blue Rocks (Daniel S. Frawley Stadium; A; Carolina League), 801 S. Madison St., Wilmington, DE 19801, tel. 302/888–2015, fax 302/888–2032

Florida

Brevard County Manatees (Space Coast Stadium; A; Florida State League), 5800 Stadium Pkwy., Melbourne, FL 32940, tel. 407/633–9200, fax 407/633–9210

Charlotte Rangers (Charlotte County Stadium; A; Florida State League), 2300 El Jobean Rd., Port Charlotte, FL 33948, tel. 941/625–9500, fax 941/624–5168

Clearwater Phillies (Jack Russell Memorial Stadium; A; Florida State League), 800 Phillies Dr., Clearwater, FL 34615, tel. 813/441–8638, fax 813/447–3924

Daytona Cubs (Jackie Robinson Ballpark; A; Florida State League), 105 E. Orange Ave., Daytona, FL 32114, tel. 904/257–3172, fax 904/257–3382

Dunedin Blue Jays (Dunedin Stadium; A; Florida State League), 311 Douglas Ave., Dunedin, FL 3469, tel. 813/733–9302, fax 813/734–7661

Florida Marlins (Joe Robbie Stadium; National League), 2267 NW 199th St., Miami, FL 33056, tel. 305/626–7400, fax 305/626–7302

Fort Myers Miracle (Bill Hammond Stadium; A; Florida State League), 14400 Six Mile Cypress Pkwy., Fort Myers, FL 33912, tel. 941/768–4210, fax 941/768–4211

Jacksonville Suns (Wolfson Park; AA; Southern League), 1201 E. Duval St., Jacksonville, FL 32202, tel. 904/358–2846, fax 904/358–2845

Kissimmee Cobras (Osceola County Stadium; A; Florida State League), 1000 Bill Beck Blvd., Kissimmee, FL 32744, tel. 407/933–5500, fax 407/847–6237

Lakeland Tigers (Joker Marchant Stadium; A; Florida State League), 2125 N. Lake Ave., Lakeland, FL 33805, tel. 941/688–7911, fax 941/688–9589

Orlando Cubs (Tinker Field; AA; Southern League), 287 S. Tampa Ave., Orlando, FL 32805, tel. 407/245–2827, fax 407/649–1637

St. Lucie Mets (Thomas J. White Stadium; A; Florida State League), 525 NW Peacock Blvd., Port St. Lucie, FL 43986, tel. 407/871–2100, fax 407/878–9802

St. Petersburg Devil Rays (Al Lang Stadium; A; Florida State League), 180 2nd Ave. SE, St. Petersburg, FL 33701, tel. 813/822–3384, fax 813/895–1556

Sarasota Red Sox (Ed Smith Stadium; A; Florida State League), 2700 12th St., Sarasota, FL 34237, tel. 941/365–4460, fax 941/365–4217

Tampa Yankees (Legends Field; A; Florida State League), 3802 Martin Luther King Blvd., Tampa, FL 33614, tel. 813/879–2244, fax 813/673–3188

Vero Beach Dodgers (Holman Stadium; A; Florida State League), 4101 26th St., Vero Beach, FL 32960, tel. 407/569–4900, fax 407/569–0819

West Palm Beach Expos (Municipal Stadium; A; Florida State League), 715 Hank Aaron Blvd., West Palm Beach, FL 33401, tel. 407/684–6801, fax 407/686–0221

Georgia

Atlanta Braves (Atlanta-Fulton County Stadium; National League), 521 Capital Ave. SW, Atlanta, GA 30312, tel. 404/522–7630, fax 404/614–1391

Augusta Greenjackets (Lake Olmstead Stadium; A; South Atlantic League), 78 Milledge Rd., Augusta, GA 30904; tel. 706/736–7846, fax 706/736–1122

Columbus Redstixx (Cougar Field; A; South Atlantic League), 100 Fourth St., Columbus, GA 31901, tel. 706/571–8866, fax 706/571–9107

Macon Braves (Luther Williams Field; A; South Atlantic League), Central City Park, 7th St., Macon, GA 31201, tel. 912/745–8943, fax 912/743–5559

Savannah Sand Gnats (Grayson Stadium; A; South Atlantic League), 1401 E. Victory Dr., Savannah, GA 31404, tel. 912/351–9150, fax 912/352–9722

Idaho

Boise Hawks (Memorial Stadium; Short Season A; Northwest League), 5600 Glenwood St., Boise, ID 83714, tel. 208/322–5000, fax 208/322–7432

Idaho Falls Braves (McDermott Field; Rookie Short Season; Pioneer League), 568 W. Elva St., Idaho Falls, ID 83402, tel. 208/522–8363, fax 208/522–9858

Illinois

Chicago Cubs (Wrigley Field; National League), 1060 W. Addison St., Chicago, IL 60613, tel. 312/404–2827, fax 312/404–4129

Chicago White Sox (Comiskey Park; American League), 333 W. 35th St., Chicago, IL 60616, tel. 312/924–1000, fax 312/451–5116

Kane County Cougars (Philip B. Elfstrom Stadium; A; Midwest League), 34W002 Cherry Ln., Geneva, IL 60134, tel. 630/232–8811, fax 630/232–8815

Peoria Chiefs (Pete Vonachen Stadium; A; Midwest League), 1524 W. Nebraska Ave., Peoria, IL 61604, tel. 309/688–1622, fax 309/686–4516

Rockford Cubbies (Marinelli Stadium; A; Midwest League), 101 15th Ave., Rockford, IL 61104, tel. 815/962–2827, fax 815/961–2002

Springfield Capitals (Robin Roberts Stadium; Independent; Frontier League), 1351 N. Gand Ave., E. Springfield, IL 62702, tel. 217/525–5500, fax 217/525–5508

Indiana

Fort Wayne Wizards (Memorial Stadium; A; Midwest League), 4000 Parnell Ave., Fort Wayne, IN 46805, tel. 219/482–6400, fax 219/471–4678

Evansville Otters (Bosse Field; Independent; Frontier League), 1701 N. Main St., Evansville, IN 47711, tel. 812/435–8686, fax 812/435–8688

Indianapolis Indians (Victory Field; AAA; American Association), Maryland and West Sts., Indianapolis, IN 46225, tel. 317/269–3545, fax 317/269–3541

Richmond Roosters (Don McBride Stadium; Independent; Frontier League), McBride Stadium, Richmond, IN 47375, tel. 317/935–7529, fax 317/962–7047

South Bend Silver Hawks (Stanley Coveleski Regional Stadium; A; Midwest League), 501 W. South St., South Bend, IN 46601, tel. 219/235–9988, fax 219/235–9950

Iowa

Burlington Bees (Community Field; A; Midwest League), 2712 Mt. Pleasant St., Burlington, IA 52601, tel. 319/754–5705, fax 319/754–5882

Cedar Rapids Kernels (Veterans Memorial Stadium; A; Midwest League), 950 Rockford Rd. SW, Cedar Rapids, IA 52404, tel. 319/363–3887, fax 319/363–5631

Clinton Lumber Kings (Riverview Stadium; A; Midwest League), 6th Ave. N and 1st St., Clinton, IA 52733, tel. 319/242–0727, fax 319/242–1433

Iowa Cubs (Sec Taylor Stadium; AAA; American Association), 350 SW 1st St., Des Moines, IA 50309, tel. 515/243–6111, fax 515/243–5152

Quad City River Bandits (John O'Donnell Stadium; A; Midwest League), 209 S. Gaines St., Davenport, IA 52802, tel. 319/324–2032, fax 319/324–3109

Sioux City Explorers (Lewis & Clark Park; Independent; Northern League), 3400 Line Dr., Sioux City, IA 51106, tel. 712/277–9467, fax 712/277–9406

Kansas

Wichita Wranglers (Lawrence-Dumont Stadium; AA; Texas League), 300 S. Sycamore St., Wichita, KS 67213, tel. 316/267–3372, fax 316/267–3382

Kentucky

Louisville Redbirds (Cardinal Stadium; AAA; American Association), Phillips Ln. and Freedom Way, Louisville, KY 40213, 502/367–9121, fax 502/368–5120

Louisiana

Alexandria Aces (Bringhurst Field; Independent; Texas-Louisiana League), 1 Babe Ruth Dr., Alexandria, LA 71307, tel. 318/473–2237, fax 318/473–2229

New Orleans Zephyrs (new stadium; AAA; American Association), Airline Hwy. and Elise Ln., Metairie, LA 70003, tel. 504/734–5155, fax 504/734–5118

Shreveport Captains (Fair Grounds Field; AA; Texas League), 2901 Pershing Blvd., Shreveport, LA 71109, tel. 318/636–5555, fax 318/636–5670

Maine

Portland Sea Dogs (Hadlock Field; AA; Eastern League), 271 Park Ave., Portland, ME 04102, tel. 207/874–9300, fax 207/780–0317

Maryland

Baltimore Orioles (Oriole Park at Camden Yards; American League), 333 W. Camden St., Baltimore, MD 21201, tel. 410/685–9800, fax 410/547–6272

Bowie Baysox (Prince George's Stadium; AA; Eastern League), 4101 NE Crain Hwy., Bowie, MD 20716, tel. 301/805–6007, fax 301/805–6008

Delmarva Shorebirds (Arthur W. Perdue Stadium; A; South Atlantic League), Hobbs Rd., Salisbury, MD 21802, tel. 410/219–3112, fax 410/219–9164

Frederick Keys (Harry Grove Stadium; A; Carolina League), 6201 New Design Rd., Frederick, MD 21702, tel. 301/662–0013, fax 301/662–0018

Hagerstown Suns (Municipal Stadium; A; South Atlantic League), 274 E. Memorial Blvd., Hagerstown, MD 21740, tel. 301/791–6266, fax 301/791–6066

Massachusetts

Boston Red Sox (Fenway Park; American League), 4 Yawkey Way, Boston, MA 02215, tel. 617/267–9440, fax 617/236–6797

Lowell Spinners (Alumni Field; Short Season A; New York–Penn League), 2 Merrimack St., Lowell, MA 01853, tel. 508/459–1702, fax 508/459–1674

Pittsfield Mets (Wahconah Park; Short Season A; New York–Penn League), 105 Waconah St., Pittsfield, MA 01201, tel. 413/499–6387, fax 413/443–7144

Michigan

Detroit Tigers (Tiger Stadium; American League), 2121 Trumbull Ave., Detroit, MI 48216, tel. 313/962–4000, fax 313/965–2138

Kalamazoo Kodiaks (Sutherland Field; Independent; Frontier League), 200 Mills St., Kalamazoo, MI 49003, tel. 616/383–4487, fax 616/383–4492

Lansing Lugnuts (Oldsmobile Park; A; Midwest League), 505 E. Michigan Ave., Lansing, MI 48933, tel. 527/485–4500, fax 517/485–4518

Michigan Battle Cats (C.O. Brown Stadium; A; Midwest League), 1392 Capital Ave. NE, Battle Creek, MI 49017, tel. 616/660–2287, fax 616/660–2288

West Michigan Whitecaps (Old Kent Park; A; Midwest League), 4500 W. River Dr., Comstock Park, MI 49321, tel. 616/784–4131, fax 616/784–4911

Minnesota

Duluth-Superior Dukes (Wade Stadium; Independent; Northern League), 34th Ave., Duluth, MN 55802, tel. 218/727–4525, fax 218/727–4533

Minnesota Twins (Hubert H. Humphrey Metrodome; American League), 501 Chicago Ave. S, Minneapolis, MN 55415, tel. 612/375–1366, fax 612/375–7473

St. Paul Saints (Midway Stadium; Independent; Northern League), 1771 Energy Park Dr., St. Paul, MN 55108, tel. 612/644–3517, fax 612/644–1627

Mississippi

Jackson Generals (Smith-Wills Stadium; AA; Texas League), 1200 Lakeland Dr., Jackson, MS 39216, tel. 601/961–4664, fax 601/981–4669

Missouri

Kansas City Royals (Kauffman Stadium; American League), One Royal Way, Kansas City, MO 64141, tel. 816/921–2200, fax 816/921–5775

St. Louis Cardinals (Busch Stadium; National League), 250 Stadium Plaza, St. Louis, MO 63102, tel. 314/421–3060, fax 314/425–0640

Montana

Billings Mustangs (Cobb Field; Rookie Short Season; Pioneer League), 901 N. 27th St., Billings, MT 59103, tel. 406/252–1241, fax 406/252–2968

Butte Copper Kings (Alumni Coliseum; Rookie Short Season; Pioneer League), Montana Tech, W. Park St., Butte, MT 59701, tel. 406/723–8206, fax 406/723–3376

Great Falls Dodgers (Legion Park; Rookie Short Season; Pioneer League), 11 5th St. N, Great Falls, MT 59401, tel. 406/452–5311, fax 406/454–0811

Helena Brewers (Kindrick Legion Field; Rookie Short Season; Pioneer League), Warren and Memorial Sts., Helena, MT 59601, tel. 406/449–7616, fax 409/449–6979

Nebraska

Omaha Royals (Rosenblatt Stadium; AAA; American Association), 1202 Bert Murphy Dr., Omaha, NE 68107, tel. 402/734–2550, fax 402/734–7166

Nevada

Las Vegas Stars (Cashman Field; AAA; Pacific Coast League), 850 Las Vegas Blvd. N, Las Vegas, NV 89101, tel. 702/386–7200, fax 702/386–7214

Reno Chukars (Moana Stadium; Independent; Western League), Moana Stadium, Reno, NV 89570, tel. 702/829–7890, fax 702/829–7895

New Jersey

New Jersey Cardinals (Skylands Park; Short Season A; New York–Penn League), 94 Championship Pl., Augusta, NJ 07822, tel. 201/579–7500, fax 201/579–7502

Trenton Thunder (Mercer County Waterfront Park; AA; Eastern League), 1 Thunder Rd., Trenton, NJ 08611, tel. 609/394–3300, fax 609/394–9666

New Mexico

Albuquerque Dukes (Albuquerque Sports Stadium; AAA; Pacific Coast League), 1601 Stadium Blvd. SE, Albuquerque, NM 87106, tel. 505/243–1791, fax 505/842–0561

New York

Auburn Doubledays (Falcon Park; Short Season A; New York–Penn League), 108 N. Division St., Auburn, NY 13021, tel. 315/255–2489, fax 315/255–2675

Batavia Clippers (Dwyer Stadium; Short Season A; New York–Penn League), 299 Bank St., Batavia, NY 14020, tel. 716/343–5454, fax 716/343–5620

Binghamton Mets (Binghamton Municipal Stadium; AA; Eastern League), 211 Henry St., Binghamton, NY 13901, tel. 607/723–6387, fax 607/723–7779

Buffalo Bisons (North AmeriCare Park; AAA; American Association), 275 Washington St., Buffalo, NY 14203, 716/846–2000, fax 716/852–6530

Hudson Valley Renegades (Dutchess Stadium; Short Season A; New York–Penn League), Rte. 90, Wappingers Falls, NY 12590, tel. 914/838–0094, fax 914/838–0014

Jamestown Jammers (College Stadium; Short Season A; New York–Penn League), 485 Falconer St., Jamestown, NY 14702, tel. 716/664–0915, fax 716/664–4175

New York Mets (Shea Stadium, National League), 123 Roosevelt Ave., Flushing, NY 11368, tel. 718/507–6387, fax 718/565–4382

New York Yankees (Yankee Stadium; American League), 161st St. and River Ave., Bronx, NY 10451, tel. 718/293–4300, fax 718/293–8431

Oneonta Yankees (Damaschke Field; Short Season A; New York–Penn League), 95 River St., Oneonta, NY 13820, tel. 607/432–6326, fax 607/432–1965

Rochester Red Wings (Silver Stadium; AAA; International League), 500 Norton St., Rochester, NY 14621, tel. 716/467–3000, fax 716/467–6732

Syracuse SkyChiefs (P & C Stadium; AAA; Independent League), Hiawatha Blvd. E and 2nd St., Syracuse, NY 13208, tel. 315/474–7833, fax 315/474–2658

Utica Blue Marlins (Donovan Stadium; Short Season A; New York–Penn League), 1700 Sunset Ave., Utica, NY 13502, tel. 315/738–0999, fax 315/738–0992

Watertown Indians (Alex T. Duffy Fairgrounds; Short Season A; New York–Penn League), 900 Coffeen St., Watertown, NY 13601, tel. 315/788–8747, fax 315/788–8841

North Carolina

Asheville Tourists (McCormick Field; A; South Atlantic League), 30 Buchanan St., Asheville, NC 28801, tel. 704/258–0428, fax 704/258–0320

Burlington Indians (Burlington Athletic Stadium; Rookie Short Season; Appalachian League), 1450 Graham St., Burlington, NC 27215, tel. 910/222–0223, fax 910/226–2498

Carolina Mudcats (Five County Stadium; AA; Southern League), 1501 Hwy. 39, Zebulon, NC 27597, tel. 919/269–2287, fax 919/269–4910

Cape Fear Crocs (J.P. Riddle Stadium; A; South Atlantic League), 2823 Legion Rd., Fayetteville, NC 28306, tel. 910/424–6500, fax 910/424–4325

Durham Bulls (Durham Bulls Athletic Park; A; Carolina League), 409 Blackwell St., Durham, NC 27701, tel. 919/687–6500, fax 919/687–6560

Greensboro Bats (War Memorial Stadium; A; South Atlantic League), 510 Yanceyville St., Greensboro, NC 27405, tel. 910/333–2287, fax 910/273–7350

Hickory Crawdads (L.P. Frans Stadium; A; South Atlantic League), 2500 Clement Blvd. NW, Hickory, NC 28601, tel. 704/322–3000, fax 704/322–6137

Kinston Indians (Grainger Stadium; A; Carolina League), 400 E. Grainer Ave., Kinston, NC 28501, tel. 919/527–9111, fax 919/527–2328

Piedmont Boll Weevils (Fieldcrest Cannon Stadium; A; South Atlantic League), 2888 Moose Rd., Kannapolis, NC 28083, tel. 704/932–3267, fax 704/938–7040

Port City Roosters (Brooks Field; AA; Southern League), 601 S. College Rd., Wilmington, NC 28403, tel. 910/350–7000, fax 910/350–7098

Winston-Salem Warthogs (Ernie Shore Field; A; Carolina League), 401 Deacon Blvd., Winston-Salem, NC 27105, tel. 910/759–2233, fax 910/759–2042

North Dakota

Fargo-Moorhead Redhawks (New Stadium; Independent; Northern League), Albrecht Blvd. at 15th Ave. N, Fargo, ND 58102, tel. 701/235–6161, fax 701/232–4108

Ohio

Canton-Akron Indians (Thurman Munson Memorial Stadium; AA; Eastern League), 2501 Allen Av. SE, Canton, OH 44707, tel. 216/456–5100, fax 216/456–5450

Chillicothe Paints (V.A. Memorial Field; Independent; Frontier League), 59 N. Paint St., Chillicothe, OH 45601, tel. 614/773–8326, fax 614/773–8338

Cincinnati Reds (Riverfront Stadium; National League), 100 Riverfront Stadium, Cincinnati, OH 45202, tel. 513/421–4510, fax 513/421–7342

Cleveland Indians (Jacobs Field; American League), 2401 Ontario St., Cleveland, OH 44115, tel. 216/420–4200, fax 216/420–4396

Columbus Clippers (Cooper Stadium; AAA; International League), 1155 W. Mound St. Columbus, OH 43223, tel. 614/462–5250, fax 614/462–3271

Toledo Mud Hens (Ned Skeldon Stadium; AAA; International League), 2901 Key St., Maumee, OH 43537, tel. 419/893–9483, fax 419/893–5847

Zanesville Greys (Gant Municipal Stadium; Independent; Frontier League), Gant Stadium Zanesville, OH 43702, tel. 614/454–7397, fax 614/454–8601

Oklahoma

Oklahoma City 89ers (All Sports Stadium; AAA; American Association State Fairgrounds, Oklahoma City, OK 73107, tel. 405/946–8989, fax 405/942–4198

Tulsa Drillers (Drillers Stadium; AA; Texas League), 4802 E. 15th St., Tulsa, OK 74112, tel. 918/744–5998, fax 918/747–3267

Oregon

Bend Bandits (Vince Genna Stadium; Independent; Western League), Genna Stadium, Bend, OR 97709, tel. 541/383–1983, fax 541/383–2004

Eugene Emeralds (Civic Stadium; Short Season A; Northwest League), 2077 Willamette St., Eugene, OR 97405, tel. 541/342–5367, fax 503/342–6089

Keizer Baseball Club (Keizer Stadium; Short Season A; Northwest League), 6535 Radiant Dr., Keizer, OR 97307, tel. 503/390–2225, fax 503/390–2227

Portland Rockies (Civic Stadium; Short Season A; Northwest League), 1844 SW Morrison Portland, OR 97207, tel. 503/223–2837, fax 503/223–2948

Southern Oregon Timberjacks (Miles Field; Short Season A; Northwest League), 1801 S. Pacific Hwy. Medford, OR 97501, tel. 541/770–5364, fax 541/772–4466

Pennsylvania

Erie Seawolves (Jerry Uht Park; Short Season A; New York–Penn League), 110 E. 10th St., Erie, PA 16507, tel. 814/456–1300, fax 814/456–7520

Harrisburg Senators (RiverSide Stadium; AA; Eastern League), City Island, Harrisburg, PA 17101, tel. 717/231–4444, fax 717/231–4445

Johnstown Steal (Johnstown Point Stadium; Independent; Frontier League), 211 Main St., Johnstown, PA 15901, tel. 814/536–8326, fax 814/539–0056

Philadelphia Phillies (Veterans Stadium; National League), 3501 S. Broad St., Philadelphia, PA 19148, tel. 215/463–6000, fax 215/389–3050

Pittsburgh Pirates (Three Rivers Stadium; National League), 600 Stadium Cir., Pittsburgh, PA 15212, tel. 412/323–5000, fax 412/323–1724

Reading Phillies (Reading Municipal Memorial Stadium; AA; Eastern League), 1900 Centre Ave., Reading, PA 19605, tel. 610/375–8469, fax 610/373–5868

Scranton/Wilkes-Barre Red Barons (Lackawanna County Stadium; AAA; International League), 235 Montage Mountain Rd., Moosic, PA 18507, tel. 717/969–2255, fax 717/963–6564

Williamsport Cubs (Bowman Field; Short Season A; New York–Penn League), 1700 W. 4th St., Williamsport, PA 17701, tel. 717/326–3389, fax 717/326–3494

Rhode Island

Pawtucket Red Sox (McCoy Stadium; AAA; International League), 1 Columbus Av., Pawtucket, RI 02860, tel. 401/724–7300, fax 401/724–2140

South Carolina

Capital City Bombers (Capital City Stadium; A; South Atlantic League), 301 S. Assembly St., Columbia, SC 29201, tel. 803/256–4110, fax 803/256–4338

Charleston Riverdogs (Charleston Ballpark; A; South Atlantic League), Lockwood Blvd. and Fishbourne St., Charleston, SC 29403, tel. 803/723–7241, fax 803/723–2641

Charlotte Knights (Knights Castle; AAA; International League), 2280 Deerfield Dr., Fort Mill, SC 29715, tel. 704/357–8071, fax 803/548–8055

Greenville Braves (Greenville Municipal Stadium; AA; Southern League), 1 Braves Ave., Greenville, SC 29607, tel. 864/299–3456, fax 864/277–7369

South Dakota

Sioux Falls Canaries (Sioux Falls Stadium; Independent; Northern League), 119 Main St., Sioux Falls, SD 57102, tel. 605/333–0179, fax 605/333–0139

Tennessee

Chattanooga Lookouts (Historic Engel Stadium; AA; Southern League), 1130 E. 3rd St., Chattanooga, TN 37402, tel. 423/267–2208, fax 423/267–4258

Elizabethton Twins (Riverside Park; Rookie Short Season; Appalachian League), Holly Ln., Elizabethton, TN 37643, tel. 423/543–4395, fax 423/542–1510

Johnson City Cardinals (Howard Johnson Field; Rookie Short Season; Appalachian League), 111 Legion St., Johnson City, TN 37601, tel. 423/461–4853, fax 423/461–4864

Kingsport Mets (Hunter Wright Stadium; Rookie Short Season; Appalachian League), 411 E. Center St., Kingsport, TN 37660, tel. 423/378–3744, fax 423/245–0467

Knoxville Smokies (Bill Meyer Stadium; AA; Southern League), 633 Jessamine St., Knoxville, TN 37917, tel. 423/637–9494, fax 423/523–9913

Memphis Chicks (Tim McCarver Stadium; AA; Southern League), 800 Home Run Ln., Memphis, TN 38104, tel. 901/272–1687, fax 901/278–3354

Nashville Sounds (Herschel Greer Stadium; AAA; American Association), 534 Chestnut St., Nashville, TN 37203, tel. 615/242–4371, fax 615/256–5684

Texas

Abilene Prairie Dogs (Crutcher-Scott Field; Independent; Texas-Louisiana League), 2249 N. Judge Ely Blvd., Abilene, TX 79601, tel. 915/673–7364, fax 915/677–3294

Amarillo Dillas (Potter County Memorial Stadium; Independent; Texas-Louisiana League), 3222 E. 3rd St., Amarillo, TX 79120, tel. 806/342–3455, fax 806/374–2269

El Paso Diablos (Cohen Stadium; AA; Texas League), 9700 Gateway N. Blvd., El Paso, TX 79924, tel. 915/755–2000, fax 915/757–0671

Houston Astros (Astrodome National League), 8400 Kirby Dr., Houston, TX 77054, tel. 713/799–9500, fax 713/799–9562

Lubbock Crickets (Dan Law Field; Independent; Texas-Louisiana League), 6th St. and Flint Ave., Lubbock, TX 79408, tel. 806/749–2225, fax 806/749–6625

Midland Angels (Christensen Stadium; AA; Texas League), 4300 N. Lamesa Rd., Midland, TX 79705, tel. 915/683–4251, fax 915/683–0994

Rio Grande Valley Whitewings (Harlingen Field; Independent; Texas-Louisiana League), 1216 Fair Park Blvd., Harlingen, TX 78550, tel. 210/412–9464, fax 210/412–9479

San Antonio Missions (Nelson Wolff Municipal Stadium; AA; Texas League), 5757 Hwy. 90 W., San Antonio, TX 78227, tel. 210/675–7275, fax 210/670–0001

Texas Rangers (Ballpark in Arlington; American League), 1000 Ballpark Way, Arlington, TX 76011, tel. 817/273–5222, fax 817/273–5206

Tyler Wildcatters (Mike Carter Field; Independent; Texas-Lousiana League), Carter Field Tyler, TX 75711, tel. 903/597–9453, fax 903/597–6464

Utah

Ogden Raptors (Serge Simmons Field; Rookie Short Season; Pioneer League), 2904 Washington Blvd., Ogden, UT 84401, tel. 801/393–2400, fax 801/393–2473

Salt Lake Buzz (Franklin Quest Field; AAA; Pacific Coast League), 77 W. 1300 S., Salt Lake City, UT 84115, tel. 801/485–3800, fax 801/485–6818

Vermont

Vermont Expos (Centennial Field; Short Season A; New York–Penn League), Champlain Mill, Winooski, VT 05404, tel. 802/655–4200, fax 802/655–5660

Virginia

Bristol White Sox (DeVault Memorial Stadium; Rookie Short Season; Appalachian League), 1501 Euclid Ave., Bristol, VA 24201, tel. 540/645–7275, fax 540/645–7377

Danville Braves (Dan Daniel Memorial Park; Rookie Short Season Appalachian League), 302 River Park Dr., Danville, VA 24541, tel. 804/791–3346, fax 804/791–3347

Lynchburg Hillcats (City Stadium; A; Carolina League), Fort Ave. and Wythe Rd., Lynchburg, VA 24501, tel. 804/528–1144, fax 804/846–0768

Martinsville Phillies (Hooker Field; Rookie Short Season; Appalachian League), Chatham Heights Rd., Martinsville, VA 24112, tel. 540/666–2000, fax 540/666–2139

Norfolk Tides (Harbor Park; AAA; International League), 150 Park Ave., Norfolk, VA 23510, tel. 804/622–2222, fax 804/624–9090

Prince William Cannons (Prince William County Stadium; A; Carolina League), 7 County Complex Ct., Woodbridge, VA 22193, tel. 703/590–2311, fax 703/590–5716

Pulaski Rangers (Calfee Park; Rookie Appalachian League), 5th St., Pulaski, VA 24301

Richmond Braves (The Diamond; AAA; International League), 3001 N. Boulevard, Richmond, VA 23230, tel. 804/359–4444, fax 804/359–0731

Salem Avalanche (Salem Memorial Baseball Complex; A; Carolina League), 1004 Texas St., Salem, VA 24153, tel. 540/389–3333, fax 540/389–9710

Washington

Everett Aquasox (Everett Memorial Stadium; Short Season A; Northwest League), 2118 Broadway, Everett, WA 98201, tel. 206/258–3673, fax 206/258–3675

Grays Harbor Gulls (Olympic Stadium; Independent; Western League), 1017 S. Boone St., Aberdeen, WA 98520, tel. 360/532–4488, fax 360/532–4122

Seattle Mariners (Kingdome; American League), 201 S. King St., Seattle, WA 98104, tel. 206/628–3555, fax 206/628–3340

Spokane Indians (Seafirst Stadium; Short Season A; Northwest League), 602 N. Havana, Spokane, WA 99202, tel. 509/535–2922, fax 509/534–5368

Tacoma Rainiers (Cheney Stadium; AAA; Pacific Coast League), 2502 S. Tyler, Tacoma, WA 98405, tel. 206/752–7707, fax 206/752–7135

Tri-City Posse (Tri-Cities Stadium; Independent; Western League), 6200 Burden Rd., Pasco, WA 99301, tel. 509/547–6773, fax 509/547–4008

Yakima Bears (Yakima County Stadium; Short Season A; Northwest League), 810 W. Nob Hill Blvd., Yakima, WA 98902, tel. 509/457–5151, fax 509/457–9909

West Virginia

Bluefield Orioles (Bowen Field; Rookie Short Season; Appalachian League), Stadium Dr., Bluefield, WV 24701, tel. 540/326–1326, fax 540/326–1318

Charleston Alley Cats (Walt Powell Park; A; South Atlantic League), 3403 MacCorkle Ave., Charleston, WV 25304, tel. 304/344–2287, fax 304/344–0083

Ohio Valley Redcoats (Bennett Stump Field; Independent; Frontier League), Stump Field, Parkersburg, WV 26102, tel. 304/485–4889, fax 304/485–7510

Princeton Reds (Hunnicutt Field; Rookie Short Season; Appalachian League), Old Bluefield-Princeton Rd., Princeton, WV 24740, tel. 304/487–2000, fax 304/425–6999

Wisconsin

Beloit Snappers (Harry Pohlman Field; A; Midwest League), 2301 Skyline Dr., Beloit, WI 53511, tel. 608/362–2272, fax 608/362–0418

Madison Black Wolf (Warner Park; Independent; Northern League), 2920 N. Sherman Ave., Madison, WI 53704, tel. 608/244–5666, fax 608/244–6996

Milwaukee Brewers (County Stadium; American League), 201 S. 46th St., Milwaukee, WI 53214, tel. 414/933–4114, fax 414/933–7323

Wisconsin Timber Rattlers (Fox Cities Stadium; A; Midwest League), 2400 N. Casaloma Dr., Appleton, WI 54911, tel. 414/733–4152, fax 414/733–8032

Canada

Calgary Cannons (Burns Stadium; AAA; Pacific Coast League), 2255 Cowchild Trail NW, Calgary, Alberta T2M 4S7, tel. 403/284–1111, fax 403/284–4343

Edmonton Trappers (TELUS Field; AAA; Pacific Coast League), 10233 96th Ave., Edmonton, Alberta T5K 0A5, tel. 403/429–2934, fax 403/426–5640

Lethbridge Black Diamonds (Henderson Stadium; Rookie Short Season; Pioneer League), 365 1st St. SE, Medicine Hat, Alberta T1A 7G2, tel. 403/526–0404, fax 403/526–4000

Montreal Expos (Olympic Stadium; National League), 4549 Pierre-de-Coubertin Ave., Montreal, Quebec H1V 3N7, tel. 514/253–3434, fax 514/253–8282

Ottawa Lynx (Ottawa Stadium; AAA; International League), 300 Chemin Coventry Rd., Ottawa, Ontario K1K 4P5, tel. 613/747–5969, fax 613/747–0003

St. Catherines Stompers (Community Park; Short Season A; New York–Penn League), 426 Merritt St., St. Catherines, Ontario L2P 1P3, tel. 905/641–5297, fax 905/641–3007

Thunder Bay Whiskey Jacks (Port Arthur Stadium; Independent; Northern League), 425 Winnipeg Ave., Thunder Bay, Ontario P7B 6B7, tel. 807/344–5225, fax 807/343–4611

Toronto Blue Jays (SkyDome; American League), 1 Blue Jays Way, Toronto, Ontario M5V 1J1, tel. 416/341–1000, fax 416/341–1250

Vancouver Canadians (Nat Bailey Stadium; AAA; Pacific Coast League), 4601 Ontario St., Vancouver, B.C. V5V 3H4, tel. 604/872–5232, fax 604/872–1714

Winnipeg Goldeyes (Winnipeg Stadium; Independent; Northern League), 1430 Maroons Rd., Winnipeg, Manitoba R3G 0L5, tel. 204/982–2273, fax 204/982–2274

Notes

2 KIDS FREE!

Present this multiple-use coupon at the box office and receive **free General Admission for two children** with two paying adults for one game of each of the following baseball teams:

Albuquerque Dukes	____	Lake Elsinore Storm	____
Arkansas Travelers	____	Louisville Redbirds	____
Bowie Baysox	____	Lynchburg Hillcats	____
Charleston RiverDogs	____	Memphis Chicks	____
Chattanooga Lookouts	____	New Haven Ravens	____
Delmarva Shorebirds	____	Portland Sea Dogs	____
Elmira Pioneers	____	Prince William Cannons	____
Everett Aquasox	____	San Bernardino Stampede	____
Frederick Keys	____	San Jose Giants	____
Greensboro Bats	____	Savannah Sand Gnats	____
Hagerstown Suns	____	Sioux City Explorers	____
Hudson Valley Renegades	____	Toledo Mud Hens	____
Jamestown Jammers	____	Williamsport Cubs	____
Kane County Cougars	____	Winston-Salem Warthogs	____

2 KIDS FREE!

This coupon entitles bearer to two free children's Upper Reserved seats with the purchase of two adult Upper Reserved seats for any SAN FRANCISCO GIANTS home game date except Opening Day. To obtain tickets, mail this coupon, a check for $18 (including $3 handling charge) payable to San Francisco Giants (1997 season; call 415/467-8000 for ticket price information for the 1998 season) for the two adult tickets, and a self-addressed, stamped envelope to: Giants Ticket Office, 3COM Park, San Francisco, California 94124.

Offers expire 10/1/98

Fodor's
BALLPARK VACATIONS
FREE COUPON

Offer expires 10/1/98

Fodor's
BALLPARK VACATIONS
FREE COUPON

Offer expires 10/1/98